Organization Theory and Design

EIGHTH EDITION

Richard L. Daft
Vanderbilt University

THOMSON
SOUTH-WESTERN

Australia · Canada · Mexico · Singapore · Spain · United Kingdom · United States

THOMSON
SOUTH-WESTERN

Organization Theory and Design   **8th Edition**
Richard L. Daft   Vanderbilt University

Vice President/Editorial Director:
Jack Calhoun

Vice President/Editor-in-Chief:
Mike Roche

Senior Publisher:
Melissa Acuña

Acquisitions Editor:
Joe Sabatino

Developmental Editor:
Emma Guttler

Marketing Manager:
Jacquelyn Carrillo

Production Editor:
Cliff Kallemeyn

Media Developmental Editor:
Kristen Meere

Media Production Editor:
Karen Schaffer

Senior Designer:
Anne Marie Rekow

Manufacturing Coordinator:
Rhonda Utley

Production House/Compositor:
DPS Associates, Inc.

Printer:
RR Donnelley & Sons Company
Willard, OH

Library of Congress Control
Number: 2003103619

ISBN: 0-324-15691-X

International Student Edition
ISBN 0-324-28278-8
(Not for Sale in the United States)

About the Author

Richard L. Daft, Ph.D., is Associate Dean for Academic Programs and the Brownlee O. Currey, Jr., Professor of Management in the Owen Graduate School of Management at Vanderbilt University. Professor Daft specializes in the study of organization theory and leadership, and enjoys applying these ideas in his role as Associate Dean. Dr. Daft is a Fellow of the Academy of Management and has served on the editorial boards of *Academy of Management Journal*, *Administrative Science Quarterly*, and *Journal of Management Education*. He was the Associate Editor-in-Chief of *Administrative Science Quarterly*.

Professor Daft has authored or co-authored 13 books, including *Management* (Thomson Learning/South Western, 2003), *The Leadership Experience* (Thomson Learning/South-Western, 2001), and *What to Study: Generating and Developing Research Questions* (Sage, 1982). He recently published *Fusion Leadership: Unlocking the Subtle Forces That Change People and Organizations* (Berrett-Koehler, 2000, with Robert Lengel). He has also published in *Administrative Science Quarterly*, *Academy of Management Journal*, *Journal of Management*, *Accounting Organizations and Society*, *Management Science*, *MIS Quarterly*, *California Management Review*, and *Organizational Behavior Teaching Review*. Professor Daft has been awarded several government research grants to pursue studies of organization design, organizational innovation and change, strategy implementation, and organizational information processing.

Dr. Daft is also an active teacher and consultant. He has taught organization design, management, leadership, change management, organizational behavior, and strategic management. He has been involved in management development and consulting for many companies and government organizations, including the American Banking Association, Bell Canada, National Transportation Research Board, USAA, Nortel, TVA, Pratt & Whitney, State Farm Insurance, Tenneco, the United States Air Force, the U.S. Army, J. C. Bradford & Co., Central Parking System, Entergy Sales and Service, Bristol-Myers Squibb, First American National Bank, and the Vanderbilt University Medical Center.

$\mathscr{B}$RIEF CONTENTS

CONTENTS

My vision for the eighth edition of *Organization Theory and Design* is to integrate contemporary thinking about organization design with classic ideas and theories in a way that is interesting and enjoyable for students. This edition has undergone a transformation. Significant changes have been made in many areas, including a new chapter, major revisions of several chapters to incorporate the most recent ideas, new case examples, new book reviews, new end-of-chapter cases, and new end-of-book integrative cases. The research and theories in the field of organization studies are rich and insightful, and will help students and managers understand their organizational world and solve real-life problems. My mission is to integrate the concepts and models from organizational theory with changing events in the real world to provide the most up-to-date view of organization design available.

DISTINGUISHING FEATURES OF THE EIGHTH EDITION

Many students in a typical organization theory course do not have extensive work experience, especially at the middle and upper levels where organization theory is most applicable. To engage students in the world of organizations, the eighth edition adds or expands significant features: a new chapter that explains how to design organizations for the global environment, a feature called Leading by Design that focuses on companies that are successfully using organization design concepts to compete in today's complex and uncertain business world, student experiential activities that engage students in applying chapter concepts, new Book Marks, new In Practice examples, and new end-of-chapter and integrative cases for student analysis. The total set of features substantially expands and improves the book's contents and accessibility. These multiple pedagogical devices enhance student involvement in text materials.

Leading by Design The Leading by Design features describe companies that have undergone major shifts in organization design, strategic direction, values, or culture as they strive to become learning organizations and be more competitive in today's turbulent global environment. Many of these companies are applying new design ideas such as modular organizing, e-business, or organizing temporary systems for flexibility and innovation. The Leading by Design examples illustrate company transformations toward knowledge sharing, empowerment of employees, new structures, new cultures, the breaking down of barriers between departments and organizations, and the joining together of employees in a common mission. Leading by Design organizations include Marriott, The Salvation Army, Motek, Corrugated Supplies, Commerce Bank, Google, Royal Dutch/Shell, and Dell Computer.

Book Marks Book Marks, a unique feature of this text, are book reviews that reflect current issues of concern for managers working in real-life organizations.

These reviews describe the varied ways companies are dealing with the challenges of today's changing environment. New Book Marks in the eighth edition include *The Company of the Future: How the Communications Revolution Is Changing Management, Cross-Cultural Business Behavior, Managing Strategic Relationships, Good to Great, Winning Decisions, Futurize Your Enterprise: Business Strategy in the Age of the E-Customer, The Myth of the Paperless Office,* and *It's Not the Big That Eat the Small . . . It's the Fast That Eat the Slow.*.

A Look Inside This feature introduces each chapter with a relevant and interesting organizational example to illustrate theoretical concepts. Many examples are international, and all are based on real organizations. New cases include Xerox, Guiltless Gourmet, Starbucks, Progressive Insurance, Interpol, and Procter and Gamble.

In Practice These cases also illustrate theoretical concepts in organizational settings. New In Practice cases used within chapters to illustrate specific concepts include UPS, Parkland Memorial Hospital, Tesco.com, JetBlue Airlines, Electronic Data Systems, Cementos Mexicanos (Cemex), Yahoo!, STMicroelectronics NV, Colgate Palmolive, Pret A Manger, Paramount Pictures, Ford Motor Corporation, and Nokia.

Briefcase Located in the chapter margins, this feature tells students how to use concepts to analyze cases and manage organizations.

Text Exhibits Frequent exhibits are used to help students visualize organizational relationships, and the artwork for these exhibits has been designed to communicate concepts clearly.

Summary and Interpretation The summary and interpretation section tells students which points are important in the broader context of organizational theory.

Case for Analysis These cases are tailored to chapter concepts and provide a vehicle for student analysis and discussion.

Integrative Cases The integrative cases at the end of the text are positioned to encourage student discussion and involvement. These cases include Custom Chip, Inc., The Audubon Zoo, Royce Consulting, and W. L. Gore & Associates.

NEW CHAPTER

The new chapter, Chapter 6, describes the complexity of the global environment and explores concepts and ideas that can help managers design their organizations to be more effective on a global scale. Interest in global trade is greater today than ever before, and many companies have to become involved in international business to survive. The chapter explores companies' motivations for going global, the stages of international development, and how managers can design organizations to fit global strategy. Specific design alternatives are explained, including the most recent thinking about the kind of complex organization needed to compete internationally. Many companies have trouble transferring successful ideas, products, services, and technologies from their home country to the international domain. This chapter describes how organizations can build global capabilities, and includes a discussion of how cultural differences affect organizations operating globally.

NEW CONCEPTS

Many concepts have been added or expanded in this edition. New material has been added on performance and effectiveness, the modular organization structure, e-business organization design, designing the integrated enterprise, virtual teams, the incident command model, managing organizational decline and downsizing, building social capital, shaping ethical values, diversity as a force for culture change, lean manufacturing, process reengineering, Six Sigma, time-based competition, social audits, creativity and idea incubators, and the point-counterpoint technique for improving decision making. Many ideas are aimed at helping students learn to design organizations for an environment characterized by uncertainty, a renewed emphasis on ethics and social responsibility, and the need for a speedy response to change, crises, or shifting customer expectations. In addition, coping with the complexity of today's global environment is explored thoroughly in Chapter 6.

CHAPTER ORGANIZATION

Each chapter is highly focused and is organized into a logical framework. Many organization theory textbooks treat material in sequential fashion, such as Here's View A, Here's View B, Here's View C, and so on. *Organization Theory and Design* shows how the various viewpoints apply in organizations. Moreover, each chapter sticks to the essential point. Students are not introduced to extraneous material or confusing methodological squabbles that occur among organizational researchers. The body of research in most areas points to a major trend, which is reported here. Several chapters develop a framework that organizes major ideas into an overall scheme.

   This book has been extensively tested on students. Feedback from students and faculty members has been used in the revision. The combination of organization theory concepts, book reviews, examples of leading organizations, case illustrations, experiential exercises, and other new teaching devices is designed to meet student learning needs, and students have responded favorably.

SUPPLEMENTS

Instructor's Resource Guide with Test Bank (0-324-15692-8)

The Resource Guide contains chapter overviews, chapter outlines, lecture enhancements, discussion questions, discussion of workbook activities, discussion of chapter cases, Internet activities, case notes for integrative cases, and a guide to the videos available for use with the text. The Test Bank consists of multiple choice, true/false, and short answer questions.

Instructor's Resource CD-ROM (IRCD) (0-324-27481-5)

Key instructor ancillaries (Instructor's Resource Guide with Test Bank, PowerPoint Lecture Presentation and ExamView) are provided on CD-ROM, giving instructors the ultimate tool for customizing lectures and presentations.

ExamView

Available on the IRCD, this computerized version of the Test Bank is available upon request. ExamView contains all of the questions in the printed Test Bank. This program is an easy-to-use test creation software compatible with Microsoft Windows. Instructors can add or edit questions, instructions, and answers, and select questions (randomly or numerically) by previewing them on the screen. Instructors can also create and administer quizzes online, whether over the Internet, a local area network (LAN), or a wide area network (WAN).

PowerPoint Lecture Presentation

Available on the IRCD and on the Web site, the PowerPoint slides are prepared in conjunction with the text and Instructor's Resource Guide. Containing approximately 150 slides, the package includes figures and tables from the text, as well as outside materials to supplement chapter concepts. Material is organized by chapter and can be modified or expanded for individual classroom use. PowerPoint presentations can also be easily printed to create customized Transparency Masters. Available on the Instructor's Resource CD-ROM and the Web site, the PowerPoint Lecture Presentation enables instructors to customize their own multimedia classroom presentations.

Turner Learning/CNN, Management and Organizations Video (0-324-28816-6)

Bring the news gathering and programming power of CNN into your classroom with the VHS cassette of high-interest clips from the world's leading 24-hour global news network. Short segments—perfect for introducing key concepts— cover a range of issues, from online anonymity to workplace privacy, affirmative action, compulsory overtime, biotechnology, and more.

Web site (http://daft.swcollege.com)

The Daft Web site is a comprehensive, resource-rich location for both instructors and students to find pertinent information. It includes a complete listing of URLs from the text, case links, interactive quizzes, InfoTrac exercises, PowerPoint Lecture Presentations, and Search the Web features with links to additional sources. The Instructor Resources section contains an Instructor's Resource Guide download, Test Bank download, PowerPoint download, case material, and PDF files of 2 chapters. The Interactive Study Center includes Interactive Quizzes, complete text glossary and key end of chapter materials for online reference.

ACKNOWLEDGEMENTS

Textbook writing is a team enterprise. The eighth edition has integrated ideas and hard work from many people to whom I am grateful. The reviewers and focus group participants of the seventh edition made an especially important contribution. They praised many features, were critical of things that didn't work well, and offered valuable suggestions. I thank the following individuals for their significant contributions to this text.

David Ackerman
University of Alaska, Southeast

Michael Bourke
Houston Baptist University

Jo Anne Duffy
Sam Houston State University

Cheryl Duvall
Mercer University

Patricia Feltes
Southwest Missouri State University

Robert Girling
Sonoma State University

John A. Gould
University of Maryland

Ralph Hanke
Pennsylvania State University

Bruce J. Hanson
Pepperdine University

Guiseppe Labianca
Tulane University

Jane Lemaster
University of Texas–Pan American

Steven Maranville
University of Saint Thomas

Rick Martinez
Baylor University

Janet Near
Indiana University

Julie Newcomer
Texas Woman's University

Asbjorn Osland
George Fox University

Laynie Pizzolatto
Nicholls State University

Samantha Rice
Abilene Christian University

Richard Saaverda
University of Michigan

W. Robert Sampson
University of Wisconsin, Eau Claire

Amy Sevier
University of Southern Mississippi

W. Scott Sherman
Pepperdine University

Thomas Terrell
Coppin State College

Jack Tucci
Southeastern Louisiana University

Judith White
Santa Clara University

Jan Zahrly
University of North Dakota

Among my professional colleagues, I am grateful to my friends and colleagues at Vanderbilt's Owen School—Bruce Barry, Ray Friedman, Neta Moye, Rich Oliver, David Owens, and Bart Victor—for their intellectual stimulation and feedback. I also owe a special debt to Dean Bill Christie for providing the time and resources for me to stay current on the organization design literature and develop the revisions for the text.

I want to extend a special thanks to my editorial associate, Pat Lane. She skillfully drafted materials on a variety of topics and special features, found resources, and did an outstanding job with the copyedited manuscript and page proofs. Pat's personal enthusiasm and care for the content of this text enabled the eighth edition to achieve its high level of excellence.

The team at South-Western also deserves special mention. Joe Sabatino, Acquisitions Editor, did a superb job of designing the project while offering ideas for improvement. Emma Guttler was superb as Developmental Editor, keeping the people and project on schedule while solving problems creatively and quickly. Cliff Kallemeyn, Production Editor, provided superb project coordination and used his creativity and management skills to facilitate the book's on-time completion. In addition, Crystal Chapin and the team at DPS Associates helped to guide me through the details of the production process.

Finally, I want to acknowledge the love and contributions of my wife, Dorothy Marcic. Dorothy has been very supportive of my textbook projects, and has created an environment in which we can grow together. She took the book a giant step forward with her creation of the Workbook and Workshop student exercises, which were a significant addition to the text. I also want to acknowledge the love and support of my daughters Danielle, Amy, Roxanne, Solange, and Elizabeth, who make my life special during our precious time together.

Introduction to Organizations

Chapter 1
Organizations and Organization Theory

part **I**

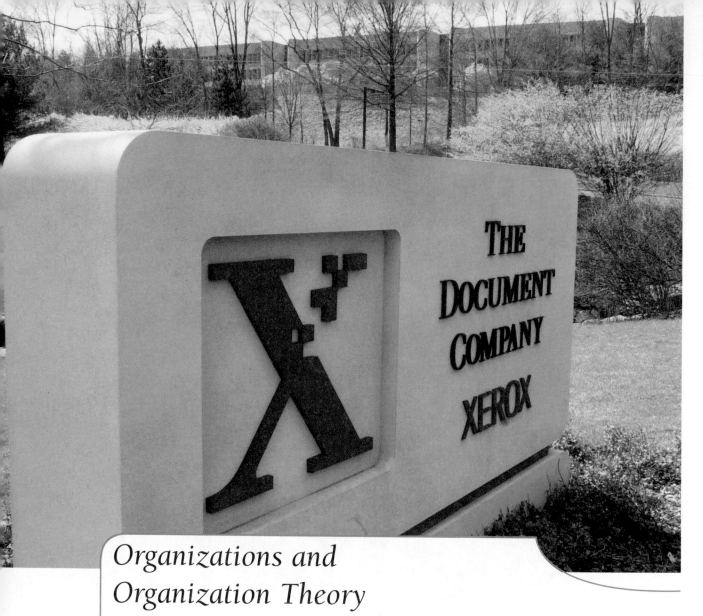

Organizations and Organization Theory

chapter 1

LOOK INSIDE

Xerox Corporation

Not so long ago, Xerox seemed on top of the world, with fast-rising earnings, a soaring stock price, and a new line of computerized copiers/printers that were technologically superior to rival products. Less than two years later, many were questioning whether the once-revered company could survive. Consider the following events in Xerox's recent history:

- Sales and earnings plummeted as rivals caught up with Xerox's high-end digital machines, offering comparable products at lower prices.
- Xerox's losses for the opening year of the twenty-first century totaled $384 million, and the company continued to bleed red ink. Debt mounted to $17 billion.
- The stock fell from a high of $64 to below $4, amid fears the company would file for federal bankruptcy protection. Over an eighteen-month period, Xerox lost $38 billion in shareholder wealth.
- Twenty-two thousand Xerox workers lost their jobs, further weakening the morale and loyalty of remaining employees. Major customers were alienated, too, by a restructuring that threw salespeople into unfamiliar territories and tied billing up in knots, leading to mass confusion and billing errors.
- The company was fined a whopping $10 million by the Securities and Exchange Commission (SEC) for accounting irregularities and alleged fraud.

What went wrong at Xerox? The company's deterioration is a classic story of organizational decline. Although Xerox appeared to fall almost overnight, the organization's recent problems are connected to a series of organizational blunders over a period of many years.

Background

Xerox was founded in 1906 as the Haloid Company, a photographic supply house that developed the world's first xerographic copier, introduced in 1959. Without a doubt, the "914" copier was a money-making machine. By the time it was retired in the early 1970s, the 914 was the best-selling industrial product of all time, and the new name of the company, Xerox, was listed in the dictionary as a synonym for photocopying.

Joseph C. Wilson, Haloid's longtime chairman and president, created a positive, people-oriented culture continued by his successor, David Kearns, who steered Xerox until 1990. The Xerox culture and its dedicated employees (sometimes called "Xeroids") were the envy of the corporate world. In addition to values of fairness and respect, Xerox's culture emphasized risk-taking and employee involvement. Wilson wrote the following for early recruiting materials: "We seek people who are willing to accept risk, willing to try new ideas and have ideas of their own . . . who are not afraid to change what they are doing from one day to the next, and from one year to the next . . . who welcome new people and new positions." Xerox continues to use these words in its recruiting efforts today, but the culture the words epitomize began to erode years ago.

"Burox" Takes Hold

Like many profitable organizations, Xerox became a victim of its own success. Leaders no doubt knew that the company needed to move beyond copiers to sustain its growth, but they found it difficult to look beyond the 70 percent gross profit margins of the 914. Xerox's Palo Alto Research Center (PARC), established in 1970, became known around the world for innovation—many of the most revolutionary technologies in the computer industry, including the personal computer, graphical user interface, Ethernet, and laser printer, were invented at PARC. But the copier bureaucracy, or *Burox* as it came to be known, blinded Xerox leaders to the enormous potential of these innovations. While Xerox was plodding along selling copy machines, younger, smaller, and hungrier companies were developing PARC technologies into tremendous money-making products and services. "At Xerox, unless there's a crisis in the organization, as long as the stock prices are acceptable, it doesn't move very fast," says a former Xerox manager.

The dangers of Burox became dramatically clear in the early 1970s, when the company's xerography patents began expiring. Suddenly, Japanese rivals such as Canon and Ricoh were selling copiers at the cost it took Xerox to make them. Market share declined from 95 percent to 13 percent by 1982. And with no new products to make up the difference, the company had to fight hard to cut costs and reclaim market share by committing to Japanese-style techniques and total quality management. Through the strength of his leadership, CEO Kearns was able to rally the troops and rejuvenate the company by 1990. However, he also set Xerox on a path to future disaster. Seeing a need to diversify, Kearns moved the company into insurance and financial services on a large scale. By the time he turned leadership over to Paul Allaire in 1990, Xerox's balance sheet was crippled by billions of dollars in insurance liabilities.

Entering the Digital Age

Allaire wisely began a methodical, step-by-step plan for extricating Xerox from the insurance and financial services business. At the same time, he initiated a mixed strategy of cost-cutting and new-product introductions to get the stodgy company moving again. Xerox had success with a line of digital presses and new high-speed digital copiers, but it fumbled again by underestimating the threat of the inkjet printer. By the time Xerox introduced its own line of desktop printers, the game was already over.

Desktop printers, combined with increasing use of the Internet and e-mail, cut heavily into Xerox's sales of copiers. People didn't need to make as many photocopies, but there was a huge increase in the number of documents being created and shared. Rebranding Xerox as "The Document Company," Allaire pushed into the digital era, hoping to remake Xerox in the image of the rejuvenated IBM, offering not just "boxes (machines)," but document management solutions.

As part of that strategy, Allaire picked Richard Thoman, who was then serving as Louis Gerstner's right-hand man at IBM, as his successor. Thoman came to Xerox as president, chief operating officer, and eventually CEO amid high hopes that the company could regain the stature of its glory years. Only thirteen months later, as revenues and the stock price continued to slide, he was fired by Allaire, who had remained as Xerox chairman.

Playing Politics

Allaire and Thoman blamed each other for failure to successfully implement the digital strategy. Outsiders, however, believe the failure had much more to do with Xerox's dysfunctional culture. The culture was already slow to adapt. Some say that under Allaire it became almost totally paralyzed by politics. Thoman was brought in to shake things up, but when he tried, the old guard rebelled. A management struggle developed, with the outsider Thoman and a few allies on one side lined up against Allaire and his group of insiders who were accustomed to doing things the Xeroid way. Recognized for his knowledge, business experience, and intensity, Thoman was also considered to be somewhat haughty and unapproachable. He was never able to exert substantial influence with key managers and employees, nor gain the support of board members, who continued to rally behind Allaire.

The failed CEO succession illustrates the massive challenge of reinventing a nearly 100-year-old company. By the time Thoman arrived, Xerox had been going through various rounds of restructuring, cost-cutting, rejuvenating, and reinventing for nearly two decades, but little had really changed. Many believe Thoman tried to do too much too soon. He saw the urgency for change but was unable to convey that urgency to others within the company and inspire them to take the difficult journey real transformation requires. Others doubt that anyone can fix Xerox because the culture has become too dysfunctional and politicized. "There was always an in-crowd and an out-crowd," says one former executive. "They change the branches, but when you look closely, the same old monkeys are sitting in the trees."

The Insider's Insider
Enter Anne Mulcahy, the consummate insider. In August 2001, Allaire turned over the CEO reins to the popular twenty-four-year veteran, who had started at Xerox as a copier saleswoman and worked her way up the hierarchy. Despite her insider status, Mulcahy says she's more than willing to challenge the status quo at Xerox.

Mulcahy is a strong decision maker. One of her first moves was to kill off several money-losing operations, including the company's belatedly launched line of inkjet printers. She personally negotiated the settlement of a long investigation into fraudulent accounting practices, insisting that her personal involvement was necessary to signal a new commitment to ethical business practices. She is searching for a partner to buy equity in the famed PARC research center, which Xerox can no longer afford to operate on its own. She has introduced new products and services that hold promise for increasing revenues and profits. And she has contracted out many functions to other organizations that can do the work more efficiently.

By getting Xerox out of some tough financial jams, Mulcahy has gained respect and admiration from employees, labor leaders, customers, and creditors. Xerox has been taken off the critical list. Yet problems remain and no one, including the CEO, is ready to declare victory just yet. Can Xerox ever regain the prestige it once held in America's corporate landscape? Can it even continue to exist as an independent organization? In the rapidly changing world of organizations, nothing is ever certain.[1]

Welcome to the real world of organization theory. The shifting fortunes of Xerox illustrate organization theory in action. Xerox managers were deeply involved in organization theory each day of their working lives—but they never realized it. Company managers didn't fully understand how the organization related to the environment or how it should function internally. Familiarity with organization theory helps managers analyze and diagnose what is happening and the changes needed to keep the company competitive. Organization theory gives us the tools to explain the decline of Xerox. It helps us understand and explain what happened in the past, as well as what may happen in the future, so that we can manage our organizations more effectively.

Organization Theory in Action

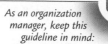

TOPICS

Each of the topics to be covered in this book is illustrated in the Xerox case. Consider, for example, Xerox's failure to respond to or control such elements as competitors, customers, and creditors in the fast-paced external environment; its inability to implement strategic and structural changes to help the organization attain effectiveness; ethical lapses within the organization; difficulties coping with the problems of large size and bureaucracy; lack of adequate cost controls; the negative use of power and politics among managers that created conflict and allowed the organization to drift further into chaos; and an outmoded corporate culture that stifled innovation and change. These are the subjects with which organization theory is concerned. Understanding organization theory can also help Anne Mulcahy and other top leaders as they strive to find the right strategy, structure, and design to revitalize the giant company.

Of course, the concepts of organization theory are not limited to Xerox. Managers at AirTran Airways have applied organization theory concepts to expand their business during a difficult time. Even as many carriers are slashing costs and seeking federal loans to combat huge losses, AirTran has maintained a course of steady growth by developing strong interorganizational partnerships.[2] EBay built a thriving business by applying a new technology to create an online flea market. Kinko's, Hewlett-Packard, and Ford Motor Company have all undergone major structural transformations using concepts based in organization theory. Organization theory also applies to nonprofit organizations such as the Girl Scouts, the American Humane Association, local arts organizations, colleges and universities, and the Make-a-Wish Foundation, which grants wishes to terminally ill children.

Organization theory draws lessons from these organizations and makes those lessons available to students and managers. The story of Xerox's decline is important because it demonstrates that even large, successful organizations are vulnerable, that lessons are not learned automatically, and that organizations are only as strong as their decision makers. Organizations are not static; they continuously adapt to shifts in the external environment. Today, many companies are facing the need to transform themselves into dramatically different organizations because of new challenges in the environment.

CURRENT CHALLENGES

Research into hundreds of organizations provides the knowledge base to make Xerox and other organizations more effective. For example, challenges facing organizations today are quite different from those of the past, and thus the concept of organizations and organization theory is evolving. For one thing, the world is changing more rapidly than ever before. In a survey of top executives, coping with rapid change emerged as the most common problem facing managers and organizations.[3] Some specific challenges are competing globally, maintaining high standards of ethics and social responsibility, responding rapidly to environmental changes and customer needs, managing the digital workplace, and supporting diversity.

Global Competition. The cliché that the world is getting smaller is dramatically true for today's organizations. With rapid advances in technology and communications, the time it takes to exert influence around the world from even the most remote locations has been reduced from years to only seconds. Business is becoming a unified global field as trade barriers fall, communication becomes faster and cheaper, and consumer tastes in everything from clothing to cellular phones converge. In the twenty-first century, organizations will have to feel "at home" anywhere in the world. Companies can locate different parts of the organization wherever it makes the most business sense: top leadership in one country, technical brainpower and production in other locales. A related trend is to contract out some functions to organizations in other countries or to partner with foreign organizations to gain global advantage. General Motors entered into a joint venture with Russian automaker Avtovaz to sell an Avtovaz-designed sport utility vehicle under the Chevrolet name in emerging markets around the world.[4] Companies such as Nortel Networks, Reebok, and American Express contract with information technology companies in India to manage activities like accounting, inventory management, payroll, billing, and credit card approvals. Korea's Samsung Electronics, which has manufacturing plants in fourteen countries, has long supplied components for U.S. computer firms, and it recently designed a new laptop that it will manufacture for Texas-based Dell Computer Corp.[5]

Although this growing interdependence brings many advantages, it also means that the environment for companies is becoming extremely complex and extremely competitive. Organizations have to learn to cross lines of time, culture, and geography in order to survive. Companies large and small are searching for the right structures and processes that can help them reap the advantages of global interdependence and minimize the disadvantages.

Ethics and Social Responsibility. Ethics and social responsibility has become one of the hottest topics in corporate America. As this text is being written, the list of major corporations involved in financial scandals continues to grow. The sordid story began when leaders at high-flying Enron Corporation admitted they inflated earnings and hid debt through a series of complex partnerships. Executives profited handsomely from the fraud, but when the company collapsed, employees and average investors lost billions. Arthur Andersen LLP, the company's auditor, was found guilty of obstruction of justice for improperly shredding tons of documents. Within months after the Enron debacle, the ethical storm hit full force. Executives at WorldCom were accused of inappropriate accounting practices that inflated company profits by a whopping $3.8 billion. Tyco's revered former CEO was charged with tax evasion and accused of secret deals to use Tyco funds for personal expenses. Adelphia Communications came under investigation for failing to properly disclose $3.9 billion in loans to its founder's family. And ImClone executives were accused of tipping off friends and family members, including domestic-style maven Martha Stewart, to sell their shares of ImClone stock after learning that the FDA would not approve ImClone's key drug.[6] The list goes on and on. This is corporate corruption on a scale never before seen, and the effects within organizations and society will be felt for years to come.

Although some executives and officials continue to insist that it is a few bad apples involved in all the wrongdoing, the "man on the street" is quickly forming the opinion that all corporate executives are crooks.[7] The public is disgusted with the whole mess, and leaders will face tremendous pressure from government and the public to hold their organizations and employees to high ethical and professional standards.

Speed of Responsiveness. A third significant challenge for organizations is to respond quickly and decisively to environmental changes, organizational crises, or shifting customer expectations. For much of the twentieth century, organizations operated in a relatively stable environment, so managers could focus on designing structures and systems that kept the organization running smoothly and efficiently. There was little need to search for new ways to cope with increased competition, volatile environmental shifts, or changing customer demands. All that began to change in the 1980s, and the situation today is dramatically different. Leaders find that their organizations must be constantly poised for change and adaptation. This chapter's Leading by Design box describes how Royal Dutch/Shell has applied new concepts to create an organization that can rapidly respond to environmental shifts.

Today's customers expect new products and services developed more often and delivered more rapidly, and organizations must respond to these new demands. In addition, people today want products and services tailored to their exact needs. Companies that relied on mass production and distribution techniques must be prepared with new computer-aided systems that can produce one-of-a-kind variations and streamlined distribution systems that deliver products directly from the manufacturer to the consumer. Another shift brought about by technology is that the financial basis of today's economy is *information*, not machines and factories. For example, fifty years ago, tangible assets represented 73 percent of the assets of nonfinancial corporations in the United States. Today, the proportion is down to about 53 percent.[8] One result of concern to organizational leaders is that the primary factor of production becomes knowledge, to which managers must respond by increasing the power of employees. Employees, not production machinery, have the power and knowledge needed to keep the company competitive.

Considering the turmoil and flux inherent in today's world, the mindset needed by organizational leaders is to expect the unexpected and be prepared for rapid change and potential crises. Crisis management has moved to the forefront in light of terrorist attacks in the United States; a tough economy, rocky stock market, and weakening consumer confidence; widespread ethical scandals; and, in general, an environment that may shift dramatically at a moment's notice.

The Digital Workplace. Many traditional managers feel particularly awkward in today's technology-driven workplace. Organizations have been engulfed by information technology that affects how they are designed and managed. In today's workplace, many employees perform much of their work on computers and may work in virtual teams, connected electronically to colleagues around the world. In addition, organizations are becoming enmeshed in electronic networks. The world of e-business is booming as more and more business takes place by digital processes over a computer network rather than in physical space. Some companies have taken e-business to very high levels to achieve amazing performance. Dell Computer Corp. pioneered the use of end-to-end digital supply-chain networks to keep in touch with customers, take orders, buy components from suppliers, coordinate with manufacturing partners, and ship customized products directly to consumers. This trend toward *disintermediation*—eliminating the middleman—is affecting every industry, prompting a group of consultants at a Harvard University conference to conclude that businesses today must either "Dell or Be Delled."[9] These advances mean that organizational leaders not only need to be technologically savvy but are also responsible for managing a web of relationships that reaches far beyond the boundaries of the physical organization, building flexible e-links between a company and its employees, suppliers, contract partners, and customers.[10]

Diversity. Diversity is a fact of life that no organization can afford to ignore. The workforce—as well as the customer base—is changing in terms of age, gender, race, national origin, sexual orientation, and physical ability. For one thing, organizations increasingly have an international face. Look at the makeup of consulting firm McKinsey & Co. In the 1970s, most consultants were American, but

LEADING BY DESIGN   *Royal Dutch/Shell*

Top managers at Royal Dutch/Shell have found a way to get almost immediate feedback from employees on the front lines and keep the whole company in touch with changes in the marketplace and customer needs. But creating a system in which frontline employees and managers work as collaborators wasn't easy.

When Steve Miller was appointed group managing director of Shell's worldwide oil products business (known in the company as *Downstream*), the group had been through two years of massive reorganizations, traumatic layoffs, and management workshops that accomplished little beyond destroying morale. Real transformation began only when Miller decided to stop treating the Downstream business like a machine to be driven and instead began thinking about it as a living system that needed to adapt and evolve.

Miller believed that the only way to achieve real and lasting change was to unleash potential from below rather than pushing solutions from above. He wanted to reach around the resistant bureaucracy and rigid culture to directly involve employees on the front lines, or, as he phrases it, "at the coal face," in determining the company's strategic direction. Senior leaders worked directly with grassroots employees in six-member cross-functional teams from operating companies around the world. Over time, these intense but informal sessions helped to define a more relaxed give-and-take culture.

Miller relied on techniques such as the "fishbowl" to create trust and establish a less hierarchical way of working. The fishbowl put Miller and other top managers in the middle of the room with one team while other team members listened in the outer circle. The group had to negotiate what they were going to do and how top management would support them. Initial resistance from

managers melted as they saw that the best ideas came from the lower ranks who were in direct contact with customers, and employee distrust dissipated as senior members followed through on their commitments.

Miller was promoted to chairman and CEO of Shell's U.S. division in 1999 and retired from the company in 2002, but the process he used in the Downstream business became an important part of a company-wide reorganization that shifted the locus of power and control closer to employees on the front lines. Today, teamwork and collaboration have become the way Shell does all its work. Managers strive to encourage full expression of individual creativity and initiative at all levels to foster new ways of doing business and solving problems.

Shell's new strategic approach can be thought of as *design for emergence.* "Top-down strategies don't win ballgames," Miller says. "Experimentation, rapid learning, and seizing the momentum of success is the better approach." Design for emergence recognizes that thousands of strategic choices have to be made every day by people closest to the action, rather than assuming that the people at the top have all the answers. Managers' responsibility is to design a learning experience, not to provide rules, solutions, and authority. "The truth is, it's scary at first," says Miller. "It's scary for me. It's scary for the team. But the track record has been incredible." Since 1995, ideas from frontline employees have led to solutions that are improving efficiency and cutting costs at a rate of $4 billion a year.

Sources: Richard T. Pascale, *Surfing the Edge of Chaos: The Laws of Nature and the New Laws of Business* (New York: Crown Publishers, 2000); "Surfing the Edge of Chaos," *Sloan Management Review* (Spring 1999), 83–94; "Change How You Define Leadership and You Change How You Run a Company," *Fast Company* (April–May 1998), 110–120; and Ian Wylie, "There Is No Alternative To . . .," *Fast Company* (July 2002), 106–110.

by 1999, McKinsey's chief partner was a foreign national (Rajat Gupta from India), only 40 percent of consultants were American, and the firm's foreign-born consultants came from forty different countries.[11] In addition, today's average worker is older, and many more women, people of color, and immigrants are seeking job and advancement opportunities.

The demographics of the U.S. population and workforce are shifting dramatically. Minorities are expected to make up 40 percent of people entering the workforce during the first decade of the twenty-first century, with many of those first-generation immigrants and almost two-thirds female. By 2020, it is estimated that women will make up fully half of the total full-time U.S. workforce. Already, white males, the majority of workers in the past, represent less than half of the workforce.[12] This growing diversity brings a variety of challenges, such as maintaining a strong corporate culture while supporting diversity, balancing work and family concerns, and coping with the conflict brought about by varying cultural styles.

People from diverse ethnic and cultural backgrounds offer varying styles, and organizations must learn to welcome and incorporate this diversity into the upper ranks. For example, recent research has indicated that women's style of doing business may hold important lessons for success in the emerging world of the twenty-first century. Yet the glass ceiling persists, keeping women from reaching positions of top leadership.[13]

PURPOSE OF THIS CHAPTER

The purpose of this chapter is to explore the nature of organizations and organization theory today. Organization theory has developed from the systematic study of organizations by scholars. Concepts are obtained from living, ongoing organizations. Organization theory can be practical, as illustrated in the Xerox case. It helps people understand, diagnose, and respond to emerging organizational needs and problems.

The next section begins with a formal definition of organization and then explores introductory concepts for describing and analyzing organizations. Next, the scope and nature of organization theory are discussed more fully. Succeeding sections examine the history of organization theory and design, the development of new organizational forms in response to changes in the environment, and how organization theory can help people manage complex organizations in today's rapidly changing world. The chapter closes with a brief overview of the themes to be covered in this book.

WHAT IS AN ORGANIZATION?

Organizations are hard to see. We see outcroppings, such as a tall building or a computer workstation or a friendly employee; but the whole organization is vague and abstract and may be scattered among several locations, even around the world. We know organizations are there because they touch us every day. Indeed, they are so common that we take them for granted. We hardly notice that we are born in a hospital, have our birth records registered in a government agency, are educated in schools and universities, are raised on food produced on corporate farms, are treated by doctors engaged in a joint practice, buy a house built by a construction company and sold by a real estate agency, borrow money from a bank, turn to police and fire departments when trouble erupts, use moving companies to change residences, receive an array of benefits from government agencies, spend forty hours a week working in an organization, and are even laid to rest by an undertaker.[14]

DEFINITION

Organizations as diverse as a church, a hospital, and Xerox have characteristics in common. The definition used in this book to describe organizations is as follows: **organizations** are (1) social entities that (2) are goal-directed, (3) are designed as deliberately structured and coordinated activity systems, and (4) are linked to the external environment.

The key element of an organization is not a building or a set of policies and procedures; organizations are made up of people and their relationships with one another. An organization exists when people interact with one another to perform essential functions that help attain goals. Recent trends in management recognize the importance of human resources, with most new approaches designed to empower employees with greater opportunities to learn and contribute as they work together toward common goals. Managers deliberately structure and coordinate organizational resources to achieve the organization's purpose. However, even though work may be structured into separate departments or sets of activities, most organizations today are striving for greater horizontal coordination of work activities, often using teams of employees from different functional areas to work together on projects. Boundaries between departments as well as those between organizations are becoming more flexible and diffuse as companies face the need to respond to changes in the external environment more rapidly. An organization cannot exist without interacting with customers, suppliers, competitors, and other elements of the external environment. Today, some companies are even cooperating with their competitors, sharing information and technology to their mutual advantage.

TYPES OF ORGANIZATIONS

Some organizations are large, multinational corporations. Others are small, family-owned shops. Some manufacture products such as automobiles or computers, whereas others provide services such as legal representation, banking, or medical services. Later in this text, Chapter 7 will look at the distinctions between manufacturing and service technologies. Chapter 9 discusses size and life cycle and describes some differences between small and large organizations.

Another important distinction is between for-profit businesses and *nonprofit organizations*. All of the topics in this text apply to nonprofit organizations such as the Salvation Army, the World Wildlife Fund, the Save the Children Foundation, and Chicago's La Rabida Hospital, which is dedicated to serving the poor, just as they do to such businesses as Starbucks Coffee, eBay, or Blockbuster Video. However, there are some important dissimilarities to keep in mind. The primary difference is that managers in businesses direct their activities toward earning money for the company, while managers in nonprofits direct their efforts toward generating some kind of social impact. The unique characteristics and needs of nonprofit organizations created by this distinction present unique challenges for organizational leaders.[15]

Financial resources for nonprofits typically come from government appropriations, grants, and donations rather than from the sale of products or services to customers. In businesses, managers focus on improving the organization's products and services to increase sales revenues. In nonprofits, however, services are typically provided to nonpaying clients, and a major problem for many organizations is securing a steady stream of funds to continue operating. Nonprofit managers, committed to serving clients with limited funds, must focus on keeping organizational costs as low as possible and demonstrating a highly efficient use of resources.[16] Another problem is that, since nonprofit organizations do not have a conventional "bottom line," managers often struggle with the question of what constitutes organizational effectiveness. It is easy to measure dollars and cents, but nonprofits have to measure intangible goals such as "improve public health" or "make a difference in the lives of the disenfranchised."

Managers in nonprofit organizations also deal with many diverse stakeholders and must market their services to attract not only clients (customers) but also volunteers and donors. This can sometimes create conflict and power struggles among organizations, as illustrated by the Make-a-Wish Foundation, which is butting heads with small, local wish-granting groups as it expands to cities across the United States. The more kids a group can count as helping, the easier it is to raise money. As charitable donations in general have declined with the economy, the issue has become serious. Small groups are charging that Make-a-Wish is abusing the power of its national presence to overwhelm or absorb the smaller groups. "We should not have to compete for children and money," says the director of the Indiana Children's Wish Fund. "They [Make-a-Wish] use all their muscle and money to get what they want."[17]

Thus, the organization design concepts discussed throughout this book, such as setting goals and measuring effectiveness, coping with environmental uncertainty, implementing effective control mechanisms, satisfying multiple stakeholders, and dealing with issues of power and conflict, apply to nonprofit organizations such as the Make-a-Wish Foundation just as they do to Xerox Corp., as described in the chapter opening. These concepts and theories are adapted and revised as needed to fit unique needs and problems.

IMPORTANCE OF ORGANIZATIONS

It may seem hard to believe today, but organizations as we know them are relatively recent in the history of humankind. Even in the late nineteenth century there were few organizations of any size or importance—no labor unions, no trade associations, and few large businesses, nonprofit organizations, or governmental departments. What a change has occurred since then! The Industrial Revolution and the development of large organizations transformed all of society. Gradually, organizations became central to people's lives and today they exert a tremendous influence in our society.[18]

Organizations are all around us and shape our lives in many ways. But what contributions do organizations make? Why are they important? Exhibit 1.1 lists seven reasons organizations are important to you and to society. First, organizations bring together resources to accomplish specific goals. Consider Northrup Grumman Newport News (formerly Newport News Shipbuilding), which builds nuclear-powered, Nimitz-class aircraft carriers. Putting together an aircraft carrier is an incredibly complex job involving 47,000 tons of precision-welded steel,

EXHIBIT 1.1   *Importance of Organizations*

Organizations exist to do the following:
1. Bring together resources to achieve desired goals and outcomes
2. Produce goods and services efficiently
3. Facilitate innovation
4. Use modern manufacturing and information technologies
5. Adapt to and influence a changing environment
6. Create value for owners, customers, and employees
7. Accommodate ongoing challenges of diversity, ethics, and the motivation and coordination of employees

more than a million distinct parts, 900 miles of wire and cable, about 40 million skilled-worker hours, and more than seven years of hard work by the organization's 17,800 employees.[19]

Organizations also produce goods and services that customers want at competitive prices. Companies look for innovative ways to produce and distribute goods and services more efficiently. Two ways are through e-business, as discussed earlier, and through the use of computer-based manufacturing technologies. Redesigning organizational structures and management practices can also contribute to increased efficiency. Organizations create a drive for innovation rather than a reliance on standard products and outmoded ways of doing things.

Organizations adapt to and influence a rapidly changing environment. The Make-a-Wish Foundation is adapting to the environment by expanding services to new locations in an effort to secure more donations during a time when charitable donations are declining. Some large businesses have entire departments charged with monitoring the external environment and finding ways to adapt to or influence that environment. One of the most significant changes in the external environment today is globalization. Organizations such as Coca-Cola, AES Corporation, Heineken Breweries, and IBM are involved in strategic alliances and partnerships with companies around the world in an effort to influence the environment and compete on a global scale.

Through all of these activities, organizations create value for their owners, customers, and employees. Managers need to understand which parts of the operation create value and which parts do not; a company can be profitable only when the value it creates is greater than the cost of resources. Gallo, which produces one of every four bottles of wine sold in the United States, made a thorough study of how to use its core competency as a low-cost producer to create better value for customers. Managers' strategic evaluation led to introduction of the new Gallo of Sonoma line, which offers upscale wines at prices from $1 to $30 less per bottle than comparable-quality competitors.[20] Finally, organizations have to cope with and accommodate today's challenges of workforce diversity and growing concerns over ethics and social responsibility, as well as find effective ways to motivate employees to work together to accomplish organizational goals.

Organizations shape our lives, and well-informed managers can shape organizations. An understanding of organization theory enables managers to design organizations to function more effectively.

Perspectives on Organizations

There are various ways to look at and think about organizations and how they function. Two important perspectives are the open systems approach and the organizational configuration framework.

Open Systems

One significant development in the study of organizations was the distinction between closed and open systems.[21] A **closed system** would not depend on its environment; it would be autonomous, enclosed, and sealed off from the outside world. Although a true closed system cannot exist, early organization studies focused on internal systems. Early management concepts, including scientific management, leadership style, and industrial engineering, were closed-system approaches because they took the environment for granted and assumed the organization could be made more effective through internal design. The management of a closed system would be quite easy. The environment would be stable and predictable and would not intervene to cause problems. The primary management issue would be to run things efficiently.

An **open system** must interact with the environment to survive; it both consumes resources and exports resources to the environment. It cannot seal itself off. It must continuously adapt to the environment. Open systems can be enormously complex. Internal efficiency is just one issue—and sometimes a minor one. The organization has to find and obtain needed resources, interpret and act on environmental changes, dispose of outputs, and control and coordinate internal activities in the face of environmental disturbances and uncertainty. Every system that must interact with the environment to survive is an open system. The human being is an open system. So is the planet earth, the city of New York, and Xerox Corp. Indeed, one problem at Xerox was that top managers seemed to forget they were part of an open system. They isolated themselves within the bureaucratic culture and failed to pay close attention to what was going on with their customers, suppliers, and competitors. The rapid changes over the past few decades, including globalization and increased competition, the explosion of the Internet and e-business, and the growing diversity of the population and workforce, have forced many managers to reorient toward an open-systems mindset and recognize their business as part of a complex, interconnected whole.

To understand the whole organization, we must view it as a system. A **system** is a set of interacting elements that acquires inputs from the environment, transforms them, and discharges outputs to the external environment. The need for inputs and outputs reflects dependency on the environment. Interacting elements mean that people and departments depend on one another and must work together.

Exhibit 1.2 illustrates an open system. Inputs to an organization system include employees, raw materials and other physical resources, information, and financial resources. The transformation process changes these inputs into something of value that can be exported back to the environment. Outputs include specific products and services for customers and clients. Outputs may also include employee satisfaction, pollution, and other by-products of the transformation process.

EXHIBIT 1.2   *An Open System and its Subsystems*

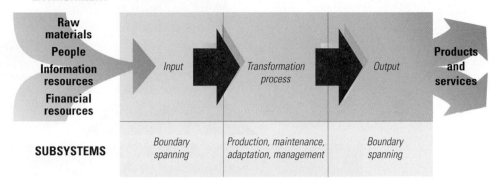

A system is made up of several **subsystems**, as illustrated at the bottom of Exhibit 1.2. These subsystems perform the specific functions required for organizational survival, such as production, boundary spanning, maintenance, adaptation, and management. The production subsystem produces the product and service outputs of the organization. Boundary subsystems are responsible for exchanges with the external environment. They include activities such as purchasing supplies or marketing products. The maintenance subsystem maintains the smooth operation and upkeep of the organization's physical and human elements. The adaptive subsystems are responsible for organizational change and adaptation. Management is a distinct subsystem, responsible for coordinating and directing the other subsystems of the organization.

ORGANIZATIONAL CONFIGURATION

Various parts of the organization are designed to perform the key subsystem functions illustrated in Exhibit 1.2. One framework proposed by Henry Mintzberg suggests that every organization has five parts.[22] These parts, illustrated in Exhibit 1.3, include the technical core, top management, middle management, technical support, and administrative support. The five parts of the organization may vary in size and importance depending on the organization's environment, technology, and other factors.

Technical Core. The technical core includes people who do the basic work of the organization. It performs the production subsystem function and actually produces the product and service outputs of the organization. This is where the primary transformation from inputs to outputs takes place. The technical core is the production department in a manufacturing firm, the teachers and classes in a university, and the medical activities in a hospital. At Xerox, the technical core produces copiers, digital presses, and document management services for customers.

Technical Support. The technical support function helps the organization adapt to the environment. Technical support employees such as engineers and researchers scan the environment for problems, opportunities, and technological developments. Technical support is responsible for creating innovations in the technical core, helping the organization change and adapt. Technical support at

EXHIBIT 1.3   *Five Basic Parts of an Organization*

Source: Based on Henry Mintzberg, *The Structuring of Organizations* (Englewood Cliffs, N.J.: Prentice-Hall, 1979), 215–297; and Henry Mintzberg, "Organization Design: Fashion or Fit?" *Harvard Business Review* 59 (January–February 1981): 103–116.

Xerox is provided by departments such as technology, research and development, and marketing research.

Administrative Support.   The administrative support function is responsible for the smooth operation and upkeep of the organization, including its physical and human elements. This includes human resource activities such as recruiting and hiring, establishing compensation and benefits, and employee training and development, as well as maintenance activities such as cleaning of buildings and service and repair of machines. Administrative support functions in a corporation such as Xerox might include the human resource department, organizational development, the employee cafeteria, and the maintenance staff.

Management.   Management is a distinct subsystem, responsible for directing and coordinating other parts of the organization. Top management provides direction, strategy, goals, and policies for the entire organization or major divisions. Middle management is responsible for implementation and coordination at the departmental level. In traditional organizations, middle managers are responsible for mediating between top management and the technical core, such as implementing rules and passing information up and down the hierarchy.

In real-life organizations, the five parts are interrelated and often serve more than one subsystem function. For example, managers coordinate and direct other parts of the system, but they may also be involved in administrative and technical support. In addition, several of the parts serve the *boundary spanning* function mentioned in the previous section. For example, in the administrative support realm, human resource departments are responsible for working with the external environment to find quality employees. Purchasing departments acquire needed materials and supplies. In the technical support area, research and development departments work directly with the external environment to learn about new technological developments. Managers perform boundary spanning as well, such as when Anne Mulcahy of Xerox negotiated directly with the SEC regarding accounting irregularities. The important boundary spanning subsystem is embraced by several areas, rather than being confined to one part of the organization.

DIMENSIONS OF ORGANIZATION DESIGN

The systems view pertains to dynamic, ongoing activities within organizations. The next step for understanding organizations is to look at dimensions that describe specific organizational design traits. These dimensions describe organizations much the same way that personality and physical traits describe people.

Organizational dimensions fall into two types: structural and contextual, illustrated in Exhibit 1.4. **Structural dimensions** provide labels to describe the internal characteristics of an organization. They create a basis for measuring and comparing organizations. **Contextual dimensions** characterize the whole organization, including its size, technology, environment, and goals. They describe the organizational setting that influences and shapes the structural dimensions. Contextual dimensions can be confusing because they represent both the organization and the environment. Contextual dimensions can be envisioned as a set of overlapping elements that underlie an organization's structure and work processes. To understand and evaluate organizations, one must examine both structural and contextual dimensions.[23] These dimensions of organization design interact with one another and can be adjusted to accomplish the purposes listed earlier in Exhibit 1.1.

STRUCTURAL DIMENSIONS   ✓

1. *Formalization* pertains to the amount of written documentation in the organization. Documentation includes procedures, job descriptions, regulations, and policy manuals. These written documents describe behavior and

EXHIBIT 1.4   *Interacting Contextual and Structural Dimensions of Organization Design*

The Organization

Goals and Strategy

Environment

Size

Culture

Structure
1. Formalization
2. Specialization
3. Hierarchy of authority
4. Centralization
5. Professionalism
6. Personnel ratios

Technology

activities. Formalization is often measured by simply counting the number of pages of documentation within the organization. Large state universities, for example, tend to be high on formalization because they have several volumes of written rules for such things as registration, dropping and adding classes, student associations, dormitory governance, and financial assistance. A small, family-owned business, in contrast, may have almost no written rules and would be considered informal.

2. *Specialization* is the degree to which organizational tasks are subdivided into separate jobs. If specialization is extensive, each employee performs only a narrow range of tasks. If specialization is low, employees perform a wide range of tasks in their jobs. Specialization is sometimes referred to as the *division of labor*.

3. *Hierarchy of authority* describes who reports to whom and the span of control for each manager. The hierarchy is depicted by the vertical lines on an organization chart, as illustrated in Exhibit 1.5. The hierarchy is related to span of control (the number of employees reporting to a supervisor). When *spans of control* are narrow, the hierarchy tends to be tall. When spans of control are wide, the hierarchy of authority will be shorter.

4. *Centralization* refers to the hierarchical level that has authority to make a decision. When decision making is kept at the top level, the organization is centralized. When decisions are delegated to lower organizational levels, it is decentralized. Organizational decisions that might be centralized or decentralized include purchasing equipment, establishing goals, choosing suppliers, setting prices, hiring employees, and deciding marketing territories.

5. *Professionalism* is the level of formal education and training of employees. Professionalism is considered high when employees require long periods of training to hold jobs in the organization. Professionalism is generally measured as the average number of years of education of employees, which could be as high as twenty in a medical practice and less than ten in a construction company.

6. *Personnel ratios* refer to the deployment of people to various functions and departments. Personnel ratios include the administrative ratio, the clerical ratio, the professional staff ratio, and the ratio of indirect to direct labor employees. A personnel ratio is measured by dividing the number of employees in a classification by the total number of organizational employees.

CONTEXTUAL DIMENSIONS

1. *Size* is the organization's magnitude as reflected in the number of people in the organization. It can be measured for the organization as a whole or for specific components, such as a plant or division. Because organizations are social systems, size is typically measured by the number of employees. Other measures such as total sales or total assets also reflect magnitude, but they do not indicate the size of the human part of the social system.

2. *Organizational technology* refers to the tools, techniques, and actions used to transform inputs into outputs. It concerns how the organization actually produces the products and services it provides for customers and includes such things as flexible manufacturing, advanced information systems, and the Internet. An automobile assembly line, a college classroom, and an overnight package delivery system are technologies, although they differ from one another.

EXHIBIT 1.5   Organization Chart Illustrating the Hierarchy of Authority for a Community Job Training Program

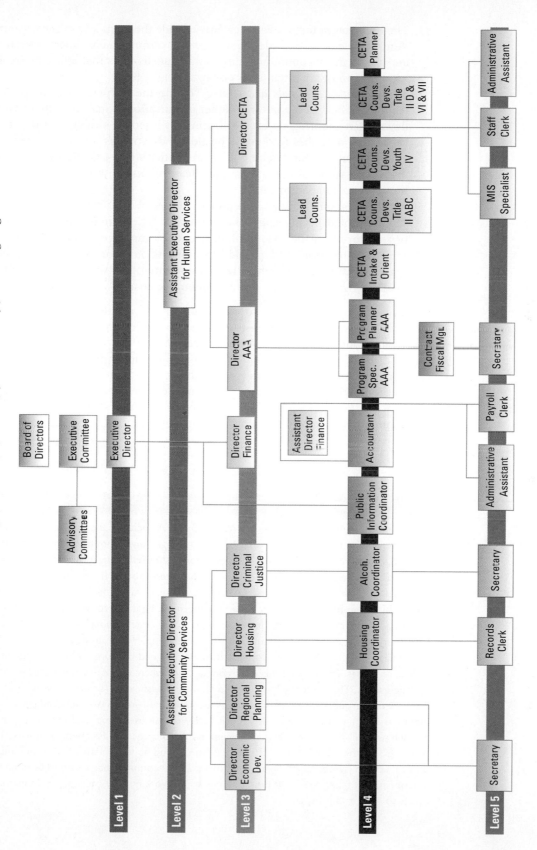

3. The *environment* includes all elements outside the boundary of the organization. Key elements include the industry, government, customers, suppliers, and the financial community. Environmental elements that affect an organization the most are often other organizations.

4. The organization's *goals and strategy* define the purpose and competitive techniques that set it apart from other organizations. Goals are often written down as an enduring statement of company intent. A strategy is the plan of action that describes resource allocation and activities for dealing with the environment and for reaching the organization's goals. Goals and strategies define the scope of operations and the relationship with employees, customers, and competitors.

5. An organization's *culture* is the underlying set of key values, beliefs, understandings, and norms shared by employees. These underlying values may pertain to ethical behavior, commitment to employees, efficiency, or customer service, and they provide the glue to hold organization members together. An organization's culture is unwritten but can be observed in its stories, slogans, ceremonies, dress, and office layout.

The eleven contextual and structural dimensions discussed here are interdependent. For example, large organization size, a routine technology, and a stable environment all tend to create an organization that has greater formalization, specialization, and centralization. More detailed relationships among the dimensions are explored in later chapters of this book.

These dimensions provide a basis for the measurement and analysis of characteristics that cannot be seen by the casual observer, and they reveal significant information about an organization. Consider, for example, the dimensions of W. L. Gore & Associates compared with those of Wal-Mart and a governmental agency.

W. L. GORE & ASSOCIATES

When Jack Dougherty began work at W. L. Gore & Associates, Inc., he reported to Bill Gore, the company's founder, to receive his first assignment. Gore told him, "Why don't you find something you'd like to do." Dougherty was shocked at the informality but quickly recovered and began interrogating various managers about their activities. He was attracted to a new product called GORE-TEX, a membrane that was waterproof but breathable when bonded to fabric. The next morning, he came to work dressed in jeans and began helping feed fabric into the maw of a large laminator. Five years later, Dougherty was responsible for marketing and advertising in the fabrics group.

Bill Gore died in 1986, but the organization he designed still runs without official titles, orders, or bosses. People are expected to find a place where they can contribute and manage themselves. The company has some six thousand associates (not employees) in forty-five locations around the world. The plants are kept small—up to two hundred people—to maintain a family atmosphere. "It's much better to use friendship and love than slavery and whips," Bill Gore said. Several professional employees are assigned to develop new products, but the administrative structure is lean. Good human relations is a more important value than is internal efficiency, and it works. The company has six times been named one of *Fortune* magazine's "100 Best Companies to Work For in America," and Gore continues to grow and prosper.

Contrast that approach to Wal-Mart, where efficiency is the goal. Wal-Mart achieves its competitive edge through employee commitment and internal cost efficiency. A standard formula is used to build each store, with uniform displays and merchandise. Wal-Mart operates about 1,600 discount stores, as well as 1,100 Supercenters, 500 Sam's Clubs, and more than 1,000 international stores. Its administrative expenses are the lowest of any chain. The distribution system is a marvel of efficiency. Goods can be delivered to any store in less than two days after an order is placed. Stores are controlled from the top, but store managers are also given some freedom to adapt to local conditions. Performance is high, and employees are satisfied because the pay is fair and more than half of them share in corporate profits.

An even greater contrast is often seen in government agencies or nonprofit organizations that rely heavily on public funding. Most state humanities and arts agencies, for example, are staffed by only a small number of highly-trained employees, but workers are overwhelmed with rules and regulations and swamped by paperwork. Employees who have to implement rule changes often don't have time to read the continuous stream of memos as well as keep up with their daily work with community arts organizations. Employees must require extensive reporting from their clients in order to make regular reports to a variety of state and federal funding sources. Agency workers are frustrated and so are the community-based organizations they seek to serve. These organizations sometimes refuse assistance because of the extensive paperwork involved.[24]

Exhibit 1.6 illustrates several structural and contextual dimensions of Gore & Associates, Wal-Mart, and the state arts agency. Gore & Associates is a medium-sized manufacturing organization that ranks very low with respect to formalization, specialization, and centralization. A number of professional staff are assigned to nonworkflow activities to do the research and development

Exhibit 1.6   *Characteristics of Three Organizations*

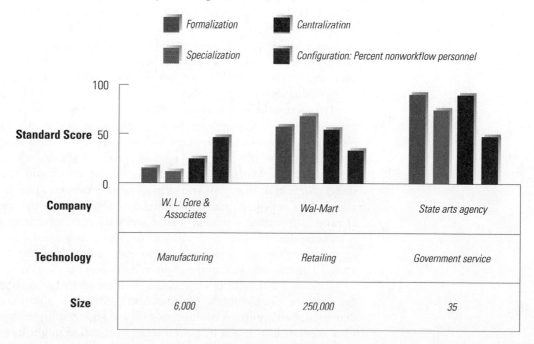

needed to stay abreast of changes in the fiber industry. Wal-Mart is much more formalized, specialized, and centralized. Efficiency is more important than new products, so most activities are guided by standard regulations. The percentage of nonworkflow personnel is kept to a minimum. The arts agency, in contrast to the other organizations, reflects its status as a small part of a large government bureaucracy. The agency is overwhelmed with rules and standard ways of doing things. Rules are dictated from the top. Most employees are assigned to workflow activities, although in normal times a substantial number of people are devoted to administration and clerical support.

Structural and contextual dimensions can thus tell a lot about an organization and about differences among organizations. Organization design dimensions are examined in more detail in later chapters to determine the appropriate level of each dimension needed to perform effectively in each organizational setting.

PERFORMANCE AND EFFECTIVENESS OUTCOMES

BRIEFCASE

As an organization manager, keep this guideline in mind:

Consider the needs and interests of all stakeholders when setting goals and designing the organization to achieve effectiveness.

The whole point of understanding varying perspectives and the structural and contextual dimensions of organizations is to design the organization in such a way as to achieve high performance and effectiveness. Managers adjust structural and contextual dimensions and organizational subsystems to most efficiently and effectively transform inputs into outputs and provide value. **Efficiency** refers to the amount of resources used to achieve the organization's goals. It is based on the quantity of raw materials, money, and employees necessary for producing a given level of output. **Effectiveness** is a broader term, meaning the degree to which an organization achieves its goals.

To be effective, organizations need clear, focused goals and appropriate strategies for achieving them. Strategy, goals, and approaches to measuring effectiveness will be discussed in detail in Chapter 2. Many organizations are using new technology to improve efficiency and effectiveness. Freddie Mac, one of the largest mortgage underwriters in the United States, uses a system that can automatically—and almost instantly—calculate whether to underwrite a home loan. Since the Loan Prospector system was launched, Freddie Mac's transaction volume has increased 200 percent, without the addition of more staff.[25] GE Power Systems has implemented systems that enable designers, customers, and suppliers to use collaboration software and the Internet to build turbines, cutting the time involved by 20 to 30 percent and reducing costly errors and last-minute changes.[26]

However, achieving effectiveness is not always a simple matter because different people want different things from the organization. For customers, the primary concern is high-quality products and services at a reasonable price, whereas employees are mostly concerned with adequate pay, good working conditions, and job satisfaction. Managers carefully balance the needs and interests of various stakeholders in setting goals and striving for effectiveness. This is referred to as the **stakeholder approach**, which integrates diverse organizational activities by looking at various organizational stakeholders and what they want from the organization. A **stakeholder** is any group within or outside of the organization that has a stake in the organization's performance. The satisfaction level of each group can be assessed as an indication of the organization's performance and effectiveness.[27]

Exhibit 1.7 illustrates various stakeholders and what each group wants from the organization. Organizations often find it difficult to simultaneously satisfy the demands of all groups. A business might have high employee satisfaction, but supplier relationships might be poor or the organization might have difficulties with

EXHIBIT 1.7   *Major Stakeholder Groups and What They Expect*

OWNERS AND STOCKHOLDERS
- *Financial return*

EMPLOYEES
- *Satisfaction*
- *Pay*
- *Supervision*

CUSTOMERS
- *High-quality goods, services*
- *Service*
- *Value*

SUPPLIERS
- *Satisfactory transactions*
- *Revenue from purchases*

CREDITORS
- *Creditworthiness*
- *Fiscal responsibility*

COMMUNITY
- *Good corporate citizen*
- *Contribution to community affairs*

ORGANIZATION

UNION
- *Worker pay*
- *Benefits*

GOVERNMENT
- *Obedience to laws and regulations*
- *Fair competition*

MANAGEMENT
- *Efficiency*
- *Effectiveness*

creditors. In addition, stakeholder interests sometimes conflict, such as when unions demand wage increases that might hurt shareholders' financial returns or require a switch to lower cost suppliers. In nonprofit organizations, the needs and interests of clients sometimes conflict with restrictions on use of government funds or contributions from donors. In reality, it is unreasonable to assume that all stakeholders can be equally satisfied. However, if an organization fails to meet the needs of several stakeholder groups, it is probably not meeting its effectiveness goals. Recall from the opening case Xerox's problems with satisfying employees, customers, creditors, stockholders, and government regulators.

Research has shown that the assessment of multiple stakeholder groups is an accurate reflection of organizational effectiveness, especially with respect to organizational adaptability.[28] Moreover, both profit and nonprofit organizations care about their reputations and attempt to shape stakeholders' perceptions of their performance.[29] Managers strive to at least minimally satisfy the interests of all stakeholders. When any one group becomes seriously dissatisfied, it may withdraw its support and hurt future organizational performance. Satisfying multiple stakeholders can be challenging, as illustrated by the following example.

KNIGHT RIDDER

In Practice

Since 1926, Knight Ridder newspapers have won eighty-three Pulitzer prizes. The name was once synonymous with integrity and concern for the public good. But the Pulitzers have been drying up lately. Journalists at the company's string of newspapers, including *The Philadelphia Inquirer* and the *Miami Herald*, are complaining that a relentless pursuit of profits by Knight Ridder is destroying journalistic excellence and overriding the central mission of freely and fairly covering the news.

CEO Tony Ridder finds himself in a tough spot. He is constantly under pressure from shareholders whose main concern is the best possible return on their investment, while at the same time his employees are pushing for less consideration of profits and more consideration of good journalism. Advertisers want better placement of ads and less emphasis on stories that might negatively affect their own companies. Readers want accurate, up-to-date news coverage and interesting stories that touch their own lives.

The battle between the pursuit of profits and the pursuit of quality journalism is one every news organization faces every day. At Knight Ridder, the situation has become critical. Ridder's delicate balancing act has ended up leaving everyone dissatisfied. When he became CEO in 1995, Ridder wanted to impose financial discipline and get the stock price moving upward yet still produce good journalism. He has successfully reduced costs and improved profits, largely by cutting labor costs, but Wall Street is pushing for still higher profit margins. Meanwhile, employees are publicly lambasting Ridder for the company's cost-cutting culture, and several key editors and writers have resigned in frustration. Readers will not be happy either if the quality of the company's newspapers declines. Today, Knight Ridder is neither the beacon of journalism it once was nor the financial triumph Tony Ridder envisioned.[30]

The story of Knight Ridder illustrates how difficult it can be for managers to satisfy multiple stakeholders. Ridder faces a need to reevaluate stakeholder concerns and establish goals that can help to achieve at least minimal satisfaction for major groups.

THE EVOLUTION OF ORGANIZATION THEORY AND DESIGN

Organization theory is not a collection of facts; it is a way of thinking about organizations. Organization theory is a way to see and analyze organizations more accurately and deeply than one otherwise could. The way to see and think about organizations is based on patterns and regularities in organizational design and behavior. Organization scholars search for these regularities, define them, measure them, and make them available to the rest of us. The facts from the research are not as important as the general patterns and insights into organizational functioning.

HISTORICAL PERSPECTIVES

Organization design and management practices have varied over time in response to changes in the larger society.

You may recall from an earlier management course that the modern era of management theory began with the classical management perspective in the late nineteenth and early twentieth century. The emergence of the factory system during the Industrial Revolution posed problems that earlier organizations had not encountered. As work was performed on a much larger scale by a larger number of workers, people began thinking about how to design and manage work in order to increase productivity and help organizations attain maximum efficiency. The classical perspective, which sought to make organizations run like efficient, well-oiled machines, is associated with the development of hierarchy and bureaucratic organizations and remains the basis of much of modern management theory and practice. In this section, we will examine the classical perspective, with its emphasis on efficiency and organization, as well as other perspectives that emerged to address new concerns, such as employee needs and the role of the environment. Elements of each perspective are still used in organization design, although they have been adapted and revised to meet changing needs.

Efficiency is Everything. Pioneered by Frederick Winslow Taylor, **scientific management** postulates that decisions about organizations and job design should be based on precise, scientific study of individual situations.[31] To use this approach, managers develop precise, standard procedures for doing each job, select workers with appropriate abilities, train workers in the standard procedures, carefully plan work, and provide wage incentives to increase output. Taylor's approach is illustrated by the unloading of iron from railcars and reloading finished steel for the Bethlehem Steel plant in 1898. Taylor calculated that with correct movements, tools, and sequencing, each man was capable of loading 47.5 tons per day instead of the typical 12.5 tons. He also worked out an incentive system that paid each man $1.85 per day for meeting the new standard, an increase from the previous rate of $1.15. Productivity at Bethlehem Steel shot up overnight. These insights helped to establish organizational assumptions that the role of management is to maintain stability and efficiency, with top managers doing the thinking and workers doing what they are told.

How to Get Organized. Another subfield of the classical perspective took a broader look at the organization. Whereas scientific management focused primarily on the technical core—on work performed on the shop floor—**administrative principles** looked at the design and functioning of the organization as a whole. For example, Henri Fayol proposed fourteen principles of management, such as "each subordinate receives orders from only one superior" (unity of command) and "similar activities in an organization should be grouped together under one manager" (unity of direction). These principles formed the foundation for modern management practice and organization design.

The scientific management and administrative principles approaches were powerful and gave organizations fundamental new ideas for establishing high productivity and increasing prosperity. Administrative principles in particular contributed to the development of **bureaucratic organizations**, which emphasized designing and managing organizations on an impersonal, rational basis through such elements as clearly defined authority and responsibility, formal recordkeeping, and uniform application of standard rules. Although the term *bureaucracy* has taken on negative connotations in today's organizations, bureaucratic characteristics worked extremely well for the needs of the Industrial Age. One problem with the classical perspective, however, is that it failed to consider the social context and human needs.

What About People? Early work on industrial psychology and human relations received little attention because of the prominence of scientific management. However, a major breakthrough occurred with a series of experiments at a Chicago electric company, which came to be known as the **Hawthorne Studies**. Interpretations of these studies concluded that positive treatment of employees improved their motivation and productivity. The publication of these findings led to a revolution in worker treatment and laid the groundwork for subsequent work examining treatment of workers, leadership, motivation, and human resource management. These human relations and behavioral approaches added new and important contributions to the study of management and organizations.

However, the hierarchical system and bureaucratic approaches that developed during the Industrial Revolution remained the primary approach to organization design and functioning well into the 1970s and 1980s. In general, this approach worked well for most organizations until the past few decades. However, during the 1980s, it began to lead to problems. Increased competition, especially on a global scale, changed the playing field.[32] North American companies had to find a better way.

The 1980s produced new corporate cultures that valued lean staff, flexibility, rapid response to the customer, motivated employees, caring for customers, and quality products.

Over the past two decades, the world of organizations has undergone even more profound and far-reaching changes. The Internet and other advances in information technology, globalization, rapid social and economic changes, and other challenges from the environment call for new management perspectives and more flexible approaches to organization design.

Don't Forget the Environment. Many problems occur when all organizations are treated as similar, which was the case with scientific management and administrative principles approaches that attempted to design all organizations alike. The structures and systems that work in the retail division of a conglomerate will not be appropriate for the manufacturing division. The organization charts and financial procedures that are best for an entrepreneurial Internet firm like eBay or MaMaMedia will not work for a large food processing plant.

Contingency means that one thing depends on other things, and for organizations to be effective, there must be a "goodness of fit" between their structure and the conditions in their external environment.[33] What works in one setting may not work in another setting. There is not one best way. Contingency theory means "it depends." For example, some organizations experience a certain environment, use a routine technology, and desire efficiency. In this situation, a management approach that uses bureaucratic control procedures, a hierarchical structure, and formal communication would be appropriate. Likewise, free-flowing management processes work best in an uncertain environment with a nonroutine technology. The correct management approach is contingent on the organization's situation.

Today, almost all organizations operate in highly uncertain environments. Thus, we are involved in a significant period of transition, in which concepts of organization theory and design are changing as dramatically as they were changed with the dawning of the Industrial Revolution.

CONTEMPORARY ORGANIZATION DESIGN

To a great extent, managers and organizations are still imprinted with the hierarchical, bureaucratic approach that arose more than a century ago. Yet the challenges presented by today's environment—global competitiveness, diversity, ethical concerns, rapid advances in technology, the rise of e-business, a shift to knowledge and information as organizations' most important form of capital, and the growing expectations of workers for meaningful work and opportunities for personal and professional growth—call for dramatically different responses from people and organizations. The perspectives of the past do not provide a road map for navigating the world of business today. Today's managers must design and orchestrate new responses for a dramatically new world. This chapter's Book Mark examines how information technology is contributing to a shift away from rigid, hierarchical structures toward more flexible, collaborative approaches.

BRIEFCASE

As an organization manager, keep this guideline in mind:

Be cautious when applying something that works in one situation to another situation. All organizational systems are not the same. Use organization theory to identify the correct structure, goals, strategy, and management systems for each organization.

BOOK MARK *1.0*   *Have You Read This Book?*

The Company of the Future: How the Communications Revolution Is Changing Management
By Frances Cairncross

Frances Cairncross, author of *The Company of the Future*, asserts that Internet technologies will have an increasingly powerful influence on the structure and management practices of organizations by changing how people share information, use knowledge, and collaborate. The Internet is an amazing tool, yet it still awaits the management innovations that will fully realize its potential as an instrument of economic efficiency and organizational change. Cairncross maintains, "Getting corporate structure right will be just as important for making the best use of Internet technologies as acquiring the right software and hardware."

RULES FOR SURVIVAL IN A NEW BUSINESS ERA

The book offers several essential rules that managers can follow to guide their companies toward a successful future:

- *Build the right structure.* Because the Internet greatly reduces the cost of finding and sharing information, being connected to suppliers and partners, and staying close to customers, companies will become less vertical and hierarchical and more horizontal and modular. Outsourcing, already a key trend, will increase, but managers have to carefully consider which activities need to be kept in-house. For example, the oil giant BP has outsourced much of the routine work of its human resource department to Exult, and everyday aspects of finance and accounting to PricewaterhouseCoopers. However, key activities that determine how the company meets its strategic goals are kept in-house.
- *Manage collaboration.* Companies and teams that are separated by geography and time zones will have new opportunities for teamwork, but virtual

teamwork is effective only when the organization builds an environment of openness, trust and shared understanding, excellent communication, and incentives for collaboration. At BP, "every accomplishment is a team accomplishment." Managers devote 15 to 20 percent of their time to activities that share knowledge—and staff—with other units.
- *Develop leadership.* The real key to success in an Internet world has less to do with technical know-how than with superior leadership that enables the organization to expedite and build on organizational change. Managers define context and standards at every level of the company and then give people freedom to act and innovate, developing leadership throughout the organization. The company of the future will be built on the intelligence, knowledge, and understanding of its employees.

THE SHAPE OF FUTURE COMPANIES

Cairncross takes an extensive look at how the communications revolution is changing organization design and comes out a sober optimist in *The Company of the Future*. Her central message is that the effect of the Internet on how managers structure and run organizations will be long lasting. Managers armed with rules for navigating the new world can recognize the Internet era as the most revolutionary period this generation has ever encountered, yet can also understand that the power of this transformation will accrue only to companies that know their real advantage lies not in technology but in good management.

The Company of the Future: How the Communications Revolution Is Changing Management, by Frances Cairncross, is published by Harvard Business School Press.

Today's organizations and managers may be seen as shifting from a mindset based on mechanical systems to one based on natural and biological systems. These changing beliefs and perceptions affect how we think about organizations and the patterns of behavior within organizations.

For most of the twentieth century, eighteenth-century Newtonian science, which suggests that the world functions as a well-behaved machine, continued to guide managers' thinking about organizations.[34] The environment was perceived as orderly and predictable and the role of managers was to maintain stability. This mindset worked quite well for the industrial age.[35] Growth was a primary criterion for organizational success. Organizations became large and complex, and boundaries between functional departments and between organizations were distinct. Internal structures grew more complex, vertical, and bureaucratic. Leadership was based on solid management principles and tended to be autocratic; communication was primarily through formal memos, letters, and reports. Managers did all the planning and "thought work," while employees did the manual labor in exchange for wages and other compensation.

The environment for today's companies, however, is anything but stable. With the turbulence of recent years, managers can no longer maintain an illusion of order and predictability. The science of **chaos theory** suggests that relationships in complex, adaptive systems—including organizations—are nonlinear and made up of numerous interconnections and divergent choices that create unintended effects and render the universe unpredictable.[36] The world is full of uncertainty, characterized by surprise, rapid change, and confusion. Managers can't measure, predict, or control in traditional ways the unfolding drama inside or outside the organization. However, chaos theory also recognizes that this randomness and disorder occurs within certain larger patterns of order. The ideas of chaos suggest that organizations should be viewed more as natural systems than as well-oiled, predictable machines.

Many organizations are shifting to flexible, decentralized structures that emphasize horizontal collaboration and widespread information sharing. In addition, boundaries between organizations are becoming diffuse, as even competitors form partnerships to compete globally, sometimes joining in virtual or modular organizations that are connected electronically.

In this new environment, many managers are redesigning their companies toward something called the **learning organization**. The learning organization promotes communication and collaboration so that everyone is engaged in identifying and solving problems, enabling the organization to continuously experiment, improve, and increase its capability. The learning organization is based on equality, open information, little hierarchy, and a culture that encourages adaptability and participation, enabling ideas to bubble up from anywhere that can help the organization seize opportunities and handle crises. In a learning organization, the essential value is problem solving, as opposed to the traditional organization designed for efficient performance.

EFFICIENT PERFORMANCE VERSUS THE LEARNING ORGANIZATION

As managers struggle toward the learning organization, they are finding that specific dimensions of the organization have to change. Exhibit 1.8 compares organizations designed for efficient performance with those designed for continuous learning by looking at five elements of organization design: structure, tasks, systems, culture, and strategy. As shown in the exhibit, all of these elements are interconnected and influence one another.

From Vertical to Horizontal Structure. Traditionally, the most common organizational structure has been one in which activities are grouped together by common work from the bottom to the top of the organization. Generally little collaboration occurs across functional departments, and the whole organization is coordinated and controlled through the vertical hierarchy, with decision-making authority

EXHIBIT 1.8   *Two Organization Design Approaches*

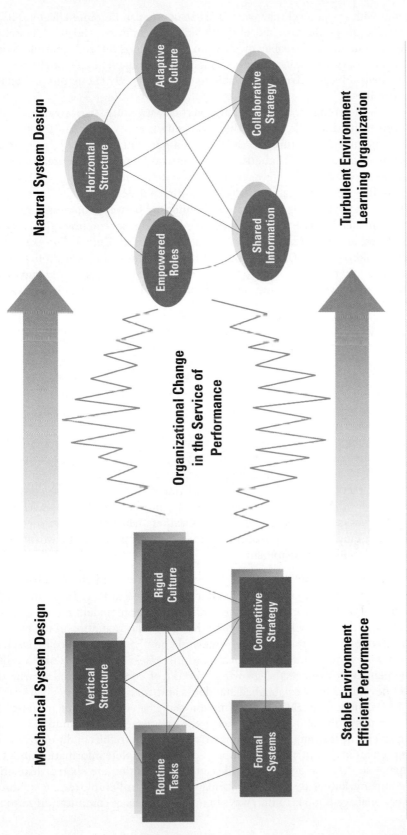

Source: Adapted from David K. Hurst, *Crisis and Renewal: Meeting the Challenge of Organizational Change* (Boston, Mass.: Harvard Business School Press, 1995).

residing with upper-level managers. This structure can be quite effective. It promotes efficient production and in-depth skill development, and the hierarchy of authority provides a sensible mechanism for supervision and control in large organizations. However, in a rapidly changing environment, the hierarchy becomes overloaded. Top executives are not able to respond rapidly enough to problems or opportunities.

In the learning organization, the vertical structure that creates distance between managers at the top of the organization and workers in the technical core is disbanded. Structure is created around horizontal workflows or processes rather than departmental functions. The vertical hierarchy is dramatically flattened, with perhaps only a few senior executives in traditional support functions such as finance or human resources. Self-directed teams are the fundamental work unit in the learning organization. Boundaries between functions are practically eliminated because teams include members from several functional areas. In some cases, organizations do away with departments altogether. For example, at Oticon Holding A/S, a Danish company that introduced the world's first digital hearing aid, there are no organization charts, no departments, no functions, and no titles. Employees are continuously forming and reforming into self-directed teams that work on specific projects.[37]

From Routine Tasks to Empowered Roles. Another shift in thinking relates to the degree of formal structure and control placed on employees in the performance of their work. Recall that scientific management advocated precisely defining each job and how it should be performed. A **task** is a narrowly defined piece of work assigned to a person. In traditional organizations, tasks are broken down into specialized, separate parts, as in a machine. Knowledge and control of tasks are centralized at the top of the organization, and employees are expected to do as they are told. A **role**, in contrast, is a part in a dynamic social system. A role has discretion and responsibility, allowing the person to use his or her discretion and ability to achieve an outcome or meet a goal. In learning organizations, employees play a role in the team or department and roles may be continually redefined or adjusted. There are few rules or procedures, and knowledge and control of tasks are located with workers rather than with supervisors or top executives. Employees are encouraged to take care of problems by working with one another and with customers.

From Formal Control Systems to Shared Information. In young, small organizations, communication is generally informal and face-to-face. There are few formal control and information systems because the top leaders of the company usually work directly with employees in the day-to-day operation of the business. However, when organizations grow large and complex, the distance between top leaders and workers in the technical core increases. Formal systems are often implemented to manage the growing amount of complex information and to detect deviations from established standards and goals.[38]

In learning organizations, information serves a very different purpose. The widespread sharing of information keeps the organization functioning at an optimum level. The learning organization strives to return to the condition of a small, entrepreneurial firm in which all employees have complete information about the company so they can act quickly. Ideas and information are shared throughout the company. Rather than using information to control employees, a significant part of a manager's job is to find ways to open channels of communication so that ideas flow in all directions. In addition, learning organizations maintain open lines of communication with customers, suppliers, and even competitors to enhance learning capability. Information technology is one way to keep people in touch. For example, at Buckman Laboratories, a computerized knowledge network called K'Netix keeps 1,200 employees in 80 countries connected with one another and brings all of the organization's brainpower to bear in serving each customer.[39]

From Competitive to Collaborative Strategy. In traditional organizations designed for efficient performance, strategy is formulated by top managers and imposed on the organization. Top executives think about how the organization can best respond to competition, efficiently use resources, and cope with environmental changes. In the learning organization, in contrast, the accumulated actions of an informed and empowered workforce contribute to strategy development. Since all employees are in touch with customers, suppliers, and new technology, they help identify needs and solutions and participate in strategy making. In addition, strategy emerges from partnerships with suppliers, customers, and even competitors. Organizations become collaborators as well as competitors, experimenting to find the best way to learn and adapt.

From Rigid to Adaptive Culture. For an organization to remain healthy, its culture should encourage adaptation to the external environment. A danger for many organizations is that the culture becomes fixed, as if set in concrete. Organizations that were highly successful in stable environments often became victims of their own success when the environment began to change dramatically. This is what happened at Xerox Corp., as described in the opening case, when managers became stuck in the Burox culture and were unable to respond to rapid changes in the technological environment. The cultural values, ideas, and practices that helped attain success were detrimental to effective performance in a rapidly changing environment.

In a learning organization, the culture encourages openness, equality, continuous improvement, and change. People in the organization are aware of the whole system, how everything fits together, and how the various parts of the organization interact with one another and with the environment. This whole-system mindset minimizes boundaries within the organization and with other companies. In addition, activities and symbols that create status differences, such as executive dining rooms or reserved parking spaces, are discarded. Each person is a valued contributor and the organization becomes a place for creating a web of relationships that allows people to develop their full potential. The emphasis on treating everyone with care and respect creates a climate in which people feel safe to experiment, take risks, and make mistakes, all of which encourages learning.

No company represents a perfect example of a learning organization, although many of today's most competitive organizations have shifted toward ideas and forms based on the concept of a living, dynamic system. Some of these organizations are spotlighted throughout this book in the Leading by Design boxes.

As illustrated in Exhibit 1.8, today's managers are involved in a struggle as they attempt to change their companies into learning organizations. The challenge for managers is to maintain some level of stability as they actively promote change toward the new way of thinking, to navigate between order and chaos.

One organization that is transforming into a learning organization is Mexico's Cementos Mexicanos (Cemex).

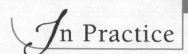

CEMENTOS MEXICANOS

Cementos Mexicanos (Cemex), based in Monterrey, Mexico, has been making and delivering concrete for nearly a century. But the organization is on the cutting edge of organization design, a model of what it takes to succeed in the complex environment of the twenty-first century.

Cemex specializes in delivering concrete in developing areas of the world, places where anything can, and usually does, go wrong. Even in Monterrey, Cemex copes with unpredictable weather and traffic conditions, spontaneous labor disruptions, building permit snafus, and arbitrary government inspections of construction sites. In addition, more than half of all orders are changed or canceled by customers, usually at the last minute. Considering that a load of concrete is never more than ninety minutes from spoiling, those chaotic conditions mean high costs, complex scheduling, and frustration for employees, managers, and customers.

To help the organization compete in this environment, managers looked for both technological and organizational innovations. Leaders call their new approach "living with chaos." Rather than trying to change the customers, Cemex resolved to do business on the customers' own terms and design a system in which last-minute changes and unexpected problems are routine.

A core element of this approach is a complex information technology system, including a global positioning satellite system and onboard computers in all delivery trucks, which is fed with streams of day-to-day data on customer orders, production schedules, traffic problems, weather conditions, and so forth. Now Cemex trucks head out every morning to cruise the streets. When a customer order comes in, an employee checks the customer's credit status, locates a nearby truck, and relays directions for delivery. If the order is cancelled, computers automatically direct the plant to scale back production.

Cemex also made managerial and organizational changes to support the new approach. The company enrolled all its drivers, who had an average of six years of formal schooling, in weekly secondary-education classes and began training them in delivering not just cement but quality service. In addition, many strict and demanding work rules were abolished so that workers had more discretion and responsibility for identifying and rapidly responding to problems and customer needs. As a result, Cemex trucks now operate as self-organizing business units, run by well-trained employees who think like businesspeople. According to Francisco Perez, operations manager at Cemex in Guadalajara, "They used to think of themselves as drivers. But anyone can deliver concrete. Now our people know that they're delivering a service that the competition cannot deliver."

Cemex has transformed the industry by combining extensive networking technology with a new management approach that taps into the mindpower of everyone in the company. People at Cemex are constantly learning—on the job, in training classes, and through visits to other organizations. As a result, the company has a startling capacity to anticipate customer needs, solve problems, and innovate quickly. In addition, Cemex freely shares what it knows with other organizations, even competitors, believing the widespread sharing of knowledge and information is the best way to keep the organization thriving in a world of complexity.[40]

FRAMEWORK FOR THE BOOK

What topic areas are relevant to organization theory and design? How does a course in management or organizational behavior differ from a course in organization theory? The answer is related to the concept called level of analysis.

LEVELS OF ANALYSIS

In systems theory, each system is composed of subsystems. Systems are nested within systems, and one **level of analysis** has to be chosen as the primary focus. Four levels of analysis normally characterize organizations, as illustrated in Exhibit 1.9. The individual human being is the basic building block of organizations. The human being is to the organization what a cell is to a biological system. The next higher system level is the group or department. These are collections of individuals who work together to perform group tasks. The next level of analysis is the organization itself. An organization is a collection of groups or departments that combine into the total organization. Organizations themselves can be grouped together into the next higher level of analysis, which is the interorganizational set and community. The interorganizational set is the group of organizations with which a single organization interacts. Other organizations in the community also make up an important part of an organization's environment.

Organization theory focuses on the organizational level of analysis but with concern for groups and the environment. To explain the organization, one should look not only at its characteristics but also at the characteristics of the environment and of the departments and groups that make up the organization. The focus of this book is to help you understand organizations by examining their specific characteristics, the nature of and relationships among groups and departments that make up the organization, and the collection of organizations that make up the environment.

Are individuals included in organization theory? Organization theory does consider the behavior of individuals, but in the aggregate. People are important, but they are not the primary focus of analysis. Organization theory is distinct from organizational behavior. **Organizational behavior** is the micro approach to organizations because it focuses on the individuals within organizations as the relevant units of analysis. Organizational behavior examines concepts such as motivation, leadership style, and personality and is concerned with cognitive and

EXHIBIT 1.9   *Levels of Analysis in Organizations*

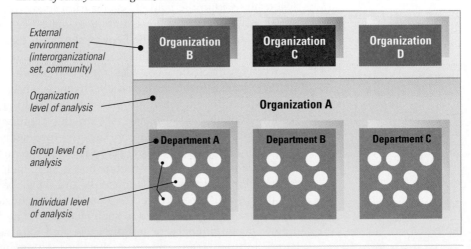

Source: Based on Andrew H. Van De Ven and Diane L. Ferry, *Measuring and Assessing Performance* (New York: Wiley, 1980), 8; and Richard L. Daft and Richard M. Steers, *Organizations: A Micro/Macro Approach* (Glenview, Ill.: Scott, Foresman, 1986), 8.

emotional differences among people within organizations. **Organization theory** is a macro examination of organizations because it analyzes the whole organization as a unit. Organization theory is concerned with people aggregated into departments and organizations and with the differences in structure and behavior at the organization level of analysis. Organization theory is the sociology of organizations, while organizational behavior is the psychology of organizations.

A new approach to organization studies is called meso theory. Most organizational research and many management courses specialize in either organizational behavior or organization theory. **Meso theory** (*meso* means "in between") concerns the integration of both micro and macro levels of analysis. Individuals and groups affect the organization and the organization in return influences individuals and groups. To thrive in organizations, managers and employees need to understand multiple levels simultaneously. For example, research may show that employee diversity enhances innovation. To facilitate innovation, managers need to understand how structure and context (organization theory) are related to interactions among diverse employees (organizational behavior) to foster innovation, because both macro and micro variables account for innovations.[41]

For its part, organization theory is directly relevant to top- and middle-management concerns and partly relevant to lower management. Top managers are responsible for the entire organization and must set goals, develop strategy, interpret the external environment, and decide organization structure and design. Middle management is concerned with major departments, such as marketing or research, and must decide how the department relates to the rest of the organization. Middle managers must design their departments to fit work-unit technology and deal with issues of power and politics, intergroup conflict, and information and control systems, each of which is part of organization theory. Organization theory is only partly concerned with lower management because this level of supervision is concerned with employees who operate machines, input data, teach classes, and sell goods. Organization theory is concerned with the big picture of the organization and its major departments.

PLAN OF THE BOOK

The topics within the field of organization theory are interrelated. Chapters are presented so that major ideas unfold in logical sequence. The framework that guides the organization of the book is shown in Exhibit 1.10. Part 1 introduces the basic idea of organizations as social systems and the nature of organization theory. This discussion provides the groundwork for Part 2, which is about strategic management, goals and effectiveness, and the fundamentals of organization structure. Organizations are open systems that exist for a purpose. This section examines how managers help the organization achieve its purpose, including the design of an appropriate structure, such as a functional, divisional, matrix, or horizontal structure. Part 3 looks at the various open system elements that influence organization structure and design, including the external environment, interorganizational relationships, and the global environment.

Parts 4 and 5 look at processes inside the organization. Part 4 describes how organization design is related to such factors as manufacturing and service technology, organizational size and life cycle, and information and control systems. Part 5 shifts to dynamic processes that exist within and between major organizational departments and includes topics such as innovation and change, culture and ethical values, decision-making processes, managing intergroup conflict, and power and politics.

Exhibit 1.10   *Framework for the Book*

Part 1 Introduction to Organizations

CHAPTER 1
Organizations and Organization Theory

Part 2 Organizational Purpose and Structural Design

CHAPTER 2
Strategy, Organization Design, and Effectiveness

CHAPTER 3
Fundamentals of Organization Structure

Part 3 Open System Design Elements

CHAPTER 4
The External Environment

CHAPTER 5
Interorganizational Relationships

CHAPTER 6
Designing Organizations for the International Environment

Part 4 Internal Design Elements

CHAPTER 7
Manufacturing and Service Technologies

CHAPTER 8
Information Technology and Control

CHAPTER 9
Organizational Size, Life Cycle, and Decline

Part 5 Managing Dynamic Processes

CHAPTER 10
Organizational Culture and Ethical Values

CHAPTER 11
Innovation and Change

CHAPTER 12
Decision-Making Processes

CHAPTER 13
Conflict, Power, and Politics

PLAN OF EACH CHAPTER

Each chapter begins with an organizational case to illustrate the topic to be covered. Theoretical concepts are introduced and explained in the body of the chapter. Several *In Practice* segments are included in each chapter to illustrate the concepts and show how they apply to real organizations. *Book Marks* are included in most chapters to present organizational issues managers face right now. These book reviews discuss current concepts and applications to deepen and enrich your understanding of organizations. The *Leading by Design* examples illustrate the dramatic changes taking place in management thinking and practice. Key points for designing and managing organizations are highlighted in the *Briefcase* items throughout the chapter. Each chapter closes with a "Summary and Interpretation" section that reviews and explains important theoretical concepts.

SUMMARY AND INTERPRETATION

One important idea in this chapter is that organizations are systems. In particular, they are open systems that must adapt to the environment to survive. Various parts of the organization are designed to perform the key subsystem functions of production, adaptation, maintenance, management, and boundary spanning. Five parts of the organization are the technical core, top management, middle management, technical support, and administrative support.

The focus of analysis for organization theory is not individual people but the organization itself. Relevant concepts include the dimensions of organization structure and context. The dimensions of formalization, specialization, hierarchy of authority, centralization, professionalism, personnel ratios, size, organizational technology, environment, goals and strategy, and culture provide labels for measuring and analyzing organizations. These dimensions vary widely from organization to organization. Subsequent chapters provide frameworks for analyzing organizations with these concepts.

Many types of organizations exist. One important distinction is between for-profit businesses, in which managers direct their activities toward earning money for the company, and nonprofit organizations, in which managers direct their efforts toward generating some kind of social impact. Managers strive to design organizations to achieve high performance and effectiveness. Effectiveness is complex because different stakeholders have different interests and needs that they want satisfied by the organization.

Turbulence and complexity have replaced stability and predictability as defining traits for today's organizations. Some of the specific challenges managers and organizations face include competing globally, maintaining high standards of ethics and social responsibility, achieving rapid response to environmental changes, organizational crises, or new customer expectations, shifting to a technology-based workplace, and supporting diversity.

These challenges are leading to changes in organization design and management practices. The trend is away from highly structured systems based on a mechanical model toward looser, more flexible systems based on a natural, biological model. Many managers are redesigning companies toward the learning organization, which is characterized by a horizontal structure, empowered employees, shared information, collaborative strategy, and an adaptive culture.

Finally, most concepts in organization theory pertain to the top- and middle-management levels of the organization. This book is concerned more with the topics of those levels than with the operational-level topics of supervision and motivation of employees, which are discussed in courses on organizational behavior.

Key Concepts

administrative principles	open system
bureaucratic organizations	organization theory
chaos theory	organizational behavior
closed system	organizations
contextual dimensions	role
contingency	scientific management
effectiveness	stakeholder
efficiency	stakeholder approach
Hawthorne Studies	structural dimensions
learning organization	subsystems
level of analysis	system
meso theory	task

Discussion Questions

1. What is the definition of *organization*? Briefly explain each part of the definition.
2. What is the difference between an open system and a closed system? Can you give an example of a closed system? How is the stakeholder approach related to this concept?
3. Explain how Mintzberg's five basic parts of the organization perform the subsystem functions shown at the bottom of Exhibit 1.2. If an organization had to give up one of these five parts, which one could it survive the longest without? Discuss.
4. Why might human organizations be considered more complex than machine-type systems? What is the implication of this complexity for managers?
5. What is the difference between formalization and specialization? Do you think an organization high on one dimension would also be high on the other? Discuss.
6. What does *contingency* mean? What are the implications of contingency theories for managers?
7. What are the primary differences between an organization designed for efficient performance and one designed for learning and change? Which type of organization do you think would be easier to manage? Discuss.
8. Why is shared information so important in a learning organization as compared to an efficient performance organization? Discuss how an organization's approach to information-sharing might be related to other elements of organization design, such as structure, tasks, strategy, and culture.
9. What are some differences one might expect among stakeholder expectations for a nonprofit organization versus a for-profit business? Do you think nonprofit managers have to pay more attention to stakeholders than do business managers? Discuss.

10. Early management theorists believed that organizations should strive to be logical and rational, with a place for everything and everything in its place. Discuss the pros and cons of this approach for today's organizations.

Chapter 1 Workbook *Measuring Dimensions of Organizations**

Analyze two organizations along the dimensions shown below. Indicate where you think each organization would fall on each of the scales. Use an X to indicate the first organization and an * to show the second.

You may choose any two organizations you are familiar with, such as your place of work, the university, a student organization, your church or synagogue, or your family.

Formalization

| Many written rules | 1 2 3 4 5 6 7 8 9 10 | Few rules |

Specialization

| Separate tasks and roles | 1 2 3 4 5 6 7 8 9 10 | Overlapping tasks |

Hierarchy

| Tall hierarchy of authority | 1 2 3 4 5 6 7 8 9 10 | Flat hierarchy of authority |

Technology

| Product | 1 2 3 4 5 6 7 8 9 10 | Service |

External Environment

| Stable | 1 2 3 4 5 6 7 8 9 10 | Unstable |

Culture

| Clear norms and values | 1 2 3 4 5 6 7 8 9 10 | Ambiguous norms and values |

Professionalism

| High professional training | 1 2 3 4 5 6 7 8 9 10 | Low professional training |

Goals

| Well-defined goals | 1 2 3 4 5 6 7 8 9 10 | Goals not defined |

Size

| Small | 1 2 3 4 5 6 7 8 9 10 | Large |

Organizational Mindset

| Mechanical system | 1 2 3 4 5 6 7 8 9 10 | Biological system |

Questions

1. What are the main differences between the two organizations you evaluated?

2. Would you recommend that one or both of the organizations have different ratings on any of the scales? Why?

CASE FOR ANALYSIS   *S-S Technologies Inc. (A)—Introduction**

In January 1994, Rick Brock and Keith Pritchard, owners of S-S Technologies Inc. (SST) were concerned with the rapid rate of growth facing their company. SST had revenues of $6.3 million in 1993 and employed thirty highly skilled workers. These numbers could double or triple in the next couple of years. To determine how well SST was structured to achieve its future goals, Brock hired a consultant he had worked with successfully in the past. The consultant's major role was to make recommendations as to the appropriate organizational design (culture, people, layers of management, and administrative systems) in the event that SST grew from 30 to 60 or even 120 employees. As a by-product of his activities at SST, the consultant also questioned whether some marketing opportunities were being missed with the current operations. In addition, questions regarding employee compensation had begun to surface, and the owners wanted to address this issue as soon as possible. Finally, the consultant wondered if a more formalized measurement system, directly tied to the company's strategic objectives, was necessary for SST's growth and prosperity.

Company Information

S-S Technologies Inc., incorporated in 1992, was a 100 percent Canadian-owned company that focused on industrial software and hardware development. Previously, the same business had operated for twelve years as a division of Sutherland-Schultz Limited, a large integrated engineering and construction company. When Sutherland-Schultz changed ownership, the new owner sold the SST portion of the company to Brock. Ultimately, SST was owned by its CEO, Rick Brock, former president of Sutherland-Schultz, and by Keith Pritchard, president of SST. A brief organization chart is provided as Exhibit 1.11.

SST had unique expertise in the factory automation market. The company brought together engineers and technicians with different but synergistic expertise to focus on projects that other systems integrators were unable or unwilling to handle. Out of these efforts, several unique communication and simulation products evolved. The company recognized the opportunities these products represented and expanded its capabilities to successfully bring these products to the global automation market. Over the last three years, SST had grown an average of 33 percent per year (the

IVEY
Richard Ivey School of Business
The University of Western Ontario

*Nancy Suttie prepared this case under the supervision of Al Mikalachki solely to provide material for class discussion. The authors do not intend to illustrate either effective or ineffective handling of a managerial situation. The authors may have disguised certain names and other identifying information to protect confidentiality. Ivey Management Services prohibits any form of reproduction, storage, or transmittal without its written permission. This material is not covered under authorization from CanCopy or any reproduction rights organization. To order copies or request permission to reproduce materials, contact Ivey Publishing, Ivey Management Services, c/o Richard Ivey School of Business, The University of Western Ontario, London, Ontario, Canada, N6A 3K7; phone 519-661-3208; fax 519-661-3882; e-mail cases@ivey.uwo.ca. Copyright © 1994, Ivey Management Service. One-time permission to reproduce Ivey cases granted by Ivey Management Services on March 20, 2003.

EXHIBIT 1.11   *S-S Technologies Organization Chart*

Products Group had grown an average of 64 percent and the Integrated Systems Group an average of 30 percent), as shown in Exhibit 1.12.

Operating Groups

As Exhibit 1.11 indicates, SST was divided into two distinct operating groups: the Products Group (PG) and the Integrated Systems Group (ISG), each with its own characteristics.

Products Group

PG was involved in the development and marketing of the company's unique hardware and software products. The products were sold around the world through licensed representatives, distributors, and direct sales. There were two key types of products:

- **Direct-Link Interface Cards** were totally programmable interfaces designed to make it easier and quicker to exchange data between personal computers and industrial computers/programmable controllers. In layperson's terms, the product allowed office computers to communicate with factory floor computers (commonly termed *PLCs* or *Programmable Logic Controllers*). SST designed and manufactured the interfaces for both the factory floor computers and desktop computers, as well as complementary diagnostic software to ensure that computer networks were performing optimally. The Direct-Link cards received the *Canada Award for Business Excellence in Innovation* from Industry, Science and Technology Canada in 1991.

- **PICS (Programmable Industrial Control Simulator)** was a hardware and software package that allowed a personal computer (PC) to simulate, in real time, an automated factory floor environment. To use PICS, a PC (running the PICS software) is connected directly to a PLC via a Direct-Link card. An experienced software developer then programs, under the PICS environment, a set of routines that send input to and receive output from the PLC, allowing the PC to act as if it were one or more automated factory machines. The PLC is, in essence, "tricked" into thinking it is actually running the automated factory floor, allowing the user to ensure that the PLC software is performing properly. The system can be used for debugging new industrial software, retooling, and employee training, all of which result in substantial time and cost savings for the user.

These products, developed by SST, were often the result of a solution to a technical problem no other company could solve. PG also had a number of other products and ideas under consideration for possible launch in 1994 or 1995.

PG's key success factors fell into two categories: products and marketing. Quality product performance was imperative. In case of faulty products, a replacement had to be provided quickly. In addition, new products were needed to maintain pace with a rapidly changing plant electronic environment. PG's growth also depended highly on marketing. Product awareness by systems integration engineers complemented by an efficient and effective distribution network was vital for PG's successful growth.

Integrated Systems Group

ISG was involved in three distinct, yet often interrelated areas of services: consulting, system engineering, and customer support. ISG employed computer professionals and engineers who were dedicated to the development of software and hardware solutions for complex factory floor systems. Clients were provided with tested, reliable, and sophisticated solutions for data collection, custom control software, batching systems, diagnostic systems, and programmable controller simulation. ISG also implemented and commissioned packaged control software and provided project management for large and technically complex projects. ISG customers

EXHIBIT 1.12   *S-S Technologies Revenue*

Year	Products	Integrated Systems	Total*
1990	$ 931,000	$1,100,000	$2,685,202
1991	$1,638,000	$1,200,000	$3,570,797
1992	$2,763,000	$1,300,000	$4,521,987
1993	$4,036,000	$2,270,000	$6,306,000
1994**	$5,200,000	$3,500,000	$8,700,000

*Includes other sources of income and expenses
**Projection

included industrial manufacturers and institutional organizations.

ISG's key success factors were to complete projects on time, on budget, and of high quality. To date, ISG had received excellent feedback from clients. ISG's performance depended highly on the quality of its employees. Its goals were for manageable growth, focusing on products within the company's scope and skills.

Environment

In early 1990, the North American economy was in a recession. Although recovery was widely predicted,

some results of the recession were permanent. Companies sought to maintain margins during this recession through downsizing and reducing production costs. SST's Products Group benefited from this trend because PICS and Direct-Link cards offered ways of reducing the cost of automating a plant, a move that often reduced production costs. The market for PG grew despite the recession. The recession also meant that many companies eliminated or drastically reduced their in-house engineering capabilities and sought to subcontract this work, a trend that benefited ISG.

CASE FOR ANALYSIS   *S-S Technologies Inc. (D) Organizational Design**

The task of designing an organization to support S-S Technologies Inc.'s (SST) growth was taken on by the company's CEO (Richard Brock), president (Keith Pritchard), and a consultant hired by Brock. They were to develop a structure and set of administrative systems (policies, performance appraisal, compensation and partnering program) that would achieve the company's key success factors (see S-S Technologies Inc. (A)—Introduction), maintain the existing culture, and attract the kind of people they wanted working for them.

SST's Top Management and Human Resources

SST was directed by its two owners:

*   Richard R. Brock, P.Eng., was the CEO of SST. During his eight years as president of Sutherland-Schultz Limited, Brock recognized and nurtured the potential of the Products Group (PG) and Integrated Systems Group (ISG), which eventually formed S-S Technologies Inc. He continued to be involved in all aspects of the new company and brought to it his extensive knowledge of business management and development.
*   Keith Pritchard was the president of SST. Pritchard had risen through the company ranks, starting as a systems analyst, becoming project manager, then group manager, and finally president in 1992. Pritchard also developed the PICS product, which accounted for $500,000 of company sales. His unique set of skills in both management and technical areas made him an excellent leader for the company.

SST had a flat organizational structure that allowed it to respond quickly to technical and market changes. Anyone who had a door, left it open; employees felt free to take their concerns to whomever they believed could help. Decisions were often made using a consultative approach that empowered those involved and that led to "ownership" of problems and their solutions

Projects were assigned to individuals or teams, depending on the size. The individuals and teams were self-managed. Responsibility for project scheduling, budgeting, and execution was left largely in team members' hands. Such responsibility created commitment to the project for those who worked on it and led to the high motivation evident within the company.

Overhead resources, such as marketing and administration, were kept to a minimum. For example, there were only four people on the marketing team, which managed more than $4 million in revenues. Administrative support was provided by two, or at times, three people. Even the controller (Doug

IVEY

Richard Ivey School of Business
The University of Western Ontario

*Nancy Suttie prepared this case under the supervision of Professor Al Mikalachki solely to provide material for class discussion. The authors do not intend to illustrate either effective or ineffective handling of a managerial situation. The authors may have disguised certain names and other identifying information to protect confidentiality. Ivey Management Services prohibits any form of reproduction, storage, or transmittal without its written permission. This material is not covered under authorization from CanCopy or any reproduction rights organization. To order copies or request permission to reproduce materials, contact Ivey Publishing, Ivey Management Services, c/o Richard Ivey School of Business, The University of Western Ontario, London, Ontario, Canada, N6A 3K7; phone 519-661-3208; fax 519-661-3882; e-mail cases@ivey.uwo.ca. Copyright © 1994, Ivey Management Services. One-time permission to reproduce Ivey cases granted by Ivey Management Services on March 20, 2003.

Winger) shared his time with two other related organizations (SAF and Wilson Gas). SST was truly a lean organization.

Resources—PG

PG had highly competent, highly motivated technical teams. The technical people were leaders in their respective fields, with extensive and varied educations and backgrounds. They worked well together to meet R&D challenges and to respond quickly and effectively to customers' inquiries. Many team members were involved in the original product development and expressed a personal commitment to PG's continued market success.

- Linda Oliver, B.Math., the lead programmer for the PICS project, had worked on the project as a designer and programmer since its inception.
- Bruce Andrews, Ph.D., was involved in the ongoing development of the PICS product, especially the communications tasks and testing; he also wrote the manuals.
- Lorne Diebel, C.E.T., developed a reputation as a communications guru. Lorne often traveled to far-off sites, on a moment's notice, to debug a customer's application problem.
- Jonathan Malton, B.Sc., a talented hardware designer, had been instrumental in advancing the Direct-Link cards from the old "through hole" format to the new "surface mount" technology.

Newer members were added to PG as the pace of R&D increased and customer support became more demanding. Newcomers brought their own areas of expertise and worked alongside the more senior team members, whose enthusiasm for their work was infectious.

As a result of its progressive and applied R&D program, the technical team members were advanced on the learning curve. This allowed SST to keep ahead of the competition. As a result, large PLC vendors often came to SST to solve their communication and simulation problems, rather than investing in the learning curve themselves.

The marketing team had grown over the past few years as PG revenues grew. People from both a marketing and a technical background combined to create a well-rounded, effective marketing department:

- Ian Suttie, P.Eng., the marketing manager, was involved in design review, marketing, distribution, and sales of all products. His main function was to set up a network of distributors and representatives to reach all major markets in the United States, Europe, and beyond.
- Colleen Richmond had experience in marketing with other high-tech firms. She handled all the trade shows, promotional material, and advertising activities.
- Steve Blakely was the inside salesperson and came to SST with a technical background. He responded to inquiries for information and was the first contact within SST for customers having technical difficulties.
- Colleen Dietrich was recently hired by SST to determine the extent to which leads generated through the various advertising media used by PG eventually resulted in sales.

The marketing team worked well together, buoyed by PG's success. However, they were stretched to the limit and team members admitted they were unable to do everything they wished to do because of personnel constraints. All known product complaints were acted upon; however, there was no formal audit of customer satisfaction.

Resources—ISG

ISG's most important resource was its people. The engineers and technicians were not only technically competent but also highly motivated and loyal. The following is a brief summary of ISG people and the unique skills they brought to the company:

- Mark Schwarz, P.Eng., an accomplished systems analyst, wrote sales proposals, estimated projects, and did most of the marketing for ISG. He was very good at business development, seeking out large, extremely complicated projects, and often helping the customer define the scope and approach to the project. Convincing a customer that you could handle their large, technically complex job was tricky business, but Schwarz exhibited a talent for it. Schwarz also had a talent for scheduling personnel and was interested in ensuring that everyone had something interesting to do.
- Vivienne Ojala, P.Eng., an experienced and talented project manager, designer, and programmer, was more than capable of handling all aspects of design and project management for the $2 million-plus projects ISG hoped to attract. She was excellent with customers who preferred her "straight" talk to the "techno-babble" others gave them. Ojala made the customer confident

that the project was in good hands, which is very important when you have asked a manufacturer to give you a production system that could determine business success or failure. Ojala was also good at training those who worked on her projects, as well as developing people in general.

- Peter Roeser, P.Eng., was a systems analyst with special skills in the area of communications and various operating systems.
- Brian Thomson, P.Eng., was an expert in the area of real-time software development. He also managed projects.
- Ted Hannah, P.Eng., was a project manager and systems analyst with extensive skills and experience.
- Bruce Travers, who marketed ISG capabilities in Ontario and provided technical direction for projects, had more than twenty years' experience with industrial applications of information systems.

Due to the diverse skills of its people, ISG was able to tackle large, complex systems integration projects that most of the competitors could not. ISG had in-house expertise covering nearly every technology that would be applied to a project. Also, because ISG was not tied to a single supplier of PLCs or PCs (as many competitors were), it was able to be more flexible and innovative in the solutions that were presented to customers.

Another important ISG resource was its excellent reputation and relationship with a large Canadian manufacturer that had given ISG substantial repeat business. As well, ISG had completed many projects for several large North American companies and had never failed to deliver on its promises.

ISG was advanced on the learning curve. New customers benefited from the fact that ISG had faced many challenges before and solved them successfully. ISG's experience was more rounded, and hence more innovative and current, than an in-house engineering department that had worked in only one type of factory.

Consultant's Interviews

The consultant interviewed all SST employees. Some of the observations that resulted from his interviews are grouped below by issues:

(i) Goals and Strategies

Other than Brock, Pritchard, Suttie, and Schwarz, few employees were aware of SST's goals and strategies or even those of their own Group. In addition,

even within top management (Pritchard, Suttie, and Schwarz), significant differences existed regarding SST's goals and strategy.

(ii) Hierarchical Structure

Pritchard viewed Suttie and Schwarz as PG and ISG managers, respectively. However, PG members generally saw themselves as reporting to Pritchard and saw Suttie as performing the marketing function. When apprised of this situation by the consultant, Pritchard said it would take time for Suttie to establish his position.

The ISG situation also proved somewhat confusing. A number of ISG members saw Schwarz as the manager. However, there was some confusion as to his position vis-à-vis Ojala, who had recently returned to SST after leaving to work for a much larger technology company in Montreal. Ojala tells the story of Pritchard begging her to return to SST, a story that Pritchard confirms. Ojala saw herself as reporting to Pritchard (and so did Pritchard). Her "formal" relationship to Schwarz had to be worked out.

Before Ojala left SST (she was away for five months), both she and Schwarz reported to Pritchard directly. When Ojala left, many of her responsibilities, such as some of the proposal writing and personnel scheduling, were given to Schwarz. Now that Ojala was back, to everyone's relief, there was the question of how to structure her role, particularly in relation to Pritchard and Schwarz. Ojala would not report to Schwarz, and Schwarz would not report to Ojala.

(iii) Physical Space

SST had outgrown the location that it shared with two other companies, Wilson Gas and SAF. Brock owned SAF, which was part of SST holdings, and rented space out to Wilson Gas. Each company had about one-third of the building they shared. SST added a trailer to house additional personnel. Any expansion in the same building required evicting SAF, Wilson, or both. Pritchard was adamant that all SST personnel be housed in one location and have easy access to one another.

(iv) Compensation

One of the most contentious issues that arose from the interviews dealt with bonuses and compensation. Historically, bonuses had been promised if the company succeeded. The amount and date of the bonus were at the discretion of Brock and Pritchard. To date, no bonuses had been paid. Given the company's growth and success, many employees were expecting a Christmas bonus. There was no policy regarding bonus or merit pay.

Both Brock and Pritchard wondered what the policy should be and how that policy should be developed. Existing compensation tended to be at the low end of the spectrum for engineers. This was particularly true for the longer-term employees in ISG.

It became apparent during the interviews that it was important to formalize the bonus plan to end the speculation, uncertainty, and disappointment caused by the present, seemingly random (to the employees at least) system. Historically, when SST was part of Sutherland-Schultz, the company had a few good years and generous bonuses were paid. However, when the recession hit, the construction side of Sutherland-Schultz slumped considerably and, although PG and ISG held their profitability, the company as a whole could not afford to pay bonuses. In fact, SST people were laid off and some of those who remained felt cheated. Now that SST was on its own, there was an opportunity to tie bonuses directly to the company's performance. Management wanted the bonus system to achieve the following goals:

- To develop a cooperative, team spirit
- To foster cooperation between ISG and PG and limit interpersonal competition
- To provide extra reward for unique contributions
- To not reward weak performance

(v) Partnering

Given the experience of losing Ojala to another firm (albeit temporarily), Brock was anxious to develop a "partnering" system in which those crucial to the company's success could participate. He wanted to make people like Suttie, Schwarz, and Ojala feel like owners or partners committed to the company, so they would not be lured away by the promise of greener pastures; after all, the job market for people of this caliber was extremely promising. This was true not only of those in management positions but also of the best systems analysts and programmers: people like Linda Oliver and Lorne Diebel.

Brock wanted part of the partners' bonus to consist of stock in the company. The problem was that these people were all young, with growing families, and could not afford to have their money tied up in stock when they had mortgage payments and day-care costs to worry about. Generally, their immediate concern was cash flow, as they knew their

long-term earning potential was excellent. Brock's concern was how to structure the partners' bonuses and compensation to keep key people on-side, while allowing room for more partners to be brought in as the company grew. The company had recently hired a half-dozen talented engineering and computer science students, all of whom had the potential to become the next Schwarz, Suttie, or Ojala. On top of all this, Brock still had his own return on equity to consider.

(vi) Commitment and Motivation

The consultant was overwhelmed by the high commitment to SST and the task motivation expressed by employees. The people loved the work environment, the lack of politics, the quick response to their technical needs (equipment and/or information), and the lack of talk-for-talk's-sake meetings. They were confident in their future and happy to come to work. For the consultant, this was a refreshing contrast to the downsizing gloom and doom that permeated many other companies he worked with in the 1990s.

The employees set their own working hours. They had to put in forty hours per week, but could do this at any time. The flexible working hours allowed them to engage in other activities that occurred between 9 and 5, such as their children's school events. Employees kept track of their overtime and were either paid straight time or took the equivalent in extra holidays. Each employee recorded his/her overtime weekly and passed on the information to Pritchard. Previously, employees had noted the overtime information mentally. Pritchard had them write it out and report it weekly because he observed that their mental calculations erred on the side of the company (they remembered fewer hours than they worked overtime).

(vii) Personnel Function and Communications

New employees were generally assigned to a project manager who informally took on the induction and training role. In that way, new employees immediately tied into a task, and it was left to them to learn the culture and expectations of SST by osmosis. Should the employees not perform well, or fit into the culture, their employment was terminated.

Periodically, Pritchard would have a meeting of all employees to inform them of SST's progress, success, and direction. Given these meetings, Pritchard was surprised to learn that only a few employees were aware of SST's goals and strategy.

EXHIBIT 1.13   *S-S Technologies' Desired Culture and People*

Culture	People
• Open communications at all levels	• Highly motivated
• Flexible working hours	• Highly skilled (tech)
• Few policies	• Entrepreneurial
• Profit sharing at all levels	• Team players
• Quick decision making	• High performers
• Encourage initiative, not bureaucracy	• Committed to SST

One issue mentioned by a couple of employees dealt with performance appraisal and company benefits. Performance appraisal was conducted by Pritchard; however, he did not keep a record of the meeting and it was not done at regular intervals. Also, anyone interested in learning about benefits or salary ranges for various jobs did not know whom to contact. In contrast, all employees knew whom to contact for technical information. In fact, performance appraisal, compensation, and benefits were managed in an ad hoc manner.

Where Do We Go from Here?

Brock, Pritchard, and the consultant wanted to design an organization that would contemplate an expansion to double or triple SST's current size. They knew the existing SST culture attracted and nurtured highly motivated and committed employees who expanded the company successfully and rapidly. They also knew that they could not manage $50 million in revenue and 120 to 150 people as they managed $6 million in revenue and 30 people.

The trio's task was to design an organization that would allow SST to grow successfully. Given SST's culture and the kind of people it wanted to attract (as shown in Exhibit 1.13), what were the best structure, performance appraisal, compensation/bonus plan, company policies, and partnering program that should be implemented?

Notes

1. This case is based on: Anthony Bianco and Pamela L. Moore, "Downfall: The Inside Story of the Management Fiasco at Xerox," *BusinessWeek* (March 5, 2001), 82–92; Robert J. Grossman, "HR Woes at Xerox," *HR Magazine* (May 2001), 34–45; Jeremy Kahn, "The Paper Jam from Hell," *Fortune* (November 13, 2000), 141–146; Pamela L. Moore, "She's Here to Fix the Xerox," *BusinessWeek* (August 6, 2001), 47–48; and Claudia H. Deutsch, "At Xerox, the Chief Earns (Grudging) Respect," *The New York Times* (June 2, 2002), section 3, 1, 12. All quotes are from Grossman, "HR Woes at Xerox."

2. Martha Brannigan, "Air Pressure: Discount Carrier Lands Partners in Ill-Served Cities," *The Wall Street Journal* (July 16, 2002), A1, A10.

3. Eileen Davis, "What's on American Managers' Minds?" *Management Review* (April 1995), 14–20.

4. David Welch, "GM Tries to Show Who's Boss," *BusinessWeek*, (March 12, 2001), 54–55.

5. William J. Holstein, "Samsung's Golden Touch," *Fortune* (April 1, 2002), 89–94.

6. "High Profiles in Hot Water," *The Wall Street Journal* (June 28, 2002), B1.

7. David Wessel, "Venal Sins: Why the Bad Guys of the Boardroom Emerged en Masse," *The Wall Street Journal* (June 20, 2002), A1, A6.

8. Greg Ip, "Mind Over Matter—Disappearing Acts: The Rapid Rise and Fall of the Intangible Asset," *The Wall Street Journal* (April 4, 2002), A1, A6.

9. Bernard Wysocki Jr., "Corporate Caveat: Dell or Be Delled," *The Wall Street Journal* (May 10, 1999), A1.

10. Andy Reinhardt, "From Gearhead to Grand High Pooh-Bah," *BusinessWeek* (August 28, 2000), 129–130.

11. G. Pascal Zachary, "Mighty is the Mongrel," *Fast Company* (July 2000), 270–284.

12. "Keeping Your Edge: Managing a Diverse Corporate Culture," Special Advertising Section, *Fortune* (June 3, 2001) S1–S17; Steven Greenhouse, N.Y. Times News Service, "Influx of Immigrants Having Profound Impact on Economy," *Johnson City Press* (September 4, 2000), 9; Richard W. Judy and Carol D'Amico, *Workforce 2020: Work and Workers in the 21st Century* (Indianapolis, Ind: Hudson Institute, 1997).

13. Debra E. Meyerson and Joyce K. Fletcher, "A Modest Manifesto for Shattering the Glass Ceiling," *Harvard Business Review* (January–February 2000), 127–136; Annie Finnigan, "Different Strokes," *Working Woman* (April 2001), 42–48; Joline Godfrey, "Been There, Doing That," *Inc.* (March 1996), 21–22; Paula Dwyer, Marsha Johnston, and Karen Lowry Miller, "Out of the Typing Pool, into Career Limbo," *BusinessWeek* (April 15, 1996), 92–94.

14. Howard Aldrich, *Organizations and Environments* (Englewood Cliffs, N.J.: Prentice-Hall, 1979), 3.

15. This section is based largely on Peter F. Drucker, *Managing the Non-Profit Organization: Principles and Practices* (New York: HarperBusiness, 1992); and Thomas Wolf, *Managing a Nonprofit Organization* (New York: Fireside/Simon & Schuster, 1990).

16. Christine W. Letts, William P. Ryan, and Allen Grossman, *High Performance Nonprofit Organizations* (New York: John Wiley & Sons, Inc., 1999), 30–35.

17. Lisa Bannon, "Dream Works: As Make-a-Wish Expands Its Turf, Local Groups Fume," *The Wall Street Journal* (July 8, 2002), A1, A8.

18. Robert N. Stern and Stephen R. Barley, "Organizations and Social Systems: Organization Theory's Neglected Mandate," *Administrative Science Quarterly* 41 (1996): 146–162.

19. Philip Siekman, "Build to Order: One Aircraft Carrier," *Fortune* (July 22, 2002), 180[B]– 180[J].

20. Bethany McLean, "Growing Up Gallo," *Fortune* (August 14, 2000), 211–232.

21. James D. Thompson, *Organizations in Action* (New York: McGraw-Hill, 1967), 4–13.

22. Henry Mintzberg, *The Structuring of Organizations* (Englewood Cliffs, N.J.: Prentice-Hall, 1979), 215-297; and Henry Mintzberg, "Organization Design: Fashion or Fit?" *Harvard Business Review* 59 (January–February 1981), 103–116.

23. The following discussion was heavily influenced by Richard H. Hall, *Organizations: Structures, Processes, and Outcomes* (Englewood Cliffs, N.J.: Prentice-Hall, 1991); D. S. Pugh, "The Measurement of Organization Structures: Does Context Determine Form?" *Organizational Dynamics* 1 (Spring 1973), 19–34; and D. S. Pugh, D. J. Hickson, C. R. Hinings, and C. Turner, "Dimensions of Organization Structure," *Administrative Science Quarterly* 13 (1968), 65–91.

24. John Huey, "The New Post-Heroic Leadership," *Fortune* (February 21, 1994), 42–50; John Huey, "Wal-Mart: Will It Take Over the World?" *Fortune* (January 30, 1989), 52–61; Howard Rudnitsky, "How Sam Walton Does It," *Forbes* (August 16, 1982), 42–44; *http://www.gore.com*, accessed on August 28, 2002; "The 100 Best Companies to Work For," *Fortune* (February 4, 2002), 60–90; and *http://www.walmartstores.com*, accessed on August 28, 2002.

25. Anna Bernasek, "Pattern for Prosperity," *Fortune* (October 2, 2000), 100–108.

26. Jennifer Reingold and Marcia Stepanek, with Diane Brady, "Why the Productivity Revolution Will Spread," *BusinessWeek* (February 14, 2000), 112–118.

27. T. Donaldson and L. E. Preston, "The Stakeholder Theory of the Corporation: Concepts, Evidence, and Implications," *Academy of Management Review* 20 (1995), 65–91; Anne S. Tusi, "A Multiple-Constituency Model of Effectiveness: An Empirical Examination at the Human Resource Subunit Level," *Administrative Science Quarterly* 35 (1990), 458–483; Charles Fombrun and Mark Shanley, "What's in a Name? Reputation Building and Corporate Strategy," *Academy of Management Journal* 33 (1990), 233–258; Terry Connolly, Edward J. Conlon, and Stuart Jay Deutsch, "Organizational Effectiveness: A Multiple-Constituency Approach," *Academy of Management Review* 5 (1980), 211–217.

28. Tusi, "A Multiple-Constituency Model of Effectiveness."

29. Fombrun and Shanley, "What's in a Name?"

30. Devin Leonard, "Tony Ridder Just Can't Win," *Fortune* (December 24, 2001), 99–106; and Felicity Barringer, "Unresolved Clash of Cultures: At Knight Ridder, Good Journalism vs. the Bottom Line," *The New York Times* (May 29, 2001), C1, C4.

31. Ann Harrington, "The Big Ideas," *Fortune* (November 22, 1999), 152–154; Robert Kanigel, *The One Best Way: Frederick Winslow Taylor and the Enigma of Efficiency* (New York: Viking, 1997); and Alan Farnham, "The Man Who Changed Work Forever," *Fortune* (July 21, 1997), 114. For a discussion of the impact of scientific management on American industry, government, and nonprofit organizations, also see Mauro F. Guillén, "Scientific Management's Lost Aesthetic: Architecture, Organization, and the Taylorized Beauty of the Mechanical," *Administrative Science Quarterly* 42 (1997), 682–715.

32. Amanda Bennett, *The Death of the Organization Man* (New York: William Morrow, 1990).

33. Johannes M. Pennings, "Structural Contingency Theory: A Reappraisal," *Research in Organizational Behavior* 14 (1992), 267–309.

34. This discussion is based in part on Toby J. Tetenbaum, "Shifting Paradigms: From Newton to Chaos," *Organizational Dynamics* (Spring 1998), 21–32.

35. William Bergquist, *The Postmodern Organization* (San Francisco: Jossey-Bass, 1993).

36. Based on Tetenbaum, "Shifting Paradigms: From Newton to Chaos" and Richard T. Pascale, "Surfing the Edge of Chaos," *Sloan Management Review* (Spring 1999), 83–94.

37. Polly LaBarre, "This Organization is Disorganization," *Fast Company* (June–July 1996), 77+.

38. David K. Hurst, *Crisis and Renewal: Meeting the Challenge of Organizational Change* (Boston, Mass.: Harvard Business School Press, 1995), 32–52.

39. Glenn Rifkin, "Nothing But Net," *Fast Company* (June–July 1996), 118–127.

40. Thomas Petzinger, *The New Pioneers: The Men and Women Who Are Transforming the Workplace and Marketplace* (New York: Simon & Schuster, 1999), 91–93; and "In Search of the New World of Work," *Fast Company* (April 1999), 214–220+; Peter Katel, "Bordering on Chaos," *Wired* (July 1997), 98–107; and Oren Harari, "The Concrete Intangibles," *Management Review* (May 1999), 30–33.

41. Robert House, Denise M. Rousseau, and Melissa Thomas-Hunt, "The Meso Paradigm: A Framework for the Integration of Micro and Macro Organizational Behavior," *Research in Organizational Behavior* 17 (1995): 71–114.

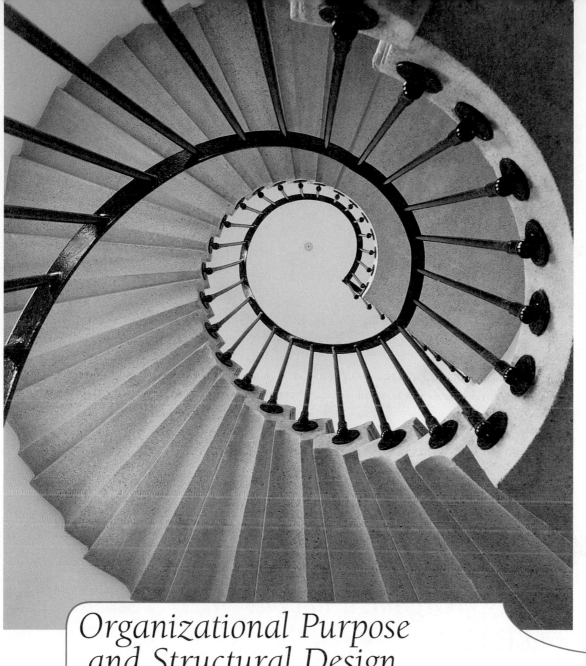

Organizational Purpose and Structural Design

part 2

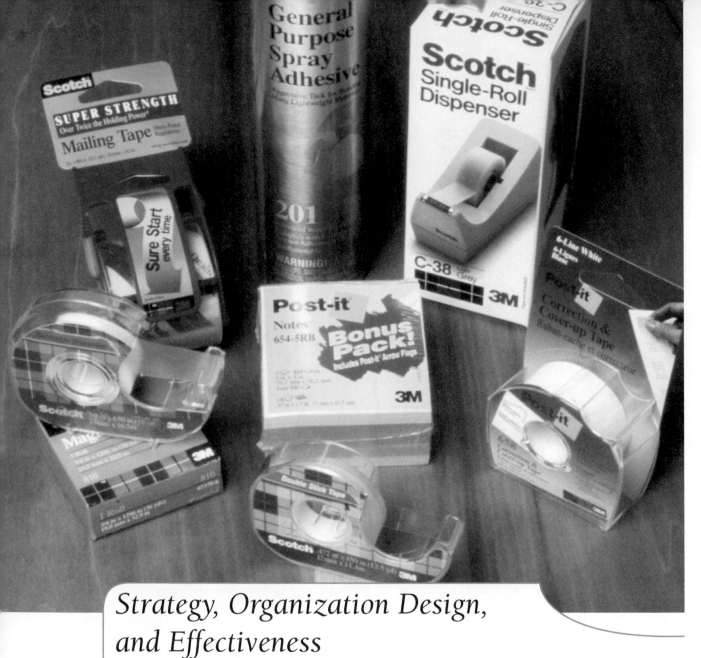

Strategy, Organization Design, and Effectiveness

chapter 2

3M Corporation

It has given us sandpaper and Post-it notes, cellophane tape and Thinsulate insulation, Scotchgard repellents and dishwashing sponges. For a century, 3M Corporation has been a leader in innovation, cranking out thousands of profitable new products. The company set a record in 2000 by generating $5.6 billion—fully one-third of its total revenues—from products that didn't exist just four years earlier.

But that accomplishment is not enough for new chairman and CEO James McNerney Jr. He's done away with the requirement that 30 percent of sales come from products introduced in the past four years in favor of revving up overall sales and earnings, which have lagged somewhat in recent years. McNerney, who came to 3M from General Electric, has set an audacious long-term goal of doubling the sales numbers of 2000 in ten years or less. His short-term goals include increasing sales by 11 percent a year and operating earnings by 12 percent—nearly twice the rate of the past decade. To accomplish his ambitious targets, McNerney plans to do the following:

- Move manufacturing to low-wage sites overseas. Combine purchasing across divisions to gain price advantages with suppliers.
- Implement Six Sigma, an aggressive quality and process-management system, to root out inefficiencies corporate-wide.
- Get new products to market much faster by focusing research and development spending in the most promising areas.
- Seek and accomplish promising acquisitions and expand beyond products into services.

So far, the declining economy has meant a slow start toward goal achievement for 3M. Sales and profits at the company have been dropping faster than at any other time in the past three decades. Critics also warn that some of McNerney's changes could destroy the very creativity the company is famous for. For example, rather than giving individual business heads free rein, top leaders now are specifying how research dollars can be spent and setting uniform performance standards for all business units.

Many 3M veterans, however, support McNerney and believe his goals and strategies are sound. McNerney has emphasized that he isn't seeking a full-scale reorganization. "It's not a matter of machine-gunning the team because I'm new and I think I'm smarter and better," he says. "This is taking a very good company and making it better."[1]

Top managers such as James McNerney are responsible for positioning their organizations for success by establishing goals and strategies that can help the company be competitive. An organizational goal is a desired state of affairs that the organization attempts to reach.[2] A goal represents a result or end point toward which organizational efforts are directed. The goals for 3M include increasing sales by 11 percent a year and operating earnings by 12 percent. The choice of goals and strategy affects organization design, as we will discuss in this chapter.

PURPOSE OF THIS CHAPTER

Top managers give direction to organizations. They set goals and develop the strategies for their organization to attain those goals. The purpose of this chapter is to help you understand the types of goals that organizations pursue and some of the competitive strategies managers develop to reach those goals. We will examine two significant frameworks for determining strategic action and look at how strategies affect organization design. The chapter also describes the most popular approaches to measuring the effectiveness of organizational efforts. To manage organizations well, managers need a clear sense of how to measure effectiveness.

THE ROLE OF STRATEGIC DIRECTION IN ORGANIZATION DESIGN

An organization is created to achieve some purpose, which is decided by the chief executive officer and the top management team. Top executives decide on the end purpose the organization will strive for and determine the direction it will take to accomplish it. It is this purpose and direction that shapes how the organization is designed and managed. Indeed, *the primary responsibility of top management is to determine an organization's goals, strategy, and design, therein adapting the organization to a changing environment.*[3] Middle managers do much the same thing for major departments within the guidelines provided by top management. The relationships through which top managers provide direction and then design are illustrated in Exhibit 2.1.

The direction-setting process typically begins with an assessment of the opportunities and threats in the external environment, including the amount of change, uncertainty, and resource availability, which we discuss in more detail in Chapter 4. Top management also assesses internal strengths and weaknesses to define the company's distinctive competence compared with other firms in the industry.[4] The assessment of internal environment often includes an evaluation of each department and is shaped by past performance and the leadership style of the CEO and top management team. The next step is to define overall mission and official goals based on the correct fit between external opportunities and internal strengths. Specific operational goals or strategies can then be formulated to define how the organization is to accomplish its overall mission.

In Exhibit 2.1, organization design reflects the way goals and strategies are implemented. Organization design is the administration and execution of the strategic plan. Organization direction is implemented through decisions about structural form, including whether the organization will be designed for a learning or an efficiency orientation, as discussed in Chapter 1, as well as choices about information and control systems, the type of production technology, human resource policies, culture, and linkages to other organizations. Changes in structure, technology, human resource policies, culture, and interorganization linkages will be discussed in subsequent chapters. Also note the arrow in Exhibit 2.1 running from organization design back to strategic direction. This means that

Exhibit 2.1   *Top Management Role in Organization Direction, Design, and Effectiveness*

External Environment
Opportunities
Threats
Uncertainty
Resource availability

CEO, Top management team

Strategic Direction
Define mission, official goals
Select operational goals, competitive strategies

Organization Design
Structural form—learning vs. efficiency
Information and control systems
Production technology
Human resource policies, incentives
Organizational culture
Interorganizational linkages

Effectiveness Outcomes
Resources
Efficiency
Goal attainment
Competing values

Internal Situation
Strengths
Weaknesses
Distinctive competence
Leader style
Past performance

Source: Adapted from Arie Y. Lewin and Carroll U. Stephens, "Individual Properties of the CEO as Determinants of Organization Design," unpublished manuscript, Duke University, 1990; and Arie Y. Lewin and Carroll U. Stephens, "CEO Attributes as Determinants of Organization Design: An Integrated Model," *Organization Studies* 15, no. 2 (1994): 183–212.

strategies are often made within the current structure of the organization, so that current design constrains or puts limits on goals and strategy. More often than not, however, the new goals and strategy are selected based on environmental needs, and then top management attempts to redesign the organization to achieve those ends.

Finally, Exhibit 2.1 illustrates how managers evaluate the effectiveness of organizational efforts—that is, the extent to which the organization realizes its goals. This chart reflects the most popular ways of measuring performance, each of which is discussed later in this chapter. It is important to note here that performance measurements feed back into the internal environment, so that past performance of the organization is assessed by top management in setting new goals and strategic direction for the future.

The role of top management is important because managers can interpret the environment differently and develop different goals. For example, the new president of Harvard University, Lawrence H. Summers (former U.S. Treasury secretary), believes Harvard needs a dramatic transformation to prepare its undergraduates to meet the challenges of today's fast-changing global economy.[5] Summers has established goals for tougher grading standards, revised tenure reviews, increased foreign study and enhanced science and technology education for undergraduates, and greater undergraduate contact with professors. Previous leaders, whose experience was often strictly academic, usually did not consider the volatile global environment in setting goals for the nation's leading university, choosing to keep it on a steady path that has proven successful in the past.

The choices top managers make about goals, strategies, and organization design have a tremendous impact on organizational effectiveness. This chapter's Book Mark discusses the need for managers to take a new approach to strategy in today's environment. Remember that goals and strategy are not fixed or taken for granted. Top managers and middle managers must select goals for their respective units, and the ability to make these choices largely determines firm success. Organization design is used to implement goals and strategy and also determines

See also "Strategy as Simple Rules" Eisenhardt & Sull

BOOK MARK 2.0   *Have You Read This Book?*

Competing on the Edge: Strategy as Structured Chaos
By Shona L. Brown and Kathleen M. Eisenhardt

In *Competing on the Edge*, Shona Brown and Kathleen Eisenhardt contend that today's companies must constantly reinvent themselves to prosper in a world of unstable markets, fierce global competition, and relentless change. Today's market leaders, the authors suggest, are those companies that find a balance between chaos and stability and allow strategy to emerge as the firm adapts to an unpredictable and rapidly changing business environment. They remain open and flexible in order to be innovative and creative, yet they maintain enough discipline and structure to successfully execute strategies and plans. As the authors explain: "The underlying insight behind competing on the edge is that strategy is the result of a firm's organizing to change constantly and letting a semicoherent strategic direction emerge from the organization. In other words, it is about combining the two parts of strategy by simultaneously addressing where you want to go and how you are going to get there."

RULES FOR COMPETING ON THE EDGE
Brown and Eisenhardt distill ten rules of strategy for competing on the edge. Some examples of these rules are:

- *Advantage is temporary.* To compete on the edge, managers should treat any strategy as temporary. Competitive advantage is fleeting, so company managers focus on constantly generating new sources of advantage. They look for opportunities in the changes going on around them rather than looking for ways to defend themselves against change.
- *Strategy is diverse, emergent, and complicated.* In a high-velocity environment, strategy should be not

a single approach but a diverse collection of strategic moves. Managers allow strategy to emerge and then shape and articulate their plans around it. They take a variety of approaches, watch what happens, learn from it, and shift strategies and plans as necessary.

- *Drive strategy from the business level.* Strategy is not something that is formulated by top managers and imposed on the organization top-down. Too many factors are changing too rapidly and unpredictably to wait for strategy to trickle down through the hierarchy. Companies that compete on the edge allow strategy to be driven by the people closest to the action. Success comes not from carefully planned ideas at the top, but from skilled, fast, and agile moves at the business level.

CONCLUSION
Although *Competing on the Edge* is inspired by scientific theories of complexity and chaos, it is firmly grounded in the practical realities facing business organizations. The authors present examples of organizations such as the Atlanta Braves, 3M, Nike, and Intel that remain market leaders in volatile industries by learning how to adapt and innovate in a business environment that is constantly in a state of flux. Through numerous detailed examples of successful and not-so-successful companies, tips on avoiding managerial traps, and explanations of new strategic concepts, Brown and Eisenhardt offer managers a valuable handbook for dealing with unpredictable change.

Competing on the Edge: Strategy as Structured Chaos, by Shona L. Brown and Kathleen M. Eisenhardt, is published by Harvard Business School Press.

organization success. We will now discuss further the concept of organizational goals and strategy, and in the latter part of this chapter, we will discuss various ways to evaluate organizational effectiveness.

ORGANIZATIONAL PURPOSE

Organizations are created and continued in order to accomplish something. All organizations, including Harvard University, New Line Cinema, the Catholic Church, the U.S. Department of Agriculture, the local dry cleaners, and the neighborhood deli, exist for a purpose. This purpose may be referred to as the overall goal, or mission. Different parts of the organization establish their own goals and objectives to help meet the overall goal, mission, or purpose of the organization.

Many types of goals exist in an organization, and each type performs a different function. One major distinction is between the officially stated goals, or mission, of the organization and the operative goals the organization actually pursues.

MISSION

BRIEFCASE

As an organization manager, keep this guideline in mind:

Establish and communicate organizational mission and goals. Communicate official goals to provide a statement of the organization's mission to external constituents. Communicate operational goals to provide internal direction, guidelines, and standards of performance for employees.

The overall goal for an organization is often called the **mission**—the organization's reason for existence. The mission describes the organization's vision, its shared values and beliefs, and its reason for being. It can have a powerful impact on an organization.[6] The mission is sometimes called the **official goals**, which refers to the formally stated definition of business scope and outcomes the organization is trying to achieve. Official goal statements typically define business operations and may focus on values, markets, and customers that distinguish the organization. Whether called a mission statement or official goals, the organization's general statement of its purpose and philosophy is often written down in a policy manual or the annual report. The mission statement for Hallmark is shown in Exhibit 2.2. Note how the overall mission, values, and goals are all defined.

One of the primary purposes of a mission statement is to serve as a communication tool.[7] The *mission statement* communicates to current and prospective employees, customers, investors, suppliers, and competitors what the organization stands for and what it is trying to achieve. A mission statement communicates legitimacy to internal and external stakeholders, who may join and be committed to the organization because they identify with its stated purpose. Most top leaders want employees, customers, competitors, suppliers, investors, and the local community to look on them in a favorable light, and the concept of legitimacy plays a critical role.[8] The corporate concern for legitimacy is real and pertinent. Consider the accounting firm Arthur Andersen, which was accused of obstructing justice by shredding tons of accounting documents related to the Enron investigation. Once the previously respected global firm lost legitimacy with clients, investors, and the public, it was all but dead.[9]

OPERATIVE GOALS

Operative goals designate the ends sought through the actual operating procedures of the organization and explain what the organization is actually trying to do.[10] Operative goals describe specific measurable outcomes and are often concerned with the short run. Operative versus official goals represent actual versus stated goals. Operative goals typically pertain to the primary tasks an organization

EXHIBIT 2.2   *Hallmark's Mission Statement*

THIS IS HALLMARK

We believe:

That our *products and services* must enrich people's lives
 and enhance their relationships.
That *creativity and quality*—in our concepts, products
 and services—are essential to our success.
That the *people* of Hallmark are our company's
 most valuable resource.
That distinguished *financial performance* is a must,
 not as an end in itself, but as a means
 to accomplish our broader mission.
That our *private ownership* must be preserved.

The values that guide us are:

Excellence in all we do.
Ethical and moral conduct at all times
 and in all our relationships.
Innovation in all areas of our business as a means
 of attaining and sustaining leadership.
Corporate social responsibility to Kansas City
 and to each community in which we operate.

These beliefs and values guide our business strategies,
 our corporate behavior, and our relationships
 with suppliers, customers, communities, and each other.

Source: Hallmark Cards, Inc. Used with permission.

must perform, similar to the subsystem activities identified in Chapter 1.[11] These
goals concern overall performance, boundary spanning, maintenance, adaptation,
and production activities. Specific goals for each primary task provide direction
for the day-to-day decisions and activities within departments.

Overall Performance.   Profitability reflects the overall performance of for-profit
organizations. Profitability may be expressed in terms of net income, earnings per
share, or return on investment. Other overall performance goals are growth and
output volume. Growth pertains to increases in sales or profits over time. Volume
pertains to total sales or the amount of products or services delivered. The opening case of 3M Corporation illustrates growth goals.

Nonprofit organizations such as social service agencies or labor unions do not have goals of profitability, but they do have goals that attempt to specify the delivery of services to clients or members within specified expense levels. Growth and volume goals also may be indicators of overall performance in nonprofit organizations. Expanding their services to new clients is a primary goal for many social service agencies, such as Contact USA, which provides helpline services to people in crisis.

Resources. Resource goals pertain to the acquisition of needed material and financial resources from the environment. They may involve obtaining financing for the construction of new plants, finding less expensive sources for raw materials, or hiring top-quality technology graduates. Resource goals for Harvard University include attracting top-notch professors and students. Honda Motor Company has resource goals of obtaining high-quality auto parts at low cost. For Contact USA, resource goals include recruiting dedicated telephone volunteers and expanding the organization's funding base.

Market. Market goals relate to the market share or market standing desired by the organization. Market goals are the responsibility of marketing, sales, and advertising departments. An example of a market goal is Honda's desire to overtake Toyota Motor Company as the number-one seller of cars in Japan. Honda recently surpassed Nissan to become number two in Japan, and its recently introduced Fit subcompact has eclipsed the Toyota Corolla as the best-selling car in that market.[12]

Employee Development. Employee development pertains to the training, promotion, safety, and growth of employees. It includes both managers and workers. Fetzer Vineyards has a primary goal to contribute to the continuous growth and development of employees. The goal includes providing a comprehensive employee education program, with classes such as English as a second language, decision making, and communication. According to Barbara Wallace, Fetzer's director of human resources, " . . . our company feels that developing people's capabilities strengthens the organization. It's a way of creating loyalty."[13] At Marriott, alleviating employee stress and burnout in the hotel business is a priority, as described in the Leading by Design box.

Innovation and Change. Innovation goals pertain to internal flexibility and readiness to adapt to unexpected changes in the environment. Innovation goals are often defined with respect to the development of specific new services, products, or production processes At General Electric, Jeffrey Immelt has signaled a new focus on innovation by setting a goal to develop 25 percent more new products.[14]

Productivity. Productivity goals concern the amount of output achieved from available resources. They typically describe the amount of resource inputs required to reach desired outputs and are thus stated in terms of "cost for a unit of production," "units produced per employee," or "resource cost per employee." Managers at Akamai Technologies, which sells Web content delivery services, keep a close eye on sales per employee to see if the company is meeting productivity goals. Akamai's chief financial officer, Timothy Weller, sees this statistic as "the single easiest measure of employee productivity." Boeing Company has installed a new moving assembly line for the 737 aircraft to increase productivity. Once the wings and landing gear are attached, each plane is dragged toward the door at two inches a minute, with workers moving along with it on a float-like apparatus. Boeing's new productivity goal is to push a 737 out the door in five days, down from the eleven it currently takes.[15]

Successful organizations use a carefully balanced set of operative goals. Although profitability is important, some of today's best companies recognize that a single-minded focus on bottom-line profits may not be the best way to achieve high performance. Innovation and change goals are increasingly important, even though they may initially cause a *decrease* in profits. Employee development goals are critical for helping to maintain a motivated, committed workforce.

LEADING BY DESIGN   *Marriott*

Hotels are open 24 hours a day, 365 days a year, and problems have to be solved immediately to keep the hotel running and make sure guests are safe and satisfied. At Marriott, as at many hotels, the pursuit of superior round-the-clock performance led to a deeply ingrained culture of "face time." The more hours a manager put in, the better, whether the manager was in food and beverage, housekeeping, finance, or human resources. Seeing and being seen by employees and guests was considered critical to the hotel's success. But this philosophy had a price. By the mid-1990s, Marriott was having a tough time recruiting talented people, and some of the best and most experienced managers were leaving, citing a desire to have more of a life outside of work.

Top executives set new employee development goals that put a priority on managers' health and well-being. A test program called *Management Flexibility* was implemented at three of the company's hotels to see if new practices could help managers strike a better balance between their work and personal lives, relieve stress, and help prevent symptoms of burnout. The senior leadership team at each hotel began looking for ways to eliminate redundant meetings and tasks. In addition, all 165 managers from the three pilot hotels attended focus groups, where they identified numerous inefficiencies as well as asked for specific technology or tools that could help them do their jobs better in less time.

Implementation of the changes occurred swiftly to keep the momentum of the focus groups going. Senior leaders had to set the tone for many changes, such as emphasizing to managers that they shouldn't feel bashful about taking off in the middle of the afternoon if they were having a slow day. That meant top leaders themselves had to make the first move, making a concerted effort to leave work early whenever they could and being sure everyone knew about it. It took only a few months for real signs of change to be evident. For one thing, people no longer told "banker's hours" jokes when someone would leave early. In the past, if someone left at 5:00 p.m., a coworker might make a remark such as, "Working just half a day?" The comments reinforced the culture of face time and often made people feel guilty for working "just a ten-hour day." Now, instead of these kinds of comments, people were beginning to show genuine interest in one another's outside lives.

Marriott's test program was a success. By the end of the test period, people were paying much less attention to the number of hours worked and more to the tasks accomplished. Surveys revealed that managers were working an average of five less hours per week, while maintaining quality service and superior financial performance. Managers also reported being happier at work, feeling significantly less stress and job burnout, and being more motivated. Management Flexibility is now being implemented at hotels in the western, south central, and mid-Atlantic regions, with a wider rollout planned for later. By helping its managers find a healthy balance, Marriott has gained happier employees and better performance. In addition, recruiting is easier because talented people want to work for a company that allows them to thrive both at work and in their personal lives.

Source: Bill Munck, "Changing a Culture of Face Time," *Harvard Business Review* (November 2001), 125–131.

THE IMPORTANCE OF GOALS

Both official goals and operative goals are important for the organization, but they serve very different purposes. Official goals and mission statements describe a value system for the organization; operative goals represent the primary tasks of the organization. Official goals legitimize the organization; operative goals are more explicit and well defined.

Operative goals serve several specific purposes, as outlined in Exhibit 2.3. For one thing, goals can provide employees with a sense of direction, so that they know what they are working toward. This can help to motivate employees toward goal accomplishment, especially if employees are involved in setting the targets. Another purpose of goals is to act as guidelines for employee decision making. Goals act as a set of constraints on individual behavior and actions.[16] They help to define the appropriate decisions concerning organization structure, innovation, employee welfare, or growth. Finally, goals provide a standard for assessment. The level of organizational performance, whether in terms of profits, units produced, degree of employee satisfaction, level of innovation, or number of customer complaints, needs a basis for evaluation. Operative goals provide this standard for measurement.

A FRAMEWORK FOR SELECTING STRATEGY AND DESIGN

To support and accomplish the direction determined by organizational mission and operative goals, managers have to select specific strategy and design options that will help the organization achieve its purpose and goals within its competitive environment. In this section, we will examine a couple of practical approaches to selecting strategy and design.

A **strategy** is a plan for interacting with the competitive environment to achieve organizational goals. Some managers think of goals and strategies as interchangeable, but for our purposes, *goals* define where the organization wants to go and *strategies* define how it will get there. For example, a goal might be to achieve 15 percent annual sales growth; strategies to reach that goal might include aggressive advertising to attract new customers, motivating salespeople to increase the average size of customer purchases, and acquiring other businesses that produce similar products. Strategies can include any number of techniques to achieve the goal. The essence of formulating strategies is choosing whether the organization will perform different activities than its competitors or will execute similar activities more efficiently than its competitors do.[17]

Two models for formulating strategies are the Porter model of competitive strategies and Miles and Snow's strategy typology. Each provides a framework for

EXHIBIT 2.3   *Goal Type and Purpose*

Type of Goals	Purpose of Goals
Official goals, mission:	Legitimacy
Operative goals:	Employee direction and motivation
	Decision guidelines
	Standard of performance

competitive action. After describing the two models, we will discuss how the choice of strategies affects organization design.

PORTER'S COMPETITIVE STRATEGIES

Michael E. Porter studied a number of businesses and introduced a framework describing three competitive strategies: low-cost leadership, differentiation, and focus.[18] The focus strategy, in which the organization concentrates on a specific market or buyer group, is further divided into *focused low cost* and *focused differentiation*. This yields four basic strategies, as illustrated in Exhibit 2.4. To use this model, managers evaluate two factors, competitive advantage and competitive scope. With respect to advantage, managers determine whether to compete through lower cost or through the ability to offer unique or distinctive products and services that can command a premium price. Managers then determine whether the organization will compete on a broad scope (competing in many customer segments) or a narrow scope (competing in a selected customer segment or group of segments). These choices determine the selection of strategies, as illustrated in Exhibit 2.4.

Differentiation. In a differentiation strategy, organizations attempt to distinguish their products or services from others in the industry. An organization may use advertising, distinctive product features, exceptional service, or new technology to achieve a product perceived as unique. This strategy usually targets customers who are not particularly concerned with price, so it can be quite profitable. Maytag appliances, Tommy Hilfiger clothing, and Jaguar automobiles are examples of products from companies using a differentiation strategy. Service

"/><parttext text="BRIEFCASE

As an organization manager, keep this guideline in mind:

After goals have been defined, select strategies for achieving those goals. Define specific strategies based on Porter's competitive strategies or Miles and Snow's strategy typology."/><parttext text="

EXHIBIT 2.4   *Porter's Competitive Strategies*

Source: Adapted with the permission of The Free Press, a Division of Simon & Schuster Adult Publishing Group, from *COMPETITIVE ADVANTAGE: Creating and Sustaining Superior Performance* by Michael E. Porter. Copyright © 1985, 1988 by Michael E. Porter.
"/>

firms such as American Express, Hilton Hotels, and Starbucks Coffee can use a differentiation strategy as well. Charles Schwab, a brokerage firm that has long succeeded with a low-cost strategy, is shifting toward a differentiation strategy in its efforts to woo wealthy clients who have become disillusioned with big Wall Street firms involved in investment banking scandals.

In Practice

CHARLES SCHWAB & COMPANY

"This is retesting what the company stands for," David Pottruck says of Charles Schwab & Company's aggressive new strategy to push itself as a financial adviser to the wealthy. Pottruck, who serves as co-CEO with Charles R. (Chuck) Schwab, is charged with making the brokerage firm's new differentiation strategy work.

There are profound changes occurring at Schwab, which began as a discount broker-age firm in the mid-1970s to exploit the end of fixed-rate commissions. Schwab's success-ful OneSource no-fee mutual fund supermarket, launched in 1992, brought dramatic changes in that business. And Schwab got an early start in online trading, a market it still dominates. The core of Schwab's new strategy, however, is to promote itself as a unique kind of financial adviser for affluent investors. The centerpiece of the plan is a computer-based stock rating system combined with a private-client service. For a flat annual fee, a client meets one-on-one with a personal advisor to work out an investment plan and then returns to the same adviser for further advice throughout the year. The service is available at any branch, but Schwab has also opened nine separate sedate, plush offices in upscale neighborhoods so wealthy clients can avoid the hustle and bustle of the regular branches.

The unique aspect of all this is how Schwab rates stocks. A computer model grades more than 3,000 stocks on a scale of A to F, based on objective measurements, and updates them weekly. Schwab believes the objectivity of its system will be welcome to investors who have lost faith in the research advice of big Wall Street firms due to invest-ment banking and commission-based sales conflicts. Schwab's advertisements carefully point out that it doesn't have an investment banking arm, so it can't be swayed by loy-alty to corporate clients. The computerized system also protects clients from the whims or personal preferences of the adviser. "We're promoting a model different from all those other firms, and we will not be shy about promoting how different we are," Chuck Schwab says.[19]

A differentiation strategy can reduce rivalry with competitors and fight off the threat of substitute products because customers are loyal to the company's brand. However, companies must remember that successful differentiation strategies require a number of costly activities, such as product research and design and extensive advertising. Companies that pursue a differentiation strat-egy need strong marketing abilities and creative employees who are given the time and resources to seek innovations.

Low-Cost Leadership.   The **low-cost leadership** strategy tries to increase mar-ket share by emphasizing low cost compared to competitors. With a low-cost leadership strategy, the organization aggressively seeks efficient facilities, pursues cost reductions, and uses tight controls to produce products more efficiently than its competitors.

This strategy is concerned primarily with stability rather than taking risks or seeking new opportunities for innovation and growth. A low-cost position means the company can undercut competitors' prices and still offer comparable quality and earn a reasonable profit. One low-cost strategy leader, Dell Computer, declared a brutal price war in mid-2001 just as the computer industry entered its worst slump ever. The company's cost efficiency enabled Dell to rack up $361 million in profits while the rest of the industry reported losses totaling $1.1 billion.[20]

A low-cost strategy can help a company defend against current competitors because customers cannot find lower prices elsewhere. In addition, if substitute products or potential new competitors enter the picture, the low-cost producer is in a better position to prevent loss of market share.

Focus. With Porter's third strategy, the **focus strategy**, the organization concentrates on a specific regional market or buyer group. The company will try to achieve either a low-cost advantage or a differentiation advantage within a narrowly defined market. A classic example of a focused low-cost strategy is Wal-Mart. Sam Walton set the company on a path to success when he implemented his strategy to "put good-sized stores into little one-horse towns which everybody else was ignoring" and offer small town and rural customers national brands at "everyday low prices."[21] Edward Jones, a St. Louis-based brokerage house, is aiming to become the "Wal-Mart of Wall Street" by using a focused differentiation strategy. The firm has succeeded by building its business in rural and small-town America and providing investors with conservative, long-term investments. Peter Drucker (the ultimate management guru, who has worked as a consultant to Edward Jones) points out that the firm's safety-first orientation means it delivers a product "that no Wall Street house has ever sold before: peace of mind."[22]

When managers fail to adopt a competitive strategy, the organization is left with no strategic advantage and performance suffers. Porter found that companies that did not consciously adopt a low-cost, differentiation, or focus strategy, for example, achieved below-average profits compared to those that used one of the three strategies. Many Internet companies have failed because they did not develop competitive strategies that would distinguish them in the marketplace.[23] On the other hand, eBay has been highly successful with its coherent differentiation strategy.

MILES AND SNOW'S STRATEGY TYPOLOGY

Another business strategy typology was developed from the study of business strategies by Raymond Miles and Charles Snow.[24] The Miles and Snow typology is based on the idea that managers seek to formulate strategies that will be congruent with the external environment. Organizations strive for a fit among internal organization characteristics, strategy, and the external environment. The four strategies that can be developed are the prospector, the defender, the analyzer, and the reactor.

Prospector. The **prospector** strategy is to innovate, take risks, seek out new opportunities, and grow. This strategy is suited to a dynamic, growing environment, where creativity is more important than efficiency. Federal Express Corporation, which innovates in both services and production technology in the rapidly changing overnight mail industry, exemplifies the prospector strategy, as do today's leading high-tech companies, such as Microsoft.

Defender. The **defender** strategy is almost the opposite of the prospector. Rather than taking risks and seeking out new opportunities, the defender strategy is concerned with stability or even retrenchment. This strategy seeks to hold onto current customers, but it neither innovates nor seeks to grow. The defender is concerned primarily with internal efficiency and control to produce reliable, high-quality products for steady customers. This strategy can be successful when the organization exists in a declining industry or a stable environment. Paramount Pictures has been using a defender strategy for several years.[25] Paramount turns out a steady stream of reliable hits but few blockbusters. Managers shun risk and sometimes turn down potentially high-profile films to keep a lid on costs. This has enabled the company to remain highly profitable while other studios have low returns or actually lose money.

Analyzer.   The **analyzer** tries to maintain a stable business while innovating on the periphery. It seems to lie midway between the prospector and the defender. Some products will be targeted toward stable environments in which an efficiency strategy designed to keep current customers is used. Others will be targeted toward new, more dynamic environments, where growth is possible. The analyzer attempts to balance efficient production for current product lines with the creative development of new product lines. Procter & Gamble illustrates an analyzer strategy. Its strategy is to maintain a stable business for strong brands such as Tide, Crest, and Pampers, while also pushing to invent entirely new categories of products, such as those developed for home dry cleaning.[26]

Reactor.   The **reactor** strategy is not really a strategy at all. Rather, reactors respond to environmental threats and opportunities in an ad hoc fashion. In a reactor strategy, top management has not defined a long-range plan or given the organization an explicit mission or goal, so the organization takes whatever actions seem to meet immediate needs. Although the reactor strategy can sometimes be successful, it can also lead to failed companies. Some large, once highly successful companies, such as Xerox and Kodak, are struggling because managers failed to adopt a strategy consistent with consumer trends. Managers at McDonald's, long one of the most successful fast-food franchises in the world, currently seem to be floundering to find the appropriate strategy. McDonald's has had a string of disappointing quarterly profits and competitors continue to steal market share. Franchisees are aggravated and discouraged by the current uncertainty and lack of clear strategic direction for the future.[27]

HOW STRATEGIES AFFECT ORGANIZATION DESIGN

Choice of strategy affects internal organization characteristics. Organization design characteristics need to support the firm's competitive approach. For example, a company wanting to grow and invent new products looks and "feels" different from a company that is focused on maintaining market share for long-established products in a stable industry. Exhibit 2.5 summarizes organizational design characteristics associated with the Porter and Miles and Snow strategies.

With a low-cost leadership strategy, managers take an efficiency approach to organization design, whereas a differentiation strategy calls for a learning approach. Recall from Chapter 1 that organizations designed for efficiency have different characteristics from those designed for learning. A low-cost leadership strategy (efficiency) is associated with strong, centralized authority and tight control, standard operating procedures, and emphasis on efficient procurement and distribution systems. Employees generally perform routine tasks under close supervision and control and are not empowered to make decisions or take action on their own. A differentiation strategy, on the other hand, requires that employees be constantly experimenting and learning. Structure is fluid and flexible, with

BRIEFCASE

As an organization manager, keep this guideline in mind:

Design the organization to support the firm's competitive strategy. With a low-cost leadership or defender strategy, select design characteristics associated with an efficiency orientation. For a differentiation or prospector strategy, on the other hand, choose characteristics that encourage learning, innovation, and adaptation. Use a balanced mixture of characteristics for an analyzer strategy.

EXHIBIT 2.5   *Organizational Design Outcomes of Strategy*

Porter's Competitive Strategies	Miles and Snow's Strategy Typology
Strategy: Differentiation **Organization Design:** · Learning orientation; acts in a flexible, loosely knit way, with strong horizontal coordination · Strong capability in research · Values and builds in mechanisms for customer intimacy · Rewards employee creativity, risk-taking, and innovation **Strategy:** Low-Cost Leadership **Organization Design:** · Efficiency orientation; strong central authority; tight cost control, with frequent, detailed control reports · Standard operating procedures · Highly efficient procurement and distribution systems · Close supervision; routine tasks; limited employee empowerment	**Strategy:** Prospector **Organization Design:** · Learning orientation; flexible, fluid, decentralized structure · Strong capability in research **Strategy:** Defender **Organization Design:** · Efficiency orientation; centralized authority and tight cost control · Emphasis on production efficiency; low overhead · Close supervision; little employee empowerment **Strategy:** Analyzer **Organization Design:** · Balances efficiency and learning; tight cost control with flexibility and adaptability · Efficient production for stable product lines; emphasis on creativity, research, risk-taking for innovation **Strategy:** Reactor **Organization Design:** · No clear organizational approach; design characteristics may shift abruptly, depending on current needs

Source: Based on Michael E. Porter, *Competitive Strategy: Techniques for Analyzing Industries and Competitors* (New York: The Free Press, 1980); Michael Treacy and Fred Wiersema, "How Market Leaders Keep Their Edge," *Fortune* (February 6, 1995), 88–98; Michael Hitt, R. Duane Ireland, and Robert E. Hoskisson, *Strategic Management* (St. Paul, Minn.: West, 1995), 100–113; and Raymond E. Miles, Charles C. Snow, Alan D. Meyer, and Henry J. Coleman, Jr., "Organizational Strategy, Structure, and Process," *Academy of Management Review* 3 (1978), 546–562.

strong horizontal coordination. Empowered employees work directly with customers and are rewarded for creativity and risk taking. The organization values research, creativity, and innovativeness over efficiency and standard procedures.

The prospector strategy requires characteristics similar to a differentiation strategy, and the defender strategy takes an efficiency approach similar to low-cost leadership. Because the analyzer strategy attempts to balance efficiency for stable product lines with flexibility and learning for new products, it is associated with a mix of characteristics, as listed in Exhibit 2.5. With a reactor strategy, managers have left the organization with no direction and no clear approach to design.

OTHER FACTORS AFFECTING ORGANIZATION DESIGN

Strategy is one important factor that affects organization design. Ultimately, however, organization design is a result of numerous contingencies, which will be discussed throughout this book. The emphasis given to efficiency and control versus learning and flexibility is determined by the contingencies of strategy, environment, size and life cycle, technology, and organizational culture. The organization is designed to "fit" the contingency factors, as illustrated in Exhibit 2.6.

Exhibit 2.6   *Contingency Factors Affecting Organization Design*

The Right Mix of Design Characteristics Fits the Contingency Factors

For example, in a stable environment, the organization can have a traditional structure that emphasizes vertical control, efficiency, specialization, standard procedures, and centralized decision making. However, a rapidly changing environment may call for a more flexible structure, with strong horizontal coordination and collaboration through teams or other mechanisms. Environment will be discussed in detail in Chapters 4 and 5. In terms of size and life cycle, young, small organizations are generally informal and have little division of labor, few rules and regulations, and ad hoc budgeting and performance systems. Large organizations such as IBM or Sears, on the other hand, have an extensive division of labor, numerous rules and regulations, and standard procedures and systems for budgeting, control, rewards, and innovation. Size and stages of the life cycle will be discussed in Chapter 9.

Design must also fit the workflow technology of the organization. For example, with mass production technology, such as a traditional automobile assembly line, the organization functions best by emphasizing efficiency, formalization, specialization, centralized decision making, and tight control. An e-business, on the other hand, might need to be informal and flexible. Technology's impact on design will be discussed in detail in Chapters 7 and 8. A final contingency that affects organizational design is corporate culture. An organizational culture that values teamwork, collaboration, creativity, and open communication among all employees and managers, for example, would not function well with a tight, vertical structure and strict rules and regulations. The role of culture is discussed in Chapter 10.

One responsibility of managers is to design organizations that fit the contingency factors of strategy, environment, size and life cycle, technology, and culture. Finding the right "fit" leads to organizational effectiveness, whereas a poor fit can lead to decline or even the demise of the organization.

ASSESSING ORGANIZATIONAL EFFECTIVENESS

Understanding organizational goals and strategies, as well as the concept of fitting design to various contingencies, is a first step toward understanding organizational effectiveness. Organizational goals represent the reason for an organization's existence and the outcomes it seeks to achieve. The next few sections of the chapter explore the topic of effectiveness and how effectiveness is measured in organizations.

Recall from Chapter 1 that organizational effectiveness is the degree to which an organization realizes its goals.[28] *Effectiveness* is a broad concept. It implicitly takes into consideration a range of variables at both the organizational and departmental levels. Effectiveness evaluates the extent to which multiple goals—whether official or operative—are attained.

Efficiency is a more limited concept that pertains to the internal workings of the organization. Organizational efficiency is the amount of resources used to produce a unit of output.[29] It can be measured as the ratio of inputs to outputs. If one organization can achieve a given production level with fewer resources than another organization it would be described as more efficient.[30]

Sometimes efficiency leads to effectiveness. In other organizations, efficiency and effectiveness are not related. An organization may be highly efficient but fail to achieve its goals because it makes a product for which there is no demand. Likewise, an organization may achieve its profit goals but be inefficient.

Overall effectiveness is difficult to measure in organizations. Organizations are large, diverse, and fragmented. They perform many activities simultaneously. They pursue multiple goals. And they generate many outcomes, some intended and some unintended.[31] Managers determine what indicators to measure in order to gauge the effectiveness of their organizations. One study found that many managers have a difficult time with the concept of evaluating effectiveness based on characteristics that are not subject to hard, quantitative measurement.[32] However, top executives at some of today's leading companies are finding new ways to measure effectiveness, using indicators such as "customer delight" and employee satisfaction. A number of approaches to measuring effectiveness look at which measurements managers choose to track. These *contingency effectiveness approaches*, discussed in the next section, are based on looking at which part of the organization managers consider most important to measure. Later, we will examine an approach that integrates concern for various parts of the organization.

CONTINGENCY EFFECTIVENESS APPROACHES

Contingency approaches to measuring effectiveness focus on different parts of the organization. Organizations bring resources in from the environment, and those resources are transformed into outputs delivered back into the environment, as shown in Exhibit 2.7. The **goal approach** to organizational effectiveness is concerned with the output side and whether the organization achieves its goals in terms of desired levels of output.[33] The **resource-based approach** assesses effectiveness by observing the beginning of the process and evaluating whether the organization effectively obtains resources necessary for high performance. The **internal process approach** looks at internal activities and assesses effectiveness by indicators of internal health and efficiency.

GOAL APPROACH

The goal approach to effectiveness consists of identifying an organization's output goals and assessing how well the organization has attained those goals.[34] This is a logical approach because organizations do try to attain certain levels of

EXHIBIT 2.7   *Contingency Approaches to the Measurement of Organizational Effectiveness*

External Environment

Resource Inputs

Organization
Internal activities and processes

Product and Service Outputs

Resource-based approach

Internal process approach

Goal approach

output, profit, or client satisfaction. The goal approach measures progress toward attainment of those goals. For example, an important measure for the Women's National Basketball Association is number of tickets sold per game. During the league's first season, President Val Ackerman set a goal of 4,000 to 5,000 tickets per game. The organization actually averaged nearly 9,700 tickets per game, indicating that the WNBA was highly effective in meeting its goal for attendance.[35]

Indicators. The important goals to consider are operative goals. Efforts to measure effectiveness have been more productive using operative goals than using official goals.[36] Official goals tend to be abstract and difficult to measure. Operative goals reflect activities the organization is actually performing.

One example of multiple goals is from a survey of U.S. business corporations.[37] Their reported goals are shown in Exhibit 2.8. Twelve goals were listed

EXHIBIT 2.8   *Reported Goals of U.S. Corporations*

Goal	% Corporations
Profitability	89
Growth	82
Market share	66
Social responsibility	65
Employee welfare	62
Product quality and service	60
Research and development	54
Diversification	51
Efficiency	50
Financial stability	49
Resource conservation	39
Management development	35

Source: Adapted from Y. K. Shetty, "New Look at Corporate Goals." *California Management Review* 22, no. 2 (1979), 71–79.

as being important to these companies. These twelve goals represent outcomes that cannot be achieved simultaneously. They illustrate the array of outcomes organizations attempt to achieve.

Usefulness.   The goal approach is used in business organizations because output goals can be readily measured. Business firms typically evaluate performance in terms of profitability, growth, market share, and return on investment. However, identifying operative goals and measuring performance of an organization are not always easy. Two problems that must be resolved are the issues of multiple goals and subjective indicators of goal attainment.

Since organizations have multiple and conflicting goals, effectiveness often cannot be assessed by a single indicator. High achievement on one goal might mean low achievement on another. Moreover, there are department goals as well as overall performance goals. The full assessment of effectiveness should take into consideration several goals simultaneously. Most organizations use a balanced approach to measuring goals.

The other issue to resolve with the goal approach is how to identify operative goals for an organization and how to measure goal attainment. For business organizations, there are often objective indicators for certain goals, such as profit or growth. However, subjective assessment is needed for other goals, such as employee welfare or social responsibility. Someone has to go into the organization and learn what the actual goals are by talking with the top management team. Once goals are identified, subjective perceptions of goal attainment have to be used when quantitative indicators are not available. Managers rely on information from customers, competitors, suppliers, and employees, as well as their own intuition, when considering these goals. Consider the case of Nortel Networks.

In Practice

NORTEL

Nortel Networks, a Canadian-based company, is one of the world's largest global providers of high-performance Internet and advanced data networks. Nortel competes in more than 150 countries and has a major corporate goal of being the leader in next-generation network evolution. In an organization the size and scope of Nortel, setting and tracking goals can seem overwhelming. Yet leaders find ways to establish goals for each department and division and measure progress towards achieving them. Nortel has a diverse set of goals, including sales and profitability goals, market goals, goals for resource acquisition and innovation, and employee development goals.

Another important goal area for Nortel concerns the company's environmental commitment, which illustrates use of the goal approach to assessing effectiveness. Nortel tracks twenty-five performance indicators, including releases of air toxics, ozone precursors, and greenhouse gases; consumption of water, electricity, and paper; and regulatory violations. Some of these indicators can be easily measured, but Nortel managers have to make subjective decisions about how to weight the various indicators in measuring overall environmental performance. However, managers believe the goal approach provides a good way to keep the company on track toward a high level of environmental responsibility. Since Nortel began tracking these measurements, performance in the areas of paper consumption, pollutant releases, and overall energy consumption have steadily declined, reflecting positive movement toward meeting the company's long-term environmental goals.[38]

Although the goal approach seems to be the most logical way to assess organizational effectiveness, managers and evaluators should keep in mind that the actual measure of effectiveness is a complex process.

RESOURCE-BASED APPROACH

The resource-based approach looks at the input side of the transformation process shown in Exhibit 2.7. It assumes organizations must be successful in obtaining and managing valued resources in order to be effective. From a resource-based perspective, organizational effectiveness is defined as the ability of the organization, in either absolute or relative terms, to obtain scarce and valued resources and successfully integrate and manage them.[39]

Indicators. Obtaining and successfully managing resources is the criterion by which organizational effectiveness is assessed. In a broad sense, indicators of effectiveness according to the resource-based approach encompass the following dimensions:

- Bargaining position—the ability of the organization to obtain from its environment scarce and valued resources, including financial resources, raw materials, human resources, knowledge, and technology
- The abilities of the organization's decision makers to perceive and correctly interpret the real properties of the external environment
- The abilities of managers to use tangible (e.g., supplies, people) and intangible (e.g., knowledge, corporate culture) resources in day-to-day organizational activities to achieve superior performance
- The ability of the organization to respond to changes in the environment

Usefulness. The resource-based approach is valuable when other indicators of performance are difficult to obtain. In many not-for-profit and social welfare organizations, for example, it is hard to measure output goals or internal efficiency. Some for-profit organizations also use a resource-based approach. For example, Mathsoft, Inc., which provides a broad range of technical calculation and analytical software for business and academia, evaluates its effectiveness partly by looking at how many top-rate Ph.D.s it can recruit. CEO Charles Digate believes Mathsoft has a higher ratio of Ph.D.s to total employees than any other software company, which directly affects product quality and the company's image.[40]

Although the resource-based approach is valuable when other measures of effectiveness are not available, it does have shortcomings. For one thing, the approach only vaguely considers the organization's link to the needs of customers in the external environment. A superior ability to acquire and use resources is important only if resources and capabilities are used to achieve something that meets a need in the environment. Critics have challenged that the approach assumes stability in the marketplace and fails to adequately consider the changing value of various resources as the competitive environment and customer needs change.[41] The resource-based approach is most valuable when measures of goal attainment cannot be readily obtained.

INTERNAL PROCESS APPROACH

In the internal process approach, effectiveness is measured as internal organizational health and efficiency. An effective organization has a smooth, well-oiled internal process. Employees are happy and satisfied. Departmental activities mesh with one another to ensure high productivity. This approach does not consider the external environment. The important element in effectiveness is what the organization does with the resources it has, as reflected in internal health and efficiency.

Indicators. One indicator of internal process effectiveness is the organization's economic efficiency. However, the best-known proponents of a process model are from the human relations approach to organizations. Such writers as Chris Argyris, Warren G. Bennis, Rensis Likert, and Richard Beckhard have all worked extensively with human resources in organizations and emphasize the connection between human resources and effectiveness.[42] Writers on corporate culture and organizational excellence have stressed the importance of internal processes. Results from a study of nearly two hundred secondary schools showed that both human resources and employee-oriented processes were important in explaining and promoting effectiveness in those organizations.[43]

There are seven indicators of an effective organization as seen from an internal process approach:

1. Strong corporate culture and positive work climate
2. Team spirit, group loyalty, and teamwork
3. Confidence, trust, and communication between workers and management
4. Decision making near sources of information, regardless of where those sources are on the organizational chart
5. Undistorted horizontal and vertical communication; sharing of relevant facts and feelings
6. Rewards to managers for performance, growth, and development of subordinates and for creating an effective working group
7. Interaction between the organization and its parts, with conflict that occurs over projects resolved in the interest of the organization[44]

BRIEFCASE

As an organization manager, keep this guideline in mind:

Use the goal approach, internal process approach, and resource-based approach to obtain specific pictures of organizational effectiveness. Assess competing values to obtain a broader, more balanced picture of effectiveness.

Usefulness. The internal process approach is important because the efficient use of resources and harmonious internal functioning are ways to measure effectiveness. Today, most managers believe that happy, committed, actively involved employees and a positive corporate culture are important measures of effectiveness. Gary White, CEO of The Gymboree Corp., for example, believes that keeping employees happy is the key to long-term success for his company, which runs parent-child play programs and operates more than 500 retail clothing stores.[45]

The internal process approach also has shortcomings. Total output and the organization's relationship with the external environment are not evaluated. Also, evaluations of internal health and functioning are often subjective, because many aspects of inputs and internal processes are not quantifiable. Managers should be aware that this approach alone represents a limited view of organizational effectiveness.

AN INTEGRATED EFFECTIVENESS MODEL

The three approaches—goal, resource-based, internal process—to organizational effectiveness described earlier all have something to offer, but each one tells only part of the story. The competing values model tries to balance a concern with various parts of the organization rather than focusing on one part. This approach to effectiveness acknowledges that organizations do many things and have many outcomes.[46] It combines several indicators of effectiveness into a single framework.

The model is based on the assumption that there is disagreement and competing viewpoints about what constitutes effectiveness. Managers sometimes disagree over which are the most important goals to pursue and measure. In addition, stakeholders have competing claims on what they want from the organization, as described in Chapter 1. The competing values model was originally developed by Robert Quinn and John Rohrbaugh to combine the diverse indicators of performance used by managers and researchers.[47] Using a comprehensive list of performance indicators, a panel of experts in organizational effectiveness rated the indicators for similarity. The analysis produced underlying dimensions of effectiveness criteria that represented competing management values in organizations.

Indicators. The first value dimension pertains to organizational **focus**, which is whether dominant values concern issues that are *internal* or *external* to the firm. Internal focus reflects a management concern for the well-being and efficiency of employees, and external focus represents an emphasis on the well-being of the organization itself with respect to the environment. The second value dimension pertains to organization **structure**, and whether *stability* versus *flexibility* is the dominant structural consideration. Stability reflects a management value for efficiency and top down control, whereas flexibility represents a value for learning and change.

The value dimensions of structure and focus are illustrated in Exhibit 2.9. The combination of dimensions provides four approaches to organizational effectiveness, which, though seemingly different, are closely related. In real organizations, these competing values can and often do exist together. Each approach reflects a different management emphasis with respect to structure and focus.[48]

EXHIBIT 2.9   *Four Approaches to Effectiveness Values*

Source: Adapted from Robert E. Quinn and John Rohrbaugh, "A Spatial Model of Effectiveness Criteria: Toward a Competing Values Approach to Organizational Analysis," *Management Science* 29 (1983), 363–377; and Robert E. Quinn and Kim Cameron, "Organizational Life Cycles and Shifting Criteria of Effectiveness: Some Preliminary Evidence," *Management Science* 29 (1983), 33–51.

A combination of external focus and flexible structure leads to an **open systems emphasis**. Management's primary goals are growth and resource acquisition. The organization accomplishes these goals through the subgoals of flexibility, readiness, and a positive external evaluation. The dominant value is establishing a good relationship with the environment to acquire resources and grow. This emphasis is similar in some ways to the resource-based approach described earlier.

The **rational goal emphasis** represents management values of structural control and external focus. The primary goals are productivity, efficiency, and profit. The organization wants to achieve output goals in a controlled way. Subgoals that facilitate these outcomes are internal planning and goal setting, which are rational management tools. The rational goal emphasis is similar to the goal approach described earlier.

The **internal process emphasis** is in the lower-left section of Exhibit 2.9; it reflects the values of internal focus and structural control. The primary outcome is a stable organizational setting that maintains itself in an orderly way. Organizations that are well established in the environment and simply want to maintain their current position would reflect this emphasis. Subgoals include mechanisms for efficient communication, information management, and decision making. Although this part of the competing values model is similar in some ways to the internal process approach described earlier, it is less concerned with human resources than with other internal processes that lead to efficiency.

The **human relations emphasis** incorporates the values of an internal focus and a flexible structure. Here, management concern is for the development of human resources. Employees are given opportunities for autonomy and development. Management works toward the subgoals of cohesion, morale, and training opportunities. Organizations adopting this emphasis are more concerned with employees than with the environment.

The four cells in Exhibit 2.9 represent opposing organizational values. Managers must decide which goal values will take priority in their organizations. The way two organizations are mapped onto the four approaches is shown in Exhibit 2.10.[49] Organization A is a young organization concerned with finding a niche and becoming established in the external environment. Primary emphasis is given to flexibility, innovation, the acquisition of resources from the environment, and the satisfaction of external constituencies. This organization gives moderate emphasis to human relations and even less emphasis to current productivity and profits. Satisfying and adapting to the environment are more important. The attention given to open systems values means that the internal process emphasis is practically nonexistent. Stability and equilibrium are of little concern.

Organization B, in contrast, is an established business in which the dominant value is productivity and profits. This organization is characterized by planning and goal setting. Organization B is a large company that is well established in the environment and is primarily concerned with successful production and profits. Flexibility and human resources are not major concerns. This organization prefers stability and equilibrium to learning and innovation because it wants to take advantage of its established customers.

Usefulness. The competing values model makes two contributions. First, it integrates diverse concepts of effectiveness into a single perspective. It incorporates the ideas of output goals, resource acquisition, and human resource development as

Exhibit 2.10   *Effectiveness Values for Two Organizations*

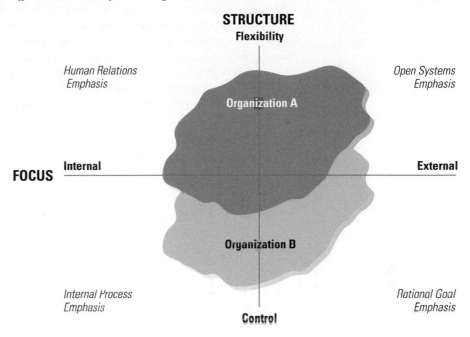

goals the organization tries to accomplish. Second, the model calls attention to effectiveness criteria as management values and shows how opposing values exist at the same time. Managers must decide which values they wish to pursue and which values will receive less emphasis. The four competing values exist simultaneously, but not all will receive equal priority. For example, a new, small organization that concentrates on establishing itself within a competitive environment will give less emphasis to developing employees than to the external environment.

The dominant values in an organization often change over time as organizations experience new environmental demands or new top leadership. Chrysler provides an example of how new values were brought in with new leadership.

In Practice

CHRYSLER CORPORATION

When Germany's Daimler-Benz AG acquired Chrysler Corporation, the American company's managers were focused on internal control, trying to maintain stability and consistency within the organization. However, costs had continued to climb, while the automaker's market share continued a downhill slide. Thus, leaders wanted to put more emphasis on the external environment in their approach to effectiveness.

New top managers at Chrysler immediately began shifting the organization toward external values of growth and profitability. CEO Dieter Zetsche has declared a goal of boosting Chrysler's annual sales by one million vehicles a year over the next five to ten years. To do that means rapidly developing hot new models of cars and trucks, requiring that the organization be flexible and in tune with the marketplace. At the same time, Zetsche and his chief operating officer, Wolfgang Bernhard, are trying to rein in costs, improve efficiency, and boost profits.

It is a balancing act that seems to be working. Consider the development of a new low-end Jeep targeting young buyers. With the focus on speed, flexibility, and efficiency, a team made up of people from across the company completed a preliminary design for the new model within about four months, a process that would have previously taken a year. To save on market research costs, team members hung out in Internet chat rooms and local sandwich shops that cater to teenagers. One team member contributed ideas from his teenage nephew. Even more important, the platform for the low-end Jeep can be scaled up to Jeep Grand Cherokee size and will be used to support four or five different models. Using a common core for multiple models is key to a new product development process that trims costs at the same time it increases the variety of models available in Chrysler showrooms.

Chrysler is still struggling, but the shift to new values holds promise for getting Detroit's number-three car maker back on track.[50]

The dominant goal at Chrysler for several years was control with a focus on internal costs, reflecting an internal process emphasis as shown in Exhibit 2.10. The new values have shifted to an external focus and include goals of flexibility and growth as well as increasing efficiency and profitability, consistent with the open systems and rational goal emphases.

SUMMARY AND INTERPRETATION

This chapter discussed organizational goals and the strategies top managers use to help organizations achieve those goals. Goals specify the mission or purpose of an organization and its desired future state; strategies define how the organization will reach its goals. The chapter also discussed the impact of strategy on organization design and how designing the organization to fit strategy and other contingencies can lead to organizational effectiveness. The chapter closed with an examination of the most popular approaches to measuring effectiveness, that is, how well the organization realizes its purpose and attains its desired future state.

Organizations exist for a purpose; top managers define a specific mission or task to be accomplished. The mission statement, or official goals, makes explicit the purpose and direction of an organization. Official and operative goals are a key element in organizations because they meet these needs—establishing legitimacy with external groups and setting standards of performance for participants.

Managers must develop strategies that describe the actions required to achieve goals. Strategies may include any number of techniques to achieve the stated goals. Two models for formulating strategies are Porter's competitive strategies and the Miles and Snow strategy typology. Organization design needs to fit the firm's competitive approach to contribute to organizational effectiveness.

Assessing organizational effectiveness reflects the complexity of organizations as a topic of study. No easy, simple, guaranteed measure will provide an unequivocal assessment of performance. Organizations must perform diverse activities well—from obtaining resource inputs to delivering outputs—to be successful. Contingency approaches use output goals, resource acquisition, or internal health and efficiency as the criteria of effectiveness. The competing values model is a balanced approach that considers multiple criteria simultaneously. Organizations can be assessed by evaluating competing values for effectiveness. No approach is suitable for every organization, but each offers some advantages that the others may lack.

From the point of view of managers, the goal approach to effectiveness and measures of internal efficiency are useful when measures are available. The attainment of output and profit goals reflects the purpose of the organization, and efficiency reflects the cost of attaining those goals. Other factors such as top-management preferences, the extent to which goals are measurable, and the scarcity of environmental resources may influence the use of effectiveness criteria. In not-for-profit organizations, where internal processes and output criteria are often not quantifiable, resource acquisition may be the best available indicator of effectiveness.

From the point of view of people outside the organization, such as academic investigators or government researchers, the competing values model of organizational effectiveness may be preferable. This model acknowledges different areas of focus (internal, external) and structure (flexibility, stability) and allows for managers to choose among approaches—human relations, open systems, rational goal, or internal process—in order to emphasize the values they wish to pursue.

Key Concepts

analyzer	mission
competing values model	official goals
defender	open systems emphasis
differentiation	operative goals
focus	organizational goal
focus strategy	prospector
goal approach	rational goal emphasis
human relations emphasis	reactor
internal process approach	resource-based approach
internal process emphasis	strategy
low-cost leadership	structure

Discussion Questions

1. Discuss the role of top management in setting organizational direction.
2. How might a company's goals for employee development be related to its goals for innovation and change? To goals for productivity? Can you discuss ways these types of goals might conflict in an organization?
3. What is a goal for the class for which you are reading this text? Who established this goal? Discuss how the goal affects your direction and motivation.
4. What is the difference between a goal and a strategy as defined in the text? Identify both a goal and a strategy for a campus or community organization with which you are involved.
5. Discuss the similarities and differences in the strategies described in Porter's competitive strategies and Miles and Snow's typology.
6. Do you believe mission statements and official goal statements provide an organization with genuine legitimacy in the external environment? Discuss.
7. Suppose you have been asked to evaluate the effectiveness of the police department in a medium-sized community. Where would you begin, and how would you proceed? What effectiveness approach would you prefer?
8. What are the advantages and disadvantages of the resource-based approach versus the goal approach for measuring organizational effectiveness?
9. What are the similarities and differences between assessing effectiveness on the basis of competing values versus the stakeholder approach described in Chapter 1? Explain.
10. A noted organization theorist once said, "Organizational effectiveness can be whatever top management defines it to be." Discuss.

Chapter 2 Workbook *Identifying Company Goals and Strategies**

Choose three companies, either in the same industry or in three different industries. Search the Internet for information on the companies, including annual reports. In each company look particularly at the goals expressed. Refer back to the goals in Exhibit 2.8 and also to Porter's competitive strategies in Exhibit 2.4.

	Goals from Exhibit 2.8 articulated	Strategies from Porter used
Company #1		
Company #2		
Company #3		

Questions

1. Which goals seem most important?
2. Look for differences in the goals and strategies of the three companies and develop an explanation for those differences.
3. Which of the goals or strategies should be changed? Why?

4. *Optional:* Compare your table with those of other students and look for common themes. Which companies seem to articulate and communicate their goals and strategies best?

CASE FOR ANALYSIS   *The University Art Museum**

Visitors to the campus were always shown the University Art Museum, of which the large and distinguished university was very proud. A photograph of the handsome neoclassical building that housed the museum had long been used by the university for the cover of its brochures and catalogs.

The building, together with a substantial endowment, was given to the university around 1912 by an alumnus, the son of the university's first president, who had become very wealthy as an investment banker. He also gave the university his own small, but high-quality, collections—one of Etruscan figurines, and one, unique in America, of English pre-Raphaelite paintings. He then served as the museum's unpaid director until his death. During his tenure he brought a few additional collections to the museum, largely from other alumni of the university. Only rarely did the museum purchase anything. As a result, the museum housed several small collections of uneven quality. As long as the founder ran the museum, none of the collections was ever shown to anybody except a few members of the university's art history faculty, who were admitted as the founder's private guests.

After the founder's death, in the late 1920s, the university intended to bring in a professional museum director. Indeed, this had been part of the agreement

---

*Case #3, "The University Art Museum: Defining Purpose and Mission"(pp. 28–35), from *Management Cases* by Peter F. Drucker. Copyright © 1977 by Peter F. Drucker. Reprinted by permission of the author.

under which the founder had given the museum. A search committee was to be appointed; but in the meantime a graduate student in art history, who had shown interest in the museum and who had spent a good many hours in it, took over temporarily. At first, Miss Kirkoff did not even have a title, let alone a salary. But she stayed on acting as the museum's director and over the next thirty years was promoted in stages to that title. But from the first day, whatever her title, she was in charge. She immediately set about changing the museum altogether. She cataloged the collections. She pursued new gifts, again primarily small collections from alumni and other friends of the university. She organized fund raising for the museum. But, above all, she began to integrate the museum into the work of the university.

When a space problem arose in the years immediately following World War II, Miss Kirkoff offered the third floor of the museum to the art history faculty, which moved its offices there. She remodeled the building to include classrooms and a modern and well-appointed auditorium. She raised funds to build one of the best research and reference libraries in art history in the country. She also began to organize a series of special exhibitions built around one of the museum's own collections, complemented by loans from outside collections. For each of these exhibitions, she had a distinguished member of the university's art faculty write a catalog. These catalogs speedily became the leading scholarly texts in the fields.

Miss Kirkoff ran the University Art Museum for almost half a century. But at the age of 68, after suffering a severe stroke, she had to retire. In her letter of resignation she proudly pointed to the museum's growth and accomplishment under her stewardship. "Our endowment," she wrote, "now compares favorably with museums several times our size. We never have had to ask the university for any money other than our share of the university's insurance policies. Our collections in the areas of our strength, while small, are of first-rate quality and importance. Above all, we are being used by more people than any museum of our size. Our lecture series, in which members of the university's art history faculty present a major subject to a university audience of students and faculty, attracts regularly three hundred to five hundred people; and if we had the seating capacity, we could easily have a larger audience. Our exhibitions are seen and studied by more visitors, most of them members of the university community, than all

but the most highly publicized exhibitions in the very big museums ever draw. Above all, the courses and seminars offered in the museum have become one of the most popular and most rapidly growing educational features of the university. No other museum in this country or anywhere else," concluded Miss Kirkoff, "has so successfully integrated art into the life of a major university and a major university into the work of a museum."

Miss Kirkoff strongly recommended that the university bring in a professional museum director as her successor. "The museum is much too big and much too important to be entrusted to another amateur such as I was forty-five years ago," she wrote. "And it needs careful thinking regarding its direction, its basis of support, and its future relationship with the university."

The university took Miss Kirkoff's advice. A search committee was duly appointed and, after one year's work, it produced a candidate whom everybody approved. The candidate was himself a graduate of the university who had then obtained his Ph.D. in art history and in museum work from the university. Both his teaching and his administrative record were sound, leading to his current museum directorship in a medium-sized city. There he converted an old, well-known, but rather sleepy museum to a lively, community-oriented museum whose exhibitions were well publicized and attracted large crowds.

The new museum director took over with great fanfare in September 1981. Less than three years later he left—with less fanfare, but still with considerable noise. Whether he resigned or was fired was not quite clear. But that there was bitterness on both sides was only too obvious.

The new director, upon his arrival, had announced that he looked upon the museum as a "major community resource" and intended to "make the tremendous artistic and scholarly resources of the museum fully available to the academic community as well as to the public." When he said these things in an interview with the college newspaper, everybody nodded in approval. It soon became clear that what he meant by "community resource" and what the faculty and students understood by these words were not the same. The museum had always been "open to the public" but, in practice, it was members of the college community who used the museum and attended its lectures, its exhibitions, and its frequent seminars.

The first thing the new director did, however, was to promote visits from the public schools in the area. He soon began to change the exhibition policy. Instead of organizing small shows, focused on a major collection of the museum and built around a scholarly catalog, he began to organize "popular exhibitions" around "topics of general interest" such as "Women Artists through the Ages." He promoted these exhibitions vigorously in the newspapers, in radio and television interviews, and, above all, in the local schools. As a result, what had been a busy but quiet place was soon knee-deep with schoolchildren, taken to the museum in special buses that cluttered the access roads around the museum and throughout the campus. The faculty, which was not particularly happy with the resulting noise and confusion, became thoroughly upset when the scholarly old chairman of the art history department was mobbed by fourth-graders who sprayed him with their water pistols as he tried to push his way through the main hall to his office.

Increasingly, the new director did not design his own shows, but brought in traveling exhibitions from major museums, importing their catalog as well rather than have his own faculty produce one.

The students, too, were apparently unenthusiastic after the first six or eight months, during which the new director had been somewhat of a campus hero. Attendance at the classes and seminars held at the art museum fell off sharply, as did attendance at the evening lectures. When the editor of the campus newspaper interviewed students for a story on the museum, he was told again and again that the museum had become too noisy and too "sensational" for students to enjoy the classes and to have a chance to learn.

What brought all this to a head was an Islamic art exhibit in late 1983. Since the museum had little Islamic art, nobody criticized the showing of a traveling exhibit, offered on very advantageous terms with generous financial assistance from some of the Arab governments. But then, instead of inviting one of the university's own faculty members to deliver the customary talk at the opening of the exhibit, the director brought in a cultural attaché of one of the Arab embassies in Washington. The speaker, it was reported, used the occasion to deliver a violent attack on Israel and on the American policy of supporting Israel against the Arabs. A week later, the university senate decided to appoint an advisory committee, drawn mostly from members of the art history faculty, which, in the future, would have to approve all plans for exhibits and lectures. The director thereupon, in an interview with the campus newspaper, sharply attacked the faculty as "elitist" and "snobbish" and as believing that "art belongs to the rich." Six months later, in June 1984, his resignation was announced.

Under the bylaws of the university, the academic senate appoints a search committee. Normally, this is pure formality. The chairperson of the appropriate department submits the department's nominees for the committee who are approved and appointed, usually without debate. But when the academic senate early the following semester was asked to appoint the search committee, things were far from "normal." The dean who presided, sensing the tempers in the room, tried to smooth over things by saying, "Clearly, we picked the wrong person the last time. We will have to try very hard to find the right one this time."

He was immediately interrupted by an economist, known for his populism, who broke in and said, "I admit that the late director was probably not the right personality. But I strongly believe that his personality was not at the root of the problem. He tried to do what needs doing, and this got him in trouble with the faculty. He tried to make our museum a community resource, to bring in the community and to make art accessible to broad masses of people, to the blacks and the Puerto Ricans, to the kids from the ghetto schools and to a lay public. And this is what we really resented. Maybe his methods were not the most tactful ones—I admit I could have done without those interviews he gave. But what he tried to do was right. We had better commit ourselves to the policy he wanted to put into effect, or else we will have deserved his attacks on us as 'elitist' and 'snobbish.'"

"This is nonsense," cut in the usually silent and polite senate member from the art history faculty. "It makes absolutely no sense for our museum to become the kind of community resource our late director and my distinguished colleague want it to be. First, there is no need. The city has one of the world's finest and biggest museums, and it does exactly that and does it very well. Secondly, we have neither the artistic resources nor the financial resources to serve the community at large. We can do something different but equally important and indeed unique. Ours is the only museum in the country, and perhaps in the world, that is fully integrated with an academic community and truly a teaching institution. We are using it, or at least we used to until the last few unfortunate years, as a major educational resource for all our students. No other museum in the country, and as far as I know in the world, is bringing undergraduates into art the way we do. All of us, in addition to our scholarly and graduate work, teach undergraduate courses for people who are not going to be art majors or art historians. We work with the engineering students and show them what we do in our conservation and restoration work. We work with architecture students and show them the development of architecture through the ages. Above all, we work with liberal arts students, who often have had no exposure to art before they came here and who enjoy our courses all the more because they are scholarly and not just 'art appreciation.' This is unique and this is what our museum can do and should do."

"I doubt that this is really what we should be doing," commented the chairman of the mathematics department. "The museum, as far as I know, is part of the graduate faculty. It should concentrate on training art historians in its Ph.D. program, on its scholarly work, and on its research. I would strongly urge that the museum be considered an adjunct to graduate and especially to Ph.D. education, confine itself to this work, and stay out of all attempts to be 'popular,' both on campus and outside of it. The glory of the museum is the scholarly catalogs produced by our faculty, and our Ph.D. graduates who are sought after by art history faculties throughout the country. This is the museum's mission, which can only be impaired by the attempts to be 'popular,' whether with students or with the public."

"These are very interesting and important comments," said the dean, still trying to pacify. "But I think this can wait until we know who the new director is going to be. Then we should raise these questions with him."

"I beg to differ, Mr. Dean," said one of the elder statesmen of the faculty. "During the summer months, I discussed this question with an old friend and neighbor of mine in the country, the director of one of the nation's great museums. He said to me: 'You do not have a personality problem; you have a management problem. You have not, as a university, taken responsibility for the mission, the direction, and the objectives of your museum. Until you do this, no director can succeed. And this is your decision. In fact, you cannot hope to get a good director until you can tell that person what your basic objectives are. If your late director is to blame—I know him and I know that he is abrasive—it is for being willing to take on a job when you, the university, had not faced up to the basic management decisions. There is no point talking about who should manage until it is clear what it is that has to be managed and for what.'"

At this point the dean realized that he had to adjourn the discussion unless he wanted the meeting to degenerate into a brawl. But he also realized that he had to identify the issues and possible decisions before the next senate meeting a month later.

CASE FOR ANALYSIS   Airstar, Inc.*

Airstar, Inc. manufactures, repairs, and overhauls pistons and jet engines for smaller, often previously owned aircraft. The company had a solid niche, and most managers had been with the founder for more than twenty years. With the founder's death five years ago, Roy Morgan took over as president at Airstar. Mr. Morgan has called you in as a consultant.

Your research indicates that this industry is changing rapidly. Airstar is feeling encroachment of huge conglomerates like General Electric and Pratt &Whitney, and its backlog of orders is the lowest in several years. The company has always been known for its superior quality, safety, and customer service. However, it has never been under threat before, and senior managers are not sure which strategic direction to take. They have considered potential acquisitions, imports and exports, more research, and additional repair lines. The organization is becoming more chaotic, which is frustrating Morgan and his vice presidents.

Before a meeting with his team, he confides to you, "Organizing is supposed to be easy. For maximum efficiency, work should be divided into simple, logical, routine tasks. These business tasks can be grouped by similar kinds of work characteristics and arranged within an organization under a particularly suited executive. So why are we having so many problems with our executives?"

*Adapted from Bernard A. Deitzer and Karl A. Shilliff, *Contemporary Management Incidents* (Columbus, Ohio: Grid, Inc., 1977), 43–46. Copyright © 1997 by John Wiley & Sons, Inc. This material is used by permission of John Wiley & Sons, Inc.

Morgan met with several of his trusted corporate officers in the executive dining room to discuss what was happening to corporate leadership at Airstar. Morgan went on to explain that he was really becoming concerned with the situation. There have been outright conflicts between the vice president of marketing and controller over merger and acquisition opportunities. There have been many instances of duplication of work, with corporate officers trying to outmaneuver each other.

"Communications are atrocious," Morgan said to the others. "Why, I didn't even get a copy of the export finance report until my secretary made an effort to find one for me. My basis for evaluation and appraisal of corporate executive performance and goal accomplishment is fast becoming obsolete. People have been working up their own job descriptions, and they all include overlapping responsibilities. Changes and decisions are being made on the basis of expediency and are perpetuating too many mistakes. We must take a good look at these organizational realities and correct the situation immediately."

Jim Robinson, vice president of manufacturing, pointed out to Morgan that Airstar is not really following the "principles of good organization." "For instance," explained Robinson, "let's review what we should be practicing as administrators." Some of the principles Robinson believed they should be following are:

1. Determine the goals, policies, programs, plans and strategies that will best achieve the desired results for our company.

2. Determine the various business tasks to be done.
3. Divide the business tasks into a logical and understandable organizational structure.
4. Determine the suitable personnel to occupy positions within the organizational structure.
5. Define the responsibility and authority of each supervisor clearly in writing.
6. Keep the number and kinds of levels of authority at a minimum.

Robinson proposed that the group study the corporate organizational chart, as well as the various corporate business tasks. After reviewing the corporate organizational chart, Robinson, Morgan, and the others agreed that the number and kinds of formal corporate authority were logical and not much different from other corporations. The group then listed the various corporate business tasks that went on within Airstar.

Robinson continued. "How did we ever decide who should handle mergers or acquisitions?" Morgan answered, "I guess it just occurred over time that the vice president of marketing should have the responsibility." "But," Robinson queried, "where is it written down? How would the controller know it?" "Aha," Morgan exclaimed. "It looks like I'm part of the problem. There isn't anything in writing. Tasks were assigned superficially, as they became problems. This has all been rather informal. I'll establish a group to decide who should have responsibility for what so things can return to our previous level of efficiency."

Chapter 2 Workshop   *Competing Values and Organizational Effectiveness* *

1. Divide into groups of four to six members.
2. Select an organization to "study" for this exercise. It should be an organization one of you has worked at, or it could be the university.
3. Using the exhibit "Four Approaches to Effectiveness Values" (Exhibit 2.9), your group should list eight potential measures that show a balanced view of performance. These should relate not only to work activities, but also to goal values for the company. Use the table on page 81.
4. How will achieving these goal values help the organization to become more effective? Which values could be given more weight than others? Why?

5. Present your competing values chart to the rest of the class. Each group should explain why it chose those particular values and which are more important. Be prepared to defend your position to the other groups, which are encouraged to question your choices.

* Adapted by Dorothy Marcic from general ideas in Jennifer Howard and Larry Miller, *Team Management*, The Miller Consulting Group, 1994, p. 92.

Goal or Subgoal		Performance Gauge	How to Measure	Source of Data	What Do You Consider Effective?
(Example) Equilibrium		Turnover rates	Compare percentages of workers who left	HRM files	25% reduction in first year
Open system	1.				
	2.				
Human relations	3.				
	4.				
Internal process	5.				
	6.				
Rational goal	7.				
	8.				

Notes

1. Michael Arndt, "3M: A Lab for Growth?" *BusinessWeek* (January 21, 2002), 50–51; and Jerry Useem, "Can McNerney Reinvent GE?" *Fortune* (August 12, 2002), 127–132.

2. Amitai Etzioni, *Modern Organizations* (Englewood Cliffs, N.J.: Prentice-Hall, 1964), 6.

3. John P. Kotter, "What Effective General Managers Really Do," *Harvard Business Review* (November–December 1982), 156–167; Henry Mintzberg, *The Nature of Managerial Work* (New York: Harper & Row, 1973).

4. Charles C. Snow and Lawrence G. Hrebiniak, "Strategy, Distinctive Competence, and Organizational Performance," *Administrative Science Quarterly* 25 (1980), 317–335.

5. William C. Symonds with Rich Miller, "Harvard," *BusinessWeek* (February 18, 2002), 72–78.

6. David L. Calfee, "Get Your Mission Statement Working!" *Management Review* (January 1993), 54–57; John A. Pearce II and Fred David, "Corporate Mission Statements: The Bottom Line," *Academy of Management Executive* 1 (1987), 109–116; and Christopher K. Bart, "Sex, Lies, and Mission Statements," *Business Horizons* (November–December 1997), 23–28.

7. Barbara Bartkus, Myron Glassman, and R. Bruce McAfee, "Mission Statements: Are They Smoke and Mirrors?" *Business Horizons* (November–December 2000), 23–28.

8. Mark C. Suchman, "Managing Legitimacy: Strategic and Institutional Approaches," *Academy of Management Review* 20, no. 3 (1995), 571–610.

9. Kurt Eichenwald, "Miscues, Missteps, and the Fall of Andersen," *The New York Times* (May 8, 2002), C1, C4.

10. Charles Perrow, "The Analysis of Goals in Complex Organizations," *American Sociological Review* 26 (1961), 854–866.

11. Johannes U. Stoelwinder and Martin P. Charns, "The Task Field Model of Organization Analysis and Design," *Human Relations* 34 (1981), 743–762; Anthony Raia, *Managing by Objectives* (Glenview, Ill.: Scott, Foresman, 1974).

12. Alex Taylor III, "Honda Goes Its Own Way," *Fortune* (July 22, 2002), 148–152.

13. Miriam Schulman, "Winery with a Mission," *Issues in Ethics* (Spring 1996): 14–15.

14. Rachel Emma Silverman, "GE Goes Back to Future," *The Wall Street Journal* (May 7, 2002), B1, B4.

15. Kim Cross, "Does Your Team Measure Up?" *Business2.com* (June 12, 2001), 22–28; J. Lynn Lunsford, "Lean Times: With Airbus on Its Tail, Boeing is Rethinking How It Builds Planes," *The Wall Street Journal* (September 5, 2001), A11.

16. James D. Thompson, *Organizations in Action* (New York: McGraw-Hill, 1967): 83–98.

17. Michael E. Porter, "What Is Strategy?" *Harvard Business Review* (November–December 1996), 61–78.

18. Michael E. Porter, *Competitive Strategy: Techniques for Analyzing Industries and Competitors* (New York: Free Press, 1980).

19. Louise Lee with Emily Thornton, "Schwab vs. Wall Street," *BusinessWeek* (June 3, 2002), 64–71.

20. Andrew Park with Peter Burrows, "Dell, The Conqueror," *BusinessWeek* (September 24, 2001), 92–102.

21. Joan Magretta, "Why Business Models Matter," *Harvard Business Review* (May 2002), 86–92.

22. Richard Teitelbaum, "The Wal-Mart of Wall Street," *Fortune* (October 13, 1997), 128–130.

23. Michael E. Porter, "Strategy and the Internet," *Harvard Business Review* (March 2001), 63–78; and Magretta, "Why Business Models Matter."

24. Raymond E. Miles and Charles C. Snow, *Organizational Strategy, Structure, and Process* (New York: McGraw-Hill, 1978).

25. Geraldine Fabrikant, "The Paramount Team Puts Profit Over Splash," *The New York Times* (June 30, 2002), Section 3, 1, 15.

26. Katrina Brooker, "Can Procter & Gamble Change Its Culture, Protect Its Market Share, and Find the Next Tide?" *Fortune* (April 26, 1999), 146–152.

27. David Stires, "Fallen Arches," *Fortune* (April 29, 2002), 74–76.

28. Etzioni, *Modern Organizations*, 8.

29. Etzioni, *Modern Organizations*, 8; Gary D. Sandefur, "Efficiency in Social Service Organizations," *Administration and Society* 14 (1983), 449–468.

30. Richard M. Steers, *Organizational Effectiveness: A Behavioral View* (Santa Monica, Calif.: Goodyear, 1977), 51.

31. Karl E. Weick and Richard L. Daft, "The Effectiveness of Interpretation Systems," in Kim S. Cameron and David A. Whetten, eds., *Organizational Effectiveness: A Comparison of Multiple Models* (New York: Academic Press, 1982).

32. David L. Blenkhorn and Brian Gaber, "The Use of 'Warm Fuzzies' to Assess Organizational Effectiveness," *Journal of General Management*, 21, no. 2 (Winter 1995), 40–51.

33. Steven Strasser, J. D. Eveland, Gaylord Cummins, O. Lynn Deniston, and John H. Romani, "Conceptualizing the Goal and Systems Models of Organizational Effectiveness—Implications for Comparative Evaluation Research," *Journal of Management Studies* 18 (1981), 321–340.

34. James L. Price, "The Study of Organizational Effectiveness," *Sociological Quarterly* 13 (1972), 3–15.

35. Lucy McCauley, ed. "Unit of One: Measure What Matters," *Fast Company* (May 1999), 97+.

36. Richard H. Hall and John P. Clark, "An Ineffective Effectiveness Study and Some Suggestions for Future Research," *Sociological Quarterly* 21 (1980), 119–134; Price, "The Study of Organizational Effectiveness"; Perrow, "Analysis of Goals."

37. George W. England, "Organizational Goals and Expected Behaviors in American Managers," *Academy of Management Journal* 10 (1967), 107–117.

38. "Tracking Nortel's Progress Toward Corporate Goals," *Measuring Up: Toward a Common Framework for Tracking Corporate Environmental Performance*, Management Institute for Environment and Business, World Resources Institute, accessed on March 5, 2003 at *http://www.wri. org/meb/measure/mup-toc.html*; and *http://www. nortelnetworks. com.*

39. The discussion of the resource-based approach is based in part on Michael V. Russo and Paul A. Fouts, "A Resource-Based Perspective on Corporate Environmental Performance and Profitability," *Academy of Management Journal* 40, no. 3 (June 1997), 534–559; and Jay B. Barney, J. L. "Larry" Stempert, Loren T. Gustafson, and Yolanda Sarason, "Organizational Identity Within the Strategic Management Conversation: Contributions and Assumptions," in I*dentity in Organizations: Building Theory through Conversations*, David A. Whetten and Paul C. Godfrey, eds. (Thousand Oaks, Calif.: Sage Publications, 1998): 83–98.

40. Lucy McCauley, "Measure What Matters."

41. Richard I. Priem, "Is the Resource-Based 'View' a Useful Perspective for Strategic Management

Research?" Academy of Management Review 26, no. 1 (2001), 22–40.

42. Chris Argyris, *Integrating the Individual and the Organization* (New York: Wiley, 1964); Warren G. Bennis, *Changing Organizations* (New York: McGraw-Hill, 1966); Rensis Likert, *The Human Organization* (New York: McGraw-Hill, 1967); Richard Beckhard, *Organization Development Strategies and Models* (Reading, Mass.: Addison-Wesley, 1969).

43. Cheri Ostroff and Neal Schmitt, "Configurations of Organizational Effectiveness and Efficiency," *Academy of Management Journal* 36 (1993), 1345–1361; Peter J. Frost, Larry F. Moore, Meryl Reise Louis, Craig C. Lundburg, and Joanne Martin, *Organizational Culture* (Beverly Hills, Calif.: Sage, 1985).

44. J. Barton Cunningham, "Approaches to the Evaluation of Organizational Effectiveness," *Academy of Management Review* 2 (1977), 463–474; Beckhard, *Organization Development*.

45. Lucy McCauley, ed., "Measure What Matters."

46. Eric J. Walton and Sarah Dawson, "Managers' Perceptions of Criteria of Organizational Effectiveness," *Journal of Management Studies* 38, no. 2 (2001), 173–199.

47. Robert E. Quinn and John Rohrbaugh, "A Spatial Model of Effectiveness Criteria: Toward a Competing Values Approach to Organizational Analysis," *Management Science* 29 (1983), 363–377.

48. Regina M. O'Neill and Robert E. Quinn, "Editor's Note: Applications of the Competing Values Framework," *Human Resource Management* 32 (Spring 1993), 1–7.

49. Robert E. Quinn and Kim Cameron, "Organizational Life Cycles and Shifting Criteria of Effectiveness: Some Preliminary Evidence," *Management Science* 29 (1983), 33–51.

50. Jeffrey Ball, "Disciplined Pizazz: Chrysler's New Bosses Give Refresher Course on Thrift and Style," *The Wall Street Journal* (January 4, 2002), A1, A9.

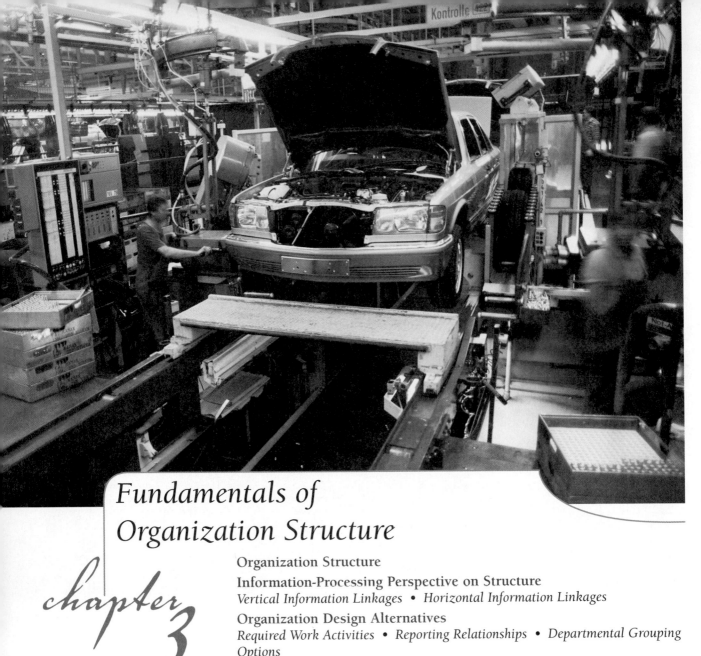

Fundamentals of
Organization Structure

chapter 3

Cunningham Motor Company

Robert Lutz isn't the first entrepreneur to dream of starting a car company from scratch. But he is the first one who plans to do it without putting a penny into building a factory. Beginning in 2004, Lutz hopes to build and sell the sleek Cunningham C7—capable of speeds of up to 200 mph and selling for about $250,000—with a company of only twenty people. How does he plan to accomplish his dream? By contracting with other organizations to handle everything from engineering to final assembly and shipping. If the plan succeeds, Cunningham Motors will be the first truly "modular" car company.

Lutz and his partner, Briggs S. Cunningham III, the son of racing legend Briggs S. Cunningham Jr., wanted to build a super-luxury American sports car to rival European prestige brands such as Ferrari and Aston Martin. But automotive history is full of romantic dreams that crashed on the rocks of financial reality. Lutz knew the only way they could reach their goals would be to keep start-up costs low by creating an organization design based on partnering with other companies. With a reasonable target of selling only about 600 cars a year, building a factory simply didn't make sense. The plan is for a network of automotive suppliers to furnish parts and assemble them into modules, which will then be shipped to one large partner that will put the modules together into a finished vehicle. Internet-based collaborative software will tie together a vast network of designers, chassis developers, parts makers, fabricators, and manufacturers throughout the United States.

Times have changed since iron ore and other raw materials went into one end of Henry Ford's factory in Dearborn, Michigan, and bright, shiny Model As came out the other end. At the beginning of the twenty-first century, vertical integration has given way to disintegration, with more and more companies farming out more of their activities to outside contractors. "The concept of a virtual car company is something everyone is thinking about," says Randy Redding, manager of the Automotive Industry Group at UGS, the partner providing collaborative software for Cunningham. Lutz and Cunningham are turning thought into action—and, they hope, into a successful new car company.[1]

Cunningham Motor Company represents a bold new approach to organization design, one in which practically all organizational functions are outsourced to other companies. Few companies have taken the concept so far, but many organizations are outsourcing various parts of their operations. Nearly all of Hewlett-Packard's printers are made by contract manufacturers, for example. About half of all Samuel Adams beer comes from contract brewers. Sun Microsystems, Apple Computer, and GlaxoSmithKline all outsource a large part of their production. Other car companies, too, are pushing the outsourcing trend further than ever before by having suppliers provide larger and larger chunks of vehicles.[2] This trend, and the modular approach to organization design, will be discussed in detail later in the chapter.

Organizations use various structural alternatives to help them achieve their purpose and goals. Nearly every firm needs to undergo reorganization at some point to help meet new challenges. Structural changes are needed to reflect new strategies or respond to changes in other contingency factors introduced in Chapter 2: environment, technology, size and life cycle, and culture. For example, at Amgen, a drug company, structural reorganization was needed when the company became so large and departmentalized that horizontal coordination began to suffer. Amgen implemented horizontal product development teams, which improved coordination across the organization because each team includes members from various functions who work together to organize and complete the whole process of bringing a new drug to market.[3]

PURPOSE OF THIS CHAPTER

This chapter introduces basic concepts of organization structure and shows how to design structure as it appears on the organization chart. First we will define structure and provide an overview of structural design. Then, an information processing perspective explains how to design vertical and horizontal linkages to provide needed information flow. The chapter will next present basic design options, followed by strategies for grouping organizational activities into functional, divisional, matrix, horizontal, modular, or hybrid structures. The final section will examine how the application of basic structures depends on the organization's situation and will outline the symptoms of structural misalignment.

ORGANIZATION STRUCTURE

There are three key components in the definition of **organization structure**:

1. Organization structure designates formal reporting relationships, including the number of levels in the hierarchy and the span of control of managers and supervisors.
2. Organization structure identifies the grouping together of individuals into departments and of departments into the total organization.
3. Organization structure includes the design of systems to ensure effective communication, coordination, and integration of effort across departments.[4]

BRIEFCASE

As an organization manager, keep this guideline in mind:

Develop organization charts that describe task responsibilities, reporting relationships, and the grouping of individuals into departments. Provide sufficient documentation so that all people within the organization know to whom they report and how they fit into the total organization picture.

These three elements of structure pertain to both vertical and horizontal aspects of organizing. For example, the first two elements are the structural *framework*, which is the vertical hierarchy.[5] The third element pertains to the pattern of *interactions* among organizational employees. An ideal structure encourages employees to provide horizontal information and coordination where and when it is needed.

Organization structure is reflected in the organization chart. It isn't possible to see the internal structure of an organization the way we might see its manufacturing tools, offices, or products. Although we might see employees going about their duties, performing different tasks, and working in different locations, the only way to actually see the structure underlying all this activity is through the organization chart. The organization chart is the visual representation of a whole set of underlying activities and processes in an organization. Exhibit 3.1 shows a sample organization chart. The organization chart can be quite useful in

Exhibit 3.1   *A Sample Organization Chart*

EXHIBIT 3.1   *A Sample Organization Chart*

understanding how a company works. It shows the various parts of an organization, how they are interrelated, and how each position and department fits into the whole.

The concept of an organization chart, showing what positions exist, how they are grouped, and who reports to whom, has been around for centuries.[6] For example, diagrams outlining church hierarchy can be found in medieval churches in Spain. However, the use of the organization chart for business stems largely from the Industrial Revolution. As we discussed in Chapter 1, as work grew more complex and was performed by greater and greater numbers of workers, there was a pressing need to develop ways of managing and controlling organizations. The growth of the railroads provides an example. After the collision of two passenger trains in Massachusetts in 1841, the public demanded better control of the operation. As a result, the board of directors of the Western Railroad took steps to outline "definite responsibilities for each phase of the company's business, drawing solid lines of authority and command for the railroad's administration, maintenance, and operation."[7]

The type of organization structure that grew out of these efforts in the late nineteenth and early twentieth centuries was one in which the CEO was placed at the top and everyone else was arranged in layers down below, as illustrated in Exhibit 3.1. The thinking and decision making is done by those at the top, and the physical work is performed by employees who are organized into distinct, functional departments. This structure was quite effective and became entrenched in the business world for most of the twentieth century. However, this type of vertical structure is not always effective, particularly in rapidly changing environments. Over the years, organizations have developed other structural designs, many of them aimed at increasing horizontal coordination and communication and encouraging adaptation to external changes. One significant change in the environment is the rise of the Internet as a place for doing business. Book Mark 3.0 describes the importance of reorganizing to a customer-led company to succeed in the world of e-commerce. In this chapter, we will examine five basic structural designs and show how they are reflected in the organization chart.

BOOK MARK *3.0*   *Have You Read This Book?*

Futurize Your Enterprise: Business Strategy in the Age of the E-Customer
By David Siegel

Organizations have experienced tremendous change over the past decade, but David Siegel, author of *Futurize Your Enterprise*, believes it is only the tip of the iceberg. Despite the crash of the dot-coms, Siegel predicts that over the next decade the Internet will totally transform organizations. E-customers, he says, are not loyal to a company or a brand but to other customers and to employees with whom they've built a relationship: "The global connectivity of 2 billion people that we will have by 2010 will change everything." According to Siegel, a customer-led company "focuses on groups of people rather than on types of products and services," which has profound implications for organization structure.

DESIGNING THE CUSTOMER-LED ORGANIZATION

Siegel's book offers guidelines for redesigning organizations to be customer-led rather than manager-led, using the Internet as a primary tool. Here are a few of them:

* *Create new positions.* Siegel advocates creating a chief Net officer (CNO) position and filling it with someone who is a future-oriented risk taker comfortable in the online world. Technological expertise is less important than intuition, judgment, and the ability to create a listening culture that pulls customers into the company through its Web site. Another important position is the customer group host, who is empowered to be a leader for a distinct customer group.
* *Design a customer-led Web site.* Using integrated, companywide teams led by the CNO, identify important customer groups and create ways to give top-tier customers whatever they want and need. In addition, give these people special status in the online community and build in ways they can interact with and help one another, which helps to build customer loyalty. Design the site so that the home page directs each customer

to the appropriate "neighborhood" tailored to that specific customer group.
* *Use empowered Web teams.* Assign at least ten full-time staff members to work in integrated teams, led by a customer group host, to focus on serving each customer group with exceptional levels of customer service. Teach and promote active listening skills so that customers become a part of the team and help determine the future direction of the organization.
* *Align the organization around customers.* Rather than creating horizontal units for different products or services, organize the online business around customer groups. For example, Office Depot is divided along three lines: individual consumers, small businesses, and contract customers. One Web division under a separate administration targets the first two groups, and a separate Web unit serves large contract customers.

FUTURIZING THE ENTERPRISE

Taken together, Siegel's principles and guidelines move a company toward a completely networked, pilotless corporate environment. The CNO hires and guides one or more customer hosts for each important customer group. These hosts build customer neighborhoods and facilitate dialogue between the company and its customers. Project managers within each customer group assemble teams as they see fit to best serve customers. New company divisions emerge as needed, following the customers' lead. The key to futurizing your enterprise, says Siegel, is to "hitch your divisions to their customer groups and let them go. Don't worry about them too much. They'll be fine without the usual amount of supervision because they're letting their customers lead the way."

Futurize Your Enterprise: Business Strategy in the Age of the E-Customer, by David Siegel, is published by John Wiley & Sons.

INFORMATION-PROCESSING PERSPECTIVE ON STRUCTURE

The organization should be designed to provide both vertical and horizontal information flow as necessary to accomplish the organization's overall goals. If the structure doesn't fit the information requirements of the organization, people either will have too little information or will spend time processing information that is not vital to their tasks, thus reducing effectiveness.[8] However, there is an inherent tension between vertical and horizontal mechanisms in an organization. Whereas vertical linkages are designed primarily for control, horizontal linkages are designed for coordination and collaboration, which usually means reducing control.

Organizations can choose whether to orient toward a traditional organization designed for efficiency, which emphasizes vertical communication and control, or toward a contemporary learning organization, which emphasizes horizontal communication and coordination. Exhibit 3.2 compares organizations designed for efficiency with those designed for learning. An emphasis on efficiency and control is associated with specialized tasks, a hierarchy of authority, rules and regulations, formal reporting systems, few teams or task forces, and **centralized** decision making, which means problems and decisions are funneled to top levels of the hierarchy for resolution. Emphasis on learning is associated with shared tasks, a relaxed hierarchy, few rules, face-to-face communication, many teams and task forces, and informal, **decentralized** decision making. Decentralized decision making means decision making authority is pushed down to lower organizational levels. Organizations may have to experiment to find the correct degree of centralization or decentralization to meet their needs. Companies such as Dow Chemical and Procter & Gamble decentralized decision making to increase speed and flexibility, but found that the organization's vertical communication and control systems were too weak to keep a huge, global corporation functioning effectively. Thus, managers at these companies are searching for the best combination of vertical control and horizontal collaboration, centralization and decentralization, for their own situations.[9]

VERTICAL INFORMATION LINKAGES

Organization design should facilitate the communication among employees and departments that is necessary to accomplish the organization's overall task. *Linkage* is defined as the extent of communication and coordination among organizational elements. **Vertical linkages** are used to coordinate activities between the top and bottom of an organization and are designed primarily for control of the organization. Employees at lower levels should carry out activities consistent

EXHIBIT 3.2   *The Relationship of Organization Design to Efficiency vs. Learning Outcomes*

with top-level goals, and top executives must be informed of activities and accomplishments at the lower levels. Organizations may use any of a variety of structural devices to achieve vertical linkage, including hierarchical referral, rules, plans, and formal management information systems.[10]

Hierarchical Referral.   The first vertical device is the hierarchy, or chain of command, which is illustrated by the vertical lines in Exhibit 3.1. If a problem arises that employees don't know how to solve, it can be referred up to the next level in the hierarchy. When the problem is solved, the answer is passed back down to lower levels. The lines of the organization chart act as communication channels.

Rules and Plans.   The next linkage device is the use of rules and plans. To the extent that problems and decisions are repetitive, a rule or procedure can be established so employees know how to respond without communicating directly with their manager. Rules provide a standard information source enabling employees to be coordinated without actually communicating about every job. A plan also provides standing information for employees. The most widely used plan is the budget. With carefully designed budget plans, employees at lower levels can be left on their own to perform activities within their resource allotment.

Vertical Information Systems.   A **vertical information system** is another strategy for increasing vertical information capacity. Vertical information systems include the periodic reports, written information, and computer-based communications distributed to managers. Information systems make communication up and down the hierarchy more efficient. Vertical information systems are an important component of vertical control at software maker Oracle.

In Practice

ORACLE CORPORATION

In an era of decentralization and empowerment, Larry Ellison, CEO of Oracle, doesn't hesitate to proclaim his belief in stronger vertical control. Oracle got in trouble some years ago because sales managers around the globe were cutting backroom deals or hammering out private individualized compensation agreements with salespeople in different countries. Today, all the terms, including sales contracts and commissions, are dictated from the top and spelled out in a global database. In addition, Ellison requires that all deals be entered into the database so they can easily be tracked by top managers.

The Internet is a central part of Ellison's plan for exerting stronger control over Oracle, by offering the power to centralize complex operations while also rapidly disseminating information all over the world. Oracle uses its own suite of Internet software applications that work together on a global basis. All employees do their work via the Internet, enabling Ellison to carefully track, analyze, and control the behavior of each unit, manager, and employee. Although many managers weren't happy with the stronger top-down control, Ellison and other top leaders believed it was necessary to effectively manage a sprawling global corporation that was beginning to behave more like a bunch of separate companies. In addition, the system helps to circulate and assure implementation of standard rules and procedures across divisions. According to Chief Marketing Officer Mark Jarvis, this ultimately provides for greater freedom for lower levels and prevents the hierarchy from becoming overloaded. "Once we have a standard set of global business practices," Jarvis notes, "the [managers] can be allowed more scope for decision making within the broad framework."[11]

In today's world of corporate financial scandals and "post-Enron" ethical concerns, many top managers are considering strengthening their organization's linkages for vertical information and control. The other major issue in organizing is to provide adequate horizontal linkages for coordination and collaboration.

HORIZONTAL INFORMATION LINKAGES

Horizontal communication overcomes barriers between departments and provides opportunities for coordination among employees to achieve unity of effort and organizational objectives. **Horizontal linkage** refers to the amount of communication and coordination horizontally across organizational departments. Its importance is articulated by comments made by Lee Iacocca when he took over Chrysler Corporation in the 1980s.

> What I found at Chrysler were thirty-five vice presidents, each with his own turf. . . . I couldn't believe, for example, that the guy running engineering departments wasn't in constant touch with his counterpart in manufacturing. But that's how it was. Everybody worked independently. I took one look at that system and I almost threw up. That's when I knew I was in really deep trouble.
> . . . Nobody at Chrysler seemed to understand that interaction among the different functions in a company is absolutely critical. People in engineering and manufacturing almost have to be sleeping together. These guys weren't even flirting![12]

During his tenure at Chrysler (now DaimlerChrysler), Iacocca pushed horizontal coordination to a high level. Everyone working on a specific vehicle project—designers, engineers, and manufacturers, as well as representatives from marketing, finance, purchasing, and even outside suppliers—worked together on a single floor so they could constantly communicate. Ford and General Motors have also enhanced horizontal communication and coordination through mechanisms such as teams, task forces, and information systems.

Horizontal linkage mechanisms often are not drawn on the organization chart, but nevertheless are part of organization structure. The following devices are structural alternatives that can improve horizontal coordination and information flow.[13] Each device enables people to exchange information.

Information Systems. A significant method of providing horizontal linkage in today's organizations is the use of cross-functional information systems. Computerized information systems can enable managers or frontline workers throughout the organization to routinely exchange information about problems, opportunities, activities, or decisions. For example, DaimlerChrysler uses an information system called FastCar that allows anyone involved in any aspect of product development to share information and track cost status, quality, manufacturability, and other details as a vehicle model moves through various stages of the design process.[14]

Some organizations also encourage employees to use the company's information systems to build relationships with others all across the organization, aiming to support and enhance ongoing horizontal coordination across projects and geographical boundaries. CARE International, one of the world's largest private international relief organizations, enhanced its personnel database to make it easy for people to find others with congruent interests, concerns, or needs. Each person in the database has listed past and current responsibilities, experience, language abilities, knowledge of foreign countries, emergency experiences, skills and competencies, and outside interests. The database makes it easy for employees working across borders to seek each other out, share ideas and information, and build enduring horizontal connections.[15]

Direct Contact. A higher level of horizontal linkage is direct contact between managers or employees affected by a problem. One way to promote direct contact is to create a special **liaison role**. A liaison person is located in one department but has the responsibility for communicating and achieving coordination with another department. Liaison roles often exist between engineering and manufacturing departments because engineering has to develop and test products to fit the limitations of manufacturing facilities.

Another approach is to locate people close together so they will have direct contact with one another on a regular basis. BMW used this tactic when it was introducing the 300 Series model. All the groups involved in the redesign efforts were temporarily moved into the prototype factory. This meant product designers, manufacturing process designers, purchasing negotiators, training program coordinators, marketing managers, and financial analysts had close daily contact throughout the design process.[16]

Task Forces. Liaison roles usually link only two departments. When linkage involves several departments, a more complex device such as a task force is required. A **task force** is a temporary committee composed of representatives from each department affected by a problem.[17] Each member represents the interest of a department and can carry information from the meeting back to that department.

Task forces are an effective horizontal linkage device for temporary issues. They solve problems by direct horizontal coordination and reduce the information load on the vertical hierarchy. Typically, they are disbanded after their tasks are accomplished.

Organizations have used task forces for everything from organizing the annual company picnic to solving expensive and complex manufacturing problems. At GE Lighting Company in Cleveland, Ohio, a task force made up of members from information technology, finance, human resources, and other functions oversaw the implementation of an ambitious systems-integration project that spanned operations in the United States and Canada. The U.S. Department of Defense set up a task force to simplify and streamline travel rules and regulations.[18]

Full-time Integrator. A stronger horizontal linkage device is to create a full-time position or department solely for the purpose of coordination. A full-time **integrator** frequently has a title, such as product manager, project manager, program manager, or brand manager. Unlike the liaison person described earlier, the integrator does not report to one of the functional departments being coordinated. He or she is located outside the departments and has the responsibility for coordinating several departments.

The brand manager for Planters Peanuts, for example, coordinates the sales, distribution, and advertising for that product. General Motors set up brand managers who are responsible for marketing and sales strategies for each of GM's new models.[19]

The integrator can also be responsible for an innovation or change project, such as developing the design, financing, and marketing of a new product. An organization chart that illustrates the location of project managers for new product development is shown in Exhibit 3.3. The project managers are drawn to the side to indicate their separation from other departments. The arrows indicate

EXHIBIT 3.3   *Project Manager Location in the Structure*

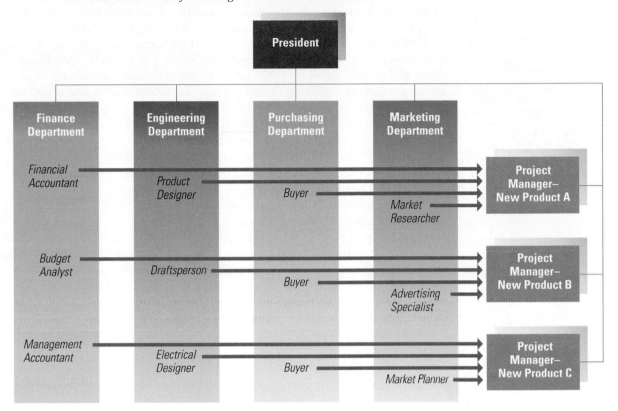

project members assigned to the new product development. New Product A, for example, has a financial accountant assigned to keep track of costs and budgets. The engineering member provides design advice, and purchasing and manufacturing members represent their areas. The project manager is responsible for the entire project. He or she sees that the new product is completed on time, is introduced to the market, and achieves other project goals. The horizontal lines in Exhibit 3.3 indicate that project managers do not have formal authority over team members with respect to giving pay raises, hiring, or firing. Formal authority rests with the managers of the functional departments, who have formal authority over subordinates.

Integrators need excellent people skills. Integrators in most companies have a lot of responsibility but little authority. The integrator has to use expertise and persuasion to achieve coordination. He or she spans the boundary between departments and must be able to get people together, maintain their trust, confront problems, and resolve conflicts and disputes in the interest of the organization.[20]

Teams. Project teams tend to be the strongest horizontal linkage mechanism. Teams are permanent task forces and are often used in conjunction with a full-time integrator. When activities among departments require strong coordination over a long period of time, a cross-functional team is often the solution. Special project teams may be used when organizations have a large-scale project, a major innovation, or a new product line.

Boeing used about 250 teams to design and manufacture the 777 aircraft. Some teams were created around sections of the plane, such as the wing, cockpit, or engines, while others were developed to serve specific customers, such as United Airlines or British Airways. Boeing's teams had to be tightly integrated and coordinated to accomplish this massive project. Hewlett-Packard's Medical Products Group uses *virtual cross-functional teams*, made up of members from various countries, to develop and market medical products and services such as electrocardiograph systems, ultrasound imaging technologies, and patient monitoring systems.[21] A **virtual team** is one that is made up of organizationally or geographically dispersed members who are linked primarily through advanced information and communications technologies. Members frequently use the Internet and collaborative software to work together, rather than meeting face to face.[22]

An illustration of how teams provide strong horizontal coordination is shown in Exhibit 3.4. Wizard Software Company develops and markets software for various applications, from videogames to financial services. Wizard uses teams to coordinate each product line across the research, programming, and marketing departments, as illustrated by the dashed lines and shaded areas in the exhibit. Members from each team meet the first thing each day as needed to resolve problems concerning customer needs, backlogs, programming changes, scheduling conflicts, and any other problem with the product line.

Some organizations, such as Nissan, also use teams of managers to implement large-scale change projects.

In Practice

NISSAN

When Carlos Ghosn arrived as the new CEO of Nissan, the company had been struggling to turn a profit for eight years. Its purchasing and manufacturing costs were too high and profit margins were notoriously low. In addition, debt had mounted to more than $11 billion. Ghosn knew he was facing a do-or-die situation—it was either turn things around or the business would cease to exist.

However, he knew that simply mandating a series of dramatic and wrenching top-down changes would create resistance, damage morale, and ultimately put the company in even more trouble. Ghosn decided to mobilize Nissan's line managers through a series of cross-functional teams that would identify and lead the radical changes that needed to be made. He believed the team approach was the best way to get managers to see beyond the functional and regional boundaries that had previously defined their jobs. Thus, he created nine management teams and charged them with creating a plan for transformation in all areas of the business. The teams were organized into these areas: Business Development; Purchasing; Manufacturing and Logistics; Research and Development; Sales and Marketing; General and Administrative; Finance and Costs; Phaseout of Products and Parts Complexity Management; and Organization. Each team was made up of members from various functional areas. For example, the Purchasing team consisted of members from purchasing, engineering, manufacturing, and finance. The Organization team had members from product planning, sales and marketing, manufacturing, engineering, finance, and purchasing. Each team was appointed two leaders drawn from the executive committee, but these leaders took a backseat in the actual functioning of the team, serving more as sponsors to smooth the process and remove administrative obstacles to the team's work.

EXHIBIT 3.4   *Teams Used for Horizontal Coordination at Wizard Software Company*

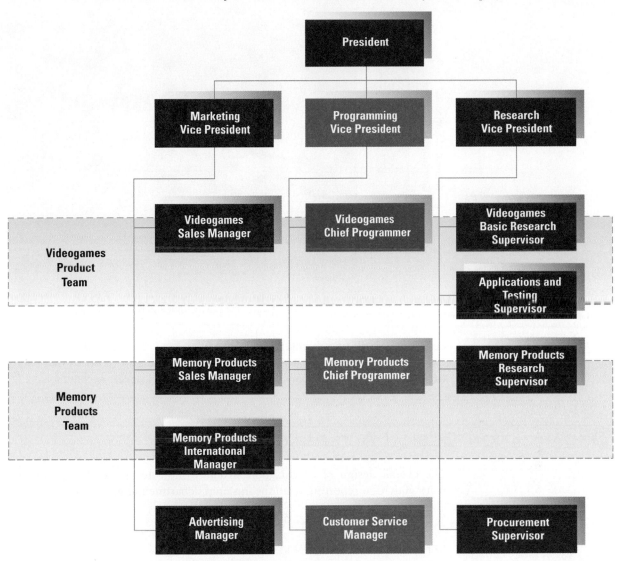

Within three months, the nine teams had created a detailed blueprint for Nissan's turnaround. Within three years, implementation of the various aspects of the plan had helped return the company to profitability. In addition, because managers throughout the company were involved in creating the plan, morale, cooperation, and company identity have grown stronger. The teams continue to operate as an integral part of Nissan's management structure, serving as overseers of the ongoing turnaround and continuing to search for new ways to improve performance.[23]

Exhibit 3.5 summarizes the mechanisms for achieving horizontal linkages. These devices represent alternatives that managers can select to increase horizontal coordination in any organization. The higher-level devices provide more horizontal information capacity, although the cost to the organization in terms of time and human resources is greater. If horizontal communication is insufficient,

EXHIBIT 3.5   *Ladder of Mechanisms for Horizontal Linkage and Coordination*

departments will find themselves out of synchronization and will not contribute to the overall goals of the organization. When the amount of horizontal coordination required is high, managers should select higher-level mechanisms.

ORGANIZATION DESIGN ALTERNATIVES

The overall design of organization structure indicates three things—required work activities, reporting relationships, and departmental groupings.

REQUIRED WORK ACTIVITIES

Departments are created to perform tasks considered strategically important to the company. For example, in a typical manufacturing company, work activities fall into a range of functions that help the organization accomplish its goals, such as a human resource department to recruit and train employees, a purchasing department to obtain supplies and raw materials, a production department to build the product, a sales department to sell products, and so forth. As organizations grow larger and more complex, more and more functions need to be performed. Organizations typically define new departments or divisions as a way to accomplish tasks deemed valuable by the organization. Today, many companies are finding it important to establish departments such as information technology or e-business to take advantage of new technology and new business opportunities.

REPORTING RELATIONSHIPS

Once required work activities and departments are defined, the next question is how these activities and departments should fit together in the organizational hierarchy. Reporting relationships, often called the chain of command, are represented by vertical lines on an organization chart. The chain of command should be an unbroken line of authority that links all persons in an organization and shows who reports to whom. In a large organization like Motorola or Ford Motor Company, one hundred or more charts are required to identify reporting relationships among thousands of employees. The definition of departments and the drawing of reporting relationships defines how employees are to be grouped into departments.

DEPARTMENTAL GROUPING OPTIONS

Options for departmental grouping, including functional grouping, divisional grouping, multifocused grouping, horizontal grouping, and modular grouping, are illustrated in Exhibit 3.6. **Departmental grouping** affects employees because they share a common supervisor and common resources, are jointly responsible for performance, and tend to identify and collaborate with one another.[24] For example, at Albany Ladder Company, the credit manager was shifted from the finance department to the marketing department. As a member of the marketing department, the credit manager started working with salespeople to increase sales, thus becoming more liberal with credit than when he was located in the finance department.

Functional grouping places employees together who perform similar functions or work processes or who bring similar knowledge and skills to bear. For example, all marketing people work together under the same supervisor, as do manufacturing and engineering people. All people associated with the assembly process for generators are grouped together in one department. All chemists may be grouped in a department different from biologists because they represent different disciplines.

Divisional grouping means people are organized according to what the organization produces. All people required to produce toothpaste—including personnel in marketing, manufacturing, and sales—are grouped together under one executive. In huge corporations such as EDS, some product or service lines may represent independent businesses, such as A. T. Kearney (management consulting) and Wendover Financial Services.

Multifocused grouping means an organization embraces two structural grouping alternatives simultaneously. These structural forms are often called *matrix* or *hybrid*. They will be discussed in more detail later in this chapter. An organization may need to group by function and product division simultaneously or perhaps by product division and geography.

Horizontal grouping means employees are organized around core work processes, the end-to-end work, information, and material flows that provide value directly to customers. All the people who work on a core process are brought together in a group rather than being separated into functional departments. For example, at field offices of the Occupational Safety and Health Administration, teams of workers representing various functions respond to complaints from American workers regarding health and safety issues, rather than having the work divided up among specialized workers.[25]

Modular grouping is the most recent approach to departmental grouping. With a modular grouping, the organization is a loosely connected cluster of separate components. In essence, departments are separate organizations that are electronically connected for the sharing of information and completion of tasks.

EXHIBIT 3.6   *Structural Design Options for Grouping Employees into Departments*

Source: Adapted from David Nadler and Michael Tushman, *Strategic Organization Design* (Glenview, Ill.: Scott Foresman, 1988), 68.

Departments can be spread all over the world rather than located together in one geographical location.

The organizational forms described in Exhibit 3.6 provide the overall options within which the organization chart is drawn and the detailed structure is designed. Each structural design alternative has significant strengths and weaknesses, to which we now turn.

FUNCTIONAL, DIVISIONAL, AND GEOGRAPHICAL DESIGNS

Functional grouping and divisional grouping are the two most common approaches to structural design.

FUNCTIONAL STRUCTURE

In a **functional structure**, activities are grouped together by common function from the bottom to the top of the organization. All engineers are located in the engineering department, and the vice president of engineering is responsible for all engineering activities. The same is true in marketing, research and development, and manufacturing. An example of the functional organization structure was shown in Exhibit 3.1 earlier in this chapter.

With a functional structure, all human knowledge and skills with respect to specific activities are consolidated, providing a valuable depth of knowledge for the organization. This structure is most effective when in-depth expertise is critical to meeting organizational goals, when the organization needs to be controlled and coordinated through the vertical hierarchy, and when efficiency is important. The structure can be quite effective if there is little need for horizontal coordination. Exhibit 3.7 summarizes the strengths and weaknesses of the functional structure.

One strength of the functional structure is that it promotes economy of scale within functions. Economy of scale results when all employees are located in the

EXHIBIT 3.7   *Strengths and Weaknesses of Functional Organization Structure*

Strengths
1. Allows economies of scale within functional departments
2. Enables in-depth knowledge and skill development
3. Enables organization to accomplish functional goals
4. Is best with only one or a few products

Weaknesses
1. Slow response time to environmental changes
2. May cause decisions to pile on top, hierarchy overload
3. Leads to poor horizontal coordination among departments
4. Results in less innovation
5. Involves restricted view of organizational goals

Source: Adapted from Robert Duncan, "What Is the Right Organization Structure? Decision Tree Analysis Provides the Answer," *Organizational Dynamics* (Winter 1979): 429.

same place and can share facilities. Producing all products in a single plant, for example, enables the plant to acquire the latest machinery. Constructing only one facility instead of separate facilities for each product line reduces duplication and waste. The functional structure also promotes in-depth skill development of employees. Employees are exposed to a range of functional activities within their own department.[26]

The main weakness of the functional structure is a slow response to environmental changes that require coordination across departments. The vertical hierarchy becomes overloaded. Decisions pile up, and top managers do not respond fast enough. Other disadvantages of the functional structure are that innovation is slow because of poor coordination, and each employee has a restricted view of overall goals.

Consider how the functional structure provides the coordination Blue Bell Creameries needs.

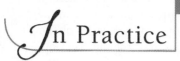

BLUE BELL CREAMERIES, INC.

Within seconds, the old-timer on the radio had taken listeners out of their bumper-to-bumper Houston world and placed them gently in Brenham, Texas, with its rolling hills and country air, in the era when the town got its first traffic light.

"You know," he said, "that's how Blue Bell Ice Cream is. Old-fashioned, uncomplicated, homemade good." He paused. "It's all made in that little creamery in Brenham."

That little creamery isn't little anymore, but the desire for first-quality homemade ice cream is stronger than when Blue Bell started in 1907. Today, Blue Bell is the third-largest ice cream maker in the United States, selling over $220 million in ice cream annually. The company has an unbelievable 60 percent share of the ice cream market in Houston, Dallas, and San Antonio—Texas's three largest cities.

The company cannot meet the demand for Blue Bell Ice Cream. It doesn't even try. Top managers have expanded slowly into Louisiana, Oklahoma, and about a dozen Southeastern states. Management refuses to compromise quality by expanding into regions that cannot be satisfactorily serviced or by growing so fast that it can't adequately train employees in the art of making ice cream.

Blue Bell's major departments are sales, quality control, production, maintenance, and distribution. There is also an accounting department and a small research and development group. Product changes are infrequent because the orientation is toward tried-and-true products. The environment is stable. The customer base is well established. The only change has been the increase in demand for Blue Bell Ice Cream.

Blue Bell's quality control department tests all incoming ingredients and ensures that only the best products go into its ice cream. Quality control also tests outgoing ice cream products. After years of experience, quality inspectors can taste the slightest deviation from expected quality. It's no wonder Blue Bell has successfully maintained the image of a small-town creamery making homemade ice cream.[27]

The functional structure is just right for Blue Bell Creameries. The organization has chosen to stay medium-sized and focus on making a single product—quality ice cream. However, as Blue Bell expands, it may have problems coordinating across departments, requiring stronger horizontal linkage mechanisms.

FUNCTIONAL STRUCTURE WITH HORIZONTAL LINKAGES

Today, there is a shift toward flatter, more horizontal structures because of the challenges introduced in Chapter 1. Very few of today's successful companies can maintain a strictly functional structure. Organizations compensate for the vertical functional hierarchy by installing horizontal linkages, as described earlier in this chapter. Managers improve horizontal coordination by using information systems, direct contact between departments, full-time integrators or project managers (illustrated in Exhibit 3.3), task forces, or teams (illustrated in Exhibit 3.4). One interesting use of horizontal linkages occurred at Karolinska Hospital in Stockholm, Sweden, which had forty-seven functional departments. Even after top executives cut that down to eleven, coordination was still woefully inadequate. The team set about reorganizing workflow at the hospital around patient care. Instead of bouncing a patient from department to department, Karolinska now envisions the illness to recovery period as a process with "pit stops" in admissions, X-ray, surgery, and so forth. The most interesting aspect of the approach is the new position of nurse coordinator. Nurse coordinators serve as full-time integrators, troubleshooting transitions within or between departments. The improved horizontal coordination dramatically improved productivity and patient care at Karolinska.[28] Karolinska is effectively using horizontal linkages to overcome some of the disadvantages of the functional structure.

DIVISIONAL STRUCTURE

The term **divisional structure** is used here as the generic term for what is sometimes called *a product structure* or *strategic business units*. With this structure, divisions can be organized according to individual products, services, product groups, major projects or programs, divisions, businesses, or profit centers. The distinctive feature of a divisional structure is that grouping is based on organizational outputs.

The difference between a divisional structure and a functional structure is illustrated in Exhibit 3.8. The functional structure can be redesigned into separate product groups, and each group contains the functional departments of R&D, manufacturing, accounting, and marketing. Coordination across functional departments within each product group is maximized. The divisional structure promotes flexibility and change because each unit is smaller and can adapt to the needs of its environment. Moreover, the divisional structure *decentralizes* decision making, because the lines of authority converge at a lower level in the hierarchy. The functional structure, by contrast, is *centralized*, because it forces decisions all the way to the top before a problem affecting several functions can be resolved.

Strengths and weaknesses of the divisional structure are summarized in Exhibit 3.9. The divisional organization structure is excellent for achieving coordination across functional departments. It works well when organizations can no longer be adequately controlled through the traditional vertical hierarchy, and when goals are oriented toward adaptation and change. Giant, complex organizations such as General Electric, Nestlé, and Johnson & Johnson are subdivided into a series of smaller, self-contained organizations for better control and coordination. In these large companies, the units are sometimes called divisions,

EXHIBIT 3.8   *Reorganization from Functional Structure to Divisional Structure at Info-Tech*

EXHIBIT 3.9   *Strengths and Weaknesses of Divisional Organization Structure*

Strengths

1. Suited to fast change in unstable environment
2. Leads to customer satisfaction because product responsibility and contact points are clear
3. Involves high coordination across functions
4. Allows units to adapt to differences in products, regions, customers
5. Best in large organizations with several products
6. Decentralizes decision making

Weaknesses

1. Eliminates economies of scale in functional departments
2. Leads to poor coordination across product lines
3. Eliminates in-depth competence and technical specialization
4. Makes integration and standardization across product lines difficult

Source: Adapted from Robert Duncan, "What Is the Right Organization Structure? Decision Tree Analysis Provides the Answer," *Organization Dynamics* (Winter 1979): 431.

businesses, or strategic business units. The structure at Johnson & Johnson includes 180 separate operating units, including McNeil Consumer Products, makers of Tylenol; Ortho Pharmaceuticals, which makes Retin-A and birth control pills; and J & J Consumer Products, the company that brings us Johnson's Baby Shampoo and Band-Aids. Each division is a separately chartered, autonomous company operating under the guidance of Johnson & Johnson's corporate headquarters.[29] Some U.S. government organizations also use a divisional structure. An example is the Internal Revenue Service, which has separate divisions that serve individual taxpayers, small businesses, large businesses, and tax-exempt organizations. Each division has its own budget, personnel, policies, and planning staffs that are focused on what is best for each particular taxpayer segment.[30]

Microsoft Corporation uses a divisional structure to focus on developing and marketing different software products.

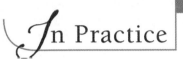

MICROSOFT

Bill Gates started Microsoft 27 years ago and built it into the most profitable technology company in the world. But as the company grew larger, the functional structure became ineffective. Employees began complaining about the growing bureaucracy and the snail's pace for decision making. A functional structure was just too slow and inflexible for a large organization operating in the fast-moving technology industry.

To speed things up and be better able to respond to environmental changes, Microsoft's top executives created eight new divisions. The Business and Enterprise Division focuses on bringing software to corporate customers, whereas the Home and Retail Division handles games, home applications, children's software, and peripherals. A Business Productivity Group targets knowledge workers, developing applications like word processing, while the Sales and Support Group focuses on customer segments such as corporate accounts, Internet service providers, and small business. Other divisions include a Developer Group (creating tools used by corporate programmers), a Consumer and Commerce Group (linking merchants via the company's MSN Web portal), and a Consumer Windows Division, whose goal is to make the PC easier to use for consumers. The final division, Microsoft Research, conducts basic research on everything from speech recognition to advanced networking.

What really makes the new structure revolutionary for Microsoft is that the heads of the eight divisions are given the freedom and authority to run the businesses and spend their budgets as they see fit, provided they meet revenue and profit goals. Previously, Gates had been involved in every decision large and small—from deciding key features in Windows 2000 to reviewing response records for customer support lines. Managers of the divisions are charged up by the new authority and responsibility. One manager said he feels "like I am running my own little company."[31]

The divisional structure has several strengths that are of benefit to Microsoft.[32] This structure is suited to fast change in an unstable environment and provides high product visibility. Since each product line has its own separate division, clients are able to contact the correct division and achieve satisfaction. Coordination across functions is excellent. Each product can adapt to requirements of individual customers or regions. The divisional structure typically works best in organizations that have multiple products or services and enough personnel to staff separate functional units. At corporations like Johnson & Johnson, PepsiCo, and Microsoft, decision making is pushed down to the lowest levels. Each division is small enough to be quick on its feet, responding rapidly to changes in the market.

One disadvantage of using divisional structuring is that the organization loses economies of scale. Instead of fifty research engineers sharing a common facility in a functional structure, ten engineers may be assigned to each of five product divisions. The critical mass required for in-depth research is lost, and physical facilities have to be duplicated for each product line. Another problem is that product lines become separate from each other, and coordination across product lines can be difficult. As one Johnson & Johnson executive said, "We have to keep reminding ourselves that we work for the same corporation."[33] There is some concern at Microsoft that the newly independent divisions might start offering products and services that conflict with one another.

Companies such as Hewlett-Packard and Xerox have a large number of divisions and have had real problems with horizontal coordination. The software division may produce programs that are incompatible with business computers sold by another division. Customers are frustrated when a sales representative from one division is unaware of developments in other divisions. Task forces and other linkage devices are needed to coordinate across divisions. A lack of technical specialization is also a problem in a divisional structure. Employees identify with the product line rather than with a functional specialty. R&D personnel, for example, tend to do applied research to benefit the product line rather than basic research to benefit the entire organization. Microsoft is avoiding this problem by creating a separate division to do basic research.

GEOGRAPHICAL STRUCTURE

Another basis for structural grouping is the organization's users or customers. The most common structure in this category is geography. Each region of the country may have distinct tastes and needs. Each geographic unit includes all functions required to produce and market products in that region. For multinational corporations, self-contained units are created for different countries and parts of the world.

Some years ago, Apple Computer reorganized from a functional to a geographical structure to facilitate manufacture and delivery of Apple computers to customers around the world. Exhibit 3.10 contains a partial organization structure illustrating the geographical thrust. Apple used this structure to focus managers and employees on specific geographical customers and sales targets. McDonald's divided its U.S. operations into five geographical divisions, each with its own president and staff functions such as human resources and legal.[34] The regional structure allows Apple and McDonald's to focus on the needs of customers in a geographical area.

The strengths and weaknesses of a geographic divisional structure are similar to the divisional organization characteristics listed in Exhibit 3.9. The organization can adapt to specific needs of its own region, and employees identify with regional goals rather than with national goals. Horizontal coordination within a region is emphasized rather than linkages across regions or to the national office.

EXHIBIT 3.10   *Geographical Structure for Apple Computer*

Source: Apple Computer, Inc. regions of the world. [Online] available *http://www.apple.com/find/areas.htm*, April 18, 2000.

MATRIX STRUCTURE

Sometimes, an organization's structure needs to be multifocused in that both product and function or product and geography are emphasized at the same time. One way to achieve this is through the **matrix structure**. The matrix can be used when both technical expertise and product innovation and change are important for meeting organizational goals. The matrix structure often is the answer when organizations find that the functional, divisional, and geographical structures combined with horizontal linkage mechanisms will not work.

The matrix is a strong form of horizontal linkage. The unique characteristic of the matrix organization is that both product division and functional structures (horizontal and vertical) are implemented simultaneously, as shown in Exhibit 3.11. The product managers and functional managers have equal authority within the organization, and employees report to both of them. The matrix structure is similar to the use of full-time integrators or product managers described earlier in this chapter (Exhibit 3.3), except that in the matrix structure the product managers (horizontal) are given formal authority equal to that of the functional managers (vertical).

CONDITIONS FOR THE MATRIX

A dual hierarchy may seem an unusual way to design an organization, but the matrix is the correct structure when the following conditions are met:[35]

- *Condition 1.* Pressure exists to share scarce resources across product lines. The organization is typically medium-sized and has a moderate number of

EXHIBIT 3.11   *Dual-Authority Structure in a Matrix Organization*

product lines. It feels pressure for the shared and flexible use of people and equipment across those products. For example, the organization is not large enough to assign engineers full-time to each product line, so engineers are assigned part-time to several products or projects.

- *Condition 2.* Environmental pressure exists for two or more critical outputs, such as for in-depth technical knowledge (functional structure) and frequent new products (divisional structure). This dual pressure means a balance of power is needed between the functional and product sides of the organization, and a dual-authority structure is needed to maintain that balance.
- *Condition 3.* The environmental domain of the organization is both complex and uncertain. Frequent external changes and high interdependence between departments require a large amount of coordination and information processing in both vertical and horizontal directions.

Under these three conditions, the vertical and horizontal lines of authority must be given equal recognition. A dual-authority structure is thereby created so the balance of power between them is equal.

Referring again to Exhibit 3.11, assume the matrix structure is for a clothing manufacturer. Product A is footwear, product B is outerwear, product C is sleepwear, and so on. Each product line serves a different market and customers. As a medium-size organization, the company must effectively use people from manufacturing, design, and marketing to work on each product line. There are not enough designers to warrant a separate design department for each product line, so the designers are shared across product lines. Moreover, by keeping the manufacturing, design, and marketing functions intact, employees can develop the in-depth expertise to serve all product lines efficiently.

The matrix formalizes horizontal teams along with the traditional vertical hierarchy and tries to give equal balance to both. However, the matrix may shift one way or the other. Many companies have found a balanced matrix hard to implement and maintain because one side of the authority structure often dominates. As a consequence, two variations of matrix structure have evolved—the **functional matrix** and the **product matrix**. In a functional matrix, the functional bosses have primary authority and the project or product managers simply coordinate product activities. In a product matrix, by contrast, the project or product managers have primary authority and functional managers simply assign technical personnel to projects and provide advisory expertise as needed. For many organizations, one of these approaches works better than the balanced matrix with dual lines of authority.[36]

All kinds of organizations have experimented with the matrix, including hospitals, consulting firms, banks, insurance companies, government agencies, and many types of industrial firms.[37] This structure has been used successfully by large, global organizations such as Procter & Gamble and Dow Chemical, which fine-tuned the matrix to suit their own particular goals and culture.

STRENGTHS AND WEAKNESSES

The matrix structure is best when environmental change is high and when goals reflect a dual requirement, such as for both product and functional goals. The dual-authority structure facilitates communication and coordination to cope with rapid environmental change and enables an equal balance between product and functional bosses. The matrix facilitates discussion and adaptation to unexpected problems. It tends to work best in organizations of moderate size with a few product lines. The matrix is not needed for only a single product line, and too many product lines make it difficult to coordinate both directions at once. Exhibit 3.12 summarizes the strengths and weaknesses of the matrix structure based on what we know of organizations that use it.[38]

The strength of the matrix is that it enables an organization to meet dual demands from customers in the environment. Resources (people, equipment) can be flexibly allocated across different products, and the organization can adapt to changing external requirements.[39] This structure also provides an opportunity for employees to acquire either functional or general management skills, depending on their interests.

One disadvantage of the matrix is that some employees experience dual authority, which can be frustrating and confusing. They need excellent interpersonal and conflict-resolution skills, which may require special training in human relations. The matrix also forces managers to spend a great deal of time in meetings.[40] If managers do not adapt to the information and power sharing required by the matrix, the system will not work. Managers must collaborate with one another rather than rely on vertical authority in decision making. The successful implementation of one matrix structure occurred at a steel company in Pittsburgh.

EXHIBIT 3.12   *Strengths and Weaknesses of Matrix Organization Structure*

Strengths
1. Achieves coordination necessary to meet dual demands from customers
2. Flexible sharing of human resources across products
3. Suited to complex decisions and frequent changes in unstable environment
4. Provides opportunity for both functional and product skill development
5. Best in medium-sized organizations with multiple products

Weaknesses
1. Causes participants to experience dual authority, which can be frustrating and confusing
2. Means participants need good interpersonal skills and extensive training
3. Is time-consuming; involves frequent meetings and conflict resolution sessions
4. Will not work unless participants understand it and adopt collegial rather than vertical type relationships
5. Requires great effort to maintain power balance

Source: Adapted from Robert Duncan, "What Is the Right Organization Structure? Decision Tree Analysis Provides the Answer," *Organizational Dynamics* (Winter 1979): 429.

WORLDWIDE STEEL

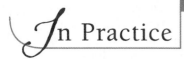
In Practice

As far back as anyone could remember, the steel industry in the United States was stable and certain. If steel manufacturers could produce quality steel at a reasonable price, that steel would be sold. However, in the 1970s and 1980s, inflation, a national economic downturn, reduced consumption of autos, and competition from steelmakers in Germany and Japan forever changed the steel industry. Steelmakers shifted to specialized steel products. They had to market aggressively, make efficient use of internal resources, and adapt to rapid-fire changes.

Worldwide Steel employed 2,500 people, made 300,000 tons of steel a year, and was 170 years old. For 160 of those years, functional structure worked fine. As the environment became more turbulent and competitive, however, Worldwide Steel managers realized they were not keeping up. Fifty percent of Worldwide's orders were behind schedule. Profits were eroded by labor, material, and energy cost increases. Market share declined.

In consultation with outside experts, the president of Worldwide Steel saw that the company had to walk a tightrope. It had to specialize in a few high-value-added products tailored for separate markets, while maintaining economies of scale and sophisticated technology within functional departments. The dual pressure led to an unusual solution for a steel company: a matrix structure.

Worldwide Steel had four product lines: open-die forgings, ring-mill products, wheels and axles, and steelmaking. A business manager was given responsibility for and authority over each line, which included preparing a business plan and developing targets for production costs, product inventory, shipping dates, and gross profit. The managers were given authority to meet those targets and to make their lines profitable. Functional vice presidents were responsible for technical decisions relating to their function. Functional managers were expected to stay abreast of the latest techniques in their areas and to keep personnel trained in new technologies that could apply to product lines. With twenty thousand recipes for specialty steels and several hundred new recipes ordered each month, functional personnel had to stay current. Two functional departments—field sales and industrial relations—were not included in the matrix because they worked independently. The final design was a hybrid matrix structure with both matrix and functional relationships, as illustrated in Exhibit 3.13.

EXHIBIT 3.13   *Matrix Structure for Worldwide Steel*

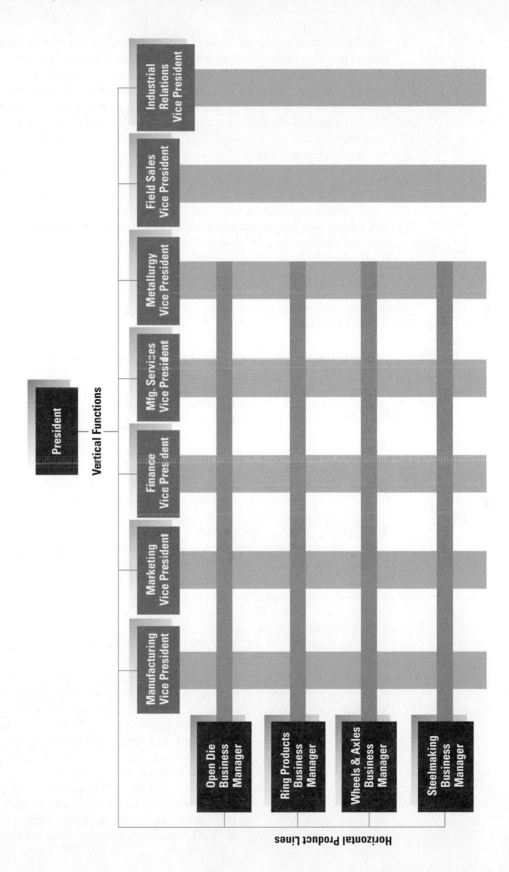

Implementation of the matrix was slow. Middle managers were confused. Meetings to coordinate across functional departments seemed to be held every day. After about a year of training by external consultants, Worldwide Steel was on track. Ninety percent of the orders were now delivered on time and market share recovered. Both productivity and profitability increased steadily. The managers thrived on matrix involvement. Meetings to coordinate product and functional decisions provided a growth experience. Middle managers began including younger managers in the matrix discussions as training for future management responsibility.[41]

This example illustrates the correct use of a matrix structure. The dual pressure to maintain economies of scale and to market four product lines gave equal emphasis to the functional and product hierarchies. Through continuous meetings for coordination, Worldwide Steel achieved both economies of scale and flexibility.

HORIZONTAL STRUCTURE

A recent approach to organizing is the **horizontal structure**, which organizes employees around core processes. Organizations typically shift toward a horizontal structure during a procedure called reengineering. **Reengineering**, or *business process reengineering*, basically means the redesign of a vertical organization along its horizontal workflows and processes. A **process** refers to an organized group of related tasks and activities that work together to transform inputs into outputs that create value for customers.[42] Reengineering changes the way managers think about how work is done. Rather than focusing on narrow jobs structured into distinct functional departments, they emphasize core processes that cut horizontally across the organization and involve teams of employees working together to serve customers. Examples of processes include order fulfillment, new product development, and customer service.

A good illustration of process is provided by claims handling at Progressive Casualty Insurance Company. In the past, a customer would report an accident to an agent, who would pass the information to a customer service representative, who, in turn, would pass it to a claims manager. The claims manager would batch the claim with others from the same territory and assign it to an adjuster, who would schedule a time to inspect the vehicle damage. Today, adjusters are organized into teams that handle the entire claims process from beginning to end. One member handles claimant calls to the office while others are stationed in the field. When an adjuster takes a call, he or she does whatever is possible over the phone. If an inspection is needed, the adjuster contacts a team member in the field and schedules an appointment immediately. Progressive now measures the time from call to inspection in hours rather than the seven to ten days it once took.[43]

When a company is reengineered to a horizontal structure, all the people throughout the organization who work on a particular process (such as claims handling or order fulfillment) have easy access to one another so they can communicate and coordinate their efforts. The horizontal structure virtually eliminates both the vertical hierarchy and old departmental boundaries. This structural approach is largely a response to the profound changes that have occurred in the workplace and the business environment over the past fifteen to twenty years. Technological progress emphasizes computer- and Internet-based integration and coordination. Customers expect faster and better service, and employees want opportunities to use their minds, learn new skills, and assume greater responsibility. Organizations mired in a vertical mindset have a hard time meeting these challenges. Thus, numerous organizations have experimented with horizontal mechanisms such as cross-functional teams to achieve coordination across departments or task forces to accomplish temporary projects. Increasingly, organizations are shifting away from hierarchical, function-based structures to structures based on horizontal processes.

CHARACTERISTICS

An illustration of a company reengineered into a horizontal structure appears in Exhibit 3.14. Such an organization has the following characteristics:[44]

- Structure is created around cross-functional core processes rather than tasks, functions, or geography. Thus, boundaries between departments are obliterated. Ford Motor Company's Customer Service Division, for example, has core process groups for business development, parts supply and logistics, vehicle service and programs, and technical support.
- Self-directed teams, not individuals, are the basis of organizational design and performance.

EXHIBIT 3.14   *A Horizontal Structure*

Source: Based on Frank Ostroff, *The Horizontal Organization* (New York: Oxford University Press, 1999); John A. Byrne, "The Horizontal Corporation," *BusinessWeek* (December 20, 1993), 76–81; and Thomas A. Stewart, "The Search for the Organization of Tomorrow," *Fortune* (May 18, 1992), 92–98.

- Process owners have responsibility for each core process in its entirety. For Ford's parts supply and logistics process, for example, a number of teams may work on jobs such as parts analysis, purchasing, material flow, and distribution, but a process owner is responsible for coordinating the entire process.
- People on the team are given the skills, tools, motivation, and authority to make decisions central to the team's performance. Team members are cross-trained to perform one another's jobs, and the combined skills are sufficient to complete a major organizational task.
- Teams have the freedom to think creatively and respond flexibly to new challenges that arise.
- Customers drive the horizontal corporation. Effectiveness is measured by end-of-process performance objectives (based on the goal of bringing value to the customer), as well as customer satisfaction, employee satisfaction, and financial contribution.
- The culture is one of openness, trust, and collaboration, focused on continuous improvement. The culture values employee empowerment, responsibility, and well being.

General Electric's Salisbury, North Carolina, plant shifted to a horizontal structure to improve flexibility and customer service.

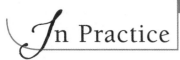

GE SALISBURY

General Electric's plant in Salisbury, North Carolina, which manufactures electrical lighting panel boards for industrial and commercial purposes, used to be organized functionally and vertically. Because no two GE customers have identical needs, each panel board has to be configured and built to order, which frequently created bottlenecks in the standard production process. In the mid-1980s, faced with high product-line costs, inconsistent customer service, and a declining market share, managers began exploring new ways of organizing that would emphasize teamwork, responsibility, continuous improvement, empowerment, and commitment to the customer.

By the early 1990s, GE Salisbury had made the transition to a horizontal structure that links sets of multiskilled teams who are responsible for the entire build-to-order process. The new structure is based on the goal of producing lighting panel boards "of the highest possible quality, in the shortest possible cycle time, at a competitive price, with the best possible service." The process consists of four linked teams, each made up of ten to fifteen members representing a range of skills and functions. A production control team serves as process owner (as illustrated earlier in Exhibit 3.14) and is responsible for order receipt, planning, coordination of production, purchasing, working with suppliers and customers, tracking inventory, and keeping all the teams focused on meeting objectives. The fabrication team cuts, builds, welds, and paints the various parts that make up the steel box that will house the electrical components panel, which is assembled and tested by the electrical components team. The electrical components team also handles shipping. A maintenance team takes care of heavy equipment maintenance that cannot be performed as part of the regular production process. Managers have become *associate advisors* who serve as guides and coaches and bring their expertise to the teams as needed.

The key to success of the horizontal structure is that all the operating teams work in concert with each other and have access to the information they need to meet team and process goals. Teams are given information about sales, backlogs, inventory, staffing needs, productivity, costs, quality, and other data, and each team regularly shares information about its part of the build-to-order process with the other teams. Joint production meetings, job rotation, and cross-training of employees are some of the mechanisms that help ensure smooth integration. The linked teams assume responsibility for setting their own production targets, determining production schedules, assigning duties, and identifying and solving problems.

Productivity and performance have dramatically improved with the horizontal structure. Bottlenecks in the workflow, which once wreaked havoc with production schedules, have been virtually eliminated. A six-week lead time has been cut to two and a half days. More subtle but just as important are the increases in employee and customer satisfaction that GE Salisbury has realized since implementing its new structure.[45]

STRENGTHS AND WEAKNESSES

As with all structures, the horizontal structure has weaknesses as well as strengths. The strengths and weaknesses of the horizontal structure are listed in Exhibit 3.15.

The most significant strength of the horizontal structure is that it can dramatically increase the company's flexibility and response to changes in customer needs because of the enhanced coordination. The structure directs everyone's attention toward the customer, which leads to greater customer satisfaction as well as improvements in productivity, speed, and efficiency. In addition, because there are no boundaries between functional departments, employees take a broader view of organizational goals rather than being focused on the goals of a single department. The horizontal structure promotes an emphasis on teamwork and cooperation, such that team members share a commitment to meeting common objectives. Finally, the horizontal structure can improve the quality of life for employees by giving them opportunities to share responsibility, make decisions, and contribute significantly to the organization.

EXHIBIT 3.15   *Strengths and Weaknesses of Horizontal Structure*

Strengths
1. Promotes flexibility and rapid response to changes in customer needs
2. Directs the attention of everyone toward the production and delivery of value to the customer
3. Each employee has a broader view of organizational goals
4. Promotes a focus on teamwork and collaboration
5. Improves quality of life for employees by offering them the opportunity to share responsibility, make decisions, and be accountable for outcomes

Weaknesses
1. Determining core processes is difficult and time consuming
2. Requires changes in culture, job design, management philosophy, and information and reward systems
3. Traditional managers may balk when they have to give up power and authority
4. Requires significant training of employees to work effectively in a horizontal team environment
5. Can limit in-depth skill development

Sources: Based on Frank Ostroff, *The Horizontal Organization: What the Organization of the Future Looks Like and How It Delivers Value to Customers* (New York: Oxford University Press, 1999); and Richard L. Daft, *Organization Theory and Design*, 6th ed. (Cincinnati, Ohio: South-Western, 1998), 253.

A weakness of the horizontal structure is that it can harm rather than help organizational performance unless managers carefully determine which core processes are critical for bringing value to customers. Simply defining the processes around which to organize can be difficult and time consuming. AT&T's Network Systems Division eventually counted 130 processes and then began working to pare them down to fewer than 15 core ones.[46] In addition, shifting to a horizontal structure is time consuming because it requires significant changes in culture, job design, management philosophy, and information and reward systems. Traditional managers may balk when they have to give up power and authority to serve instead as coaches and facilitators of teams. Employees have to be trained to work effectively in a team environment. Finally, because of the cross-functional nature of work, a horizontal structure can limit in-depth knowledge and skill development unless measures are taken to give employees opportunities to maintain and build technical expertise.

MODULAR STRUCTURE

The modular structure extends the concept of horizontal coordination and collaboration beyond the boundaries of the traditional organization. With a **modular structure**, the firm subcontracts many or most of its major processes to separate companies and coordinates their activities from a small headquarters organization.[47]

HOW THE STRUCTURE WORKS

BRIEFCASE

As an organization manager, keep this guideline in mind:

Use a modular structure for extreme flexibility and rapid response to changing market conditions. Focus on key activities that give the organization its competitive advantage and outsource other activities to carefully selected partners.

The modular organization may be viewed as a central hub surrounded by a network of outside specialists. Rather than being housed under one roof or located within one organization, services such as accounting, design, manufacturing, marketing, and distribution are outsourced to separate companies that are connected electronically to a central office. Organizational partners located in different parts of the world may use networked computers or the Internet to exchange data and information so rapidly and smoothly that a loosely connected network of suppliers, manufacturers, and distributors can look and act like one seamless company. The modular form incorporates a free-market style to replace the traditional vertical hierarchy. Subcontractors may flow into and out of the system as needed to meet changing needs.

With a modular structure, the hub maintains control over processes in which it has world-class or difficult-to-imitate capabilities and then transfers other activities—along with the decision making and control over them—to other organizations. These partner organizations organize and accomplish their work using their own ideas, assets, and tools.[48] The idea is that a firm can concentrate on what it does best and contract out everything else to companies with distinctive competence in those specific areas, enabling the organization to do more with less.[49] Cunningham Motors, described in the chapter opening, is an example of a modular structure, in which Cunningham will maintain control over the design of luxury sports cars while almost everything else is handled by other organizations. Exhibit 3.16 illustrates a simplified modular structure for Premiere Plus Publishing, a publisher of travel and recreation books. Premiere's small staff focuses its energy on acquisitions, finding authors who have written or want to write manuscripts that would make a contribution to Premiere's list of

EXHIBIT 3.16   *Modular Structure at Premiere Plus Publishing Company*

high-quality travel books. Everything else is outsourced. An editorial services module handles securing permissions for photographs or other artwork, copyediting, writing blurbs for the book jacket, and other services needed to get the manuscript ready for publication. A design module creates a design for the book and formats the manuscript into pages, which are sent to the printing module, which prints and ships the books. Premiere also contracts with a public relations firm to promote the book through book tours, signings in bookstores, interviews, and attempts to get the book reviewed in newspapers and magazines.

STRENGTHS AND WEAKNESSES

Exhibit 3.17 summarizes the strengths and weaknesses of the modular structure. One of the major strengths is that the organization, no matter how small, can be truly global, drawing on resources worldwide to achieve the best quality and

EXHIBIT 3.17   *Strengths and Weaknesses of Modular Structure*

Strengths
1. Enables even small organizations to obtain talent and resources worldwide
2. Gives a company immediate scale and reach without huge investments in factories, equipment, or distribution facilities
3. Enables the organization to be highly flexible and responsive to changing needs
4. Reduces administrative overhead costs

Weaknesses
1. Managers do not have hands-on control over many activities and employees
2. Requires a great deal of time to manage relationships and potential conflicts with contract partners
3. There is a risk of organizational failure if a partner fails to deliver or goes out of business
4. Employee loyalty and corporate culture might be weak because employees feel they can be replaced by contract services

price and then selling products or services worldwide just as easily through subcontractors. The modular structure also enables a new or small company to develop products or services and get them to market rapidly without huge investments in factories, equipment, warehouses, or distribution facilities. The ability to arrange and rearrange resources to meet changing needs and best serve customers gives the modular structure greater flexibility and rapid response. New technologies can be developed quickly by tapping into a worldwide network of experts. The organization can continually redefine itself to meet changing product or market opportunities. A final strength is reduced administrative overhead. Large teams of staff specialists and administrators are not needed. Managerial and technical talent can be focused on key activities that provide competitive advantage while other activities are outsourced.[50]

The modular structure also has a number of weaknesses.[51] The primary weakness is a lack of control. The modular structure takes decentralization to the extreme. Managers do not have all operations under their jurisdiction and must rely on contracts, coordination, and negotiation to hold things together. This also means increased time spent managing relationships with partners and resolving conflicts. At Internet service provider Juno, which has used a modular structure from its beginning, the CEO says he spends at least 25 percent of his time managing partnerships.[52] Juno has only a few hundred employees, but it has thousands of people in other organizations working on content, customer service, and other activities that support the company.

A problem of equal importance is the risk of failure if one organizational partner fails to deliver, has a plant burn down, or goes out of business. Managers in the headquarters organization have to act quickly to spot problems and find new arrangements. Finally, from a human resource perspective, employee loyalty can be weak in a modular organization because of concerns over job security. Employees may feel that they can be replaced by contract services. In addition, it is more difficult to develop a cohesive corporate culture. Turnover may be higher because emotional commitment between the organization and employees is low. With changing products, markets, and partners, the organization may need to reshuffle employees at any time to get the correct mix of skills and capabilities.

HYBRID STRUCTURE

As a practical matter, many structures in the real world do not exist in the pure forms we have outlined in this chapter. Organizations often use a **hybrid structure** that combines characteristics of various approaches tailored to specific strategic needs. Most companies combine characteristics of functional, divisional, geographical, horizontal, or modular structures to take advantage of the strengths of various structures and to avoid some of the weaknesses. Hybrid structures tend to be used in rapidly changing environments because they offer the organization greater flexibility.

One type of hybrid that is often used is to combine characteristics of the functional and divisional structures. When a corporation grows large and has several products or markets, it typically is organized into self-contained divisions of some type. Functions that are important to each product or market are decentralized to the self-contained units. However, some functions that are relatively stable and require economies of scale and in-depth specialization are also centralized at headquarters. Sun Petroleum Products (SPPC) reorganized to a hybrid structure to be more responsive to changing markets. The hybrid organization structure adopted by SPPC is illustrated in part 1 of Exhibit 3.18. Three major product divisions—fuels, lubricants, and chemicals—were created, each serving a different market and requiring a different strategy and management style. Each product-line vice president is now in charge of all functions for that product, such as marketing, planning, supply and distribution, and manufacturing. However, activities such as human resources, legal, technology, and finance were centralized as functional departments at headquarters in order to achieve economies of scale. Each of these departments provides services for the entire organization.[53]

A second hybrid approach that is increasingly used today is to combine characteristics of functional and horizontal structures. Ford Motor Company's Customer Service Division, a global operation made up of 12,000 employees serving nearly 15,000 dealers, provides an example of this type of hybrid. Beginning in 1995, when Ford launched its "Ford 2000" initiative to become the world's leading automotive firm in the twenty-first century, top executives grew increasingly concerned about complaints regarding customer service. They decided that the horizontal model offered the best chance to gain a faster, more efficient, integrated approach to customer service. Part 2 of Exhibit 3.18 illustrates a portion of the Customer Service Division's hybrid structure. Several horizontally aligned groups, made up of multiskilled teams, focus on core processes such as parts supply and logistics (acquiring parts and getting them to dealers quickly and efficiently), vehicle service and programs (collecting and disseminating information about repair problems), and technical support (ensuring that every service department receives updated technical information). Each group has a process owner who is responsible for seeing that the teams meet overall objectives. Ford's Customer Service Division retained a functional structure for finance, strategy and communication, and human resources departments. Each of these departments provides services for the entire division.[54]

In a huge organization such as Ford, managers may use a variety of structural characteristics to meet the needs of the total organization. Like many large organizations, for example, Ford outsources some non-core activities. A hybrid structure is often preferred over the pure functional, divisional, horizontal, or modular structure because it can provide some of the advantages of each and overcome some of the disadvantages.

EXHIBIT 3.18   *Two Hybrid Structures*

Part 1. Sun Petrochemical Products

Functional Structure

President

Chief Counsel | Human Resources Director | Technology Vice President | Financial Services Vice President

Product Structure

Fuels Vice President | Lubricants Vice President | Chemicals Vice President

Part 2. Ford Customer Service Division

Functional Structure

Vice President and General Manager

Finance | Strategy and Communication | Human Resources

Horizontal Structure

Director and Process Owner — Teams — **Parts Supply / Logistics Group**

Director and Process Owner — Teams — **Vehicle Service Group**

Director and Process Owner — Teams — **Technical Support Group**

Sources: Based on Linda S. Ackerman, "Transition Management: An In-Depth Look at Managing Complex Change," *Organizational Dynamics* (Summer 1982): 46–66; and Frank Ostroff, *The Horizontal Organization* (New York: Oxford University Press, 1999), Fig 2.1., 34.

APPLICATIONS OF STRUCTURAL DESIGN

Each type of structure is applied in different situations and meets different needs. In describing the various structures, we touched briefly on conditions such as environmental stability or change and organizational size that are related to structure. Each form of structure—functional, divisional, matrix, horizontal, modular, hybrid—represents a tool that can help managers make an organization more effective, depending on the demands of its situation.

STRUCTURAL ALIGNMENT

Ultimately, the most important decision that managers make about structural design is to find the right balance between vertical control and horizontal coordination, depending on the needs of the organization. Vertical control is associated with goals of efficiency and stability, while horizontal coordination is associated with learning, innovation, and flexibility. Exhibit 3.19 shows a simplified continuum that illustrates how structural approaches are associated with vertical control versus horizontal coordination. The functional structure is appropriate when the organization needs to be coordinated through the vertical hierarchy and when efficiency is important for meeting organizational goals. The functional structure uses task specialization and a strict chain of command to gain efficient use of scarce resources, but it does not enable the organization to be flexible or innovative. At the opposite end of the scale, the horizontal structure is appropriate when the organization has a high need for coordination among functions to achieve innovation and promote learning. The horizontal structure enables organizations to differentiate themselves and respond quickly to changes, but at the expense of efficient resource use. The modular structure offers even greater flexibility and potential for rapid response by allowing the organization to add or subtract pieces as needed to adapt and meet changing needs from the environment and marketplace. Exhibit 3.19 also shows how other types of structure defined in this chapter—functional with horizontal linkages, divisional,

EXHIBIT 3.19   *Relationship of Structure to Organization's Need for Efficiency vs. Learning*

and matrix—represent intermediate steps on the organization's path to efficiency or innovation and learning. The exhibit does not include all possible structures, but it illustrates how organizations attempt to balance the needs for efficiency and vertical control with innovation and horizontal coordination. In addition, as described in the chapter, many organizations use a hybrid structure to combine characteristics of these structural types.

SYMPTOMS OF STRUCTURAL DEFICIENCY

Top executives periodically evaluate organization structure to determine whether it is appropriate to changing organization needs. Many organizations try one organization structure and then reorganize to another structure in an effort to find the right fit between internal reporting relationships and the needs of the external environment. Compaq Computer Corporation, for example, switched from a functional structure to a divisional structure for about a year to develop new products and then switched back to a functional structure to reduce competition among its product lines.[55]

As a general rule, when organization structure is out of alignment with organization needs, one or more of the following **symptoms of structural deficiency** appear.[56]

- *Decision making is delayed or lacking in quality.* Decision makers may be overloaded because the hierarchy funnels too many problems and decisions to them. Delegation to lower levels may be insufficient. Another cause of poor-quality decisions is that information may not reach the correct people. Information linkages in either the vertical or horizontal direction may be inadequate to ensure decision quality.
- *The organization does not respond innovatively to a changing environment.* One reason for lack of innovation is that departments are not coordinated horizontally. The identification of customer needs by the marketing department and the identification of technological developments in the research department must be coordinated. Organization structure also has to specify departmental responsibilities that include environmental scanning and innovation.
- *Too much conflict is evident.* Organization structure should allow conflicting departmental goals to combine into a single set of goals for the entire organization. When departments act at cross-purposes or are under pressure to achieve departmental goals at the expense of organizational goals, the structure is often at fault. Horizontal linkage mechanisms are not adequate.

SUMMARY AND INTERPRETATION

Organization structure must accomplish two things for the organization. It must provide a framework of responsibilities, reporting relationships, and groupings, and it must provide mechanisms for linking and coordinating organizational elements into a coherent whole. The structure is reflected on the organization chart. Linking the organization into a coherent whole requires the use of information systems and linkage devices in addition to the organization chart.

It is important to understand the information-processing perspective on structure. Organization structure can be designed to provide vertical and horizontal information linkages based on the information processing required to meet the organization's overall goal. Managers can choose whether to orient toward a traditional organization designed for efficiency, which emphasizes vertical linkages such as hierarchy, rules and plans, and formal information systems, or toward a contemporary learning organization, which emphasizes horizontal communication and coordination. Vertical linkages are not sufficient for most organizations today. Organizations provide horizontal linkages through cross-functional information systems, direct contact between managers across department lines, temporary task forces, full-time integrators, and teams.

Alternatives for grouping employees and departments into overall structural design include functional grouping, divisional grouping, multifocused grouping, horizontal grouping, and modular grouping. The choice among functional, divisional, and horizontal structures determines where coordination and integration will be greatest. With functional and divisional structures, managers also use horizontal linkage mechanisms to complement the vertical dimension and achieve integration of departments and levels into an organizational whole. With a horizontal structure, activities are organized horizontally around core work processes. A modular structure extends the concept of horizontal coordination and collaboration beyond the boundaries of the organization. Core activities are performed by a central hub while other functions and activities are outsourced to contract partners. The matrix structure attempts to achieve an equal balance between the vertical and horizontal dimensions of structure. Most organizations do not exist in these pure forms, using instead a hybrid structure that incorporates characteristics of two or more types of structure. Ultimately, managers attempt to find the correct balance between vertical control and horizontal coordination.

Finally, an organization chart is only so many lines and boxes on a piece of paper. The purpose of the organization chart is to encourage and direct employees into activities and communications that enable the organization to achieve its goals. The organization chart provides the structure, but employees provide the behavior. The chart is a guideline to encourage people to work together, but management must implement the structure and carry it out.

Key Concepts

centralized	matrix structure
decentralized	modular grouping
departmental grouping	modular structure
divisional grouping	multifocused grouping
divisional structure	organization structure
functional grouping	process
functional matrix	product matrix
functional structure	reengineering
horizontal grouping	symptoms of structural deficiency
horizontal linkage	task force
horizontal structure	teams
hybrid structure	vertical information system
integrator	vertical linkages
liaison role	virtual team

Discussion Questions

1. What is the definition of *organization structure*? Does organization structure appear on the organization chart? Explain.
2. How do rules and plans help an organization achieve vertical integration?
3. When is a functional structure preferable to a divisional structure?
4. Large corporations tend to use hybrid structures. Why?
5. What are the primary differences between a traditional organization designed for efficiency and a more contemporary organization designed for learning?
6. What is the difference between a task force and a team? Between liaison role and integrating role? Which of these provides the greatest amount of horizontal coordination?
7. What conditions usually have to be present before an organization should adopt a matrix structure?
8. The manager of a consumer products firm said, "We use the brand manager position to train future executives." Do you think the brand manager position is a good training ground? Discuss.
9. Why do companies using a horizontal structure have cultures that emphasize openness, employee empowerment, and responsibility? What do you think a manager's job would be like in a horizontally organized company?
10. How is structure related to the organization's need for efficiency versus its need for learning and innovation? How can managers tell if structure is out of alignment with the organization's needs?
11. Describe the modular structure. Why do you think this is becoming a good structural alternative for some of today's organizations?

Chapter 3 Workbook   *You and Organization Structure**

To better understand the importance of organization structure in your life, do the following assignment.

Select one of the following situations to organize:

- A copy and printing shop
- A travel agency
- A sports rental (such as jet skis or snowmobiles) in a resort area
- A bakery

Background

Organization is a way of gaining some power against an unreliable environment. The environment provides the organization with inputs, which include raw materials, human resources, and financial resources. There is a service or product to produce that involves technology. The output goes to clients, a group that must be nurtured. The complexities of the environment and the technology determine the complexity of the organization.

Planning Your Organization

1. Write down the mission or purpose of the organization in a few sentences.
2. What are the specific tasks to be completed to accomplish the mission?
3. Based on the specifics in number 2, develop an organization chart. Each position in the chart will perform a specific task or is responsible for a certain outcome.
4. You are into your third year of operation, and your business has been very successful. You want to add a second location a few miles away. What issues will you face running the business at two locations? Draw an organization chart that includes the two business locations.

5. Five more years go by and the business has grown to five locations in two cities. How do you keep in touch with it all? What issues of control and coordination have arisen? Draw an up-to-date organization chart and explain your rationale for it.

6. Twenty years later you have seventy-five business locations in five states. What are the issues and problems that have to be dealt with through organizational structure? Draw an organization chart for this organization, indicating such factors as who is responsible for customer satisfaction, how you will know if customer needs are met, and how information will flow within the organization.

Adapted by Dorothy Marcic from "Organizing," in Donald D. White and H. William Vroman, *Action in Organizations*, 2nd ed. (Boston: Allyn and Bacon, 1982), 154, and Cheryl Harvey and Kim Morouney, "Organization Structure and Design: The Club Ed Exercise," *Journal of Management Education* (June 1985), 425–429.

CASE FOR ANALYSIS   *C & C Grocery Stores, Inc.**

The first C & C grocery store was started in 1947 by Doug Cummins and his brother Bob. Both were veterans who wanted to run their own business, so they used their savings to start the small grocery store in Charlotte, North Carolina. The store was immediately successful. The location was good, and Doug Cummins had a winning personality. Store employees adopted Doug's informal style and "serve the customer" attitude. C & C's increasing circle of customers enjoyed an abundance of good meats and produce.

By 1997, C & C had over 200 stores. A standard physical layout was used for new stores. Company headquarters moved from Charlotte to Atlanta in 1985. The organization chart for C & C is shown in Exhibit 3.20. The central offices in Atlanta handled personnel, merchandising, financial, purchasing, real estate, and legal affairs for the entire chain. For management of individual stores, the organization was divided by regions. The southern, southeastern, and northeastern regions each had about seventy stores. Each region was divided into five districts of ten to fifteen stores each. A district director was responsible for supervision and coordination of activities for the ten to fifteen district stores.

Each district was divided into four lines of authority based on functional specialty. Three of these lines reached into the stores. The produce department manager within each store reported directly to the produce specialist for the division, and the same was true for the meat department manager, who reported directly to the district meat specialist. The meat and produce managers were responsible for all activities associated with the acquisition and sale of perishable products. The store manager's responsibility included the grocery line, front-end departments, and store operations. The store manager was responsible for appearance of personnel, cleanliness, adequate checkout service, and price accuracy. A grocery manager reported to the store manager, maintained inventories, and restocked shelves for grocery items. The district merchandising office was responsible for promotional campaigns, advertising circulars, district advertising, and attracting customers into the stores. The grocery merchandisers were expected to coordinate their activities with each store in the district.

Business for the C & C chain has dropped off in all regions in recent years—partly because of a declining economy, but mostly because of increased competition from large discount retailers such as Wal-Mart, Target, and Costco Wholesale. When these large discounters entered the grocery business, they brought a level of competition unlike any C & C had seen before. C & C had managed to hold its own against larger supermarket chains, but now even the big chains were threatened by Wal-Mart, which became No. 1 in grocery sales in 2001. C & C managers knew they couldn't compete on price, but they were considering ways they could use advanced information technology to improve service and customer satisfaction and distinguish the store from the large discounters.

However, the most pressing problem was how to improve business with the resources and stores they now had. A consulting team from a major university was hired to investigate store structure and operations.

The consultants visited several stores in each region, talking to about fifty managers and employees. The consultants wrote a report that pinpointed four problem areas to be addressed by store executives.

*Prepared by Richard L. Daft, from Richard L. Daft and Richard Steers, *Organizations: A Micro/Macro Approach* (Glenview, Ill.: Scott, Foresman, 1986). Reprinted with permission.

EXHIBIT 3.20   *Organization Structure for C & C Grocery Stores, Inc.*

1. *The chain was slow to adapt to change.* Store layout and structure were the same as had been designed fifteen years ago. Each store did things the same way, even though some stores were in low-income areas and other stores in suburban areas. A new computerized supply chain management system for ordering and stocking had been developed, but after two years it was only partially implemented in the stores. Other proposed IT initiatives were still "on the back burner," not yet even in the development stage.

2. *Roles of the district store supervisor and the store manager were causing dissatisfaction.* The store managers wanted to learn general management skills for potential promotion into district or regional management positions. However, their jobs restricted them to operational activities and they learned little about merchandising, meat, and

produce. Moreover, district store supervisors used store visits to inspect for cleanliness and adherence to operating standards rather than to train the store manager and help coordinate operations with perishable departments. Close supervision on the operational details had become the focus of operations management rather than development, training, and coordination.

3. *Cooperation within stores was low and morale was poor. The informal, friendly atmosphere originally created by Doug Cummins was gone.* One example of this problem occurred when the grocery merchandiser and store manager in a Louisiana store decided to promote Coke and Diet Coke as a loss leader. Thousands of cartons of Coke were brought in for the sale, but the stockroom was not prepared and did not have room. The store manager wanted to use floor area in the meat

and produce sections to display Coke cartons, but those managers refused. The produce department manager said that Diet Coke did not help his sales and it was okay with him if there was no promotion at all.

4. *Long-term growth and development of the store chain would probably require reevaluation of long-term strategy.* The percent of market share going to traditional grocery stores was declining nationwide due to competition from large super stores and discount retailers. In the near future, C & C might need to introduce nonfood items into the stores for one-stop shopping, add specialty or gourmet sections within stores, and investigate how new technology could help distinguish the company, such as through targeted marketing and promotion, providing superior service and convenience, and offering their customers the best product assortment and availability.

To solve the first three problems, the consultants recommended reorganizing the district and the store structure as illustrated in Exhibit 3.21. Under this reorganization, the meat, grocery, and produce department managers would all report to the store manager. The store manager would have complete store control and would be responsible for coordination of all store activities. The district supervisor's role would be changed from supervision to training and development. The district supervisor would head a team that included himself and several meat, produce, and merchandise specialists who would visit area stores as a team to provide advice and help for the store managers and other employees. The team would act in a liaison capacity between district specialists and the stores.

The consultants were enthusiastic about the proposed structure. With the removal of one level of district operational supervision, store managers would

EXHIBIT 3.21   *Proposed Reorganization of C & C Grocery Stores, Inc.*

have more freedom and responsibility. The district liaison team would establish a cooperative team approach to management that could be adopted within stores. The focus of store responsibility on a single manager would encourage coordination within stores and adaptation to local conditions. It would also provide a focus of responsibility for storewide administrative changes.

The consultants also believed that the proposed structure could be expanded to accommodate non-grocery lines and gourmet units if these were included in C & C's future plans. Within each store, a new department manager could be added for pharmacy, gourmet/specialty items, or other major departments. The district team could be expanded to include specialists in these lines, as well as an information technology coordinator to act as liaison for stores in the district.

CASE FOR ANALYSIS   *Aquarius Advertising Agency**

The Aquarius Advertising Agency is a middle-sized firm that offered two basic services to its clients: (1) customized plans for the content of an advertising campaign (for example, slogans and layouts) and (2) complete plans for media (such as radio, TV, newspapers, billboards, and magazines). Additional services included aid in marketing and distribution of products and marketing research to test advertising effectiveness.

Its activities were organized in a traditional manner. The organization chart is shown in Exhibit 3.22. Each department included similar functions.

Each client account was coordinated by an account executive who acted as a liaison between the client and the various specialists on the professional staff of the operations and marketing divisions. The number of direct communications and contacts between clients and Aquarius specialists, clients and account executives, and Aquarius specialists and account executives is indicated in Exhibit 3.23. These sociometric data were gathered by a consultant who conducted a study of the patterns of formal and informal communication. Each intersecting cell of Aquarius personnel and the clients contains an index of the direct contacts between them.

Although an account executive was designated to be the liaison between the client and specialists within the agency, communications frequently occurred directly between clients and specialists and bypassed the account executive. These direct contacts involved a wide range of interactions, such as meetings, telephone calls, letters, and so on. A large number of direct communications occurred between agency specialists and their counterparts in the client organization. For example, an art specialist working as one member of a team on a particular client account would often be contacted directly by the client's in-house art specialist, and agency research personnel had direct communication with research people of the client firm. Also, some of the unstructured contacts often led to more formal meetings with clients in which agency personnel made presentations, interpreted and defended agency policy, and committed the agency to certain courses of action.

Both hierarchical and professional systems operated within the departments of the operations and marketing divisions. Each department was organized hierarchically with a director, an assistant director, and several levels of authority. Professional communications were widespread and mainly concerned with sharing knowledge and techniques, technical evaluation of work, and development of professional interests. Control in each department was exercised mainly through control of promotions and supervision of work done by subordinates. Many account executives, however, felt the need for more influence, and one commented:

> Creativity and art. That's all I hear around here. It is hard as hell to effectively manage six or seven hot-shots who claim they have to do their own thing. Each of them tries to sell his or her idea to the client, and most of the time I don't know what has happened until a week later. If I were a despot, I would make all of them check with me first to get approval. Things would sure change around here.

The need for reorganization was made more acute by changes in the environment. Within a short period of time, there was a rapid turnover in the major accounts handled by the agency. It was typical for advertising agencies to gain or lose clients quickly, often with no advance warning as consumer

*Adapted from John F. Veiga and John N. Yanouzas, "Aquarius Advertising Agency," *The Dynamics of Organization Theory* (St. Paul, Minn.: West, 1984), 212–217, with permission.

EXHIBIT 3.22   *Aquarius Advertising Agency Organization Chart*

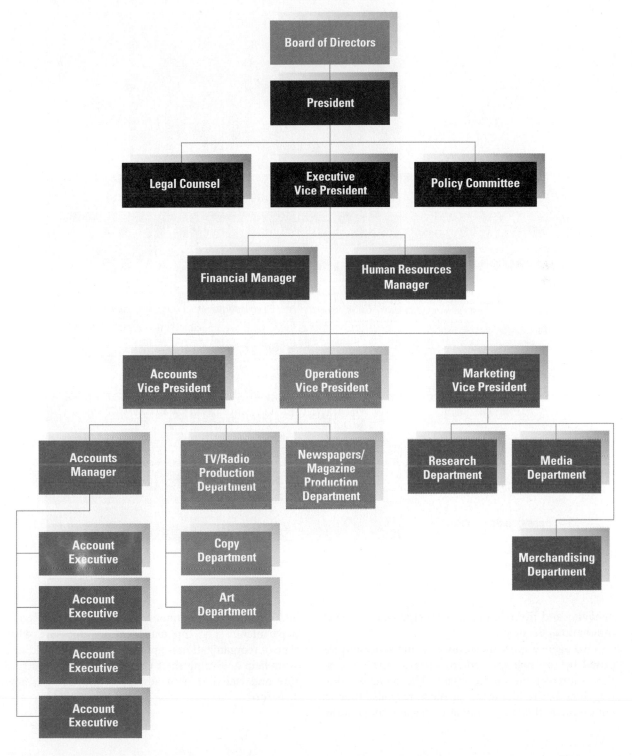

EXHIBIT 3.23   Sociometric Index of Aquarius Personnel and Clients

	Clients	Account Manager	Account Executives	TV/Radio Specialists	Newspaper/Magazine Specialists	Copy Specialists	Art Specialists	Merchandising Specialists	Media Specialists	Research Specialists
Clients	X	F	F	N	N	O	O	O	O	O
Account Manager		X	F	N	N	N	N	N	N	N
Account Executives			X	F	F	F	F	F	F	F
TV/Radio Specialists				X	N	O	O	N	N	O
Newspaper/Magazine Specialists					X	O	O	N	O	O
Copy Specialists						X	N	O	O	O
Art Specialists							X	O	O	O
Merchandising Specialists								X	F	F
Media Specialists									X	F
Research Specialists										X

F = Frequent—daily
O = Occasional—once or twice per project
N = None

behavior and lifestyle changes emerged and product innovations occurred.

An agency reorganization was one solution proposed by top management to increase flexibility in this unpredictable environment. The reorganization was aimed at reducing the agency's response time to environmental changes and at increasing cooperation and communication among specialists from different departments. The top managers are not sure what type of reorganization is appropriate. They would like your help analyzing their context and current structure and welcome your advice on proposing a new structure.

Notes

1. Based on David Welch, "Bob Lutz: The First Virtual Carmaker?" *BusinessWeek* (June 18, 2001), 66–70; Kerry A. Dolan and Robyn Meredith, "Ghost Cars, Ghost Brands," *Forbes.com* (April 30, 2001), accessed at *http://www.forbes.com/global/2001/0430/068* on July 29, 2002; "USG Software to Help Legendary Automotive Manufacturer Implement 'Virtual Car Company' Business Model," accessed at *http://www.edsplmsolutions.co.uk/press/* on March 2, 2003; and "GM Invests in Cunningham Motor Co." *Automotive Intelligence News*, (December 27, 2001), *http://www.autointell.com/news.htm*.

2. Dolan and Meredith, "Ghost Cars, Ghost Brands."

3. A. Erdman, "How to Keep That Family Feeling," *Fortune* (April 6, 1992), 95–96.

4. John Child, *Organization* (New York: Harper & Row, 1984).

5. Stuart Ranson, Bob Hinings, and Royston Greenwood, "The Structuring of Organizational Structures," *Administrative Science Quarterly* 25 (1980): 1–17; Hugh Willmott, "The Structuring of Organizational Structure: A Note," *Administrative Science Quarterly* 26 (1981): 470–474.

6. This section is based on Frank Ostroff, *The Horizontal Organization: What the Organization of the Future Looks Like and How It Delivers Value to Customers* (New York: Oxford University Press, 1999).

7. Stephen Salsbury, *The State, the Investor, and the Railroad: The Boston & Albany, 1825–1867* (Cambridge: Harvard University Press, 1967), 186–187.

8. David Nadler and Michael Tushman, *Strategic Organization Design* (Glenview, Ill.: Scott Foresman, 1988).

9. "Country Managers: From Baron to Hotelier," *The Economist* (May 11, 2002), 55–56.

10. Based on Jay R. Galbraith, *Designing Complex Organizations* (Reading, Mass.: Addison-Wesley, 1973), and *Organization Design* (Reading, Mass.: Addison-Wesley, 1977), 81–127.

11. G. Christian Hill, "Dog Eats Dog Food. And Damn If It Ain't Tasty," *Ecompany Now* (November 2000), 169–178; and "Country Managers: From Baron to Hotelier."

12. Lee Iacocca with William Novak, *Iacocca: An Autobiography* (New York: Phantom Books, 1984), 152–153.

13. Based on Galbraith, *Designing Complex Organizations*.

14. Tim Stevens, "Integrated Product Development" (Part II of the "Factories of the Future" series), *Industry Week* (June 2002), 21–28.

15. Jay Galbraith, Diane Downey, and Amy Kates, "How Networks Undergird the Lateral Capability of an Organization—Where the Work Gets Done," *Journal of Organizational Excellence* (Spring 2002) 67–78.

16. Ibid.

17. Walter Kiechel III, "The Art of the Corporate Task Force," *Fortune* (January 28, 1991), 104–105; William J. Altier, "Task Forces: An Effective Management Tool," *Management Review* (February 1987), 52–57.

18. Laton McCartney, "A Team Effort," *Industry Week* (December 18, 1995), 65–72; Richard Koonce, "Reengineering the Travel Game," *Government Executive* (May 1995), 28–34, 69–70.

19. Keith Naughton and Kathleen Kerwin, "At GM, Two Heads May Be Worse Than One," *Business Week* (August 14, 1995), 46.

20. Paul R. Lawrence and Jay W. Lorsch, "New Managerial Job: The Integrator," *Harvard Business Review* (November–December 1967): 142–151.

21. Jay R. Galbraith, *Competing with Flexible Lateral Organizations*, 2nd ed. (Reading, Mass.: Addison-Wesley, 1994), 17–18; ; Thomas L. Legare, "How Hewlett-Packard Used Virtual Cross-Functional Teams to Deliver Healthcare Industry Solutions," *Journal of Organizational Excellence* (Autumn 2001), 29–37.

22. Anthony M. Townsend, Samuel M. DeMarie, and Anthony R. Hendrickson, "Virtual Teams: Technology and the Workplace of the Future," *Academy of Management Executive* 12, no. 3 (August 1998), 17–29.

23. Carlos Ghosn, "Saving the Business Without Losing the Company," *Harvard Business Review* (January 2002), 37–45.

24. Henry Mintzberg, *The Structuring of Organizations* (Englewood Cliffs, N.J.: Prentice-Hall, 1979).

25. Frank Ostroff, "Stovepipe Stomper," *Government Executive* (April 1999), 70.

26. Based on Robert Duncan, "What Is the Right Organization Structure?" *Organizational Dynamics* (Winter 1979), 59–80; W. Alan Randolph and Gregory G. Dess, "The Congruence Perspective

of Organization Design: A Conceptual Model and Multivariate Research Approach," *Academy of Management Review* 9 (1984), 114–127.

27. Toni Mack, "The Ice Cream Man Cometh," *Forbes* (January 22, 1990), 52–56; David Abdalla, J. Doehring, and Ann Windhager, "Blue Bell Creameries, Inc.: Case and Analysis" (Unpublished manuscript, Texas A&M University, 1981); Jorjanna Price, "Creamery Churns Its Ice Cream into Cool Millions," *Parade* (February 21, 1982), 18–22; and Art Chapman, "Lone Star Scoop–Blue Bell Ice Cream Is a Part of State's Culture," *http://www.bluebell. com/press/FtWorthStar-july2002.htm.*

28. Rahul Jacob, "The Struggle to Create an Organization for the 21st Century," *Fortune* (April 3, 1995), 90–99.

29. Joseph Weber, "A Big Company That Works," *Business Week* (May 4, 1992), 124–132; and Elyse Tanouye, "Johnson & Johnson Stays Fit by Shuffling Its Mix of Businesses," *The Wall Street Journal* (December 22, 1992), A1, A4.

30. Brian Friel, "Hierarchies and Networks," *Government Executive* (April 2002), 31–39.

31. Michael Moeller, with Steve Hamm and Timothy J. Mullaney, "Remaking Microsoft," *Business-Week* (May 17, 1999), 106–114.

32. Based on Duncan, "What Is the Right Organization Structure?"

33. Weber, "A Big Company That Works."

34. John Markoff, "John Sculley's Biggest Test," *The New York Times* (February 26, 1989), sec. 3, 1, 26; and Shelly Branch, "What's Eating McDonald's?" *Fortune* (October 13, 1997), 122–125.

35. Stanley M. Davis and Paul R. Lawrence, *Matrix* (Reading, Mass.: Addison–Wesley, 1977), 11–24.

36. Eric W. Larson and David H. Gobeli, "Matrix Management: Contradictions and Insight," *California Management Review* 29 (Summer 1987), 126–138.

37. Davis and Lawrence, *Matrix,* 155–180.

38. Robert C. Ford and W. Alan Randolph, "Cross-Functional Structures: A Review and Integration of Matrix Organizations and Project Management," *Journal of Management* 18 (June 1992): 267–294; Duncan, "What Is the Right Organization Structure?"

39. Lawton R. Burns, "Matrix Management in Hospitals: Testing Theories of Matrix Structure and Development," *Administrative Science Quarterly* 34 (1989): 349–368.

40. Christopher A. Bartlett and Sumantra Ghoshal, "Matrix Management: Not a Structure, a Frame of Mind," *Harvard Business Review* (July–August 1990), 138–145.

41. This case was inspired by John E. Fogerty, "Integrative Management at Standard Steel" (Unpublished manuscript, Latrobe, Pennsylvania, 1980); Bill Saporito, "Allegheny Ludlum Has Steel Figured Out," *Fortune* (June 25, 1984), 40–44; "The Worldwide Steel Industry: Reshaping to Survive," *BusinessWeek* (August 20, 1984), 150–154; Stephen Baker, "The Brutal Brawl Ahead in Steel," *BusinessWeek* (March 13, 1995), 88–90, and "Why Steel Is Looking Sexy," *BusinessWeek* (April 4, 1994), 106–108.

42. Michael Hammer, "Process Management and the Future of Six Sigma," *Sloan Management Review* (Winter 2002), 26–32; and Michael Hammer and Steve Stanton, "How Process Enterprises *Really* Work," *Harvard Business Review* 77 (November–December 1999), 108–118.

43. Hammer, "Process Management and the Future of Six Sigma."

44. Based on Ostroff, *The Horizontal Organization*, and Richard L. Daft, *Organization Theory and Design*, 6th ed. (Cincinnati, Ohio: South-Western, 1998), 250–253.

45. Frank Ostroff, *The Horizontal Organization*, 102–114.

46. John A. Byrne, "The Horizontal Corporation," *BusinessWeek* (December 20, 1993), 76–81.

47. Melissa A. Schilling and H. Kevin Steensma, "The Use of Modular Organizational Forms: An Industry-Level Analysis," *Academy of Management Journal* 44, no. 6 (2001), 1149–1168; Raymond E. Miles and Charles C. Snow, "The New Network Firm: A Spherical Structure Built on a Human Investment Philosophy," *Organizational Dynamics* (Spring 1995), 5–18; and R. E. Miles, C. C. Snow, J. A. Matthews, G. Miles, and H. J. Coleman Jr., "Organizing in the Knowledge Age: Anticipating the Cellular Form," *Academy of Management Executive* 11, no. 4 (1997), 7–24.

48. Paul Engle, "You *Can* Outsource Strategic Processes," *Industrial Management* (January–February 2002), 13–18.

49. Don Tapscott, "Rethinking Strategy in a Networked World," *Strategy & Business* 24 (Third Quarter, 2001), 34–41.

50. Miles and Snow, "The New Network Firm"; Gregory G. Dess, Abdul M. A. Rasheed, Kevin J. McLaughlin, and Richard L. Priem, "The New Corporate Architecture," *Academy of Management Executive* 9, no. 2 (1995), 7–20; and Engle, "You *Can* Outsource Strategic Processes."

51. The discussion of weaknesses is based on Engle, "You *Can* Outsource Strategic Processes"; Henry W. Chesbrough and David J. Teece, "Organizing for Innovation: When Is Virtual Virtuous?" *Harvard Business Review* (August 2002), 127–134; Dess et al., "The New Corporate Architecture"; and N. Anand, "Modular, Virtual, and Hollow Forms of Organization Design," working paper, London Business School, 2000.

52. John A. Byrne, "Management By Web," *BusinessWeek* (August 28, 2000), 84–96

53. Linda S. Ackerman, "Transition Management: An In-depth Look at Managing Complex Change," *Organizational Dynamics* (Summer 1982): 46–66.

54. Based on Ostroff, *The Horizontal Organization*, 29–44.

55. Jo Ellen Davis, "Who's Afraid of IBM?" *BusinessWeek* (June 29, 1987), 68–74.

56. Based on Child, *Organization*, ch. 1.

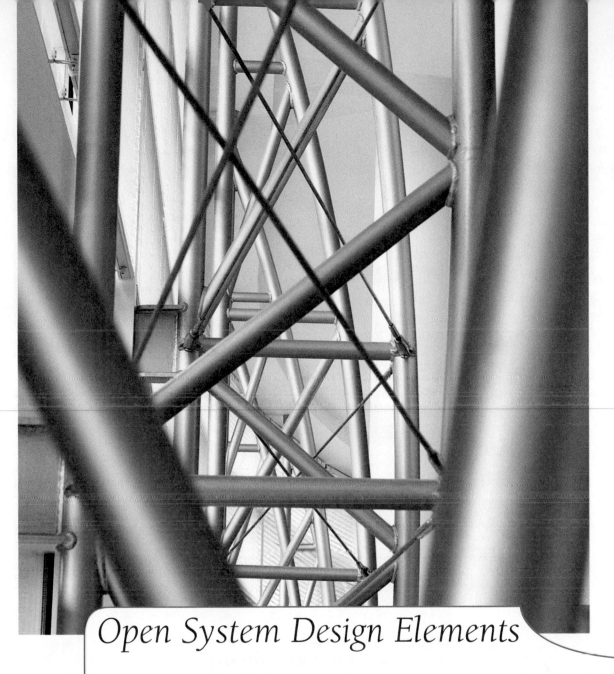

Open System Design Elements

part 3

The External Environment

chapter 4

Guiltless Gourmet

It was the early 1990s, and fat phobia was rampant across America. People were shunning artery-clogging potato chips, movie popcorn, and cookies, searching for alternative munchies that offered taste without the high fat content. The trend made Guiltless Gourmet of Austin, Texas, one of the hottest small companies in America. Within five years, Guiltless Gourmet, the maker of baked fat-free tortilla chips, grew from the founder's kitchen into a $23 million enterprise operating out of an 18,000-square-foot factory. The company was gobbling up market share from its local, domestic, and international snack food competitors. But by the turn of the century, Guiltless Gourmet was all but dead.

Guiltless Gourmet was started by an entrepreneur who had a good idea and the commitment and fortitude to make his dream come true. The company grew quickly, but leaders failed to notice the shifting landscape around them and the changes in the environment that could put Guiltless Gourmet on a fast-track to extinction. When the company was started in 1989, nobody else was making baked, low-fat chips, and the distinctive product had a wide-open market. However, by 1994, Frito-Lay, the giant of the snack-food industry, rolled out the new, low-fat Baked Tostitos with a flood of publicity and an army of 13,000 salespeople, many of whom were in stores every day promoting the new product. Guiltless Gourmet's orders plummeted 25 percent within six months. The company tried to compete, improving the taste of the chips and developing new packaging and promotion methods. But another problem was lurking just around the corner and Guiltless Gourmet failed to notice it: Americans just got downright tired of dieting. The country's low-fat craze peaked in 1996 and has been steadily declining ever since. The shift in consumer tastes wasn't a crisis for a large organization such as Frito-Lay, which has many other products, but for Guiltless Gourmet, it was devastating. By 2000, the company was fighting for its life. Its share of the tortilla chip market was down to 0.5 percent, and its revenues had sunk to below $9 million.[1]

Many companies, like Guiltless Gourmet, are surprised by the environment and are unable to quickly adapt to new competition, shifting consumer interests and social trends, or innovative technologies. Today, Guiltless Gourmet is still alive partly because it picked up on a new social trend—the concern over pesticides and genetically altered crops. The company downplays its low-fat claims in favor of emphasizing the use of all-organic corn in its products. It has also expanded its product line to nine different tortilla flavors and a range of low-fat dips and salsas.

Numerous factors in the external environment cause turbulence and uncertainty for organizations. Sales for manufacturers of cold cereal are down because of social and demographic changes. For example, many people want a convenient breakfast on the go, aging baby boomers want products that provide some medicinal benefit, and fewer people than ever are eating the first meal of the day. Following the September 11, 2001, terrorist attacks in the United States, many companies canceled or scaled back holiday parties, causing problems for companies such as Pear Tree Catering of Chicago, which lost about 30 percent of its business.[2] Traditional booksellers such as Barnes & Noble were slow to adopt new Internet technology, enabling Amazon.com to get a tremendous head start in online book sales. The external environment, including international competition and events, is the source of major threats confronting today's organizations. The environment often imposes significant constraints on the choices that managers make for an organization.

PURPOSE OF THIS CHAPTER

The purpose of this chapter is to develop a framework for assessing environments and how organizations can respond to them. First, we will identify the organizational domain and the sectors that influence the organization. Then, we will explore two major environmental forces on the organization—the need for information and the need for resources. Organizations respond to these forces through structural design, planning systems, and attempts to change and control elements in the environment.

THE ENVIRONMENTAL DOMAIN

In a broad sense the environment is infinite and includes everything outside the organization. However, the analysis presented here considers only the aspects of the environment to which the organization is sensitive and must respond to survive. Thus, **organizational environment** is defined as all elements that exist outside the boundary of the organization and have the potential to affect all or part of the organization.

The environment of an organization can be understood by analyzing its domain within external sectors. An organization's **domain** is the chosen environmental field of action. It is the territory an organization stakes out for itself with respect to products, services, and markets served. Domain defines the organization's niche and defines those external sectors with which the organization will interact to accomplish its goals. Guiltless Gourmet failed to pay attention to a critical part of its domain and was unprepared when Frito-Lay entered the low-fat tortilla chip market.

The environment comprises several **sectors** or subdivisions of the external environment that contain similar elements. Ten sectors can be analyzed for each organization: industry, raw materials, human resources, financial resources, market, technology, economic conditions, government, sociocultural, and international. The sectors and a hypothetical organizational domain are illustrated in Exhibit 4.1. For most companies, the sectors in Exhibit 4.1 can be further subdivided into the task environment and general environment.

TASK ENVIRONMENT

The **task environment** includes sectors with which the organization interacts directly and that have a direct impact on the organization's ability to achieve its goals. The task environment typically includes the industry, raw materials, and market sectors, and perhaps the human resources and international sectors.

The following examples illustrate how each of these sectors can affect organizations:

BRIEFCASE

As an organization manager, keep this guideline in mind:

Organize elements in the external environment into ten sectors for analysis: industry, raw materials, human resources, financial resources, market, technology, economic conditions, government, sociocultural, and international. Focus on sectors that may experience significant change at any time.

Exhibit 4.1   *An Organization's Environment*

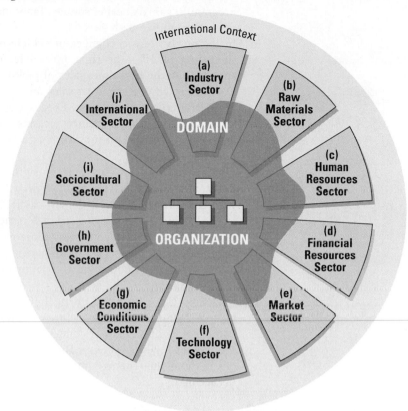

(a) Competitors, industry size and competitiveness, related industries

(b) Suppliers, manufacturers, real estate,
   services

(c) Labor market, employment agencies,
   universities, training schools, employees
   in other companies, unionization

(d) Stock markets, banks, savings and
   loans, private investors

(e) Customers, clients, potential users of
   products and services

(f) Techniques of production, science,
   computers, information technology,
   e-commerce

(g) Recession, unemployment rate, inflation rate, rate of investment, economics, growth

(h) City, state, federal laws and regulations,
   taxes, services, court system, political
   processes

(i) Age, values, beliefs, education, religion,
   work ethic, consumer and green movements

(j) Competition from and acquisition by
   foreign firms, entry into overseas markets, foreign customs, regulations,
   exchange rate

• In the *industry sector*, Home Depot, which revolutionized the home improvement retail industry with its huge warehouse stores, has been increasingly
  threatened by number-two Lowe's, which is building even larger stores on
  Home Depot's turf and slowly stealing market share. To fight back, Home
  Depot recently added appliances to its product mix to compete with Lowe's
  appliance business.[3]

• An interesting example in the *raw materials sector* concerns the beverage can
  industry. Steelmakers owned the beverage can market until the mid-1960s,

when Reynolds Aluminum Company launched a huge aluminum recycling program to gain a cheaper source of raw materials and make aluminum cans price-competitive with steel.[4]

- In the *market sector*, changes in vehicle-buying patterns have automakers struggling to offer the right mix of features that appeal to today's consumers. For the first time, sales of pickup trucks and sport utility vehicles have outpaced passenger car sales, but today's buyers aren't looking for the hard-driving rigs of the past. Ford, General Motors, and DaimlerChrysler are offering high-performance pickups that look tough but feature cushy leather seats, cruise control, sunroofs, and center armrests that can double as laptop workstations.[5]
- The *human resources sector* is of significant concern to every business. Research groups say U.S. businesses will soon face a shortage of skilled workers. Princeton, New Jersey–based Educational Testing Service, for example, found that the literacy of American adults ranks tenth out of seventeen industrialized countries. Moreover, younger adults underperform Americans over forty, leading researchers to warn that without improved adult training and education U.S. companies will fall further behind in the global economy.[6]
- For many U.S. companies today, the *international sector* is also a part of the task environment because of intense foreign competition. Even a low-tech company such as Dixon Ticonderoga Company, which makes pencils, feels the pinch of overseas competition. Today, more than 50 percent of the pencils in the United States come from overseas, compared to only 16 percent a decade ago.[7]

GENERAL ENVIRONMENT

The **general environment** includes those sectors that might not have a direct impact on the daily operations of a firm but will indirectly influence it. The general environment often includes the government, sociocultural, economic conditions, technology, and financial resources sectors. These sectors affect all organizations eventually. Consider the following examples:

- In the *government sector*, a new Securities and Exchange Commission regulation implemented in the wake of financial scandals at Enron, WorldCom, and numerous other organizations requires top executives of large corporations to personally swear under oath that their financial reports are accurate. In addition, President George W. Bush has signed far-reaching accounting reform legislation that will impact organizations.
- Shifting demographics is a significant element in the *sociocultural sector*. The huge baby-boom generation is aging and losing some of its interest in high-cost, brand-name goods. Meanwhile, the sons and daughters of baby boomers, sometimes called "Generation Y," disdain such once-favored brands as Nike and Levi Strauss. Companies are struggling to build loyalty among this new generation, which rivals the baby-boom generation in size and will soon rival it in buying clout.[8]
- General *economic conditions* often affect the way a company does business. The weak economy in the United States has led many organizations to shed jobs, defer raises, and reduce spending on new equipment or product development. Yet, to keep consumers buying, companies knocked down prices

and offered promotions such as no-interest financing on new cars. One Volvo dealership offered two free airline tickets to buyers who would pick up their new car at the factory in Europe, saving the import fees.[9]

- The *technology sector* is an area in which massive changes have occurred in recent years, from the explosion of the Internet, to advances in cloning technology and stem-cell research, to digital entertainment systems with hard drives that allow people to tap into the Internet, tie together all their entertainment options, and record hundreds of hours of programs for later viewing. Another interesting technological advance is the use of tiny microchips embedded in products that enable manufacturers to reduce inventories and retailers to track exactly what customers buy and where they buy it.[10]

- All businesses have to be concerned with *financial resources*, but this sector is often first and foremost in the minds of entrepreneurs starting a new business. Scott Blum started Buy.com, which resells computers and other products at or below cost over the Internet, with money out of his own savings. A couple of years later, Blum raised $60 million from Japanese tech company Softbank in return for a 20 percent equity stake in the company.[11]

INTERNATIONAL CONTEXT

The international sector can directly affect many organizations, and it has become extremely important in the last few years. In addition, all domestic sectors can be affected by international events. Despite the significance of international events for today's organizations, many students fail to appreciate the importance of international events and still think domestically. Think again. Even if you stay in your hometown, your company may be purchased tomorrow by the English, Canadians, Japanese, or Germans. For example, General Shale Brick, with headquarters in a small community in East Tennessee, was recently bought by Wienerberger Baustoffindustrie AG, a Vienna, Austria, company that is the world's largest brickmaker. The Japanese alone own more than one thousand U.S. companies, including steel mills, rubber and tire factories, automobile assembly plants, and auto parts suppliers.[12]

The distinctions between foreign and domestic operations have become increasingly irrelevant. For example, in the auto industry, Ford owns Sweden's Volvo, while Chrysler, still considered one of America's Big Three automakers, is owned by Germany's DaimlerChrysler and builds its PT Cruiser in Mexico. Toyota is a Japanese company, but it has built more than 10 million vehicles in North American factories. In addition, U.S. based companies are involved in thousands of partnerships and alliances with firms all around the world. These increasing global interconnections have both positive and negative implications for organizations. Because of the significance of the international sector and its tremendous impact on organization design, this topic will be covered in detail in Chapter 6.

The growing importance of the international sector means that the environment for all organizations is becoming extremely complex and extremely competitive. However, every organization faces uncertainty domestically as well as globally. Consider how changing elements in the various environmental sectors have created uncertainty for Ford Motor Company.

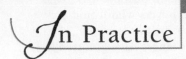

FORD MOTOR COMPANY

The business world has changed dramatically since Henry Ford first started building Model As and Model Ts a century ago. Today, Ford Motor Company is facing enormous challenges as a result of a complex, competitive, and constantly changing environment. Ford nearly suffered a blowout in 2000 when some of its standard tires—those manufactured by supplier Bridgestone/Firestone and installed on the top-selling Explorer—began coming apart on the road, causing severe injuries and fatalities. Ford goofed by failing to immediately accept its share of responsibility. The two companies instead engaged in denial and finger-pointing, damaging relationships with customers and ultimately ending Ford's century-old supplier relationship with Firestone.

As if the tire debacle wasn't enough, other elements of the environment were also creating havoc for Ford. The company had always been a model of efficiency, but as the twenty-first century dawned, that was no longer enough. Technology, consumer tastes, and financial markets were all changing at unprecedented speed, and Ford missed some key turns needed to keep in step with the environment. Instead of factories that efficiently cranked out high volumes of one standard vehicle, automakers now needed flexible factories that allowed for production of two or three different sizes and shapes of cars in one plant, capable of changing from one model to another over a weekend. Foreign and domestic rivals who had a technological edge were leaving Ford in the dust. For example, General Motors' revamped line of trucks and SUVs and Toyota's popular new models cut heavily into Ford's market share. At the same time, Ford's quality, which was top-notch during the late 1980s and 1990s, began to suffer, increasing the cost of its warranties and further eroding consumer confidence. The economic downturn in Europe, and more recently in the United States, created further woes for the car company.

Today, William Clayton Ford Jr., the first family member to lead the company since 1979, is struggling just to get Ford back on track. He's announced a serious five-year retrenchment plan that involves closing five North American plants and eliminating thousands of jobs worldwide. Ford will cease production of four models—the Lincoln Continental, Mercury Villager, Mercury Cougar, and Ford Escort—and implement new technologies to make its remaining factories more flexible. "For most of the last decade, Ford Motor Co. was on a roll," Ford said. "But the auto industry is fiercely competitive and things can change very quickly."[13]

In the following sections, we will discuss in greater detail how companies such as Ford cope with and respond to environmental uncertainty and instability.

ENVIRONMENTAL UNCERTAINTY

How does the environment influence an organization? The patterns and events occurring in the environment can be described along several dimensions, such as whether the environment is stable or unstable, homogeneous or heterogeneous, concentrated or dispersed, simple or complex; the extent of turbulence; and the amount of resources available to support the organization.[14] These dimensions boil down to two essential ways the environment influences organizations: (1) the need for information about the environment and (2) the need for resources from the environment. The environmental conditions of complexity and change create a greater need to gather information and to respond based on that information.

The organization also is concerned with scarce material and financial resources and with the need to ensure availability of resources.

Environmental uncertainty pertains primarily to those sectors that an organization deals with on a regular, day-to-day basis. Recall the earlier discussion of the general environment and the task environment. Although sectors of the general environment—such as economic conditions, social trends, or technological changes—can create uncertainty for organizations, determining an organization's environmental uncertainty generally means focusing on sectors of the *task environment*, such as how many elements the organization deals with regularly, how rapidly these elements change, and so forth. To assess uncertainty, each sector of the organization's task environment can be analyzed relative to the three analytical categories of change, complexity, and need for resources. The total amount of uncertainty felt by an organization is the uncertainty accumulated across environmental sectors. The remainder of this section will discuss the information perspective, which is concerned with the uncertainty that environmental complexity and change create for the organization. Later in the chapter, we will discuss how organizations control the environment to acquire needed resources.

Organizations must cope with and manage uncertainty to be effective. **Uncertainty** means that decision makers do not have sufficient information about environmental factors, and they have a difficult time predicting external changes. Uncertainty increases the risk of failure for organizational responses and makes it difficult to compute costs and probabilities associated with decision alternatives.[15] Characteristics of the environmental domain that influence uncertainty are the extent to which the external domain is simple or complex and the extent to which events are stable or unstable.[16]

SIMPLE COMPLEX DIMENSION

The **simple–complex dimension** concerns environmental complexity, which refers to heterogeneity, or the number and dissimilarity of external elements relevant to an organization's operations. The more external factors that regularly influence the organization and the greater number of other companies in an organization's domain, the greater the complexity. A complex environment is one in which the organization interacts with and is influenced by numerous diverse external elements. In a simple environment, the organization interacts with and is influenced by only a few similar external elements.

Aerospace firms such as Boeing Co. and Europe's Airbus operate in a complex environment, as do universities. Universities span a large number of technologies and are continually buffeted by social, cultural, and value changes. Universities also must cope with numerous ever-changing government regulations, competition for quality students and highly educated employees, and scarce financial resources for many programs. They deal with granting agencies, professional and scientific associations, alumni, parents, foundations, legislators, community residents, international agencies, donors, corporations, and athletic teams. This large number of external elements thus make up the organization's domain, creating a complex environment. On the other hand, a family-owned hardware store in a suburban community is in a simple environment. The store does not have to deal with complex technologies or extensive government regulations, and cultural and social changes have little impact. Human resources is not a problem because the store is run by family members and part-time help. The only external elements of real importance are a few competitors, suppliers, and customers.

STABLE–UNSTABLE DIMENSION

The **stable–unstable dimension** refers to whether elements in the environment are dynamic. An environmental domain is stable if it remains the same over a period of months or years. Under unstable conditions, environmental elements shift abruptly. Instability may occur when competitors react with aggressive moves and countermoves regarding advertising and new products. Wireless phone companies such as Verizon, Suncom, and Cingular are continuously going after each other's customers, advertising new plans offering more minutes, wider geographical coverage, or lower costs. Sometimes specific, unpredictable events—such as reports that "foul-smelling" soft drinks were making Coca-Cola's European customers ill, accounts of anthrax–laced letters being sent through the U.S. Postal Service, or charges by Greenpeace that Gerber's baby foods contained genetically altered corn that produced dangerous toxins—create unstable conditions. Today, "hate sites" on the World Wide Web, such as Ihatemcdonalds.com and Walmartsucks.com, are an important source of instability for scores of companies, from Allstate Insurance to Toys "R" Us. Microsoft critics can visit more than twenty hate sites.[17]

Although environments are becoming more unstable for most organizations today, an example of a traditionally stable environment is a public utility.[18] In the rural Midwest, demand and supply factors for a public utility are stable. A gradual increase in demand may occur, which is easily predicted over time. Toy companies, by contrast, have an unstable environment. Hot new toys are difficult to predict, a problem compounded by the fact that toys are subject to fad buying. The hottest toy of the holidays in 1996, Tickle Me Elmo, was quickly replaced by new fads such as Furby, Pokémon, Poochie the robotic dog, and Sony's Playstation 2. Toys tied to major motion pictures, such as *Star Wars* and *Harry Potter and the Chamber of Secrets*, can produce millions of dollars in sales, but they also dry up quickly. For example, Hasbro sold $500 million worth of Star Wars toys, but another $125 million worth were left gathering dust on retailers' shelves.[19]

FRAMEWORK

The simple–complex and stable–unstable dimensions are combined into a framework for assessing environmental uncertainty in Exhibit 4.2. In the *simple, stable* environment, uncertainty is low. There are only a few external elements to contend with, and they tend to remain stable. The *complex, stable* environment represents somewhat greater uncertainty. A large number of elements have to be scanned, analyzed, and acted upon for the organization to perform well. External elements do not change rapidly or unexpectedly in this environment.

Even greater uncertainty is felt in the *simple, unstable* environment.[20] Rapid change creates uncertainty for managers. Even though the organization has few external elements, those elements are hard to predict, and they react unexpectedly to organizational initiatives. The greatest uncertainty for an organization occurs in the *complex, unstable* environment. A large number of elements impinge upon the organization, and they shift frequently or react strongly to organizational initiatives. When several sectors change simultaneously, the environment becomes turbulent.[21]

A beer distributor functions in a simple, stable environment. Demand for beer changes only gradually. The distributor has an established delivery route,

EXHIBIT 4.2   *Framework for Assessing Environmental Uncertainty*

	Simple	**Complex**
Stable	**Simple + Stable = Low Uncertainty** 1. Small number of external elements, and elements are similar 2. Elements remain the same or change slowly Examples: Soft drink bottlers, beer distributors, container manufacturers, food processors	**Complex + Stable = Low-Moderate Uncertainty** 1. Large number of external elements, and elements are dissimilar 2. Elements remain the same or change slowly Examples: Universities, appliance manufacturers, chemical companies, insurance companies
Unstable	**Simple + Unstable = High-Moderate Uncertainty** 1. Small number of external elements, and elements are similar 2. Elements change frequently and unpredictably Examples: E-commerce, fashion clothing, music industry, toy manufacturers	**Complex + Unstable = High Uncertainty** 1. Large number of external elements, and elements are dissimilar 2. Elements change frequently and unpredictably Examples: Computer firms, aerospace firms, telecommunications firms, airlines

ENVIRONMENTAL CHANGE

ENVIRONMENTAL COMPLEXITY

Source: Adapted and reprinted from "Characteristics of Perceived Environments and Perceived Environmental Uncertainty" by Robert B. Duncan, published in *Administrative Science Quarterly* 17 (1972): 313–327, by permission of *The Administrative Science Quarterly*. Copyright © 1972 by Cornell University.

and supplies of beer arrive on schedule. State universities, appliance manufacturers, and insurance companies are in somewhat stable, complex environments. A large number of external elements are present, but although they change, changes are gradual and predictable.

Toy manufacturers are in simple, unstable environments. Organizations that design, make, and sell toys, as well as those that are involved in the clothing or music industry, face shifting supply and demand. Most e-commerce companies focus on a specific competitive niche and, hence, operate in simple but unstable environments as well. Although there may be few elements to contend with—e.g., technology, competitors—they are difficult to predict and change abruptly and unexpectedly.

The telecommunications industry and the airline industry face complex, unstable environments. Many external sectors are changing simultaneously. In the case of airlines, in just a few years they were confronted with an air-traffic controller shortage, price cuts from low-cost carriers such as Southwest Airlines, soaring fuel prices, the entry of new competitors such as JetBlue and AirTran, a series of major air traffic disasters, and a drastic decline in customer demand following the 2001 terrorist attacks.

ADAPTING TO ENVIRONMENTAL UNCERTAINTY

Once you see how environments differ with respect to change and complexity, the next question is, "How do organizations adapt to each level of environmental uncertainty?" Environmental uncertainty represents an important contingency for organization structure and internal behaviors. Recall from Chapter 3 that organizations facing uncertainty generally have a more horizontal structure that encourages cross-functional communication and collaboration to help the company adapt to changes in the environment. In this section we will discuss in more detail how the environment affects organizations. An organization in a certain environment will be managed and controlled differently from an organization in an uncertain environment with respect to positions and departments, organizational differentiation and integration, control processes, and future planning and forecasting. Organizations need to have the right fit between internal structure and the external environment.

POSITIONS AND DEPARTMENTS

As the complexity in the external environment increases, so does the number of positions and departments within the organization, which in turn increases internal complexity. This relationship is part of being an open system. Each sector in the external environment requires an employee or department to deal with it. The human resource department deals with unemployed people who want to work for the company. The marketing department finds customers. Procurement employees obtain raw materials from hundreds of suppliers. The finance group deals with bankers. The legal department works with the courts and government agencies. Today, many companies are adding e-business departments to handle electronic commerce and information technology departments to deal with the increasing complexity of computerized information and knowledge management systems.

The U.S. government has also responded to environmental uncertainty by creating new positions and departments. Soon after the 2001 terrorist attacks in the United States, President George W. Bush created the position of Director of Homeland Security to craft a "coordinated, integrated, and comprehensive national strategy to combat domestic terrorism."[22] Congress has created a Department of Homeland Security that will merge all or parts of various agencies to focus on protecting Americans against terrorism at home.

BUFFERING AND BOUNDARY SPANNING

The traditional approach to coping with environmental uncertainty was to establish buffer departments. The purpose of **buffering roles** is to absorb uncertainty from the environment.[23] The technical core performs the primary production activity of an organization. Buffer departments surround the technical core and exchange materials, resources, and money between the environment and the organization. They help the technical core function efficiently. The purchasing department buffers the technical core by stockpiling supplies and raw materials. The human resource department buffers the technical core by handling the uncertainty associated with finding, hiring, and training production employees.

A newer approach some organizations are trying is to drop the buffers and expose the technical core to the uncertain environment. These organizations no longer create buffers because they believe being well connected to customers and suppliers is more important than internal efficiency. For example, John Deere has assembly-line workers visiting local farms to determine and respond to customer concerns. Whirlpool pays hundreds of customers to test computer-simulated products and features.[24] Opening up the organization to the environment makes it more fluid and adaptable.

Boundary-spanning roles link and coordinate an organization with key elements in the external environment. Boundary spanning is primarily concerned with the exchange of information to (1) detect and bring into the organization information about changes in the environment and (2) send information into the environment that presents the organization in a favorable light.[25]

Organizations have to keep in touch with what is going on in the environment so that managers can respond to market changes and other developments. A study of high-tech firms found that 97 percent of competitive failures resulted from lack of attention to market changes or the failure to act on vital information.[26] To detect and bring important information into the organization, boundary personnel scan the environment. For example, a market research department scans and monitors trends in consumer tastes. Boundary spanners in engineering and research and development (R&D) departments scan new technological developments, innovations, and raw materials. Boundary spanners prevent the organization from stagnating by keeping top managers informed about environmental changes. Often, the greater the uncertainty in the environment, the greater the importance of boundary spanners.[27]

One of the fastest-growing areas of boundary spanning is competitive intelligence (CI). Membership in the Society of Competitive Intelligence Professionals has more than doubled since 1997, and colleges are setting up master's degree programs in CI to respond to the growing demand for these professionals in organizations.[28] Competitive intelligence gives top executives a systematic way to collect and analyze public information about rivals and use it to make better decisions.[29] Using techniques that range from Internet surfing to digging through trash cans, intelligence professionals dig up information on competitors' new products, manufacturing costs, or training methods and share it with top leaders. For example, Nutrasweet's competitive intelligence department helped the company delay a costly advertising campaign when it learned that a rival sweetener was at least five years away from FDA approval.[30] In today's uncertain environment, competitive intelligence is a trend that is likely to increase. In addition, a growing number of software applications aid in competitive intelligence searches on the Internet, and some entrepreneurs have started new businesses aimed solely at monitoring the Internet for large corporations to see how they are perceived in the environment. The "mystery shopper" industry has also dramatically grown, expanding from retail stores to banks, hotels, and medical facilities. Organizations such as Mystery Shoppers in Knoxville, Tennessee, send employees posing as customers to evaluate a client's firm or its competitors, and provide this intelligence to top leaders.[31]

The boundary task of sending information into the environment to represent the organization is used to influence other people's perception of the organization. In the marketing department, advertising and sales people represent the organization to customers. Purchasers may call on suppliers and describe purchasing needs. The legal department informs lobbyists and elected officials about the organization's needs or views on political matters. Many companies set up their own Web pages to present the organization in a favorable light. To counteract hate sites that criticize their labor practices in Third World countries, Nike and Unocal both created Web sites specifically to tell their side of the story.[32]

All organizations have to keep in touch with the environment. Here's how Tommy Hilfiger spans the boundary in the shifting environment of the fashion industry to stay ahead of the style curve.

In Practice

TOMMY HILFIGER

Twenty years ago, the number-one brand of jeans and casual clothes among young, hip consumers was Levi's. Today, that brand barely registers in customers' minds—or at the checkout—as new brands have taken over. One company that succeeded in recent years by keeping in touch with youth fashion trends is Tommy Hilfiger.

The torrent of high-speed information available on the Internet means teen fashion changes faster than ever, and Tommy Hilfiger wants to stay ahead of the curve. So, when Hilfiger's distinctive logo-laden shirts and jackets first began showing up on urban rappers in the early 1990s, the company started sending researchers into music clubs all across America to see how this influential group of consumers was wearing the styles. This gave executives information they needed to keep shifting Hilfiger styles to keep up with the times. Hilfiger also used the information to bolster its traditional mass-media ads with unusual promotions such as giving free clothing to stars on MTV and VH1. Recognizing its customers' passion for computer games, the company sponsored a Nintendo competition and installed Nintendo terminals in its stores. Hilfiger's efforts to stay close to the coveted youth fashion market worked

But nothing lasts forever in the fashion business, and today Hilfiger itself is struggling to maintain its popularity as young consumers increasingly turn away from status-conscious clothing and behavior. Hilfiger managers continue to look for ways to stay in touch with teenagers and keep tabs on emerging trends in the ever-changing fashion world.[33]

DIFFERENTIATION AND INTEGRATION

Another response to environmental uncertainty is the amount of differentiation and integration among departments. Organization **differentiation** is "the differences in cognitive and emotional orientations among managers in different functional departments, and the difference in formal structure among these departments."[34] When the external environment is complex and rapidly changing, organizational departments become highly specialized to handle the uncertainty in their external sector. Success in each sector requires special expertise and behavior. Employees in a research and development department thus have unique attitudes, values, goals, and education that distinguish them from employees in manufacturing or sales departments.

A study by Paul Lawrence and Jay Lorsch examined three organizational departments—manufacturing, research, and sales—in ten corporations.[35] This study found that each department evolved toward a different orientation and structure to deal with specialized parts of the external environment. The market, scientific, and manufacturing subenvironments identified by Lawrence and Lorsch are illustrated in Exhibit 4.3. Each department interacted with different external groups. The differences that evolved among departments within the organizations are shown in Exhibit 4.4. To work effectively with the scientific subenvironment, R&D had a goal of quality work, a long time horizon (up to five years), an informal structure, and task-oriented employees. Sales was at the opposite extreme. It had a goal of customer satisfaction, was oriented toward the short term (two weeks or so), had a very formal structure, and was socially oriented.

One outcome of high differentiation is that coordination among departments becomes difficult. More time and resources must be devoted to achieving coordination when attitudes, goals, and work orientation differ so widely. **Integration** is the quality of collaboration among departments.[36] Formal integrators are often required to coordinate departments. When the environment is highly uncertain, frequent changes require more information processing to achieve horizontal coordination, so integrators become a necessary addition to the organization structure. Sometimes integrators are called liaison personnel, project managers, brand managers, or coordinators. As illustrated in Exhibit 4.5, organizations with highly uncertain environments and a highly differentiated structure assign about 22 percent of management personnel to integration activities, such as serving on committees, on task forces, or in liaison roles.[37] In organizations characterized by very simple, stable environments, almost no managers are assigned to integration roles. Exhibit 4.5 shows that, as environmental uncertainty increases, so does differentiation among departments; hence, the organization must assign a larger percentage of managers to coordinating roles.

Lawrence and Lorsch's research concluded that organizations perform better when the levels of differentiation and integration match the level of uncertainty in the environment. Organizations that performed well in uncertain environments had high levels of both differentiation and integration, while those performing well in less uncertain environments had lower levels of differentiation and integration.

EXHIBIT 4.3   *Organizational Departments Differentiate to Meet Needs of Subenvironments*

EXHIBIT 4.4   *Differences in Goals and Orientations Among Organizational Departments*

Characteristic	R&D Department	Manufacturing Department	Sales Department
Goals	New developments, quality	Efficient production	Customer satisfaction
Time horizon	Long	Short	Short
Interpersonal orientation	Mostly task	Task	Social
Formality of structure	Low	High	High

Source: Based on Paul R. Lawrence and Jay W. Lorsch, *Organization and Environment* (Homewood, Ill.: Irwin, 1969), 23–29.

ORGANIC VERSUS MECHANISTIC MANAGEMENT PROCESSES

Another response to environmental uncertainty is the amount of formal structure and control imposed on employees. Tom Burns and G. M. Stalker observed twenty industrial firms in England and discovered that external environment was related to internal management structure.[38] When the external environment was stable, the internal organization was characterized by rules, procedures, and a clear hierarchy of authority. Organizations were formalized. They were also centralized, with most decisions made at the top. Burns and Stalker called this a **mechanistic** organization system.

In rapidly changing environments, the internal organization was much looser, free-flowing, and adaptive. Rules and regulations often were not written down or, if written down, were ignored. People had to find their own way through the system to figure out what to do. The hierarchy of authority was not clear. Decision-making authority was decentralized. Burns and Stalker used the term **organic** to characterize this type of management structure.

Exhibit 4.6 summarizes the differences in organic and mechanistic systems. As environmental uncertainty increases, organizations tend to become more organic, which means decentralizing authority and responsibility to lower levels, encouraging employees to take care of problems by working directly with one another, encouraging teamwork, and taking an informal approach to assigning tasks and responsibility. Thus, the organization is more fluid and is able to adapt continually to changes in the external environment.[39]

The learning organization, described in Chapter 1, and the horizontal and modular structures, described in Chapter 3, are organic organizational forms that are used by companies to compete in rapidly changing environments. Guiltless Gourmet, described in the chapter opening, has shifted to a flexible

BRIEFCASE

As an organization manager, keep this guideline in mind:

Match internal organization structure to the external environment. If the external environment is complex, make the organization structure complex. Associate a stable environment with a mechanistic structure and an unstable environment with an organic structure. If the external environment is both complex and changing, make the organization highly differentiated and organic, and use mechanisms to achieve coordination across departments.

EXHIBIT 4.5   *Environmental Uncertainty and Organizational Integrators*

Industry	Plastics	Foods	Container
Environmental uncertainty	High	Moderate	Low
Departmental differentiation	High	Moderate	Low
Percent management in integrating roles	22%	17%	0%

Source: Based on Jay W. Lorsch and Paul R. Lawrence, "Environmental Factors and Organizational Integration," *Organizational Planning: Cases and Concepts* (Homewood, Ill.: Irwin and Dorsey, 1972), 45.

EXHIBIT 4.6   *Mechanistic and Organic Forms*

Mechanistic	Organic
1. Tasks are broken down into specialized, separate parts.	1. Employees contribute to the common tasks of the department.
2. Tasks are rigidly defined.	2. Tasks are adjusted and redefined through employee teamwork.
3. There is a strict hierarchy of authority and control, and there are many rules.	3. There is less hierarchy of authority and control, and there are few rules.
4. Knowledge and control of tasks are centralized at the top of the organization.	4. Knowledge and control of tasks are located anywhere in the organization.
5. Communication is vertical.	5. Communication is horizontal.

Source: Adapted from Gerald Zaltman, Robert Duncan, and Johnny Holbek, *Innovations and Organizations* (New York: Wiley, 1973), 131.

modular structure to remain competitive. The company has redesigned itself to become basically a full-time marketing organization, while production and other activities are outsourced. The 18,000-square-foot plant in Austin has been closed and the workforce has been cut from 125 to about 10 core people who will handle marketing and sales promotions. The flexible structure allows Guiltless Gourmet to adapt quickly to changing market conditions. Another excellent example of a company that shifted to a more organic system to cope with change and uncertainty is Rowe Furniture Company, described in the Leading by Design box.

PLANNING, FORECASTING, AND RESPONSIVENESS

The whole point of increasing internal integration and shifting to more organic processes is to enhance the organization's ability to quickly respond to sudden changes in an uncertain environment. It might seem that in an environment where everything is changing all the time, planning is useless. However, in uncertain environments, planning and environmental forecasting actually become *more* important as a way to keep the organization geared for a coordinated, speedy response. Japanese electronics giants such as Toshiba and Fujitsu, for example, were caught off guard by a combination of nimble new competitors, rapid technological change, deregulation, the declining stability of Japan's banking system, and the sudden end of the 1990s technology boom. Lulled into complacency by years of success, Japan's industrial electronics companies were unprepared to respond to these dramatic changes and lost billions.[40]

When the environment is stable, the organization can concentrate on current operational problems and day-to-day efficiency. Long-range planning and forecasting are not needed because environmental demands in the future will be the same as they are today.

With increasing environmental uncertainty, planning and forecasting become necessary.[41] Planning can soften the adverse impact of external shifting. Organizations that have unstable environments often establish a separate planning department. In an unpredictable environment, planners scan environmental elements and analyze potential moves and countermoves by other organizations. Planning can be extensive and may forecast various *scenarios* for environmental contingencies. As time passes, plans are updated through replanning. Shell Oil uses a concept called TINA (There is no alternative) to keep its scenario planning anchored during times of rapid change and uncertainty. It does extensive research to isolate the forces in the environment that seem unstoppable (TINA for the late 1990s, for example, included the forces of globalization, liberalization, and technology) and then builds its potential scenarios around them. Shell has been a leader in speedy response to massive changes that other organizations failed to perceive until it was too late.[42]

Planning, however, cannot substitute for other actions, such as effective boundary spanning and adequate internal integration and coordination. The

---

LEADING BY DESIGN   *Rowe Furniture Company*

Nestled in the foothills of the Appalachian Mountains, the Rowe Furniture Company has been cranking out sofas, loveseats, and easy chairs for more than forty years. For most of that time, Rowe's workers punched their time cards, turned off their brains, and did exactly what the boss told them to do. When Charlene Pedrolie came to Rowe as the plant's new manufacturing chief, she found five hundred people working on a traditional assembly line, performing the same boring tasks over and over—one person cutting, another sewing, another gluing, and so forth. Rowe had been successful with this approach so far, but the marketplace was changing and top executives knew Rowe needed to change to keep pace.

Furniture shoppers used to be content to buy what was on the showroom floor or else wait months for a custom-made product. But not any longer—customers were demanding custom-designed pieces, but in today's fast-paced world, most wouldn't tolerate the long lead times, which could be up to six months. Rowe executives responded by installing a network of showroom computers, which allowed customers to select fabrics and furniture designs to their individual tastes and promised delivery within a month. To meet that difficult challenge Rowe needed a hyper-efficient assembly process, and Pedrolie believed the solution resided in the collective minds of the people out on the shop floor. She eliminated most supervisory positions, cross-trained employees to perform the different tasks required to build a piece of furniture, and then asked frontline workers to form horizontal clusters, or *cells*, and design the new production system. Each group selected its own members from the various functional areas and then created the processes, schedules, and routines for a particular product line. The assembly line was a thing of the past. Five hundred workers who had been accustomed to standing

in one place and having the furniture come to them were suddenly wandering from one partially assembled piece to another, performing a variety of tasks. For a while, it was sheer chaos, and some workers walked off the job and never came back. However, within a few weeks, the pieces fell into place. And when they did, productivity and quality shot through the roof. Before long, the factory was delivering custom-made pieces within thirty days. Only a few months later, that lead time had decreased to a mere ten days.

A key to Rowe's new system is open information. Every member of every team has instant access to current information about order flows, output, productivity, and quality. Data that were once closely guarded by management are now the common property of the shop floor. The sense of personal control and responsibility eventually led to a dramatic change in workers, who began holding impromptu meetings to discuss problems, check each other's progress, or talk about new ideas and better ways of doing things. One group came together as a "down-pillow task force" to invent a better stuffing process. Another came up with a way to increase the capacity of the drying kilns by feeding in sawdust as fuel. As the kilns became more and more efficient, the company began selling the excess drying capacity to outside lumber treaters through their own marketing program, thereby creating an entirely new business for itself.

The shift to an organic system at Rowe was not easy, but managers believe the results were worth the effort, creating an environment in which workers are constantly learning, solving problems, and creating new and better operational procedures.

Source: Thomas Petzinger, Jr., *The New Pioneers: The Men and Women Who Are Transforming the Workplace and Marketplace* (New York: Simon & Schuster, 1999), 27–32.

organizations that are most successful in uncertain environments are those that keep everyone in constant touch with the environment so they can spot threats and opportunities, enabling the organization to respond immediately. Honing the ability to anticipate the future and spot trends is the first step toward creating a superfast organization, as described in this chapter's Book Mark.

BOOK MARK 4.0   *Have You Read This Book?*

It's Not the Big That Eat the Small . . . It's the Fast That Eat the Slow
By Jason Jennings and Laurence Haughton

Speed is critical in today's business environment, and Jason Jennings and Laurence Haughton, authors of *It's Not the Big That Eat the Small . . . It's the Fast That Eat the Slow*, have provided managers with a guidebook for turning their companies into speed demons. To quickly bring new products, ideas, and services to the market, the authors argue that the organization has to learn to be swift on its feet in every area, from research and development to human resource management. Using real-life examples from their selected "fastest companies in the world," the book illustrates twenty-five tactics for moving faster. The first critical step is to learn *fast thinking*.

THINK FAST TO BE FAST
Speed without a destination in mind is merely haste, the authors point out, and will eventually land you in trouble. But organizations can gain an advantage by honing leaders' ability to interpret the environment, anticipate what the future is going to look like, and quickly and accurately assess new ideas and situations. Here are three aspects of fast thinking:

1. *The ability to anticipate.* Leopoldo Fernando Pujals, a sales manager for Johnson & Johnson in Spain, noticed the droves of women entering the Spanish workforce in the early 1990s and anticipated that siestas, late-night dinners, and heavy Spanish cuisine would soon be a thing of the past, and people would be needing home-delivered food. He founded Telepizza and ten years later was running an empire with 1,000 restaurants worth $2 billion. Leaders can anticipate what the future might be like by employing a number of techniques, such as looking backward to past cycles and trends for clues to the future, questioning everything, having empathy with customers, and developing "what if" scenarios to encourage forward thinking.

2. *The ability to spot trends.* Managers must learn to understand the environmental drivers of change, such as advances in technology, demographic shifts, government regulations, and financial changes. In addition, they continuously scan the environment for clues—not just by reading industry journals, but by watching television, listening to new music, traveling, studying how people in different communities live, and attending popular events that give them insight into people's interests.

3. *Let the best idea win.* Managers learn to quickly assess an idea's potential for success by "putting it through the grinder." The authors offer a series of questions to ask of every idea, such as "Will you be swimming upstream?" "Has someone done the math?" "Will it sidetrack the company?" and "Can it be done for less?" Managers also create an environment where ideas bubble up from all over and the best idea—whether it comes from the executive suite or the mailroom—wins the day.

MOVING ON
The remainder of the book builds on the idea of fast thinking to offer guidelines for making fast decisions, acceleration into the marketplace, and sustaining speed over the long term. In an era when the fear of eating competitors' dust is always present, *It's Not the Big That Eat the Small . . . It's the Fast That Eat the Slow* provides step-by-step advice for increasing a company's speed. Short, snappy summaries and an abundance of interesting examples make this a stimulating read for managers who want to get their organizations in the fast lane.

It's Not the Big That Eat the Small . . . It's the Fast That Eat the Slow, by Jason Jennings and Laurence Haughton, is published by HarperBusiness.

FRAMEWORK FOR ORGANIZATIONAL RESPONSES TO UNCERTAINTY

The ways environmental uncertainty influences organizational characteristics are summarized in Exhibit 4.7. The change and complexity dimensions are combined and illustrate four levels of uncertainty. The low uncertainty environment is simple and stable. Organizations in this environment have few departments and a mechanistic structure. In a low-moderate uncertainty environment, more departments are needed along with more integrating roles to coordinate the departments. Some planning may occur. Environments that are high-moderate uncertainty are unstable but simple. Organization structure is organic and decentralized. Planning is emphasized and managers are quick to make internal changes as needed. The high uncertainty environment is both complex and unstable and is the most difficult environment from a management perspective.

EXHIBIT 4.7   *Contingency Framework for Environmental Uncertainty and Organizational Responses*

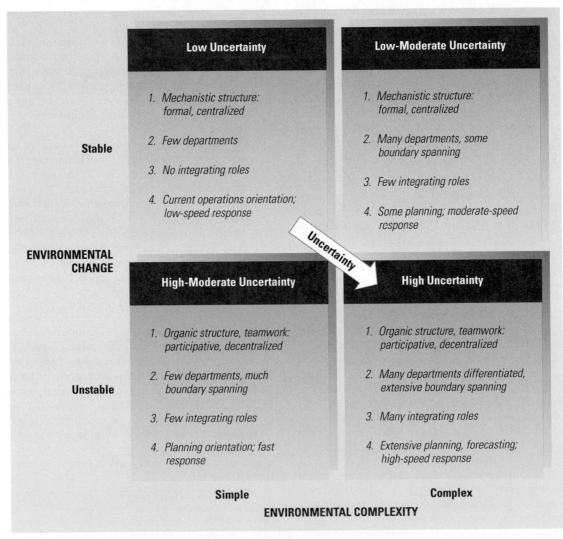

Organizations are large and have many departments, but they are also organic. A large number of management personnel are assigned to coordination and integration, and the organization uses boundary spanning, planning, and forecasting to enable a high-speed response to environmental changes.

RESOURCE DEPENDENCE

Thus far, this chapter has described several ways in which organizations adapt to the lack of information and to the uncertainty caused by environmental change and complexity. We turn now to the third characteristic of the organization-environment relationship that affects organizations, which is the need for material and financial resources. The environment is the source of scarce and valued resources essential to organizational survival. Research in this area is called the resource dependence perspective. **Resource dependence** means that organizations depend on the environment but strive to acquire control over resources to minimize their dependence.[43] Organizations are vulnerable if vital resources are controlled by other organizations, so they try to be as independent as possible. Organizations do not want to become too vulnerable to other organizations because of negative effects on performance. For example, when a fire at a Philips Electronics plant delayed production of computer chips, makers of cellular phones such as Nokia and Ericsson that relied on the supplier were left scrambling.

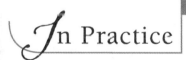

NOKIA CORPORATION

A lightning bolt in Albuquerque, New Mexico, was felt around the world after it started a fire that sparked a crisis for Nokia Corporation of Finland and neighboring Sweden's Telefon AB L. M. Ericsson. The blaze at a computer chip-making plant owned by Philips Electronics NV of the Netherlands burned for only ten minutes, but it would take weeks to get the factory back up to capacity.

Nokia and Ericsson, which used those chips in cell phones, couldn't afford to wait. Nokia was poised to meet the challenge with a speedy response. Its boundary–spanning mechanisms were so agile that a chief component-purchasing manager detected a slow-down in the flow of chips even before Philips notified Nokia of the problem. The flexible, organic structure at Nokia encourages bad news to travel fast, so top managers quickly learned of the situation and sprang into action. The company's motto, "Connecting People," applies internally as well as to customers. Within hours of learning just how serious the situation was, a team of supply engineers, chip designers, and top managers from China, Finland, and the United States were crafting a solution. They redesigned some chips so they could be produced elsewhere, sped up a project to develop new ways to boost chip production, and used their muscle to squeeze more out of other suppliers in a hurry. The crisis frayed nerves at Nokia, but production stayed on target.

The situation wasn't handled so smoothly at rival Ericsson, which lost about $400 million in potential revenue as a result of the crisis. Managers failed to detect the problem early and moved much more slowly once they did learn of it. In addition, Ericsson didn't have other potential suppliers to turn to. Ultimately, Ericsson came up millions of chips short of what it needed to produce a key product. Since then, the company has overhauled the way it procures parts, including making sure key components come from more than one supplier. "We will never be exposed like this again," said one top manager.[44]

Although companies like to minimize their dependence, when costs and risks are high they also team up to share scarce resources and be more competitive on a global basis. For example, the chip crisis combined with other component problems led Ericsson to announce that it would get out of the phone handset production market and begin outsourcing all handset manufacturing to a partner, Flextronics International Ltd. However, this also leaves the company vulnerable if Flextronics fails to perform as expected.

Formal relationships with other organizations present a dilemma to managers. Organizations seek to reduce vulnerability with respect to resources by developing links with other organizations, but they also like to maximize their own autonomy and independence. Organizational linkages require coordination,[45] and they reduce the freedom of each organization to make decisions without concern for the needs and goals of other organizations. Interorganizational relationships thus represent a tradeoff between resources and autonomy. To maintain autonomy, organizations that already have abundant resources will tend not to establish new linkages. Organizations that need resources will give up independence to acquire those resources.

Dependence on shared resources gives power to other organizations. Once an organization relies on others for valued resources, those other organizations can influence managerial decision making. When a large company like Nokia, Motorola, or Ford Motor Co. forges a partnership with a supplier for parts, both sides benefit, but each loses a small amount of autonomy. For example, some of these large companies are now putting strong pressure on vendors to lower costs, and the vendors have few alternatives but to go along.[46] In much the same way, dependence on shared resources gives advertisers power over print and electronic media companies. For example, as newspapers face increasingly tough financial times, they are less likely to run stories that are critical of advertisers. Though newspapers insist advertisers don't get special treatment, some editors admit there is growing talk around the country of the need for "advertiser-friendly" newspapers.[47]

In another industry, Microsoft is so large and powerful that it has a virtual monopoly in personal computer operating systems, so its every technical change adversely affects producers of application software. Microsoft has been accused of abusing this power and of squashing small competitors that would like to link up with it.[48]

CONTROLLING ENVIRONMENTAL RESOURCES

In response to the need for resources, organizations try to maintain a balance between linkages with other organizations and their own independence. Organizations maintain this balance through attempts to modify, manipulate, or control other organizations.[49] To survive, the focal organization often tries to reach out and change or control elements in the environment. Two strategies can be adopted to manage resources in the external environment: (1) establish favorable linkages with key elements in the environment and (2) shape the environmental domain.[50] Techniques to accomplish each of these strategies are summarized in Exhibit 4.8. As a general rule, when organizations sense that valued resources are scarce, they will use the strategies in Exhibit 4.8 rather than go

EXHIBIT 4.8   *Organizing Strategies for Controlling the External Environment*

Establishing Interorganizational Linkages	Controlling the Environmental Domain
1. Ownership	1. Change of domain
2. Contracts, joint ventures	2. Political activity, regulation
3. Cooptation, interlocking directorates	3. Trade associations
4. Executive recruitment	4. Illegitimate activities
5. Advertising, public relations	

it alone. Notice how dissimilar these strategies are from the responses to environmental change and complexity described in Exhibit 4.7. The dissimilarity reflects the difference between responding to the need for resources and responding to the need for information.

ESTABLISHING INTERORGANIZATIONAL LINKAGES

Ownership. Companies use ownership to establish linkages when they buy a part of or a controlling interest in another company. This gives the company access to technology, products, or other resources it doesn't currently have.

A greater degree of ownership and control is obtained through acquisition or merger. An *acquisition* involves the purchase of one organization by another so that the buyer assumes control. A *merger* is the unification of two or more organizations into a single unit.[51] AT&T Broadband and Comcast recently merged to create the nation's largest cable company. In the pharmaceuticals industry, Sweden's Pharmacia and the Upjohn Co. of Kalamazoo, Michigan, merged to form Pharmacia & Upjohn Inc. Acquisition occurred when IBM bought software developer Lotus Development Corp. and when Wal-Mart purchased Britain's ASDA Group. These forms of ownership reduce uncertainty in an area important to the acquiring company.

Formal Strategic Alliances. When there is a high level of complementarity between the business lines, geographical positions, or skills of two companies, the firms often go the route of a strategic alliance rather than ownership through merger or acquisition.[52] Such alliances are formed through contracts and joint ventures.

Contracts and joint ventures reduce uncertainty through a legal and binding relationship with another firm. Contracts come in the form of *license agreements* that involve the purchase of the right to use an asset (such as a new technology) for a specific time and *supplier arrangements* that contract for the sale of one firm's output to another. Contracts can provide long-term security by tying customers and suppliers to specific amounts and prices. For example, McDonald's contracts for an entire crop of russet potatoes to be certain of its supply of french fries. McDonald's also gains influence over suppliers through these contracts and has changed the way farmers grow potatoes and the profit margins they earn, which is consistent with the resource dependence perspective.[53] Large retailers such as Wal-Mart, Target, and Home Depot are gaining so much clout that they can almost dictate contracts telling manufacturers what to make, how to make it, and how much to charge for it. For example, CD companies edit songs and visual covers to cut out "offensive material" in order to get their products on the shelves of Wal-Mart, which sells more than 50 million

CDs annually. As one manufacturing rep put it, "Most suppliers would do absolutely anything to sell Wal-Mart."[54]

Joint ventures result in the creation of a new organization that is formally independent of the parents, although the parents will have some control.[55] In a joint venture, organizations share the risk and cost associated with large projects or innovations. AOL created a joint venture with Venezuela's Cisneros Group to smooth its entry into the Latin American online market. IBM recently announced a joint venture with USA Technologies Inc. to test Web-enabled washers and dryers at colleges and universities. Traditional coin-operated technology will be replaced with an IBM micropayment system that allows students to pay by swiping an ID card or pushing a code on a cell phone. They can log onto a Web site to see if a machine is available and have an e-mail sent when a load is done.[56]

Cooptation, Interlocking Directorates. **Cooptation** occurs when leaders from important sectors in the environment are made part of an organization. It takes place, for example, when influential customers or suppliers are appointed to the board of directors, such as when the senior executive of a bank sits on the board of a manufacturing company. As a board member, the banker may become psychologically coopted into the interests of the manufacturing firm. Community leaders also can be appointed to a company's board of directors or to other organizational committees or task forces. These influential people are thus introduced to the needs of the company and are more likely to include the company's interests in their decision making.

An **interlocking directorate** is a formal linkage that occurs when a member of the board of directors of one company sits on the board of directors of another company. The individual is a communications link between companies and can influence policies and decisions. When one individual is the link between two companies, this is typically referred to as a **direct interlock**. An **indirect interlock** occurs when a director of company A and a director of company B are both directors of company C. They have access to one another but do not have direct influence over their respective companies.[57] Recent research shows that, as a firm's financial fortunes decline, direct interlocks with financial institutions increase. Financial uncertainty facing an industry also has been associated with greater indirect interlocks between competing companies.[58]

Executive Recruitment. Transferring or exchanging executives also offers a method of establishing favorable linkages with external organizations. For example, each year the aerospace industry hires retired generals and executives from the Department of Defense. These generals have personal friends in the department, so the aerospace companies obtain better information about technical specifications, prices, and dates for new weapon systems. They can learn the needs of the defense department and are able to present their case for defense contracts in a more effective way. Companies without personal contacts find it nearly impossible to get a defense contract. Having channels of influence and communication between organizations serves to reduce financial uncertainty and dependence for an organization.

Advertising and Public Relations. A traditional way of establishing favorable relationships is through advertising. Organizations spend large amounts of money to influence the taste of consumers. Advertising is especially important in highly competitive consumer industries and in industries that experience variable demand. In the fashion industry, Gap Inc. is trying to reconnect with customers and revive sales with new ads featuring jeans with the tag line "For Every Generation," while Wrangler hopes to capitalize on the current patriotic fervor with flag-waving television commercials for its Five Star Denim jeans.

Public relations is similar to advertising, except that stories often are free and aimed at public opinion. Public relations people cast an organization in a favorable light in speeches, in press reports, and on television. Public relations attempts to shape the company's image in the minds of customers, suppliers, and government officials. For example, in an effort to survive in this antismoking era, tobacco companies have launched an aggressive public relations campaign touting smokers' rights and freedom of choice.

CONTROLLING THE ENVIRONMENTAL DOMAIN

In addition to establishing favorable linkages to obtain resources, organizations often try to change the environment. There are four techniques for influencing or changing a firm's environmental domain.

Change of Domain. The ten sectors described earlier in this chapter are not fixed. The organization decides which business it is in, the market to enter, and the suppliers, banks, employees, and location to use, and this domain can be changed.[59] An organization can seek new environmental relationships and drop old ones. An organization may try to find a domain where there is little competition, no government regulation, abundant suppliers, affluent customers, and barriers to keep competitors out.

Acquisition and divestment are two techniques for altering the domain. Canada's Bombardier, maker of Ski-Doo snowmobiles, began a series of acquisitions to alter its domain when the snowmobile industry declined. CEO Laurent Beaudoin gradually moved the company into the aerospace industry by negotiating deals to purchase Canadair, Boeing's deHaviland unit, business-jet pioneer Learjet, and Short Brothers of Northern Ireland. Deere & Co. felt vulnerable with the declining customer base for agricultural machinery, so Chairman and CEO Hans Becherer began reallocating resources into other lines of business, such as health care and financial services. Entering these new domains is helping Deere weather uncertain times and take some pressure off the machinery business.[60] An example of divestment is when Sears redefined its domain by selling off its financial services divisions, including Coldwell Banker, Allstate, and Dean Witter, to focus the company on retailing.

Political Activity, Regulation. Political activity includes techniques to influence government legislation and regulation. For example, General Motors used political activity to successfully settle a battle with the U.S. Transportation Department over the safety of some of its pickup trucks. The settlement requires that GM spend $51 million on safety programs over a five-year period but saved the company the cost of a $1 billion recall.[61] Large pharmaceutical companies frequently engage in political activity, as illustrated by the following example.

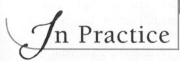

SCHERING–PLOUGH CORPORATION

Well-known patent medicines produce billions in annual sales for pharmaceutical companies like Schering-Plough Corp. So, when the patent on these drugs is nearing expiration, Schering-Plough begins looking for ways to delay regulatory approval of low-price generic pills that will cut into its lucrative market. One approach the company has used is to file suit against generic manufacturers, arguing that the selling of knockoff pills will violate a separate chemical compound patent. The defense typically does not prevail in court, but it achieves its purpose of significantly delaying government approval of generic equivalents to brand-name drugs.

This is just one in an increasingly aggressive string of legal and political maneuverings that large drug companies use to slow regulatory approval of generic drugs. One of the most common is filing so-called *citizen petitions* raising safety concerns. The practice is acceptable under a 1977 regulation that allows anyone to raise concerns about the safety of drugs or other items the Food and Drug Administration is reviewing. Most of the petitions filed by large drug companies are eventually rejected by the FDA, but they effectively hold up the approval of a competing generic drug by six months or longer, allowing the larger companies to reap more profits from brand-name drugs.

Now, drug makers are facing another threat following a recent study that says splitting pills to save money on many prescription drugs is safe. Many drug companies charge essentially the same price per tablet regardless of the dose. Thus, prescribing forty-milligram tablets of a drug such as Zocor for patients who need only twenty milligrams a day allows the patient to split the pill in half and save more than $700 a year. This is welcome news to patients and health insurers, but the drug companies are already fighting back with lawsuits and arguments that the practice isn't consistent with FDA labeling. The companies would like to see regulation that would limit the practice and prevent large health maintenance organizations from encouraging it.[62]

Pharmaceutical firms and other organizations frequently use lobbying to influence government actions. Some pay lobbyists to express their views to members of federal and state legislatures. Many CEOs, however, believe they should do their own lobbying. CEOs have easier access than lobbyists and can be especially effective when they do the politicking. Political activity is so important that "informal lobbyist" is an unwritten part of almost any CEO's job description.[63]

Political strategy can be used to erect regulatory barriers against new competitors or to squash unfavorable legislation. Corporations also try to influence the appointment to agencies of people who are sympathetic to their needs.

Trade Associations. Much of the work to influence the external environment is accomplished jointly with other organizations that have similar interests. For example, the pharmaceutical industry's trade group, Pharmaceutical Research and Manufacturers of America, is actively involved in the debate over pill splitting. Most manufacturing companies are part of the National Association of Manufacturers and also belong to associations in their specific industry. By pooling resources, these organizations can pay people to carry out activities such as lobbying legislators, influencing new regulations, developing public relations campaigns, and making campaign contributions. The National Tooling and Machining Association (NTMA) devotes a quarter of a million dollars each year to lobbying, mainly on issues that affect small business, such as taxes, health insurance, or government mandates. NTMA also gives its members statistics and information that help them become more competitive in the global marketplace.[64]

Illegitimate Activities. Illegitimate activities represent the final technique companies sometimes use to control their environmental domain. Certain conditions, such as low profits, pressure from senior managers, or scarce environmental resources, may lead managers to adopt behaviors not considered legitimate.[65] Many well-known companies have been found guilty of unlawful or unethical activities. Examples include payoffs to foreign governments, illegal political contributions, promotional gifts, and wiretapping. At formerly high-flying companies such as Enron and WorldCom, pressure for financial performance encouraged managers to disguise financial problems through complex partnerships or questionable accounting practices. In the defense industry, the intense competition for declining contracts for major weapon systems led some companies to do almost anything to get an edge, including schemes to peddle inside information and to pay off officials.[66] One study found that companies in industries with low demand, shortages, and strikes were more likely to be convicted for illegal activities, implying that illegal acts are an attempt to cope with resource scarcity.[67] In another study, social movement organizations such as Earth First! and the AIDS Coalition to Unleash Power (ActUp) were found to have acted in ways considered illegitimate or even illegal to bolster their visibility and reputation.[68]

ORGANIZATION–ENVIRONMENT INTEGRATIVE FRAMEWORK

The relationships illustrated in Exhibit 4.9 summarize the two major themes about organization–environment relationships discussed in this chapter. One theme is that the amount of complexity and change in an organization's domain influences the need for information and hence the uncertainty felt within an organization. Greater information uncertainty is resolved through greater structural flexibility and the assignment of additional departments and boundary roles. When uncertainty is low, management structures can be more mechanistic, and the number of departments and boundary roles can be fewer. The second theme pertains to the scarcity of material and financial resources. The more dependent an organization is on other organizations for those resources, the more important it is to either establish favorable linkages with those organizations or control entry into the domain. If dependence on external resources is low, the organization can maintain autonomy and does not need to establish linkages or control the external domain.

SUMMARY AND INTERPRETATION

The external environment has an overwhelming impact on management uncertainty and organization functioning. Organizations are open social systems. Most are involved with hundreds of external elements. The change and complexity in environmental domains have major implications for organizational design and action. Most organizational decisions, activities, and outcomes can be traced to stimuli in the external environment.

Organizational environments differ in terms of uncertainty and resource dependence. Organizational uncertainty is the result of the stable–unstable and simple–complex dimensions of the environment. Resource dependence is the result of scarcity of the material and financial resources needed by the organization.

Organization design takes on a logical perspective when the environment is considered. Organizations try to survive and achieve efficiencies in a world characterized by uncertainty and scarcity. Specific departments and functions

EXHIBIT 4.9   *Relationship Between Environmental Characteristics and Organizational Actions*

are created to deal with uncertainties. The organization can be conceptualized as a technical core and departments that buffer environmental uncertainty. Boundary-spanning roles provide information about the environment.

The concepts in this chapter provide specific frameworks for understanding how the environment influences the structure and functioning of an organization. Environmental complexity and change, for example, have specific impact on internal complexity and adaptability. Under great uncertainty, more resources are allocated to departments that will plan, deal with specific environmental elements, and integrate diverse internal activities. Moreover, when risk is great or resources are scarce, the organization can establish linkages through the acquisition of ownership and through strategic alliances, interlocking directorates, executive recruitment, or advertising and public relations that will minimize risk and maintain a supply of scarce resources. Other techniques for controlling the environment include a change of the domain in which the organization operates, political activity, participation in trade associations, and perhaps illegitimate activities.

Two important themes in this chapter are that organizations can learn and adapt to the environment and that organizations can change and control the environment. These strategies are especially true for large organizations that command many resources. Such organizations can adapt when necessary but can also neutralize or change problematic areas in the environment.

Key Concepts

boundary-spanning roles   mechanistic
buffering roles   organic
cooptation   organizational environment
differentiation   resource dependence
direct interlock   sectors
domain   simple–complex dimension
general environment   stable–unstable dimension
indirect interlock   task environment
integration   uncertainty
interlocking directorate

Discussion Questions

1. Define *organizational environment*. Would the task environment for a new Internet-based company be the same as that of a government welfare agency? Discuss.
2. What are some forces that influence environmental uncertainty? Which typically has the greatest impact on uncertainty—environmental complexity or environmental change? Why?
3. Why does environmental complexity lead to organizational complexity? Explain.
4. Discuss the importance of the international sector for today's organizations, compared to domestic sectors. What are some ways in which the international sector affects organizations in your city or community?
5. Describe differentiation and integration. In what type of environmental uncertainty will differentiation and integration be greatest? Least?
6. Under what environmental conditions is organizational planning emphasized? Is planning an appropriate response to a turbulent environment?
7. What is an organic organization? A mechanistic organization? How does the environment influence organic and mechanistic structures?
8. Why do organizations become involved in interorganizational relationships? Do these relationships affect an organization's dependency? Performance?
9. Assume you have been asked to calculate the ratio of staff employees to production employees in two organizations—one in a simple, stable environment and one in a complex, shifting environment. How would you expect these ratios to differ? Why?
10. Is changing the organization's domain a feasible strategy for coping with a threatening environment? Explain.

Chapter 4 Workbook   *Organizations You Rely On**

Below, list eight organizations you somehow rely on in your daily life. Examples might be a restaurant, a clothing or CD store, a university, your family, the post office, the telephone company, an airline, a pizzeria that delivers, your place of work, and so on. In the first column, list those eight organizations. Then, in column 2, choose another organization you could use in case the ones in column 1 were not available. In column 3, evaluate your level of dependence on the organizations listed in column 1 as Strong, Medium, or Weak. Finally, in column 4, rate the certainty of that organization being able to meet your needs as High (certainty), Medium, or Low.

Column 1 Organization	Column 2 Backup	Column 3 Level of dependence	Column 4 Level of certainty
1.			
2.			
3.			
4.			
5.			
6.			
7.			
8.			

*Adapted by Dorothy Marcic from "Organizational Dependencies," in Ricky W. Griffin and Thomas C. Head, *Practicing Management*, 2nd ed. (Dallas: Houghton Mifflin), 2–3.

Questions

1. Do you have adequate backup organizations for those of high dependence? How might you create even more backups?
2. What would you do if an organization you rated high for dependence and high for certainty suddenly became high-dependence and low-certainty?

How would your behavior relate to the concept of resource dependence?

3. Have you ever used any behaviors similar to those in Exhibit 4.8 to manage your relationships with the organizations listed in column 1?

CASE FOR ANALYSIS   *The Paradoxical Twins: Acme and Omega Electronics* *

Part I

In 1980, Technological Products of Erie, Pennsylvania, was bought out by a Cleveland manufacturer. The Cleveland firm had no interest in the electronics division of Technological Products and subsequently sold to different investors two plants that manufactured computer chips and printed circuit boards. Integrated circuits, or chips, were the first step into microminiaturization in the electronics industry, and both plants had developed some expertise in the technology, along with their superior capabilities in manufacturing printed circuit boards. One of the plants, located in nearby Waterford, was renamed Acme Electronics; the other plant, within the city limits of Erie, was renamed Omega Electronics, Inc.

Acme retained its original management and upgraded its general manager to president. Omega hired a new president who had been a director of a large electronic research laboratory and upgraded several of the existing personnel within the plant. Acme and Omega often competed for the same contracts. As subcontractors, both firms benefited from the electronics boom and both looked forward to future growth and expansion. The world was going digital, and both companies began producing digital microprocessors along with the production of circuit boards. Acme had annual sales of $100 million and employed 550 people. Omega had annual sales of $80 million and employed 480 people. Acme regularly achieved greater net profits, much to the chagrin of Omega's management.

Inside Acme

The president of Acme, John Tyler, was confident that, had the demand not been so great, Acme's competitor would not have survived. "In fact," he said, "we have been able to beat Omega regularly for the most profitable contracts, thereby increasing our profit." Tyler credited his firm's greater effectiveness

to his managers' abilities to run a "tight ship." He explained that he had retained the basic structure developed by Technological Products because it was most efficient for high-volume manufacturing. Acme had detailed organization charts and job descriptions. Tyler believed everyone should have clear responsibilities and narrowly defined jobs, which would lead to efficient performance and high company profits. People were generally satisfied with their work at Acme; however, some of the managers voiced the desire to have a little more latitude in their jobs.

Inside Omega

Omega's president, Jim Rawls, did not believe in organization charts. He felt his organization had departments similar to Acme's, but he thought Omega's plant was small enough that things such as organization charts just put artificial barriers between specialists who should be working together. Written memos were not allowed since, as Rawls expressed it, "the plant is small enough that if people want to communicate, they can just drop by and talk things over."

The head of the mechanical engineering department said, "Jim spends too much of his time and mine making sure everyone understands what we're doing and listening to suggestions." Rawls was concerned with employee satisfaction and wanted everyone to feel part of the organization. The top management team reflected Rawls's attitudes. They also believed that employees should be familiar with activities throughout the organization so that cooperation between departments would be increased. A newer member of the industrial engineering department said, "When I first got here, I wasn't sure what I was supposed to do. One day I worked with some mechanical engineers and the next day I helped the shipping department design some packing cartons.

*Adapted from John F. Veiga, "The Paradoxical Twins: Acme and Omega Electronics," in John F. Veiga and John N. Yanouzas, *The Dynamics of Organizational Theory* (St. Paul: West, 1984), 132–138.

The first months on the job were hectic, but at least I got a real feel for what makes Omega tick."

Part II

In the 1990s, mixed analog and digital devices began threatening the demand for the complex circuit boards manufactured by Acme and Omega. This "system-on-a-chip" technology combined analog functions, such as sound, graphics, and power management, together with digital circuitry, such as logic and memory, making it highly useful for new products such as cellular phones, and wireless computers. Both Acme and Omega realized the threat to their futures and began aggressively to seek new customers.

In July 1992, a major photocopier manufacturer was looking for a subcontractor to assemble the digital memory units of its new experimental copier. The projected contract for the job was estimated to be $7 million to $9 million in annual sales.

Both Acme and Omega were geographically close to this manufacturer, and both submitted highly competitive bids for the production of one hundred prototypes. Acme's bid was slightly lower than Omega's; however, both firms were asked to produce one hundred units. The photocopier manufacturer told both firms speed was critical because its president had boasted to other manufacturers that the firm would have a finished copier available by Christmas. This boast, much to the designer's dismay, required pressure on all subcontractors to begin prototype production before the final design of the copier was complete. This meant Acme and Omega would have at most two weeks to produce the prototypes or would delay the final copier production.

Part III

Inside Acme

As soon as John Tyler was given the blueprints (Monday, July 11, 1992), he sent a memo to the purchasing department asking to move forward on the purchase of all necessary materials. At the same time, he sent the blueprints to the drafting department and asked that it prepare manufacturing prints. The industrial engineering department was told to begin methods design work for use by the production department supervisors. Tyler also sent a memo to all department heads and executives indicating the critical time constraints of this job and how he expected that all employees would perform as efficiently as they had in the past.

The departments had little contact with one another for several days, and each seemed to work at its own speed. Each department also encountered problems. Purchasing could not acquire all the parts on time. Industrial engineering had difficulty arranging an efficient assembly sequence. Mechanical engineering did not take the deadline seriously and parceled its work to vendors so the engineers could work on other jobs scheduled previously. Tyler made it a point to stay in touch with the photocopier manufacturer to let it know things were progressing and to learn of any new developments. He traditionally worked to keep important clients happy. Tyler telephoned someone at the photocopier company at least twice a week and got to know the head designer quite well.

On July 15, Tyler learned that mechanical engineering was far behind in its development work, and he "hit the roof." To make matters worse, purchasing had not obtained all the parts, so the industrial engineers decided to assemble the product without one part, which would be inserted at the last minute. On Thursday, July 21, the final units were being assembled, although the process was delayed several times. On Friday, July 22, the last units were finished while Tyler paced around the plant. Late that afternoon, Tyler received a phone call from the head designer of the photocopier manufacturer, who told Tyler that he had received a call on Wednesday from Jim Rawls of Omega. He explained that Rawls's workers had found an error in the design of the connector cable and taken corrective action on their prototypes. He told Tyler that he had checked out the design error and that Omega was right. Tyler, a bit overwhelmed by this information, told the designer that he had all the memory units ready for shipment and that, as soon as they received the missing component on Monday or Tuesday, they would be able to deliver the final units. The designer explained that the design error would be rectified in a new blueprint he was sending over by messenger and that he would hold Acme to the Tuesday delivery date.

When the blueprint arrived, Tyler called in the production supervisor to assess the damage. The alterations in the design would call for total disassembly and the unsoldering of several connections. Tyler told the supervisor to put extra people on the alterations first thing Monday morning and to try to finish the job by Tuesday. Late Tuesday afternoon, the alterations were finished and the missing components were delivered. Wednesday morning, the production supervisor discovered that the units would have to be torn apart again to install the missing component. When John Tyler was told this, he again "hit the roof." He called industrial engineering and asked if it could help out. The production supervisor and the methods engineer couldn't agree on how to install the component. John Tyler settled the argument by ordering that all units be taken apart again and the missing component installed. He told shipping to prepare cartons for delivery on Friday afternoon.

On Friday, July 29, fifty prototypes were shipped from Acme without final inspection. John Tyler was concerned about his firm's reputation, so he waived the final inspection after he personally tested one unit and found it operational. On Tuesday, August 2, Acme shipped the last fifty units.

Inside Omega

On Friday, July 8, Jim Rawls called a meeting that included department heads to tell them about the potential contract they were to receive. He told them that as soon as he received the blueprints, work could begin. On Monday, July 11, the prints arrived and again the department heads met to discuss the project. At the end of the meeting, drafting had agreed to prepare manufacturing prints, while industrial engineering and production would begin methods design.

Two problems arose within Omega that were similar to those at Acme. Certain ordered parts could not be delivered on time, and the assembly sequence was difficult to engineer. The departments proposed ideas to help one another, however, and department heads and key employees had daily meetings to discuss progress. The head of electrical engineering knew of a Japanese source for the components that could not be purchased from normal suppliers. Most problems were solved by Saturday, July 16.

On Monday, July 18, a methods engineer and the production supervisor formulated the assembly plans, and production was set to begin on Tuesday morning. On Monday afternoon, people from mechanical engineering, electrical engineering, production, and industrial engineering got together to produce a prototype just to ensure that there would be no snags in production. While they were building the unit, they discovered an error in the connector cable design. All the engineers agreed, after checking and rechecking the blueprints, that the cable was erroneously designed. People from mechanical engineering and electrical engineering spent Monday night redesigning the cable, and on Tuesday morning, the drafting department finalized the changes in the manufacturing prints. On Tuesday morning, Rawls was a bit apprehensive about the design changes and decided to get formal approval. Rawls received word on Wednesday from the head designer at the photocopier firm that they could proceed with the design changes as discussed on the phone. On Friday, July 22, the final units were inspected by quality control and were then shipped.

Part IV

Ten of Acme's final memory units were defective, while all of Omega's units passed the photocopier firm's tests. The photocopier firm was disappointed with Acme's delivery delay and incurred further delays in repairing the defective Acme units. However, rather than give the entire contract to one firm, the final contract was split between Acme and Omega with two directives added: (1) maintain zero defects and (2) reduce final cost. In 1982, through extensive cost-cutting efforts, Acme reduced its unit cost by 20 percent and was ultimately awarded the total contract.

Notes

1. Dennis K. Berman, "Crunch Time," *BusinessWeek Frontier* (April 24, 2000), F28–F38.
2. Kim Severson, "Cereal Crunch: Manufacturers Struggle to Keep Us Loyal to the Bowl," *The San Francisco Chronicle*, August 29, 2001, WB1; Dave Carpenter, "Lavish Office Parties Rare This Year," AP story in *Johnson City Press* (December 1, 2001), 21.
3. Rick Brooks, "Home Depot Turns Copycat in Its Efforts to Stoke New Growth," *The Wall Street Journal* (November 21, 2000), A1.
4. Dana Milbank, "Aluminum Producers, Aggressive and Agile, Outfight Steelmakers," *The Wall Street Journal* (July 1, 1992), A1.
5. Jonathan Welsh, "Prettifying the Pickup Truck," *The Wall Street Journal* (August 30, 2002), B1, B4.

6. Aaron Bernstein, "The Time Bomb in the Workforce: Illiteracy," *BusinessWeek* (February 25, 2002), 122.

7. Ann Carrns, "Point Taken: Hit Hard by Imports, American Pencil Icon Tries to Get a Grip," *The Wall Street Journal* (November 24, 1999), A1, A6.

8. Michael Hickins, "Brand Names Losing Luster for Affluent Customers," *Management Review* (June 1999), 9; and Ellen Neuborne with Kathleen Kerwin, "Generation Y," *BusinessWeek*, (February 15, 1999), 80–88.

9. Greg Ip and Russell Gold, "Open Wallets: In Uneasy Times, Consumers Boost a Fragile U.S. Economy," *The Wall Street Journal* (September 3, 2002), A1, A8.

10. Arlene Weintraub with Faith Keenan, "The Clone Wars," *BusinessWeek* (March 25, 2002), 94–96; Devin Leonard, "The Most Valuable Square Foot in America," *Fortune* (April 1, 2002), 118–124; Chana R. Schoenberger, "The Internet of Things," *Forbes* (March 18, 2002), 155.

11. Eric Nee, "Meet Mister buy(everything).com," *Fortune* (May 29, 1999), 119–124.

12. Andrew Kupfer, "How American Industry Stacks Up," *Fortune* (March 9, 1992), 36–46.

13. Norihiko Shirouzu, Gregory L. White, and Joseph B. White, "Driving Lessons: Beyond Explorer Woes, Ford Misses Key Turns in Buyers, Technology," *The Wall Street Journal* (January 14, 2002), A1, A8; and "Tire Trouble: The Ford-Firestone Blowout," *Forbes* (June 20, 2001), *http://www.forbes.com*.

14. Allen C. Bluedorn, "Pilgrim's Progress: Trends and Convergence in Research on Organizational Size and Environment," *Journal of Management* 19 (1993), 163–191; Howard E. Aldrich, *Organizations and Environments* (Englewood Cliffs, N.J.: Prentice-Hall, 1979); Fred E. Emery and Eric L. Trist, "The Casual Texture of Organizational Environments," *Human Relations* 18 (1965), 21–32.

15. Christine S. Koberg and Gerardo R. Ungson, "The Effects of Environmental Uncertainty and Dependence on Organizational Structure and Performance: A Comparative Study," *Journal of Management* 13 (1987), 725–737; Frances J. Milliken, "Three Types of Perceived Uncertainty About the Environment: State, Effect, and Response Uncertainty," *Academy of Management Review* 12 (1987), 133–143.

16. Robert B. Duncan, "Characteristics of Organizational Environment and Perceived Environmental Uncertainty," *Administrative Science Quarterly* 17 (1972), 313–327; Gregory G. Dess and Donald W. Beard, "Dimensions of Organizational Task Environments," *Administrative Science Quarterly* 29 (1984), 52–73; Ray Jurkovich, "A Core Typology of Organizational Environments," *Administrative Science Quarterly* 19 (1974), 380–394.

17. Mike France with Joann Muller, "A Site for Soreheads," *BusinessWeek* (April 12, 1999), 86–90.

18. J. A. Litterer, *The Analysis of Organizations,* 2d ed. (New York: Wiley, 1973), 335.

19. Adam Throne, "Why He Who Dies with the Hottest Toy Wins," BrandEra.com, accessed at *http://www.brandera.com/features/01/03/14/trendset.html* on September 3, 2002; and Julian E. Barnes, "Toy Makers Hope to Keep *Harry Potter* Magic," *Houston Chronicle* (November 1, 2001), *http://www. HoustonChronicle.com*.

20. Rosalie L. Tung, "Dimensions of Organizational Environments: An Exploratory Study of Their Impact on Organizational Structure," *Academy of Management Journal* 22 (1979), 672–693.

21. Joseph E. McCann and John Selsky, "Hyperturbulence and the Emergence of Type 5 Environments," *Academy of Management Review* 9 (1984), 460–470.

22. Katherine McIntire Peters, "The War at Home," *Government Executive* (November 2001), 27–31.

23. James D. Thompson, *Organizations in Action* (New York: McGraw-Hill, 1967), 20–21.

24. Sally Solo, "Whirlpool: How to Listen to Consumers," *Fortune* (January 11, 1993), 77–79.

25. David B. Jemison, "The Importance of Boundary Spanning Roles in Strategic Decision-Making," *Journal of Management Studies* 21 (1984): 131–152; Mohamed Ibrahim Ahmad At-Twaijri and John R. Montanari, "The Impact of Context and Choice on the Boundary-Spanning Process: An Empirical Extension," *Human Relations* 40 (1987), 783–798.

26. Michelle Cook, "The Intelligentsia," *Business 2.0* (July 1999), 135–136.

27. Robert C. Schwab, Gerardo R. Ungson, and Warren B. Brown, "Redefining the Boundary-Spanning Environment Relationship," *Journal of Management* 11 (1985), 75–86.

Chapter 4   The External Environment

167

28. Pia Nordlinger, "Know Your Enemy," *Working Woman* (May 2001), 16.</cite></cite>

29.</cite> Ken Western, "Ethical Spying," *Business Ethics* (September/October 1995), 22–23; Stan Crock, Geoffrey Smith, Joseph Weber, Richard A. Melcher, and Linda Himelstein, "They Snoop to Conquer," *BusinessWeek* (October 28, 1996), 172–176; Kenneth A. Sawka, "Demystifying Business Intelligence," *Management Review* (October 1996), 47–51.

30. Crock et al., "They Snoop to Conquer."

31. Jory Des Jardins, "Spies Who Buy," *Working Woman* (May 1999), 76.

32. France with Muller, "A Site for Soreheads."

33. Neuborne with Kerwin, "Generation Y."

34. Jay W. Lorsch, "Introduction to the Structural Design of Organizations," in Gene W. Dalton, Paul R. Lawrence, and Jay W. Lorsch, eds., *Organizational Structure and Design* (Homewood, Ill.: Irwin and Dorsey, 1970), 5.

35. Paul R. Lawrence and Jay W. Lorsch, *Organization and Environment* (Homewood, Ill.: Irwin, 1969).

36. Lorsch, "Introduction to the Structural Design of Organizations," 7.

37. Jay W. Lorsch and Paul R. Lawrence, "Environmental Factors and Organizational Integration," in J. W. Lorsch and Paul R. Lawrence, eds., *Organizational Planning: Cases and Concepts* (Homewood, Ill.: Irwin and Dorsey, 1972), 45.

38. Tom Burns and G. M. Stalker, *The Management of Innovation* (London: Tavistock, 1961).

39. John A. Courtright, Gail T. Fairhurst, and L. Edna Rogers, "Interaction Patterns in Organic and Mechanistic Systems," *Academy of Management Journal* 32 (1989), 773–802.

40. Robert A. Guth, "Eroding Empires: Electronics Giants of Japan Undergo Wrenching Change," *The Wall Street Journal* (June 20, 2002), A1, A9.

41. Thomas C. Powell, "Organizational Alignment as Competitive Advantage," *Strategic Management Journal* 13 (1992), 119–134. Mansour Javidan, "The Impact of Environmental Uncertainty on Long-Range Planning Practices of the U.S. Savings and Loan Industry," *Strategic Management Journal* 5 (1984), 381–392; Tung, "Dimensions of Organizational Environments," 672–693; Thompson, *Organizations in Action.*

42. Ian Wylie, "There Is No Alternative To . . .," *Fast Company* (July 2002), 106–110.

43. David Ulrich and Jay B. Barney, "Perspectives in Organizations: Resource Dependence, Efficiency, and Population," *Academy of Management Review* 9 (1984), 471–481; Jeffrey Pfeffer and Gerald Salancik, *The External Control of Organizations: A Resource Dependent Perspective* (New York: Harper & Row, 1978).

44. Almar Latour, "Trial by Fire: A Blaze in Albuquerque Sets Off Major Crisis for Cell-Phone Giants," *The Wall Street Journal* (January 29, 2001), A1, A8.

45. Andrew H. Van de Ven and Gordon Walker, "The Dynamics of Interorganizational Coordination," *Administrative Science Quarterly* (1984), 598–621; Huseyin Leblebici and Gerald R. Salancik, "Stability in Interorganizational Exchanges: Rulemaking Processes of the Chicago Board of Trade," *Administrative Science Quarterly* 27 (1982): 227–242.

46. Kevin Kelly and Zachary Schiller with James B. Treece, "Cut Costs or Else: Companies Lay Down the Law to Suppliers," *BusinessWeek* (March 22, 1993), 28–29.

47. G. Pascal Zachary, "Many Journalists See a Growing Reluctance to Criticize Advertisers," *The Wall Street Journal* (February 6, 1992), A1, A9.

48. Richard Brandt, "Microsoft Is Like an Elephant Rolling Around, Squashing Ants," *BusinessWeek* (October 30, 1989), 148–152.

49. Judith A. Babcock, *Organizational Responses to Resource Scarcity and Munificence: Adaptation and Modification in Colleges within a University* (Ph.D. diss., Pennsylvania State University, 1981).

50. Peter Smith Ring and Andrew H. Van de Ven, "Developmental Processes of Corporative Interorganizational Relationships," *Academy of Management Review* 19 (1994), 90–118; Jeffrey Pfeffer, "Beyond Management and the Worker: The Institutional Function of Management," *Academy of Management Review* 1 (April 1976), 36–46; John P. Kotter, "Managing External Dependence," *Academy of Management Review* 4 (1979), 87–92.

51. Bryan Borys and David B. Jemison, "Hybrid Arrangements as Strategic Alliances: Theoretical Issues in Organizational Combinations," *Academy of Management Review* 14 (1989), 234–249.

52. Julie Cohen Mason, "Strategic Alliances: Partnering for Success," *Management Review* (May 1993), 10–15.

53. John F. Love, *McDonald's: Behind the Arches* (New York: Bantam Books, 1986).

54. Zachary Schiller and Wendy Zellner with Ron Stodghill II and Mark Maremont, "Clout! More and More, Retail Giants Rule the Marketplace," *BusinessWeek* (December 21, 1992), 66–73.

55. Borys and Jemison, "Hybrid Arrangements as Strategic Alliances."

56. Ian Katz and Elisabeth Malkin, "Battle for the Latin American Net," *BusinessWeek* (November 1, 1999), 194–200; "IBM Joint Venture to Put Laundry on Web," *The Wall Street Journal* (August 30, 2002), B4.

57. Donald Palmer, "Broken Ties: Interlocking Directorates and Intercorporate Coordination," *Administrative Science Quarterly* 28 (1983), 40–55; F. David Shoorman, Max H. Bazerman, and Robert S. Atkin, "Interlocking Directorates: A Strategy for Reducing Environmental Uncertainty," *Academy of Management Review* 6 (1981), 243–251; Ronald S. Burt, *Toward a Structural Theory of Action* (New York: Academic Press, 1982).

58. James R. Lang and Daniel E. Lockhart, "Increased Environmental Uncertainty and Changes in Board Linkage Patterns," *Academy of Management Journal* 33 (1990), 106–128; Mark S. Mizruchi and Linda Brewster Stearns, "A Longitudinal Study of the Formation of Interlocking Directorates," *Administrative Science Quarterly* 33 (1988), 194–210.

59. Kotter, "Managing External Dependence."

60. William C. Symonds, with Farah Nayeri, Geri Smith, and Ted Plafker, "Bombardier's Blitz," *BusinessWeek* (February 6, 1995), 62–66; Joseph Weber, with Wendy Zellner and Geri Smith, "Loud Noises at Bombardier," *BusinessWeek* (January 26, 1998), 94–95; and Anita Lienert, "Plowing Ahead in Uncertain Times," *Management Review* (December 1998), 16–21.

61. Daniel Pearl and Gabriella Stern, "How GM Managed to Wring Pickup Pact and Keep on Truckin'," *The Wall Street Journal* (December 5, 1994), A1.

62. Gardiner Harris and Chris Adams, "Delayed Reaction: Drug Manufacturers Step Up Legal Attacks That Slow Generics," *The Wall Street Journal* (July 12, 2001), A1, A10; Ron Winslow, "Study Finds Splitting Pills Usually Is Safe," *The Wall Street Journal* (August 30, 2002), B1, B4.

63. David B. Yoffie, "How an Industry Builds Political Advantage," *Harvard Business Review* (May–June 1988), 82–89; Jeffrey H. Birnbaum, "Chief Executives Head to Washington to Ply the Lobbyist's Trade," *The Wall Street Journal* (March 19, 1990), A1, A16.

64. David Whitford, "Built By Association," *Inc.* (July 1994), 71–75.

65. Anthony J. Daboub, Abdul M. A. Rasheed, Richard L. Priem, and David A. Gray, "Top Management Team Characteristics and Corporate Illegal Activity," *Academy of Management Review* 20, no. 1 (1995), 138–170.

66. Stewart Toy, "The Defense Scandal," *Business Week* (July 4, 1988), 28–30.

67. Barry M. Staw and Eugene Szwajkowski, "The Scarcity-Munificence Component of Organizational Environments and the Commission of Illegal Acts," *Administrative Science Quarterly* 20 (1975), 345–354.

68. Kimberly D. Elsbach and Robert I. Sutton, "Acquiring Organizational Legitimacy through Illegitimate Actions: A Marriage of Institutional and Impression Management Theories," *Academy of Management Journal* 35 (1992), 699–738.

Interorganizational Relationships

chapter
5

U.S. Army, Anniston, Alabama, Depot

The U.S. Army's depots employ about 9,500 civilians to perform in-house maintenance, repair, and upgrading of the service's fighting equipment. But at the Anniston, Alabama, depot, it is sometimes hard to tell who works for the depot and who works for General Dynamics or General Motors. Employees from the three companies are working side by side to jointly produce at least two-thirds of the Army's next-generation armored vehicles. The deal marks the first time the Army will be involved in building its own combat vehicles—and a whole new era in the previously distant, often adversarial, relationship between Army depots and defense contractors.

For years, the depots and contractors had well-defined roles in building and maintaining huge equipment such as tanks. Depot and contractor managers rarely talked to one another, never visited each other's facilities, and frequently competed for the same repair jobs. But a funny thing happened at the end of the Cold War: Managers at Anniston began to realize that, with Defense Department dollars dwindling, they needed a new strategy. "We could either build the fences higher and fight to keep what we had, or we could work with them," said Jesse Poor, deputy commander at Anniston. Partnership offered a way to cut costs and improve efficiency for both sides while still meeting strict combat readiness requirements.

Anniston has gone from no partnerships in the early 1990s to more than thirty alliances with companies such as General Dynamics Land Systems, United Defense, and Honeywell that have generated $240 million in revenue. The most recent deal to produce next-generation combat vehicles is the biggest and boldest. This time, General Dynamics came courting Anniston because of their positive working relationships over the past decade. Before the alliances, contractors were wary of the depots. "We were adversarial," said Richard Kaelin, General Dynamics' Anniston-based manager. "We spent time and money developing programs to compete with Anniston." Today, competition has turned to collaboration—and a new $7 billion partnership.[1]

Organizations of all sizes in all industries are rethinking how they do business in response to today's chaotic environment. One of the most widespread trends is to reduce boundaries and increase collaboration between companies—even competitors—as was done at the Anniston depot. High-tech companies such as Nokia and Cisco Systems depend on strategic partnerships with other organizations. Global semiconductor makers have been collaborating while competing for years because of the high costs and risks associated with creating and marketing a new generation of semiconductors.

International competition and rapid advances in technology, communications, and transportation have created amazing new opportunities for organizations, but they have also raised the cost of doing business and made it increasingly difficult for any company to take advantage of those opportunities on its own. In this new economy, webs of organizations are emerging. A large company like Wal-Mart develops a special relationship with a supplier such as Procter & Gamble that eliminates middlemen by sharing complete information and reducing the costs of salespersons and distributors. Several small companies may join together to produce and market noncompeting products. You can see the results of interorganizational collaboration when movies such as *Star Wars: Episode II—Attack of the Clones*, *Harry Potter and the Chamber of Secrets*, or *Spider-Man* are launched. Prior to seeing the movie, you might read a cover story in *People* or *Entertainment Weekly*, see a preview clip or chat live with the stars at an online site such as E online, find action toys being given away at a fast-food franchise, and notice retail stores loaded with movie-related merchandise. For a movie like *Spider-Man*, coordinated action among companies can yield millions in addition to box-office and DVD profits. In the new economy, organizations think of themselves as teams that create value jointly rather than as autonomous companies that are in competition with all others.

PURPOSE OF THIS CHAPTER

This chapter explores the most recent trend in organizing, which is the increasingly dense web of relationships among organizations. Companies have always been dependent on other organizations for supplies, materials, and information. The question is how these relationships are managed. At one time it was a matter of a large, powerful company like General Motors tightening the screws on small suppliers. Today a company can choose to develop positive, trusting relationships. Or a large company like General Motors might find it difficult to adapt to the environment and create a new organizational form, such as Saturn, to operate with a different structure and culture. The notion of horizontal relationships described in Chapter 3, and the understanding of environmental uncertainty in Chapter 4, are leading to the next stage of organizational evolution, which is horizontal relationships *across* organizations. Organizations can choose to build relationships in many ways, such as appointing preferred suppliers, establishing agreements, business partnering, joint ventures, or even mergers and acquisitions.

Interorganizational research has yielded perspectives such as resource dependence, networks, population ecology, and institutionalism. The sum total of these ideas can be daunting, because it means managers no longer can rest in the safety of managing a single organization. They have to figure out how to manage a whole set of interorganizational relationships, which is a great deal more challenging and complex.

ORGANIZATIONAL ECOSYSTEMS

Interorganizational relationships are the relatively enduring resource transactions, flows, and linkages that occur among two or more organizations.[2] Traditionally, these transactions and relationships have been seen as a necessary evil to obtain what an organization needs. The presumption has been that the world is composed of distinct businesses that thrive on autonomy and compete for supremacy. A company may be forced into interorganizational relationships depending on its needs and the stability of the environment.

A new view described by James Moore argues that organizations are now evolving into business ecosystems. An **organizational ecosystem** is a system formed by the interaction of a community of organizations and their environment. An ecosystem cuts across traditional industry lines. A company can create its own ecosystem. Microsoft travels in four major industries: consumer electronics, information, communications, and personal computers. Its ecosystem also includes hundreds of suppliers, including Hewlett-Packard and Intel, and millions of customers across many markets.[3] Traditional boundaries are dissolving. Circuit City uses its expertise gained from selling televisions and stereos to sell used cars. Shell Oil is the largest seller of packaged sausages in the Scandinavian countries. Wal-Mart created an ecosystem based on well-known brands and low prices in rural and small-town markets. Today, Wal-Mart cannot be categorized simply as a retailer. It is also a wholesaler, a logistics company, and an information services company. Wal-Mart, like other business ecosystems, develops relationships with hundreds of organizations cutting across traditional business boundaries.

IS COMPETITION DEAD?

No company can go it alone under a constant onslaught of international competitors, changing technology, and new regulations. Organizations around the world are embedded in complex networks of confusing relationships—collaborating in some markets, competing fiercely in others. Indeed, research indicates that a large percentage of new alliances in recent years have been between competitors. These alliances influence organizations' competitive behavior in varied ways.[4]

Traditional competition, which assumes a distinct company competing for survival and supremacy with other stand-alone businesses, no longer exists because each organization both supports and depends on the others for success, and perhaps for survival. However, most managers recognize that the competitive stakes are higher than ever in a world where market share can crumble overnight and no industry is immune from almost instant obsolescence.[5] In today's world, a new form of competition is in fact intensifying.[6]

For one thing, companies now need to coevolve with others in the ecosystem so that everyone gets stronger. Consider the wolf and the caribou. Wolves cull weaker caribou, which strengthens the herd. A strong herd means that wolves must become stronger themselves. With coevolution, the whole system becomes stronger. In the same way, companies coevolve through discussion with each other, shared visions, alliances, and managing complex relationships, as we saw with the partnership between the Anniston, Alabama depot, General Dynamics, and General Motors described in the opening case. Exhibit 5.1 illustrates the complexity of an ecosystem by showing the myriad overlapping relationships in which high-tech companies were involved in 1999. Since then, many of these companies have merged, been acquired, or gone out of business during the dot-com crash of 2000 and 2001. Ecosystems constantly change and evolve, with some relationships growing stronger while others weaken or are terminated. The changing pattern of relationships and interactions in an ecosystem contributes to the health and vitality of the system as an integrated whole.[7]

In an organizational ecosystem, conflict and cooperation frequently exist at the same time. Consider a recent fight between Disney and Time Warner (now AOL Time Warner). In early 2000, Time Warner Cable abruptly dropped Disney's ABC network in New York, Los Angeles, and several other large cities because of an ongoing dispute over fees for the Disney Channel. The two companies engaged in all-out war that included front-page headlines and calls for the Federal

EXHIBIT 5.1   *An Organizational Ecosystem*

The largest companies (those with more than 10,000 employees) are, not surprisingly, the hubs of the digital universe: they tend to have the most strategic partnerships (black lines) and investments (red lines).*

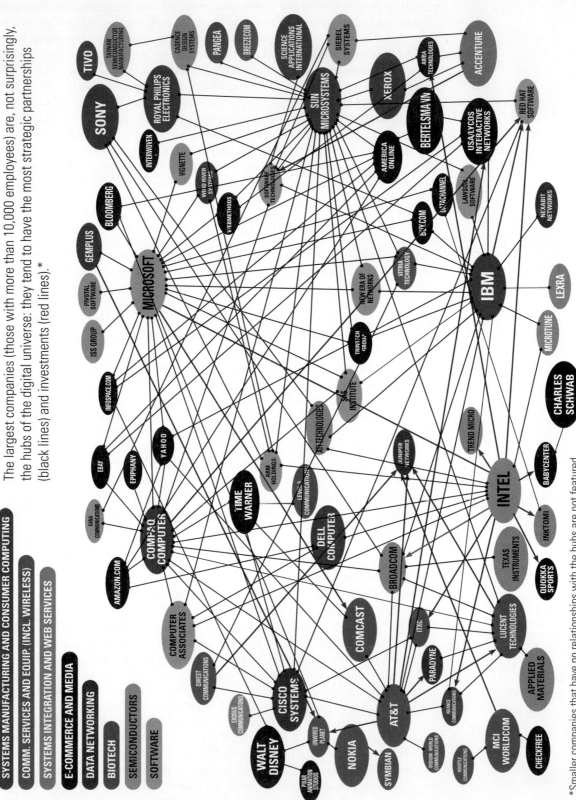

SYSTEMS MANUFACTURING AND CONSUMER COMPUTING

COMM. SERVICES AND EQUIP. (INCL. WIRELESS)

SYSTEMS INTEGRATION AND WEB SERVICES

E-COMMERCE AND MEDIA

DATA NETWORKING

BIOTECH

SEMICONDUCTORS

SOFTWARE

*Smaller companies that have no relationships with the hubs are not featured.

Communications Commission to step in.[8] The conflict, however, masked a simple fact: The two companies can't live without each other. Disney and Time Warner are wedded to one another in separate business deals around the world. They will never let competition in one area upset their larger interdependence on a global scale. Disney's ABC network, for example, is a major buyer of shows produced by Warner Brothers, while Time Warner's WB network carries Disney-produced programs. Mutual dependencies and partnerships have become a fact of life in business ecosystems. Companies today may use their strength to win conflicts and negotiations, but ultimately cooperation carries the day.

THE CHANGING ROLE OF MANAGEMENT

Within business ecosystems managers learn to move beyond traditional responsibilities of corporate strategy and designing hierarchical structures and control systems. If a top manager looks down to enforce order and uniformity, the company is missing opportunities for new and evolving external relationships.[9] In this new world, managers think about horizontal processes rather than vertical structures. Important initiatives are not just top down; they cut across the boundaries separating organizational units. Moreover, horizontal relationships, as described in Chapter 3, now include linkages with suppliers and customers, who become part of the team. Business leaders can learn to lead economic coevolution. Managers learn to see and appreciate the rich environment of opportunities that grow from cooperative relationships with other contributors to the ecosystem. Rather than trying to force suppliers into low prices or customers into high prices, managers strive to strengthen the larger system evolving around them, finding ways to understand this big picture and how to contribute.

This is a broader leadership role than ever before. For example, Donovan Neale-May, president of Neale-May & Partners, formed an international alliance of forty independent high-tech public relations agencies, called GlobalFluency, to share information and market their services to acquire business that small, owner-run agencies have trouble winning on their own. "We have companies— our own neighbors here in Colorado—that won't hire us because we don't have offices in sixty-five countries," says John Metzger, CEO of a Boulder firm. Now, with the power of GlobalFluency behind them, small firms such as Metzger's are winning accounts that once went only to large competitors. Alliance members still maintain their independence for small jobs but can join together to pitch for regional projects or international campaigns.[10]

INTERORGANIZATIONAL FRAMEWORK

Understanding this larger organizational ecosystem is one of the most exciting areas of organization theory. The models and perspectives for understanding interorganizational relationships ultimately help managers change their role from top-down management to horizontal management across organizations. A framework for analyzing the different views of interorganizational relationships is in Exhibit 5.2. Relationships among organizations can be characterized by whether the organizations are dissimilar or similar and whether relationships are competitive or cooperative. By understanding these perspectives, managers can assess their environment and adopt strategies to suit their needs. The first perspective is called resource dependence theory, which was briefly described in Chapter 4. It describes rational ways organizations deal with each other to reduce

EXHIBIT 5.2   *A Framework of Interorganizational Relationships**

Thanks to Anand Narasimhan for suggesting this framework.

dependence on the environment. The second perspective is about collaborative networks, wherein organizations allow themselves to become dependent on other organizations to increase value and productivity for both. The third perspective is population ecology, which examines how new organizations fill niches left open by established organizations, and how a rich variety of new organizational forms benefits society. The final approach is called institutionalism and explains why and how organizations legitimate themselves in the larger environment and design structures by borrowing ideas from each other. These four approaches to the study of interorganizational relationships will be described in the remainder of this chapter.

RESOURCE DEPENDENCE

Resource dependence represents the traditional view of relationships among organizations. As described in Chapter 4, **resource dependence** theory argues that organizations try to minimize their dependence on other organizations for the supply of important resources and try to influence the environment to make resources available.[11] Organizations succeed by striving for independence and autonomy. When threatened by greater dependence, organizations will assert control over external resources to minimize that dependence. Resource dependence theory argues that organizations do not want to become vulnerable to other organizations because of negative effects on performance.

The amount of dependence on a resource is based on two factors. First is the importance of the resource to the firm, and second is how much discretion or monopoly power those who control a resource have over its allocation and use.[12] For example, a Wisconsin manufacturer made scientific instruments with internal electronics. It acquired parts from a supplier that provided adequate quality at the lowest price. The supplier was not involved in the manufacturer's product design but was able to provide industry-standard capacitors at fifty cents each. As industry standards changed, other suppliers of the capacitor switched to other products, and in one year the cost of the capacitors increased to $2 each. The Wisconsin firm had no choice but to pay the higher price. Within eighteen months, the price of the capacitors increased to $10 each, and then the supplier discontinued production altogether. Without capacitors, production came to a halt for six months. The scientific instruments manufacturer allowed itself to become dependent on a single supplier and made no plans for redesign to use substitute capacitors or to develop new suppliers. A single supplier had sufficient power to increase prices beyond reason and to almost put the Wisconsin firm out of business.[13]

Organizations aware of resource dependence tend to develop strategies to reduce their dependence on the environment and learn how to use their power differences.

RESOURCE STRATEGIES

When organizations feel resource or supply constraints, the resource dependence perspective says they maneuver to maintain their autonomy through a variety of strategies, several of which were described in Chapter 4. One strategy is to adapt to or alter the interdependent relationships. This could mean purchasing ownership in suppliers, developing long-term contracts or joint ventures to lock in necessary resources, or building relationships in other ways. Some large contract manufacturers such as Flextronics International Ltd. are buying parts suppliers and stakes in distribution companies to be sure they have the resources they need to manufacture and ship products for such companies as Cisco, 3Com, and Ericsson Electronics.[14] Another technique is to use interlocking directorships, which means boards of directors include members of the boards of supplier companies. Organizations may also join trade associations to coordinate their needs, sign trade agreements, or merge with another firm to guarantee resource and material supplies. Some organizations may take political action, such as lobbying for new regulations or deregulation, favorable taxation, tariffs, or subsidies, or push for new standards that make resource acquisition easier. Organizations operating under the resource dependence philosophy will do whatever is needed to avoid excessive dependence on the environment to maintain control of resources and hence reduce uncertainty.

POWER STRATEGIES

In resource dependence theory, large, independent companies have power over small suppliers.[15] For example, power in consumer products has shifted from vendors such as Rubbermaid and Procter & Gamble to the big discount retail chains such as Wal-Mart and Target, which can demand—and receive—special pricing deals. As another example, large grocery distributors and wholesalers have power over suppliers because the suppliers have access to independent and smaller grocers only through the distributor. These companies routinely deduct small amounts from suppliers' bills, citing such reasons as incomplete or damaged orders, and the practice is accepted as the price of keeping the customer. But suppliers say the nation's largest grocery distributor, Fleming Co., has abused its power and pushed the practice to extremes, deducting larger and larger amounts and threatening to halt its purchases if suppliers complain.[16] Suppliers typically have no choice but to go along with these demands if they want to reach many stores, including those Kmarts that sell groceries.

Similarly, health maintenance organizations have growing power to dictate terms to pharmaceutical companies because they may account for 40 percent or more of a drugmaker's U.S. sales. Group Health Cooperative of Puget Sound ordered its doctors to stop prescribing all but an essential handful of drugs from Merck and Pfizer because the two drugmakers refused to discount their prices. The Seattle-based HMO instead began using equivalent drugs from rival suppliers who were willing to cut prices 10 to 20 percent. The loss in revenues prompted Merck's president to personally visit Group Health and begin offering discounts.[17] When one company has power over another, it can ask suppliers to absorb more costs, ship more efficiently, and provide more services than ever before, often without a price increase. Often the suppliers have no choice but to go along, and those who fail to do so may go out of business.

COLLABORATIVE NETWORKS

Traditionally, the relationship between organizations and their suppliers has been an adversarial one. Indeed, North American companies typically have worked alone, competing with each other and believing in the tradition of individualism and self-reliance. Today, however, thanks to an uncertain international environment, a realignment in corporate relationships is taking place. The **collaborative network** perspective is an emerging alternative to resource dependence theory. Companies join together to become more competitive and to share scarce resources. Thirty-four companies from a variety of industries have formed an alliance to develop an alternative to Microsoft's Web site authentication service.[18] Large pharmaceutical companies join with small biotechnology firms to share resources and knowledge and spur innovation. Consulting firms, investment companies, and accounting firms may join in an alliance to meet customer demands for expanded services.[19] As companies move into their own uncharted territory, they are also racing into alliances.

WHY COLLABORATION?

Why all this interest in interorganizational collaboration? Major reasons are sharing risks when entering new markets, mounting expensive new programs and reducing costs, and enhancing organizational profile in selected industries or technologies. Cooperation is a prerequisite for greater innovation, problem solving, and performance.[20] In addition, partnerships are a major avenue for entering global markets, with both large and small firms developing partnerships overseas and in North America.

North Americans have learned from their international experience just how effective interorganizational relationships can be. Both Japan and Korea have long traditions of corporate clans or industrial groups that collaborate and assist each other. North Americans typically have considered interdependence a bad thing, believing it would reduce competition. However, the experience of collaboration in other countries has shown that competition among companies can be fierce in some areas even as they collaborate in others. It is as if the brothers and sisters of a single family went into separate businesses and want to outdo one another, but they still love one another and will help each other when needed.

Interorganizational linkages provide a kind of safety net that encourages long-term investment and risk taking. Companies can achieve higher levels of

innovation and performance as they learn to shift from an adversarial to a partnership mindset.[21] In many cases companies are learning to work closely
together. Consider the following examples:

- IBM is reaching out everywhere, dropping the old do-it-from-scratch
  approach to team up with major software companies such as SAP, PeopleSoft,
  and Siebel Systems, as well as smaller software developers in country and
  regional markets. Rather than trying to develop its own software solutions,
  Big Blue has since 1999 formed 140 strategic alliances with other companies
  that can influence businesses to run their software on IBM equipment and
  call on IBM services.[22]

- The pharmaceuticals giant Pfizer collaborates with more than four hundred
  companies on research and development projects and co-marketing campaigns. For example, Pfizer has earned billions from co-promotion of
  Warner-Lambert's Lipitor, for treating elevated cholesterol, and Pharmacia's
  Celebrex, the leading prescription drug for arthritis pain.[23]

- With corporate research budgets under pressure and technologies increasingly
  complex, the hottest R&D trend is collaboration. Companies are figuring out
  how to fruitfully connect with outside experts in other companies, consor-
  tiums, universities, and government labs. GE Aircraft Engines teamed up with
  arch-rival Pratt & Whitney to share the $1 billion cost of designing a new jet
  engine. Texas Instruments and Hitachi joined their semiconductor businesses
  to share the best design and engineering abilities of both companies.[24]

- Small companies are banding together to compete against much larger
  firms. Forty local microbreweries formed the Oregon Brewers Guild to gain
  the resources needed to compete against craft brews from Miller and
  Anheuser-Busch.[25]

FROM ADVERSARIES TO PARTNERS

BRIEFCASE

As an organization manager, keep this guideline in mind:

Seek collaborative partnerships that enable mutual dependence and enhance value and gain for both sides. Get deeply involved in your partner's business, and vice versa, to benefit both.

Fresh flowers are blooming on the battle-scarred landscape where once-bitter
rivalries among suppliers, customers, and competitors took place. In North
America, collaboration among organizations initially occurred in not-for-profit
social service and mental health organizations where public interest was
involved. Community organizations collaborated to achieve greater effectiveness
and better utilize scarce resources.[26] With the push from international competitors and international examples, hard-nosed American business managers began
shifting to a new partnership paradigm on which to base their relationships.

A summary of this change in mindset is in Exhibit 5.3. More companies are
changing from a traditional adversarial mindset to a partnership orientation. More
and more evidence from studies of such companies as General Electric, Amoco,
and Whirlpool indicate that partnering allows reduced cost and increased value for
both parties in a predatory world economy.[27] The new model is based on trust and
the ability of partners to develop equitable solutions to conflicts that inevitably
arise. Managing strategic relationships with other firms has become a critical management skill, as discussed in this chapter's Book Mark. In the new orientation,
people try to add value to both sides and believe in high commitment rather than
suspicion and competition. Companies work toward equitable profits for both
sides rather than just for their own benefit. The new model is characterized by lots
of shared information, including electronic linkages for automatic ordering and
face-to-face discussions to provide corrective feedback and solve problems.
Sometimes people from other companies are on site to enable very close coordination. Partners are involved in each other's product design and production, and they

EXHIBIT 5.3   *Changing Characteristics of Interorganizational Relationships*

Traditional Orientation: Adversarial	New Orientation: Partnership
Suspicion, competition, arm's length	Trust, addition of value to both sides, high commitment
Price, efficiency, own profits	Equity, fair dealing, both profit
Limited information and feedback	Electronic linkages to share key information, problem feedback, and discussion
Legal resolution of conflict	Mechanisms for close coordination, people on site
Minimal involvement and up-front investment, separate resources	Involvement in partner's product design and production, shared resources
Short-term contracts	Long-term contracts
Contract limiting the relationship	Business assistance beyond the contract

Source: Based on Jeffrey H. Dyer, "How Chrysler Created an American *Keiretsu*," *Harvard Business Review* (July–August 1996), 42–56; Myron Magnet, "The New Golden Rule of Business," *Fortune*, (February 21, 1994), 60–64; and Peter Grittner, "Four Elements of Successful Sourcing Strategies," *Management Review* (October 1995), 41–45.

invest for the long term. It's not unusual for business partners to help each other outside whatever is specified in the contract.[28]

For example, AMP, a manufacturer of electronic and electrical connectors, was contacted by a customer about a broken connector that posed serious problems. It wasn't even AMP's connector, but the vice president and his sales manager went to a warehouse on a weekend and found replacement parts to get the customer back on line. They provided the service with no charge as a way to enhance the relationship. Indeed, this kind of teamwork treats partner companies almost like departments of one's own organization.[29]

Companies like DaimlerChrysler intimately involve suppliers in the product development stage for new vehicles. Microsoft hired contract manufacturer Flextronics to not only build but also help design the electronic game console, Xbox.[30] Outsourcing partnerships have ballooned in recent years. Amtrak decided to outsource its e-business operations after the September 11, 2001, terrorist attacks in the United States drove hundreds of would-be travelers to Amtrak and its Web site. The site and call centers were overwhelmed, causing the company to turn customers away. Akamai Technologies, a Cambridge, Massachusetts-based company, stepped in and offered to allow Amtrak to reroute Web traffic through its servers for free for one month following the attacks. The arrangement eventually turned into a partnership with Akamai to manage e-business operations. "They literally saved our site," says Amtrak's Mary Cortina.[31]

In this new view of partnerships, dependence on another company is seen to reduce rather than increase risks. Greater value can be achieved by both parties. By being embedded in a system of interorganizational relationships, everyone does better by helping each other. This is a far cry from the belief that organizations do best by being autonomous and independent. Sales representatives may have a desk on the customer's factory floor, and they have access to information systems and the research lab.[32] Coordination is so intimate that it's sometimes hard to tell one organization from another. Consider how Canada's Bombardier and its suppliers are linked together almost like one organization in building the new Continental, a "super-midsize" business jet that can comfortably fly eight passengers nonstop from coast to coast.

BOOK MARK 5·0   *Have You Read This Book?*

Managing Strategic Relationships: The Key to Business Success
By Leonard Greenhalgh

What determines organizational success in the twenty-first century? According to Leonard Greenhalgh, author of *Managing Strategic Relationships: The Key to Business Success*, it's how successfully they support, foster and protect collaborative relationships, both inside and outside the firm. In separate chapters, the book offers strategies for managing relationships between people and groups within the company and with other organizations. Effectively managing relationships generates a sense of commonwealth and consensus, which ultimately results in competitive advantage.

MANAGING RELATIONSHIPS IN A NEW ERA

Greenhalgh says managers need a new way of thinking to fit the realities of the new era. Here are a few guidelines:

- *Recognize that detailed legal contracts can undermine trust and goodwill.* Greenhalgh stresses the need to build relationships that are based on honesty, trust, understanding, and common goals instead of on narrowly defined legal contracts that concentrate on what one business can give to the other.
- *Treat partners like members of your own organization.* Members of partner organizations need to be active participants in the learning experience by becoming involved in training, team meetings, and other activities. Giving a partner organization's employees a chance to make genuine contributions promotes deeper bonds and a sense of commonwealth.
- *Top managers must be champions for the alliance.* Managers from both organizations have to act in ways that signal to everyone inside and outside the organization a new emphasis on partnership and collaboration. Using ceremony and symbols can help instill a commitment to partnership in the company culture.

CONCLUSION

To succeed in today's environment, old-paradigm management practices based on power, hierarchy, and adversarial relationships must be traded for new-era commonwealth practices that emphasize collaboration and communal forms of organization. The companies that will thrive, Greenhalgh believes, "are those that really have their act together—those that can successfully integrate strategy, processes, business arrangements, resources, systems, and empowered workforces." That can be accomplished, he argues, only by effectively creating, shaping, and sustaining strategic relationships.

Managing Strategic Relationships: The Key to Business Success, by Leonard Greenhalgh, is published by The Free Press.

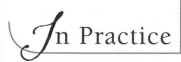

BOMBARDIER

In an assembly plant on the edge of Mid-Continent Airport in Wichita, a new plane is taking shape as great chunks of it are rolled in and joined together. Not counting rivets, it takes just a dozen big parts—all manufactured elsewhere—to put Bombardier's new Continental together. Those big subassemblies come from all over the world—the engines from Phoenix in the United States, the nose and cockpit from Montreal, Canada, the mid-fuselage from Belfast, Northern Ireland, the tail from Taichung, Taiwan, the wings from Nagoya, Japan, and other parts from Australia, France, Germany, and Austria. When production is up to full speed, it will take just four days to put a plane together and get it in the air.

In the past, most executive-jet companies have made major parts in-house. Canada's Bombardier, instead, relies heavily on suppliers for design support and the sharing of development costs and market risks. The company is intertwined with about thirty suppliers, a dozen or so of which have been involved since the design stage. At one point, about 250 team members from Bombardier and 250 from outsider suppliers worked together in

Montreal to make sure the design was going to be good for everyone involved. Bombardier has so far invested about $250 million in the Continental, but suppliers have probably equaled that amount in development costs. In addition to sharing costs, the supplier companies also share the risks. "They haven't got a contract that says, 'You're going to sell us twenty-five wings a year for the next ten years.' If the market's there, it's there, and if it's not, it's not," says John Holding, who is in charge of Bombardier's engineering and product development.

Integrating partners so that everyone benefits from and depends on the others—and managing this multinational, multicompany endeavor—is no easy task, but with development costs for a new plane reaching more than $1 billion, the partnership approach just makes sense.[33]

By breaking down boundaries and becoming involved in partnerships with an attitude of fair dealing and adding value to both sides, today's organization's are changing the concept of what makes an organization. The type of collaborative network illustrated by Bombardier is also being used by a growing number of automotive companies, including Volkswagen and General Motors. These companies are pushing the idea of partnership further than ever before, moving somewhat toward a modular approach to organization design, as described in Chapter 3.

POPULATION ECOLOGY

This section introduces a different perspective on relationships among organizations. The **population ecology** perspective differs from the other perspectives because it focuses on organizational diversity and adaptation within a population of organizations.[34] A **population** is a set of organizations engaged in similar activities with similar patterns of resource utilization and outcomes. Organizations within a population compete for similar resources or similar customers, such as financial institutions in the Seattle area.

Within a population, the question asked by ecology researchers is about the large number and variation of organizations in society. Why are new organizational forms constantly appearing that create such diversity? Their answer is that individual organizational adaptation is severely limited compared to the changes demanded by the environment. Innovation and change in a population of organizations take place through the birth of new forms and kinds of organizations more so than by the reform and change of existing organizations. Indeed, organizational forms are considered relatively stable, and the good of a whole society is served by the development of new forms of organization through entrepreneurial initiatives. New organizations meet the new needs of society more so than established organizations that are slow to change.[35]

What does this theory mean in practical terms? It means that large established organizations often become dinosaurs. Established booksellers, for example, have had tremendous difficulty adapting to a rapidly changing environment. Hence, new organizational forms that fit the current environment will emerge, such as Amazon.com, that fill a new niche and over time take away business from established companies.

Why do established organizations have such a hard time adapting to a rapidly changing environment? Michael Hannan and John Freeman, originators of the population ecology model of organization, argue that there are many limitations on the ability of organizations to change. The limitations come from heavy investment in plant, equipment, and specialized personnel, limited information, established viewpoints of decision makers, the organization's own successful history that justifies current procedures, and the difficulty of changing corporate culture. True transformation is a rare and unlikely event in the face of all these barriers.[36]

At this very moment, new organizational forms are emerging. Consider Asset Recovery Center, which buys leftover routers, servers, and other networking equipment from dead or bankrupt corporations for pennies on the dollar and then resells it at a profit. There are thousands of such operations in business today because of the tremendous opportunities—organizations are cutting capital spending, while at the same time widespread corporate troubles have created a glut of nearly new equipment for sale. Large equipment makers such as Cisco, Nortel Networks, and Sun Microsystems are feeling the pinch as they lose million-dollar deals to used equipment brokers.[37] Another recent change is the development of corporate universities within large companies like Motorola and FedEx. There are more than two thousand corporate universities, compared to just two hundred a few years ago. One reason they've developed so fast is that companies can't get desired services from established universities, which are too stuck in traditional ways of thinking and teaching.[38]

According to the population ecology view, when looking at an organizational population as a whole, the changing environment determines which organizations survive or fail. The assumption is that individual organizations suffer from structural inertia and find it difficult to adapt to environmental changes. Thus, when rapid change occurs, old organizations are likely to decline or fail, and new organizations emerge that are better suited to the needs of the environment.

The population ecology model is developed from theories of natural selection in biology, and the terms *evolution* and *selection* are used to refer to the underlying behavioral processes. Theories of biological evolution try to explain why certain life forms appear and survive whereas others perish. Some theories suggest the forms that survive are typically best fitted to the immediate environment.

A few years ago, *Forbes* magazine reported a study of American businesses over seventy years, from 1917 to 1987. Do you recall Baldwin Locomotive, Studebaker, or Lehigh Coal & Navigation? These companies were among 78 percent of the top one hundred in 1917 that did not see 1987. Of the twenty-two that remained in the top one hundred, only eleven did so under their original names. The environment of the 1940s and 1950s was suitable to Woolworth, but new organizational forms like Wal-Mart and Kmart became dominant in the 1980s. In 1917, most of the top one hundred companies were huge steel and mining industrial organizations, which were replaced by high-technology companies such as IBM and Merck.[39] Two companies that seemed to prosper over a long period were Ford and General Motors, but they are now being threatened by world changes in the automobile industry. No company is immune to the processes of social change. From just 1979 to 1989, 187 of the companies on the *Fortune* 500 list ceased to exist as independent companies. Some were acquired, some merged, and some were liquidated.[40] Meanwhile, technology was changing the environment again. AT&T, once the dominant long-distance carrier and the biggest, healthiest, and wealthiest company in the United States, has steadily declined in importance, while cellular technology has made Verizon Communications almost a household name.

BRIEFCASE

As an organization manager, keep this guideline in mind:

Adapt your organization to new variations being selected and retained in the external environment. If you are starting a new organization, find a niche that contains a strong environmental need for your product or service, and be prepared for a competitive struggle over scarce resources.

The expansion of the Internet into the everyday consumer's household brought a proliferation of new companies such as Expedia.com, America Online (now part of AOL Time Warner), and the still-growing eBay.

ORGANIZATIONAL FORM AND NICHE

The population ecology model is concerned with organizational forms. **Organizational form** is an organization's specific technology, structure, products, goals, and personnel, which can be selected or rejected by the environment. Each new organization tries to find a **niche** (a domain of unique environmental resources and needs) sufficient to support it. The niche is usually small in the early stages of an organization but may increase in size over time if the organization is successful. If a niche is not available, the organization will decline and may perish.

From the viewpoint of a single firm, luck, chance, and randomness play important parts in survival. New products and ideas are continually being proposed by both entrepreneurs and large organizations. Whether these ideas and organizational forms survive or fail is often a matter of chance—whether external circumstances happen to support them. A woman who started a small electrical contracting business in a rapidly growing Florida community would have an excellent chance of success. If the same woman were to start the same business in a declining community elsewhere in the United States, the chance of success would be far less. Success or failure of a single firm thus is predicted by the characteristics of the environment as much as by the skills or strategies used by the organization.

PROCESS OF ECOLOGICAL CHANGE

The population ecology model assumes that new organizations are always appearing in the population. Thus, organization populations are continually undergoing change. The process of change in the population is defined by three principles that occur in stages: **variation**, **selection**, and **retention**. These stages are summarized in Exhibit 5.4.

- *Variation.* New organizational forms continually appear in a population of organizations. They are initiated by entrepreneurs, established with venture capital by large corporations, or set up by a government seeking to provide new services. Some forms may be conceived to cope with a perceived need in the external environment. In recent years, a large number of new firms have been initiated to develop computer software, to provide consulting and other services to large corporations, and to develop products and technologies for Internet commerce. Other new organizations produce a traditional

EXHIBIT 5.4   *Elements in the Population Ecology Model of Organizations*

Variation	Selection	Retention
Large number of variations appear in the population of organizations	Some organizations find a niche and survive	A few organizations grow large and become institutionalized in the environment

product such as steel, but do it using minimal technology and new management techniques that make the new companies, such as the steel company Nucor, far more able to survive. Organizational variations are analogous to mutations in biology, and they add to the scope and complexity of organizational forms in the environment. This chapter's Leading by Design box describes a new organizational form conceived by a British entrepreneur to capitalize on advances in information technology and wireless text messaging.

- *Selection.* Some variations will suit the external environment better than others. Some prove beneficial and thus are able to find a niche and acquire the resources from the environment necessary to survive. Other variations fail to meet the needs of the environment and perish. When there is insufficient demand for a firm's product and when insufficient resources are available to the organization, that organization will be "selected out." Only a few variations are "selected in" by the environment and survive over the long term. For example, Shazam, described in the Leading by Design box, was launched only in mid-2002. If demand for the new service is low, or if the company cannot obtain needed resources, the company will be selected out and cease to exist.

LEADING BY DESIGN   *Shazam——It's Magic!*

Many people have had the experience of hearing a song they like on the radio and waiting in vain for the DJ to identify it, or finding themselves hopelessly addicted to a tune they hear in an advertisement, with no way to learn the title and artist. Shazam, a new mobile phone service launched in the United Kingdom in August 2002, has come to the rescue. The next time a cell phone user hears that mystery tune, all he or she has to do is dial a four-digit number on the cell phone, let the music play into the machine, and moments later receive a text message with the artist and title of the song. The user can then forward a thirty-second clip of the track to friends, along with a text message. With today's technological advances, it's an almost blindingly obvious idea, but it remains to be seen if Shazam can build a business out of it.

Shazam's magic happens through the use of a pattern-recognition software algorithm developed by the company's chief scientist. The algorithm picks out the salient characteristics of a tune and matches them against a massive music database. The company, founded by entrepreneur Chris Barton, calls the process "tagging," and users can log onto the company's Web site to see a list of all the songs they've tagged, buy CDs, or be directed to the nearest music store with the product available. Shazam's success will depend on developing collaborative partnerships with mobile phone companies, major record labels, music stores, and others. The mobile phone companies will have to agree to offer tagging as a premium service to

their customers and pay Shazam a cut of the profits. Since tagging promises to drive up call times, mobile phone companies are likely to be interested. And the record labels' interests will be served by getting new music in front of consumers. Word-of-mouth recommendations are a powerful means of driving music sales, so the idea of people all over Britain forwarding thirty-second clips of their new songs has music companies paying attention. Since Shazam wants to sell CDs over its Web site rather than letting customers download the music for free, it is unlikely to provoke the kind of resistance some other Web-based music services have encountered.

Shazam is one of the brightest new ideas in the world of technology. However, managers still have a lot of work to do negotiating the complicated partnerships and music rights, making sure everyone has an equal share in the benefits. Negotiations are being kept under close wraps, but right now, Shazam seems willing to take a small cut just to stay in business and build the alliances it will need to grow and expand its service globally. Time will tell if Barton and his colleagues have found a new niche that will build a lasting organization.

Sources: Michael Parsons, "I Got Music, I Got Algorithm," *Red Herring* (May 2002), 54–57; Owen Gibson, "Name That Tune," *Media Guardian* (July 8, 2002), downloaded at *http://www.shazamentertainment.com/press_they_mg2. shtml* on September 9, 2002; and "Mobiles Guess that Song," *BBC News* (August 19, 2002), downloaded at *http://news.bbc.co.uk/1/hi/entertainment/ music/2202830.stm* on September 9, 2002.

- *Retention*. Retention is the preservation and institutionalization of selected organizational forms. Certain technologies, products, and services are highly valued by the environment. The retained organizational form may become a dominant part of the environment. Many forms of organization have been institutionalized, such as government, schools, churches, and automobile manufacturers. McDonald's, which owns 43 percent of the fast-food market and provides the first job for many teenagers, has become institutionalized in American life.

Institutionalized organizations like McDonald's seem to be relatively permanent features in the population of organizations, but they are not permanent in the long run. The environment is always changing, and, if the dominant organizational forms do not adapt to external change, they will gradually diminish and be replaced by other organizations. McDonald's is struggling because chains such as Burger King and Wendy's continue to offer fresher, hotter, higher-quality food at lower prices with faster service. In an annual consumer satisfaction survey, McDonald's has scored dead last among fast-food restaurants every year since 1992.[41] In the fourth quarter of 2002, McDonald's posted its first-ever quarterly loss, in part because of its decision to close 719 poorly performing restaurants.[42] Unless it adapts, McDonald's might no longer be competitive in the fast-food market.

From the population ecology perspective, the environment is the important determinant of organizational success or failure. The organization must meet an environmental need, or it will be selected out. The process of variation, selection, and retention leads to the establishment of new organizational forms in a population of organizations.

STRATEGIES FOR SURVIVAL

Another principle that underlies the population ecology model is the **struggle for existence**, or competition. Organizations and populations of organizations are engaged in a competitive struggle over resources, and each organizational form is fighting to survive. The struggle is most intense among new organizations, and both the birth and survival frequencies of new organizations are related to factors in the larger environment. Factors such as size of urban area, percentage of immigrants, political turbulence, industry growth rate, and environmental variability have influenced the launching and survival of newspapers, telecommunication firms, railroads, government agencies, labor unions, and even voluntary organizations.[43]

In the population ecology perspective, **generalist** and **specialist** strategies distinguish organizational forms in the struggle for survival. Organizations with a wide niche or domain, that is, those that offer a broad range of products or services or that serve a broad market, are generalists. Organizations that provide a narrower range of goods or services or that serve a narrower market are specialists.

In the natural environment, a specialist form of flora and fauna would evolve in protective isolation in a place like Hawaii, where the nearest body of land is two thousand miles away. The flora and fauna are heavily protected. In contrast, a place like Costa Rica, which experienced wave after wave of external influences, developed a generalist set of flora and fauna that has better resilience and flexibility for adapting to a broad range of circumstances. In the business world, Amazon.com started with a specialist strategy, selling books over the Internet, but evolved to a generalist strategy with the addition of music, video, greeting cards, and other products, plus links to sites selling drugstore goods, pet supplies, and flowers. A company such as Olmec Corporation, which sells African-American and Hispanic dolls, would be considered a specialist, whereas Mattel is a generalist, marketing a broad range of toys for boys and girls of all ages.[44]

Specialists are generally more competitive than generalists in the narrow area in which their domains overlap. However, the breadth of the generalist's domain serves to protect it somewhat from environmental changes. Though demand may decrease for some of the generalist's products or services, it usually increases for others at the same time. In addition, because of the diversity of products, services, and customers, generalists are able to reallocate resources internally to adapt to a changing environment, whereas specialists are not. However, because specialists are often smaller companies, they can sometimes move faster and be more flexible in adapting to a changing environment.[45]

Managerial impact on company success often comes from selecting a strategy that steers a company into an open niche. One organization that has been selected and retained by the environment is Starbucks Coffee, where managers turned coffee drinking into a cultural phenomenon.

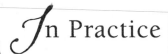

In Practice

STARBUCKS COFFEE

Chatting with friends over a cup of coffee has always been a favorite social pastime for Americans, from colleagues sharing a coffee break to retirees sitting around a table at the local diner. But until Howard Schultz came along, no one saw coffee as more than a commodity product. Schultz believed he could exploit the idea of combining coffee and community by offering a chic café atmosphere, a variety of gourmet coffees, and well-trained employees who served customers not just a cup of coffee but a cultural experience.

It was a whole new approach to selling coffee, and it caught on fast. Beginning with nine Starbucks stores in Seattle in 1987, Schultz parlayed the concept into a worldwide phenomenon. Today, Starbucks boasts more than 5,000 outlets around the world. Starbucks recruits most of its "baristas," who prepare coffee drinks, from colleges and community groups and provides them with extensive training in coffeemaking and lore. Employees' knowledge and their ability to interact with customers are key to the company's hip image and quality service that keeps people coming back for more. Starbucks stores are also arranged for comfort. A lone customer wanting to escape the hustle and bustle of the outside world for a half hour can find a quiet spot. A group wanting to chat for a while might settle in one of the cushy seating areas or at an outdoor table. Two colleagues working on a business project can take a regular table and spread out their notes. No one is ever rushed at Starbucks. The company wants people to linger, even if they don't buy anything. Friends sometimes use Starbucks as a central meeting place, where they join up to travel together to a soccer game or even move on to another restaurant—they might not buy anything at all, but it's almost certain they will at another time. "Our most successful stores turn out to be the ones with the most loitering," says Darren Huston, senior vice president for new initiatives. "We think it's great if people want to stay awhile. It creates a sense of community."[46]

Howard Schultz spotted an open niche and created a whole new type of organization, the gourmet coffeehouse. He used a specialist strategy to offer a new approach to selling coffee, and it worked. After less than twenty years, Starbucks has become almost as recognizable a brand name as Coca-Cola.

Institutionalism

The institutional perspective provides yet another view of interorganizational relationships.[47] Organizations are highly interconnected. Just as companies need efficient production to survive, the institutional view argues that organizations need legitimacy from their stakeholders. Companies perform well when they are perceived by the larger environment to have a legitimate right to exist. Thus, the **institutional perspective** describes how organizations survive and succeed through congruence between an organization and the expectations from its environment. The **institutional environment** is composed of norms and values from stakeholders (customers, investors, associations, boards, government, collaborating organizations). Thus the institutional view believes that organizations adopt structures and processes to please outsiders, and these activities come to take on rule-like status in organizations. The institutional environment reflects what the greater society views as correct ways of organizing and behaving.[48]

Legitimacy is defined as the general perspective that an organization's actions are desirable, proper, and appropriate within the environment's system of norms, values, and beliefs.[49] Institutional theory thus is concerned with the set of intangible norms and values that shape behavior, as opposed to the tangible elements of technology and structure. Organizations must fit within the cognitive and emotional expectations of their audience. For example, people will not deposit money in a bank unless it sends signals of compliance with norms of wise financial management. Consider also your local government and whether it could raise property taxes for increased school funding if community residents did not approve of the school district's policies and activities. Big accounting firms such as Deloitte Touche Tohmatsu and PricewaterhouseCoopers are searching for new ways to bolster their legitimacy in the wake of the Arthur Andersen accounting scandal. When news came out that employees at Arthur Andersen's Houston office had shredded tons of documents related to the Enron investigation, the public outrage and corporate fear spread to the entire accounting industry.[50] In the turbulent airline industry, new low-cost carriers are emerging to compete with established airlines, consistent with the population ecology view described earlier. Now, the new carriers, such as JetBlue, are concerned with signaling that they provide safety and comfort as well as an economical price.

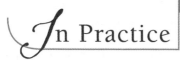

JetBlue

The environment had begun changing for airlines even before the September 11, 2001, terrorist attacks. However, that day was a serious blow to large, established carriers that have had a hard time adapting to changing conditions. Domestic passenger traffic has been declining for the major carriers, while it has increased for smaller, low-fare rivals such as JetBlue, a New York–based airline that in May of 2002 saw its passenger traffic increase by more than 100 percent.

JetBlue has succeeded by offering low-cost, high-touch service for today's harried travelers. However, with customer concerns over safety, managers knew they had to go above and beyond the call of duty to gain legitimacy in the minds of the public. Some of the company's previous selling points, such as all-leather seats and real-time television beamed to screens on the backs of seats, seemed frivolous in the aftermath of September 11. Within hours of the attacks, founder and CEO David Neeleman was on the phone to aircraft supplier Airbus asking for prototype doors that would secure pilots from intruders. Long before the FAA issued a mandate, JetBlue set out on a mission to become the first national carrier to install bulletproof, dead-bolted cockpit doors on all its aircraft. Because the company is small and nimble, it was able to do a fleetwide upgrade in weeks rather than the months it took larger carriers.

"We do it first because we think it's the right thing to do," Neeleman says. "But then, for that, you're perceived as a company that can move quickly and that understands what needs to be done."[51]

Managers at JetBlue know that how the company is perceived by customers and the public plays a big role in establishing legitimacy and laying a foundation for long-term success. Other organizations are concerned with legitimacy as well, as reflected in the annual *Fortune* magazine survey that ranks corporations based on their reputation.[52]

The notion of legitimacy answers an important question for institutional theorists. Why is there so much homogeneity in the forms and practices of established organizations? For example, visit banks, high schools, hospitals, government departments, or business firms in a similar industry, in any part of the country, and they will look strikingly similar. When an organizational field is just getting started, such as in e-commerce, then diversity is the norm. New organizations fill emerging niches. However, once an industry becomes established, there is an invisible push toward similarity. *Isomorphism* is the term used to describe this move toward similarity.

THE INSTITUTIONAL VIEW AND ORGANIZATION DESIGN

The institutional view also sees organizations as having two essential dimensions—technical and institutional. The technical dimension is the day-to-day work technology and operating requirements. The institutional structure is that part of the organization most visible to the outside public. Moreover, the technical dimension is governed by norms of rationality and efficiency, but the institutional dimension is governed by expectations from the external environment. As a result of pressure to do things in a proper and correct way, the formal structures of many organizations reflect the expectations and values of the environment rather than the demand of work activities. This means that an organization may incorporate positions or activities (equal employment officer, e-commerce division) perceived as important by the larger society and thus increase its legitimacy and survival prospects, even though these elements may decrease efficiency. For example, many small companies set up Web sites, even though the benefits gained from the site are sometimes outweighed by the costs of maintaining it. Having a dot-com division is perceived as essential by the larger society today. The formal structure and design of an organization may not be rational with respect to workflow and products or services, but it will ensure survival in the larger environment.

Organizations adapt to the environment by signaling their congruence with the demands and expectations stemming from cultural norms, standards set by professional bodies, funding agencies, and customers. Structure is something of a facade disconnected from technical work through which the organization obtains approval, legitimacy, and continuing support. The adoption of structures thus might not be linked to actual production needs, and might occur regardless of whether specific internal problems are solved. Formal structure is separated from technical action in this view.[53]

INSTITUTIONAL SIMILARITY

Organizations have a strong need to appear legitimate. In so doing, many aspects of structure and behavior may be targeted toward environmental acceptance rather than toward internal technical efficiency. Interorganizational relationships thus are characterized by forces that cause organizations in a similar population to look like one another. **Institutional similarity**, called *institutional isomorphism* in the academic literature, is the emergence of a common structure and approach among organizations in the same field. Isomorphism is the process that causes one unit in a population to resemble other units that face the same set of environmental conditions.[54]

Exactly how does increasing similarity occur? How are these forces realized? A summary of three mechanisms for institutional adaptation appears in Exhibit 5.5. These three core mechanisms are mimetic forces, which result from responses to uncertainty, coercive forces, which stem from political influence, and normative forces, which result from common training and professionalism.[55]

Mimetic Forces. Most organizations, especially business organizations, face great uncertainty. It is not clear to senior executives exactly what products, services, or technologies will achieve desired goals, and sometimes the goals themselves are not clear. In the face of this uncertainty, **mimetic forces**, the pressure to copy or model other organizations, occur.

Executives see an innovation in a firm generally regarded as successful, so the management practice is quickly copied. This modeling is done without any clear proof that performance will be improved. Mimetic processes explain why fads and fashions occur in the business world. Once a new idea starts, many organizations grab onto it, only to learn that the application is difficult and may cause more problems than it solves. This was the case with the recent merger wave that swept many industries. The past two decades have seen the largest merger and acquisition wave in history, but evidence shows that many of these mergers did not produce the expected financial gains and other benefits. The sheer momentum of the trend was so powerful that many companies chose to merge not because of potential increases in efficiency or profitability but simply

EXHIBIT 5.5   *Three Mechanisms for Institutional Adaptation*

	Mimetic	Coercive	Normative
Reason to become similar:	Uncertainty	Dependence	Duty, obligation
Events:	Innovation visibility	Political law, rules, sanctions	Professionalism—certification, accreditation
Social basis:	Culturally supported	Legal	Moral
Example:	Reengineering, benchmarking	Pollution controls, school regulations	Accounting standards, consultant training

Source: Adapted from W. Richard Scott, *Institutions and Organizations* (Thousand Oaks, Calif.: Sage, 1995).

because it seemed like the right thing to do.[56] Downsizing of the workforce is another trend that can be attributed partly to mimetic forces. Despite some evidence that massive downsizing actually hurts organizations, managers perceive it as a legitimate and effective means of improving performance.[57] Techniques such as outsourcing, reengineering, Six Sigma quality programs, and the balanced scorecard have all been adopted without clear evidence for efficiency or effectiveness. The one certain benefit is that management's feelings of uncertainty will be reduced, and the company's image will be enhanced because the firm is seen as using the latest management techniques. A recent study of one hundred organizations confirmed that those companies associated with using popular management techniques were more admired and rated higher in quality of management, even though these organizations did not reflect higher economic performance.[58]

Perhaps the clearest example of official copying is the technique of benchmarking that occurs as part of the total quality movement. Benchmarking means identifying who's best at something in an industry and then duplicating the technique for creating excellence, perhaps even improving it in the process.

The mimetic process works because organizations face continuous high uncertainty, they are aware of innovations occurring in the environment, and the innovations are culturally supported, thereby giving legitimacy to adopters. This is a strong mechanism by which a group of banks, or high schools, or manufacturing firms begin to look and act like one another.

Coercive Forces. All organizations are subject to pressure, both formal and informal, from government, regulatory agencies, and other important organizations in the environment, especially those on which a company is dependent. **Coercive forces** are the external pressures exerted on organizations to adopt structures, techniques, or behaviors similar to other organizations. As with other changes, those brought about because of coercive forces may not make the organization more effective, but it will look more effective and will be accepted as legitimate in the environment. Some pressures may have the force of law, such as government mandates to adopt new pollution control equipment. Health and safety regulations may demand that a safety officer be appointed. New regulations and government oversight boards have been set up for the accounting industry following widespread accounting scandals.[59]

Coercive pressures may also occur between organizations where there is a power difference, as described in the resource dependence section earlier in this chapter. It is not unusual for a large retailer like Wal-Mart or a manufacturer like General Motors to insist on certain policies, procedures, and techniques used by its suppliers. When Honda picked Donnelly Corporation to make all the mirrors for its U.S.-manufactured cars, Honda insisted that Donnelly empower its workers. Unless an organization knows how to foster collaborative relationships internally, Honda believes the company won't be good at making a partnership work between the two companies.

Organizational changes that result from coercive forces occur when an organization is dependent on another, when there are political factors such as rules, laws, and sanctions involved, or when some other contractual or legal basis defines the relationship. Organizations operating under those constraints will adopt changes and relate to one another in a way that increases homogeneity and limits diversity.

Normative Forces. The third reason organizations change according to the institutional view is normative. **Normative forces** are pressures to change to achieve standards of professionalism, and to adopt techniques that are considered by the professional community to be up to date and effective. Changes may be in any area, such as information technology, accounting requirements, or marketing techniques. Professionals share a body of formal education based on university degrees and professional networks through which ideas are exchanged by consultants and professional leaders. Universities, consulting firms, and professional training institutions develop norms among professional managers. People are exposed to similar training and standards and adopt shared values, which are implemented in organizations with which they work. Business schools teach finance, marketing, and human resource majors that certain techniques are better than others, so using those techniques becomes a standard in the field. In one study, for example, a radio station changed from a functional to a multidivisional structure because a consultant recommended it as a "higher standard" of doing business. There was no proof that this structure was better, but the radio station wanted legitimacy and to be perceived as fully professional and up to date in its management techniques.

Companies accept normative pressure to become like one another through a sense of obligation or duty to high standards of performance based on professional norms shared by managers and specialists in their respective organizations. These norms are conveyed through professional education and certification and have almost a moral or ethical requirement based on the highest standards accepted by the profession at that time. In some cases, though, normative forces that maintain legitimacy break down, as they recently did in the accounting industry, and coercive forces are needed to shift organizations back toward acceptable standards.

A company may use any or all of the mechanisms of mimetic, coercive, or normative forces to change itself for greater legitimacy in the institutional environment. Firms tend to use these mechanisms when they are acting under conditions of dependence, uncertainty, ambiguous goals, and reliance on professional credentials. The outcome of these processes is that organizations become far more homogeneous than would be expected from the natural diversity among managers and environments.

BRIEFCASE

As an organization manager, keep this guideline in mind:

Enhance legitimacy by borrowing good ideas from other firms, complying with laws and regulations, and following procedures considered best for your company.

SUMMARY AND INTERPRETATION

This chapter has been about the important evolution in interorganizational relationships. At one time organizations considered themselves autonomous and separate, trying to outdo other companies. Today more organizations see themselves as part of an ecosystem. The organization may span several industries and will be anchored in a dense web of relationships with other companies. In this ecosystem, collaboration is as important as competition. Indeed, organizations may compete and collaborate at the same time depending on the location and issue. In this business ecosystem, the role of management is changing to include the development of horizontal relationships with other organizations.

Four perspectives have been developed to explain relationships among organizations. The resource dependence perspective is the most traditional, arguing that organizations try to avoid excessive dependence on other organizations. In this view, organizations devote considerable effort to controlling the environment to ensure ample resources while maintaining independence.

Moreover, powerful organizations will exploit the dependence of small companies. The collaborative network perspective is an emerging alternative. Organizations welcome collaboration and interdependence with other organizations to enhance value for both. Many executives are changing mindsets away from autonomy toward collaboration, often with former corporate enemies. The new mindset emphasizes trust, fair dealing, and achieving profits for all parties in a relationship.

The population ecology perspective explains why organizational diversity continuously increases with the appearance of new organizations filling niches left open by established companies. This perspective says that large companies usually cannot adapt to meet a changing environment; hence, new companies emerge with the appropriate form and skills to serve new needs. Through the process of variation, selection, and retention, some organizations will survive and grow while others perish. Companies may adopt a generalist or specialist strategy to survive in the population of organizations.

The institutional perspective argues that interorganizational relationships are shaped as much by a company's need for legitimacy as by the need for providing products and services. The need for legitimacy means that the organization will adopt structures and activities that are perceived as valid, proper, and up to date by external stakeholders. In this way, established organizations copy techniques from one another and begin to look very similar. The emergence of common structures and approaches in the same field is called institutional similarity or institutional isomorphism. There are three core mechanisms that explain increasing organizational homogeneity: mimetic forces, which result from responses to uncertainty; coercive forces, which stem from power differences and political influences; and normative forces, which result from common training and professionalism.

Each of the four perspectives is valid. They represent different lenses through which the world of interorganizational relationships can be viewed: organizations experience a competitive struggle for autonomy; they can thrive through collaborative relationships with others; the slowness to adapt provides openings for new organizations to flourish; and organizations seek legitimacy as well as profits from the external environment. The important thing is for managers to be aware of interorganizational relationships and to consciously manage them.

Key Concepts

coercive forces
collaborative network
generalist
institutional environment
institutional perspective
institutional similarity
interorganizational relationships
legitimacy
mimetic forces
niche
normative forces

organizational ecosystem
organizational form
population
population ecology
resource dependence
retention
selection
specialist
struggle for existence
variation

Discussion Questions

1. The concept of business ecosystems implies that organizations are more interdependent than ever before. From personal experience do you agree? Explain.
2. How do you feel about the prospect of becoming a manager and having to manage a set of relationships with other companies rather than just managing your own company? Discuss.
3. Assume you are the manager of a small firm that is dependent on a large computer manufacturing customer that uses the resource dependence perspective. Put yourself in the position of the small firm, and describe what actions you would take to survive and succeed. What actions would you take from the perspective of the large firm?
4. Many managers today were trained under assumptions of adversarial relationships with other companies. Do you think operating as adversaries is easier or more difficult than operating as partners with other companies? Discuss.
5. Discuss how the adversarial versus partnership orientations work among students in class. Is there a sense of competition for grades? Is it possible to develop true partnerships in which your work depends on others?
6. The population ecology perspective argues that it is healthy for society to have new organizations emerging and old organizations dying as the environment changes. Do you agree? Why would European countries pass laws to sustain traditional organizations and inhibit the emergence of new ones?
7. Explain how the process of variation, selection, and retention might explain innovations that take place within an organization.
8. Do you believe that legitimacy really motivates organizations? Is acceptance by other people a motivation for individuals? Explain.
9. How does the desire for legitimacy result in organizations becoming more similar over time?
10. How do mimetic forces differ from normative forces? Give an example of each.

Chapter 5 Workbook *Management Fads**

Look up one or two articles on current trends or fads in management. Then, find one or two articles on a management fad from several years ago. Finally, surf the Internet for information on both the current and previous fads.

Questions

1. How were these fads used in organizations? Use real examples from your readings.

2. Why do you think the fads were adopted? To what extent were the fads adopted to truly improve productivity and morale versus the company's desire to appear current in its management techniques compared to the competition?

3. Give an example in which a fad did not work as expected. Explain the reason it did not work.

Oxford Plastics manufactures high-quality plastics and resins for use in a variety of products, from lawn ornaments and patio furniture to automobiles. The Oxford plant located near Beatty, a town of about 45,000 in a southeastern state, employs about 3,000 workers. It plays an important role in the local economy and, indeed, that of the entire state, which offers few well-paying factory jobs.

In early 1995, Sam Henderson, plant manager of the Beatty facility, notified Governor Tom Winchell that Oxford was ready to announce plans for a major addition to the factory—a state-of-the-art color lab and paint shop that would enable better and faster matching of colors to customer requirements. The new shop would keep Oxford competitive in the fast-paced global market for plastics, as well as bring the Beatty plant into full compliance with U.S. Environmental Protection Agency (EPA) regulations due to take effect within two years.

Plans for the new facility were largely complete. The biggest remaining task was identifying the specific location. The new color lab and paint shop would cover approximately 25 acres, requiring Oxford to purchase some additional land adjacent to its 100-acre factory campus. Henderson was somewhat concerned with top management's preferred site because it fell outside the current industrial zoning boundary, and, moreover, would necessitate destruction of several 400- to 500-year old beech trees. The owner of the property, a nonprofit agency, was ready to sell, whereas property located on the other side of the campus might be more difficult to obtain in a timely manner. Oxford was on a tight schedule to get the project completed. If the new facility wasn't up and running by the time the new EPA regulations went into effect, there was a chance the EPA could force Oxford to stop using its old process—in effect, shutting down the factory.

The governor was thrilled with Oxford's decision to build the new shop in Beatty and he urged Henderson to immediately begin working closely with local and state officials to circumvent any potential problems. It was essential, he stressed, that the project not be bogged down or thwarted by conflict among different interest groups, as it was too important to the economic development of the region. Governor Winchell assigned Beth Friedlander, director of the Governor's Office of Economic Development, to work

closely with Henderson on the project. However, Winchell was not willing to offer his commitment to help push through the rezoning, as he had been an enthusiastic public supporter of environmental causes.

Following his conversation with Governor Winchell, Henderson sat down to identify the various people and organizations that would have an interest in the new color lab project and need to collaborate in order for it to proceed in a smooth and timely manner. They are:

Oxford Plastics
- Mark Thomas, Vice President of North American Operations. Thomas would be flying in from Oxford's Michigan headquarters to oversee land purchase and negotiations regarding the expansion.
- Sam Henderson, Beatty Plant Manager, who has spent his entire career at the Beatty facility, beginning on the factory floor fresh out of high school.
- Wayne Talbert, local union president. The union is strongly in favor of the new shop being located in Beatty because of the potential for more and higher-wage jobs.

State Government
- Governor Tom Winchell, who can exert pressure on local officials to support the project.
- Beth Friedlander, Director of the Governor's Office of Economic Development.
- Manu Gottlieb, Director of the State Department of Environmental Quality.

City Government
- Mayor Barbara Ott, a political newcomer, who has been in office for less than a year and who campaigned on environmental issues.
- Major J. Washington, the Chamber of Commerce chair of local economic development.

Source: Based on "Mammoth Motors' New Paint Shop," a role-play originally prepared by Arnold Howitt, Executive Director of the A. Alfred Taubman Center for State and Local Government at the Kennedy School of Government, Harvard University, and subsequently edited by Gerald Cormick, a principal in the CSE Group, and Senior Lecturer for the Graduate School of Public Affairs at the University of Washington.

Public

- May Pinelas, Chairman of Historic Beatty, who argues vociferously that the future of the region lies in historic and natural preservation and tourism.
- Tommy Tompkins, President of the Save Our Future Foundation, a coalition of private individuals and representatives from the local university who have long been involved in public environmental issues and have successfully thwarted at least one previous expansion project.

Henderson is feeling torn about how to proceed. He thinks to himself, "To move forward, how will I build a coalition among these diverse organizations and groups?" He understands the need for Oxford to move quickly, but he wants Oxford to have a good relationship with the people and organizations that will surely oppose destruction of more of Beatty's natural beauty. Henderson has always liked finding a win-win compromise, but there are so many groups with an interest in this project that he's not sure where to start. Maybe he should begin by working closely with Beth Friedlander from the Governor's office—there's no doubt this is an extremely important project for the state's economic development. On the other hand, it's the local people who are going to be most affected and most involved in the final decisions. Oxford's vice president has suggested a press conference to announce the new shop at the end of the week, but Henderson is worried about putting the news out cold. Perhaps he should call a meeting of interested parties now and let everyone get their feelings out into the open? He knows it could get emotional, but he wonders if things won't get much uglier later on if he doesn't.

CASE FOR ANALYSIS   *Hugh Russel, Inc.**

The following story is a personal recollection by David Hurst of the experience of a group of managers in a mature organization undergoing profound change. . . . The precipitating event in this change was a serious business crisis. . . .

When I joined Hugh Russel Inc. in 1979, it was a medium-sized Canadian distributor of steel and industrial products. With sales of CDN$535 million and three thousand employees, the business was controlled by the chairman, Archie Russel, who owned 16 percent of the common shares. The business consisted of four groups—the core steel distribution activities (called "Russelsteel"), industrial bearings and valves distribution, a chain of wholesalers of hardware and sporting goods, and a small manufacturing business. . . .

The company was structured for performance. . . . The management was professional, with each of the divisional hierarchies headed by a group president reporting to Peter Foster in his capacity as president of the corporation. Jobs were described in job descriptions, and their mode of execution was specified in detailed standard operating procedures. Three volumes of the corporate manual spelled out policy on everything from accounting to vacation pay. Extensive accounting and data processing systems allowed managers to track the progress of individual operations against budgets and plans. Compensation was performance-based, with return on net assets (RONA) as the primary measure and large bonuses (up to 100 percent of base) for managers who made their targets.

At the senior management level, the culture was polite but formal. The board of directors consisted of Archie's friends and associates together with management insiders. Archie and Peter ran the organization as if they were majority owners. Their interaction with management outside of the head office was restricted to the occasional field trip. . . .

Crisis

Nine months after I joined the company as a financial planner, we were put "in play" by a raider and, after a fierce bidding war, were acquired in a hostile takeover. Our acquirer was a private company controlled by the eldest son of an entrepreneur of legendary wealth and ability, so we had no inkling at the time of the roller-coaster ride that lay ahead of us. We were unaware that not only did the son not have the support of his father in this venture but also he had neglected to consult his two brothers, who were joint owners of the acquiring company! As he had taken on $300 million of debt to do the deal, this left each of the brothers on the hook for a personal guarantee of $100 million. They were not amused, and it showed!

Source: Reprinted by permission of Harvard Business School Press. From *Crisis and Renewal: Meeting the Challenge of Organizational Change* by David K. Hurst, Boston, MA 1995, p. 53–73. Copyright ©1995 by the Harvard Business School Publishing Corporation; all rights reserved.

Within days of the deal, we were inundated by waves of consultants, lawyers, and accountants: each shareholder seemed to have his or her own panel of advisers. After six weeks of intensive analysis, it was clear that far too much had been paid for us and that the transaction was vastly overleveraged. At the start of the deal, the acquirer had approached our bankers and asked them if they wanted a piece of the "action." Concerned at the possible loss of our banking business and eager to be associated with such a prominent family, our bankers had agreed to provide the initial financing on a handshake. Now, as they saw the detailed numbers for the first time and became aware of the dissent among the shareholders, they withdrew their support and demanded their money back. We needed to refinance $300 million of debt—fast. . . .

Change

The takeover and the subsequent merger of our new owner's moribund steel-fabricating operations into Hugh Russel changed our agenda completely. We had new shareholders (who fought with each other constantly), new bankers, and new businesses in an environment of soaring interest rates and plummeting demand for our products and services. Almost overnight, the corporation went from a growth-oriented, acquisitive, earnings-driven operation to a broken, cash-starved company, desperate to survive. Closures, layoffs, downsizing, delayering, asset sales, and "rationalization" became our new priorities. . . . At the head office, the clarity of jobs vanished. For example, I had been hired to do financial forecasting and raise capital in the equity markets, but with the company a financial mess, this clearly could not be done. For all of us, the future looked dangerous and frightening as bankruptcy, both personal and corporate, loomed ahead.

And so it was in an atmosphere of crisis that Wayne Mang, the new president (Archie Russel and Peter Foster left the organization soon after the deal), gathered the first group of managers together to discuss the situation. Wayne Mang had been in the steel business for many years and was trusted and respected by the Hugh Russel people. An accountant by training, he used to call himself the "personnel manager" to underscore his belief in both the ability of people to make the difference in the organization and the responsibility of line management to make this happen. The hastily called first meeting consisted of people whom Wayne respected and trusted from all over the organization. They had been selected without regard for their position in the old hierarchy.

The content and style of that first meeting were a revelation to many! Few of them had ever been summoned to the head office for anything but a haranguing over their budgets. Now they were being told the complete gory details of the company's situation and, for the first time, being treated as if they had something to contribute. Wayne asked for their help.

During that first meeting, we counted nineteen major issues confronting the corporation. None of them fell under a single functional area. We arranged ourselves into task forces to deal with them. I say "arranged ourselves" because that was the way it seemed to happen. Individuals volunteered without coercion to work on issues in which they were interested or for which their skills were relevant. They also volunteered others who were not at the meeting but, it was thought, could help. There was some guidance—each task force had one person from the head office whose function it was to report what was happening back to the "center"—and some members found themselves on too many task forces, which required that substitutes be found. But that was the extent of the conscious management of the process.

The meeting broke up at 2:00 A.M., when we all went home to tell our incredulous spouses what had happened. . . .

The cross-functional project team rapidly became our preferred method of organizing new initiatives, and at the head office, the old formal structure virtually disappeared. The teams could be formed at a moment's notice to handle a fast-breaking issue and dissolved just as quickly. We found, for example, that even when we weren't having formal meetings, we seemed to spend most of our time talking to each other informally. Two people would start a conversation in someone's office, and almost before you knew it, others had wandered in and a small group session was going. Later on, we called these events "bubbles"; they became our equivalent of campfire meetings. . . .

Later, when I became executive vice president, Wayne and I deliberately shared an office so we could each hear what the other was doing in real time and create an environment in which "bubbles" might form spontaneously. As people wandered past our open door, we would wave them in to talk; others would wander in after them. The content of these sessions always had to do with our predicament, both corporate and personal. It was serious stuff, but the atmosphere was light and open. Our fate was potentially a bad one, but at least it would be shared.

All of us who were involved then cannot remember ever having laughed so much. We laughed at ourselves and at the desperate situation. We laughed at the foolishness of the bankers in having financed such a mess, and we laughed at the antics of the feuding shareholders, whose outrageous manners and language we learned to mimic to perfection.

I think it was the atmosphere from these informal sessions that gradually permeated all our interactions—with employees, bankers, suppliers, everyone with whom we came into contact. Certainly, we often had tough meetings, filled with tension and threat, but we were always able to "bootstrap" ourselves back up emotionally at the informal debriefings afterward. . . .

Perhaps the best example of both the change in structure and the blurring of the boundaries of the organization was our changing relationships with our bankers. In the beginning, at least for the brief time that the loan was in good standing, the association was polite and at arm's length. Communication was formal. As the bank realized the full horror of what it had financed (a process that took about eighteen months), the relationship steadily grew more hostile. Senior executives of the bank became threatening, spelling out what actions they might take if we did not solve our problem. This hostility culminated in an investigation by the bank for possible fraud (a standard procedure in many banks when faced with a significant loss).

Throughout this period, we had seen a succession of different bankers, each of whom had been assigned to our account for a few months. As a result of our efforts to brief every new face that appeared, we had built a significant network of contacts within the bank with whom we had openly shared a good deal of information and opinion. When no fraud was found, the bank polled its own people on what to do. Our views presented so coherently by our people (because everyone knew what was going on), and shared so widely with so many bankers, had an enormous influence on the outcome of this process. The result was the formation of a joint company-bank team to address a shared problem that together we could solve. The boundary between the corporation and the bank was now blurred: to an outside observer, it would have been unclear where the corporation ended and the bank began. . . .

Our corporation had extensive formal reporting systems to allow the monitoring of operations on a regular basis. After the takeover, these systems required substantial modifications. For example . . .

we had to report our results to the public every quarter at a time when we were losing nearly two million dollars a week! We knew that unless we got to our suppliers ahead of time, they could easily panic and refuse us credit. Hasty moves on their part could have had fatal consequences for the business.

In addition, our closure plans for plants all over Canada and the United States brought us into contact with unions and governments in an entirely different way. We realized that we had no option but to deal with these audiences in advance of events.

I have already described how our relationship with the bankers changed as a result of our open communication. We found exactly the same effect with these new audiences. Initially, our major suppliers could not understand why we had told them we were in trouble before we had to. We succeeded, however, in framing the situation in a way that enlisted their cooperation in our survival, and by the time the "war story" was news, we had their full support. Similarly, most government and union organizations were so pleased to be involved in the process before announcements were made that they bent over backward to be of assistance. Just as had been the case with the bank, we set up joint task forces with these "outside" agencies to resolve what had become shared problems. A significant contributor to our ability to pull this off was the high quality of our internal communication. Everyone on the teams knew the complete, up-to-date picture of what was happening. An outside agency could talk to anyone on a team and get the same story. In this way, we constructed a formidable network of contacts, many of whom had special skills and experience in areas that would turn out to be of great help to us in the future.

The addition of multiple networks to our information systems enhanced our ability both to gather and to disseminate information. The informality and openness of the networks, together with the high volume of face-to-face dialogues, gave us an early warning system with which to detect hurt feelings and possible hostile moves on the part of shareholders, suppliers, nervous bankers, and even customers. This information helped us head off trouble before it happened. The networks also acted as a broadcast system through which we could test plans and actions before announcing them formally. In this way, not only did we get excellent suggestions for improvement, but everyone felt that he or she had been consulted before action was taken. . . .

We had a similar experience with a group of people outside the company during the hectic last six months of 1983, when we were trying to finalize a deal for the shareholders and bankers to sell the steel distribution business to new owners. The group of people in question comprised the secretaries of the numerous lawyers and accountants involved in the deal. . . .

We made these secretaries part of the network, briefing them in advance on the situation, explaining why things were needed, and keeping them updated on the progress of the deal. We were astounded at the cooperation we received: our calls were put through, our messages received prompt responses, and drafts and opinions were produced on time. In the final event, a complex deal that should have taken nine months to complete was done in three. All of this was accomplished by ordinary people going far beyond what might have been expected of them. . . .

We had been thrust into crisis without warning, and our initial activities were almost entirely reactions to issues that imposed themselves upon us. But as we muddled along in the task forces, we began to find that we had unexpected sources of influence over what was happening. The changing relationship with the bank illustrates this neatly. Although we had no formal power in that situation, we found that by framing a confusing predicament in a coherent way, we could, via our network, influence the outcomes of the bank's decisions. The same applied to suppliers: by briefing them ahead of time and presenting a reasonable scenario for the recovery of their advances, we could influence the decisions they would make.

Slowly we began to realize that, although we were powerless in a formal sense, our networks, together with our own internal coherence, gave us an ability to get things done invisibly. As we discussed the situation with all the parties involved, a strategy began to emerge. A complicated financial/tax structure would allow the bank to "manage" its loss and give it an incentive not to call on the shareholders' personal guarantees. The core steel distribution business could be refinanced in the process and sold to new owners. The wrangle between the shareholders could be resolved, and each could go his or her own way. All that had to be done was to bring all the parties together, including a buyer for the steel business, and have them agree that this was the best course to follow. Using our newfound skills, we managed to pull it off.

It was not without excitement: at the last minute, the shareholders raised further objections to the deal. Only the bank could make them sell, and they were reluctant to do so, fearful that they might attract a lawsuit. Discreet calls to the major suppliers, several of whose executives were on the board of the bank, did the trick. "This business needs to be sold and recapitalized," the suppliers were told. "If the deal does not go through, you should probably reduce your credit exposure." The deal went through. By the end of 1983, we had new owners, just in time to benefit from the general business recovery. The ordeal was over. . . .

Chapter 5 Workshop *Ugli Orange Case**

1. Form groups of three members. One person will be Dr. Roland, one person will be Dr. Jones, and the third person will be an observer.
2. Roland and Jones will read only their own roles, but the observer will read both.
3. Role-play: Instructor announces, "I am Mr./Ms. Cardoza, the owner of the remaining Ugli oranges. My fruit export firm is based in South America. My country does not have diplomatic relations with your country, although we do have strong trade relations."

    The groups will spend about ten minutes meeting with the other firm's representative and will decide on a course of action. Be prepared to answer the following questions:

    a. What do you plan to do?
    b. If you want to buy the oranges, what price will you offer?
    c. To whom and how will the oranges be delivered?
4. The observers will report the solutions reached. The groups will describe the decision-making process used.
5. The instructor will lead a discussion on the exercise addressing the following questions:
    a. Which groups had the most trust? How did that influence behavior?
    b. Which groups shared more information? Why?
    c. How are trust and disclosure important in negotiations?

*By Dr. Robert House, University of Toronto. Used with permission.

Role of "Dr. Jones"

You are Dr. John W. Jones, a biological research scientist employed by a pharmaceutical firm. You have recently developed a synthetic chemical useful for curing and preventing Rudosen. Rudosen is a disease contracted by pregnant women. If not caught in the first four weeks of pregnancy, the disease causes serious brain, eye, and ear damage to the unborn child. Recently there has been an outbreak of Rudosen in your state, and several thousand women have contracted the disease. You have found, with volunteer patients, that your recently developed synthetic serum cures Rudosen in its early stages. Unfortunately, the serum is made from the juice of the Ugli orange, which is a very rare fruit. Only a small quantity (approximately four thousand) of these oranges were produced last season. No additional Ugli oranges will be available until next season, which will be too late to cure the present Rudosen victims.

You've demonstrated that your synthetic serum is in no way harmful to pregnant women. Consequently, there are no side effects. The Food and Drug Administration has approved production and distribution of the serum as a cure for Rudosen. Unfortunately, the current outbreak was unexpected, and your firm had not planned on having the compound serum available for six months. Your firm holds the patent on the synthetic serum, and it is expected to be a highly profitable product when it is generally available to the public.

You have recently been informed on good evidence that Mr. R. H. Cardoza, a South American fruit exporter, is in possession of three thousand Ugli oranges in good condition. If you could obtain the juice of all three thousand you would be able to both cure present victims and provide sufficient inoculation for the remaining pregnant women in the state. No other state currently has a Rudosen threat.

You have recently been informed that Dr. P. W. Roland is also urgently seeking Ugli oranges and is also aware of Mr. Cardoza's possession of the three thousand available. Dr. Roland is employed by a competing pharmaceutical firm. He has been working on biological warfare research for the past several years. There is a great deal of industrial espionage in the pharmaceutical industry. Over the past several years, Dr. Roland's firm and yours have sued each other for infringement of patent rights and espionage law violations several times.

You've been authorized by your firm to approach Mr. Cardoza to purchase the three thousand Ugli oranges. You have been told he will sell them to the highest bidder. Your firm has authorized you to bid as high as $250,000 to obtain the juice of the three thousand available oranges.

Role of "Dr. Roland"

You are Dr. P. W. Roland. You work as a research biologist for a pharmaceutical firm. The firm is under contract with the government to do research on methods to combat enemy uses of biological warfare.

Recently several World War II experimental nerve gas bombs were moved from the United States to a small island just off the U.S. coast in the Pacific. In the process of transporting them, two of the bombs developed a leak. The leak is currently controlled by government scientists, who believe that the gas will permeate the bomb chambers within two weeks. They know of no method of preventing the gas from getting into the atmosphere and spreading to other islands and very likely to the West Coast as well. If this occurs, it is likely that several thousand people will incur serious brain damage or die.

You've developed a synthetic vapor that will neutralize the nerve gas if it is injected into the bomb chamber before the gas leaks out. The vapor is made with a chemical taken from the rind of the Ugli orange, a very rare fruit. Unfortunately, only four thousand of these oranges were produced this season.

You've been informed on good evidence that a Mr. R. H. Cardoza, a fruit exporter in South America, is in possession of three thousand Ugli oranges. The chemicals from the rinds of all three thousand oranges would be sufficient to neutralize the gas if the serum is developed and injected efficiently. You have been informed that the rinds of these oranges are in good condition.

You have learned that Dr. J.W. Jones is also urgently seeking to purchase Ugli oranges and that he is aware of Mr. Cardoza's possession of the three thousand available. Dr. Jones works for a firm with which your firm is highly competitive. There is a great deal of industrial espionage in the pharmaceutical industry. Over the years, your firm and Dr. Jones's have sued each other for violations of industrial espionage laws and infringement of patent rights several times. Litigation on two suits is still in process.

The federal government has asked your firm for assistance. You've been authorized by your firm to approach Mr. Cardoza to purchase three thousand Ugli oranges. You have been told he will sell them to the highest bidder. Your firm has authorized you to bid as high as $250,000 to obtain the rinds of the oranges.

Before approaching Mr. Cardoza, you have decided to talk to Dr. Jones to influence him so that he will not prevent you from purchasing the oranges.

Notes

1. George Cahlink, "Partners for Life," *Government Executive* (October 2001), 31–36.

2. Christine Oliver, "Determinants of Interorganizational Relationships: Integration and Future Directions," *Academy of Management Review* 15 (1990), 241–265.

3. James Moore, *The Death of Competition: Leadership and Strategy in the Age of Business Ecosystems* (New York: HarperCollins, 1996).

4. Howard Muson, "Friend? Foe? Both? The Confusing World of Corporate Alliances," *Across the Board* (March–April 2002), 19–25; Devi R. Gnyawali and Ravindranath Madhavan, "Cooperative Networks and Competitive Dynamics: A Structural Embeddedness Perspective," *Academy of Management Review* 26, no. 3 (2001), 431–445.

5. Thomas Petzinger, Jr., *The New Pioneers: The Men and Women Who Are Transforming the Workplace and Marketplace* (New York: Simon & Schuster, 1999): 53–54.

6. James Moore, "The Death of Competition," *Fortune* (April 15, 1996), 142–144.

7. Brian Goodwin, *How the Leopard Changed Its Spots: The Evolution of Complexity* (New York: Touchstone, 1994), 181, quoted in Petzinger, *The New Pioneers*, 53.

8. Joe Flint, "Disney–Time Warner Cable Dispute Turns Many TV Screens Black," *The Wall Street Journal* (May 2, 2000), B1, B4; and Bruce Orwall, Joe Flint, and Martin Peers, "Sparring Partners—Moral of Disney's War Against Time Warner: Don't Dis Distribution," *The Wall Street Journal* (May 3, 2000), A1, A12.

9. Sumantra Ghoshal and Christopher A. Bartlett, "Changing the Role of Top Management: Beyond Structure and Process," *Harvard Business Review* (January–February 1995), 86–96.

10. Susan Greco and Kate O'Sullivan, "Independents' Day," *Inc.* (August 2002), 76–83.

11. J. Pfeffer and G. R. Salancik, *The External Control of Organizations: A Resource Dependence Perspective* (New York: Harper & Row, 1978).

12. Derek S. Pugh and David J. Hickson, *Writers on Organizations*, 5th ed. (Thousand Oaks, Calif.: Sage, 1996).

13. Peter Grittner, "Four Elements of Successful Sourcing Strategies," *Management Review* (October 1996), 41–45.

14. Pete Engardio, "The Barons of Outsourcing," *BusinessWeek*, August 28, 2000, 177–178.

15. This discussion is based on Matthew Schifrin, "The Big Squeeze," *Forbes* (March 11, 1996), 45–46; Wendy Zellner with Marti Benedetti, "CLOUT!" *BusinessWeek* (December 21, 1992), 62–73; Kevin Kelly and Zachary Schiller with James B. Treece, "Cut Costs or Else," *BusinessWeek* (March 22, 1993), 28–29; Lee Berton, "Push From Above," *The Wall Street Journal* (May 23, 1996), R24.

16. Ann Zimmerman, "'Shared Savings'—Grocery Distributor Squeezes Suppliers at Bill-Paying Time," *The Wall Street Journal* (September 5, 2002), A1, A10.

17. Joseph Weber with Sunita Wadekar Bhargava, "Drugmakers Get a Taste of Their Own Medicine," *BusinessWeek* (April 26, 1993), 104.

18. Jay Greene with Stephen Baker and Peter Burrows, "Ganging Up to Compete with Microsoft," *BusinessWeek* (December 3, 2001), 70.

19. Mitchell P. Koza and Arie Y. Lewin, "The Co-Evolution of Network Alliances: A Longitudinal Analysis of an International Professional Service Network," Center for Research on New Organizational Forms, Working Paper 98-09-02; Kathy Rebello with Richard Brandt, Peter Coy, and Mark Lewyn, "Your Digital Future," *BusinessWeek* (September 7, 1992), 56–64.

20. Christine Oliver, "Determinants of Interorganizational Relationships: Integration and Future Directions," *Academy of Management Review*, 15 (1990), 241–265; Ken G. Smith, Stephen J. Carroll, and Susan Ashford, "Intra- and Interorganizational Cooperation: Toward a Research Agenda," *Academy of Management Journal*, 38 (1995), 7–23. Ken G. Smith, Stephen

J. Carroll, and Susan Ashford, "Intra- and Interorganizational Cooperation: Toward a Research Agenda," *Academy of Management Journal* 38 (1995), 7–23.

21. Timothy M. Stearns, Alan N. Hoffman, and Jan B. Heide, "Performance of Commercial Television Stations as an Outcome of Interorganizational Linkages and Environmental Conditions," *Academy of Management Journal* 30 (1987), 71–90; David A. Whetten and Thomas K. Kueng, "The Instrumental Value of Interorganizational Relations: Antecedents and Consequences of Linkage Formation," *Academy of Management Journal* 22 (1979), 325–344.

22. Muson, "Friend? Foe? Both?"

23. Ibid.

24. Lee Berton, "Shall We Dance?" *CFO* (January 1998), 28–35.

25. Donna Fenn, "Sleeping with the Enemy," *Inc.* (November 1997), 78–88.

26. Keith G. Provan and H. Brinton Milward, "A Preliminary Theory of Interorganizational Network Effectiveness: A Comparative of Four Community Mental Health Systems," *Administrative Science Quarterly* 40 (1995), 1–33.

27. Myron Magnet, "The New Golden Rule of Business," *Fortune* (February 21, 1994), 60–64; Grittner, "Four Elements of Successful Sourcing Strategies."

28. Peter Smith Ring and Andrew H. Van de Ven, "Developmental Processes of Corporate Interorganizational Relationships," *Academy of Management Review* 19 (1994), 90–118; Jeffrey H. Dyer, "How Chrysler Created an American Keiretsu" *Harvard Business Review* (July–August 1996), 42–56; Magnet, "The New Golden Rule of Business"; Grittner, "Four Elements of Successful Sourcing Strategies."

29. Magnet, "The New Golden Rule of Business"; Grittner, "Four Elements of Successful Sourcing Strategies."

30. "FastCar Speeds Design Decisions," in Tim Stevens, "Integrated Product Development, Part II," *IndustryWeek* (June 2002), 21–28; Engardio, "The Barons of Outsourcing."

31. Alix Nybert, "Should It Stay or Should It Go?" *CFO* (February 2002), 61–64.

32. Fred R. Blekley, "Some Companies Let Suppliers Work on Site and Even Place Orders," *The Wall Street Journal* (January 13, 1995), A1, A6.

33. Philip Siekman, "The Snap-Together Business Jet," *Fortune* (January 21, 2002), 104[A]–104[H].

34. This section draws from Joel A. C. Baum, "Organizational Ecology," in Steward R. Clegg, Cynthia Hardy, and Walter R. Nord, eds, *Handbook of Organization Studies* (Thousand Oaks, Calif.: Sage, 1996); Jitendra V. Singh, *Organizational Evolution: New Directions* (Newbury Park, Calif.: Sage, 1990); Howard Aldrich, Bill McKelvey, and Dave Ulrich, "Design Strategy from the Population Perspective," *Journal of Management* 10 (1984), 67–86; Howard E. Aldrich, *Organizations and Environments* (Englewood Cliffs, N.J.: Prentice Hall, 1979); Michael Hannan and John Freeman, "The Population Ecology of Organizations," *American Journal of Sociology* 82 (1977), 929–964; Dave Ulrich, "The Population Perspective: Review, Critique, and Relevance," *Human Relations* 40 (1987), 137–152; Jitendra V. Singh and Charles J. Lumsden, "Theory and Research in Organizational Ecology," *Annual Review of Sociology* 16 (1990), 161–195; Howard E. Aldrich, "Understanding, Not Integration: Vital Signs from Three Perspectives on Organizations," in Michael Reed and Michael D. Hughes, eds., *Rethinking Organizations: New Directions in Organizational Theory and Analysis* (London: Sage, 1992); Jitendra V. Singh, David J. Tucker, and Robert J. House, "Organizational Legitimacy and the Liability of Newness," *Administrative Science Quarterly* 31 (1986), 171–193; Douglas R. Wholey and Jack W. Brittain, "Organizational Ecology: Findings and Implications," *Academy of Management Review* 11 (1986), 513–533.

35. Derek S. Pugh and David J. Hickson, *Writers on Organizations*; Lex Donaldson, *American Anti-Management Theories of Organization* (New York: Cambridge University Press, 1995).

36. Michael T. Hannan and John Freeman, "The Population Ecology of Organizations."

37. Julie Creswell, "Cisco's Worst Nightmare (And Sun's and IBM's and Nortel's and . . .)," *Fortune* (February 4, 2002), 114–116.

38. Thomas Moore, "The Corporate University: Transforming Management Education" (Presentation in August, 1996. Thomas Moore is the Dean of the Arthur D. Little University).

39. Peter Newcomb, "No One is Safe," *Forbes* (July 13, 1987), 121; "It's Tough Up There," *Forbes* (July 13, 1987), 145–160.

40. Stewart Feldman, "Here One Decade, Gone the Next," *Management Review* (November 1990), 5–6.

41. David Stires, "Fallen Arches," *Fortune* (April 29, 2002), 74–76.

42. Shirley Leung, "McDonald's Has First Ever Loss During a Quarter," *The Wall Street Journal* (January 24, 2003), A2.

43. David J. Tucker, Jitendra V. Singh, and Agnes G. Meinhard, "Organizational Form, Population Dynamics, and Institutional Change: The Founding Patterns of Voluntary Organizations," *Academy of Management Journal* 33 (1990), 151–178; Glenn R. Carroll and Michael T. Hannan, "Density Delay in the Evolution of Organizational Populations: A Model and Five Empirical Tests," *Administrative Science Quarterly* 34 (1989), 411–430; Jacques Delacroix and Glenn R. Carroll, "Organizational Foundings: An Ecological Study of the Newspaper Industries of Argentina and Ireland," *Administrative Science Quarterly* 28 (1983), 274–291; Johannes M. Pennings, "Organizational Birth Frequencies: An Empirical Investigation," *Administrative Science Quarterly* 27 (1982), 120–144; David Marple, "Technological Innovation and Organizational Survival: A Population Ecology Study of Nineteenth-Century American Railroads," *Sociological Quarterly* 23 (1982), 107–116; Thomas G. Rundall and John O. McClain, "Environmental Selection and Physician Supply," *American Journal of Sociology* 87 (1982), 1090–1112.

44. Robert D. Hof and Linda Himelstein, "eBay vs. Amazon.com," *BusinessWeek* (May 31, 1999), 128–132; and Maria Mallory with Stephanie Anderson Forest, "Waking Up to a Major Market," *BusinessWeek* (March 23, 1992), 70–73.

45. Arthur G. Bedeian and Raymond F. Zammuto, *Organizations: Theory and Design* (Orlando, Fla.: Dryden Press, 1991); Richard L. Hall, *Organizations: Structure, Process and Outcomes* (Englewood Cliffs, N.J.: Prentice-Hall, 1991).

46. Nelson D. Schwartz, "Still Perking After All These Years," *Fortune* (May 24, 1999); Ken Belson, "As Starbucks Grows, Japan, Too, Is Awash," *The New York Times* (October 21, 2001), C3; and George Anders, "Starbucks Brews a New Strategy," *Fast Company* (August 2001), 145–146.

47. M. Tina Dacin, Jerry Goodstein, and W. Richard Scott, "Institutional Theory and Institutional Change: Introduction to the Special Research Forum," *Academy of Management Journal* 45, no. 1 (2002), 45–47. Thanks to Tina Dacin for her material and suggestions for this section of the chapter.

48. J. Meyer and B. Rowan, "Institutionalized Organizations: Formal Structure as Myth and Ceremony," *American Journal of Sociology* 83 (1990), 340–363.

49. Mark C. Suchman, "Managing Legitimacy: Strategic and Institutional Approaches," *Academy of Management Review* 20 (1995), 571–610.

50. Jeremy Kahn, "Deloitte Restates Its Case," *Fortune* (April 29, 2002), 64–72.

51. Melanie Trottman and Scott McCartney, "Executive Flight: The Age of 'Wal-Mart' Airlines Crunches the Biggest Carriers," *The Wall Street Journal* (June 18, 2002), A1, A8; and Paul C. Judge, "How Will Your Company Adapt?" *Fast Company* (December 2001), 128–139.

52. Matthew Boyle, "America's Most Admired: The Shiniest Reputations in Tarnished Times," *Fortune* (March 4, 2002), 70–72.

53. Pamela S. Tolbert and Lynne G. Zucker, "The Institutionalization of Institutional Theory," in Stewart R. Clegg, Cynthia Hardy, and Walter R. Nord, eds., *Handbook of Organization Studies* (Thousand Oaks, Calif.: Sage, 1996).

54. Pugh and Hickson, *Writers on Organizations*; Paul J. DiMaggio and Walter W. Powell, "The Iron Cage Revisited: Institutional Isomorphism and Collective Rationality in Organizational Fields," *American Sociological Review* 48 (1983), 147–160.

55. This section is based largely on DiMaggio and Powell, "The Iron Cage Revisited"; Pugh and Hickson, *Writers on Organizations*; and W. Richard Scott, *Institutions and Organizations* (Thousand Oaks, Calif.: Sage, 1995).

56. Ellen R. Auster and Mark L. Sirower, "The Dynamics of Merger and Acquisition Waves," *The Journal of Applied Behavioral Science* 38, no. 2 (June 2002), 216–244.

57. William McKinley, Jun Zhao, and Kathleen Garrett Rust, "A Sociocognitive Interpretation of Organizational Downsizing," *Academy of Management Review* 25, no. 1 (2000), 227–243.

58. Barry M. Staw and Lisa D. Epstein, "What Bandwagons Bring: Effects of Popular Management Techniques on Corporate Performance, Reputation, and CEO Pay," *Administrative Science Quarterly* 45, no. 3 (September 2000): 523–560.

59. Kahn, "Deloitte Restates Its Case."

Designing Organizations for the International Environment

chapter 6

Starbucks

Every major city in the United States seems to have a Starbucks on every corner. With more than 4,200 stores scattered across the United States and Canada, the domestic market is quickly becoming saturated. Seattle now has a Starbucks store for every 9,400 people, and the saturation point in Manhattan and other cities isn't far behind. And that's not the only problem Starbucks leaders face. Throughout the 1990s, successful baby boomers lapped up the company's hip image along with their lattes and cappuccinos, but younger consumers are turned off by the power, image, and high prices of the ubiquitous brand. Although Starbucks has plans for opening new U.S. stores, its potential for significant sales growth at home looks dim.

Chairman Howard Schultz and other top leaders aren't worried, though. There's a whole world just waiting to be colonized. Global opportunities are astounding, and Starbucks is aggressively exporting its brand and concept internationally. The emphasis on international business is reflected in Schultz's new title—chairman and chief global strategist—which he assumed in 2000, leaving the day-to-day management of the chain to other leaders.

Consider this: In 1999, Starbucks had 281 international stores. By September 2002, it had 1,200, including recently opened stores in Vienna, Zurich, Madrid, Berlin, and Jakarta. That still leaves plenty of room for growth, and the company already has plans for at least 400 new international outlets. The brand's sparkle might have dimmed in the United States, but overseas the Starbucks package is shiny and new, considered cool by young consumers who can keep the company's sales growing for years. For example, the company has been a hit among the young in Vienna, which is teeming with its own local coffeehouses. "The coffeehouses in Vienna are nice, but they are old," says a business editor for the paper *Der Standard*. "Starbucks is considered hip."

Despite the opportunities, Starbucks' global expansion is fraught with risk. To succeed, the company has to adapt to varied market needs, cultural values, and government regulations. Accustomed to going it alone in the Unites States, managers are having to partner with local companies to gain the insight and experience they need to translate the concept for each new market they enter. Starbucks is determined to become a global as well as a national powerhouse, but managers have to make decisions about global strategy, the best type of structure to use to meet international and organizational goals, and how to most efficiently and effectively serve a broad global market.[1]

Companies based in the United States have long been involved in international business, but interest in global trade is greater today than ever before. Thousands of U.S.-based companies have set up foreign operations to produce goods and services needed by consumers in other countries, as well as to obtain lower costs for producing products to sell at home. In return, companies from Japan, Germany, and the United Kingdom compete with American companies on their own turf as well as abroad. Domestic markets for many companies, like Starbucks, are becoming saturated, and the only potential for growth lies overseas. For e-commerce companies, expanding internationally is becoming a priority. The United States' share of total worldwide e-commerce is falling as foreign companies set up their own e-commerce ventures that better respond to local needs.[2] Succeeding on a global scale isn't easy. Organizations have to make decisions about strategic approach, how best to get involved in international markets, and how to design the organization to reap the benefits of international expansion.

PURPOSE OF THIS CHAPTER

This chapter will explore how managers design the organization for the international environment. We begin by looking at some of the primary motivations for organizations to expand internationally, the typical stages of international development, and the use of strategic alliances as a means for international expansion. Then, the chapter will examine global strategic approaches and the application of various structural designs for global advantage. Next, we will discuss some of the specific challenges global organizations face, mechanisms for addressing them, and cultural differences that influence the organization's approach to designing and managing a global firm. Finally, the chapter takes a look at an emerging type of global organization, the *transnational model*, that achieves high levels of the varied capabilities needed to succeed in a complex and volatile international environment.

ENTERING THE GLOBAL ARENA

As recently as twenty years ago, many companies could afford to ignore the international environment. Today's companies must think globally or get left behind. The world is becoming a unified global field. Extraordinary advancements in communications, technology, and transportation have created a new, highly competitive landscape. Products can be made and sold anywhere in the world, communications are instant, and product development and life cycles are growing shorter. No company is isolated from global influence. Some large so-called American companies such as Coca-Cola, Procter & Gamble, and Exxon rely on international sales for a substantial portion of their sales and profits. And even the smallest companies can be actively involved in international business through exports and online business.

MOTIVATIONS FOR GLOBAL EXPANSION

Economic, technological, and competitive forces have combined to push many companies from a domestic to a global focus. In some industries, being successful in today's environment means succeeding on a global scale. Three primary factors motivate companies to expand internationally: economies of scale, economies of scope, and cheaper production factors.[3]

Economies of Scale. Building a global presence expands an organization's scale of operations, enabling it to realize **economies of scale**. The trend toward large organizations was initially sparked by the Industrial Revolution, which created pressure in many industries for larger factories that could seize the benefits of economies of scale offered by new technologies and production methods.

Through large-volume production, these industrial giants were able to achieve the lowest possible cost per unit of production. However, for many companies, domestic markets no longer provide the high level of sales needed to maintain enough volume to achieve scale economies. In an industry such as automobile manufacturing, for example, a company would need a tremendous share of the domestic market to achieve scale economies. Thus, an organization such as Ford Motor Company is forced to become international in order to survive. Economies of scale also enable companies to obtain volume discounts from suppliers, lowering the organization's cost of production.

Economies of Scope.   A second factor is the enhanced potential for exploiting **economies of scope**. *Scope* refers to the number and variety of products and services a company offers, as well as the number and variety of regions, countries, and markets it serves. Having a presence in multiple countries provides marketing power and synergy compared to the same size firm that has presence in fewer countries. For example, an advertising agency with a presence in several global markets gains a competitive edge serving large companies that span the globe. Or consider the case of McDonald's, which has to obtain nearly identical mustard and ketchup packets for its restaurants around the world. A supplier that has a presence in every country McDonald's serves has an advantage because it provides cost, consistency, and convenience benefits to McDonald's, which does not have to deal with a number of local suppliers in each country. Economies of scope can also increase a company's market power as compared to competitors, because the company develops broad knowledge of the cultural, social, economic, and other factors that affect its customers in varied locations and can provide specialized products and services to meet those needs.

Low-Cost Production Factors.   The third major force motivating global expansion relates to **factors of production**. One of the earliest, and still one of the most powerful, motivations for U.S. companies to invest abroad is the opportunity to obtain raw materials and other resources at the lowest possible cost. Organizations have long turned overseas to secure raw materials that were scarce or unavailable in their home country. For example, in the early twentieth century, tire companies went abroad to develop rubber plantations to supply tires for America's growing automobile industry. More recently, many companies have seen other countries as a source of cheap labor. Textile manufacturing in the United States continues to decline as companies shift more and more production to Mexico, Latin America, and the Caribbean where labor costs are much lower. Software companies are setting up development centers in India, apparel and shoe companies outsource production to Asian manufacturers, and document processing for U.S. credit-card applications is handled by workers in India and Mexico. Other organizations have gone international in search of lower costs of capital, sources of cheap energy, reduced government restrictions, or other factors that lower the company's total production costs. Companies can locate facilities wherever it makes the most economic sense in terms of needed employee education and skill levels, labor and raw materials costs, and other production factors. Automobile manufacturers such as Toyota, Ford, and BMW have built plants in South Africa, Brazil, and Thailand, where they can pay workers less than one-tenth of what workers earn in higher-wage, developed countries. In addition, these countries typically offer dramatically lower costs for factors such as land, water, and electricity.[4]

STAGES OF INTERNATIONAL DEVELOPMENT

No company can become a global giant overnight. The shift from domestic to global usually occurs through stages of development, as illustrated in Exhibit 6.1.[5] In stage one, the **domestic stage**, the company is domestically oriented, but managers are aware of the global environment and may want to consider initial foreign involvement to expand production volume and realize economies of scale. Market potential is limited and is primarily in the home country. The structure of the company is domestic, typically functional or divisional, and initial foreign sales are handled through an export department. The details of freight forwarding, customs problems, and foreign exchange are handled by outsiders.

In stage two, the **international stage**, the company takes exports seriously and begins to think multidomestically. **Multidomestic** means competitive issues in each country are independent of other countries; the company deals with each country individually. The concern is with international competitive positioning compared with other firms in the industry. At this point, an international division has replaced the export department, and specialists are hired to handle sales, service, and warehousing abroad. Multiple countries are identified as a potential market.

In stage three, the **multinational stage**, the company has extensive experience in a number of international markets and has established marketing, manufacturing, or research and development facilities in several foreign countries. The organization obtains a large percentage of revenues from sales outside the home country. Explosion occurs as international operations take off, and the company has business units scattered around the world along with suppliers, manufacturers, and distributors.

The fourth and ultimate stage is the **global stage**, which means the company transcends any single country. The business is not merely a collection of domestic industries; rather, subsidiaries are interlinked to the point where competitive position in one country significantly influences activities in other countries.[6] Truly **global companies** no longer think of themselves as having a single home country, and, indeed, have been called *stateless corporations*.[7] This represents a new and dramatic evolution from the multinational company of the 1960s and 1970s.

Global companies operate in truly global fashion, and the entire world is their marketplace. Organization structure at this stage can be extremely complex

EXHIBIT 6.1   *Four Stages of International Evolution*

	I. Domestic	II. International	III. Multinational	IV. Global
Strategic Orientation	Domestically oriented	Export-oriented multidomestic	Multinational	Global
Stage of Development	Initial foreign involvement	Competitive positioning	Explosion	Global
Structure	Domestic structure, plus export department	Domestic structure, plus international division	Worldwide geographic, product	Matrix, transnational
Market Potential	Moderate, mostly domestic	Large, multidomestic	Very large, multinational	Whole world

Source: Based on Nancy J. Adler, *International Dimensions of Organizational Behavior*, 4th ed. (Cincinnati, Ohio: South-Western, 2002), 8–9; and Theodore T. Herbert, "Strategy and Multinational Organization Structure: An Interorganizational Relationships Perspective," *Academy of Management Review* 9 (1984): 259–271.

and often evolves into an international matrix or transnational model, which will be discussed later in this chapter.

Global companies such as Royal Dutch/Shell, Unilever, and Matsushita Electric may operate in more than a hundred countries. The structural problem of holding together this huge complex of subsidiaries scattered thousands of miles apart is immense.

GLOBAL EXPANSION THROUGH INTERNATIONAL STRATEGIC ALLIANCES

One of the most common ways companies get involved in international operations is through strategic alliances. The average large U.S. corporation, which had no alliances in the early 1990s, now has more than thirty, many of those with international firms. Companies in rapidly changing industries such as media and entertainment, pharmaceuticals, biotechnology, and software might have hundreds of these relationships.[8]

Typical alliances include licensing, joint ventures, and consortia.[9] For example, pharmaceutical companies such as Merck, Eli Lilly, Pfizer, and Warner-Lambert cross-license their newest drugs to one another to support industrywide innovation and marketing and offset the high fixed costs of research and distribution.[10] A **joint venture** is a separate entity created with two or more active firms as sponsors. This is a popular approach to sharing development and production costs and penetrating new markets. Joint ventures may be with either customers or competitors.[11] A joint venture led by Sprint, Deutsche Telecom, and Telecom France, and involving several smaller firms, serves sixty-five countries and functions as a single company to meet the telecommunications needs of global corporations.[12] MTV Networks has joint ventures with companies in Brazil, Australia, and other countries to expand its media presence globally.[13]

Manufacturing companies often seek joint ventures to achieve production cost savings through economies of scale or to distribute new technologies and products through another country's distribution channels. The agreement between Toyota and General Motors to construct a Chevrolet plant in California was Toyota's way of distributing its technology to the United States. Caterpillar Inc. and Mitsubishi Heavy Industries Ltd. established a joint venture that enabled Caterpillar to manufacture and sell in Japan and expanded Mitsubishi's export markets.[14]

Another growing approach is for companies to become involved in **consortia**, groups of independent companies—including suppliers, customers, and even competitors—that join together to share skills, resources, costs, and access to one another's markets. Airbus Industrie, for example, is a consortium made up of French, British, and German aerospace companies to successfully compete with Boeing on a global scale.[15] Consortia are often used in other parts of the world, such as the *keiretsu* family of corporations in Japan. In Korea, these interlocking company arrangements are called *chaebol*.

A type of consortia, the global *virtual organization*, is increasingly being used in the United States and offers a promising approach to meeting worldwide competition. The virtual organization refers to a continually evolving set of company relationships that exist temporarily to exploit temporary opportunities or attain specific strategic advantages. A company may be involved in multiple alliances at any one time. Oracle, a software company, is involved in as many as 15,000 short-term organizational partnerships at any time.[16] Some executives believe shifting to a consortia or virtual approach is the best way for U.S. companies to remain competitive in the global marketplace.[17]

Managers and organizations all over the world are learning to cooperate to achieve competitive advantage on a global scale. STMicroelectronics NV rapidly grew from two to twenty-seven countries based on the strength of its partnerships with customer organizations.

STMicroelectronics NV

In Practice

Based in Geneva, Switzerland, STMicroelectronics NV was created in 1987 by the merger of two money-losing state-owned companies: SGS Microelettronica of Italy and Thomson Semiconductors of France. Since that inauspicious beginning, the company has partnered its way to a position as the world's third-largest computer chip maker and a leader in one of the hottest segments of the chip industry, manufacturing a "system-on-a-chip" that combines analog functions (such as sound and graphics) together with digital circuitry (such as logic and memory) on a single chip. The system-on-a-chip approach opened a huge market opportunity that very few other companies were prepared to exploit.

Success for STMicroelectronics came, however, not from designing and producing the system-on-a-chip in isolation, but from developing close partnerships with customers to gain a deep understanding of their system designs and unique needs. Partnering began out of necessity, as ST needed to convince customers to replace their complex circuit boards with its system-on-a-chip. One of the earliest major alliances was with California-based Seagate Corporation, the world's largest maker of disk drives. By understanding the company's needs, ST was able to shrink all the components on Seagate's hard disk drive onto one or two custom chips. Being able to produce smaller, cheaper, and less power-hungry disk drives enabled Seagate to enter entirely new markets such as laptops and handheld computers. ST's partnership with Seagate has continued, and the company has since established similar close relationships with twelve other telecommunications, computer, automotive, and consumer products companies in multiple countries. The partnership between Nokia and ST, for example, has a governance committee made up of senior executives from both companies that meets quarterly to set and measure objectives and evaluate the partnership's performance. Teams from both companies meet regularly to coordinate development, marketing, and sourcing of components, and engineers participate in regular *dream days*, where they get together and create wish-list products without interference from management.

By taking a partnership approach, STMicroelectronics now has operations in twenty-seven countries and is able to draw on technological expertise and market understanding from around the world. ST's top managers are working on forming alliances with partners in Asia, where it has very few, to expand its presence in that part of the world.[18]

Using strategic alliances helped STMicroelectronics move from a money-losing operation to year 2000 profits of $1.4 billion on sales of $7.8 billion. Over the past two decades, ST has evolved into a highly sophisticated global firm that is adept at tapping into knowledge around the world to develop innovative solutions to customers' problems. STMicroelectronics has truly achieved the global stage of development described in Exhibit 6.1; the word *country* no longer even appears in the company's vocabulary. Units around the world carry the name of the city where they're located, and each is viewed as part of a unified global system.[19]

DESIGNING STRUCTURE TO FIT GLOBAL STRATEGY

As we discussed in Chapter 3, an organization's structure must fit its situation by providing sufficient information processing for coordination and control while focusing employees on specific functions, products, or geographic regions. Organization design for international structure follows a similar logic, with special interest in global versus local strategic opportunities.

MODEL FOR GLOBAL VERSUS LOCAL OPPORTUNITIES

When organizations venture into the international domain, managers strive to formulate a coherent global strategy that will provide synergy among worldwide operations for the purpose of achieving common organizational goals. One dilemma they face is choosing whether to emphasize global integration versus national responsiveness. Managers must decide whether they want each global affiliate to act autonomously or whether activities should be standardized across countries. These decisions are reflected in the choice between a *globalization* versus a *multidomestic* global strategy.

The **globalization strategy** means that product design, manufacturing, and marketing strategy are standardized throughout the world.[20] For example, the Japanese took business away from Canadian and American companies by developing similar high-quality, low-cost products for all countries. The Canadian and American companies incurred higher costs by tailoring products to specific countries. Black & Decker became much more competitive internationally when it standardized its line of power hand tools. Other products, such as Coca-Cola, are naturals for globalization, because only advertising and marketing need to be tailored for different regions.

A globalization strategy can help an organization reap economy-of-scale efficiencies by standardizing product design and manufacturing, using common suppliers, introducing products around the world faster, coordinating prices, and eliminating overlapping facilities. By sharing technology, design, suppliers, and manufacturing standards worldwide in a coordinated global automotive operation, Ford saved $5 billion during the first three years.[21] Similarly, Gillette Company, which makes grooming products such as the Mach3 shaving system for men and the Venus razor for women, has large production facilities that use common suppliers and processes to manufacture products whose technical specifications are standardized around the world.[22]

A **multidomestic strategy** means that competition in each country is handled independently of competition in other countries. Thus, a multidomestic strategy would encourage product design, assembly, and marketing tailored to the specific needs of each country. Some companies have found that their products do not thrive in a single global market. The French do not drink orange juice for breakfast, and laundry detergent is used to wash dishes, not clothes, in parts of Mexico. Procter & Gamble tried to standardize diaper design, but discovered that cultural values in different parts of the world required style adjustments to make the product acceptable to many mothers. For example, in Italy, designing diapers to cover the baby's navel was critical to successful sales.[23]

Different global organization designs, as well, are better suited to the need for either global integration or national responsiveness. Recent research on more than 100 international firms based in Spain has provided further support for the connection between international structure and strategic focus.[24] The model in Exhibit 6.2 illustrates how organization design and international strategy fit the needs of the environment.[25]

Companies can be characterized by whether their product and service lines have potential for globalization, which means advantages through worldwide standardization. Companies that sell diverse products or services across many countries have a globalization strategy. On the other hand, some companies have products and services appropriate for a multidomestic strategy, which means local-country advantages through differentiation and customization.

As indicated in Exhibit 6.2, when forces for both global integration and national responsiveness in many countries are low, simply using an international division with the domestic structure is an appropriate way to handle international business. For some industries, however, technological, social, or economic forces may create a situation in which selling standardized products worldwide provides a basis for competitive advantage. In these cases, a global product structure is appropriate. This structure provides product managers with authority to handle their product lines on a global basis and enables the company to take advantage of a unified global marketplace. In other cases, a company can gain competitive advantages through national responsiveness—by responding to unique needs in the various countries in which it does business. For example, people in different countries have very different expectations regarding personal care products such as deodorant or toothpaste. For companies in these industries, a worldwide geographic structure is appropriate. Each country or region will have subsidiaries modifying products and services to fit that locale. The advertising firm of Ogilvy & Mather divides its operations into four primary geographical regions because advertising approaches need to be modified to fit the tastes, preferences, cultural

EXHIBIT 6.2   *Model to Fit Organization Structure to International Advantages*

Source: Roderick E. White and Thomas A. Poynter, "Organizing for Worldwide Advantage," *Business Quarterly* (Summer 1989), 84–89. Adapted by permission of *Business Quarterly*, published by the Western Business School, the University of Western Ontario, London, Ontario, Canada.

values, and government regulations in different parts of the world.[26] Children are frequently used to advertise products in the United States, but this approach in France is against the law. The competitive claims of rival products regularly seen on U.S. television would violate government regulations in Germany.[27]

In many instances, companies will need to respond to both global and local opportunities simultaneously, in which case the global matrix structure can be used. Part of the product line may need to be standardized globally, and other parts tailored to the needs of local countries. Let's discuss each of the structures in Exhibit 6.2 in more detail.

INTERNATIONAL DIVISION

As companies begin to explore international opportunities, they typically start with an export department that grows into an **international division**. The international division has a status equal to the other major departments or divisions within the company and is illustrated in Exhibit 6.3. Whereas the domestic divisions are typically organized along functional or product lines, the international

EXHIBIT 6.3   *Domestic Hybrid Structure with International Division*

division is organized according to geographic interests, as illustrated in the exhibit. The international division has its own hierarchy to handle business (licensing, joint ventures) in various countries, selling the products and services created by the domestic divisions, opening subsidiary plants, and in general moving the organization into more sophisticated international operations.

Although functional structures are often used domestically, they are less frequently used to manage a worldwide business.[28] Lines of functional hierarchy running around the world would extend too long, so some form of product or geographical structure is used to subdivide the organization into smaller units. Firms typically start with an international department and, depending on their strategy, later use product or geographic divisional structures.

GLOBAL PRODUCT DIVISION STRUCTURE

In a **global product structure**, the product divisions take responsibility for global operations in their specific product area. This is one of the most commonly used structures through which managers attempt to achieve global goals because it provides a fairly straightforward way to effectively manage a variety of businesses and products around the world. Managers in each product division can focus on organizing for international operations as they see fit and directing employees' energy toward their own division's unique set of global problems or opportunities.[29] In addition, the structure provides top managers at headquarters with a broad perspective on competition, enabling the entire corporation to respond more rapidly to a changing global environment.[30]

With a global product structure, each division's manager is responsible for planning, organizing, and controlling all functions for the production and distribution of its products for any market around the world. The product-based structure works best when a division handles products that are technologically similar and can be standardized for marketing worldwide. As we saw in Exhibit 6.2, the global product structure works best when the company has opportunities for worldwide production and sale of standard products for all markets, thus providing economies of scale and standardization of production, marketing, and advertising.

Eaton Corporation has used a form of worldwide product structure, as illustrated in Exhibit 6.4. In this structure, the automotive components group, industrial group, and so on are responsible for manufacture and sale of products worldwide. The vice president of international is responsible for coordinators in each region, including a coordinator for Japan, Australia, South America, and northern Europe. The coordinators find ways to share facilities and improve production and delivery across all product lines sold in their region. These coordinators provide the same function as integrators described in Chapter 3.

The product structure is great for standardizing production and sales around the globe, but it also has problems. Often the product divisions do not work well together, competing instead of cooperating in some countries; and some countries may be ignored by product managers. The solution adopted by Eaton Corporation of using country coordinators who have a clearly defined role is a superb way to overcome these problems.

GLOBAL GEOGRAPHIC DIVISION STRUCTURE

A regionally based organization is well suited to companies that want to emphasize adaptation to regional or local market needs through a multidomestic strategy, as illustrated in Exhibit 6.2. The **global geographic structure** divides the world into

EXHIBIT 6.4   *Partial Global Product Structure Used by Eaton Corporation*

Source: Based on *New Directions in Multinational Corporate Organization* (New York: Business International Corp., 1981).

geographical regions, with each geographical division reporting to the CEO. Each division has full control of functional activities within its geographical area.

Companies that use this type of structure have typically been those with mature product lines and stable technologies. They can find low-cost manufacturing within countries, as well as meeting different needs across countries for marketing and sales. However, several business and organizational trends have led to a broadening of the kinds of companies that use the global geographic structure.[31] The growth of service organizations has outpaced manufacturing for several years, and services by their nature must occur on a local level. In addition, to meet new competitive threats, many manufacturing firms are emphasizing the ability to customize their products to meet specific needs, which requires a greater emphasis on local and regional responsiveness. All organizations are compelled by current environmental and competitive challenges to develop closer relationships with customers, which may lead companies to shift from a product-based to a geographic-based structure.

The problems encountered by senior management using a global geographic structure result from the autonomy of each regional division. For example, it is difficult to do planning on a global scale—such as new-product R&D—because each division acts to meet only the needs of its region. New domestic technologies and products can be difficult to transfer to international markets because each division thinks it will develop what it needs. Likewise, it is difficult to rapidly introduce products developed offshore into domestic markets; and there is often duplication of line and staff managers across regions. Companies such as Dow Chemical, Gerber Products Company, and Colgate-Palmolive find ways to take advantages of the global geographic structure while overcoming these problems.

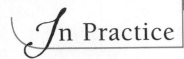

COLGATE-PALMOLIVE COMPANY

For several years, Colgate-Palmolive Company, which manufacturers and markets personal care, household, and specialty products, used a global geographic structure of the form illustrated in Exhibit 6.5. Colgate has a long, rich history of international involvement and has relied on regional divisions in North America, Europe, Latin America, the Far East, and the South Pacific to stay on the competitive edge. Well over half of the company's total sales are generated outside of the United States.

The regional approach supports Colgate's cultural values that emphasize individual autonomy, an entrepreneurial spirit, and the ability to act locally. Each regional president reports directly to the chief operating officer, and each division has its own staff functions

EXHIBIT 6.5   *Global Geographic Structure of Colgate-Palmolive Company*

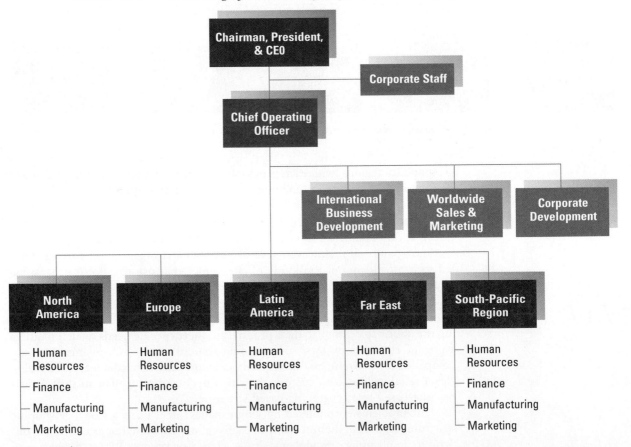

Source: Based on Robert J. Kramer, *Organizing for Global Competitiveness: The Geographic Design* (New York: The Conference Board, 1993), 30.

such as human resources, finance, manufacturing, and marketing. Colgate handled the problem of coordination across geographic divisions by creating an *international business development group* that has responsibility for long-term company planning and worldwide product coordination and communication. It used several product team leaders, many of whom had been former country managers with extensive experience and knowledge. The product leaders are essentially coordinators and advisors to the geographic divisions; they have no power to direct, but they have the ability and the organizational support needed to exert substantial influence. The addition of this business development group quickly reaped positive results in terms of more rapid introduction of new products across all countries and better, lower-cost marketing.

The success of the international business development group prompted Colgate's top management to add two additional coordinating positions, a *vice president of corporate development* to focus on acquisitions, and a *worldwide sales and marketing group* that coordinates sales and marketing initiatives across all geographic locations. With these worldwide positions added to the structure, Colgate maintains its focus on each region and achieves global coordination for overall planning, faster product introductions, and enhanced sales and marketing efficiency.[32]

GLOBAL MATRIX STRUCTURE

We've discussed how Eaton used a global product division structure and found ways to coordinate across worldwide divisions. Colgate-Palmolive used a global geographic division structure and found ways to coordinate across geographical regions. Each of these companies emphasized a single dimension. Recall from Chapter 3 that a matrix structure provides a way to achieve vertical and horizontal coordination simultaneously along two dimensions. A **global matrix structure** is similar to the matrix described in Chapter 3, except that for multinational corporations the geographical distances for communication are greater and coordination is more complex.

The matrix works best when pressure for decision-making balances the interests of both product standardization and geographical localization and when coordination to share resources is important. For many years, Asea Brown Boveri (ABB), an electrical equipment corporation headquartered in Zurich, used a global matrix structure that worked extremely well to coordinate a 200,000-employee company operating in more than 140 countries.

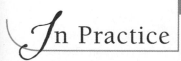

ASEA BROWN BOVERI LTD. (ABB)

ABB has given new meaning to the notion of "being local worldwide." ABB owns 1,300 subsidiary companies, divided into 5,000 profit centers located in 140 countries. ABB's average plant has fewer than 200 workers and most of the company's 5,000 profit centers contain only forty to fifty people, meaning almost everyone stays close to the customer. For many years, ABB used a complex global matrix structure similar to Exhibit 6.6 to achieve worldwide economies of scale combined with local flexibility and responsiveness.

At the top are the chief executive officer and an international committee of eight top managers, who hold frequent meetings around the world. Along one side of the matrix are sixty-five or so business areas located worldwide, into which ABB's products and services are grouped. Each business area leader is responsible for handling business on a global

EXHIBIT 6.6   *Global Matrix Structure*

scale, allocating export markets, establishing cost and quality standards, and creating mixed-nationality teams to solve problems. For example, the leader for power transformers is responsible for twenty-five factories in sixteen countries.

Along the other side of the matrix is a country structure; ABB has more than one hundred country managers, most of them citizens of the country in which they work. They run national companies and are responsible for local balance sheets, income statements, and career ladders. The German president, for example, is responsible for 36,000 people across several business areas that generate annual revenues in Germany of more than $4 billion.

The matrix structure converges at the level of the 1,300 local companies. The presidents of local companies report to two bosses—the business area leader, who is usually located outside the country, and the country president, who runs the company of which the local organization is a subsidiary.

ABB's philosophy is to decentralize things to the lowest levels. Global managers are generous, patient, and multilingual. They must work with teams made up of different nationalities and be culturally sensitive. They craft strategy and evaluate performance for people and subsidiaries around the world. Country managers, by contrast, are regional line managers responsible for several country subsidiaries. They must cooperate with business area managers to achieve worldwide efficiencies and the introduction of new products. Finally, the presidents of local companies have both a global boss—the business area manager—and a country boss, and they learn to coordinate the needs of both.[33]

ABB is a large, successful company that achieved the benefits of both product and geographic organizations through this matrix structure. However, over the past several years, as ABB has faced increasingly complex competitive issues, leaders have transformed the company toward a complex structure called the *transnational model*, which will be discussed later in this chapter.

In the real world, as with the domestic hybrid structure described in Chapter 3, many international firms apply a *global hybrid* or *mixed structure*, in which two or more different structures or elements of different structures are used. Hybrid structures are typical in highly volatile environments. AT&T's Network Wireless Systems Business Unit, for example, combines functional, geographical, and product divisions to respond to the dynamic conditions of the wireless telecommunications industry.[34]

Now, let's look at some of the specific challenges organizations face in the global arena and mechanisms for successfully confronting them.

BUILDING GLOBAL CAPABILITIES

There are many instances of well-known companies that have trouble transferring successful ideas, products, and services from their home country to the international domain. In the early 1990s, PepsiCo., Inc., set a five-year goal to triple its international soft-drink revenues and boldly expanded its presence in international markets. Yet by 1997, the company had withdrawn from some of those markets and had to take a nearly $1 billion loss from international beverage operations.[35] Wal-Mart's first foray into South America was a disaster, with the company losing $48 billion in its first two years.[36] Hundreds of American companies that saw Vietnam as a tremendous international opportunity in the mid-1990s are now calling it quits amid heavy losses. Political and cultural differences sidetracked most of the ventures. Only a few companies, such as Citigroup's Citibank unit and Caterpillar's heavy-equipment business, have found success in that country.[37] Managers taking their companies international face a tremendous challenge in how to capitalize on the incredible opportunities that global expansion presents.

THE GLOBAL ORGANIZATIONAL CHALLENGE

Exhibit 6.7 illustrates the three primary segments of the global organizational challenge: greater complexity and differentiation, the need for integration, and

EXHIBIT 6.7   *The Global Organizational Challenge*

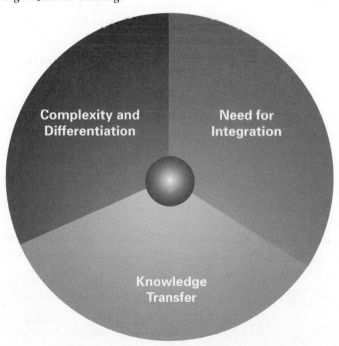

the problem of transferring knowledge across a global firm. Organizations have to accept an extremely high level of environmental complexity in the international domain and address the many differences that occur among countries, requiring greater organizational differentiation. At the same time, they must find ways to effectively achieve coordination and collaboration among far-flung units and facilitate the development and transfer of organizational knowledge for global learning.[38] Although many small companies are involved in international business, most international companies grow very large, creating a huge coordination problem. Exhibit 6.8 provides some understanding of the size and impact of international firms by comparing the sales of several large international firms with the gross national income (GNI) of selected countries.

Increased Complexity and Differentiation. When organizations enter the international arena, they encounter a greater level of internal and external complexity than anything experienced on the domestic front. Companies have to create a structure to operate in numerous countries that differ in economic development, language, political systems and government regulations, cultural norms and values, and infrastructure such as transportation and communication facilities. For example, although most international firms have their headquarters in wealthier, economically advanced countries, smart managers are investing heavily in less developed countries in Asia, Eastern Europe, and Latin America, which offer huge new markets for their goods and services. In the area of e-commerce, the number of Internet users and the amount of online sales are both expected to zoom in Latin America over the next couple of years, so companies such as Dell and America Online are establishing online stores and services for customers in that region.[39]

In addition, a growing number of global consumers are rejecting the notion of homogenized products and services, calling for greater response to local preferences. Even McDonald's, perhaps the ultimate example of standardization for a world market, has recently felt the need to be more responsive to local and national differences. In France, where consumers have been resentful of the fast-food chain's incursion, McDonald's has boosted sales by remodeling restaurants to include features such as hardwood floors, wood-beam ceilings, and comfortable

EXHIBIT 6.8   *Comparison of Country Gross National Income (GNI) and Company Sales (in millions of U.S. dollars)*

Company	Fiscal 2001 Sales*	Country	Annual GNI**
Wal-Mart Stores	$217,799	Austria	$194,463
Exxon Mobil	$213,488	Turkey	$168,335
BP	$174,218	Denmark	$166,345
General Electric	$126,102	South Africa	$125,486
Toyota Motor Co.	$114,702	Iran, Islamic Republic	$112,855
Philip Morris	$89,924	Malaysia	$86,510
Siemens	$77,413	Chile	$66,915
Sony	$57,542	Czech Republic	$54,108

*March 31, 2002, results used for Japanese companies

**Formerly referred to as gross national product, or GNP

Sources: Company sales figures are from data reported in "The Global Giants," *The Wall Street Journal* (October 14, 2002), R10, R11. GNI data are from the World Development Indicators database, World Bank, August 2002, *http://www.worldbank.org/data/,* accessed on November 15, 2002.

armchairs, and by adding menu items such as espresso, brioche, and more upscale sandwiches.[40]

All this complexity in the international environment is mirrored in a greater internal organizational complexity. Recall from Chapter 4 that as environments become more complex and uncertain, organizations grow more highly differentiated, with many specialized positions and departments to cope with specific sectors in the environment. Top management might need to set up specialized departments to deal with the diverse government, legal, and accounting regulations in various countries, for example. More boundary-spanning departments are needed to sense and respond to the external environment. In addition, organizations might implement a variety of strategies, a broader array of activities, and a much larger number of products and services on an international level in order to meet the needs of a diverse market.

Need for Integration. As organizations become more differentiated, with multiple products, divisions, departments, and positions scattered across numerous countries, managers face a tremendous integration challenge. As described in Chapter 4, *integration* refers to the quality of collaboration across organizational units. The question is how to achieve the coordination and collaboration that is necessary for a global organization to reap the benefits of economies of scale, economies of scope, and labor and production cost efficiencies that international expansion offers. Even in a domestic firm, high differentiation among departments requires that more time and resources be devoted to achieving coordination because employees' attitudes, goals, and work orientations differ widely. Imagine what it must be like for an international organization, whose operating units are divided not only by goals and work attitudes but by geographical distance, time differences, cultural values, and perhaps even language as well. Recall how Colgate-Palmolive created several specific units to achieve coordination and integration among regional divisions. Other companies, too, must find ways to share information, ideas, new products, and technologies across the organization.

Knowledge Transfer. The third piece of the international challenge is for organizations to learn from their international experiences and exploit that learning to create and leverage global organizational knowledge. The diversity of the international environment offers extraordinary opportunities for learning and the development of diverse capabilities. Organizational units in each location acquire the skills and knowledge to meet environmental challenges that arise in that particular locale. Much of that knowledge, which may be related to product improvements, operational efficiencies, technological advancements, or myriad other competencies, is relevant across multiple countries, so organizations need systems that promote the transfer of knowledge across the global enterprise. One good example comes from Procter & Gamble. Liquid Tide was one of P&G's most successful U.S. product launches in the 1980s, but the product came about from the sharing of diverse international knowledge. Liquid Tide incorporated a technology for helping to suspend dirt in wash water from P&G headquarters in the United States, the formula for its cleaning agents from P&G technicians in Japan, and special ingredients for fighting mineral salts present in hard water from company scientists in Brussels.[41]

Most organizations tap only a fraction of the potential that is available from the cross-border transfer of knowledge.[42] There are several reasons for this:

* Knowledge often remains hidden in various units because language, cultural, and geographic distances prevent top managers from recognizing it exists.

- Divisions sometimes view knowledge as power and want to hold onto it as a way to gain an influential position within the global firm.
- The "not-invented-here" syndrome makes some managers reluctant to tap into the know-how and expertise of other units.
- Much of an organization's knowledge is in the minds of employees and cannot easily be written down and shared with other units.

Organizations have to find ways to encourage both the development and sharing of knowledge and implement systems for tapping into knowledge wherever it exists to create innovative responses to new challenges.

GLOBAL COORDINATION MECHANISMS

Managers meet the global challenge of coordination and transferring knowledge across highly differentiated units in a variety of ways. Some of the most common are the use of global teams, stronger headquarters planning and control, and specific coordination roles.

Global Teams. The popularity and success of teams on the domestic front allowed managers to see firsthand how this mechanism can achieve strong horizontal coordination, as described in Chapter 3, and thus recognize the promise teams held for coordination across a global firm as well. **Global teams**, also called *transnational teams*, are cross-border work groups made up of multiskilled, multinational members whose activities span multiple countries.[43] Typically, teams are of two types: intercultural teams, whose members come from different countries and meet face to face, and virtual global teams, whose members remain in separate locations around the world and conduct their work electronically.[44] Heineken formed the European Production Task Force, a thirteen-member team made up of multinational members, to meet regularly and come up with ideas for optimizing the company's production facilities across Europe.[45] The research unit of BT Labs has 660 researchers spread across the United Kingdom and several other countries who work in global virtual teams to investigate virtual reality, artificial intelligence, and other advanced information technologies.[46] The team approach enables technologies, ideas, and learning in one country to rapidly spread across the firm via the constant sharing of information among team members.

The most advanced and competitive use of global teams involves simultaneous contributions in three strategic areas.[47] First, global teams help companies address the differentiation challenge, enabling them to be more locally responsive by providing knowledge to meet the needs of different regional markets, consumer preferences, and political and legal systems. At the same time, teams provide integration benefits, helping organizations achieve global efficiencies by developing regional or worldwide cost advantages and standardizing designs and operations across countries. Finally, these teams contribute to continuous organizational learning, knowledge transfer, and adaptation on a global level.

Headquarters Planning. A second approach to achieving stronger global coordination is for headquarters to take an active role in planning, scheduling, and control to keep the widely distributed pieces of the global organization working together and moving in the same direction. In one survey, 70 percent of global companies reported that the most important function of corporate headquarters was to "provide enterprise leadership."[48] Without strong leadership, highly autonomous divisions can begin to act like independent companies rather than coordinated parts of a global whole. To counteract this, top management may delegate responsibility and decision-making authority in some areas, such as adapting products or services to meet local needs, while maintaining strong control through centralized management and information systems that enable headquarters to keep track of what's going on and that serve to coordinate activities across divisions and countries. Plans, schedules, and formal rules and procedures can help ensure greater communication among divisions and with headquarters and foster cooperation and synergy among far-flung units to achieve the organization's goals in a cost-efficient way. Top managers can provide clear strategic direction, guide far-flung operations, and resolve competing demands from various units.

Expanded Coordination Roles.   Organizations may also implement structural solutions to achieve stronger coordination and collaboration.[49] Creating specific organizational roles or positions for coordination is a way to integrate all the pieces of the enterprise to achieve a strong competitive position. In successful international firms, the role of top *functional managers*, for example, is expanded to include responsibility for coordinating across countries, identifying and linking the organization's expertise and resources worldwide. In an international organization, the manufacturing manager has to be aware of and coordinate with manufacturing operations of the company in various other parts of the world so that the company achieves manufacturing efficiency and shares technology and ideas across units. A new manufacturing technology developed to improve efficiency in Ford's Brazilian operations may be valuable for European and North American plants as well. Manufacturing managers are responsible for being aware of new developments wherever they occur and for using their knowledge to improve the organization. Similarly, marketing managers, human resource managers, and other functional managers at an international company are involved not only in activities for their particular location but in coordinating with their sister units in other countries as well.

Whereas functional managers coordinate across countries, *country managers* coordinate across functions. A country manager for an international firm has to coordinate all the various functional activities to meet the problems, opportunities, needs, and trends in the local market, enabling the organization to achieve multinational flexibility and rapid response. The country manager in Venezuela for a global consumer products firm such as Colgate-Palmolive would coordinate everything that goes on in that country, from manufacturing to human resources to marketing, to ensure that activities meet the language, cultural, government, and legal requirements of Venezuela. Similarly, the country manager in Ireland or Canada would do the same for those countries. Country managers also help with the transfer of ideas, trends, products, and technologies that arise in one country and might have significance on a broader scale.

Some organizations create formal *network coordinator* positions to coordinate information and activities related to key customer accounts. These coordinators would enable a manufacturing organization, for example, to provide knowledge and integrated solutions across multiple businesses, divisions, and countries for a large customer such as Wal-Mart.[50] Top managers in successful global firms also encourage and support informal networks and relationships to keep information flowing in all directions. Much of an organization's information exchange occurs not through formal systems or structures but through informal channels and relationships. By supporting these informal networks, giving people across boundaries opportunities to get together and develop relationships and then ways to keep in close touch, executives enhance organizational coordination.

CULTURAL DIFFERENCES IN COORDINATION AND CONTROL

Just as social and cultural values differ from country to country, the management values and organizational norms of international companies tend to vary depending on the organization's home country. Organizational norms and values are influenced by the values in the larger national culture, and these in turn influence the organization's structural approach and the ways managers coordinate and control an international firm.

NATIONAL VALUE SYSTEMS

Studies have attempted to determine how national value systems influence management and organizations. One of the most influential was conducted by Geert Hofstede, who identified several dimensions of national value systems that vary widely across countries.[51] For example, two dimensions that seem to have a strong impact within organizations are *power distance* and *uncertainty avoidance*. High **power distance** means that people accept inequality in power among institutions, organizations, and people. Low power distance means that people expect equality in power. High **uncertainty avoidance** means that members of a society feel uncomfortable with uncertainty and ambiguity and thus support beliefs that promise certainty and conformity. Low uncertainty avoidance means that people have a high tolerance for the unstructured, the unclear, and the unpredictable.

These value dimensions are reflected within organizations in terms of beliefs regarding the need for hierarchy, centralized decision making and control, formal rules and procedures, and specialized jobs.[52] In countries that value high power distance, for example, organizations tend to be more hierarchical and centralized, with greater control and coordination from the top levels of the organization. On the other hand, organizations in countries that value low power distance are more likely to be decentralized. A low tolerance for uncertainty tends to be reflected in a preference for coordination through rules and procedures. Organizations in countries where people have a high tolerance for uncertainty typically have fewer rules and formal systems, relying more on informal networks and personal communication for coordination. This chapter's Book Mark further examines how cultural value patterns influence international organizations.

Although organizations do not always reflect the dominant cultural values, studies have found rather clear patterns of different management structures when comparing countries in Europe, the United States, and Asia.

THREE NATIONAL APPROACHES TO COORDINATION AND CONTROL

Let's look at three primary approaches to coordination and control as represented by Japanese, American, and European companies.[53] It should be noted that companies in each country use tools and techniques from each of the three coordination methods. However, there are broad, general patterns that illustrate cultural differences.

BOOK MARK *6.0*   *Have You Read This Book?*

Cross-Cultural Business Behavior: Marketing, Negotiating and Managing Across Cultures
By Richard R. Gesteland

Richard Gesteland maintains that heeding the "two iron rules of international business" is crucial to success in today's global business environment: "In International Business, the Seller Is Expected to Adapt to the Buyer," and "In International Business, the Visitor Is Expected to Observe Local Customs." In his book *Cross-Cultural Business Behavior*, Gesteland explains and categorizes various cultural patterns of behavior that can help managers follow these rules.

LOGICAL CULTURAL PATTERNS
Gesteland outlines four major cultural value patterns, which he calls *logical patterns*, that characterize countries around the world:

- *Deal-Focused vs. Relationship-Focused.* Deal-focused cultures, such as those in North America, Australia, and Northern Europe, are task-oriented, while relationship-focused cultures, including those in Arabia, Africa, Latin America, and Asia, are typically people-oriented. Deal-focused individuals approach business in an objective and impersonal way. Relationship-focused individuals believe in building close personal relationships as the appropriate way to conduct business.

- *Informal vs. Formal.* Informal cultures place a low value on status and power differences, whereas formal cultures are typically hierarchical and status-conscious. The unconstrained values of informal cultures, such as those in the United States and Australia, may insult people from formal, hierarchical societies, just as the class-consciousness of formal groups, such as cultures in most of Europe and Latin America, may offend the egalitarian ideals of people in informal cultures.

- *Rigid-Time vs. Fluid-Time.* One part of the world's societies is flexible about time and scheduling, while the other group is more rigid and dedicated to clock-time. Conflicts may occur because rigid-time types often consider fluid-time people undisciplined and irresponsible, while fluid-time people regard rigid-time folks as arrogant, demanding, and enslaved by meaningless deadlines.

- *Expressive vs. Reserved.* Expressive cultures include those in Latin America and the Mediterranean. Reserved cultures are those in East and Southeast Asia as well as Germanic Europe. This distinction can create a major communication gap. People from expressive cultures tend to talk louder and use more hand gestures and facial expressions. Reserved cultures may interpret raised voices and gesturing as signals of anger or instability.

A PRACTICAL GUIDE
Geographical-cultural differences, and the potential problems that cross-cultural communication can create, "impact our business success throughout the global marketplace," argues Gesteland. *Cross-Cultural Business Behavior* "is intended as a practical guide for the men and women in the front lines of world trade, those who face every day the frustrating differences in global business customs and practices." By understanding Gesteland's logical patterns of behavior, managers can adapt to varied cultural values and improve their chances for international success.

Cross-Cultural Business Behavior: Marketing, Negotiating and Managing Across Cultures, by Richard R. Gesteland, is published by Copenhagen Business School Press.

Centralized Coordination in Japanese Companies. When expanding internationally, Japanese companies have typically developed coordination mechanisms that rely on centralization. Top managers at headquarters actively direct and control overseas operations, whose primary focus is to implement strategies handed down from headquarters. This approach enables Japanese companies to leverage the knowledge and resources located at the corporate center, attain global efficiencies, and coordinate across units to obtain synergies and avoid turf battles. Top managers use strong structural linkages to ensure that managers at headquarters remain up-to-date and fully involved in all strategic decisions. However, centralization has its limits. As the organization expands and divisions grow larger, headquarters can become overloaded and decision making slows. The quality of decisions may also suffer as greater diversity and complexity make it difficult for headquarters to understand and respond to local needs in each region.

European Firms' Decentralized Approach. A different approach has typically been taken by European companies. Rather than relying on strong, centrally directed coordination and control, international units tend to have a high level of independence and decision-making autonomy. Companies rely on a strong mission, shared values, and informal personal relationships for coordination. Thus, great emphasis is placed on careful selection, training, and development of key managers throughout the international organization. Formal management and control systems are used primarily for financial rather than technical or operational control. With this approach, each international unit focuses on its local markets, enabling the company to excel in meeting diverse needs. One disadvantage is the cost of ensuring, through training and development programs, that managers throughout a huge, global firm share goals, values, and priorities. Decision making can also be slow and complex, and disagreements and conflicts among divisions are more difficult to resolve.

The United States: Coordination and Control through Formalization. U.S.-based companies that have expanded into the international arena have taken still a third direction. Typically, these organizations have delegated responsibility to international divisions, yet retained overall control of the enterprise through the use of sophisticated management control systems and the development of specialist headquarters staff. Formal systems, policies, standards of performance, and a regular flow of information from divisions to headquarters are the primary means of coordination and control. Decision making is based on objective data, policies, and procedures, which provides for many operating efficiencies and reduces conflict among divisions and between divisions and headquarters. However, the cost of setting up complex systems, policies, and rules for an international organization may be quite high. The approach also requires a larger headquarters staff for reviewing, interpreting, and sharing information, thus increasing overhead costs. Finally, standard routines and procedures don't always fit the needs of new problems and situations. Flexibility is limited when managers may pay so much attention to systems that they fail to recognize opportunities and threats in the environment.

Clearly, each of these approaches has advantages. But as international organizations grow larger and more complex, the disadvantages of each tend to become more pronounced. Because traditional approaches have been inadequate to meet the demands of a rapidly changing, complex international environment, many large international companies are moving toward a new kind of organization form, the *transnational model*—that is highly differentiated to address environmental complexity yet offers very high levels of coordination, learning, and transfer of organizational knowledge.

THE TRANSNATIONAL MODEL OF ORGANIZATION

The **transnational model** represents the most advanced kind of international organization. It reflects the ultimate in both organizational complexity, with many diverse units, and organizational coordination, with mechanisms for integrating the varied parts. The transnational model is useful for large, multinational companies with subsidiaries in many countries that try to exploit both global and local advantages as well as technological advancements, rapid innovation, and global learning and knowledge sharing. Rather than building capabilities primarily in one area, such as global efficiency, national responsiveness, or global learning, the transnational model seeks to achieve all three simultaneously. Dealing with multiple, interrelated, complex issues requires a complex form of organization and structure.

The transnational model represents the most current thinking about the kind of structure needed by complex global organizations such as Philips NV, illustrated in Exhibit 6.9. Headquartered in the Netherlands, Philips has hundreds of operating units all over the world and is typical of global companies such as Unilever, Matsushita, or Procter & Gamble.[54]

The units in Exhibit 6.9 are far-flung. Achieving coordination, a sense of participation and involvement by subsidiaries, and a sharing of information, knowledge, new technology, and customers is a tremendous challenge. For example, a global corporation like Philips is so large that size alone is a huge problem in coordinating global operations. In addition, some subsidiaries become so large that they no longer fit a narrow strategic role defined by headquarters. While being part of a larger organization, individual units need some autonomy for themselves and need the ability to have an impact on other parts of the organization.

The transnational model addresses these challenges by creating an integrated network of individual operations that are linked together to achieve the multidimensional goals of the overall organization.[55] The management philosophy is based on *interdependence* rather than either full divisional independence or total dependence of these units on headquarters for decision making and control. The transnational model is more than just an organization chart. It is a managerial state of mind, a set of values, a shared desire to make a worldwide learning system work, and an idealized structure for effectively managing such a system. Several characteristics distinguish the transnational organization from other global organization forms such as the matrix, described earlier.

1. *Assets and resources are dispersed worldwide into highly specialized operations that are linked together through interdependent relationships.* Resources and capabilities are widely distributed to help the organization sense and respond to diverse stimuli such as market needs, technological developments, or consumer trends that emerge in different parts of the world. However, managers forge interdependent relationships among the various product, functional, or geographic units. Mechanisms such as cross-subsidiary teams, for example, compel units to work together for the good of their own unit as well as the overall organization. Rather than being completely self-sufficient, each group has to cooperate to achieve its own goals. Such interdependencies encourage the collaborative sharing of information and resources, cross-unit problem solving, and collective implementation demanded by today's competitive international environment. Materials, people, products, ideas, resources, and information are continually flowing among the dispersed parts of the integrated network. In addition, managers actively shape, manage, and reinforce informal information networks that cross functions, products, divisions, and countries.

EXHIBIT 6.9   *International Organizational Units and Interlinkages within Philips NV*

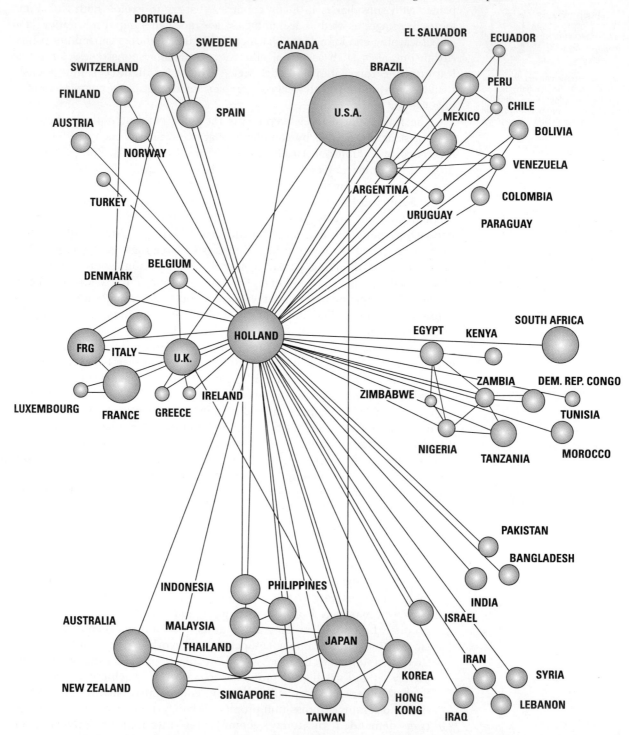

Source: Sumantra Ghoshal and Christopher A. Bartlett, "The Multinational Corporation as an Interorganizational Network," *Academy of Management Review* 15 (1990), 605. Used by permission.

2. *Structures are flexible and ever-changing.* The transnational operates on a principle of *flexible centralization*. It may centralize some functions in one country, some in another, yet decentralize still other functions among its many geographically dispersed operations. An R&D center may be centralized in Holland and a purchasing center located in Sweden, while financial accounting responsibilities are decentralized to operations in many countries. A unit in Hong Kong may be responsible for coordinating activities across Asia, while activities for all other countries are coordinated by a large division headquarters in London. The transnational requires that managers be flexible in determining structural needs based on the benefits to be gained. Some functions, products, and geographic regions by their nature may need more central control and coordination than others. In addition, coordination and control mechanisms will change over time to meet new needs or competitive threats.

3. *Subsidiary managers initiate strategy and innovations that become strategy for the corporation as a whole.* In traditional structures, managers have a strategic role only for their division. In a transnational, various centers and subsidiaries can shape the company from the bottom up by developing creative responses and initiating programs in response to local needs and dispersing those innovations worldwide. Transnational companies recognize each of the worldwide units as a source of capabilities and knowledge that can be used to benefit the entire organization. In addition, environmental demands and opportunities vary from country to country, and exposing the whole organization to this broader range of environmental stimuli triggers greater learning and innovation.

4. *Unification and coordination are achieved primarily through corporate culture, shared vision and values, and management style rather than through formal structures and systems.* The transnational is essentially a horizontal structure. It is diverse and extended, and it exists in a fluctuating environment so that hierarchy, standard rules, procedures, and close supervision are not appropriate. Achieving unity and coordination in an organization where employees come from a variety of different national backgrounds, are separated by time and geographical distance, and have different cultural norms is more easily accomplished through shared understanding than through formal systems. Top leaders build a context of shared vision, values, and perspectives among managers who in turn cascade these elements through all parts of the organization. Selection and training of managers emphasizes flexibility and open-mindedness. In addition, people are often rotated through different jobs, divisions, and countries to gain broad experience and become socialized into the corporate culture. Achieving coordination in a transnational organization is a much more complex process than simple centralization or decentralization of decision making and requires shaping and adapting beliefs, culture, and values so that everyone participates in information sharing and learning.

Taken together, these characteristics facilitate strong coordination, organizational learning, and knowledge sharing on a broad global scale. The transnational model is truly a complex and messy way to conceptualize organization structure, but it is becoming increasingly relevant for large, global firms that treat the whole world as their playing field and do not have a single country base. The autonomy of organizational parts gives strength to smaller units and allows the firm to be flexible in responding to rapid change and competitive opportunities on a local level, while the emphasis on interdependency enables global efficiencies and organizational learning. Each part of the transnational company is aware of and closely integrated with the organization as a whole so local actions complement and enhance other company parts.

SUMMARY AND INTERPRETATION

This chapter has examined how managers design organizations for a complex international environment. Almost every company today is affected by significant global forces, and many are developing overseas operations to take advantage of global markets. Three primary motivations for global expansion are to realize economies of scale, exploit economies of scope, and achieve scarce or low-cost factors of production such as labor, raw materials, or land. One popular way to become involved in international operations is through strategic alliances with international firms. Alliances include licensing, joint ventures, and consortia.

Organizations typically evolve through four stages, beginning with a domestic orientation, shifting to an international orientation, then changing to a multinational orientation, and finally moving to a global orientation that sees the whole world as a potential market. Organizations typically use an export department, then use an international department, and eventually develop into a worldwide geographic or product structure. Geographic structures are most effective for organizations that can benefit from a multidomestic strategy, meaning that products and services will do best if tailored to local needs and cultures. A product structure supports a globalization strategy, which means that products and services can be standardized and sold worldwide. Huge global firms might use a matrix structure to respond to both local and global forces simultaneously. Many firms use hybrid structures, by combining elements of two or more different structures to meet the dynamic conditions of the global environment.

Succeeding on a global scale is not easy. Three aspects of the global organizational challenge are addressing environmental complexity through greater organizational complexity and differentiation, achieving integration and coordination among the highly differentiated units, and implementing mechanisms for global learning and knowledge transfer. Common ways to address the problem of integration and knowledge transfer are through global teams, stronger headquarters planning and control, and specific coordination roles. Managers also recognize that diverse national and cultural values influence the organization's approach to coordination and control. Three varied national approaches are the centralized coordination and control typically found in many Japanese-based firms, a decentralized approach common among European firms, and the formalization approach often used by U.S.-based international firms. Most companies, however, no matter their home country, use a combination of elements from each of these approaches.

Many are also finding a need to broaden their coordination methods and are moving toward the transnational model of organization. The transnational model is based on a philosophy of interdependence. It is highly differentiated yet offers very high levels of coordination, learning, and transfer of knowledge across far-flung divisions. The transnational represents the ultimate in terms of both organizational complexity and organizational integration. Each part of the transnational organization is aware of and closely integrated with the organization as a whole so that local actions complement and enhance other company parts.

Key Concepts

consortia
domestic stage
economies of scale
economies of scope
factors of production
global companies
global geographic structure
global matrix structure
global product structure
global stage
global teams

globalization strategy
international division
international stage
joint venture
multidomestic
multidomestic strategy
multinational stage
power distance
transnational model
uncertainty avoidance

Discussion Questions

1. Under what conditions should a company consider adopting a global geographic structure as opposed to a global product structure?
2. Name some companies that you think could succeed today with a globalization strategy and explain why you selected those companies. How does the globalization strategy differ from a multidomestic strategy?
3. Why would a company want to join a strategic alliance rather than go it alone in international operations? What do you see as the potential advantages and disadvantages of international alliances?
4. Why is knowledge sharing so important to a global organization?
5. What are some of the primary reasons a company decides to expand internationally? Identify a company in the news that has recently built a new overseas facility. Which of the three motivations for global expansion described in the chapter do you think best explains the company's decision? Discuss.
6. When would an organization consider using a matrix structure? How does the global matrix differ from the domestic matrix structure described in Chapter 3?
7. Name some of the elements that contribute to greater complexity for international organizations. How do organizations address this complexity? Do you think these elements apply to an online company such as eBay that wants to grow internationally? Discuss.
8. Traditional values in Mexico support high power distance and a low tolerance for uncertainty. What would you predict about a company that opens a division in Mexico and tries to implement global teams characterized by shared power and authority and the lack of formal guidelines, rules, and structure?
9. Do you believe it is possible for a global company to simultaneously achieve the goals of global efficiency and integration, national responsiveness and flexibility, and worldwide learning and knowledge sharing? Discuss.
10. Compare the description of the transnational model in this chapter to the elements of the learning organization described in Chapter 1. Do you think the transnational model seems workable for a huge global firm? Discuss.
11. What does it mean to say that the transnational model is based on a philosophy of interdependence?

Chapter 6 Workbook *Made in the U.S.A.?*

Find three different consumer products, such as a shirt, a toy, and a shoe. Try to find out the following information for each product, as shown in the table. To find this information, use Web sites, articles on the company from various business newspapers and magazines, and the labels on the items. You could also try calling the company and talking with someone there.

Product	What country do materials come from?	Where is it manufactured or assembled?	Which country does the marketing and advertising	In what different countries is the product sold?
1.				
2.				
3.				

What can you conclude about international products and organizations based on your analysis?

CASE FOR ANALYSIS   *TopDog Software*

At the age of 39, after working for nearly 15 years at a leading software company on the West Coast, Ari Weiner and his soon-to-be-wife, Mary Carpenter, had cashed in their stock options, withdrawn all their savings, maxed out their credit cards, and started their own business, naming it TopDog Software after their beloved Alaskan malamute. The two had developed a new software package for customer relationship management (CRM) applications that they were certain was far superior to anything on the market at that time. TopDog's software was particularly effective for use in call centers because it provided a highly efficient way to integrate massive amounts of customer data and make it almost immediately accessible to call center representatives as they worked the phones. The software, which could be used as a stand-alone product or easily integrated with other major CRM software packages, dramatically expedited customer identification and verification, rapidly selected pertinent bits of data, and provided them in an easily interpreted format so that call center or customer service reps could provide fast, friendly, and customized service.

The timing proved to be right on target. CRM was just getting hot, and TopDog was poised to take advantage of the trend as a niche player in a growing market. Weiner and Carpenter brought in two former colleagues as partners and were soon able to catch the attention of a venture capitalist firm to gain additional funding. Within a couple of years, TopDog had 28 employees and sales had reached nearly $4 million.

Now, though, the partners are facing the company's first major problem. TopDog's head of sales, Samantha Jenkins, has learned of a new company based in London that is beta-testing a new CRM package that promises to outpace TopDog's—and the London-based company, FastData, has been talking up its global aspirations in the press. "If we stay focused on the United States and they start out as a global player, they'll kill us within months!" Sam moaned. "We've got to come up with an international strategy to deal with this kind of competition."

In a series of group meetings, off-site retreats, and one-on-one conversations, Weiner and Carpenter have gathered opinions and ideas from their partners, employees, advisors, and friends. Now they have to make a decision—should TopDog go global? And if so, what approach would be most effective? There's a growing market for CRM software overseas, and new companies such as FastData will soon be cutting into TopDog's U.S. market share as well. Samantha Jenkins isn't alone in her belief that TopDog has no choice but to enter new international markets or get eaten alive. Others, however, are concerned that TopDog isn't ready for that step. The company's resources are already stretched to the limit, and some advisors have warned that rapid global expansion could spell disaster. TopDog isn't even well established in the United

Source: Based on Walter Kuemmerle, "Go Global—Or No?" *Harvard Business Review* (June 2001), 37–49.

States, they argue, and expanding internationally could strain the company's capabilities and resources. Others have pointed out that none of the managers has any international experience and the company would have to hire someone with significant global exposure to even think about entering new markets.

Although Mary tends to agree that TopDog for the time being should stay clearly focused on building its business in the United States, Ari has come to believe that global expansion of some type is a necessity. But if Top Dog does eventually decide on global expansion, he wonders how on earth they should proceed in such a huge, complex environment. Sam, the sales manager, is arguing that the company should set up its own small foreign offices from scratch and staff them primarily with local people. Building a UK office and an Asian office, she asserts, would give TopDog an ideal base for penetrating markets around the world. However, it would be quite expensive, not to mention the complexities of dealing with language and cultural differences, legal and government regulations, and other matters. Another option would be to establish alliances or joint ventures with small European and Asian companies that could benefit from adding CRM applications to their suite of products. The companies could share expenses in setting up foreign production facilities and a global sales and distribution network. This would be a much less costly operation and would give TopDog the benefit of the expertise of the foreign partners. However, it might also require lengthy negotiations and would certainly mean giving up some control to the partner companies.

One of TopDog's partners is urging still a third, even lower-cost approach, that of licensing TopDog's software to foreign distributors as a route to international expansion. By giving foreign software companies rights to produce, market, and distribute its CRM software, TopDog could build brand identity and customer awareness while keeping a tight rein on expenses. Ari likes the low-cost approach, but he wonders if licensing would give TopDog enough participation and control to successfully develop its international presence. As another day winds down, Weiner and Carpenter are no closer to a decision about global expansion than they were when the sun came up.

CASE FOR ANALYSIS   *Rhodes Industries*

David Javier was reviewing the consulting firm's proposed changes in organization structure for Rhodes Industries (RI). As Javier read the report, he wondered whether the changes recommended by the consultants would do more harm than good for Rhodes Industries. Javier had been president of RI for 18 months, and he was keenly aware of the organizational and coordination problems that needed to be corrected in order for RI to improve profits and growth in its international businesses.

Company Background

Rhodes Industries was started in the 1950s in Southern Ontario, Canada, by Robert Rhodes, an engineer who was an entrepreneur at heart. He started the business by first making pipe and then glass for industrial uses, but as soon as the initial business was established, he quickly branched into new areas such as industrial sealants, coatings, and cleaners, and even into manufacturing mufflers and parts for the trucking industry. Much of this expansion occurred by acquiring small firms in Canada and the United States during the 1960s. RI had a conglomerate-type structure with rather diverse subsidiaries scattered around North America, all reporting directly to the Ontario headquarters. Each subsidiary was a complete local business and was allowed to operate independently so long as it contributed profits to RI.

During the 1970s and 1980s, the president at the time, Clifford Michaels, brought a strong international focus to RI. His strategy was to acquire small companies worldwide with the belief they could be formed into a cohesive unit that would bring RI synergies and profits through low cost of manufacturing and by serving businesses in international markets. Some of RI's businesses were acquired simply because they were available at a good price, and RI found itself in new lines of business such as consumer products (paper and envelopes) and electrical equipment (switchboards, lightbulbs, and security systems), in addition to its previous lines of business. Most of these products had local brand names or were manufactured for major international companies such as General Electric or Corning Glass.

During the 1990s, a new president of RI, Sean Rhodes, the grandson of the founder, took over the business and adopted the strategy of focusing RI on three lines of business—Industrial Products,

Consumer Products, and Electronics. He led the acquisition of more international businesses that fit these three categories, and divested a few businesses that didn't fit. Each of the three divisions had manufacturing plants as well as marketing and distribution systems in North America, Asia, and Europe.

The Industrial Products division included pipe, glass, industrial sealants and coatings, cleaning equipment, and truck parts. The Electronics Division included specialty lightbulbs, switchboards, computer chips, and resistors and capacitors for original equipment manufacturers. Consumer Products included dishes and glassware, paper and envelopes, and pencils and pens.

Structure

In 2002 David Javier replaced Sean Rhodes as president. He was very concerned about whether a new organization structure was needed for RI. The current structure was based on three major geographic areas—North America, Asia, and Europe—as illustrated in Exhibit 6.10. The various autonomous units within those regions reported to the office of the regional vice president. When several units existed in a single country, one of the subsidiary presidents was also responsible for coordinating the various businesses in that country, but most coordination was done through the regional vice president. Businesses were largely independent, which provided flexibility and motivation for the subsidiary managers.

The headquarters functional departments in Ontario are rather small. The three central departments—Corporate Relations and Public Affairs, Finance and Acquisitions, and Legal & Administrative—serve the corporate business worldwide. Other functions such as human resource management, new product development, marketing, and manufacturing all exist within individual subsidiaries and there is little coordination of these functions across geographical regions. Each business devises its own way to develop, manufacture, and market its products in its own country and region.

Organizational Problems

The problems Javier faces at RI, which are confirmed in the report on his desk, fall into three areas. First, each subsidiary acts as an independent business, using its own reporting systems and acting to maximize its own profits. This autonomy makes it increasingly hard to consolidate financial reports worldwide, and to gain the efficiencies of uniform information and reporting systems.

EXHIBIT 6.10   *Rhodes Industries Organization Chart*

Second, major strategic decisions are made to benefit individual businesses, or for a country's or region's local interests. Local projects and profits receive more time and resources than do projects that benefit RI worldwide. For example, an electronics manufacturer in Singapore refused to increase production of chips and capacitors for sale in the U.K. because it would hurt the bottom line of the Singapore operation. However, the economies of scale in Singapore would more than offset shipping costs to the U.K. and would enable RI to close expensive manufacturing facilities in Europe, increasing RI's efficiency and profits.

Third, there has been no transfer of technology, new product ideas, or other innovations within RI. For example, a cost-saving technology for manufacturing lightbulbs in Canada has been ignored in Asia and Europe. A technical innovation that provides homeowners with cell-phone access to home security systems developed in Europe has been ignored in North America. The report on Javier's desk stresses that RI is failing to disperse important innovations throughout the organization. These ignored innovations could provide significant improvements in both manufacturing and marketing worldwide. The report said, "No one at RI understands all the products and locations in a way that allows RI to capitalize on manufacturing improvements and new product opportunities." The report also said that better worldwide coordination would reduce RI's costs by 7 percent each year and increase market potential by 10 percent. These numbers were too big to ignore.

Recommended Structure

The report from the consultant recommended that RI try one of two options for improving RI's structure. The first alternative is to create a new international department at headquarters with the responsibility to coordinate technology transfer and product manufacturing and marketing worldwide (Exhibit 6.11). This department would have a Product Director for each major product line—Industrial, Consumer, and Electronics—who would have authority to coordinate activities and innovations worldwide. Each Director would have a team that would travel to each region and carry information on innovations and improvements to subsidiaries in other parts of the world.

EXHIBIT 6.11   *Proposed Product Director Structure*

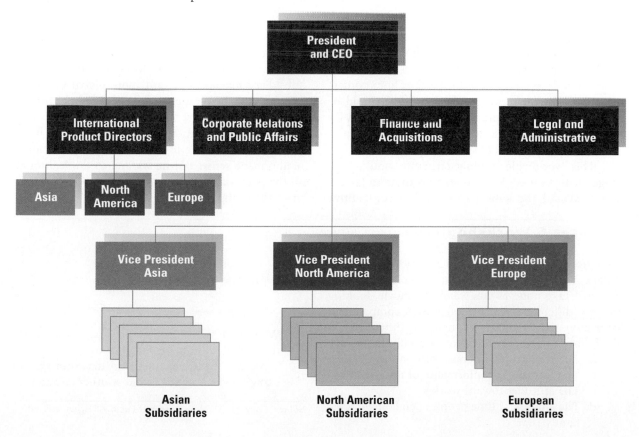

EXHIBIT 6.12   *Proposed Worldwide Business Manager Structure*

The second recommendation is to reorganize into a worldwide product structure, as shown in Exhibit 6.12. All subsidiaries worldwide associated with a product line would report to the product line Business Manager. The Business Manager and staff would be responsible for developing business strategies and for coordinating all manufacturing efficiencies and product developments worldwide for its product line.

This worldwide product structure would be a huge change for RI. Many questions came to Javier's mind. Would the subsidiaries still be competitive and adaptive in local markets if forced to coordinate with other subsidiaries around the world? Would Business Managers be able to change the habits of subsidiary managers toward more global behavior? Would it be a better idea to appoint Product Director coordinators as a first step, or jump to the Business Manager product structure right away? Javier had a hunch that the move to worldwide product coordination made sense, but he wanted to think through all the potential problems and how RI would implement the changes.

Chapter 6 Workshop *Comparing Cultures*

As a group, rent a video of a foreign movie (or, alternately, go to the cinema when a foreign movie is shown). Take notes as you watch the movie, looking for any differences in cultural norms compared to your own. For example, are there any differences in the following compared to your own cultural norms:

    a. The way people interact with one another
    b. The formality or informality of relationships
    c. The attitudes toward work
    d. The amount of time people spend on work vs. family

    e. The connection to family
    f. How people have fun

Questions
1. What were the key differences you observed in the movie's culture versus your own?
2. What are the advantages and disadvantages of using movies to understand another culture?

Notes

1. Stanley Holmes with Drake Bennett, Kate Carlisle, and Chester Dawson, "Planet Starbucks," *BusinessWeek* (September 9, 2002), 100–110.

2. Jim Rose and Salim Teja, "The Americans Are Coming!" *Business 2.0* (May 2000), 215; and Mohanbir Sawhney and Sumant Mandal, "What Kind of Global Organization Should You Build?" *Business 2.0* (May 2000), 213.

3. This discussion is based heavily on Christopher A. Bartlett and Sumantra Ghoshal, *Transnational Management: Text, Cases, and Readings in Cross-Border Management*, 3rd ed. (Boston: Irwin McGraw-Hill, 2000), 94–96; and Anil K. Gupta and Vijay Govindarajan, "Converting Global Presence into Global Competitive Advantage," *Academy of Management Executive* 15, no. 2 (2001), 45–56.

4. Todd Zaun, Gregory L. White, Norihiko Shirouzu, and Scott Miller, "More Mileage. Auto Makers Look for Another Edge Farther from Home," *The Wall Street Journal* (July 31, 2002), A1, A8.

5. Based on Nancy J. Adler, *International Dimensions of Organizational Behavior*, 4th ed. (Cincinnati, Ohio: South-Western, 2002), Theodore T. Herbert, "Strategy and Multinational Organizational Structure: An Interorganizational Relationships Perspective," *Academy of Management Review* 9 (1984), 259–271; and Laura K. Rickey, "International Expansion—U.S. Corporations: Strategy, Stages of Development, and Structure" (unpublished manuscript, Vanderbilt University, 1991).

6. Michael E. Porter, "Changing Patterns of International Competition," *California Management Review* 28 (Winter 1986) 9–40.

7. William J. Holstein, "The Stateless Corporation," *BusinessWeek* (May 14, 1990), 98–115.

8. Debra Sparks, "Partners," *BusinessWeek*, Special Report: Corporate Finance (October 25, 1999), 106–112.

9. David Lei and John W. Slocum, Jr., "Global Strategic Alliances: Payoffs and Pitfalls," *Organizational Dynamics* (Winter 1991), 17–29.

10. Joseph Weber with Amy Barrett, "Volatile Combos," *BusinessWeek*, Special Report: Corporate Finance (October 25, 1999), 122; and Lei and Slocum, "Global Strategic Alliances."

11. Stratford Sherman, "Are Strategic Alliances Working?" *Fortune* (September 21, 1992), 77–78; David Lei, "Strategies for Global Competition," *Long-Range Planning* 22 (1989), 102-109.

12. Cyrus F. Freidheim, Jr., *The Trillion-Dollar Enterprise: How the Alliance Revolution Will Transform Global Business* (New York: Perseus Books, 1998).

13. Ron Grover and Richard Siklos, "When Old Foes Need Each Other" *BusinessWeek*, Special Report: Corporate Finance (October 25, 1999), 114, 118.

14. Lei, "Strategies for Global Competition"; Sherman, "Are Strategic Alliances Working?"

15. Sparks, "Partners."

16. Sparks, "Partners."

17. Kevin Kelly and Otis Port, with James Treece, Gail DeGeorge, and Zachary Schiller, "Learning from Japan," *BusinessWeek*, (January 27, 1992), 52-60; Gregory G. Dess, Abdul M. A. Rasheed, Kevin J. McLaughlin, and Richard L. Priem, "The New Corporate Architecture," *Academy of Management Executive* 9, no. 3 (1995), 7–20.

18. Lawrence A. Fisher, "STMicroelectronics: The Metaphysics of a Metanational Pioneer," *Strategy & Business* 28 (Third Quarter 2002), 81–89.

19. Yves Doz, José Santos, and Peter Williamson, *From Global to Metanational: How Companies Win in the Knowledge Economy* (Boston: Harvard Business School Press, 2001), 13–15.

20. Kenichi Ohmae, "Managing in a Borderless World," *Harvard Business Review* (May–June 1989), 152–161.

21. Cesare R. Mainardi, Martin Salva, and Muir Sanderson, "Label of Origin: Made on Earth," *Strategy & Business* 15 (Second Quarter 1999), 42–53; Joann S. Lublin, "Place vs. Product: It's Tough to Choose a Management Model," *The Wall Street Journal* (June 27, 2001), A1, A4.

22. Mainardi, Salva, and Sanderson, "Label of Origin."

23. Gupta and Govindarajan, "Converting Global Presence into Global Competitive Advantage."

24. José Pla-Barber, "From Stopford and Wells's Model to Bartlett and Ghoshal's Typology: New Empirical Evidence," *Management International Review* 42, no. 2 (2002), 141–156.

25. Sumantra Ghoshal and Nitin Nohria, "Horses for Courses: Organizational Forms for Multinational Corporations," *Sloan Management Review*

(Winter 1993), 23–35; Roderick E. White and Thomas A. Poynter, "Organizing for Worldwide Advantage," *Business Quarterly* (Summer 1989), 84–89.

26. Robert J. Kramer, *Organizing for Global Competitiveness: The Country Subsidiary Design* (New York: The Conference Board, 1997), 12.

27. Laura B. Pincus and James A. Belohlav, "Legal Issues in Multinational Business: To Play the Game, You Have to Know the Rules," *Academy of Management Executive* 10, no. 3 (1996), 52–61.

28. John D. Daniels, Robert A. Pitts, and Marietta J. Tretter, "Strategy and Structure of U.S. Multinationals: An Exploratory Study," *Academy of Management Journal* 27 (1984), 292–307.

29. Robert J. Kramer, *Organizing for Global Competitiveness: The Product Design* (New York: The Conference Board, 1994).

30. Robert J. Kramer, *Organizing for Global Competitiveness: The Business Unit Design* (New York: The Conference Board, 1995), 18–19.

31. Based on Robert J. Kramer, *Organizing for Global Competitiveness: The Geographic Design* (New York: The Conference Board, 1993).

32. Kramer, *Organizing for Global Competitiveness: The Geographic Design*, 29–31.

33. William Taylor, "The Logic of Global Business: An Interview with ABB's Percy Barnevik," *Harvard Business Review* (March–April 1991), 91–105; Carla Rappaport, "A Tough Swede Invades the U.S.," *Fortune* (January 29, 1992), 76–79; Raymond E. Miles and Charles C. Snow, "The New Network Firm: A Spherical Structure Built on a Human Investment Philosophy," *Organizational Dynamics* (Spring 1995), 5–18; Manfred F. R. Kets de Vries, "Making a Giant Dance," *Across the Board* (October 1994), 27–32.

34. Kramer, *Organizing for Global Competitiveness: The Business Unit Design*, 30–32.

35. Gupta and Govindarajan, "Converting Global Presence into Global Competitive Advantage."

36. Jonathan Friedland and Louise Lee, "The Wal-Mart Way Sometimes Gets Lost in Translation Overseas," *The Wall Street Journal* (October 8, 1997), A1, A12.

37. Robert Frank, "Withdrawal Pains: In Paddies of Vietnam, Americans Once Again Land in a Quagmire," *The Wall Street Journal* (April 21, 2000), A1, A6.

38. The discussion of these challenges is based on Bartlett and Ghoshal, *Transnational Management*.

39. Ian Katz and Elisabeth Malkin, "Battle for the Latin American Net," *BusinessWeek* (November 1, 1999), 194–200; and Pamela Drukerman and Nick Wingfield, "Lost in Translation: AOL's Big Assault in Latin America Hits Snags in Brazil," *The Wall Street Journal* (July 11, 2000), A1.

40. Shirley Leung, "McHaute Cuisine: Armchairs, TVs, and Espresso—Is It McDonald's?" *The Wall Street Journal* (August 30, 2002), A1, A6.

41. P. Ingrassia, "Industry is Shopping Abroad for Good Ideas to Apply to Products," *The Wall Street Journal* (April 29, 1985), A1.

42. Based on Gupta and Govindarajan, "Converting Global Presence into Global Competitive Advantage."

43. Vijay Govindarajan and Anil K. Gupta, "Building an Effective Global Business Team," *MIT Sloan Management Review* 42, no. 4 (Summer 2001), 63–71.

44. Charlene Marmer Solomon, "Building Teams Across Borders," *Global Workforce* (November 1998), 12–17.

45. Charles C. Snow, Scott A. Snell, Sue Canney Davison, and Donald C. Hambrick, "Use Transnational Teams to Globalize Your Company," *Organizational Dynamics* 24, no. 4 (Spring 1996), 50–67.

46. Jane Pickard, "Control Freaks Need Not Apply," *People Management* (February 5, 1998), 49.

47. Snow et al., "Use Transnational Teams to Globalize Your Company."

48. Robert J. Kramer, *Organizing for Global Competitiveness: The Corporate Headquarters Design* (New York: The Conference Board, 1999).

49. These roles are based on Christopher A. Bartlett and Sumantra Ghoshal, *Managing Across Borders: The Transnational Solution*, 2nd ed. (Boston: Harvard Business School Press, 1998), Chapter 11, 231–249.

50. See Jay Galbraith, "Building Organizations Around the Global Customer," *Ivey Business Journal* (September–October 2001), 17–24, for a discussion of both formal and informal lateral networks used in multinational companies.

51. Geert Hofstede, "The Interaction Between National and Organizational Value Systems," *Journal of Management Studies* 22 (1985), 347–357; Geert Hofstede, *Cultures and Organizations: Software of the Mind* (London: McGraw-Hill, 1991).

52. This discussion is based on "Culture and Organization," Reading 2-2 in Christopher A. Bartlett and Sumantra Ghoshal, *Transnational Management*, 3rd ed. (Boston: Irwin McGraw-Hill, 2000), 191–216, excerpted from Susan Schneider and Jean-Louis Barsoux, *Managing Across Cultures* (London: Prentice-Hall, 1997).

53. Based on Bartlett and Ghoshal, *Managing Across Borders*, 181–201.

54. Sumantra Ghoshal and Christopher Bartlett, "The Multinational Corporation as an Inter-organizational Network," *Academy of Management Review* 15 (1990), 603–625.

55. The description of the transnational organization is based on Bartlett and Ghoshal, *Transnational Management* and *Managing Across Borders*.

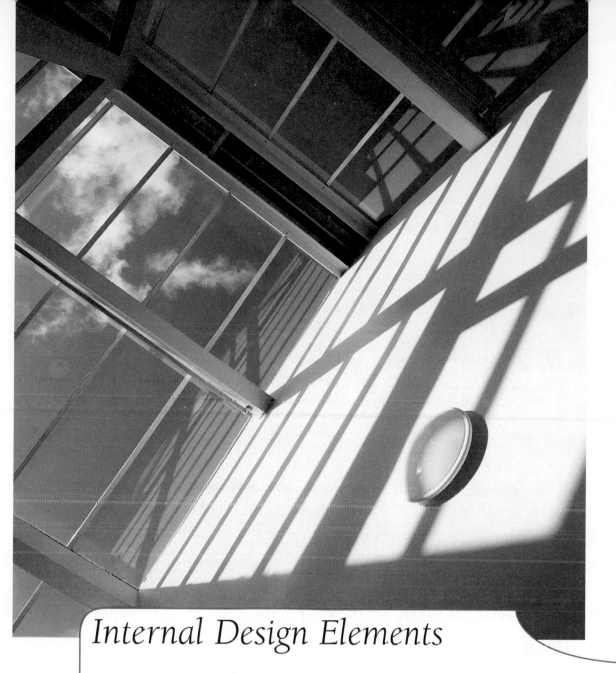

Internal Design Elements

part 4

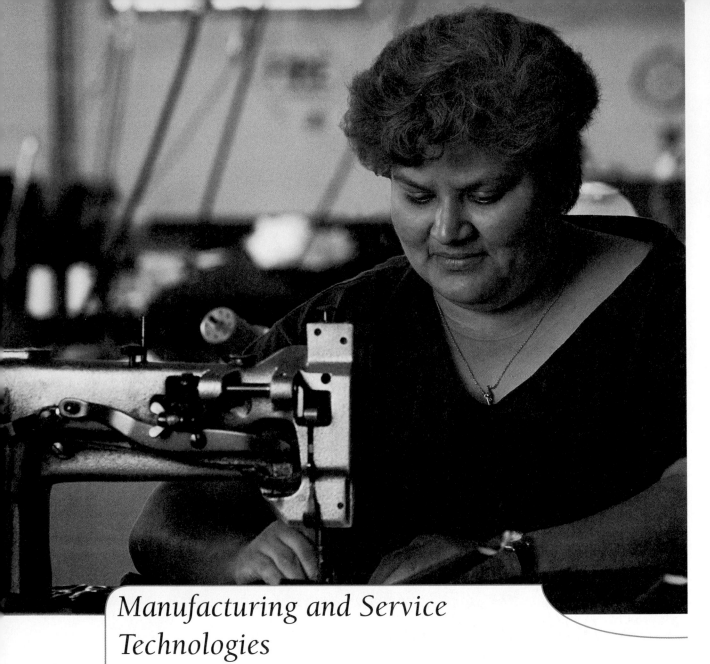

Manufacturing and Service Technologies

chapter 7

French Rags

In 1978, Brenda French started a scarf-making company in a spare bedroom of her home. Ten years later, leading department stores like Neiman Marcus, Lord & Taylor, and Bloomingdale's were showcasing her line of custom-made knitwear. French Rags seemed, to outsiders, like a booming success, but Brenda French knew better. Her business was beset by a multitude of problems and had difficulty competing against mass manufacturers with greater resources selling at lower prices. French Rags could offer customers the variety they wanted but production output was limited and costs were high.

Faced with closing the business, French began looking into new technology that offered a dazzling possibility: mass customization. She invested in a German-made Stoll knitting machine that combines new technology and timeless craft by using thousands of precisely angled needles to make clothes one stitch at a time. Today, the factory is entirely computerized. In-house computer-aided design and manufacturing software smoothly translates French's original designs into finished garments. The technology enables French Rags to produce custom-made garments at virtually the same speed—and the same cost—as the cookie-cutter offerings of mass producers. Custom software produces knit-by-numbers templates that enable fast and easy switching from one garment to another. About one hundred employees at French Rags's Los Angeles factory augment the automated knitting line with the necessary human touch. The next step French took was to create a sales force of her most affluent customers, who sell French Rags out of their homes . . . or at trunk shows held at luxury hotels. After a customer places an order, choosing her styles, fabrics, colors, and trim variations, individual measurements are taken and the order is faxed or sent over the Internet to the French Rags factory. The custom-made garments are shipped directly to the customer's home within six weeks. In addition, the company now has stores in Los Angeles, Santa Fe, and Austin, where customers get the same personal one-on-one guidance from a wardrobe consultant. An online store is also in the works.

Combining new technology with new ways of thinking turned Brenda French's small company into a full-line clothing manufacturer with more than $8 million in sales, and put French Rags on the cutting edge of a revolution in manufacturing.[1]

French Rags is among the growing number of small companies that are combining craftsmanship with advanced manufacturing technology. These companies, sometimes called *craftories*, produce individualized products and respond quickly to the specific needs of retailers and customers. Overall, manufacturing has been on the decline in the United States and other developed countries, with services becoming an increasingly greater part of the economy. However, small companies such as French Rags have led the way in gaining a new competitive edge in manufacturing.

This chapter explores both service and manufacturing technologies and how technology is related to organizational structure. **Technology** refers to the work processes, techniques, machines, and actions used to transform organizational inputs (materials, information, ideas) into outputs (products and services).[2]

Technology is an organization's production process and includes work procedures as well as machinery.

An organization's **core technology** is the work process that is directly related to the organization's mission, such as teaching in a high school, medical services in a health clinic, or manufacturing at General Motors. For example, at French Rags the core technology begins with raw materials (e.g., the 30,000 lbs. of yarn that French Rags keeps in stock). Employees take action on the raw material to make a change in it (they knit the yarn into fabric and manufacture garments), thus transforming the raw material into the output of the organization (custom-made clothing). For a service organization like FedEx, the core technology includes the production equipment (sorting machines, airplanes) and procedures for delivering overnight mail. In addition, as at companies like FedEx and French Rags, computers and new information technology have revolutionized work processes in both manufacturing and service organizations. The specific impact of new information technology on organizations will be described in Chapter 8.

Exhibit 7.1 features an example of core technology for a manufacturing plant. Note how the core technology consists of raw material inputs, a transformation work process (milling, inspection, assembly) that changes and adds value to the raw material and produces the ultimate product or service output that is sold to consumers in the environment. In today's large, complex organizations, core work processes vary widely and sometimes can be hard to pinpoint. A core technology can be partly understood by examining the raw materials flowing into the organization,[3] the variability of work activities,[4] the degree to which the production process is mechanized,[5] the extent to which one task depends on another in the workflow,[6] or the number of new product or service outputs.[7]

An important theme in this chapter is how core technology influences organizational structure. Thus, understanding core technology provides insight into how an organization can be structured for efficient performance.[8]

EXHIBIT 7.1   *Core Transformation Process for a Manufacturing Company*

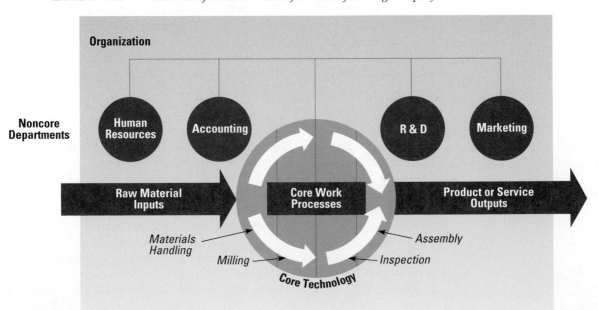

Organizations are made up of many departments, each of which may use a different work process (technology) to provide a good or service within an organization. A **noncore technology** is a department work process that is important to the organization but is not directly related to its primary mission. In Exhibit 7.1, noncore work processes are illustrated by the departments of human resources, accounting, R&D, and marketing. Thus, research and development transforms ideas into new products, and marketing transforms inventory into sales, each using a somewhat different kind of work process. The output of the HR department is people to work in the organization, and accounting produces accurate statements about the organization's financial condition.

PURPOSE OF THIS CHAPTER

In this chapter, we will discuss both core and noncore work processes and their relationship to designing organization structure. The nature of the organization's work processes must be considered in designing the organization for maximum efficiency and effectiveness. The optimum organization design is based on a variety of elements. Exhibit 7.2 illustrates that forces affecting organization design come from both outside and inside the organization. External strategic needs, such as environmental conditions, strategic direction, and organizational goals, create top-down pressure for designing the organization in such a way as to fit the environment and accomplish goals. These pressures on design have been discussed in previous chapters. However decisions about design should also take into consideration pressures from the bottom up—from the work processes that are performed to produce the organization's products or services. The operational work processes will influence the structural design associated with both the core technology and noncore departments. Thus, the subject with which this chapter is concerned is, "How should the organization be designed to accommodate and facilitate its operational work processes?"

The remainder of the chapter will unfold as follows. First, we will examine how the technology for the organization as a whole influences organization

EXHIBIT 7.2   *Pressures Affecting Design Decisions*

Source: Based on David A. Nadler and Michael L. Tushman, with Mark B. Nadler, *Competing by Design: The Power of Organizational Architecture* (New York: Oxford University Press, 1997), 54.

structure and design. This discussion will include both manufacturing and service technologies. Next, we will examine differences in departmental technologies and how the technologies influence the design and management of organizational subunits. Third, we will explore how interdependence—flow of materials and information—among departments affects structure.

CORE ORGANIZATION MANUFACTURING TECHNOLOGY

Manufacturing technologies include traditional manufacturing processes and new flexible manufacturing systems.

MANUFACTURING FIRMS

Woodward's Study. The first and most influential study of manufacturing technology was conducted by Joan Woodward, a British industrial sociologist. Her research began as a field study of management principles in south Essex. The prevailing management wisdom at the time (1950s) was contained in what was known as universal principles of management. These principles were "one best way" prescriptions that effective organizations were expected to adopt. Woodward surveyed one hundred manufacturing firms firsthand to learn how they were organized.[9] She and her research team visited each firm, interviewed managers, examined company records, and observed the manufacturing operations. Her data included a wide range of structural characteristics (span of control, levels of management) and dimensions of management style (written versus verbal communications, use of rewards) and the type of manufacturing process. Data were also obtained that reflected commercial success of the firms.

Woodward developed a scale and organized the firms according to technical complexity of the manufacturing process. **Technical complexity** represents the extent of mechanization of the manufacturing process. High technical complexity means most of the work is performed by machines. Low technical complexity means workers play a larger role in the production process. Woodward's scale of technical complexity originally had ten categories, as summarized in Exhibit 7.3. These categories were further consolidated into three basic technology groups:

- *Group I: Small-batch and unit production.* These firms tend to be job shop operations that manufacture and assemble small orders to meet specific needs of customers. Custom work is the norm. **Small-batch production** relies heavily on the human operator; it is thus not highly mechanized. Rockwell Collins, which makes electronic equipment for airplanes and other products, provides an example of small-batch manufacturing. Although sophisticated computerized machinery is used for part of the production process, final assembly requires highly skilled human operators to ensure absolute reliability of products used by aerospace companies, defense contractors, and the U.S. military. The company's workforce is divided into manufacturing cells, some of which produce only ten units a day. In one plant, 140 workers build Joint Tactical Information Distribution Systems, for managing battlefield communications from a circling plane, at a rate of ten a month.[10]

- *Group II: Large-batch and mass production.* **Large-batch production** is a manufacturing process characterized by long production runs of standardized parts. Output often goes into inventory from which orders are filled, because

EXHIBIT 7.3   *Woodward's Classification of One Hundred British Firms According to Their Systems of Production*

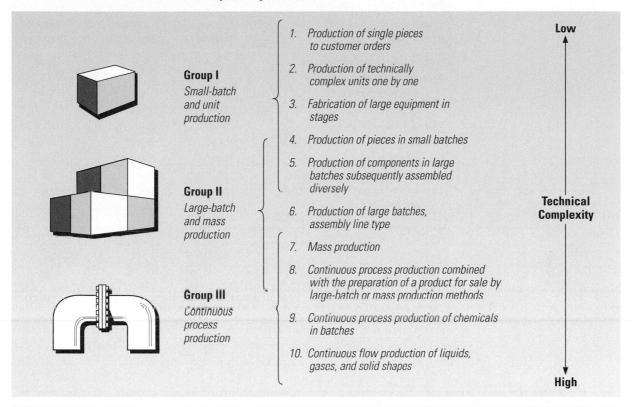

Low

Group I
Small-batch and unit production

1. Production of single pieces to customer orders

2. Production of technically complex units one by one

3. Fabrication of large equipment in stages

4. Production of pieces in small batches

5. Production of components in large batches subsequently assembled diversely

Group II
Large-batch and mass production

Technical Complexity

6. Production of large batches, assembly line type

7. Mass production

8. Continuous process production combined with the preparation of a product for sale by large-batch or mass production methods

Group III
Continuous process production

9. Continuous process production of chemicals in batches

10. Continuous flow production of liquids, gases, and solid shapes

High

Source: Adapted from Joan Woodward, *Management and Technology* (London: Her Majesty's Stationery Office, 1958). Used with permission of Her Britannic Majesty's Stationery Office.

customers do not have special needs. Examples include most assembly lines, such as for automobiles or trailer homes.

- *Group III: Continuous process production.* In **continuous process production**, the entire process is mechanized. There is no starting and stopping. This represents mechanization and standardization one step beyond those in an assembly line. Automated machines control the continuous process, and outcomes are highly predictable. Examples would include chemical plants, oil refineries, liquor producers, pharmaceuticals, and nuclear power plants.

Using this classification of technology, Woodward's data made sense. A few of her key findings are given in Exhibit 7.4. The number of management levels and the manager/total personnel ratio, for example, show definite increases as technical complexity increases from unit production to continuous process. This indicates that greater management intensity is needed to manage complex technology. Direct/indirect labor ratio decreases with technical complexity because more indirect workers are required to support and maintain complex machinery. Other characteristics, such as span of control, formalized procedures, and centralization, are high for mass production technology because the work is standardized but low for other technologies. Unit production and continuous process technologies require highly skilled workers to run the machines and verbal communication to adapt to changing conditions. Mass production is standardized

EXHIBIT 7.4   *Relationship Between Technical Complexity and Structural Characteristics*

Structural Characteristic	Technology		
	Unit Production	Mass Production	Continuous Process
Number of management levels	3	4	6
Supervisor span of control	23	48	15
Direct/indirect labor ratio	9:1	4:1	1:1
Manager/total personnel ratio	Low	Medium	High
Workers' skill level	High	Low	High
Formalized procedures	Low	High	Low
Centralization	Low	High	Low
Amount of verbal communication	High	Low	High
Amount of written communication	Low	High	Low
Overall structure	Organic	Mechanistic	Organic

Source: Joan Woodward, *Industrial Organization: Theory and Practice* (London: Oxford University Press, 1965). Used with permission.

and routinized, so few exceptions occur, little verbal communication is needed, and employees are less skilled.

Overall, the management systems in both unit production and continuous process technology are characterized as organic, as defined in Chapter 4. They are more free-flowing and adaptive, with fewer procedures and less standardization. Mass production, however, is mechanistic, with standardized jobs and formalized procedures. Woodward's discovery about technology thus provided substantial new insight into the causes of organization structure. In Joan Woodward's own words, "Different technologies impose different kinds of demands on individuals and organizations, and those demands had to be met through an appropriate structure."[11]

Strategy, Technology, and Performance. Another portion of Woodward's study examined the success of the firms along dimensions such as profitability, market share, stock price, and reputation. As indicated in Chapter 2, the measurement of effectiveness is not simple or precise, but Woodward was able to rank firms on a scale of commercial success according to whether they displayed above-average, average, or below-average performance on strategic objectives.

Woodward compared the structure-technology relationship against commercial success and discovered that successful firms tended to be those that had complementary structures and technologies. Many of the organizational characteristics of the successful firms were near the average of their technology category, as shown in Exhibit 7.4. Below-average firms tended to depart from the structural characteristics for their technology type. Another conclusion was that structural characteristics could be interpreted as clustering into organic and mechanistic management systems. Successful small-batch and continuous process organizations had organic structures, and successful mass production organizations had mechanistic structures. Subsequent research has replicated her findings.[12]

What this illustrates for today's companies is that strategy, structure, and technology need to be aligned, especially when competitive conditions change.[13] Computer makers had to realign strategy, structure, and technology to compete

BRIEFCASE

As an organization manager, keep this guideline in mind:

When adopting a new technology, realign strategy, structure, and management processes to achieve top performance.

with Dell in the personal computer market. Manufacturers such as IBM that once tried to differentiate their products and charge a premium price switched to a low-cost strategy, adopted new technology to enable them to customize PCs, revamped supply chains, and began outsourcing manufacturing to other companies that could do the job more efficiently.

Today, many manufacturers farm production out to other companies. Printronix, a publicly owned company in Irvine, California, however, has gone in the opposite direction and achieved success by carefully aligning technology, structure, and management processes to achieve strategic objectives.

In Practice

PRINTRONIX

Printronix makes 60 percent of the electromechanical line printers used in the world's factories and warehouses. To maintain the reliability that makes Printronix products worth $2,600 to $26,000 each, the company does almost everything in-house—from design, to making hundreds of parts, to final assembly, to research on new materials. In the 1970s, Printronix began by making a high-speed line printer that could run with the minicomputers then being used on factory floors. Though it was not the first line printer, it was rugged enough to use in industrial settings and incorporated pioneering software that could print graphics such as charts, graphs, and bar code labels.

Printronix started as a traditional mass production operation, but the company faced a tremendous challenge in the late 1980s when factories began switching from minicomputers to PCs and servers. Within two years, sales and profits plunged, and founder and CEO Robert A. Kleist realized Printronix needed new ideas, new technology, and new methods to adapt to a world where printers were no longer stand-alone products but parts of emerging enterprise networks. One change Kleist made was to switch from mass-producing printers that were kept in inventory to a small-batch or unit production system that built printers to order. Products were redesigned and assembly work reorganized so that small groups of workers could configure each printer to a customer's specific needs. Many workers had to be trained in new skills and to take more responsibility than they had on the traditional assembly line. Highly skilled workers were needed to make some of the precision parts needed in the new machines as well. Besides internal restructuring, Kleist decided to pick up on the outsourcing trend and go after the computer industry's factory printer business, winning orders to produce under the labels of IBM, Hewlett-Packard, and Siemens. Kleist doubled the R&D budget to be sure the company kept pace with new technological developments. In 2000, Printronix began building thermal printers as well as specialized laser printers that can print adhesive bar-code labels at lightning speed.

By making changes in technology, design, and management methods, Printronix has continued to meet its strategic objectives of differentiating its products from the competition. "The restructuring made us a stronger company in both manufacturing and engineering," says Kleist.[14]

Failing to adopt appropriate new technologies to support strategy, or adopting a new technology and failing to realign strategy to match it, can lead to poor performance. Today's increased global competition means more volatile markets, shorter product life cycles, and more sophisticated and knowledgeable consumers; and flexibility to meet these new demands has become a strategic imperative for many companies.[15] Manufacturing companies can adopt new technologies to support the strategy of flexibility. However, organization structures and management processes must also be realigned, as a highly mechanistic structure hampers flexibility and prevents the company from reaping the benefits of the new technology.[16] Managers should always remember that the technological and human systems of an organization are intertwined. This chapter's Book Mark provides a different perspective on technology by looking at the dangers of failing to understand the human role in managing technological advances.

FLEXIBLE MANUFACTURING

In the years since Woodward's research, new developments have occurred in manufacturing technology. New manufacturing technologies include robots, numerically controlled machine tools, and computerized software for product design, engineering analysis, and remote control of machinery. The ultimate automated factories are referred to as **flexible manufacturing systems** (FMS).[17] Also called *computer-integrated manufacturing*, *smart factories*, *advanced manufacturing technology, agile manufacturing,* or *the factory of the future*, FMS links together manufacturing components that previously stood alone. Thus, robots, machines, product design, and engineering analysis are coordinated by a single computer.

The result has already revolutionized the shop floor, enabling large factories to deliver a wide range of custom-made products at low mass production costs.[18] As illustrated by the chapter opening case, flexible manufacturing also enables small companies to go toe-to-toe with large factories and low-cost foreign competitors. Techknits, Inc., a small manufacturer located in New York City, competes successfully against low-cost sweater-makers in the Far East by using $8 million worth of computerized looms and other machinery. The work of designing sweaters, which once took two days, can now be accomplished in two hours. Looms operate round-the-clock and crank out 60,000 sweaters a week, enabling Techknits to fill customer orders faster than foreign competitors.[19]

Flexible manufacturing is typically the result of three subcomponents.

- *Computer-aided design (CAD).* Computers are used to assist in the drafting, design, and engineering of new parts. Designers guide their computers to draw specified configurations on the screen, including dimensions and component details. Hundreds of design alternatives can be explored, as can scaled-up or scaled-down versions of the original.[20]
- *Computer-aided manufacturing (CAM).* Computer-controlled machines in materials handling, fabrication, production, and assembly greatly increase the speed at which items can be manufactured. CAM also permits a production line to shift rapidly from producing one product to any variety of other products by changing the instruction tapes or software in the computer. CAM enables the production line to quickly honor customer requests for changes in product design and product mix.[21]
- *Integrated Information Network.* A computerized system links all aspects of the firm—including accounting, purchasing, marketing, inventory control, design, production, and so forth. This system, based on a common data and information base, enables managers to make decisions and direct the manufacturing process in a truly integrated fashion.

The combination of CAD, CAM, and integrated information systems represents the highest level of flexible manufacturing. A new product can be designed on the computer, and a prototype can be produced untouched by human hands. The

BOOK MARK 7.0   *Have You Read This Book?*

Inviting Disaster: Lessons from the Edge of Technology
By James R. Chiles

Dateline: Paris, France, July 25, 2000. Less than two minutes after Air France Concorde Flight 4590 departs Charles DeGaulle Airport, something goes horribly wrong. Trailing fire and billowing black smoke, the huge plane rolls left and crashes into a hotel, killing all 109 people aboard and 4 more on the ground. It's just one of the technological disasters James R. Chiles describes in his book, *Inviting Disaster: Lessons from the Edge of Technology*, which was published before the 2003 crash of the space shuttle *Columbia*. One of Chiles's main points is that advancing technology makes possible the creation of machines that strain the human ability to understand and safely operate them. Moreover, he asserts, the margins of safety are drawing thinner as the energies we harness become more powerful and the time between invention and use grows shorter. Chiles believes that today, "for every twenty books on the pursuit of success, we need a book on how things fly into tiny pieces despite enormous effort and the very highest ideals."

HOW THINGS FLY INTO PIECES: EXAMPLES OF SYSTEM FRACTURES

Chiles uses historical calamities such as the sinking of the *Titanic* and modern disasters such as the explosion of the space shuttle *Challenger* to illustrate the dangers of *system fracture*, a chain of events that involves human error in response to malfunctions in complex machinery. Disaster begins when one weak point links up with others.

- *Sultana* (American steamboat on the Mississippi River near Memphis, Tennessee), April 25, 1865. The boat, designed to carry a maximum of 460 people, was carrying more than 2,000 Union ex-prisoners north—as well as 200 additional crew and passengers—when three of the four boilers exploded, killing 1,800 people. One of the boilers had been temporarily patched to cover a crack,

but the patch was too thin. Operators failed to compensate by resetting the safety valve.

- *Piper Alpha* (offshore drilling rig in the North Sea), July 6, 1988. The offshore platform processed large volumes of natural gas from other rigs via pipe. A daytime work crew, which didn't complete repairing a gas-condensate pump, relayed a verbal message to the next shift, but workers turned the pump on anyway. When the temporary seal on the pump failed, a fire trapped crewmen with no escape route, killing 167 crew and rescue workers.

- *Union Carbide (India) Ltd.* (release of highly toxic chemicals into a community), Bhopal, Mahdya Pradesh, India, December 3, 1984. There are three competing theories for how water got into a storage tank, creating a violent reaction that sent highly toxic methyl isocyanate for herbicides into the environment, causing an estimated 7,000 deaths: (1) poor safety maintenance, (2) sabotage, or (3) worker error.

WHAT CAUSES SYSTEM FRACTURES?

There is a veritable catalog of causes that lead to such disasters, from design errors, insufficient operator training, and poor planning to greed and mismanagement. Chiles wrote this book as a reminder that technology takes us into risky locales, whether it be outer space, up a 2,000-foot tower, or into a chemical processing plant. Chiles also cites examples of disasters that were averted by quick thinking and appropriate response. To help prevent system fractures, managers can create organizations where people throughout the company are expert at picking out the subtle signals of real problems—and where they are empowered to report them and take prompt action.

Inviting Disaster: Lessons from the Edge of Technology, by James R. Chiles, is published by HarperBusiness.

ideal factory can switch quickly from one product to another, working fast and with precision, without paperwork or recordkeeping to bog down the system.[22]

A company can adopt CAD in its engineering design department and/or CAM in its production area and make substantial improvements in efficiency and quality. However, when all three components are brought together in a truly advanced plant, the results are breathtaking. Companies such as Texas Instruments, Hewlett-Packard, and Boeing are leading the way. Boeing's 777, the largest twin-engine plane ever built, has been called the first "paperless" jetliner.

The company designed the plane with eight IBM mainframe computers supporting 2,200 workstations that eventually handled 3,500 billion bits of information. The digital design system reduced the possibility of human error and cut engineering changes and reworking of ill-fitting components by more than 50 percent over previous plane projects.[23]

Flexible manufacturing reaches its ultimate level to improve quality, customer service, and cost cutting when all parts are used interdependently and combined with flexible management processes in a system referred to as lean manufacturing. **Lean manufacturing** uses highly trained employees at every stage of the production process, who take a painstaking approach to details and problem solving to cut waste and improve quality. The heart of lean manufacturing is not machines, but employee involvement. Employees are trained to "think lean," which means attacking waste and striving for continuous improvement in all areas.[24]

Japan's Toyota Motor Corporation, which pioneered lean manufacturing, is often considered the premier manufacturing organization in the world. The famed Toyota Production System (TPS) combines techniques such as just-in-time inventory, continuous-flow production, quick changeover of assembly lines, continuous improvement, and preventive maintenance with a management system that encourages employee involvement and problem solving. Any employee can stop the production line at any time to solve a problem. In addition, designing equipment to stop automatically so that a defect can be fixed is a key element of the system.[25]

Many North American organizations have studied the Toyota Production System and seen dramatic improvements in productivity, inventory reduction, and quality. In addition, the integration of flexible manufacturing systems with flexible work processes has paved the way for **mass customization**, whereby factories are able to mass-produce products designed to exact customer specification. Today, you can buy jeans customized for your body, glasses molded to precisely fit and flatter your face, CDs with music tracks that you select, and pills with the exact blend of vitamins and minerals you want.[26] Dell Computer Corporation, one of the first companies to offer computers assembled to a customer's exact specifications, is a model of the flexible factory, as described in the Leading by Design box.

Oshkosh Truck Company has thrived during an industrywide slump in sales by offering customized fire, cement, garbage, and military trucks. Firefighters often travel to the plant to watch their new vehicle take shape, sometimes bringing paint chips to customize the color of their fleet.[27] Auto manufacturers, too, are moving toward mass customization. Sixty percent of the cars BMW sells in Europe are built to order.[28] Plant efficiency experts believe the trend toward mass customization will grow as flexible manufacturing systems become more sophisticated and adaptive. Manufacturers such as Deere & Co., Boeing, Intel, and General Motors are exploring the use of new software applications at various levels to improve mass customization productivity and efficiency.

Performance.   The awesome advantage of FMS is that products of different sizes, types, and customer requirements freely intermingle on the assembly line. Bar codes imprinted on a part enable machines to make instantaneous changes—such as putting a larger screw in a different location—without slowing the production line. A manufacturer can turn out an infinite variety of products in unlimited batch sizes, as illustrated in Exhibit 7.5. In traditional manufacturing systems studied by Woodward, choices were limited to the diagonal. Small batch allowed for high product flexibility and custom orders, but because of the "craftsmanship" involved

EXHIBIT 7.5   *Relationship of Flexible Manufacturing Technology to Traditional Technologies*

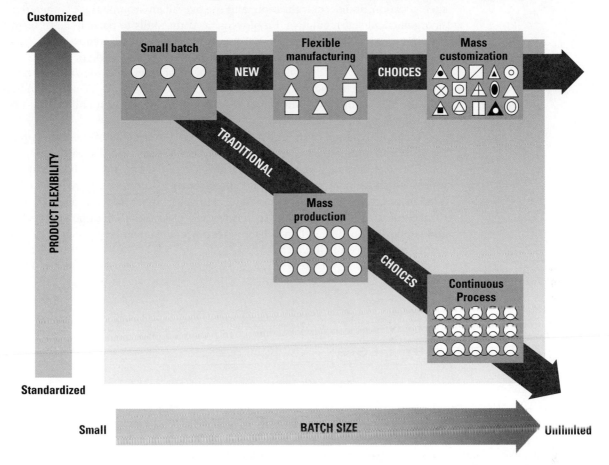

Source: Based on Jack Meredith, "The Strategic Advantages of New Manufacturing Technologies for Small Firms," *Strategic Management Journal* 8 (1987), 249–258; Paul Adler, "Managing Flexible Automation," *California Management Review* (Spring 1988), 34–56; and Otis Port, "Custom-made Direct from the Plant," *BusinessWeek/21st Century Capitalism* (November 18, 1994), 158–159.

in custom-making products, batch size was necessarily small. Mass production could have large batch size, but offered limited product flexibility. Continuous process could produce a single standard product in unlimited quantities. Flexible manufacturing allows plants to break free of this diagonal and to increase both batch size and product flexibility at the same time. When taken to its ultimate level, FMS allows for mass customization, with each specific product tailored to customer specification. This high-level use of FMS has been referred to as *computer-aided craftsmanship.*[29]

Studies suggest that with FMS, machine utilization is more efficient, labor productivity increases, scrap rates decrease, and product variety and customer satisfaction increase.[30] Many U.S. manufacturing companies are reinventing the factory using FMS and associated management systems to increase productivity.

Structural Implications. Research into the relationship between FMS and organizational characteristics is beginning to emerge, and the patterns are summarized in Exhibit 7.6. Compared with traditional mass production technologies,

FMS has a narrow span of control, few hierarchical levels, adaptive tasks, low specialization, and decentralization, and the overall environment is characterized as organic and self-regulative. Employees need the skills to participate in teams, training is broad (so workers are not overly specialized) and frequent (so workers are up-to-date). Expertise tends to be cognitive so workers can process abstract ideas and solve problems. Interorganizational relationships in FMS firms are characterized by changing demand from customers—which is easily handled with the new technology—and close relationships with a few suppliers that provide top-quality raw materials.[31]

Technology alone cannot give organizations the benefits of flexibility, quality, increased production, and greater customer satisfaction. Research suggests that FMS can become a competitive burden rather than a competitive advantage unless organizational structures and management processes are redesigned to take advantage of the new technology.[32] However, when top managers make a commitment to implement new structures and processes that empower workers and support a learning and knowledge-creating environment, FMS can help companies be more competitive.[33]

LEADING BY DESIGN   *Dell Computer*

It's a tough time in the computer industry, but Dell Computer, like the Energizer bunny, just keeps going and going and going. Even competitors agree that there is just no better way to make, sell, and deliver PCs than the way Dell does it. Dell PCs are made to order and are delivered directly to the customer. Each customer gets exactly the machine he or she wants—and gets it faster and cheaper than he or she could from the competition.

Dell's speedy, flexible, cost-efficient system is illustrated by the company's OptiPlex factory in Austin, Texas, where Dell created a new way of making PCs that helped spur the company from number three to number one in PC sales. The process combines just-in-time delivery of parts from suppliers with a complicated, integrated computer manufacturing system that practically hands a worker the right part—whether it be any of a dozen different microprocessors or a specific combination of software—at just the right moment. The goal is not only to slash costs but also to save time by reducing the number of worker-touches per machine. Dell used to build computers in progressive assembly-line fashion, with up to 25 different people building one machine. Now, very small teams of workers build a complete computer by following precise guidelines and using the components that arrive in

carefully indicated racks in front of them. The combination of baskets, racks, and traffic signals that keeps the whole operation moving is called the Pick-to-Light system. Pick-to-Light is based on an up-to-the minute database and software tying it to a stockroom system. That means the system can make sure teams have everything they need to complete an order, whether it be for one PC or two hundred. The system keeps track of which materials need replenishing and makes sure the racks and baskets are supplied with the proper components.

Dell's new system has dramatically improved productivity, increasing manufacturing speed and throughput of custom-made computers by 150 percent. Employees are happier too because they now use more skills and build a complete machine within the team rather than performing the same boring, repetitive task on an assembly line. The system that began at one cutting-edge Austin factory has been adopted at all of the company's manufacturing plants. With this kind of flexibility, no wonder Dell is number one.

Source: Stewart Deck, "Fine Line," *CIO* (February 1, 2000), 88–92; Andy Serwer, "Dell Does Domination," *Fortune* (January 21, 2002), 71–75; and Betsy Morris, "Can Michael Dell Escape the Box?" *Fortune* (October 16, 2000), 93–110.

EXHIBIT 7.6   *Comparison of Organizational Characteristics Associated with Mass Production and Flexible Manufacturing Systems*

Characteristic	Mass Production	FMS
Structure		
Span of control	Wide	Narrow
Hierarchical levels	Many	Few
Tasks	Routine, repetitive	Adaptive, craftlike
Specialization	High	Low
Decision making	Centralized	Decentralized
Overall	Bureaucratic, mechanistic	Self-regulating, organic
Human Resources		
Interactions	Standalone	Teamwork
Training	Narrow, one time	Broad, frequent
Expertise	Manual, technical	Cognitive, social
		Solve problems
Interorganizational		
Customer demand	Stable	Changing
Suppliers	Many, arm's length	Few, close relations

Source: Based on Patricia L. Nemetz and Louis W. Fry, "Flexible Manufacturing Organizations: Implications for Strategy Formulation and Organization Design," *Academy of Management Review* 13 (1988), 627–638; Paul S. Adler, "Managing Flexible Automation," *California Management Review* (Spring 1988), 34–56; and Jeremy Main, "Manufacturing the Right Way," *Fortune* (May 21, 1990) 54–64.

CORE ORGANIZATION SERVICE TECHNOLOGY

One of the biggest changes occurring in the technology of organizations is the growing service sector. The percentage of the workforce employed in manufacturing continues to decline, not only in the United States, but in Canada, France, Germany, the United Kingdom, and Sweden as well.[34] The service sector has increased three times as fast as the manufacturing sector in the North American economy. More than two-thirds of the U.S. workforce is employed in services, such as hospitals, hotels, financial services, or telecommunications. Service technologies are different from manufacturing technologies and, in turn, require a specific organization structure.

SERVICE FIRMS

Definition. Whereas manufacturing organizations achieve their primary purpose through the production of products, service organizations accomplish their primary purpose through the production and provision of services, such as education, health care, transportation, banking, and hospitality. Studies of service organizations have focused on the unique dimensions of service technologies. The characteristics of **service technology** are compared to those of manufacturing technology in Exhibit 7.7.

The most obvious difference is that service technology produces an *intangible output*, rather than a tangible product, such as a refrigerator produced by a manufacturing firm. A service is abstract and often consists of knowledge and ideas rather than a physical product. Thus, whereas manufacturers' products can be

BRIEFCASE

As an organization manager, keep this guideline in mind:

Use the concept of service technology to evaluate the production process in non-manufacturing firms. Service technologies are intangible and must be located close to the customer. Hence, service organizations may have an organization structure with fewer boundary roles, greater geographical dispersion, decentralization, highly skilled employees in the technical core, and generally less control than in manufacturing organizations.

EXHIBIT 7.7   *Differences Between Manufacturing and Service Technologies*

Service Technology
1. *Intangible output*
2. *Production and consumption take place simultaneously*
3. *Labor- and knowledge-intensive*
4. *Customer interaction generally high*
5. *Human element very important*
6. *Quality is perceived and difficult to measure*
7. *Rapid response time is usually necessary*
8. *Site of facility is extremely important*

Manufacturing Technology
1. *Tangible product*
2. *Products can be inventoried for later consumption*
3. *Capital asset-intensive*
4. *Little direct customer interaction*
5. *Human element may be less important*
6. *Quality is directly measured*
7. *Longer response time is acceptable*
8. *Site of facility is moderately important*

Service	**Product and Service**	**Product**
Airlines	*Fast-food outlets*	*Soft drink companies*
Hotels	*Cosmetics*	*Steel companies*
Consultants	*Real estate*	*Automobile manufacturers*
Health care	*Stockbrokers*	*Mining corporations*
Law firms	*Retail stores*	*Food processing plants*

Source: Based on F. F. Reichheld and W. E. Sasser, Jr., "Zero Defections: Quality Comes to Services," *Harvard Business Review* 68 (September–October 1990) 105–111; and David E. Bowen, Caren Siehl, and Benjamin Schneider, "A Framework for Analyzing Customer Service Orientations in Manufacturing," *Academy of Management Review* 14 (1989), 75–95.

inventoried for later sale, services are characterized by *simultaneous production and consumption*. A client meets with a doctor or attorney, for example, and students and teachers come together in the classroom. A service is an intangible product that does not exist until it is requested by the customer. It cannot be stored, inventoried, or viewed as a finished good. If a service is not consumed immediately upon production, it disappears.[35] This typically means that service firms are *labor- and knowledge-intensive*, with many employees needed to meet the needs of customers, whereas manufacturing firms tend to be capital-intensive, relying on mass production, continuous process, and flexible manufacturing technologies.[36]

Direct interaction between customer and employee is generally very high with services, while there is little direct interaction between customers and employees in the technical core of a manufacturing firm. This direct interaction means that the *human element* (employees) becomes extremely important in service firms. Whereas most people never meet the workers who manufactured their cars, they interact directly with the salesperson who sold them their Subaru Forester or Dodge Neon. The treatment received from the salesperson—or from a doctor, lawyer, or hairstylist—affects the perception of the service received and the customer's level of satisfaction. The *quality of a service is perceived* and cannot be directly measured and compared in the same way that the quality of a tangible product can. Another characteristic that affects customer satisfaction and perception of quality service is *rapid response time*. A service must be provided when the customer wants and needs it. When you take a friend to dinner, you want to be seated and served in a timely manner; you would not be very satisfied if the host or manager told you to come back tomorrow when there would be more tables or servers available to accommodate you.

The final defining characteristic of service technology is that *site selection is often much more important* than with manufacturing. Because services are intangible, they have to be located where the customer wants to be served. Services are dispersed and located geographically close to customers. For example, fast-food franchises usually disperse their facilities into local stores. Most towns of even moderate size today have two or more McDonald's restaurants rather than one huge one in order to provide service where customers want it.

In reality, it is difficult to find organizations that reflect 100 percent service or 100 percent manufacturing characteristics. Some service firms take on characteristics of manufacturers, and vice versa. Many manufacturing firms are placing a greater emphasis on customer service to differentiate themselves and be more competitive, which is one reason for the increased use of flexible manufacturing systems. In addition, manufacturing organizations have departments such as purchasing, human resources, and marketing that are based on service technology. On the other hand, organizations such as gas stations, stockbrokers, retail stores, and fast-food restaurants may belong to the service sector, even though the provision of a product is a significant part of the transaction. The vast majority of organizations involve some combination of products and services. The important point is that all organizations can be classified along a continuum that includes both manufacturing and service characteristics, as illustrated in Exhibit 7.7.

New Directions in Services. Service firms have always tended toward providing *customized output*—that is, providing exactly the service each customer wants and needs. For example, when you visit a hairstylist, you don't automatically get the same cut the stylist gave the three previous clients. The stylist cuts your hair the way you request it. However, the trend toward mass customization that is revolutionizing manufacturing has had a significant impact on the service sector as well. Customer expectations of what constitutes good service are rising.[37] Service companies such as the Ritz-Carlton Hotels, USAA (an insurance and financial services company), and Wells Fargo Bank are using new technology to keep customers coming back. All Ritz-Carlton hotels are linked to a database filled with the preferences of half a million guests, allowing any desk clerk or bellhop to find out what your favorite wine is, whether you're allergic to feather pillows, and how many extra towels you want in your room. At Wells Fargo, customers can apply over the Internet and get a three-second decision on a loan structured specifically for them.[38]

DESIGNING THE SERVICE ORGANIZATION

The feature of service technologies with a distinct influence on organizational structure and control systems is the need for technical core employees to be close to the customer.[39] The differences between service and product organizations necessitated by customer contact are summarized in Exhibit 7.8.

The impact of customer contact on organization structure is reflected in the use of boundary roles and structural disaggregation.[40] Boundary roles are used extensively in manufacturing firms to handle customers and to reduce disruptions for the technical core. They are used less in service firms because a service is intangible and cannot be passed along by boundary spanners, so service customers must interact directly with technical employees, such as doctors or brokers.

A service firm deals in information and intangible outputs and does not need to be large. Its greatest economies are achieved through disaggregation into small units that can be located close to customers. Stockbrokers, doctors'

EXHIBIT 7.8   *Configuration and Structural Characteristics of Service Organizations Versus Product Organizations*

Structure	Service	Product
1. Separate boundary roles	Few	Many
2. Geographical dispersion	Much	Little
3. Decision making	Decentralized	Centralized
4. Formalization	Lower	Higher
Human Resources		
1. Employee skill level	Higher	Lower
2. Skill emphasis	Interpersonal	Technical

clinics, consulting firms, and banks disperse their facilities into regional and local offices. Some fast-food chains, such as Taco Bell, are taking this a step further, selling chicken tacos and bean burritos anywhere people gather—airports, supermarkets, college campuses, or street corners. Manufacturing firms, on the other hand, tend to aggregate operations in a single area that has raw materials and an available workforce. A large manufacturing firm can take advantage of economies derived from expensive machinery and long production runs.

Service technology also influences internal organization characteristics used to direct and control the organization. For one thing, the skills of technical core employees need to be higher. These employees need enough knowledge and awareness to handle customer problems rather than just enough to perform a single, mechanical task. Employees also need social and interpersonal skills as well as technical skills.[41] Because of higher skills and structural dispersion, decision making often tends to be decentralized in service firms, and formalization tends to be low. In general, employees in service organizations have more freedom and discretion on the job. However, some service organizations, such as many fast-food chains, have set rules and procedures for customer service. The London-based chain Pret A Manger hopes to differentiate itself in the fast-food market by taking a different approach.

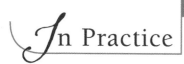

In Practice

PRET A MANGER

"Would you like fries with that?" The standard line is rattled off by fast-food workers who have been taught to follow a script in serving customers. But at Pret A Manger, a fast-growing chain based in London, you won't hear any standard lines. Employees aren't given scripts for serving customers or pigeonholed into performing the same repetitious tasks all day long. Managers want people to let their own personalities come through in offering each customer the best service possible. "Our customers say, 'I like to be served by human beings,'" explains Ewan Stickley, head of employee training. London's *Sunday Times* recently ranked Pret A Manger as one of the top fifty companies to work for in Britain—the only restaurant to make the cut.

Pret A Manger (faux French for "ready to eat") operates 118 outlets in the United Kingdom and is expanding into the United States. "Nobody has ever gone to America, the home of fast food, with a concept that turned out to be a successful national chain. We think we can do that," says chairman and CEO Andrew Rolfe. Pret's concept is based on organizing a mass-market service business around innovation rather than standardization. The menu is based on salads, fresh-made sandwiches, hot soups, sushi, and a variety of yogurt parfaits and blended juices. Menu items are constantly changing, based on what sells and what customers want. Pret A Manger has built in a number of mechanisms for getting fast feedback. The CEO reviews customer and employee comments every Friday. Employees who send in the best ideas for changes to products or procedures can win up to $1,500. Managers spend one day each quarter working in a store to keep in touch with customers and see how their policies affect employees.

In its native England, Pret A Manger has been a huge hit. Translating that success to the United States has been more of a struggle. To help make the transition, Pret has allied itself with a powerful partner—McDonald's. Some worry that McDonald's might corrupt the company's values and emphasis on fresh, healthy food and individualized service, but Rolfe believes he and his employees are up to the challenge.[42]

Understanding the nature of its service technology helps managers at Pret A Manger align strategy, structure, and management processes that are quite different from those for a product-based or traditional manufacturing technology. For example, the concept of separating complex tasks into a series of small jobs and exploiting economies of scale is a cornerstone of traditional manufacturing, but researchers have found that applying it to service organizations often does not work so well.[43] Some service firms have redesigned jobs to separate low- and high-customer contact activities, with more rules and standardization in the low-contact jobs. High-touch service jobs, like those at Pret A Manger, need more freedom and less control to satisfy customers.

Understanding service technology is important for manufacturing firms, too, especially as they put greater emphasis on service. Managers can use these concepts and ideas to strengthen their company's service orientation.

Now let's turn to another perspective on technology, that of production activities within specific organizational departments. Departments often have characteristics similar to those of service technology, providing services to other departments within the organization.

NONCORE DEPARTMENTAL TECHNOLOGY

This section shifts to the department level of analysis for departments not necessarily within the technical core. Each department in an organization has a production process that consists of a distinct technology. General Motors has departments for engineering, R&D, human resources, advertising, quality control, finance, and dozens of other functions. This section analyzes the nature of departmental technology and its relationship with departmental structure.

The framework that has had the greatest impact on the understanding of departmental technologies was developed by Charles Perrow.[44] Perrow's model has been useful for a broad range of technologies, which made it ideal for research into departmental activities.

VARIETY

Perrow specified two dimensions of departmental activities that were relevant to organization structure and process. The first is the number of exceptions in the work. This refers to task **variety**, which is the frequency of unexpected and novel events that occur in the conversion process. When individuals encounter a large number of unexpected situations, with frequent problems, variety is considered high. When there are few problems, and when day-to-day job requirements are repetitive, technology contains little variety. Variety in departments can range from repeating a single act, such as on an assembly line, to working on a series of unrelated problems or projects.

ANALYZABILITY

The second dimension of technology concerns the **analyzability** of work activities. When the conversion process is analyzable, the work can be reduced to mechanical steps and participants can follow an objective, computational procedure to solve problems. Problem solution may involve the use of standard procedures, such as instructions and manuals, or technical knowledge, such as that in a textbook or handbook. On the other hand, some work is not analyzable. When problems arise, it is difficult to identify the correct solution. There is no store of techniques or procedures to tell a person exactly what to do. The cause of or solution to a problem is not clear, so employees rely on accumulated experience, intuition, and judgment. The final solution to a problem is often the result of wisdom and experience and not the result of standard procedures. Philippos Poulos, a tone regulator at Steinway & Sons, has an unanalyzable technology. Tone regulators carefully check each piano's hammers to be sure they produce the proper Steinway sound.[45] These quality control tasks require years of experience and practice. Standard procedures will not tell a person how to do such tasks.

FRAMEWORK

The two dimensions of technology and examples of departmental activities on Perrow's framework are shown in Exhibit 7.9. The dimensions of variety and analyzability form the basis for four major categories of technology: routine, craft, engineering, and nonroutine.

Routine technologies are characterized by little task variety and the use of objective, computational procedures. The tasks are formalized and standardized. Examples include an automobile assembly line and a bank teller department.

Craft technologies are characterized by a fairly stable stream of activities, but the conversion process is not analyzable or well understood. Tasks require extensive training and experience because employees respond to intangible factors on the basis of wisdom, intuition, and experience. Although advances in machine technologies seem to have reduced the number of craft technologies in organizations, a few craft technologies remain. For example, steel furnace engineers continue to mix steel based on intuition and experience, pattern makers at apparel firms still convert rough designers' sketches into salable garments, and gas and oil explorationists use their internal divining rod to determine where millions will be spent on drilling operations.

Engineering technologies tend to be complex because there is substantial variety in the tasks performed. However, the various activities are usually handled on the basis of established formulas, procedures, and techniques. Employees normally refer to a well-developed body of knowledge to handle problems. Engineering and accounting tasks usually fall in this category.

Nonroutine technologies have high task variety, and the conversion process is not analyzable or well understood. In nonroutine technology, a great deal of effort is devoted to analyzing problems and activities. Several equally acceptable options typically can be found. Experience and technical knowledge are used to

EXHIBIT 7.9   *Framework for Department Technologies*

Departmental Technologies

Low	Performing arts Trades Fine goods manufacturing	University teaching General management	Strategic planning Social science research Applied research
	Craft	ROUTINE — NONROUTINE	**Nonroutine**
High	Sales Clerical Drafting Auditing		Legal Engineering Tax accounting General accounting
	Routine		**Engineering**

ANALYZABILITY

Low   High

VARIETY

Source: Adapted with permission from Richard Daft and Norman Macintosh, "A New Approach to Design and Use of Management Information," *California Management Review* 21 (1978), 82–92. Copyright © 1978 by the Regents of the University of California. Reprinted by permission of the Regents.

solve problems and perform the work. Basic research, strategic planning, and other work that involves new projects and unexpected problems are nonroutine.

Routine Versus Nonroutine. Exhibit 7.9 also illustrates that variety and analyzability can be combined into a single dimension of technology. This dimension is called routine versus nonroutine technology, and it is the diagonal line in Exhibit 7.9. The analyzability and variety dimensions are often correlated in departments, meaning that technologies high in variety tend to be low in analyzability, and technologies low in variety tend to be analyzable. Departments can be evaluated along a single dimension of routine versus nonroutine that combines both analyzability and variety, which is a useful shorthand measure for analyzing departmental technology.

The following questions show how departmental technology can be analyzed for determining its placement on Perrow's technology framework in Exhibit 7.9.[46] Employees normally circle a number from one to seven in response to each question.

Variety
1. To what extent would you say your work is routine?
2. Does most everyone in this unit do about the same job in the same way most of the time?
3. Are unit members performing repetitive activities in doing their jobs?

Analyzability
1. To what extent is there a clearly known way to do the major types of work you normally encounter?

2. To what extent is there an understandable sequence of steps that can be followed in doing your work?

3. To do your work, to what extent can you actually rely on established procedures and practices?

If answers to the above questions indicate high scores for analyzability and low scores for variety, the department would have a routine technology. If the opposite occurs, the technology would be nonroutine. Low variety and low analyzability indicate a craft technology, and high variety and high analyzability indicate an engineering technology. As a practical matter, most departments fit somewhere along the diagonal and can be most easily characterized as routine or nonroutine.

DEPARTMENT DESIGN

Once the nature of a department's technology has been identified, then the appropriate structure can be determined. Department technology tends to be associated with a cluster of departmental characteristics, such as the skill level of employees, formalization, and pattern of communication. Definite patterns do exist in the relationship between work unit technology and structural characteristics, which are associated with departmental performance.[47] Key relationships between technology and other dimensions of departments are described in this section and are summarized in Exhibit 7.10.

The overall structure of departments may be characterized as either organic or mechanistic. Routine technologies are associated with a mechanistic structure and processes, with formal rules and rigid management processes. Nonroutine technologies are associated with an organic structure, and department management is more flexible and free-flowing. The specific design characteristics of formalization, centralization, worker skill level, span of control, and communication and coordination vary, depending on work unit technology.

1. *Formalization.* Routine technology is characterized by standardization and division of labor into small tasks that are governed by formal rules and procedures. For nonroutine tasks, the structure is less formal and less standardized. When variety is high, as in a research department, fewer activities are covered by formal procedures.[48]

2. *Decentralization.* In routine technologies, most decision making about task activities is centralized to management.[49] In engineering technologies, employees with technical training tend to acquire moderate decision authority because technical knowledge is important to task accomplishment. Production employees who have long experience obtain decision authority in craft technologies because they know how to respond to problems. Decentralization to employees is greatest in nonroutine settings, where many decisions are made by employees.

3. *Worker skill level.* Work staff in routine technologies typically require little education or experience, which is congruent with repetitious work activities. In work units with greater variety, staff are more skilled and often have formal training in technical schools or universities. Training for craft activities, which are less analyzable, is more likely to be through job experience. Nonroutine activities require both formal education and job experience.[50]

EXHIBIT 7.10   *Relationship of Department Technology to Structural and Management Characteristics*

Mostly Organic Structure
1. *Moderate formalization*
2. *Moderate centralization*
3. *Work experience*
4. *Moderate to wide span*
5. *Horizontal, verbal communications*

CRAFT

Organic Structure
1. *Low formalization*
2. *Low centralization*
3. *Training plus experience*
4. *Moderate to narrow span*
5. *Horizontal communications, meetings*

NONROUTINE

Mechanistic Structure
1. *High formalization*
2. *High centralization*
3. *Little training or experience*
4. *Wide span*
5. *Vertical, written communications*

ROUTINE

Mostly Mechanistic Structure
1. *Moderate formalization*
2. *Moderate centralization*
3. *Formal training*
4. *Moderate span*
5. *Written and verbal communications*

ENGINEERING

Key
1. *Formalization*
2. *Centralization*
3. *Staff qualifications*
4. *Span of control*
5. *Communication and coordination*

4. *Span of control.* Span of control is the number of employees who report to a single manager or supervisor. This characteristic is normally influenced by departmental technology. The more complex and nonroutine the task, the more problems arise in which the supervisor becomes involved. Although the span of control may be influenced by other factors, such as skill level of employees, it typically should be smaller for complex tasks because on such tasks the supervisor and subordinate must interact frequently.[51]

5. *Communication and coordination.* Communication activity and frequency increase as task variety increases.[52] Frequent problems require more information sharing to solve problems and ensure proper completion of activities. The direction of communication is typically horizontal in nonroutine work units and vertical in routine work units.[53] The form of communication varies by task analyzability.[54] When tasks are highly analyzable, statistical and written forms of communication (memos, reports, rules, and procedures) are frequent. When tasks are less analyzable, information typically is conveyed face-to-face, over the telephone, or in group meetings.

Two important points are reflected in Exhibit 7.10. First, departments do differ from one another and can be categorized according to their workflow technology.[55] Second, structural and management processes differ based on departmental technology. Managers should design their departments so that requirements based on technology can be met. Design problems are most visible when the design is clearly inconsistent with technology. Studies have found that when structure and communication characteristics did not reflect technology, departments tended to be less effective.[56] Employees could not communicate with the frequency needed to solve problems. Consider how the design characteristics of Parkland Memorial Hospital's Labor and Delivery unit contribute to a smoothly functioning department.

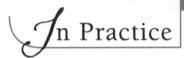

PARKLAND MEMORIAL HOSPITAL

Parkland Memorial Hospital in Dallas, Texas, delivered 16,597 babies in 2001—more than any other hospital in the United States, forty or fifty babies a day. The hospital's stillbirth and neonatal death rates are lower than the national average, despite the fact that 95 percent of the women who come into the labor and delivery unit (L&D) are indigent and many have drug or alcohol problems. As the county hospital, Parkland takes everyone—from private patients to illegal immigrants—and manages to deliver high-quality care on a shoestring. "We don't have fancy birthing rooms, hardwood floors, and pretty wallpaper," says RN Reina Duerinckx. "But we have the important stuff."

Part of the important stuff that helps Parkland achieve such phenomenal results with limited staff and money is L&D's design. Although L&D operates within a set of carefully codified protocols regarding medical care, the rules are applied in a relaxed, informal, and flexible way. The structure gives people a sense of order among the chaos, but flexibility and teamwork by L&D's highly trained professionals translate the rules into appropriate action. Decision making is decentralized so that employees can respond on their own initiative based on problems that arise. "The protocols are not recipes," says Miriam Sibley, senior VP of Parkland's Women and Children's Services. "They give us a way to organize a tremendous amount of work."

Another mechanism for maintaining a sense of order is an elaborate hierarchy that precisely defines duties and authority at every level. This ensures that each patient is served by the person best-qualified for each step of service. However, the L&D unit has an egalitarian, all-hands-on-deck feel to it. It's not unusual to see a doctor mopping out a delivery room to get ready for the next mother. When shifts change at 7 A.M., clerks, nurses, and doctors are all briefing the incoming staff. People call each other by their first (or last) names and everyone wears the same blue scrubs and shares the same locker rooms. Although Parkland managers believe it's important to have defined roles, they make clear that there should be no boundaries. Communication is frequent, face-to-face, and flowing in all directions. It has to be when as many as fourteen babies are delivered in a single hour and the next crisis might be right around the corner.[57]

WORKFLOW INTERDEPENDENCE AMONG DEPARTMENTS

So far, this chapter has explored how organization and department technologies influence structural design. The final characteristic of technology that influences structure is called interdependence. **Interdependence** means the extent to which departments depend on each other for resources or materials to accomplish their tasks. Low interdependence means that departments can do their work independently of each other and have little need for interaction, consultation, or exchange of materials. High interdependence means departments must constantly exchange resources.

TYPES

James Thompson defined three types of interdependence that influence organization structure.[58] These interdependencies are illustrated in Exhibit 7.11 and are discussed in the following sections.

Pooled. **Pooled interdependence** is the lowest form of interdependence among departments. In this form, work does not flow between units. Each department is part of the organization and contributes to the common good of the organization, but works independently. Subway restaurants or branch banks are examples of pooled interdependence. An outlet in Chicago need not interact with an outlet in Urbana. Pooled interdependence may be associated with the relationships within a *divisional structure*, defined in Chapter 3. Divisions or branches share financial resources from a common pool, and the success of each division contributes to the success of the overall organization.

Thompson proposed that pooled interdependence would exist in firms with what he called a mediating technology. A **mediating technology** provides products or services that mediate or link clients from the external environment and, in so doing, allows each department to work independently. Banks, brokerage firms, and real estate offices all mediate between buyers and sellers, but the offices work independently within the organization.

The management implications associated with pooled interdependence are quite simple. Thompson argued that managers should use rules and procedures

EXHIBIT 7.11   *Thompson's Classification of Interdependence and Management Implications*

Form of Interdependence	Demands on Horizontal Communication, Decision Making	Type of Coordination Required	Priority for Locating Units Close Together
Pooled (bank) Clients	Low communication	Standardization, rules, procedures Divisional structure	Low
Sequential (assembly line) Client	Medium communication	Plans, schedules, feedback Task forces	Medium
Reciprocal (hospital) Client	High communication	Mutual adjustment, cross-departmental meetings, teamwork Horizontal structure	High

to standardize activities across departments. Each department should use the same procedures and financial statements so the outcomes of all departments can be measured and pooled. Very little day-to-day coordination is required among units.

Sequential. When interdependence is of serial form, with parts produced in one department becoming inputs to another department, then it is called **sequential interdependence**. The first department must perform correctly for the second department to perform correctly. This is a higher level of interdependence than pooled, because departments exchange resources and depend upon others to perform well. Sequential interdependence creates a greater need for horizontal mechanisms such as integrators or task forces.

Sequential interdependence occurs in what Thompson called **long-linked technology**, which "refers to the combination in one organization of successive stages of production; each stage of production uses as its inputs the production of the preceding stage and produces inputs for the following stage."[59] Large organizations that use assembly line production, such as in the automobile industry, use long-linked technologies and are characterized by sequential interdependence between plants or departments. For example, a United Auto Workers' strike at two General Motors parts plants eventually halted production at all but one of GM's assembly plants in North America. Assembly plants were unable to continue work because they could not get the parts they needed.

The management requirements for sequential interdependence are more demanding than for pooled interdependence. Coordination among the linked plants or departments is required. Since the interdependence implies a one-way flow of materials, extensive planning and scheduling are generally needed. Plant B needs to know what to expect from Plant A so both can perform effectively. Some day-to-day communication among plants is also needed to handle unexpected problems and exceptions that arise.

Reciprocal. The highest level of interdependence is **reciprocal interdependence**. This exists when the output of operation A is the input to operation B, and the output of operation B is the input back again to operation A. The outputs of departments influence those departments in reciprocal fashion.

Reciprocal interdependence tends to occur in organizations with what Thompson called **intensive technologies**, which provide a variety of products or services in combination to a client. Hospitals are an excellent example because they provide coordinated services to patients. A patient may move back and forth between x-ray, surgery, and physical therapy as needed to be cured. A firm developing new products is another example. Intense coordination is needed between design, engineering, manufacturing, and marketing to combine all their resources to suit the customer's product need.

Management requirements are greatest in the case of reciprocal interdependence. Because reciprocal interdependence requires that departments work together intimately and be closely coordinated, a horizontal structure may be appropriate. The structure must allow for frequent horizontal communication and adjustment as at Parkland Memorial Hospital. Extensive planning is required, but plans will not anticipate or solve all problems. Daily interaction and mutual adjustment among departments are required. Managers from several departments are jointly involved in face-to-face coordination, teamwork, and decision making. Reciprocal interdependence is the most complex interdependence for organizations to handle.

STRUCTURAL PRIORITY

As indicated in Exhibit 7.11, since decision making, communication, and coordination problems are greatest for reciprocal interdependence, reciprocal interdependence should receive first priority in organization structure. New product development is one area of reciprocal interdependence that is of growing concern to managers as companies face increasing pressure to get new products to market fast. Many firms are revamping the design-manufacturing relationship by closely integrating computer-aided design (CAD) and computer-aided manufacturing (CAM) technologies discussed earlier in this chapter.[60] Activities that are reciprocally interdependent should be grouped close together in the organization so managers have easy access to one another for mutual adjustment. These units should report to the same person on the organization chart and should be physically close so the time and effort for coordination can be minimized. A horizontal structure, with linked sets of teams working on core processes, can provide the close coordination needed to support reciprocal interdependence. Poor coordination will result in poor performance for the organization. If reciprocally interdependent units are not located close together, the organization should design mechanisms for coordination, such as daily meetings between departments or an intranet to facilitate communication. The next priority is given to sequential interdependencies, and finally to pooled interdependencies.

This strategy of organizing keeps the communication channels short where coordination is most critical to organizational success. For example, Boise Cascade Corporation experienced poor service to customers because customer service reps located in New York City were not coordinating with production planners in Oregon plants. Customers couldn't get delivery as needed. Boise was reorganized, and the two groups were consolidated under one roof, reporting to the same supervisor at division headquarters. Now customer needs are met because customer service reps work with production planning to schedule customer orders.

STRUCTURAL IMPLICATIONS

Most organizations experience various levels of interdependence, and structure can be designed to fit these needs, as illustrated in Exhibit 7.12.[61] In a manufacturing firm, new product development entails reciprocal interdependence among the design, engineering, purchasing, manufacturing, and sales departments. Perhaps a horizontal structure or cross-functional teams could be used to handle the back-and-forth flow of information and resources. Once a product is designed, its actual manufacture would be sequential interdependence, with a flow of goods from one department to another, such as among purchasing, inventory, production control, manufacturing, and assembly. The actual ordering and delivery of products is pooled interdependence, with warehouses working independently. Customers could place an order with the nearest facility, which would not require coordination among warehouses, except in unusual cases such as a stock outage.

The three levels of interdependence are illustrated by a study of athletic teams that examined interdependency among players and how it influences other aspects of baseball, football, and basketball teams.

Exhibit 7.12   *Primary Means to Achieve Coordination for Different Levels of Task Interdependence in a Manufacturing Firm*

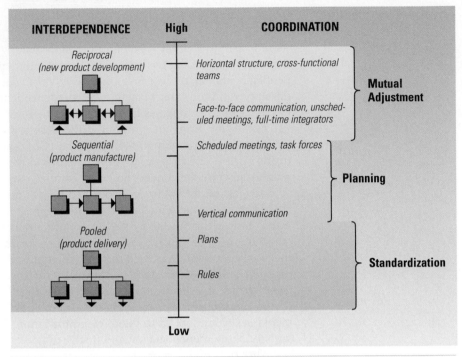

Source: Adapted from Andrew H. Van de Ven, Andre Delbecq, and Richard Koenig, "Determinants of Communication Modes Within Organizations," *American Sociological Review* 41 (1976), 330.

ATHLETIC TEAMS

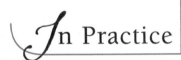

A major difference among baseball, football, and basketball is the interdependence among players. Baseball is low in interdependence, football is medium, and basketball represents the highest player interdependence. The relationships among interdependence and other characteristics of team play are illustrated in Exhibit 7.13.

Pete Rose said, "Baseball is a team game, but nine men who reach their individual goals make a nice team." In baseball, interdependence among team players is low and can be defined as pooled. Each member acts independently, taking a turn at bat and playing his or her own position. When interaction does occur, it is between only two or three players, as in a double play. Players are physically dispersed, and the rules of the game are the primary means of coordinating players. Players practice and develop their skills individually, such as by taking batting practice and undergoing physical conditioning. Management's job is to select good players. If each player is successful as an individual, the team should win.

In football, interdependence among players is higher and tends to be sequential. The line first blocks the opponents to enable the backs to run or pass. Plays are performed sequentially from first down to fourth down. Physical dispersion is medium, which allows players to operate as a coordinated unit. The primary mechanism for coordinating players is developing a game plan along with rules that govern the behavior of team members. Each player has an assignment that fits with other assignments, and management designs the game plan to achieve victory.

In basketball, interdependence tends to be reciprocal. The game is free-flowing, and the division of labor is less precise than in other sports. Each player is involved in both offense

Exhibit 7.13   Relationships Among Interdependence and Other Characteristics of Team Play

	Baseball	Football	Basketball
Interdependence	Pooled	Sequential	Reciprocal
Physical dispersion of players	High	Medium	Low
Coordination	Rules that govern the sport	Game plan and position roles	Mutual adjustment and shared responsibility
Key management job	Select players and develop their skills	Prepare and execute game	Influence flow of game

Source: Based on William Passmore, Carol E. Francis, and Jeffrey Haldeman, "Sociotechnical Systems: A North American Reflection on the Empirical Studies of the 70s," *Human Relations* 35 (1982), 1179–1204.

and defense, handles the ball, and attempts to score. The ball flows back and forth among players. Team members interact in a dynamic flow to achieve victory. Management skills involve the ability to influence this dynamic process, either by substituting players or by working the ball into certain areas. Players must learn to adapt to the flow of the game and to one another as events unfold.

Interdependence among players is a primary factor explaining the difference among the three sports. Baseball is organized around an autonomous individual, football around groups that are sequentially interdependent, and basketball around the free flow of reciprocal players.[62]

IMPACT OF TECHNOLOGY ON JOB DESIGN

So far, this chapter has described models for analyzing how manufacturing, service, and department technologies influence structure and management processes. The relation between a new technology and organization seems to follow a pattern, beginning with immediate effects on the content of jobs followed (after a longer period) by impact on design of the organization. The ultimate impact of technology on employees can be partially understood through the concepts of job design and sociotechnical systems.

JOB DESIGN

Job design includes the assignment of goals and tasks to be accomplished by employees. Managers may consciously change job design to improve productivity or worker motivation. For example, when workers are involved in performing boring, repetitive tasks, managers may introduce **job rotation**, which means moving employees from job to job to give them a greater variety of tasks. However, managers may also unconsciously influence job design through the introduction of new technologies, which can change how jobs are done and the very nature of jobs.[63] Managers should understand how the introduction of a new technology may affect employees' jobs. The common theme of new technologies in the workplace is that they in some way substitute machinery for human labor in transforming inputs into outputs. Automated teller machines

(ATMs) have replaced thousands of human bank tellers, for example. IBM has even built a plant in Austin, Texas, that can produce laptop computers without the help of a single worker.[64]

In addition to actually replacing human workers, technology may have several different effects on the human jobs that remain. Research has indicated that mass production technologies tend to produce **job simplification**, which means that the variety and difficulty of tasks performed by a single person are reduced. The consequence is boring, repetitive jobs that generally provide little satisfaction. More advanced technology, on the other hand, tends to cause **job enrichment**, meaning that the job provides greater responsibility, recognition, and opportunities for growth and development. These technologies create a greater need for employee training and education because workers need higher-level skills and greater competence to master their tasks. For example, ATMs took most the routine tasks (deposits and withdrawals) away from bank tellers and left them with the more complex tasks that require higher-level skills. Studies of flexible manufacturing found that it produces three noticeable results for employees: more opportunities for intellectual mastery and enhanced cognitive skills for workers; more worker responsibility for results; and greater interdependence among workers, enabling more social interaction and the development of teamwork and coordination skills.[65] Flexible manufacturing technology may also contribute to **job enlargement**, which is an expansion of the number of different tasks performed by an employee. Because fewer workers are needed with the new technology, each employee has to be able to perform a greater number and variety of tasks.

With advanced technology, workers have to keep learning new skills because technology is changing so rapidly. Advances in *information technology*, to be discussed in detail in the next chapter, are having a significant effect on jobs in the service industry, including doctors' offices and medical clinics, law firms, financial planners, and libraries. Workers may find that their jobs change almost daily because of new software programs, increased use of the Internet, and other advances in information technology.

Advanced technology does not always have a positive effect on employees, but research findings in general are encouraging, suggesting that jobs for workers are enriched rather than simplified, engaging their higher mental capacities, offering opportunities for learning and growth, and providing greater job satisfaction.

SOCIOTECHNICAL SYSTEMS

The **sociotechnical systems approach** recognizes the interaction of technical and human needs in effective job design, combining the needs of people with the organization's need for technical efficiency. The *socio* portion of the approach refers to the people and groups that work in organizations and how work is organized and coordinated. The *technical* portion refers to the materials, tools, machines, and processes used to transform organizational inputs into outputs.

Exhibit 7.14 illustrates the three primary components of the sociotechnical systems model.[66] The *social system* includes all human elements—such as individual and team behaviors, organizational culture, management practices, and degree of communication openness—that can influence the performance of work. The *technical system* refers to the type of production technology, the level of interdependence, the complexity of tasks, and so forth. The goal of the sociotechnical systems approach is to design the organization for **joint optimization**, which means that an organization functions best only when the social and

EXHIBIT 7.14   *Sociotechnical Systems Model*

The Social System
- Individual and team behaviors
- Organizational/team culture
- Management practices
- Leadership style
- Degree of communication openness
- Individual needs and desires

Design for Joint Optimization

Work roles, tasks, workflow

Goals and values

Skills and abilities

The Technical System
- Type of production technology (small batch, mass production, FMS, etc.)
- Level of interdependence (pooled, sequential, reciprocal)
- Physical work setting
- Complexity of production process (variety and analyzability)
- Nature of raw materials
- Time pressure

Sources: Based on T. Cummings, "Self-Regulating Work Groups: A Socio-Technical Synthesis," *Academy of Management Review* 3 (1978) 625–634; Don Hellriegel, John W. Slocum, and Richard W. Woodman, *Organizational Behavior*, 8th ed. (Cincinnati, Ohio: South-Western, 1998), 492; and Gregory B. Northcraft and Margaret A. Neale, *Organizational Behavior: A Management Challenge*, 2nd ed. (Fort Worth, Tex.: The Dryden Press, 1994), 551.

technical systems are designed to fit the needs of one another. Designing the organization to meet human needs while ignoring the technical systems, or changing technology to improve efficiency while ignoring human needs, may inadvertently cause performance problems. The sociotechnical systems approach attempts to find a balance between what workers want and need and the technical requirements of the organization's production system.[67]

One example comes from a museum that installed a closed-circuit TV system. Rather than having several guards patrolling the museum and grounds, the television could easily be monitored by a single guard. Although the technology saved money because only one guard was needed per shift, it led to unexpected performance problems. Guards had previously enjoyed the social interaction provided by patrolling; monitoring a closed-circuit television led to alienation and boredom. When a federal agency did an eighteen-month test of the system, only 5 percent of several thousand experimental covert intrusions were detected by the guard.[68] The system was inadequate because human needs were not taken into account.

Sociotechnical principles evolved from the work of the Tavistock Institute, a research organization in England, during the 1950s and 1960s.[69] Examples of organizational change using sociotechnical systems principles have occurred in numerous organizations, including General Motors, Volvo, the Tennessee Valley Authority (TVA), and Procter & Gamble.[70] Although there have been failures, in many of these applications, the joint optimization of changes in technology and structure to meet the needs of people as well as efficiency improved performance, safety, quality, absenteeism, and turnover. In some cases, work design was not the most efficient based on technical and scientific principles, but worker involvement and commitment more than made up for the difference. Thus, once again research shows that new technologies need not have a negative impact on workers, because the technology often requires higher-level mental and social skills and can be organized to encourage the involvement and commitment of employees, thereby benefiting both the employee and the organization.

The sociotechnical systems principle that people should be viewed as resources and provided with appropriate skills, meaningful work, and suitable rewards becomes even more important in today's world of growing technological complexity.[71] One study of paper manufacturers found that organizations that put too much faith in machines and technology and pay little attention to the appropriate management of people do not achieve advances in productivity and flexibility. Today's most successful companies strive to find the right mix of machines, computer systems, and people and the most effective way to coordinate them.[72]

Although many principles of sociotechnical systems theory are still valid, current scholars and researchers are also arguing for an expansion of the approach to capture the dynamic nature of today's organizations, the chaotic environment, and the shift from routine to nonroutine jobs brought about by advances in technology.[73]

SUMMARY AND INTERPRETATION

This chapter reviewed several frameworks and key research findings on the topic of organizational technology. The potential importance of technology as a factor in organizational structure was discovered during the 1960s. Since then, a flurry of research activity has been undertaken to understand more precisely the relationship of technology to other characteristics of organizations.

Five ideas in the technology literature stand out. The first is Woodward's research into manufacturing technology. Woodward went into organizations and collected practical data on technology characteristics, organization structure, and management systems. She found clear relationships between technology and structure in high-performing organizations. Her findings are so clear that managers can analyze their own organizations on the same dimensions of technology and structure. In addition, technology and structure can be co-aligned with organizational strategy to meet changing needs and provide new competitive advantages.

The second important idea is that service technologies differ in a systematic way from manufacturing technologies. Service technologies are characterized by intangible outcomes and direct client involvement in the production process. Service firms do not have the fixed, machine-based technologies that appear in manufacturing organizations; hence, organization design often differs as well.

The third significant idea is Perrow's framework applied to department technologies. Understanding the variety and analyzability of a technology tells one about the management style, structure, and process that should characterize that department. Routine technologies are characterized by mechanistic structure and nonroutine technologies by organic structure. Applying the wrong management system to a department will result in dissatisfaction and reduced efficiency.

The fourth important idea is interdependence among departments. The extent to which departments depend on each other for materials, information, or other resources determines the amount of coordination required between them. As interdependence increases, demands on the organization for coordination increase. Organization design must allow for the correct amount of communication and coordination to handle interdependence across departments.

The fifth important idea is that new flexible manufacturing systems are being adopted by organizations and having impact on organization design. For the most part, the impact is positive, with shifts toward more organic structures both on the shop floor and in the management hierarchy. These technologies replace routine jobs, give employees more autonomy, produce more challenging jobs, encourage teamwork, and let the organization be more flexible and responsive. The new technologies are enriching jobs to the point where organizations are happier places to work.

Several principles of sociotechnical systems theory, which attempts to design the technical and human aspects of an organization to fit one another, are increasingly important as advances in technology alter the nature of jobs and social interaction in today's companies.

Key Concepts

analyzability	long-linked technology
continuous process production	mass customization
core technology	mediating technology
craft technologies	noncore technology
engineering technologies	nonroutine technologies
flexible manufacturing systems	pooled interdependence
intensive technologies	reciprocal interdependence
interdependence	routine technologies
job design	sequential interdependence
job enlargement	service technology
job enrichment	small-batch production
job rotation	sociotechnical systems approach
job simplification	technical complexity
joint optimization	technology
large-batch production	variety
lean manufacturing	

Discussion Questions

1. Where would your university or college department be located on Perrow's technology framework? Look for the underlying variety and analyzability characteristics when making your assessment. Would a department devoted exclusively to teaching be put in a different quadrant from a department devoted exclusively to research?

2. Explain Thompson's levels of interdependence. Identify an example of each level of interdependence in the university or college setting. What kinds of coordination mechanisms should an administration develop to handle each level of interdependence?

3. Describe Woodward's classification of organizational technologies. Explain why each of the three technology groups is related differently to organization structure and management processes.

4. What relationships did Woodward discover between supervisor span of control and technological complexity?

5. How do flexible manufacturing systems differ from other manufacturing technologies? What is the primary advantage of FMS?

6. What is a service technology? Are different types of service technologies likely to be associated with different structures? Explain.

7. Mass customization of products has become a common approach in manufacturing organizations. Discuss ways in which mass customization can be applied to service firms as well.

8. In what primary ways does the design of service firms typically differ from that of product firms? Why?

9. A top executive claimed that top-level management is a craft technology because the work contains intangibles, such as handling personnel, interpreting the environment, and coping with unusual situations that have to be learned through experience. If this is true, is it appropriate to teach management in a business school? Does teaching management from a textbook assume that the manager's job is analyzable, and hence that formal training rather than experience is most important?

10. In which quadrant of Perrow's framework would a mass production technology be placed? Where would small-batch and continuous process technologies be placed? Why? Would Perrow's framework lead to the same recommendation about organic versus mechanistic structures that Woodward made?

11. To what extent does the development of new technologies simplify and routinize the jobs of employees? How can new technology lead to job enlargement? Discuss.

12. Describe the sociotechnical systems model. Why might some managers oppose a sociotechnical systems approach?

Chapter 7 Workbook *Bistro Technology*

You will be analyzing the technology used in three different restaurants—McDonald's, Subway, and a typical family restaurant. Your instructor will tell you whether to do this assignment as individuals or in a group.

You must visit all three restaurants and infer how the work is done, according to the following criteria. You are not allowed to interview any employees, but instead you will be an observer. Take lots of notes when you are there.

*Adapted loosely by Dorothy Marcic from "Hamburger Technology," in Douglas T. Hall et al., *Experiences in Management and Organizational Behavior*, 2nd ed. (New York: Wiley, 1982) 244–247, as well as "Behavior, Technology, and Work Design" in A. B. Shani and James B. Lau, *Behavior in Organizations* (Chicago: Irwin, 1996), M16–23 to M16–26.

	McDonald's	Subway	Family Restaurant
Organization goals: Speed, service, atmosphere, etc.			
Authority structure			
Type of technology using Woodward's model			
Organization structure: Mechanistic or organic?			
Team versus individual: Do people work together or alone?			

	McDonald's	Subway	Family Restaurant
Interdependence: How do employees depend on each other?			
Tasks: Routine versus nonroutine			
Specialization of tasks by employees			
Standardization: How varied are tasks and products?			
Expertise required: Technical versus social			
Decision making: Centralized versus decentralized			

Questions

1. Is the technology used the best one for each restaurant, considering its goals and environment?

2. From the preceding data, determine if the structure and other characteristics fit the technology.

3. If you were part of a consulting team assigned to improve the operations of each organization, what recommendations would you make?

CASE FOR ANALYSIS *Acetate Department*

The acetate department's product consisted of about twenty different kinds of viscous liquid acetate used by another department to manufacture transparent film to be left clear or coated with photographic emulsion or iron oxide.

Before the change: The department was located in an old four-story building as in Exhibit 7.15. The workflow was as follows:

1. Twenty kinds of powder arrived daily in 50-pound paper bags. In addition, storage tanks of liquid would be filled weekly from tank trucks.

2. Two or three acetate helpers would jointly unload pallets of bags into the storage area using a lift truck.

3. Several times a shift, the helpers would bring the bagged material up in the elevator to the third floor, where it would be temporarily stored along the walls.

4. Mixing batches was under the direction of the group leader and was rather like baking a cake. Following a prescribed formula, the group leader, mixers, and helpers operated valves to feed in the proper solvent and manually dump in the proper weight and mixture of solid material. The glob would be mixed by giant eggbeaters and heated according to the recipe.

5. When the batch was completed, it was pumped to a finished product storage tank.

6. After completing each batch, the crew would thoroughly clean the work area of dust and empty bags, because cleanliness was extremely important to the finished product.

*From "Redesigning the Acetate Department," by David L. Hampton, Charles E. Summer, and Ross A. Webber, *Organizational Behavior and the Practice of Management* (Glenview, Ill.: Scott, Foresman and Company, 1982), 751–755. Used with permission.

EXHIBIT 7.15   *Elevation View of Acetate Department Before Change*

Solvent Storage

Elevator

Department offices and testing laboratory

Work floor

Mixing and product storage vats

Material storage

100 feet

To accomplish this work, the department was structured as in Exhibit 7.16.

The helpers were usually young men 18 to 25 years of age, the mixers, 25 to 40, and the group leaders and foremen, 40 to 60. Foremen were on salary, group leaders, mixers, and helpers, on hourly pay.

To produce 20,000,000 pounds of product per year, the department operated 24 hours a day, 7 days a week. Four crews rotated shifts: for example, shift foreman A and his two group leaders and crews would work two weeks on the day shift (8 A.M. to 4 P.M.), then two weeks on the evening shift (4 P.M. to midnight), then two weeks on the night shift (midnight to 8 A.M. There were two days off between shift changes.

During a typical shift, a group leader and his crew would complete two or three batches. A batch would frequently be started on one shift and completed by

EXHIBIT 7.16   *Organizational Chart of Acetate Department Before Change*

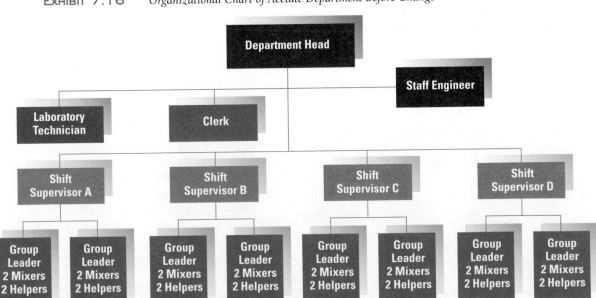

the next shift crew. There was slightly less work on the evening and night shifts because no deliveries were made, but these crews engaged in a little more cleaning. The shift foreman would give instructions to the two group leaders at the beginning of each shift as to the status of batches in process, batches to be mixed, what deliveries were expected, and what cleaning was to be done. Periodically throughout the shift, the foreman would collect samples in small bottles, which he would leave at the laboratory technicians' desk for testing.

The management and office staff (department head, staff engineer, lab technician, and department clerk) only worked on the day shift, although if an emergency arose on the other shifts, the foreman might call.

All in all, the department was a pleasant place in which to work. The work floor was a little warm, but well-lighted, quiet, and clean. Substantial banter and horseplay occurred when the crew wasn't actually loading batches, particularly on the evening and night shifts. The men had a dartboard in the work area and competition was fierce and loud. Frequently a crew would go bowling right after work, even at 1 A.M., for the community's alleys were open 24 hours a day. Department turnover and absenteeism were low. Most employees spent their entire career with the company, many in one department. The corporation was large, paternalistic, and well-paying and offered

attractive fringe benefits including large, virtually automatic bonuses for all. Then came the change.

The new system: To improve productivity, the acetate department was completely redesigned; the technology changed from batches to continuous processing. The basic building was retained but substantially modified as in Exhibit 7.17. The modified workflow is as follows:

1. Most solid raw materials are delivered via trucks in large aluminum bins holding 500 pounds.
2. One handler (formerly helper) is on duty at all times on the first floor to receive raw materials and to dump the bins into the semiautomatic screw feeder.
3. The head operator (former group leader) directs the mixing operations from his control panel on the fourth floor located along one wall across from the department offices. The mixing is virtually an automatic operation once the solid material has been sent up the screw feed; a tape program opens and closes the necessary valves to add solvent, heat, mix, etc. Sitting at a table before his panel, the head operator monitors the process to see that everything is operating within specified temperatures and pressures.

This technical change allowed the department to greatly reduce its workforce. The new structure is illustrated in Exhibit 7.18. One new position was

EXHIBIT 7.17   *Elevation View of Acetate Department After Change*

EXHIBIT 7.18   *Organizational Chart of Acetate Department After Change*

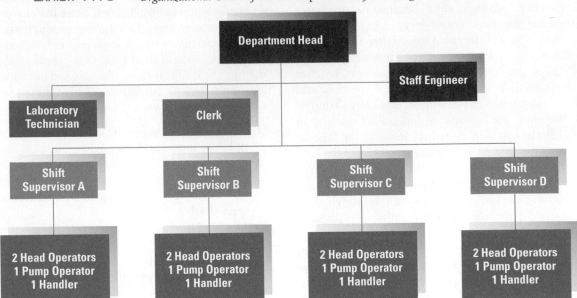

created, that of a pump operator who is located in a small separate shack about 300 feet from the main building. He operates pumps and valves that move the finished product among various storage tanks.

Under the new system, production capacity was increased to 25 million pounds per year. All remaining employees received a 15 percent increase in pay. Former personnel not retained in the acetate department were transferred to other departments in the company. No one was dismissed.

Unfortunately, actual output has lagged well below capacity in the several months since the construction work and technical training were completed. Actual production is virtually identical with that under the old technology. Absenteeism has increased markedly, and several judgmental errors by operators have resulted in substantial losses.

Notes

1. Hal Plotkin, "Riches From Rags," *Inc.* (Summer 1995), 62–67; Joel Kotkin, "Tailor-Made in America," *Inc.* (August 1996), 25–26; and *http://www.frenchrags.com*, accessed on September 11, 2002.

2. Charles Perrow, "A Framework for the Comparative Analysis of Organizations," *American Sociological Review* 32 (1967), 194–208; R. J. Schonberger, *World Class Manufacturing: The Next Decade* (New York: The Free Press, 1996).

3. Linda Argote, "Input Uncertainty and Organizational Coordination in Hospital Emergency Units," *Administrative Science Quarterly* 27 (1982), 420–434; Charles Perrow, *Organizational Analysis: A Sociological Approach* (Belmont, Calif.: Wadsworth, 1970); William Rushing, "Hardness of Material as Related to the Division of Labor in Manufacturing Industries," *Administrative Science Quarterly* 13 (1968), 229–245.

4. Lawrence B. Mohr, "Organizational Technology and Organization Structure," *Administrative Science Quarterly* 16 (1971), 444–459; David Hickson, Derek Pugh, and Diana Pheysey, "Operations Technology and Organization Structure: An Empirical Reappraisal," *Administrative Science Quarterly* 14 (1969), 378–397.

5. Joan Woodward, *Industrial Organization: Theory and Practice* (London: Oxford University Press, 1965); Joan Woodward, *Management and Technology* (London: Her Majesty's Stationery Office, 1958).

6. Hickson, Pugh, and Pheysey, "Operations Technology and Organization Structure"; James D. Thompson, *Organizations in Action* (New York: McGraw-Hill, 1967).

7. Edward Harvey, "Technology and the Structure of Organizations," *American Sociological Review* 33 (1968), 241–259.

8. Wanda J. Orlikowski, "The Duality of Technology: Rethinking the Concept of Technology in Organizations," *Organization Science* 3 (1992), 398–427.

9. Based on Woodward, *Industrial Organization* and *Management and Technology*.

10. Philip Siekman, "A Big Maker of Tiny Batches," *Fortune* (May 27, 2002), 152[A]–152[H].

11. Woodward, *Industrial Organization*, vi.

12. William L. Zwerman, *New Perspectives on Organizational Theory* (Westport, Conn.: Greenwood, 1970); Harvey, "Technology and the Structure of Organizations," 241–259.

13. Dean M. Schroeder, Steven W. Congden, and C. Gopinath, "Linking Competitive Strategy and Manufacturing Process Technology," *Journal of Management Studies* 32, no. 2 (March 1995), 163–189.

14. Gene Bylinsky, "Heroes of U.S. Manufacturing," *Fortune* (March 18, 2002), 130[A]–130[L].

15. Fernando F. Suarez, Michael A. Cusumano, and Charles H. Fine, "An Empirical Study of Flexibility in Manufacturing," *Sloan Management Review* (Fall 1995), 25–32.

16. Raymond F. Zammuto and Edward J. O'Connor, "Gaining Advanced Manufacturing Technologies' Benefits: The Roles of Organization Design and Culture," *Academy of Management Review* 17, no. 4 (1992), 701–728; Schroeder, Congden, and Gopinath, "Linking Competitive Strategy and Manufacturing Process Technology."

17. Jack R. Meredith, "The Strategic Advantages of the Factory of the Future," *California Management Review* 29 (Spring 1987), 27–41; Jack Meredith, "The Strategic Advantages of the New Manufacturing Technologies for Small Firms," *Strategic Management Journal* 8 (1987), 249–258; Althea Jones and Terry Webb, "Introducing Computer Integrated Manufacturing," *Journal of General Management* 12 (Summer 1987), 60–74.

18. Raymond F. Zammuto and Edward J. O'Connor, "Gaining Advanced Manufacturing Technologies' Benefits: The Roles of Organization Design and Culture," *Academy of Management Review* 17 (1992), 701–728.

19. John S. DeMott, "Small Factories' Big Lessons," *Nation's Business* (April 1995), 29–30.

20. Paul S. Adler, "Managing Flexible Automation," *California Management Review* (Spring 1988), 34–56.

21. Bela Gold, "Computerization in Domestic and International Manufacturing," *California Management Review* (Winter 1989), 129–143.

22. Graham Dudley and John Hassard, "Design Issues in the Development of Computer Integrated Manufacturing (CIM)," *Journal of General Management* 16 (1990), 43–53.

23. John Holusha, "Can Boeing's New Baby Fly Financially?" *The New York Times* (March 27, 1994), Section 3, 1, 6.

24. Fara Warner, "Think Lean," *Fast Company* (February 2002), 40, 42.

25. Peter Strozniak, "Toyota Alters Face of Production," *IndustryWeek* (August 13, 2001), 46–48.

26. Joel D. Goldhar and David Lei, "Variety is Free: Manufacturing in the Twenty-First Century," *Academy of Management Executive* 9, no. 4 (1995), 73–86; Justin Martin, "Give 'Em *Exactly* What They Want," *Fortune* (October 10, 1997), 283–285.

27. Mark Tatge, "Red Bodies, Black Ink," *Forbes* (September 18, 2000), 114–115.

28. Erick Schonfeld, "The Customized, Digitized, Have-It-Your-Way Economy," *Fortune* (September 28, 1998), 115–124.

29. Goldhar and Lei, "Variety is Free: Manufacturing in the Twenty-First Century."

30. Meredith, "The Strategic Advantages of the Factory of the Future."

31. Patricia L. Nemetz and Louis W. Fry, "Flexible Manufacturing Organizations: Implementations for Strategy Formulation and Organization Design," *Academy of Management Review* 13 (1988), 627–638; Paul S. Adler, "Managing Flexible Automation," *California Management Review* (Spring 1988), 34–56; Jeremy Main, "Manufacturing the Right Way," *Fortune* (May 21, 1990), 54–64; Frank M. Hull and Paul D. Collins, "High-Technology Batch Production Systems: Woodward's Missing Type," *Academy of Management Journal* 30 (1987), 786–797.

32. Goldhar and Lei, "Variety Is Free: Manufacturing in the Twenty-First Century"; P. Robert Duimering, Frank Safayeni, and Lyn Purdy, "Integrated Manufacturing: Redesign the Organization before

Implementing Flexible Technology," *Sloan Management Review* (Summer 1993), 47–56; Zammuto and O'Connor, "Gaining Advanced Manufacturing Technologies' Benefits."

33. Goldhar and Lei, "Variety is Free: Manufacturing in the Twenty-First Century."

34. "Manufacturing's Decline," *Johnson City Press* (July 17, 1999), 9; Ronald Henkoff, "Service Is Everybody's Business," *Fortune* (June 27, 1994), 48–60; Ronald Henkoff, "Finding, Training, and Keeping the Best Service Workers," *Fortune* (October 3, 1994), 110–122.

35. Byron J. Finch and Richard L. Luebbe, *Operations Management: Competing in a Changing Environment* (Fort Worth, Tex.: The Dryden Press, 1995), 51.

36. David E. Bowen, Caren Siehl, and Benjamin Schneider, "A Framework for Analyzing Customer Service Orientations in Manufacturing," *Academy of Management Review* 14 (1989), 79–95; Peter K. Mills and Newton Margulies, "Toward a Core Typology of Service Organizations," *Academy of Management Review* 5 (1980), 255–265; Peter K. Mills and Dennis J. Moberg, "Perspectives on the Technology of Service Operations," *Academy of Management Review* 7 (1982), 467–478; G. Lynn Shostack, "Breaking Free from Product Marketing," *Journal of Marketing* (April 1977), 73–80.

37. Ron Zemke, "The Service Revolution: Who Won?" *Management Review* (March 1997), 10–15; Wayne Wilhelm and Bill Rossello, "The Care and Feeding of Customers," *Management Review* (March 1997), 19–23.

38. Schonfeld, "The Customized, Digitized, Have-It-Your-Way Economy."

39. Richard B. Chase and David A. Tansik, "The Customer Contact Model for Organization Design," *Management Science* 29 (1983), 1037–1050.

40. Ibid.

41. David E. Bowen and Edward E. Lawler III, "The Empowerment of Service Workers: What, Why, How, and When," *Sloan Management Review* (Spring 1992), 31–39: Gregory B. Northcraft and Richard B. Chase, "Managing Service Demand at the Point of Delivery," *Academy of Management Review* 10 (1985), 66–75; Roger W. Schmenner, "How Can Service Businesses Survive and Prosper?" *Sloan Management Review* 27 (Spring 1986), 21–32.

42. Scott Kirsner, "Recipe for Reinvention," *Fast Company* (April 2002), 38–42.

43. Richard Metters and Vincente Vargas, "Organizing Work in Service Firms," *Business Horizons* (July–August 2000), 23–32.

44. Perrow, "A Framework for Comparative Analysis" and *Organizational Analysis*.

45. Jim Morrison, "Grand Tour. Making Music: The Craft of the Steinway Piano," *Spirit* (February 1997), 42–49, 100.

46. Michael Withey, Richard L. Daft, and William C. Cooper, "Measures of Perrow's Work Unit Technology: An Empirical Assessment and a New Scale," *Academy of Management Journal* 25 (1983), 45–63.

47. Christopher Gresov, "Exploring Fit and Misfit with Multiple Contingencies," *Administrative Science Quarterly* 34 (1989), 431–453; Dale L. Goodhue and Ronald L. Thompson, "Task-Technology Fit and Individual Performance," *MIS Quarterly* (June 1995), 213–236.

48. Gresov, "Exploring Fit and Misfit with Multiple Contingencies"; Charles A. Glisson, "Dependence of Technological Routinization on Structural Variables in Human Service Organizations," *Administrative Science Quarterly* 23 (1978), 383–395; Jerald Hage and Michael Aiken, "Routine Technology, Social Structure and Organizational Goals," *Administrative Science Quarterly* 14 (1969), 368–379.

49. Gresov, "Exploring Fit and Misfit with Multiple Contingencies"; A. J. Grimes and S. M. Kline, "The Technological Imperative: The Relative Impact of Task Unit, Modal Technology, and Hierarchy on Structure," *Academy of Management Journal* 16 (1973), 583–597; Lawrence G. Hrebiniak, "Job Technologies, Supervision and Work Group Structure," *Administrative Science Quarterly* 19 (1974), 395–410; Jeffrey Pfeffer, *Organizational Design* (Arlington Heights, Ill.: AHM, 1978), ch. 1.

50. Patrick E. Connor, *Organizations: Theory and Design* (Chicago: Science Research Associates, 1980); Richard L. Daft and Norman B. Macintosh, "A Tentative Exploration into Amount and Equivocality of Information Processing in Organizational Work Units," *Administrative Science Quarterly* 26 (1981), 207–224.

51. Paul D. Collins and Frank Hull, "Technology and Span of Control: Woodward Revisited,"

Journal of Management Studies 23 (1986), 143–164; Gerald D. Bell, "The Influence of Technological Components of Work upon Management Control," *Academy of Management Journal* 8 (1965), 127–132; Peter M. Blau and Richard A. Schoenherr, *The Structure of Organizations* (New York: Basic Books, 1971).

52. W. Alan Randolph, "Matching Technology and the Design of Organization Units," *California Management Review* 22–23 (1980–81), 39–48; Daft and Macintosh, "Tentative Exploration into Amount and Equivocality of Information Processing"; Michael L. Tushman, "Work Characteristics and Subunit Communication Structure: A Contingency Analysis," *Administrative Science Quarterly* 24 (1979), 82–98.

53. Andrew H. Van de Ven and Diane L. Ferry, *Measuring and Assessing Organizations* (New York: Wiley, 1980); Randolph, "Matching Technology and the Design of Organization Units."

54. Richard L. Daft and Robert H. Lengel, "Information Richness: A New Approach to Managerial Behavior and Organization Design," in Barry Staw and Larry L. Cummings, eds., *Research in Organizational Behavior*, vol. 6 (Greenwich, Conn.: JAI Press, 1984), 191–233; Richard L. Daft and Norman B. Macintosh, "A New Approach into Design and Use of Management Information," *California Management Review* 21 (1978), 82–92; Daft and Macintosh, "A Tentative Exploration into Amount and Equivocality of Information Processing"; W. Alan Randolph, "Organizational Technology and the Media and Purpose Dimensions of Organizational Communication," *Journal of Business Research* 6 (1978), 237–259; Linda Argote, "Input Uncertainty and Organizational Coordination in Hospital Emergency Units," *Administrative Science Quarterly* 27 (1982), 420–434; Andrew H. Van de Ven and Andre Delbecq, "A Task Contingent Model of Work Unit Structure," *Administrative Science Quarterly* 19 (1974), 183–197.

55. Peggy Leatt and Rodney Schneck, "Criteria for Grouping Nursing Subunits in Hospitals," *Academy of Management Journal* 27 (1984), 150–165; Robert T. Keller, "Technology-Information Processing," *Academy of Management Journal* 37, no. 1 (1994), 167–179.

56. Gresov, "Exploring Fit and Misfit with Multiple Contingencies"; Michael L. Tushman, "Technological Communication in R&D Laboratories: The Impact of Project Work Characteristics," *Academy of Management Journal* 21 (1978), 624–645; Robert T. Keller, "Technology-Information Processing Fit and the Performance of R&D Project Groups: A Test of Contingency Theory," *Academy of Management Journal* 37, no. 1 (1994), 167–179.

57. Charles Fishman, "Miracle of Birth," *Fast Company* (October 2002), 106–116.

58. James Thompson, *Organizations in Action* (New York: McGraw-Hill, 1967).

59. Ibid., 40.

60. Paul S. Adler, "Interdepartmental Interdependence and Coordination: The Case of the Design/Manufacturing Interface," *Organization Science* 6, no. 2 (March-April 1995), 147–167.

61. Christopher Gresov, "Effects of Dependence and Tasks on Unit Design and Efficiency," *Organization Studies* 11 (1990), 503–529; Andrew H. Van de Ven, Andre Delbecq, and Richard Koenig, "Determinants of Coordination Modes within Organizations," *American Sociological Review* 41 (1976), 322–338; Linda Argote, "Input Uncertainty and Organizational Coordination in Hospital Emergency Units", Jack K. Ito and Richard B. Peterson, "Effects of Task Difficulty and Interdependence on Information Processing Systems," *Academy of Management Journal* 29 (1986), 139–149; Joseph L. C. Cheng, "Interdependence and Coordination in Organizations: A Role-System Analysis," *Academy of Management Journal* 26 (1983), 156–162.

62. Robert W. Keidel, "Team Sports Models as a Generic Organizational Framework," *Human Relations* 40 (1987), 591–612; Robert W. Keidel, "Baseball, Football, and Basketball: Models for Business," *Organizational Dynamics* (Winter 1984), 5–18; and Nancy Katz, "Sports Teams as a Model for Workplace Teams: Lessons and Liabilities," *Academy of Management Executive* 15, no. 3 (2001), 56–67.

63. Michele Liu, Héléné Denis, Harvey Kolodny, and Benjt Stymne, "Organization Design for Technological Change," *Human Relations* 43 (January 1990), 7–22.

64. Stephen P. Robbins, *Organizational Behavior*, (Upper Saddle River, N.J.: Prentice-Hall, 1998) 521.

65. Gerald I. Susman and Richard B. Chase, "A Sociotechnical Analysis of the Integrated Factory," *Journal of Applied Behavioral Science* 22 (1986), 257–270; Paul Adler, "New Technologies, New Skills," *California Management Review* 29 (Fall 1986), 9–28.

66. Based on Don Hellriegel, John W. Slocum, Jr., and Richard W. Woodman, *Organizational Behavior*, 8th ed. (Cincinnati, Ohio: South-Western, 1998), 491–495; Gregory B. Northcraft and Margaret A. Neale, *Organizational Behavior: A Management Challenge*, 2nd ed. (Fort Worth, Tex.: The Dryden Press, 1994), 550–553.

67. F. Emery, "Characteristics of Sociotechnical Systems," Tavistock Institute of Human Relations, document 527, 1959; William Passmore, Carol Francis, and Jeffrey Haldeman, "Sociotechnical Systems: A North American Reflection on Empirical Studies of the 70s," *Human Relations* 35 (1982), 1179–1204; William M. Fox, "Sociotechnical System Principles and Guidelines: Past and Present," *Journal of Applied Behavioral Science* 31, no. 1 (March 1995), 91–105.

68. W. S. Cascio, *Managing Human Resources* (New York: McGraw-Hill, 1986), 19.

69. Eric Trist and Hugh Murray, eds., *The Social Engagement of Social Science: A Tavistock Anthology*, vol. II (Philadelphia: University of Pennsylvania Press, 1993); William A. Passmore, "Social Science Transformed: The Socio-Technical Perspective," *Human Relations* 48, no. 1 (1995), 1–21.

70. R. E. Walton, "From Control to Commitment in the Workplace," *Harvard Business Review* 63, no. 2 (1985), 76–84; E. W. Lawler, III, *High Involvement Management* (London: Jossey-Bass, 1986), 84; Hellriegel, Slocum, and Woodman, *Organizational Behavior*, 491.

71. William A. Passmore, "Social Science Transformed: The Socio-Technical Perspective," *Human Relations* 48, no. 1 (1995), 1–21.

72. David M. Upton, "What Really Makes Factories Flexible?" *Harvard Business Review* (July–August 1995), 74–84.

73. Passmore, "Social Science Transformed: The Socio-Technical Perspective"; H. Scarbrough, "Review Article: *The Social Engagement of Social Science: A Tavistock Anthology*, Vol. II," *Human Relations* 48, no. 1 (1995), 23–33.

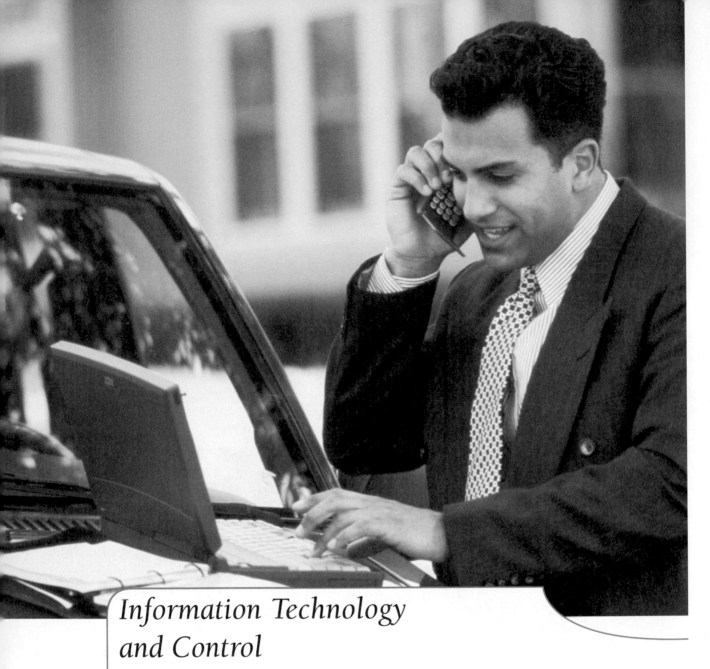

Information Technology and Control

chapter 8

A LOOK INSIDE

Progressive Insurance

Progressive Insurance is one of the fastest-growing auto insurers in the country, ranked fourth behind State Farm, Allstate, and Farmers. Yet, less than twenty years ago, Progressive was a small company providing insurance only to very high-risk drivers, who were willing to pay almost any price just to get coverage. How did a small, specialized firm compete with giant insurance companies in the larger market for standard auto insurance? By using information technology to gain a strategic advantage.

The traditional way of selling insurance has been through local agents. To get competitive quotes, customers had to call a series of agents who gathered information and passed it on to underwriters. Customers typically waited several days for a price quote. Then the process of completing a policy would take up to two more weeks. Progressive managers found a way to give customers more rapid service though the creative use of information technology. By the early 1990s, the company had begun using database management software that integrated the sales, underwriting, and price quoting process into a convenient, one-stop shopping center that customers could access over the phone. Insurance shoppers could call a toll-free number twenty-four hours a day, seven days a week, and get a quote from Progressive and up to three of its competitors, a first in the industry. Telephone sales agents (called *business development representatives*) were trained in a streamlined process using information technology tools that could gather pertinent information and complete a policy within fifteen minutes. Within a couple of years, Progressive had expanded AUTOPRO to become the first company to offer auto insurance over the Internet.

Information technology was also creatively applied to the claims process through Progressive's Immediate Response Program. Now, claims representatives use laptop computers and intelligent software to download information, record claims details, make decisions, and cut a check right on the spot. All information goes into the database, enabling managers back at headquarters to monitor expenses and make better pricing and policy decisions.[1]

Insurance isn't the only industry being transformed by information technology and the Internet. Effectively using information technology in knowledge-based firms such as consulting firm KPMG Peat Marwick, Reuters Group PLC, which provides financial information, and Business Wire, a provider of business and corporate information, has long been fundamental to the business. Today, information technology has become a crucial weapon helping companies in all industries maintain a competitive edge in the face of growing global competition and rising customer demands for speed, convenience, quality, and value. Weyerhaeuser's door factory in Marshfield, Wisconsin, uses an information technology system called DoorBuilder to track inventory, calculate prices, schedule production, and automate order taking. The sophisticated system has cut manufacturing costs, doubled production, and improved customer service and profitability.[2] Olive Garden, a restaurant chain, uses computerized systems to measure and control everything from bathroom cleanliness to food preparation time. And Memorial Health Services in Long Beach, California, uses medical identification cards (available over the Internet) that can be swiped into a computer to speed registration and give emergency room personnel immediate access to vital patient information.[3]

The rapidly growing use of the Internet has provided new avenues for commercial activity, as well as new ways to gather and disseminate information across a global network. This presents new challenges for managers. For one thing, the balance of power has shifted to the customer. With the unlimited access to information provided by the Internet, customers are much better informed and much more demanding, making customer loyalty harder to build.[4] In addition, the concept of electronically linking suppliers, partners, and customers is forcing companies to rethink their strategies, organization design, and business processes. The pace of business is moving at "warp speed."[5] Planning horizons have become shorter, expectations of customers change rapidly, and new competitors spring up almost overnight. All this means managers, as well as employees throughout the organization, need quality information at their fingertips.

Highly successful organizations today are typically those that most effectively collect, store, distribute, and use information. More than facilities, equipment, or even products, it is the information a company has and how it uses it that defines organization success—some would say even organization survival.[6] Top managers look for ways to manage, leverage, and protect what is rapidly becoming the most valuable asset of any organization: information and knowledge.

PURPOSE OF THIS CHAPTER

Information technology is an essential component of successful organizations. Managers spend at least 80 percent of their time actively exchanging information. They need this information to hold the organization together. For example, the vertical and horizontal information linkages described in Chapter 3 are designed to provide managers with relevant information for decision making, evaluation, and control. This chapter examines the evolution of information technology. The chapter begins by looking at information technology systems applied to organizational operations and then examines how information technology is used for decision making and control of the organization. The next sections consider how information technology can be used as a strategic weapon by looking at internal coordination applications such as intranets, enterprise resource planning, and knowledge management systems, as well as applications for external collaboration, such as extranets and EDI networks, e-business, and the integrated enterprise. The final section of the chapter presents an overview of how information technology affects organization design and interorganizational relationships.

INFORMATION TECHNOLOGY EVOLUTION

The evolution of information technology is illustrated in Exhibit 8.1. First-line management is typically concerned with well-defined problems about operational issues and past events. Top management, by contrast, deals mostly with uncertain, ambiguous issues, such as strategy and planning. As the complexity of computer-based information technology systems has increased, applications have grown to support effective top management control and decision making about complex and uncertain problems.

EXHIBIT 8.1   Evolution of Organizational Applications of Information Technology

TOP
(strategy, plans,
nonprogrammed)

MANAGEMENT LEVEL

FIRST-LINE
(operational,
past, programmed)

3. Strategic Weapon

Internal Coordination	**External Relationships**
• Intranets	• Extranets, EDI
• Enterprise resource planning	• Integrated enterprise
• Knowledge management	• E-business

2. Decision Making and Control

• Management information systems
• Decision support systems
• Executive information systems
• Management control systems
• Balanced scorecard

1. Operations

• Transaction processing systems
• Data warehousing

Direction of Information System Evolution

Low   **SYSTEM COMPLEXITY**   High

Initially, information technology systems in organizations were applied to operations. These initial applications were based on the notion of machine room efficiency—that is, current operations could be performed more efficiently with the use of computer technology. The goal was to reduce labor costs by having computers take over some tasks. These systems became known as **transaction processing systems** (TPS), which automate the organization's routine, day-to-day business transactions. A TPS collects data from transactions such as sales, purchases from suppliers, and inventory changes and stores them in a database. For example, Starbucks Coffee uses a transaction processing system to keep track of sales in all its stores worldwide. As data from transactions accumulate, they may be stored in various company databases.

In recent years, the concept of data warehousing and data mining has expanded the usefulness of these accumulated data. **Data warehousing** is the use of huge databases that combine all of a company's data and allow users to access the data directly, create reports, and obtain responses to what-if questions. Building a database at a large corporation is a huge undertaking that includes defining hundreds of gigabytes of data from many existing systems, providing a means of continually updating the data, making it all compatible, and linking it to other software that makes it possible for users to search and analyze the data and produce helpful reports. Software for **data mining** helps users make sense of all this data. Data mining tools use sophisticated decision-making processes to search raw data for patterns and relationships that may be significant. State governments in Virginia, Texas, and Iowa are using data mining software to find people and corporations that aren't paying their fair share of taxes. By comparing tax payments with millions of records from other sources, such as unemployment insurance, customs declarations, aircraft registrations, and various other transactions, officials can identify out-of-state corporations that may be doing business in the state but not paying taxes there.[7]

Thus, information technology has evolved to more complex systems for managerial decision making and control of the organization, the second stage illustrated in Exhibit 8.1 Further advancements have also contributed to the use of information technology as a strategic weapon, the highest level of application. The remainder of this chapter will focus on these two stages in the evolution of information technology.

INFORMATION FOR DECISION MAKING AND CONTROL

Through the application of more sophisticated computer-based systems, managers have tools to improve the performance of departments and the organization as a whole. These applications use information stored in corporate databases to help managers control the organization and make important decisions. Exhibit 8.2 illustrates the various elements of information systems used for decision making and control. Management information systems—including information reporting systems, decision support systems, and executive information systems—facilitate rapid and effective decision making. Elements for control include various management control systems and a procedure known as the balanced scorecard. In an organization, these systems are interconnected, as illustrated by the dashed lines in Exhibit 8.2. The systems for decision making and control often share the same

EXHIBIT 8.2   *Information Systems for Managerial Control and Decision Making*

basic data, but the data and reports are designed and used for a primary purpose of decision making versus control.

ORGANIZATIONAL DECISION-MAKING SYSTEMS

A **management information system** is a computer-based system that provides information and support for managerial decision making. The MIS is supported by the organization's transaction processing systems and by organizational databases (and frequently databases of external data as well). The **information reporting system**, the most common form of MIS, provides mid-level managers with reports that summarize data and support day-to-day decision making. For example, when managers need to make decisions about production scheduling, they can review the data on the anticipated number of orders within the next month, inventory levels, and availability of human resources.

At Harrah's casinos, personalized player cards with a magnetic stripe that are inserted into gaming machines collect detailed information on each player that goes into a massive customer database. Information reporting systems enable managers to offer customers just the right combination of services to keep them coming back rather than moving on to another casino. In addition, the system can calculate an individual customer's "potential value," helping managers create customized marketing programs that retain low-end players and turn some of them into high rollers.[8]

An **executive information system** (EIS) is a higher-level application that facilitates decision making at the highest levels of management. These systems are typically based on software that can convert large amounts of complex data into pertinent information and provide that information to top managers in a timely fashion. For example, Motorola's Semiconductor Products Sector, based in Austin, Texas, had massive amounts of stored data, but users couldn't easily find what they needed. The company implemented an EIS using online analytical processing software so that more than a thousand senior executives, as well as managers and project analysts in finance, marketing, sales, and accounting departments around the world, could quickly and easily get information about customer buying trends, manufacturing, and so forth, right from their desktop computers, without having to learn complex and arcane search commands.[9]

A **decision support system** (DSS) provides specific benefits to managers at all levels of the organization. These interactive, computer-based systems rely on decision models and integrated databases. Using decision support software, users can pose a series of what-if questions to test possible alternatives. Based on assumptions used in the software or specified by the user, managers can explore various alternatives and receive information to help them choose the alternative that will likely have the best outcome.

Wal-Mart uses an EIS and a DSS that rely on a massive database to make decisions about what to stock, how to price and promote it, and when to reorder. Department managers at each store can keep track of which items are top sellers in their department and make sure those items are in stock. Handheld scanners enable managers to keep close tabs on inventory. Back at headquarters, top managers use executive information systems to analyze buying patterns and other information, enabling them to spot problems or opportunities. For example, executives discovered that particular items are frequently purchased together, so they spotted an opportunity to cross-promote those items and increase sales.[10]

FEEDBACK CONTROL MODEL

Another primary use of information in organizations is for control. Effective control systems involve the use of feedback to determine whether organizational performance meets established standards to help the organization attain its goals. Managers set up systems for organizational control that consist of the four key steps in the **feedback control model** illustrated in Exhibit 8.3.

The cycle of control includes setting strategic goals for departments or the organization as a whole, establishing standards of performance, measuring actual performance and comparing it to the standards, and correcting or changing activities as needed. Feedback control helps managers make needed adjustments in work activities, standards of performance, or goals to help the organization be successful. For example, Frito-Lay establishes targets in each region of the country for snack food sales. Thousands of salespeople use handheld computers to send daily information on actual sales levels to the company database. The data are compared, and feedback is used to change strategies, products, or marketing approaches to improve sales as needed.[11]

We will discuss two commonly used methods that operate as feedback control systems: management control systems and the balanced scorecard.

MANAGEMENT CONTROL SYSTEMS

Management control systems are broadly defined as the formal routines, reports, and procedures that use information to maintain or alter patterns in organization activities.[12] These control systems include the formalized information-based activities for planning, budgeting, performance evaluation, resource allocation, and employee rewards. Targets are set in advance, outcomes compared to targets, and variance reported to managers for corrective

EXHIBIT 8.3   *A Simplified Feedback Control Model*

action. Advances in information technology have dramatically improved the efficiency and effectiveness of these systems. For example, SmithKline Beecham Pharm (now GlaxoSmithKline) developed something it calls the *executive dashboard*, a proprietary software system built on Excel. When top managers turn on their computer each morning, key control indicators, such as sales in relation to targets, appear right on the screen.[13]

Exhibit 8.4 lists four control system elements that are often considered the core of management control systems: the budget and financial reports; periodic nonfinancial statistical reports; reward systems; and quality control systems.[14]

The *budget* is typically used to set targets for the organization's expenditures for the year and then report actual costs on a monthly or quarterly basis. As a means of control, budgets report actual as well as planned expenditures for cash, assets, raw materials, salaries, and other resources so that managers can take action to correct variances. Sometimes, the variance between budgeted and actual amounts for each line item is listed as a part of the budget. Managers also rely on a variety of other financial reports. The *balance sheet* shows a firm's financial position with respect to assets and liabilities at a specific point in time. An *income statement*, sometimes called a *profit and loss statement (P&L)* summarizes the company's financial performance for a given time interval, such as for the week, month, or year. This statement shows revenues coming into the organization from all sources and subtracts all expenses, such as cost of goods sold, interest, taxes, and depreciation. The *bottom line* indicates the net income—profit or loss—for the given time period.

Managers use periodic statistical reports to evaluate and monitor nonfinancial performance, such as customer satisfaction, employee performance, or rate of staff turnover. For e-commerce organizations, important measurements of nonfinancial performance include *stickiness*—that is, the frequency with which customers come back to the site and the length of time they spend there—and the *conversion rate*, the ratio of buyers to site visitors.[15] E-commerce managers regularly review reports on stickiness, conversion rates, and other metrics to identify problems and improve their Web pages. For all organizations, nonfinancial reports typically are computer-based and may be available daily, weekly, or monthly. Managers at TNT UK, for example, regularly review statistical reports on customer satisfaction and use this information to improve service.

EXHIBIT 8.4   *Management Control Systems*

Subsystem	Content and Frequency
Budget, financial reports	Financial, resource expenditures, profit and loss; monthly
Statistical reports	Nonfinancial outputs; weekly or monthly, often computer-based
Reward systems	Evaluation of managers based on department goals and performance, set rewards; yearly
Quality control systems	Participation, benchmarking guidelines, Six Sigma goals; continuous

Source: Based on Richard L. Daft and Norman B. Macintosh, "The Nature and Use of Formal Control Systems for Management Control and Strategy Implementation," *Journal of Management* 10 (1984), 43–66.

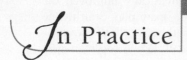

TNT UK's management control systems track performance so regularly and in such detail that every manager is constantly aware of existing problems and every employee has the information to help correct them. When most delivery companies measure customer satisfaction, they look at whether packages are delivered on time, assuming that customers are happy when this standard is met. Not TNT—it tracks every aspect of the service it provides. One biannual customer satisfaction survey asks 4,000 randomly selected customers to rank key delivery attributes—such as reliability, price, staff professionalism, range of services, and so forth—in order of importance and then to score the company's performance on each attribute. Targets are set each year to exceed the company's previous best performance. TNT managers develop tight definitions of what quality service means for every aspect of the business, providing employees with clear guidelines that spell out how to make improvements.

Far from feeling constrained by the tight measurements and procedures, employees are energized and motivated to meet service targets. For example, the company's thirty-three depots, which submit their results to top management each week, have an intense rivalry. Each wants to top the ranking charts. As a result, the proportion of perfect transactions—meaning the package is delivered on time and intact, the delivery documentation is completed on a clean invoice, and payment is received by TNT by the due date—increased from 57 percent in 1995 to 87 percent three years later. Managers are careful not to let number-crunching get in the way of meeting the needs and goals of staff members. Alan Jones, managing director of TNT UK, motivates van drivers with personal telephone calls or notes congratulating them on particular achievements. And low scores, rather than leading to a reprimand, bring a note encouraging the team to keep their chins up. As Jones points out, without the data provided by computerized management control systems, he wouldn't be able to provide that level of continuous feedback to his employees.[16]

TNT UK also effectively uses the third element listed in Exhibit 8.4—reward systems. Reward systems offer incentives for managers and employees to improve performance and meet departmental goals. Managers and employees evaluate how well previous goals were met, set new goals for the year, and establish rewards for meeting the new targets. Rewards are often tied to the annual performance appraisal process, during which managers assess employee performance and provide feedback to help the employee improve performance and obtain rewards.

The final control element listed in Exhibit 8.4 is quality control systems, which managers use to train employees in quality control methods, set targets for employee participation, establish benchmarking guidelines, and assign and measure *Six Sigma* goals. **Benchmarking** means the process of continually measuring products, services, and practices against tough competitors or other organizations recognized as industry leaders.[17] **Six Sigma**, originally conceived by Motorola Corp., is a highly ambitious quality standard that specifies a goal of no more than 3.4 defects per million parts.[18] However, Six Sigma has deviated from its precise definition to become a generic term for a whole set of control procedures that emphasize a relentless pursuit of higher quality and lower costs. The discipline is based on a methodology referred to as DMAIC (Define, Measure, Analyze, Improve, and Control), which provides a structured way for organizations to approach and solve problems.[19] Companies such as General Electric, Dow Chemical, and 3M have saved millions of dollars by rooting out inefficiencies and waste through Six Sigma processes.[20]

One finding from research into management control systems is that each of the four control systems focuses on a different aspect of the production process. These four systems thus form an overall management control system that provides middle managers with control information about resource inputs, process efficiency, and output.[21] Moreover, the use of and reliance on control systems depends on the strategic targets set by top management.

The budget is used primarily to allocate resource inputs. Managers use the budget for planning the future and reducing uncertainty about the availability of human and material resources needed to perform department tasks. Computer-based statistical reports are used to control outputs. These reports contain data about output volume and quality and other indicators that provide feedback to middle management about departmental results. The reward system and quality control systems are directed at the production process. Quality control systems specify standards for employee participation, teamwork, and problem solving. Reward systems provide incentives to meet goals and can help guide and correct employee behavior. Managers also use direct supervision to keep departmental work activities within desired limits.

THE BALANCED SCORECARD

In the past, most organizations relied largely on financial accounting measures as the primary basis for measuring organizational performance, but today's companies realize that a balanced view of both financial and operational measures is needed for successful organizational control.

The four control elements listed in Exhibit 8.4 help provide managers with a balanced view. In addition, a recent innovation is to integrate internal financial measurements and statistical reports with a concern for markets and customers as well as employees. The **balanced scorecard** is a comprehensive management control system that balances traditional financial measures with operational measures relating to a company's critical success factors.[22] A balanced scorecard contains four major perspectives, as illustrated in Exhibit 8.5: financial performance, customer service, internal business processes, and the organization's capacity for learning and growth.[23] Within these four areas, managers identify key performance indicators the organization will track. The *financial perspective* reflects a concern that the organization's activities contribute to improving short- and long-term financial performance. It includes traditional measures such as net income and return on investment. *Customer service indicators* measure such things as how customers view the organization, as well as customer retention and satisfaction. *Business process indicators* focus on production and operating statistics, such as order fulfillment or cost per order. The final component looks at the organization's *potential for learning and growth*, focusing on how well resources and human capital are being managed for the company's future. Measurements include such things as employee retention, business process improvements, and the introduction of new products. The components of the scorecard are designed in an integrative manner so that they reinforce one another and link short-term actions with long-term strategic goals, as illustrated in Exhibit 8.5.

The balanced scorecard helps managers focus on the key strategic measures that define the success of a particular organization over time and communicate them clearly throughout the organization. The scorecard has become the core management system for many organizations today, including Tenneco, Allstate, KPMG Peat Marwick, Nationwide Financial Services, Cigna Insurance, and Bell

EXHIBIT 8.5   *Major Perspectives of the Balanced Scorecard*

Source: Based on Robert S. Kaplan and David P. Norton, "Using the Balanced Scorecard as a Strategic Management System," *Harvard Business Review* (January–February 1996), 75–85; Chee W. Chow, Kamal M. Haddad, and James E. Williamson, "Applying the Balanced Scorecard to Small Companies," *Management Accounting* 79, no. 2 (August 1997), 21–27; and Cathy Lazere, "All Together Now," *CFO* (February 1998), 28–36.

Emergis (a division of Bell Canada). Managers can use the scorecard to set goals, allocate resources, plan budgets, and determine rewards.[24]

Executive information systems facilitate use of the balanced scorecard by enabling top managers to easily track measurements in multiple areas, rapidly analyze the data, and convert huge amounts of data into clear information reports.

Following the use of information systems for managerial decision making and control, information technology (IT) has evolved further to become a strategic weapon for organizations such as Wal-Mart, Harrah's Entertainment, and Progressive Insurance. This is the highest level of application, as illustrated in Exhibit 8.1 at the beginning of the chapter. Information technology can help build and enhance strategy by providing better data and information within the organization (internal coordination) as well as help the organization redefine and support relationships with customers, suppliers, and other organizations (external relationships).

INFORMATION AS A STRATEGIC WEAPON: NETWORKING FOR INTERNAL COORDINATION

Three primary information technology tools for internal coordination are intranets, enterprise resource planning (ERP), and knowledge management systems.

INTRANETS

Networking, which links people and departments within a particular building or even across corporate offices, enabling them to share information and cooperate on projects, has become an important strategic weapon for many companies. Networks may take many forms, but the fastest-growing form of corporate networking is the **intranet**, a private, company-wide information system that uses the communications protocols and standards of the Internet and the World Wide Web but is accessible only to people within the company. To view files and information, users simply navigate the site with a standard Web browser, clicking on links.[25] Because intranets are Web-based, they can be accessed from any type of computer or workstation.

Today, most companies with intranets have moved their management information systems, executive information systems, and so forth over to the intranet so they can easily be accessed by anyone who needs them. In addition, having these systems as part of the intranet means new features and applications can easily be added and accessed through a standard browser.

Intranets can improve internal communications and unlock hidden information. They enable employees to keep in touch with what's going on around the organization, quickly and easily find information they need, share ideas, and work on projects collaboratively. The most advanced intranets, such as those at SPS, Ford Motor Company, Nike, and Weyerhaeuser, are linked into the proprietary systems that govern a company's business functions. Ford's global intranet connects more than 100,000 workstations to thousands of sites offering proprietary information such as market research, analyses of competitor's components, and product development.[26] Frito-Lay's intranet enables salespeople to rapidly access sales-related customer and corporate information, brainstorm with their colleagues about the best approach for a sales pitch, or locate an expert within the company to assist with promotion planning, costing, or new product announcements.[27]

ENTERPRISE RESOURCE PLANNING

Another recent approach to information management helps pull together various types of information to see how decisions and actions in one part of the organization affect other parts of the firm. A growing number of companies are setting up broad-scale information systems that take a comprehensive view of the organization's activities. These **enterprise resource planning** (ERP) systems collect, process, and provide information about a company's entire enterprise, including order processing, product design, purchasing, inventory, manufacturing, distribution, human resources, receipt of payments, and forecasting of future demand.[28] An ERP can serve as the backbone for an entire organization by integrating and optimizing all the various business processes across the entire firm.[29]

Such a system links all of these areas of activity into a network, as illustrated in Exhibit 8.6. When a salesperson takes an order, the ERP system checks to see how the order impacts inventory levels, scheduling, human resources, purchasing, and distribution. The system replicates organizational processes in software, guides employees through the processes step-by-step, and automates as many of them as possible. For example, ERP software can automatically cut an accounts payable check as soon as a clerk confirms that goods have been received in inventory, send an online purchase order immediately after a manager has authorized a purchase, or schedule production at the most appropriate plant after an order is received.[30]

By implementing ERP, Lockport, Louisiana-based Bollinger Shipyards shaved an average of 15 percent off the time it takes to build a boat, translating into huge savings for the company. Each of nine Bollinger shipyards used to require two employees to handle administration, purchasing, and payroll; now they get by with one part-time person at each yard because the ERP system automates these processes. Freed from mundane chores, employees have been reassigned to more knowledge-intensive jobs.[31]

In addition, because the system integrates data about all aspects of operations, managers and employees at all levels can see how decisions and actions in one part of the organization affect other parts, using this information to make better decisions. ERP can provide the kind of information furnished by transaction processing systems, as well as that provided by information reporting systems, decision support systems, or executive information systems. The key is that ERP weaves all of these systems together so people can see the big picture and act quickly, helping the organization be smarter and more competitive.

EXHIBIT 8.6   *Example of an ERP Network*

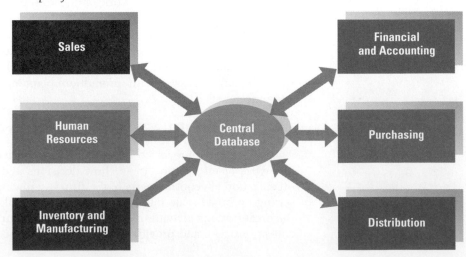

KNOWLEDGE MANAGEMENT

A primary goal for information technology systems today is to support efforts to manage and leverage organizational knowledge. Having greater access to information is useless unless that information is put to use to further the goals and success of the organization. Increasingly, intellectual capital is the primary way in which businesses measure their value.[32] Therefore, managers see knowledge as an important resource to manage, just as they manage cash flow, raw materials, or other resources. A survey of CEOs attending the World Economic Forum's annual meeting found that 97 percent of senior executives see knowledge management as a critical issue for their organizations.[33] To learn and change, organizations must effectively acquire, create, and transfer knowledge across the company and modify their activities to reflect new knowledge and insight.[34]

Knowledge management is a new way to think about organizing and sharing an organization's intellectual and creative resources. It refers to the efforts to systematically find, organize, and make available a company's intellectual capital and to foster a culture of continuous learning and knowledge sharing so that organizational activities build on what is already known.[35] The company's **intellectual capital** is the sum of its knowledge, experience, understanding, relationships, processes, innovations, and discoveries. Although most of a company's knowledge is within the formal boundaries of the organization, tapping into the knowledge of outside experts is also important because it brings new knowledge into the organization that can be combined with existing knowledge to highlight problems or opportunities and make the organization more competitive.[36]

Although information technology plays an important role in knowledge management by enabling the storage and dissemination of data and information across the organization, information technology is only one piece of a larger puzzle.[37] A complete knowledge management system includes not only processes for capturing and storing knowledge and organizing it for easy access, but also ways to generate new knowledge through learning and to share knowledge throughout the organization. As discussed in this chapter's Book Mark, old-fashioned paper might play just as important a role in knowledge work as computer technology.

What Is Knowledge? Knowledge is not the same thing as data or information, although it uses both. **Data** are simple, absolute facts and figures that, in and of themselves, may be of little use. A company might have data that show 30 percent of a particular product is sold to customers in Florida. To be useful to the organization, the data are processed into finished *information* by connecting them with other data—for example, nine out of ten of the products sold in Florida are bought by people over the age of sixty. **Information** is data that have been linked with other data and converted into a useful context for specific use. **Knowledge** goes a step further; it is a conclusion drawn from the information after it is linked to other information and compared to what is already known. Knowledge, as opposed to information and data, always has a human factor. Books can contain information, but the information becomes knowledge only when a person absorbs it and puts it to use.[38]

Organizations deal with both explicit knowledge and implicit, or tacit, knowledge.[39] **Explicit knowledge** is formal, systematic knowledge that can be codified, written down, and passed on to others in documents or general instructions. Tacit knowledge, on the other hand, is often difficult to put into words. **Tacit knowledge** is based on personal experience, rules of thumb, intuition, and

The Myth of the Paperless Office
By Abigail J. Sellen and Richard H. R. Harper

At first glance, it seems like a great idea. Get rid of all the paper that clutters desktops and put everything on computers. Especially with the proliferation of handheld gadgets, paper seems redundant. Yet paper sales increase every year because paper is woven into the fabric of our lives and organizations—and for very good reasons, argue Abigail Sellen and Richard Harper, authors of *The Myth of the Paperless Office*. Paper actually enables a certain kind of information processing, as well as supporting collaborative knowledge work. People simply can't *think* the same way when looking at a document on a computer screen.

WHY PAPER PERSISTS
Sellen and Harper offer a number of reasons why paper persists. Paper has many advantages, they assert, for performing certain kinds of cognitive tasks and supporting certain kinds of collaboration.

- *Paper is flexible and easily manipulated for reading.* Most people still prefer to read newspapers or documents on paper rather than on a computer screen. The authors cite four primary reasons for this: Paper allows people to flexibly navigate through documents, it facilitates the cross-referencing of more than one document at a time, it allows for easy annotation, and it enables the interweaving of reading and writing. Paper allows one to pick up a document or newspaper, flip through it, read bits here and there, and quickly get a sense of the overall piece.
- *Paper is a tool for managing and coordinating action among coworkers.* The authors cite a fascinating example of air traffic controllers who, despite the

availability and use of highly sophisticated technology, continue to use paper flight strips to support a seamless teamwork, enable easy manipulation to indicate flight variations, give everyone on the team information at a glance, and facilitate the rapid pace of work required in this high-pressure environment.

- *Paper supports collaboration and sharing of knowledge.* Paper has interactional properties that are not easy to duplicate with digital media and collaborative tools. People working on collaborative documents that require the professional judgment and contributions of many people typically print drafts to read, mark up, and discuss with others while flipping though the pages. Sellen and Harper argue that, without paper drafts, collaborative, iterative knowledge work is much more difficult and time consuming. Paper, they say, "is a versatile medium that can be co-opted, shaped, and adapted to meet the needs of the work."

THE BEST OF BOTH WORLDS
The authors emphasize that digital technologies have their own advantages. Their point in *The Myth of the Paperless Office* is that managers should understand what paper can do and what computers can do and should know how to get the most out of each medium. "The real issue for organizations . . . is not to get rid of paper for its own sake, but to have sufficient motivation to understand their own work process and the ways paper plays a role."

The Myth of the Paperless Office, by Abigail Sellen and Richard Harper, is published by MIT Press.

judgment. It includes professional know-how and expertise, individual insight and experience, and creative solutions that are difficult to communicate and pass on to others. Explicit knowledge may be equated with *knowing about*; whereas tacit knowledge is equated with *knowing how*.[40]

Finding ways to transfer both explicit and tacit knowledge—the knowing about and the knowing how—across the organization is critical. Knowledge that accumulates in individuals' heads and within various organizational units is of limited value until it is shared with other parts of the organization, both vertically and horizontally.[41] Although explicit knowledge can easily be captured and shared in documents and through information technology systems, as much as 80 percent of an organization's valuable knowledge may be tacit knowledge that is not easily captured and transferred.[42]

Approaches to Knowledge Management. Two distinct approaches to knowledge management are outlined in Exhibit 8.7. Critical to both approaches is a cultural mindset that encourages collaboration and knowledge sharing. Since knowledge gives people power within the organization, there is a strong impulse to hoard rather than share it. Thus, knowledge management often requires major culture change. For example, to meet new strategic goals, insurance underwriter CNA built a sophisticated Web-based knowledge network so employees could share knowledge over the corporate intranet. However, the most difficult part of the process was shifting to a culture of collaboration and knowledge sharing. Gordon Larson, CNA's chief knowledge officer, spurred culture change primarily by telling stories, a powerful means of helping people understand their new roles and responsibilities and how sharing knowledge could benefit them and the organization. Larson recruited *knowledge champions* in twenty or so functional areas who would collect and pass his way stories that demonstrated the new cultural values in action.[43]

The first approach to knowledge management outlined in Exhibit 8.7 deals primarily with the collection and sharing of explicit knowledge, largely through the use of sophisticated information technology systems.[44] Explicit knowledge may include intellectual properties such as patents and licenses, work processes such as policies and procedures, specific information on customers, markets, suppliers or competitors, competitive intelligence reports, benchmark data, and so forth. When an organization uses this approach, the focus is on collecting and codifying knowledge and storing it in databases where it can easily be accessed and reused by anyone in the organization. With this "people-to-documents" approach, knowledge is gathered from the individuals who possess it and is organized into documents that others can access and reuse. The second approach focuses on leveraging individual expertise and know-how—tacit knowledge—by connecting people face-to-face or through interactive media. Tacit knowledge includes professional know-how, individual insights and creativity, and personal experience and intuition. With this approach, managers concentrate on developing personal networks that link people together for the sharing of tacit knowledge.

EXHIBIT 8.7   *Two Approaches to Knowledge Management*

Explicit Provide high-quality, reliable, and fast information systems for access of codified, reusable knowledge		**Tacit** Channel individual expertise to provide creative advice on strategic problems
People-to-documents approach *Develop an electronic document system that codifies, stores, disseminates, and allows reuse of knowledge*	**Knowledge Management Strategy**	**Person-to-person approach** *Develop networks for linking people so that tacit knowledge can be shared*
Invest heavily in information technology, with a goal of connecting people with reusable, codified knowledge	**Information Technology Approach**	*Invest moderately in information technology, with a goal of facilitating conversations and the personal exchange of tacit knowledge*

Source: Based on Morten T. Hansen, Nitin Nohria, and Thomas Tierney, "What's Your Strategy for Managing Knowledge?" *Harvard Business Review* (March–April 1999), 106–116.

The organization uses information technology systems primarily for facilitating conversation and person-to-person sharing of experience, insight, and ideas. For example, intranets are important for helping employees, especially those who are geographically dispersed, share ideas and tap into expert knowledge throughout the organization. At CNA, when an employee needs to locate someone with expertise in a particular industry, he or she simply types in a query that is automatically sent out to all employees on the intranet. "Our knowledge network is a high-tech geographically neutral water cooler that enables access to thousands of people," says CNA's Bob James.[45] Organizations also try to find ways to get people together via face-to-face team meetings or through videoconferencing for intensive conversations.

Organizations typically combine several methods and technologies to facilitate the sharing and transfer of both explicit and tacit knowledge. Consider the example of DPR Construction, Inc., one of the fastest-growing and most successful general contracting businesses in the United States.

DPR CONSTRUCTION, INC.

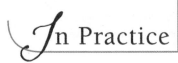

Doug Woods, Peter Nosler, and Ronald Davidowski didn't set out to reinvent the construction industry. They just wanted to build a great company that worked in an industry where many companies don't work very well. They succeeded—DPR worked so well that it grew from twelve people to 2,000 and from annual revenues of less than $1 million to more than $1.3 billion in only eight years. The company, whose motto is "DPR Exists to Build Great Things," specializes in building for six industries—biotechnology, pharmaceuticals, microelectronics, entertainment, health care, and corporate-office development. Part of the reason DPR has become so successful is that it absorbed many of the ideas that drive its fast-moving clients—companies such as Novell, Charles Schwab, Sun Microsystems, and Genentech. One of those ideas is managing and transferring knowledge.

At the start of any project, DPR uses in-house facilitators to align the interests of the project's numerous constituencies, including architects, contractors, subcontractors, clients, and suppliers. This emphasis on team building makes sure everyone has an opportunity to have input from the beginning—and DPR has a rich mechanism for acquiring new knowledge. When DPR contracted to build lab facilities for Stanford University, it brought students into the process to learn from them how the facilities could better meet their needs. The process was so successful that DPR now tries to learn everything it can from the intended users on all its projects. This kind of learning and tacit knowledge sharing is evident throughout DPR. Regular team meetings focus on solving specific problems. Regional and national meetings involve employees in deep conversations about how to improve performance in seven critical areas that DPR has identified as essential to organizational success.

However, DPR also uses computer-based information technology to give employees broad access to explicit knowledge. On almost every project, the company sets up a communications trailer, complete with servers, routers, and cellular connections. Every new hire gets a state-of-the-art laptop with core applications for estimating and project management as well as for communicating with colleagues. To harness organizational brainpower, DPR encourages employees—or anyone on a job site—to submit OFI (opportunity for improvement) forms. These may be suggestions for how to do a task more quickly, how to solve a specific problem, or how to complete a segment of a project more efficiently. The OFIs get logged into a database so that any employee can search through every project and find where others did things better, more efficiently, faster, or more safely. The database can be searched by keyword, by cost, or by one of DPR's seven critical success factors. "It's just one hell of a resource," says Jim Webb, superintendent for a renovation project at Summit Medical Center in Oakland, California. "No one at this company has done everything. But a lot of us have specialties. So when you find a problem that's beyond your expertise, you get on the computer and draw on other resources."[46]

INFORMATION AS A STRATEGIC WEAPON: STRENGTHENING EXTERNAL RELATIONSHIPS

External applications of information technology for strengthening relationships with customers, suppliers, and partners include extranets and electronic data interchange networks, systems for supply chain management and the integrated enterprise, and e-business.

ELECTRONIC DATA INTERCHANGE AND EXTRANETS

BRIEFCASE

As an organization manager, keep this guideline in mind:

Use information technology applications such as extranets and EDI networks, systems for supply chain management and enterprise integration, and e-business systems to strengthen relationships with customers, suppliers, and business partners.

Many organizations have long used one specific type of interorganizational linkage, called **electronic data interchange** (EDI), which ties businesses with suppliers. EDI, which links a computer at one company to a computer at another for the transmission of business data, such as sales statistics, without human interference, can enable businesses to achieve *rapid resupply*. Companies can save millions of dollars by using EDI to coordinate materials movement. Exhibit 8.8 shows how EDI can electronically connect several organizations to facilitate trade on both domestic and international levels. One of the earliest users of EDI was Wal-Mart, which entered into a continuous replenishment relationship with Procter & Gamble in the 1980s whereby P&G would automatically ship Pampers to Wal Mart stores without managers ever having to place an order.[47] Today, Wal-Mart

EXHIBIT 8.8   *Electronic Data Interchange for International Transactions*

requires every manufacturer it works with to manage its own in-store inventory and use EDI networks connected to Wal-Mart's private collaborative trading hub, called SupplierLink.[48]

One problem with EDI, especially for small suppliers, is the cost of setting up an EDI system. "The guy who supplies our wood pallets has five employees," says Ray Hill of Pitney Bowes. "He's not going to go out and buy a mainframe just to do business with us."[49] Advances using the Internet, however, enable small companies to transmit data over the Web. Today, many organizations use extranets for the sharing of data and information with suppliers, customers, and organizational partners. An **extranet** is an external communications system that uses the Internet and is shared by two or more organizations. Each organization moves certain data outside of its private intranet, but makes the data available only to the other companies sharing the extranet. For example, Pitney Bowes' extranet enables the small supplier of wood pallets to use a PC to tap into its site and see how many of its products Pitney Bowes has on hand and how many it will need in the next few days.

Extranets can improve communication and enhance the interorganizational relationships described in Chapter 5. An extranet helped McKesson Corp., the large San Francisco-based pharmaceutical supply business, cut costs and improve customer service. The company ships to more than 30,000 hospitals, pharmacies, and retail stores, but most belong to huge chains that pay bills from a central office. McKesson used to fax hundreds of billing statements to its customers' central accounting offices, but now uses an invoice inquiry system on the extranet. Customers can see bills from all their varied locations in one place, dramatically reducing communications and labor costs.[50] At Enterprise Rent-A-Car, insurance companies and auto body shops can access a Web-based system called Automated Rental Management System (ARMS) via an extranet.

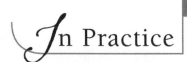

ENTERPRISE RENT-A-CAR

Enterprise Rent-A-Car gets a huge portion of its business from replacement rentals paid for by auto insurers while the driver's car is in the repair shop, making insurance companies Enterprise's most important customers. So, when a couple of major insurers asked Enterprise to develop an automated system that would streamline the cumbersome, paper-laden manual rental process, managers didn't need to think twice.

Today, the Automated Rental Management System (ARMS) enables insurance companies, Enterprise branch offices, and auto repair shops to manage the entire rental cycle online. In the past, an insurance adjuster might have had to call a local branch two or three times before finally processing a reservation. Now, the adjuster just logs onto the Web site and, using a secure extranet connection, enters required data, automatically creating a reservation and notifying the auto repair shop, which can send daily electronic updates on the status of repairs. When the rental car is returned, the system automatically generates an invoice and sends it to the insurance company.

Enterprise already had a commanding lead in the market for insurance replacement rentals, and its effective use of information technology has solidified that position. Twenty-two of the nation's 25 largest auto insurers, and 150 companies in all, are using ARMS; Enterprise processes more than $1 billion in transactions a year through the system. By making it easier for customers to do business with Enterprise, the organization has more than doubled its business with some insurance companies.[51]

THE INTEGRATED ENTERPRISE

Extranets and EDI play a critical role in today's **integrated enterprise**. The integrated enterprise is an organization that uses advanced information technology
to enable close coordination within the company as well as with suppliers, customers, and partners. One good example of the integrated enterprise is
Corrugated Supplies, which has linked its entire factory to the Internet, as
described in the Leading by Design box. An important aspect of the integrated
enterprise is *supply chain management*, which means managing the sequence of
suppliers and purchasers covering all stages of processing from obtaining raw
materials to distributing finished goods to consumers.[52] For organizations to
operate efficiently and provide high-quality items that meet customer needs, the
company must have reliable deliveries of high-quality, reasonably priced supplies
and materials. It also requires an efficient and reliable system for distributing finished products, making them readily accessible to customers.

Information Linkages.   The most recent advances involve the use of extranets
or EDI networks to achieve the right balance of low inventory levels and customer responsiveness. Exhibit 8.9 illustrates horizontal information linkages in
the integrated enterprise. By establishing electronic linkages between the organization and key partners for the sharing and exchange of data, the integrated
enterprise creates a seamless, integrated line stretching from end consumers to
raw materials suppliers.[53] For example, in the exhibit, as consumers purchase
products in retail stores, the data are automatically fed into the retail chain's
information system. In turn, the chain gives access to this constantly updated
data to the manufacturing company through a secure extranet or EDI link. With
knowledge of this demand data, the manufacturer can produce and ship products
when needed. As products are made by the manufacturer, data about raw materials used in the production process, updated inventory information, and
updated forecasted demand are electronically provided to the manufacturer's
suppliers, and the suppliers automatically replenish the manufacturer's raw
materials inventory as needed.

Horizontal Relationships.   The purpose of integrating the supply chain is for
everyone to work closely together, moving in lockstep to meet customers' product and time demands. Honeywell Garrett Engine Boosting Systems, which

EXHIBIT 8.9   *The Integrated Enterprise*

Source: Based on Jim Turcotte, Bob Silveri, and Tom Jobson, "Are You Ready for the E-Supply Chain?" *APICS—The Performance Advantage*
(August 1998), 56–59.

makes turbochargers for cars, trucks, and light aircraft, has used an extranet to give suppliers access to its inventory and production data so they can respond rapidly to the manufacturer's need for parts. Now, Honeywell is working with big customers such as Ford and Volkswagen to integrate their systems so the company will have better information about turbocharger demands from customers as well. "Our goal," says Honeywell's Paul Hopkins, "is seamless value-chain connectivity from customer demand to suppliers."[54]

As with the newer organization designs described in Chapter 3, horizontal relationships get more emphasis than vertical relationships for the integrated enterprise to work. Enterprise integration can create a level of cooperation not previously imaginable if managers approach the practice with an attitude of trust and partnership, as in the interorganizational relationships described in Chapter 5. For example, Wal-Mart and Procter & Gamble started simply by sharing sales data so P&G goods could be automatically replaced as they were sold off Wal-Mart's shelves. However, the computer-to-computer tool evolved into a horizontal relationship that involved sharing customer information, shopper loyalty information, and other data that provided strategic advantages for both sides of the trading partnership.[55]

LEADING BY DESIGN   *Corrugated Supplies*

Rick Van Horne had a vision. What would happen if all his plant's equipment continually fed data to the Internet, where the rest of the company, as well as suppliers and customers, could keep track of what was happening on the factory floor in real time? By using a password, customers could peek into the company's internal workings at any time, calling up Corrugated's production schedules to see exactly where their orders were in the process and when they would arrive. Suppliers could tap into the system to manage their own inventory—inventory they were selling to Corrugated as well as materials stored at Corrugated's plant to sell to someone else.

It cost him millions of dollars, but Van Horne's vision became a reality, making Corrugated one of the world's first completely Web-based production plants. The idea behind the new system is to connect all the plant's manufacturing equipment and then link it to the Web; the integrated system is available to everyone, from machinists on the plant floor to customers and suppliers off-site. The diagram on the next page illustrates how the system works for a customer placing an order: The customer logs onto the Web site and types in an order for corrugated paper precisely cut and folded for 20,000 boxes. Computers at Corrugated's factory go to work immediately to determine the best way to blend that order with numerous other orders ranging from a few dozen boxes to 50,000. The computer comes up with the optimum schedule—that is, the

one that gets the most orders out of a single roll with little leftover paper. A human operator checks the schedule on one of the numerous linked computer screens scattered around the plant and hits the Send button. Computer software directs the massive corrugators, trimmers, slitters, and other equipment, which begin spewing out paper orders at 800 feet per minute. Computer-controlled conveyor belts carry the order to the loading dock, where forklifts equipped with wireless PCs take the load to the designated trailer. Truck drivers log onto the Web site and are told which trailer to haul to maximize their trip's efficiency. The order is usually delivered to the customer the very next day.

Today, about 70 percent of Corrugated's orders are submitted via the Internet and routed electronically to the plant floor. The system saves time and money for Corrugated by automatically scheduling special-order details and cutting out paper waste. For customers, it means faster service and fewer mix-ups. One customer, Gene Mazurek, co-owner of Suburban Corrugated Box Co., says the first thing he does each morning is log onto Corrugated's Web site to see what's running, what's broken, where his order is, and when it should arrive. The new system has cut Mazurek's delivery time to his own customers from a week down to two days, something larger competitiors can't match. It's "the best thing that's ever happened so far," says Mazurek. "It's like Rick put his corrugating machine right inside my plant."

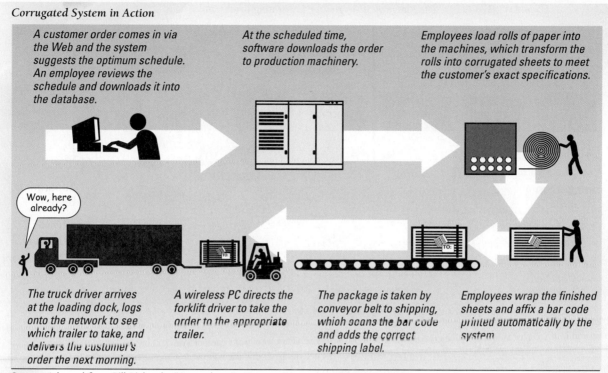

Corrugated System in Action

A customer order comes in via the Web and the system suggests the optimum schedule. An employee reviews the schedule and downloads it into the database.

At the scheduled time, software downloads the order to production machinery.

Employees load rolls of paper into the machines, which transform the rolls into corrugated sheets to meet the customer's exact specifications.

Wow, here already?

The truck driver arrives at the loading dock, logs onto the network to see which trailer to take, and delivers the customer's order the next morning.

A wireless PC directs the forklift driver to take the order to the appropriate trailer.

The package is taken by conveyor belt to shipping, which scans the bar code and adds the correct shipping label.

Employees wrap the finished sheets and affix a bar code printed automatically by the system

Source: Adapted from Bill Richards, "Superplant," *eCompany* (November 2000), 182–196.

E-BUSINESS ORGANIZATION DESIGN

Because they facilitate the integrated enterprise, extranets and EDI exchange networks are important components of e-business. **E-business** can be defined as any business that takes place by digital processes over a computer network rather than in physical space. Most commonly, it refers to electronic linkages over the Internet with customers, partners, suppliers, employees, or other key constituents. Many traditional organizations are setting up Internet operations to strengthen and improve these external relationships, but managers have to make a decision about how best to integrate *bricks and clicks*—that is, how to blend their traditional operations with an Internet initiative.

The range of basic strategies for setting up an Internet operation is illustrated in Exhibit 8.10. At one end of the spectrum, companies can set up an in-house division that is closely integrated with the traditional business. The opposite approach is to create a spin-off company that is totally separate from the traditional organization. Many companies take a middle road by forging strategic partnerships with other organizations for their Internet initiative. Each of these options presents distinct advantages and disadvantages.[56]

In-House Division. An in-house division offers tight integration between the Internet operation and the organization's traditional operation. The organization creates a separate unit within the company that functions within the structure and guidance of the traditional organization. This approach gives the new division several advantages by piggybacking on the established company. These include brand recognition, purchasing leverage with suppliers, shared customer information and marketing opportunities, and distribution efficiencies. Tesco

EXHIBIT 8.10   *The Range of Strategies for Integrating Bricks and Clicks*

In-House Division

Company A

Division 1 · Division 2 · E-Business Division

Partnership

Company A · Company B

Division 1 · Division 2 · Division 1 · Division 2

E-Business Partnership

Spin-Off

Separate E-Business Company

Integration Benefits

- *Broad recognition*
- *Purchasing leverage*
- *Shared information*
- *Distribution efficiencies*

Separation Benefits

- *Focus*
- *Flexibility*
- *Responsiveness*
- *Entrepreneurial culture*

Source: Based on Ranjay Gulati and Jason Garino, "Get the Right Mix of Bricks and Clicks," *Harvard Business Review* (May–June 2000), 107–114.

achieved success in online grocery delivery by keeping Tesco.com closely integrated with the existing grocery chain.

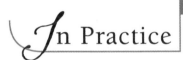

TESCO.COM

When Britain's number-one supermarket chain, Tesco, decided to launch a dot-com division, creating an electronic version of a 1950s delivery boy, managers evaluated options and decided to set up an in-house division to avoid the huge start-up costs that would be required for a spin-off company. The idea was to start slowly and keep close control over the new operation to maintain profitability.

By being part of the greater Tesco enterprise, Tesco.com was able to ride on the back of the parent company, leveraging its brand, suppliers, advertising, and customer database. Tesco started by offering delivery from just one store, gradually rolling out services to other areas. Today, more than a third of Tesco's 690 British supermarkets offer online service, putting them in reach of 91 percent of the British population. By integrating the new operation with the traditional stores, Tesco didn't have to build new warehouses; the Internet division simply used the established warehouses and distribution systems of the chain and picked goods off supermarket shelves to fill customer orders. Using the store-based picking approach kept start-up costs low. Tesco spent only $58 million on its Internet operation during the first four years, and the operation was profitable from the beginning. Managers forecast revenues of more than $2.2 billion for 2004, with net profits of nearly $200 million.[57]

Tesco's success illustrates many of the advantages of the in-house approach. A potential problem with an in-house division, however, is that the new operation doesn't have the flexibility and autonomy needed to move quickly in the Internet world.

Spin-Off. To give the Internet operation greater organizational autonomy, flexibility, and focus, some organizations choose to create a separate spin-off company.

For example, Barnes & Noble created a separate division, barnesandnoble.com, which it ultimately spun off as a stand-alone company to compete with Amazon. Whirlpool created a spin-off called Brandwise.com, a site designed to help consumers find the best products and value—even if that means from other manufacturers. Advantages of a spin-off include faster decision making, increased flexibility and responsiveness to changing market conditions, an entrepreneurial culture, and management that is totally focused on the success of the online operation. Potential disadvantages are the loss of brand recognition and marketing opportunities, higher start-up costs, and loss of leverage with suppliers.

Strategic Partnership. Partnerships, whether through joint ventures or alliances, offer a middle ground, enabling organizations to attain some of the advantages and overcome some of the disadvantages of the purely in-house or spin-off options. For example, after initially blundering in the online world, Toys "R" Us partnered with an established e-commerce company, Amazon.com, to capitalize on the advantages of both integration and separation. Partner Amazon brought e-commerce experience and an entrepreneurial mindset, while Toys "R" Us provided purchasing leverage, brand recognition in the toy industry, and an established customer base. Each company can provide its core strengths— Amazon handles customer service, warehousing, order fulfillment, and maintenance of the Web site, while Toys "R" Us does all inventory management, merchandising, purchasing, and marketing for the co-branded site.[18] A primary disadvantage of partnerships is time spent managing relationships, potential conflicts between partners, and a possibility that one company will fail to deliver as promised or go out of business. For example, if Amazon.com should fail, it would take Toysrus.com's entire business with it.

IT IMPACT ON ORGANIZATION DESIGN

BRIEFCASE

As an organization manager, keep this guideline in mind:

With greater use of information technology, consider smaller organizational units, decentralized structures, improved internal coordination, and greater interorganizational collaboration, including the possibility of outsourcing or a modular structure.

Not every organization will become involved in e-business like Tesco, Corrugated Supplies, or Barnes & Noble. However, advances in information technology are having a tremendous impact on all organizations in every industry. Some specific implications of these advances for organization design are smaller organizations, decentralized structures, improved internal and external coordination, and new modular organization structures.

1. *Smaller organizations.* Some Internet-based businesses exist almost entirely in cyberspace; there is no formal organization in terms of a building with offices, desks, and so forth. One or a few people may maintain the site from their homes or a rented work space. Even for traditional businesses, new information technology enables the organization to do more work with fewer people. At Progressive Insurance, described in the chapter opening, customers can buy insurance without ever speaking to an agent or sales rep. In addition, ERP and other information technology systems automatically handle many administrative duties, reducing the need for clerical staff. The Michigan Department of Transportation (MDOT) used to need an army of workers to verify contractors' work; large projects often required as many as twenty inspectors on-site every day to keep track of thousands of work items. Today, MDOT rarely sends more than one field technician to a site.

The employee enters data into a laptop computer using road construction management software tied to computers at headquarters. The system can automatically generate payment estimates and handle other administrative processes that used to take hours of labor.[59] Companies can also outsource many functions and thus use fewer in-house resources.

2. *Decentralized organizational structures.* Advanced information technology enables organizations to reduce layers of management and decentralize decision making. Information that may have previously been available only to top managers at headquarters can be quickly and easily shared throughout the organization, even across great geographical distances. Managers in varied business divisions or offices have the information they need to make important decisions quickly rather than waiting for decisions from headquarters. Technologies that enable people to meet and coordinate online can facilitate communication and decision making among distributed, autonomous groups of workers. In addition, technology allows for telecommuting, whereby individual workers can perform work that was once done in the office from their computers at home or other remote locations. People and groups no longer have to be located under one roof to collaborate and share information. An organization might be made up of numerous small teams or even individuals who work autonomously but coordinate electronically. Although management philosophy and corporate culture have a substantial impact on whether information technology is used to decentralize information and authority or to reinforce a centralized authority structure,[60] most organizations today use technology to further decentralization.

3. *Improved horizontal coordination.* Perhaps one of the greatest outcomes of advanced information technology is its potential to improve coordination and communication within the firm. Intranets and other networks can connect people even when their offices, factories, or stores are scattered around the world. For example, General Motors' intranet, dubbed Socrates on the basis that the Greek philosopher would be recognizable worldwide, connects some 100,000 staff members around the globe. Managers use the intranet to communicate with one another and to stay aware of organizational activities and outcomes.[61] They can also provide key information to employees throughout the organization with just a few keystrokes.

4. *Improved interorganizational relationships.* Information technology can also improve horizontal coordination and collaboration with external parties such as suppliers, customers, and partners. Extranets are increasingly important for linking companies with contract manufacturers and outsourcers, as well as for supporting the integrated enterprise, as described earlier. Studies have shown that interorganizational information networks tend to heighten integration, blur organizational boundaries, and create shared strategic contingencies among firms.[62] Exhibit 8.11 shows differences between traditional interorganizational relationship characteristics and emerging relationship characteristics.

Traditionally, organizations had an arm's-length relationship with suppliers. However, as we discussed in Chapter 5, suppliers are becoming closer partners, tied electronically to the organization for orders, invoices, and payments. In addition, relationships with customers are changing dramatically. New information technology has increased the power of consumers by giving

EXHIBIT 8.11   *Key Characteristics of Traditional vs. Emerging Interorganizational Relationships*

	Traditional Interorganizational Relationships	**Emerging Interorganizational Relationships**
Suppliers	*Arm's-length relationship* *Use of telephone, mail, some EDI for ordering, invoicing, payments*	*Interactive, electronic relationship* *Electronic ordering, invoicing, payments*
Customers	*Limited communication with manufacturer* *Mix of phone response, mail, hard copy information*	*Direct access to manufacturer, real-time information exchange* *Electronic access to product information, consumer ratings, customer service data*

Source: Based on Charles V. Callahan and Bruce A. Pasternack, "Corporate Strategy in the Digital Age," *Strategy & Business*, Issue 15 (Second Quarter 1999), 10–14.

them electronic access to a wealth of information from thousands of companies just by clicking a mouse. In addition, by giving consumers direct access to manufacturers, the Internet has radically altered customer expectations about convenience, speed, and service. Continually evolving information technology both responds to and expands the trend toward connectivity and cooperation among organizations and with consumers.

5. *Enhanced modular structures.* A high level of interorganizational collaboration is needed in modular organization structures, described in Chapter 3, and it would not be possible without the use of advanced information technology. In the business world, these are also sometimes called *network structures* or *virtual organizations.* Outsourcing has become a major trend, thanks to computer technology that can tie companies together into a seamless information flow. For example Hong Kong's Li & Fung is one of the biggest providers of clothing for retailers such as Abercrombie & Fitch, Guess, Ann Taylor, the Limited, and Disney, but the company doesn't own any factories, machines, or fabrics. Li & Fung specializes in managing information, relying on an electronically connected web of 7,500 partners in thirty-seven countries to provide raw materials and assemble the clothes. Using an extranet allows Li & Fung to stay in touch with worldwide partners and move items quickly from factories to retailers. It also lets retailers track orders as they move through production and make last-minute changes and additions.[63] With a modular structure, most activities are outsourced, so that different companies perform the various functions needed by the organization. The speed and ease of electronic communication makes the modular structure a viable option for companies that want to keep costs low but expand activities or market presence.

SUMMARY AND INTERPRETATION

This chapter covered a number of important topics related to information technology. The information revolution has had a tremendous impact on organizations in all industries. Highly successful organizations today are generally those that most effectively collect, store, distribute, and use information. Information technology systems have evolved to a variety of applications to meet organizations' information needs. Operations applications are applied to well-defined tasks at lower organization levels and help to improve efficiency. These include transaction processing systems, data warehousing, and data mining. Advanced computer-based systems are also used for better decision making and control of the organization. Decision-making systems include management information systems, reporting systems, decision support systems, and executive information systems, which are typically used at middle and upper levels of the organization. Management control systems include budgets and financial reports, periodic nonfinancial statistical reports, reward systems, and quality control systems. An innovation called the *balanced scorecard* provides managers with a balanced view of the organization by integrating traditional financial measurements and statistical reports with a concern for markets, customers, and employees.

Today, all the various computer-based systems have begun to merge into an overall information technology (IT) system that can be used as a strategic weapon. Intranets, enterprise resource planning (ERP), and knowledge management systems are used primarily to support greater internal coordination and flexibility. Systems that support and strengthen external relationships include extranets and EDI networks, the integrated enterprise, and e-business. The integrated enterprise uses advanced information technology to enable close coordination among a company and its suppliers, partners, and customers. To establish an e-business, companies can choose among an in-house division, a spin-off, or a strategic partnership. Each has strengths and weaknesses.

Advanced information technology is having a significant impact on organization design. Technology has enabled creation of the modular organization structure, in which a company subcontracts most of its major functions to separate companies that are connected electronically to the headquarters organization. Even organizations that do not use a modular structure are rapidly evolving toward greater interorganizational collaboration. Other specific implications of advances in technology for organization design include smaller organizations, decentralized organization structures, and improved internal and external coordination

Key Concepts

balanced scorecard	executive information system
benchmarking	explicit knowledge
data	extranet
data mining	feedback control model
data warehousing	information
decision support system	information reporting system
e-business	integrated enterprise
electronic data interchange	intellectual capital
enterprise resource planning	intranet

knowledge	networking
knowledge management	Six Sigma
management control systems	tacit knowledge
management information system	transaction processing systems

Discussion Questions

1. Do you think technology will eventually enable top managers to do their job with little face-to-face communication? Discuss.
2. Why might a company consider using an intranet rather than traditional management and executive information systems?
3. How might an enterprise resource planning system be used to improve strategic management of a manufacturing organization?
4. Discuss some ways a large insurance company such as Progressive, described in the chapter opening, might use MIS to improve decision making.
5. Describe how the four management control system elements discussed in the chapter might be used for feedback control within organizations. Compare and contrast this four-part system with use of the balanced scorecard.
6. Describe your use of explicit knowledge when you research and write a term paper. Do you also use tacit knowledge regarding this activity? Discuss.
7. Why is knowledge management particularly important to a company that wants to become a learning organization?
8. What is meant by the *integrated enterprise*? Describe how organizations can use extranets to extend and enhance horizontal relationships required for enterprise integration.
9. What are some competitive issues that might lead a company to take a partnership approach to e-business rather than setting up an in-house Internet division? What are the advantages and disadvantages of each approach?
10. How might the adoption of information technology affect how an organization is designed?

Chapter 8 Workbook *Are You Fast Enough to Succeed in Internet Time?**

Does your business have what it takes to move at Internet speed?

What is an Internet year? It's the time in which an e-company needs to accomplish the kind of business goals that once took a year. Conventional wisdom puts an Internet year anywhere from 60 to 90 days. Regardless, few will argue that companies need to move faster now than ever imagined.

Can you afford the luxury of in-depth analysis, full due diligence, building consensus, test marketing—all the cornerstones of responsible corporate management? Does their value change when you weigh it against the cost to your company's scarcest commodity—time? Kelsey Biggers, executive vice president of Micro Modeling Associates (MMA), offers the following scenarios to help determine whether you are capable of operating at Internet speed. Choose the best course of action from the choices given (answers below):

1. You have met a company that can be a potential strategic partner for marketing your service to a new industry online. The vibes are good, and you want to map out the potential relationship, but to do so you need to share client and billing

*"Are you fast enough to succeed in Internet time? Does your business have what it takes to move at Internet speed?" Reprinted with permission from *Entrepreneur Magazine*, September 1999, http://www.entrepreneur.com.

information. A nondisclosure agreement is necessary, and the company hands you its standard agreement. What do you do?

a. Get a copy of your company's standard nondisclosure agreement and submit it to your potential partner as an alternative to its NDA.

b. Fax the agreement to your lawyer and ask him or her to get back to you ASAP with any amendments so you can continue the conversation.

c. Look over the agreement and sign it right away.

2. You're looking for a creative director for your Web site, and you know the position will be critical to your whole look and feel online. You hope to have three or four excellent candidates to choose from and have considered doing a retained search for the position. Out of nowhere your old college roommate, whom you respect enormously, refers you to an associate for the position. You meet the candidate for breakfast and you are blown away by the person's credentials and personality. You have three choices:

a. Offer the candidate the job before the check arrives.

b. Give the candidate a strong "warm and fuzzy" about the job while you initiate a quick search for a couple of alternate candidates.

c. Schedule a round of interviews with your senior colleagues back in the office to confirm your positive instincts, while also identifying one or two alternative candidates for comparison.

3. Your online strategy calls for targeting two vertical markets for your service in the next nine months. Your service can be tailored to meet the buying needs of companies in several industries, so it's a matter of picking the right industries to target. High-growth, dynamic industries are obviously preferred. Which approach would you select?

a. Hire an MBA with expertise in finance and marketing to create high-level screening criteria for target industries and identify the five best fits for your services.

b. Hire your neighbor, who happens to be a doctor, knows the health-care industry, and can make several introductions to HMOs and pharmaceutical companies.

c. Ask an intern to research publicly available information from Gartner Group, Forrester Research, and other industry analyst organizations for online spending habits in different industries and make recommendations.

4. Your company has been looking to merge with a strategic partner for some time. You have identified three companies that would be good fits, but each has its advantages and disadvantages. Which would you choose:

a. Company A offers a service that is perfectly complementary to your own, and the price is right. However, the company has indicated that it doesn't think it has enough scale to do a merger now and would rather wait nine months until after the holiday selling season to complete the transaction.

b. Company B is smaller and dynamic, but has grown too fast and has a bad balance sheet. It could be picked up immediately, but your company would have to assume some unwanted debt along with the merger.

c. Company C has a great off-line presence in its space, but has not yet executed its e-commerce plan. The two companies might be a great fit once Company C has established its online presence by midsummer.

5. Your e-commerce strategy requires a real-time fulfillment system that can process orders straight through and provide data on client buying patterns. You have looked outside your firm for technology support to help bring this capability online and have been presented with three alternatives:

a. A senior programmer from your prior firm is now a freelance consultant. He can get started immediately and hire a dozen coders who promise to get a capability up and running in sixty days and grow out the functionality.

b. Your internal technology group can staff a team of a dozen people to build out the system in a year and will then have the ability to support and grow the service when it goes live.

c. An e-solutions consultancy can project manage and build the entire system, but would want to take sixty days to design the technical architecture before starting development. The consultancy insists this time is necessary to ensure a scalable service.

Answers: (Each correct answer is worth one point.)

Question 1

c. The objective is to make a decision quickly and to move the process forward without a great deal of red tape and delay. The legal process can oftentimes slow decision making—whether by three weeks or three months—and time is of the essence in the online world. Moreover, when was the last time an NDA about client information materially affected your business? Better to spend your time building trust than protecting against an unlikely downside.

Question 2

a. Offer the candidate the job while waiting for the check. If this person has been vouched for by someone you trust and you love the person's work, grab the candidate while he or she is available and put that person to work. If you think the candidate is a great hire, chances are, so will your competitors.

Question 3

b. Hire your neighbor. Any list of dynamic industries you put together is bound to include health care, and your biggest challenge is to find a credible person with industry know-how and contacts who can take you into the industry. Your neighbor can do that. Now start looking for the other industries you want to focus on.

Question 4

b. Buy Company B. Company B has proven itself fast-moving and dynamic, and its balance sheet issues makes it open to a favorable price. Companies A and C are both tying their success to future events—a strong holiday selling season or a successful online launch—either of which might not happen and both of which are in the distant Internet future.

Question 5

c. The one area a company cannot afford to get wrong is its technical architecture. It must scale and be reliable, or your whole business will be at risk. Programmers without a blueprint cannot ensure a successful online environment, and staffing internally is time-consuming and uncertain. Better to outsource the project immediately while building an internal team to take it over after its launch.

CASE FOR ANALYSIS   *Century Medical**

Sam Nolan clicked the mouse for one more round of solitaire on the computer in his den. He'd been at it for more than an hour, and his wife had long ago given up trying to persuade him to join her for a movie or a rare Saturday night on the town. The mind-numbing game seemed to be all that calmed Sam down enough to stop thinking about work and how his job seemed to get worse every day.

Nolan was chief information officer at Century Medical, a large medical products company based in Connecticut. He had joined the company four years ago, and since that time Century had made great progress integrating technology into its systems and processes. Nolan had already led projects to design and build two highly successful systems for Century. One was a benefits-administration system for the company's human resources department. The other was a complex Web-based purchasing system that streamlined the process of purchasing supplies and capital goods. Although the system had been up and running for only a few months, modest projections were that it would save Century nearly $2 million annually.

Previously, Century's purchasing managers were bogged down with shuffling and processing paper. The purchasing process would begin when an employee filled out a materials request form. Then the form would travel through various offices for approval and signatures before eventually being converted into a purchase order. The new Web-based system allowed employees to fill out electronic request forms that were automatically e-mailed to everyone whose approval was needed. The time for processing request forms was cut from weeks to days or even hours. When authorization was complete, the system would automatically launch a purchase order to the appropriate supplier. In addition, because the new system had dramatically cut the time purchasing managers spent shuffling paper, they now had more time to work collaboratively with key stakeholders to identify and select the best suppliers and negotiate better deals.

---

*Based on Carol Hildebrand, "New Boss Blues," *CIO Enterprise*, Section 2 (November 15, 1998): 53–58; and Megan Santosus, "Advanced Micro Devices' Web-Based Purchasing System," *CIO*, Section 1 (May 15, 1998): 84.

Nolan thought wearily of all the hours he had put in developing trust with people throughout the company and showing them how technology could not only save time and money but also support team-based work and give people more control over their own jobs. He smiled briefly as he recalled one long-term HR employee, 61-year-old Ethel Moore. She had been terrified when Nolan first began showing her the company's intranet, but she was now one of his biggest supporters. In fact, it had been Ethel who had first approached him with an idea about a Web-based job posting system. The two had pulled together a team and developed an idea for linking Century managers, internal recruiters, and job applicants using artificial intelligence software on top of an integrated Web-based system. When Nolan had presented the idea to his boss, executive vice president Sandra Ivey, she had enthusiastically endorsed it, and within a few weeks the team had authorization to proceed with the project.

But everything began to change when Ivey resigned her position six months later to take a plum job in New York. Ivey's successor, Tom Carr, seemed to have little interest in the project. During their first meeting, Carr had openly referred to the project as a waste of time and money. He immediately disapproved several new features suggested by the company's internal recruiters, even though the project team argued that the features could double internal hiring and save millions in training costs. "Just stick to the original plan and get it done. All this stuff needs to be handled on a personal basis anyway," Carr countered. "You can't learn more from a computer than you can talking to real people—and as for internal recruiting, it shouldn't be so hard to talk to people if they're already working right here in the company." Carr seemed to have no

understanding of how and why technology was being used. He became irritated when Ethel Moore referred to the system as "Web-based." He boasted that he had never visited Century's intranet site and suggested that "this Internet fad" would blow over in a year or so anyway. Even Ethel's enthusiasm couldn't get through to him. She tried to show him some of the HR resources available on the intranet and explain how it had benefited the department and the company, but he waved her away. "Technology is for those people in the IS department. My job is people, and yours should be too." Ethel was crushed, and Nolan realized it would be like beating his head against a brick wall to try to persuade Carr to the team's point of view. Near the end of the meeting, Carr even jokingly suggested that the project team should just buy a couple of filing cabinets and save everyone some time and money.

Just when the team thought things couldn't get any worse, Carr dropped the other bomb. They would no longer be allowed to gather input from users of the new system. Nolan feared that without the input of potential users, the system wouldn't meet their needs, or even that users would boycott the system because they hadn't been allowed to participate. No doubt that would put a great big "I told you so" smile right on Carr's face.

Nolan sighed and leaned back in his chair. The project had begun to feel like a joke. The vibrant and innovative human resources department his team had imagined now seemed like nothing more than a pipe dream. But despite his frustration, a new thought entered Nolan's mind: "Is Carr just stubborn and narrow-minded or does he have a point that HR is a people business that doesn't need a high-tech job posting system?"

CASE FOR ANALYSIS   *Product X* *

Several years ago the top management of a multibillion-dollar corporation decided that Product X was a failure and should be disbanded. The losses involved exceeded $100 million. At least five people knew that Product X was a failure six years before the decision was made to stop producing it. Three of those people were plant managers who lived daily with the production problems. The other two were marketing officials who realized that the manufacturing problems were

not solvable without expenditures that would raise the price of the product to the point where it would no longer be competitive in the market.

*Excerpted from C. Argyris and D. Schon, *Organizational Learning: A Theory of Action Perspective*. Argyris/Schon, *Organizational Learning*, © 1978, Addison–Wesley Publishing Co., Inc., Reading, Massachusetts. Pages 1–2. Reprinted with permission. Case appeared in Gareth Morgan, *Creative Organization Theory* (1989), Sage Publications.

There are several reasons why this information did not get to the top sooner. At first, the subordinates believed that with exceptionally hard work they might turn the errors into successes. But the more they struggled, the more they realized the massiveness of the original error. The next task was to communicate the bad news upward so that it would be heard. They knew that in their company bad news would not be well received at the upper levels if it was not accompanied with suggestions for positive action. They also knew that the top management was enthusiastically describing Product X as a new leader in its field. Therefore, they spent much time composing memos that would communicate the realities without shocking top management.

Middle management read the memos and found them too open and forthright. Since they had done the production and marketing studies that resulted in the decision to produce X, the memos from lower-level management questioned the validity of their analysis. They wanted time to really check these gloomy predictions and, if they were accurate, to design alternative corrective strategies. If the pessimistic information was to be sent upward, middle management wanted it accompanied with optimistic action alternatives. Hence further delay.

Once middle management was convinced that the gloomy predictions were valid, they began to release some of the bad news to the top—but in carefully measured doses. They managed the releases carefully to make certain they were covered if top management became upset. The tactic they used was to cut the memos drastically and summarize the findings. They argued that the cuts were necessary because top management was always complaining about receiving long memos; indeed, some top executives had let it be known that good memos were memos of one page or less. The result was that top management received fragmented information underplaying the intensity of the problem (not the problem itself) and overplaying the degree to which middle management and the technicians were in control of the problem.

Top management therefore continued to speak glowingly about the product, partially to ensure that it would get the financial backing it needed from within the company. Lower-level management became confused and eventually depressed because they could not understand this continued top management support, nor why studies were ordered to evaluate the production and marketing difficulties that they had already identified. Their reaction was to reduce the frequency of their memos and the intensity of their alarm, while simultaneously turning over the responsibility for dealing with the problem to middle-management people. When local plant managers, in turn, were asked by their foremen and employees what was happening, the only response they gave was that the company was studying the situation and continuing its support. This information bewildered the foremen and led them to reduce their own concern.

Notes

1. Lisa A. Lewins and Tim R. V. Davis, "Progressive Insurance Competes with the Strategic Application of Information Technology," *Journal of Organizational Excellence* (Spring 2002), 31–38.
2. Marcia Stepanek, "How an Intranet Opened Up the Door to Profits," *BusinessWeek E.Biz* (July 26, 1999), EB32–EB38; Bill Richards, "A Total Overhaul," *The Wall Street Journal* (December 7, 1998), R30.
3. James Cox, "Changes at Olive Garden Have Chain Living 'La Dolce Vita,'" *USA Today*, (December 18, 2000), B1; Bernard Wysocki Jr., "Hospitals Cut ER Waits," *The Wall Street Journal* (July 3, 2002), D1, D3.
4. Charles V. Callahan and Bruce R. Pasternack, "Corporate Strategy in the Digital Age," *Strategy & Business*, Issue 15 (Second Quarter 1999), 10–14.
5. Ibid.
6. Richards, "A Total Overhaul."
7. Robert Gavin, "States Turn Super Tax Sleuths," *The Wall Street Journal* (May 8, 2002), B6.
8. Joe Ashbrook Nickell, "Welcome to Harrah's," *Business 2.0* (April 2002), 48–54.
9. Megan Santosus, "Motorola's Semiconductor Products Sector's EIS," (Working Smart column), *CIO*, Section 1 (November 15, 1998), 84.
10. Christopher Palmeri, "Believe in Yourself, Believe in the Merchandise," *Continental* (December 1997), 49–51.
11. Esther Shein, "The Knowledge Crunch," *CIO* (May 1, 2001), 128–132; Jeffrey Rothfeder, Jim Bartimo, and Lois Therrien, "How Software is Making Food Sales a Piece of Cake," *BusinessWeek* (July 2, 1990), 54–55.

12. Robert Simons, "Strategic Organizations and Top Management Attention to Control Systems," *Strategic Management Journal* 12 (1991), 49–62.

13. Reported in "Tracking Vital Signs," box in "Measuring Up," an advertising supplement to *Canadian Business*.

14. Richard L. Daft and Norman B. Macintosh, "The Nature and Use of Formal Control Systems for Management Control and Strategy Implementation," *Journal of Management* 10 (1984), 43–66.

15. Matt Cutler, "Emetrics: How to Measure Stickiness," *Business2.com* (March 20, 2001), 134; Ramin Jaleshgari, "The End of the Hit Parade," *CIO* (May 14, 2000), 183–190.

16. Trevor Merriden, "Measured for Success," *Management Review* (April 1999), 27–32.

17. Howard Rothman, "You Need Not Be Big to Benchmark," *Nation's Business* (December 1992), 64–65.

18. Tom Rancour and Mike McCracken, "Applying 6 Sigma Methods for Breakthrough Safety Performance," *Professional Safety* 45, no. 10 (October 2000), 29–32; Lee Clifford, "Why You Can Safely Ignore Six Sigma," *Fortune* (January 22, 2001), 140.

19. Michael Hammer and Jeff Goding, "Putting Six Sigma in Perspective," *Quality* (October 2001), 58–62; Michael Hammer, "Process Management and the Future of Six Sigma," *Sloan Management Review* (Winter 2002), 26–32.

20. Michael Arndt, "Quality Isn't Just for Widgets," *BusinessWeek* (July 22, 2002), 72–73.

21. Daft and Macintosh, "The Nature and Use of Formal Control Systems for Management Control and Strategy Implementation"; Scott S. Cowen and J. Kendall Middaugh II, "Matching an Organization's Planning and Control System to Its Environment," *Journal of General Management* 16 (1990), 69–84.

22. "On Balance," a CFO Interview with Robert Kaplan and David Norton, *CFO* (February 2001), 73–78; Chee W. Chow, Kamal M. Haddad, and James E. Williamson, "Applying the Balanced Scorecard to Small Companies," *Management Accounting* 79, No. 2 (August 1997), 21–27; Robert Kaplan and David Norton, "The Balanced Scorecard: Measures That Drive Performance," *Harvard Business Review* (January–February 1992), 71–79.

23. Based on Kaplan and Norton, "The Balanced Scorecard"; Chow, Haddad, and Williamson, "Applying the Balanced Scorecard"; Cathy Lazere, "All Together Now," *CFO* (February 1998), 28–36.

24. Debby Young, "Score It a Hit," *CIO Enterprise*, Section 2 (November 15, 1998), 27+.

25. Wayne Kawamoto, "Click Here for Efficiency," *BusinessWeek Enterprise* (December 7, 1998), Ent. 12–Ent. 14.

26. Mary J. Cronin, "Ford's Intranet Success," *Fortune* (March 30, 1998), 158; Eryn Brown, "9 Ways to Win on the Web," *Fortune* (May 24, 1999), 112–125.

27. Shein, "The Knowledge Crunch."

28. Derek Slater, "What is ERP?" *CIO Enterprise*, Section 2 (May 15, 1999), 86; Jeffrey Zygmont, "The Ties That Bind," *Inc. Tech* no. 3 (1998), 70–84.

29. Vincent A. Mabert, Ashok Soni, and M. A. Venkataramanan, "Enterprise Resource Planning: Common Myths Versus Evolving Reality," *Business Horizons* (May–June 2001), 69–76.

30. Derek Slater, "What Is ERP?"

31. Owen Thomas, "E-Business Software: Bollinger Shipyards," *eCompany* (May 2001), 119–120.

32. Research reported in Eric Seubert, Y. Balaji, and Mahesh Makhija, "The Knowledge Imperative," *CIO Advertising Supplement* (March 15, 2000), S1–S4.

33. Andrew Mayo, "Memory Bankers," *People Management* (January 22, 1998), 34–38; Gary Abramson, "On the KM Midway," *CIO Enterprise*, Section 2 (May 15, 1999), 63–70.

34. David A. Garvin, "Building a Learning Organization," in *Harvard Business Review on Knowledge Management* (Boston, Mass.: President and Fellows of Harvard College, 1998), 47–80.

35. Based on Andrew Mayo, "Memory Bankers"; William Miller, "Building the Ultimate Resource," *Management Review* (January 1999), 42–45; Todd Datz, "How to Speak Geek," *CIO Enterprise*, Section 2 (April 15, 1999), 46–52.

36. Vikas Anand, William H. Glick, and Charles C. Manz, "Thriving on the Knowledge of Outsiders: Tapping Organizational Social Capital," *Academy of Management Executive* 16, no. 1 (2002), 87–101.

37. Louisa Wah, "Behind the Buzz," *Management Review* (April 1999), 17–26.

38. Richard McDermott, "Why Information Technology Inspired But Cannot Deliver Knowledge Management," *California Management Review* 41, no. 4 (Summer 1999), 103–117.

39. Based on Ikujiro Nonaka and Hirotaka Takeuchi, *The Knowledge-Creating Company: How Japanese Companies Create the Dynamics of Innovation* (New York: Oxford University Press, 1995), 8–9; Robert M. Grant, "Toward a Knowledge-Based Theory of the Firm," *Strategic Management Journal* 17 (Winter 1996), 109–122.

40. Grant, "Toward a Knowledge-Based Theory of the Firm."

41. Martin Schulz, "The Uncertain Relevance of Newness: Organizational Learning and Knowledge Flows," *Academy of Management Journal* 44, no. 4 (2001), 661–681.

42. C. Jackson Grayson Jr. and Carla S. O'Dell, "Mining Your Hidden Resources," *Across the Board* (April 1998), 23–28.

43. Megan Santosus, "Underwriting Knowledge," *CIO* (September 1, 2002), 85–91.

44. Based on Morten T. Hansen, Nitin Nohria, and Thomas Tierney, "What's Your Strategy for Managing Knowledge?" *Harvard Business Review* (March–April 1999), 106–116.

45. Santosus, "Underwriting Knowledge."

46. Eric Ransdell, "Building the New Economy," *Fast Company* (December 1998), 222–236.

47. Christopher Koch, "It All Began with Drayer," *CIO* (August 1, 2002), 56–60.

48. Steve Konicki, "Shopping for Savings," *Information Week* (July 1, 2002), 37–48.

49. Eryn Brown, "9 Ways to Win on the Web."

50. Andy Raskin, "The ROIght Stuff," *CIO Web Business*, Section 2 (February 1, 1999), 49–54.

51. Eric Berkman, "How to Stay Ahead of the Curve," *CIO* (February 1, 2002), 72–80.

52. Steven A. Melnyk and David R. Denzler, *Operations Management: A Value-Driven Approach* (Burr Ridge, Ill.: Richard D. Irwin, 1996), 613.

53. Jim Turcotte, Bob Silveri, and Tom Jobson, "Are You Ready for the E-Supply Chain?" *APICS—The Performance Advantage* (August 1998), 56–59.

54. Sandra Swanson, "Get Together," *Information Week* (July 1, 2002), 47–48.

55. Koch, "It All Began with Drayer."

56. This discussion is based on Ranjay Gulati and Jason Garino, "Get the Right Mix of Bricks and Clicks," *Harvard Business Review* (May–June 2000), 107–114.

57. Andy Reinhardt, "Tesco Bets Small—and Wins Big," *BusinessWeek E.Biz* (October 1, 2001), EB26–EB32.

58. Kris Frieswick, "You've Got to Have Friends," *CFO* (August 2001), 50–53.

59. Stephanie Overby, "Paving Over Paperwork," *CIO* (February 1, 2002), 82–86.

60. Siobhan O'Mahony and Stephen R. Barley, "Do Digital Telecommunications Affect Work and Organization? The State of Our Knowledge," *Research in Organizational Behavior* 21 (1999), 125–161.

61. Sari Kalin, "Overdrive," *CIO Web Business*, Section 2 (July 2, 1999), 36–40.

62. O'Mahony and Barley, "Do Digital Telecommunications Affect Work and Organization?"

63. Joanne Lee-Young and Megan Barnett, "Furiously Fast Fashions," *The Industry Standard* (June 11, 2001), 72–79.

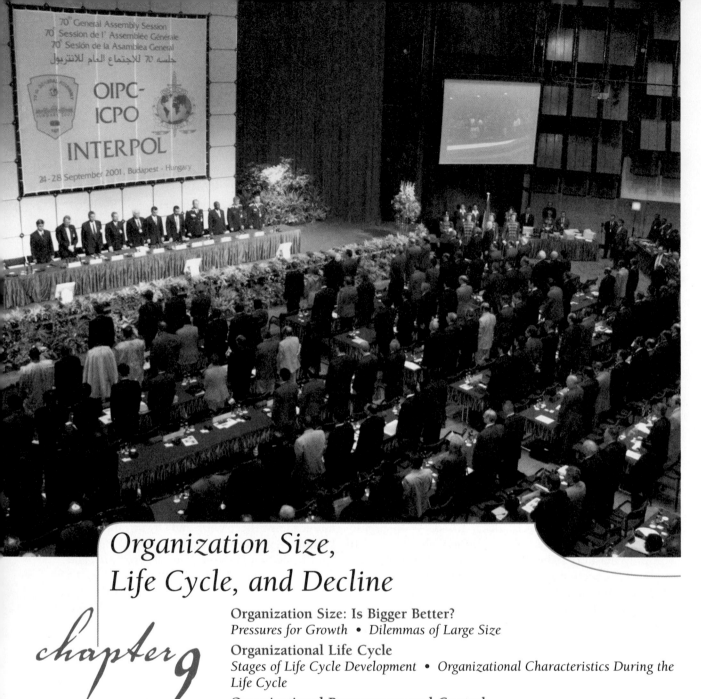

Organization Size, Life Cycle, and Decline

chapter 9

Interpol

Ron Noble, secretary general of Interpol, is managing one of the most complex organizations in the world. Interpol has to work with countries from every corner of the globe, fostering cooperation among people with different cultural values, languages, and legal and political systems. Moreover, it must do it all with a budget about one-tenth the size of the New York City Police Department's.

When Interpol works, it works very well, leading to the quick capture of international terrorists, murderers, and other fugitives. But in recent years, this international police organization, which serves largely as a clearinghouse for crime information, hasn't been working well. When Noble took over at Interpol, he found a clumsy, slow-moving, bureaucratic agency that was ill-equipped to respond to the massive challenges of a world increasingly reliant on worldwide coordinated law enforcement to prevent tragedies such as the World Trade Center attacks of September 2001. If a request for assistance and information on Mohammed Atta, one of the terrorist leaders, for example, came into Interpol on a weekend, too bad—the agency was closed until Monday morning. Interpol "Red Notices" (urgent global wanted-persons alerts) took up to six months to process. Notices had to be reviewed for accuracy, translated into Interpol's four official languages (English, French, Spanish, and Arabic), printed, and mailed to law enforcement agencies around the world. Notices were sent third class to save postage costs.

Noble knew that kind of slow response had to change. Since stepping into the role of secretary general, Noble has made it his mission to reduce bureaucracy and transform Interpol into a modern, fast-moving organization. Keeping Interpol open twenty-four hours, seven days a week, was one of his first changes. A policy of issuing red alerts for terrorists within twenty-four hours and notices for less threatening criminals within seventy-two hours was scheduled to go into effect on September 17, 2001. Instead, it went into effect immediately after the U.S. attacks on September 11. Noble has reorganized Interpol to increase speed, flexibility, and focus on the "customer" (law enforcement groups in 179 member countries). Today, the most critical notices get translated immediately, posted online, and then sent via express delivery service.

The reorganization also includes mechanisms for better coordination and information gathering. Noble hopes that eventually every police officer, customs agent, or other crime fighter will have instant access to an up-to-the-minute Interpol database whenever and wherever stopping a suspect—at the border, on the street, at the airport—before it is too late.[1]

As organizations grow large and complex, they need more complex systems and procedures for guiding and controlling the organization. Unfortunately, these characteristics can also cause problems of inefficiency, rigidity, and slow response time. Every organization—from international agencies like Interpol to locally owned restaurants and auto body shops—wrestles with questions about organizational size, bureaucracy, and control. Most entrepreneurs who start a business want their company to grow. Yet, as organizations become larger and more complex, they often find it difficult to respond quickly to changes in the environment. Today's organizations, just like Interpol, are looking for ways to be more flexible and responsive to a rapidly changing marketplace.

During the twentieth century, large organizations became widespread, and bureaucracy has become a major topic of study in organization theory.[2] Most large organizations have bureaucratic characteristics. These organizations provide us with abundant goods and services and accomplish astonishing feats—explorations of Mars, overnight delivery of packages to any location in the world, the scheduling and coordination of 20,000 airline flights a day in the United States—that are testimony to their effectiveness. On the other hand, bureaucracy is also accused of many sins, including inefficiency, rigidity, and demeaning routinized work that alienates both employees and the customers an organization tries to serve.

PURPOSE OF THIS CHAPTER

In this chapter, we will explore the question of large versus small organizations and how size is related to structure and control. Organization size is a contextual variable that influences organizational design and functioning just as do the contextual variables—technology, environment, goals—discussed in previous chapters. In the first section, we will look at the advantages of large versus small size. Then, we will explore what is called an organization's life cycle and the structural characteristics at each stage. Next, we will examine the historical need for bureaucracy as a means to control large organizations and compare bureaucratic control to various other control strategies. Finally, the chapter will look at the causes of organizational decline and discuss some methods for dealing with downsizing. By the end of this chapter, you should be able to recognize when bureaucratic control can make an organization effective, as well as when other types of control are more appropriate.

ORGANIZATION SIZE: IS BIGGER BETTER?

The question of big versus small begins with the notion of growth and the reasons so many organizations feel the need to grow large.

PRESSURES FOR GROWTH

The dream of practically every businessperson is to have his or her company become a member of the *Fortune* 500 list—to grow fast and to grow large.[3] Sometimes this goal is more urgent than to make the best products or show the greatest profits. A decade ago, analysts and management scholars were heralding a shift away from "bigness" toward small, nimble companies that could quickly respond in a fast-changing environment. Yet, despite the proliferation of new, small organizations, the giants such as Procter & Gamble, General Motors, Nortel Networks, and Wal-Mart continued to grow. Today, the business world has entered an era of the mega-corporation. Over the past decade, merger mania has given rise to behemoths such as DaimlerChrysler AG and Citigroup.[4] The advertising industry is controlled by four giant agencies—the Omnicom Group and the Interpublic Group of Companies, both with headquarters in New York, London's WPP Group, and Publicis Groupe, based in Paris.[5] These huge conglomerates own scores of companies that soak up more than half the ad industry's revenues and reach into the advertising, direct-mail marketing, and public relations of every region on the planet. Moreover, these agencies grew primarily to better serve their clients, who were themselves growing larger and more global. Companies in all industries, from aerospace to consumer products to media, strive for growth to acquire the size and resources needed to compete on a global scale, to invest in new technology, and to control distribution channels and guarantee access to markets.[6]

There are other pressures for organizations to grow. Many executives have found that firms must grow to stay economically healthy. To stop growing is to stagnate. To be stable means that customers may not have their demands met fully or that competitors will increase market share at the expense of your company. Scale is crucial to economic health in marketing-intensive companies such as Coca-Cola and Anheuser-Busch. Greater size gives these companies power in the marketplace and thus increased revenues.[7] In addition, growing organizations are vibrant, exciting places to work, which enables these companies to attract and keep quality employees. When the number of employees is expanding, the company can offer many challenges and opportunities for advancement

DILEMMAS OF LARGE SIZE

Organizations feel compelled to grow, but how much and how large? What size organization is better poised to compete in a global environment? The arguments are summarized in Exhibit 9.1.

Large. Huge resources and economies of scale are needed for many organizations to compete globally. Only large organizations can build a massive pipeline in Alaska. Only a large corporation like Boeing can afford to build a 747, and only a large American Airlines can buy it. Only a large Johnson & Johnson can invest hundreds of millions in new products such as bifocal contact lenses and a patch that delivers contraceptives through the skin. In addition, large organizations have the resources to be a supportive economic and social force in difficult times. When a 1995 earthquake hit Kobe, Japan, knocking out a key Procter & Gamble plant and displacing the families of a thousand employees, the company was able to rapidly lease new space, transfer production, find housing for displaced workers, and raise money for victims of the disaster, while P&G shipped in goods from around the world to provide further assistance.[8] Similarly, following the 2001 terrorist attacks in the United States, American Express had the resources to help stranded customers get home and waive delinquent fees on late payments.[9] Large organizations were also able to get back to business more quickly, giving employees a sense of security and belonging during an uncertain time.

Large companies are standardized, often mechanistically run, and complex. The complexity offers hundreds of functional specialties within the organization to perform complex tasks and to produce complex products. Moreover, large organizations, once established, can be a presence that stabilizes a market for years. Managers can join the company and expect a career reminiscent of the "organization men" of the 1950s and 1960s. The organization can provide longevity, raises, and promotions.

EXHIBIT 9.1   *Differences Between Large and Small Organizations*

Source: Based on John A. Byrne, "Is Your Company Too Big?" *BusinessWeek* (March 27, 1989), 84–94.

Small. The competing argument says small is beautiful because the crucial requirements for success in a global economy are responsiveness and flexibility in fast-changing markets. Although the U.S. economy contains many large organizations, research shows that as global trade has accelerated, smaller organizations have become the norm. Since the mid-1960s, most of the then-existing large businesses have lost market share worldwide.[10] Many large companies have grown even larger through merger or acquisition in recent years, yet research indicates that few of these mergers live up to their expected performance levels. A study of ten of the largest mergers of all time, including AOL/Time Warner, Glaxo/SmithKline, and Daimler/Chrysler, showed a significant decline in shareholder value for eight of the ten combined companies, as illustrated in Exhibit 9.2. Only two, Exxon/Mobil and Travelers/Citicorp, actually increased in value.[11] Although there are numerous factors involved in the decline in value, many researchers and analysts agree that frequently, bigness just doesn't add up to better performance.[12] This chapter's Book Mark argues that one reason large companies sometimes fail is that top leaders get too far away from the nuts and bolts of running the business. Any major strategic initiative, such as a merger, will falter without proper execution.

Despite the increasing size of many companies, the economic vitality of the United States, as well as most of the rest of the developed world, is tied to small and midsized businesses. There are an estimated 15 to 17 million small businesses

EXHIBIT 9.2   *Effect of Ten Recent Mega-Mergers on Shareholder Wealth*

Merger	Year of Deal	Value Created or Destroyed As of July 1, 2002
AOL/Time Warner	2001	–$148 billion
Vodafone/Mannesmann	2000	–$299 billion
Pfizer/Warner-Lambert	2000	–$78 billion
Glaxo/SmithKline	2000	–$40 billion
Chase/J.P. Morgan	2000	–$26 billion
Exxon/Mobil	1999	+$8 billion
SBC/Ameritech	1999	–$68 billion
WorldCom/MCI	1998	–$94 billion
Travelers/Citicorp	1998	+$109 billion
Daimler/Chrysler	1998	–$36 billion

Source: Reported in Keith Hammonds, "Size Is Not a Strategy," *Fast Company* (September 2002), 78–86.

in the United States, which account for a tremendous portion of goods and services provided. In addition, a large percentage of exporters are small businesses.[13] The growth of the Internet and other information technologies is making it easier for small companies to act big, as described in the previous chapter. The growing service sector also contributes to a decrease in average organization size, as many service companies remain small to better serve customers. The percentage of employees working in large organizations continues to decrease. According to the Internal Revenue Service, only about 16,000 businesses in the United States employ more than 500 people, and the majority employ fewer than 100.[14]

Small organizations have a flat structure and an organic, free-flowing management style that encourages entrepreneurship and innovation. Today's leading biotechnological drugs, for example, were all discovered by small firms, such as Chiron, which developed the hepatitis B vaccines, rather than by huge pharmaceutical companies, such as Merck.[15] Moreover, the personal involvement of employees in small firms encourages motivation and commitment because employees personally identify with the company's mission.

Big-Company/Small-Company Hybrid. The paradox is that the advantages of small companies sometimes enable them to succeed and, hence, grow large. *Fortune* magazine reports that the fastest-growing companies in America are small firms characterized by an emphasis on putting the customer first and being fast and flexible in responding to the environment.[16] Small companies, however, can become victims of their own success as they grow large, shifting to a mechanistic structure emphasizing vertical hierarchies and spawning "organization men" rather than entrepreneurs. Giant companies are "built for optimization, not innovation."[17] Big companies become committed to their existing products and technologies and have a hard time supporting innovation for the future.

The solution is what Jack Welch, recently retired chairman of General Electric, called the "big-company/small-company hybrid" that combines a large corporation's resources and reach with a small company's simplicity and flexibility. The divisional structure, described in Chapter 3, is one way organizations

BOOK MARK *9·0*   *Have You Read This Book?*

Execution: The Discipline of Getting Things Done
By Larry Bossidy and Ram Charan, with Charles Burke

Why do so many grand strategies fail and so many large companies go wrong? This is the central question addressed by Larry Bossidy, chairman and former CEO of Allied Signal, and management consultant Ram Charan in their book, *Execution: The Discipline of Getting Things Done*. Success for any organization, large or small, is found in the details. *Execution* offers a practical guide for translating great ideas into successful action. Companies that deliver on their promises year after year are those whose CEOs are skilled in the discipline of execution.

BASIC BUILDING BLOCKS
The discipline of execution is based on three basic building blocks.

- *Essential leadership behaviors.* The authors emphasize that execution is the primary job of a leader. This doesn't mean leaders should micromanage, but they must be actively and passionately involved, putting in place a culture, structure, and the right people to make things happen. Seven essential leader behaviors form the first basic building block of execution: (1) Know your people and your business; (2) insist on realism and confronting problems head-on; (3) set clear goals and priorities; (4) follow through; (5) reward the "doers"; (6) expand people's capabilities; and (7) know yourself.
- *A corporate culture that reinforces a discipline of execution.* Leaders focus on changing people's beliefs and behaviors so that they produce *results*, not just ideas, plans, and strategies. To shift toward a results-oriented culture, leaders make clear the results they want, coach people on how to

achieve them, and reward them for doing so. When people consistently fail to achieve results, leaders need the courage to give them other jobs or let them go. Consistently acting in this manner produces a culture of getting things done.

- *The right people in the right place.* One job no leader should delegate, the authors insist, is recruiting, hiring, promoting, and developing the right people. Even though most leaders claim that "people are our most important asset," they pay very little attention to this aspect of their business, choosing instead to pass it off to the human resources department. Having the right people in the right place, particularly those in the leadership pool, is a key element of successful companies, and one leaders can directly control. As CEO of Allied Signal, Larry Bossidy devoted as much as 40 percent of his day to hiring and developing leaders throughout the company.

THE IMPORTANCE OF EXECUTION
Execution is not simply getting things done; it means understanding the elements that have to be in place in order to get things done. As the authors put it: "Execution is a systematic process of rigorously discussing hows and whats, questioning, tenaciously following through, and ensuring accountability." By having the right people—individually and collectively—focusing on the right details at the right time, organizations can effectively execute and accomplish amazing results.

Execution: The Discipline of Getting Things Done, by Larry Bossidy and Ram Charan, is published by Crown Business.

such as General Electric and Johnson & Johnson attain this. By reorganizing into groups of small companies, these huge corporations capture the mindset and advantages of smallness. Johnson & Johnson is actually a group of 180 separate companies. When a new product is created in one of J&J's fifty-six labs, a new company is created along with it.[18]

Another approach to creating a big-company/small-company hybrid is called the front/back approach. Rather than dividing the company into separate businesses, each with its own products and customers, the company is divided into units with different *roles*. The "back" part of the organization focuses on creating and producing products and services, while the "front" focuses on integrating and delivering products and services to customers. This approach is becoming increasingly popular among financial services companies such as Merrill Lynch and Fidelity, as well as multiple-product technology firms such as Sun Microsystems and Hewlett-Packard.[19]

Full-service, global firms need a strong resource base and sufficient complexity and hierarchy to serve clients around the world. The development of new organization forms, with an emphasis on decentralizing authority and cutting out layers of the hierarchy, combined with the increasing use of information technology described in the previous chapter, is making it easier than ever for companies to be simultaneously large and small, thus capturing the advantages of each. Retail giants Home Depot and Wal-Mart, for example, use the advantage of size in areas such as advertising, purchasing, and raising capital; however, they also give each individual store the autonomy needed to serve customers as if it were a small, hometown shop.[20] To encourage innovation, the giant corporation Royal Dutch/Shell created a strategy in its exploration-and-production division called GameChanger. GameChanger sets aside 10 percent of the division's research budget for "crazy" ideas; anyone can apply for the funds, and decisions are made not by managers but by a small group of non-conformist employees.[21] Small companies that are growing can also use these ideas to help their organizations retain the flexibility and customer focus that fueled their growth.

ORGANIZATIONAL LIFE CYCLE

A useful way to think about organizational growth and change is the concept of an organizational **life cycle**,[22] which suggests that organizations are born, grow older, and eventually die. Organization structure, leadership style, and administrative systems follow a fairly predictable pattern through stages in the life cycle. Stages are sequential in nature and follow a natural progression.

STAGES OF LIFE CYCLE DEVELOPMENT

Research on organizational life cycle suggests that four major stages characterize organizational development.[23] These stages are illustrated in Exhibit 9.3, along with the problems associated with transition to each stage. Growth is not easy. Each time an organization enters a new stage in the life cycle, it enters a whole new ball game with a new set of rules for how the organization functions internally and how it relates to the external environment.[24] For technology companies today, life cycles are getting shorter; to stay competitive, companies have to successfully progress through stages of the cycle faster.

1. *Entrepreneurial stage.* When an organization is born, the emphasis is on creating a product and surviving in the marketplace. The founders are entrepreneurs, and they devote their full energies to the technical activities of production and marketing. The organization is informal and nonbureaucratic. The hours of work are long. Control is based on the owners' personal supervision. Growth is from a creative new product or service. Apple Computer was in the **entrepreneurial stage** when it was created by Steve Jobs and Stephen Wozniak in Wozniak's parents' garage.

EXHIBIT 9.3   *Organizational Life Cycle*

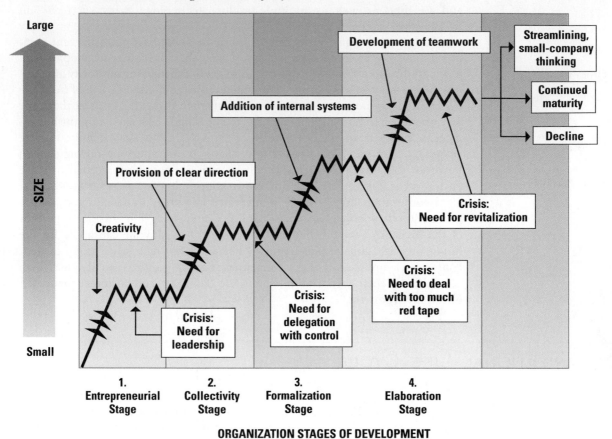

ORGANIZATION STAGES OF DEVELOPMENT

Source: Adapted from Robert E. Quinn and Kim Cameron, "Organizational Life Cycles and Shifting Criteria of Effectiveness: Some Preliminary Evidence," *Management Science* 29 (1983), 33–51; and Larry E. Greiner, "Evolution and Revolution as Organizations Grow," *Harvard Business Review* 50 (July–August 1972), 37–46.

Crisis: Need for leadership. As the organization starts to grow, the larger number of employees causes problems. The creative and technically oriented owners are confronted with management issues, but they may prefer to focus their energies on making and selling the product or inventing new products and services. At this time of crisis, entrepreneurs must either adjust the structure of the organization to accommodate continued growth or else bring in strong managers who can do so. When Apple began a period of rapid growth, A. C. Markkula was brought in as a leader because neither Jobs nor Wozniak was qualified or cared to manage the expanding company.

2. *Collectivity stage.* If the leadership crisis is resolved, strong leadership is obtained and the organization begins to develop clear goals and direction. Departments are established along with a hierarchy of authority, job assignments, and a beginning division of labor. Web search engine Google has quickly moved from the entrepreneurial to the collectivity stage. Founders Larry Page and Sergey Brin devoted their full energy to making sure Google is the most powerful, fastest, and simplest search engine available, then

brought in a skilled manager, former Novell CEO Eric Schmidt, to run the company. Google is currently hiring other experienced executives to manage various functional areas and business units as the organization grows.[25] In the collectivity stage, employees identify with the mission of the organization and spend long hours helping the organization succeed. Members feel part of a collective, and communication and control are mostly informal although a few formal systems begin to appear. Apple Computer was in the **collectivity stage** during the rapid growth years from 1978 to 1981. Employees threw themselves into the business as the major product line was established and more than two thousand dealers signed on.

> *Crisis: Need for delegation.* If the new management has been successful, lower-level employees gradually find themselves restricted by the strong top-down leadership. Lower-level managers begin to acquire confidence in their own functional areas and want more discretion. An autonomy crisis occurs when top managers, who were successful because of their strong leadership and vision, do not want to give up responsibility. Top managers want to make sure that all parts of the organization are coordinated and pulling together. The organization needs to find mechanisms to control and coordinate departments without direct supervision from the top.

3. *Formalization stage.* The **formalization stage** involves the installation and use of rules, procedures, and control systems. Communication is less frequent and more formal. Engineers, human resource specialists, and other staff may be added. Top management becomes concerned with issues such as strategy and planning and leaves the operations of the firm to middle management. Product groups or other decentralized units may be formed to improve coordination. Incentive systems based on profits may be implemented to ensure that managers work toward what is best for the overall company. When effective, the new coordination and control systems enable the organization to continue growing by establishing linkage mechanisms between top management and field units. Apple Computer was in the formalization stage in the mid-1980s.

> *Crisis: Too much red tape.* At this point in the organization's development, the proliferation of systems and programs may begin to strangle middle-level executives. The organization seems bureaucratized. Middle management may resent the intrusion of staff people. Innovation may be restricted. The organization seems too large and complex to be managed through formal programs. It was at this stage of Apple's growth that Jobs resigned from the company and a new CEO took control to face his own management challenges.

4. *Elaboration stage.* The solution to the red tape crisis is a new sense of collaboration and teamwork. Throughout the organization, managers develop skills for confronting problems and working together. Bureaucracy may have reached its limit. Social control and self-discipline reduce the need for additional formal controls. Managers learn to work within the bureaucracy without adding to it. Formal systems may be simplified and replaced by manager teams and task forces. To achieve collaboration, teams are often formed across functions or divisions of the company. The organization may also be split into multiple divisions to maintain a small-company philosophy. Apple

Computer is currently in the **elaboration stage** of the life cycle, as are such large companies as Caterpillar and Motorola.

Crisis: Need for revitalization. After the organization reaches maturity, it may enter periods of temporary decline.[26] A need for renewal may occur every ten to twenty years. The organization shifts out of alignment with the environment or perhaps becomes slow-moving and overbureaucratized and must go through a stage of streamlining and innovation. Top managers are often replaced during this period. At Apple, the top spot has changed hands a number of times as the company struggled to revitalize. CEOs John Sculley, Michael Spindler, and Gilbert Amelio were each ousted by the board as Apple's problems deepened. Steve Jobs returned in mid-1997 to run the company he had founded nearly twenty-five years earlier. During those twenty-five years, Jobs had gained management skills and experience he needed to help Apple through its problems. An older and smarter Jobs quickly reorganized the company, weeded out inefficiencies, and refocused Apple on innovative products for the consumer market, introducing a sleek new iMac in one of the hottest new product launches ever. However, although Jobs brought Apple back to life, he still faces numerous challenges to jump-start growth and keep the organization healthy as the personal computer industry constantly changes.[27] All mature organizations have to go through periods of revitalization or they will decline, as shown in the last stage of Exhibit 9.3.

Summary. Eighty-four percent of businesses that make it past the first year still fail within five years because they can't make the transition from the entrepreneurial stage.[28] The transitions become even more difficult as organizations progress through future stages of the life cycle. Organizations that do not successfully resolve the problems associated with these transitions are restricted in their growth and may even fail. From within an organization, the life cycle crises are very real. The Internet company Yahoo!, like Google, moved quickly to the collectivity stage. However, Yahoo! seemed to get stuck in a prolonged adolescence and has had trouble resolving the need for delegation and installation of more formal control systems.

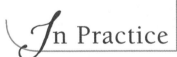

YAHOO!

It all started in 1994 when Jerry Yang and David Filo, two Stanford graduate students, came up with one of the first Internet directory services to help Web surfers find their way around. The two began the venture as a hobby, working out of a temporary building on the Stanford campus. Spurred by the service's instant popularity, though, they quickly turned the hobby into a business called Yahoo!, bringing in a few other employees, mostly other Stanford students, who worked long hours to get the business off the ground. Growth was rapid, and both Yang and Filo knew from the beginning that they didn't want to actually run the company, preferring to focus on the technology. Tim Koogle, who was then running a $400 million company that made automated data collection and communications equipment, was brought in as CEO in the summer of 1995.

With a core group of six employees, including a skilled businessperson as CEO, Yahoo! took off like a rocket, becoming one of the best-known brand names on the Internet. Six employees quickly turned into a thousand, then three thousand. Yahoo! was buying smaller companies right and left. The problem was, the company was still being run like an entrepreneurial start-up. As CEO, Koogle did a great job of rallying people around a vision, but he easily and naturally blended with the company's early anticorporate management style and failed to set up the formal systems needed for control of a fast-growing organization. Moreover, insiders say the biggest problem Yahoo! had was managers' inability to delegate authority. The "gang of six" early hires became like a secret club that no one else could join. Most top executives brought in as a result of Yahoo!'s acquisitions ended up leaving the company. Scores of middle managers began leaving as well, frustrated by the inability to make decisions and take action without funneling everything to the top for approval. "You can't run a 3,000 person company, a $2 billion company, with a core management team of four or five people," says Bill Bishop, cofounder and executive vice president of CBS Marketwatch Inc., a Yahoo! advertiser. "It doesn't work."

Yahoo! fell as quickly as it rose. The antimanagement management style had worked fine as long as the economy was booming and new dot-com companies were springing up every day begging to advertise on Yahoo!'s site. But when "old economy" realities began hitting the company, the loss of experienced management talent really began to hurt. In early 2001, Tim Koogle resigned as CEO (remaining as chairman) to let someone else step in and help the company through its growing pains. Terry Semel, a former Warner Brothers executive who came on board as CEO in May of 2001, quickly set up formal rules and control systems and delegated authority to numerous new executives he brought in to impose a healthy dose of discipline on the struggling organization. Although some longtime employees aren't happy with the more bureaucratic style, Semel's changes have had a significant positive effect on sales and profits. Cofounders Yang and Filo seem more than willing to take advice and have someone guide Yahoo! with a firmer hand.

"Everything [Yahoo!] did as a start-up company was brilliant in the climate that existed up to that point in time. . . .," Semel says. "But times change; companies change." Semel has stabilized Yahoo! and helped it move well into the formalization stage of the life cycle. It remains to be seen whether he can help the company thrive as it matures.[29]

ORGANIZATIONAL CHARACTERISTICS DURING THE LIFE CYCLE

As organizations evolve through the four stages of the life cycle, changes take place in structure, control systems, innovation, and goals. The organizational characteristics associated with each stage are summarized in Exhibit 9.4.

Entrepreneurial. Initially, the organization is small, nonbureaucratic, and a one-person show. The top manager provides the structure and control system. Organizational energy is devoted to survival and the production of a single product or service.

Collectivity. This is the organization's youth. Growth is rapid, and employees are excited and committed to the organization's mission. The structure is still mostly informal, although some procedures are emerging. Strong charismatic leaders like Tim Koogle at Yahoo! or Steve Jobs of Apple provide direction and goals for the organization. Continued growth is a major goal.

Formalization. At this point, the organization is entering midlife. Bureaucratic characteristics emerge. The organization adds staff support groups, formalizes procedures, and establishes a clear hierarchy and division of labor. Innovation

Exhibit 9.4   *Organization Characteristics During Four Stages of Life Cycle*

Characteristic	1. Entrepreneurial Nonbureaucratic	2. Collectivity Prebureaucratic	3. Formalization Bureaucratic	4. Elaboration Very Bureaucratic
Structure	Informal, one-person show	Mostly informal, some procedures	Formal procedures, division of labor, new specialties added	Teamwork within bureaucracy, small-company thinking
Products or services	Single product or service	Major product or service, with variations	Line of products or services	Multiple product or service lines
Reward and control systems	Personal, paternalistic	Personal, contribution to success	Impersonal, formalized systems	Extensive, tailored to product and department
Innovation	By owner-manager	By employees and managers	By separate innovation group	By institutionalized R&D department
Goal	Survival	Growth	Internal stability, market expansion	Reputation, complete organization
Top management style	Individualistic, entrepreneurial	Charismatic, direction-giving	Delegation with control	Team approach, attack bureaucracy

Source: Adapted from Larry E. Greiner, "Evolution and Revolution as Organizations Grow," *Harvard Business Review* 50 (July–August 1972), 37–46; G. L. Lippitt and W. H. Schmidt, "Crises in a Developing Organization," *Harvard Business Review* 45 (November–December 1967), 102–112; B. R. Scott, "The Industrial State: Old Myths and New Realities," *Harvard Business Review* 51 (March–April 1973), 133–148; Robert E. Quinn and Kim Cameron, "Organizational Life Cycles and Shifting Criteria of Effectiveness," *Management Science* 29 (1983), 33–51.

may be achieved by establishing a separate research and development department. Major goals are internal stability and market expansion. Top management has to delegate, but it also implements formal control systems.

At this stage, for example, Michael Dell hired a cadre of experienced managers to help him develop and implement formal planning, management, and budgeting systems at Dell Computer. According to vice chairman Kevin B. Rollins, "Michael realized that he needed professionals to run this company, so that he could continue to be a visionary."[30] At the formalization stage, organizations may also develop complementary products to offer a complete product line.

Elaboration.   The mature organization is large and bureaucratic, with extensive control systems, rules, and procedures. Organization managers attempt to develop a team orientation within the bureaucracy to prevent further bureaucratization. Top managers are concerned with establishing a complete organization. Organizational stature and reputation are important. Innovation is institutionalized through an R&D department. Management may attack the bureaucracy and streamline it.

Summary.   Growing organizations move through stages of a life cycle, and each stage is associated with specific characteristics of structure, control systems, goals, and innovation. The life cycle phenomenon is a powerful concept used for understanding problems facing organizations and how managers can respond in a positive way to move an organization to the next stage.

ORGANIZATIONAL BUREAUCRACY AND CONTROL

As organizations progress through the life cycle, they usually take on bureaucratic characteristics as they grow larger and more complex. The systematic study of bureaucracy was launched by Max Weber, a sociologist who studied government organizations in Europe and developed a framework of administrative characteristics that would make large organizations rational and efficient.[31] Weber wanted to understand how organizations could be designed to play a positive role in the larger society.

WHAT IS BUREAUCRACY?

Although Weber perceived **bureaucracy** as a threat to basic personal liberties, he also recognized it as the most efficient possible system of organizing. He predicted the triumph of bureaucracy because of its ability to ensure more efficient functioning of organizations in both business and government settings. Weber identified a set of organizational characteristics, listed in Exhibit 9.5, that could be found in successful bureaucratic organizations.

Rules and standard procedures enabled organizational activities to be performed in a predictable, routine manner. Specialized duties meant that each employee had a clear task to perform. Hierarchy of authority provided a sensible mechanism for supervision and control. Technical competence was the basis by which people were hired rather than friendship, family ties, and favoritism, which dramatically reduced work performance. The separation of the position from the position holder meant that individuals did not own or have an inherent right to the job, which promoted efficiency. Written records provided an organizational memory and continuity over time.

Although bureaucratic characteristics carried to an extreme are widely criticized today, the rational control introduced by Weber was a significant idea and a new form of organization. Bureaucracy provided many advantages over organization forms based upon favoritism, social status, family connections, or graft. For example, in Mexico, a retired American lawyer had to pay a $500 bribe to purchase a telephone and then discovered that a government official had sold his telephone number to another family. In China, the tradition of giving government posts to relatives is widespread even under communism. China's emerging class of educated people doesn't like seeing the best jobs going to children and other relatives of officials.[32] By comparison, the logical and rational form of organization described by Weber allows work to be conducted efficiently and according to established rules.

EXHIBIT 9.5   *Weber's Dimensions of Bureaucracy and Bases of Organizational Authority*

Bureaucracy	Legitimate Bases of Authority
1. Rules and procedures	1. Rational-legal
2. Specialization and division of labor	2. Traditional
3. Hierarchy of authority	3. Charismatic
4. Technically qualified personnel	
5. Separate position and incumbent	
6. Written communications and records	

The bureaucratic characteristics listed in Exhibit 9.5 can have a positive impact on many large firms. Consider UPS, one of the most efficient large organizations in the United States and Canada.

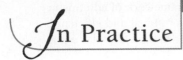

UNITED PARCEL SERVICE

United Parcel Service, sometimes called Big Brown for the color of employee uniforms and the trucks that deliver packages, is the largest package-distribution company in the world. Despite a crippling strike in 1997 that allowed competitors such as the U.S. Postal Service and FedEx to grab some of its business, UPS's 300,000 worldwide employees deliver 13 million packages every business day. Long the leader in ground delivery, UPS is rapidly catching up with competitors in the fast-growing market for air service. In addition, the company's logistics division is booming since UPS built the Internet's dominant logistics hub.

How did UPS become so successful? Many efficiencies were realized through adoption of the bureaucratic model of organization. UPS is bound up in rules and regulations. It teaches drivers an astounding 340 precise steps for how to correctly deliver a package. For example, it tells them how to load their trucks (neatly and evenly, like a stack of bricks), how to fasten their seat belts (with the left hand while simultaneously putting the key in the ignition with their right), how to walk (briskly, but no running allowed), and how to carry their keys (key ring on the pinkie finger so they don't have to fumble in their pockets). Strict dress codes are enforced—clean uniforms (called "browns") every day, black or brown polished shoes with nonslip soles, no shirt unbuttoned below the first button, no hair below the shirt collar, no beards, no smoking in front of customers, and so on. The company still conducts three-minute physical inspections of its drivers each day, a practice begun by the founder in the early 1900s. There are safety rules for drivers, loaders, clerks, and managers. Employees are asked to clean off their desks at the end of each day so they can start fresh the next morning. Each manager is given copies of policy books with the expectation that they will be regularly used, and memos on various policies and rules circulate by the hundreds every day.

Despite the strict rules, employees are satisfied and UPS has a retention rate of more than 90 percent. Employees are treated well and paid well, and the company has maintained a sense of equality and fairness. Everyone is on a first-name basis. The policy book states, "A leader does not have to remind others of his authority by use of a title. Knowledge, performance, and capacity should be adequate evidence of position and leadership." Technical qualification, not favoritism, is the criterion for hiring and promotion. Top executives started at the bottom—the current chief executive, James Kelly, for example, began as a temporary holiday-rush driver. The emphasis on equality, fairness, and a promote-from-within mentality inspires loyalty and commitment throughout the ranks.

UPS has also been a leader in using new technology to enhance reliability and efficiency. Drivers use a computerized clipboard, called DIAD (Delivery Information Acquisition Device) to record everything from driver's miles per gallon to data on parcel delivery. Technology is enabling UPS to expand its services and become a global mover of knowledge and information as well as packages. Top managers know the new technology means some of UPS's rigid procedures may have to bend. However, it's likely they won't bend too far. When you're moving more than 13 million items a day, predictability and stability are the watchwords, whether you're using the company's first Model T Ford or its latest technological wizardry.[33]

UPS illustrates how bureaucratic characteristics increase with large size. UPS is so productive and dependable that it dominates the small package delivery market. As it expands and transitions into a global, knowledge-based logistics business, UPS managers will likely need to find effective ways to reduce the bureaucracy. The new technology and new services place more demands on workers, who may need more flexibility and autonomy to perform well. Now, let's look at some specific ways size affects organizational structure and control.

SIZE AND STRUCTURAL CONTROL

In the field of organization theory, organization size has been described as an important variable that influences structural design and methods of control. Should an organization become more bureaucratic as it grows larger? In what size organizations are bureaucratic characteristics most appropriate? More than one hundred studies have attempted to answer these questions.[34] Most of these studies indicate that large organizations are different from small organizations along several dimensions of bureaucratic structure, including formalization, centralization, and personnel ratios.

Formalization and Centralization. **Formalization**, as described in Chapter 1, refers to rules, procedures, and written documentation, such as policy manuals and job descriptions, that prescribe the rights and duties of employees.[35] The evidence supports the conclusion that large organizations are more formalized, as at UPS. The reason is that large organizations rely on rules, procedures, and paperwork to achieve standardization and control across their large numbers of employees and departments, whereas top managers can use personal observation to control a small organization.[36]

Centralization refers to the level of hierarchy with authority to make decisions. In centralized organizations, decisions tend to be made at the top. In decentralized organizations, similar decisions would be made at a lower level.

Decentralization represents a paradox because, in the perfect bureaucracy, all decisions would be made by the top administrator, who would have perfect control. However, as an organization grows larger and has more people and departments, decisions cannot be passed to the top, or senior managers would be overloaded. Thus, the research on organization size indicates that larger organizations permit greater decentralization.[37] Johnson & Johnson decentralizes almost every aspect of its business to speed up decision making. In small start-up organizations, on the other hand, the founder or top executive is often involved in every decision, large and small.

Personnel Ratios. Another characteristic of bureaucracy is **personnel ratios** for administrative, clerical, and professional support staff. The most frequently studied ratio is the administrative ratio.[38] Two patterns have emerged. The first is that the ratio of top administration to total employees is actually smaller in large organizations,[39] indicating that organizations experience administrative economies as they grow larger. The second pattern concerns clerical and professional support staff ratios.[40] These groups tend to *increase* in proportion to organization size. The clerical ratio increases because of the greater communication and reporting requirements needed as organizations grow larger. The professional staff ratio increases because of the greater need for specialized skills in larger, complex organizations.

Exhibit 9.6 illustrates administrative and support ratios for small and large organizations. As organizations increase in size, the administrative ratio declines

EXHIBIT 9.6   *Percentage of Personnel Allocated to Administrative and Support Activities*

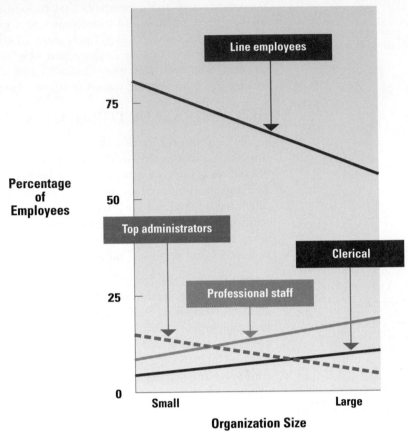

and the ratios for other support groups increase.[41] The net effect for direct workers is that they decline as a percentage of total employees. In summary, while top administrators do not make up a disproportionate number of employees in large organizations, the idea that proportionately greater overhead is required in large organizations is supported. Although large organizations reduced overhead during the difficult economic years of the 1980s, overhead costs for many American corporations began creeping back up again as revenues soared during the late 1990s.[42] With the declining U.S. economy following the crash of the technology sector, threats of war and terrorism, and general feelings of uncertainty, many companies have again been struggling to cut overhead costs. Keeping costs for administrative, clerical, and professional support staff low represents an ongoing challenge for large organizations.[43]

BUREAUCRACY IN A CHANGING WORLD

Weber's prediction of the triumph of bureaucracy proved accurate. Bureaucratic characteristics have many advantages and have worked extremely well for many of the needs of the industrial age.[44] By establishing a hierarchy of authority and specific rules and procedures, bureaucracy provided an effective way to bring order to large groups of people and prevent abuses of power. Impersonal relationships based on roles rather than people reduced the favoritism and nepotism characteristic of many preindustrial organizations. Bureaucracy also provided for systematic and rational ways to organize and manage tasks too complex to be understood and handled by a few individuals, thus greatly improving the efficiency and effectiveness of large organizations.

The world is rapidly changing, however, and the machinelike bureaucratic system of the industrial age no longer works so well as organizations face new challenges. With global competition and uncertain environments, many organizations are fighting against increasing formalization and professional staff ratios. The problems caused by over-bureaucratization are evident in the inefficiencies of some U.S. government organizations. Some agencies have so many clerical staff members and confusing job titles that no one is really sure who does what. Richard Cavanagh, once an aide to President Jimmy Carter, reports his favorite federal title as the "administrative assistant to the assistant administrator for administration of the General Services Administration."[45] Many business organizations, too, need to reduce formalization and bureaucracy. Narrowly defined job descriptions, for example, tend to limit the creativity, flexibility, and rapid response needed in today's knowledge-based organizations. One sales consultant tells a story of giving a presentation on a new media product to a company whose managers admitted it was exactly what they needed, but the extensive formalization and precise job descriptions in the organization meant no one had the authority to make the purchase for that type of product.[46]

ORGANIZING TEMPORARY SYSTEMS FOR FLEXIBILITY AND INNOVATION

How can organizations overcome the problems of bureaucracy in rapidly changing environments? Some are implementing innovative structural solutions. One structural concept, called the *incident command system* (ICS), is commonly used by organizations that have to respond rapidly to emergency or crisis situations, such as police and fire departments or other emergency management agencies. The **incident command system** was developed to maintain the efficiency and control benefits of bureaucracy yet prevent the problem of slow response to crises.[47] The approach is being adapted by other types of organizations to help them respond quickly to new opportunities, unforeseen competitive threats, or organizational crises.

The basic idea behind ICS is that the organization can glide smoothly between a highly formalized, hierarchical structure that is effective during times of stability and a more flexible, loosely structured one needed to respond well to unexpected and demanding environmental conditions. The hierarchical side with its rules, procedures, and chain of command helps maintain control and ensure adherence to rules that have been developed and tested over many years to cope with well-understood problems and situations. However, during times of complexity and high uncertainty, the most effective structure is one that loosens the lines of command and enables people to work across departmental and hierarchical lines to anticipate, avoid, and solve unanticipated problems within a context of a clearly understood mission and guidelines.

The approach can be seen on the deck of a nuclear aircraft carrier, where there is a rigid chain of command and people are expected to follow orders promptly and without question.[48] Formalization is high, with manuals detailing proper procedures for every known situation. However, at times of high uncertainty, such as the launching and recovery of planes during real or simulated warfare, an important shift occurs. The rigid hierarchy seems to dissolve, and a loosely organized, collaborative structure in which sailors and officers work together as colleagues takes its place. People discuss the best procedures to use, and everyone typically follows the lead of whoever has the most experience and knowledge in a particular area. During this time, no one is thinking about job titles, authority, or chain of command; they are just thinking about the best way to accomplish the mission safely.

A variety of mechanisms ensure smooth functioning of the incident command system.[49] For example, despite the free-flowing and flexible nature of crisis response, someone is always in charge. The *incident commander* is ultimately responsible for all activities that occur, and everyone knows clearly who is in charge of what aspect of the situation. This helps maintain order in a chaotic environment. The key is that, while formal authority relationships are fixed, decision-making authority is dispersed to individuals who best understand the particular situation. The system is based on trust that lower-level workers have a clear understanding of the mission and will make decisions and take actions within guidelines that support the organization's goals. Developing an incident command system requires a significant commitment of time and resources, but it offers great potential for organizations that require extremely high reliability as well as flexibility and innovation. One organization that effectively uses the incident command model is The Salvation Army, as described in this chapter's Leading by Design box.

OTHER APPROACHES TO REDUCING BUREAUCRACY

Today's large organizations are taking a number of other, less dramatic steps to reduce bureaucracy. Many are cutting layers of the hierarchy, keeping headquarters staff small, and giving lower-level workers greater freedom to make decisions rather than burdening them with excessive rules and regulations. Centex Corporation, which has annual revenues of about $3.8 billion, is run from a modest headquarters in Dallas by a staff of fewer than one hundred. Centex decentralizes authority and responsibility to the operating divisions.[50] The point is to not overload headquarters with lawyers, accountants, and financial analysts who will inhibit the flexibility and autonomy of divisions.

Of course, many companies must be large to have sufficient resources and complexity to produce products for a global environment; but companies such as Wal-Mart, 3M, Coca-Cola, Emerson Electric, and Heinz are striving toward greater decentralization and leanness. They are giving frontline workers more authority and responsibility to define and direct their own jobs, often by creating self-directed teams that find ways to coordinate work, improve productivity, and better serve customers.

Another attack on bureaucracy is from the increasing professionalism of employees. Professionalism is defined as the length of formal training and experience of employees. More employees need college degrees, MBAs, and other professional degrees to work as attorneys, researchers, or doctors at General Motors, Kmart, and Bristol-Myers Squibb Company. In addition, Internet-based companies may be staffed entirely by well-educated knowledge workers. Studies of professionals show that formalization is not needed because professional training regularizes a high standard of behavior for employees that acts as a substitute for bureaucracy.[51] Companies also enhance this trend when they provide ongoing training for *all* employees, from the front office to the shop floor, in a push for continuous individual and organizational learning. Increased training substitutes for bureaucratic rules and procedures that can constrain the creativity of employees in solving problems and increases organizational capability.

A form of organization called the *professional partnership* has emerged that is made up completely of professionals.[52] These organizations include medical practices, law firms, and consulting firms, such as McKinsey & Co. and PricewaterhouseCoopers. The general finding concerning professional partnerships is that branches have substantial autonomy and decentralized authority to make necessary decisions. They work with a consensus orientation rather than the top-down direction typical of traditional business and government organizations.

LEADING BY DESIGN *The Salvation Army*

The Salvation Army has been called "the most effective organization in the world" by a leading management scholar. One reason the organization is so effective and powerful is its approach to organizing, which makes use of the incident command system to provide the right amount of structure, control, and flexibility to meet the requirements of each situation. The Salvation Army refers to its approach as "organizing to improvise."

The Salvation Army provides day-to-day assistance to the homeless and economically disadvantaged. In addition, the organization rushes in whenever there is a major disaster—whether it be a tornado, flood, hurricane, airplane crash, or terrorist attack—to network with other agencies to provide disaster relief. Long after the most desperate moments of the initial crisis have passed, The Salvation Army continues helping people rebuild their lives and communities, offering financial assistance, meeting physical needs for food, clothing, and housing, and providing emotional and spiritual support to inspire hope and help people build a foundation for the future. The Army's management realizes that emergencies demand high flexibility. At the same time, the organization must have a high level of control and accountability to ensure its continued existence and meet its day-to-day responsibilities. As a former national commander puts it: "We have to have it both ways. We can't choose to be flexible and reckless or to be accountable and responsive. . . . We have to be several different kinds of organizations at the same time." The key is that every decision and action, everything the Army does, is based on and evaluated in terms of whether it fulfills the organization's mission.

In the early emergency moments of a crisis, The Salvation Army deploys a temporary organization that has its own command structure. People need to have a clear sense of who's in charge to prevent the rapid response demands from generating into chaos. For example, if the Army responds to a flood in Tennessee or a tornado in Oklahoma, manuals clearly specify in advance who will be responsible for talking to the media, who will be in charge of supply inventories, who has liaison duties with other agencies, and so forth. This model for the temporary organization keeps The Salvation Army responsive and consistent. In the later recovery and rebuilding phases of a crisis, supervisors frequently give people general guidelines and allow them to improvise the best solutions. There isn't time for supervisors to review and sign off on every decision that needs to be made to get families and communities reestablished.

Thus, The Salvation Army actually has people simultaneously working in all different types of organizational structures, from traditional vertical command structures, to horizontal teams and networks, to a sort of modular form that relies on collaboration with other agencies. Operating in such a fluid way enables the organization to accomplish amazing results. In one recent year, the Army assisted more than 2.3 million people caught up in disasters in the United States, in addition to many more served by regular day-to-day programs. It has been recognized as a leader in putting money to maximum use, meaning donors are willing to give because they trust the organization to be responsible and accountable at the same time it is flexible and innovative in meeting human needs.

Source: Robert A. Watson and Ben Brown, *The Most Effective Organization in the U.S.: Leadership Secrets of The Salvation Army* (New York: Crown Business, 2001), 159–181.

Thus, the trend of increasing professionalism combined with rapidly changing environments is leading to less bureaucracy in corporate North America.

ORGANIZATIONAL CONTROL STRATEGIES

Even though many organizations are trying to decrease bureaucracy and reduce rules and procedures that constrain employees, every organization needs systems for guiding and controlling the organization. Employees may have more freedom in today's companies, but control is still a major responsibility of management.

Managers at the top and middle levels of an organization can choose among three overall control strategies. These strategies come from a framework for organizational control proposed by William Ouchi of the University of California at Los Angeles. Ouchi suggested three control strategies that organizations could adopt—bureaucratic, market, and clan.[53] Each form of control uses different types of information. However, all three types may appear simultaneously in an organization. The requirements for each control strategy are given in Exhibit 9.7.

BUREAUCRATIC CONTROL

Bureaucratic control is the use of rules, policies, hierarchy of authority, written documentation, standardization, and other bureaucratic mechanisms to standardize behavior and assess performance. Bureaucratic control uses the bureaucratic characteristics defined by Weber and illustrated in the UPS case. The primary purpose of bureaucratic rules and procedures is to standardize and control employee behavior.

Recall that as organizations progress through the life cycle and grow larger, they become more formalized and standardized. Within a large organization, thousands of work behaviors and information exchanges take place both vertically and horizontally. Rules and policies evolve through a process of trial and error to regulate these behaviors. Some degree of bureaucratic control is used in virtually every organization. Rules, regulations, and directives contain information about a range of behaviors.

To make bureaucratic control work, managers must have the authority to maintain control over the organization. Weber argued that legitimate, rational authority granted to managers was preferred over other types of control (for example, favoritism or payoffs) as the basis for organizational decisions and activities. Within the larger society, however, Weber identified three types of authority that could explain the creation and control of a large organization.[54]

EXHIBIT 9.7   *Three Organizational Control Strategies*

Type	Requirements
Bureaucracy	Rules, standards, hierarchy, legitimate authority
Market	Prices, competition, exchange relationship
Clan	Tradition, shared values and beliefs, trust

Source: Based on William G. Ouchi, "A Conceptual Framework for the Design of Organizational Control Mechanisms," *Management Science* 25 (1979), 833–848.

Rational-legal authority is based on employees' belief in the legality of rules and the right of those elevated to positions of authority to issue commands. Rational-legal authority is the basis for both creation and control of most government organizations and is the most common base of control in organizations worldwide. **Traditional authority** is the belief in traditions and in the legitimacy of the status of people exercising authority through those traditions. Traditional authority is the basis for control for monarchies and churches and for some organizations in Latin America and the Persian Gulf. **Charismatic authority** is based on devotion to the exemplary character or to the heroism of an individual person and the order defined by him or her. Revolutionary military organizations are often based on the leader's charisma, as are North American organizations led by charismatic individuals such as Michael Dell or Steve Jobs. The organization reflects the personality and values of the leader.

More than one type of authority—such as long tradition and the leader's special charisma—may exist in organizations, but rational-legal authority is the most widely used form to govern internal work activities and decision making, particularly in large organizations.

MARKET CONTROL

Market control occurs when price competition is used to evaluate the output and productivity of an organization. The idea of market control originated in economics.[55] A dollar price is an efficient form of control because managers can compare prices and profits to evaluate the efficiency of their corporation. Top managers nearly always use the price mechanism to evaluate performance in corporations. Corporate sales and costs are summarized in a profit and-loss statement that can be compared against performance in previous years or with that of other corporations.

The use of market control requires that outputs be sufficiently explicit for a price to be assigned and that competition exist. Without competition, the price will not accurately reflect internal efficiency. Even some government and traditionally not-for-profit organizations are turning to market control. For example, the U.S. Federal Aviation Administration took bids to operate its payroll computers (the Department of Agriculture beat out IBM and two other private companies to win the bid). Seventy-three percent of local governments now use private janitorial services and 54 percent use private garbage collectors.[56] The city of Indianapolis requires all its departments to bid against private companies. When the transportation department was underbid by a private company on a contract to fill potholes, the city's union workers made a counterproposal that involved eliminating most of the department's middle managers and reengineering union jobs to save money. Eighteen supervisors were laid off, costs were cut by 25 percent, and the department won the bid.[57]

Market control was once used primarily at the level of the entire organization, but it is increasingly used in product divisions. Profit centers are self-contained product divisions, such as those described in Chapter 3. Each division contains resource inputs needed to produce a product. Each division can be evaluated on the basis of profit or loss compared with other divisions. Asea Brown Boveri (ABB), a multinational electrical contractor and manufacturer of electrical equipment, includes three different types of profit centers, all operating according to their own bottom line and all interacting through buying and selling with one another and with outside customers.[58] The modular organization, also described in Chapter 3, illustrates market control as well. Different companies compete on price to provide the functions and services required by the hub organization. The organization typically contracts with the company that offers the best price and value.

Some firms require that individual departments interact with one another at market prices—buying and selling products or services among themselves at prices equivalent to those quoted outside the firm. To make the market control system work, internal units also have the option to buy and sell with outside companies. Imperial Oil Limited of Canada (formerly Esso) transformed its R&D department into a semiautonomous profit center several years ago.

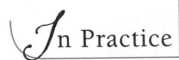

IMPERIAL OIL LIMITED

In the early 1990s, Imperial Oil's R&D was a monopoly service provider allocated an annual budget of about $45 million. Imperial felt that this method of operating gave the two hundred scientists and staff little incentive to control costs or advance quality. Today, R&D receives a much smaller budget and essentially supports itself through applied research and lab-services contracts negotiated with internal and external customers. Contracts spell out the costs of each program, analysis, or other service, and cost-conscious Imperial managers can shop for lower prices among external labs.

R&D has even introduced competition within its own small unit. For example, research teams are free to buy some lab services outside the company if they feel their own laboratories are overpriced or inefficient. However, quality and efficiency have dramatically improved at Imperial R&D, and the unit's high-quality, low-cost services are attracting a great deal of business from outside the company. Canadian companies routinely send samples of used motor oil to the R&D labs for analysis. Manufacturers use R&D to autopsy equipment failures. Vehicle makers like GM and Ford test new engines at Imperial R&D's chassis dynamometer lab. According to John Charlton, Imperial's corporate strategic planning manager, applying market control to R&D has led to an increase in the amount of work the unit does, as well as a 12 percent reduction in internal costs.[59]

Market control can only be used when the output of a company, division, or department can be assigned a dollar price and when there is competition. Companies are finding that they can apply the market control concept to internal departments such as accounting, data processing, legal, and information services.

CLAN CONTROL

Clan control is the use of social characteristics, such as corporate culture, shared values, commitment, traditions, and beliefs, to control behavior. Organizations that use clan control require shared values and trust among employees.[60] Clan control is important when ambiguity and uncertainty are high. High uncertainty means the organization cannot put a price on its services, and things change so fast that rules and regulations are not able to specify every correct behavior. Under clan control, people may be hired because they are committed to the organization's purpose, such as in a religious organization. New employees may be subjected to a long period of socialization to gain acceptance by colleagues. Clan control is most often used in small, informal organizations or in organizations with a strong culture, because of personal involvement in and commitment to the organization's purpose. For example, St. Luke's Communications Ltd., a London advertising firm committed to equal employee ownership, is especially careful to bring in only new employees who believe in the agency's philosophy and mission. The company even turned down a $90 million contract because it would mean rapidly recruiting new employees who might not fit with St. Luke's distinctive culture. Clan control works for St. Luke's; the agency is highly respected and its revenues continue to grow.[61]

The growing use of computer networks and the Internet, which often leads to a democratic spread of information throughout the organization, may force many companies to depend less on bureaucratic control and more on shared values that guide individual actions for the corporate good.[62]

Traditional control mechanisms based on strict rules and close supervision are ineffective for controlling behavior in conditions of high uncertainty and rapid change.[63] Today's companies that are trying to become learning organizations often use clan control or *self-control* rather than relying on rules and regulations. Self-control is similar to clan control, but whereas clan control is a function of being socialized into a group, self-control stems from individual values, goals, and standards. The organization attempts to induce a change such that individual employees' own internal values and work preferences are brought in line with the organization's values and goals.[64] With self-control, employees generally set their own goals and monitor their own performance, yet companies relying on self-control need strong leaders who can clarify boundaries within which employees exercise their own knowledge and discretion.

Clan or self-control may also be used in some departments, such as strategic planning, where uncertainty is high and performance is difficult to measure. Managers of departments that rely on these informal control mechanisms must not assume that the absence of written, bureaucratic control means no control is present. Clan control is invisible yet very powerful. One recent study found that the actions of employees were controlled even more powerfully and completely with clan control than with a bureaucratic hierarchy.[65] When clan control works, bureaucratic control is not needed, as in the following case.

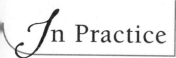

COLUMBUS MILLS

Martha Thomas was proud of being the first woman to work her way up through the manufacturing ranks at Columbus Mills, a large producer of fabrics, carpets, and specialty rugs. She was accustomed to using lengthy budgets and statistical reports, in which almost every manufacturing activity was counted and evaluated weekly. When Thomas was promoted to executive vice-president of Columbus, one of the first things she wanted to do was get the research and development department "under control." She had noticed that the department was run very loosely and people had the freedom to do as they pleased, even working at night instead of during regular business hours if they preferred.

Thomas's first step was to install a detailed budget system. A budget was established for each research project. Even minor expenditures had to be budgeted. The research and development director was expected to keep each expense category on target. Statistical reports were implemented to keep track of all nonfinancial items, such as how employees spent their time and the productivity level for each project. The amount of computer time used, travel, and use of equipment were all measured and monitored.

As the detail and intensity of the bureaucratic control system increased, satisfaction and productivity within the department decreased. At least once a week the executive vice president and the R&D director battled over differences between actual expenditures and budget or over the interpretation of activity reports. After about a year, the director resigned. This was followed by the resignations of several key researchers.

The board of directors asked that a management consultant examine the problems in the department. She found that the control procedures were not appropriate in an R&D department characterized by a long time horizon, frequent change, and uncertainty. Precise, detailed reports may work for a stable manufacturing department, but they do not capture the uncertain nature of R&D activities. Minor deviations from budget are the rule rather than the exception. A less precise control system used just to plan future projects and keep output consistent with company goals would be more effective. The consultant recommended that the bureaucratic control be reduced so that the shared values and commitment of professional employees would regulate behavior.

Martha Thomas had spent many years successfully using bureaucratic control mechanisms in the manufacturing unit of Columbus, and she failed to recognize and understand the strong system of clan control that was operating in the R&D department. Employees were socialized into professional norms and practices and shared a strong departmental culture. Most researchers worked extra hours at night to finish projects because they were deeply committed and liked the chance to talk informally among themselves about ideas they were exploring. The lack of bureaucratic control mechanisms did not mean lack of control.

ORGANIZATIONAL DECLINE AND DOWNSIZING

Earlier in the chapter, we discussed the organizational life cycle, which suggests that organizations are born, grow older, and eventually die. Every organization goes through periods of temporary decline. In addition, a reality in today's environment is that for some companies, continual growth and expansion may not be possible.

All around, we see evidence that some organizations have stopped growing, and many are declining. Huge organizations such as Enron, WorldCom, and Arthur Andersen have collapsed, partly as a result of rapid growth and ineffective control. The Catholic Church continues to lose membership following growing reports of child molestation by priests and the failure in higher levels of the organization to remove molesters and prevent further abuse. Local governments have been forced to close schools and lay off teachers as tax revenues have declined. Since the economy began a downhill slide, DaimlerChrysler, Nortel Networks, General Electric, Motorola, and Cisco Systems are just a few of the large companies that have had significant job cuts. And hundreds of Internet companies that once looked poised for rapid growth have gone out of business.

In this section, we will examine the causes and stages of organizational decline and then discuss how leaders can effectively manage the downsizing that is a reality in today's companies.

DEFINITION AND CAUSES

The term **organizational decline** is used to define a condition in which a substantial, absolute decrease in an organization's resource base occurs over a period of time.[66] Organizational decline is often associated with environmental decline in the sense that an organizational domain experiences either a reduction in size (such as shrinkage in customer demand or erosion of a city's tax base) or a reduction in shape (such as a shift in customer demand). In general, three factors are considered to cause organizational decline:

1. *Organizational atrophy.* Atrophy occurs when organizations grow older, become inefficient and overly bureaucratized, and lose muscle tone. The organization's ability to adapt to its environment deteriorates. Often, atrophy follows a long period of success, because an organization takes success for granted, becomes attached to practices and structures that worked in the past, and fails to adapt to changes in the environment.[67] Warning signals for organizational atrophy include excess staff personnel, cumbersome administrative procedures, lack of effective communication and coordination, and outdated organizational structure.[68]

2. *Vulnerability.* Vulnerability reflects an organization's strategic inability to prosper in its environment. This often happens to small organizations that are not yet fully established. They are vulnerable to shifts in consumer tastes or in the economic health of the larger community. Small e-commerce companies that had not yet become established were the first to go out of business when the technology sector began to decline. Some organizations are vulnerable because they are unable to define the correct strategy to fit the environment. Vulnerable organizations typically need to redefine their environmental domain to enter new industries or markets.

3. *Environmental decline or competition.* Environmental decline refers to reduced energy and resources available to support an organization. When the environment has less capacity to support organizations, the organization has to either scale down operations or shift to another domain.[69] For example, advertising agencies suffered as customer demand shrank following the 2001 terrorist attacks in the United States and a slump in the economy. As companies looked to cut costs, advertising was one of the easiest places to cut. In addition, many clients feared that aggressive promotional efforts would turn off buyers in the wake of economic anxieties, threats of layoffs, and security concerns.[70] Large organizations such as Interpublic Group of Companies, the world's largest advertising holding company, had to scale back operations by laying off employees and cutting costs, while many small and midsized agencies couldn't weather the downturn and closed their doors. Moreover, companies that rely heavily on advertising for revenue—TV stations, magazines, and newspapers, for example—also suffered financially.

A MODEL OF DECLINE STAGES

Based on an extensive review of organizational decline research, a model of decline stages has been proposed and is summarized in Exhibit 9.8. This model suggests that decline, if not managed properly, can move through five stages resulting in organizational dissolution.[71]

EXHIBIT 9.8   *Stages of Decline and the Widening Performance Gap*

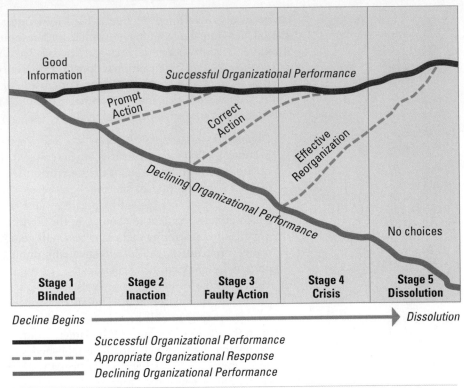

Source: Reprinted from "Decline in Organizations: A Literature Integration and Extension," by William Weitzel and Ellen Jonsson, published in *Administrative Science Quarterly*, 34, no. 1 (March 1989), by permission of *Administrative Science Quarterly*. © Johnson Graduate School of Management, Cornell University.

BRIEFCASE

As an organization manager, keep this guideline in mind:

Understand the causes and stages of decline. Be vigilant to detect signs of decline in the organization and take action as quickly as possible to reverse course. Quick action in the early stages prevents the organization from deteriorating to a stage 4 crisis, when a turnaround becomes much more difficult.

1. *Blinded stage.* The first stage of decline is the internal and external change that threatens long-term survival and might require the organization to tighten up. The organization might have excess personnel, cumbersome procedures, or lack of harmony with customers. Leaders often miss the signals of decline at this point, and the solution is to develop effective scanning and control systems that indicate when something is wrong. With timely information, alert executives can bring the organization back to top performance.

2. *Inaction stage.* The second stage of decline is called inaction, in which denial occurs despite signs of deteriorating performance. Leaders may try to persuade employees that all is well. Creative accounting may make things look fine during this period. The solution is for leaders to acknowledge decline and take prompt action to realign the organization with the environment. Leadership actions may include new problem-solving approaches, increasing decision-making participation, and encouraging expression of dissatisfaction to learn what is wrong.

3. *Faulty action stage.* In the third stage, the organization is facing serious problems, and indicators of poor performance cannot be ignored. Failure to adjust to the declining spiral at this point can lead to organizational failure. Leaders are forced by severe circumstances to consider major changes. Actions may involve retrenchment, including downsizing personnel. Leaders should reduce employee uncertainty by clarifying values and providing

information. A major mistake at this stage decreases the organization's chance for a turnaround.

4. *Crisis stage.* In stage 4, the organization still has not been able to deal with decline effectively and is facing a panic. The organization may experience chaos, efforts to go back to basics, sharp changes, and anger. It is best for managers to prevent a stage 4 crisis, and the only solution is major reorganization. The social fabric of the organization is eroding, and dramatic actions, such as replacing top administrators and revolutionary changes in structure, strategy, and culture, are necessary. Workforce downsizing may be severe.

5. *Dissolution stage.* This stage of decline is irreversible. The organization is suffering loss of markets and reputation, the loss of its best personnel, and capital depletion. The only available strategy is to close down the organization in an orderly fashion and reduce the separation trauma of employees.

The following example of a once-respected accounting firm shows how failure to respond appropriately to signs of decline can lead to disaster.

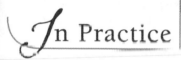

ARTHUR ANDERSEN

The accounting firm Arthur Andersen began the year of 2002 as a $9 billion enterprise. Within six months, the company was all but dead. Top executives failed to recognize the first signals of decline (*blinded stage*) as some of the firm's auditors became involved in complex and potentially illegal accounting machinations for clients such as Sunbeam, Waste Management Inc., and Enron. As signs of difficulty became unavoidably clear following the Enron collapse, managers initially resisted, denying that Andersen was part of the problem (*inaction stage*). However, when lawyers discovered that thousands of e-mails and documents related to Enron were missing, executives were quick to come forward with the information.

The next stage (*faulty action*) is where things really started to go downhill for Andersen. Top executives met with their lawyers to come up with ideas for salvaging Andersen's reputation. They sought the counsel of outsiders known for their honesty and integrity, but then argued among themselves over what these advisors should do and how much authority they should have. Ultimately, the advisors' ability to help management reverse the firm's decline was severely constrained by the limits placed on them.

After Andersen was indicted for obstruction of justice, lawyers suggested the firm consider pleading guilty and get the incident behind them as quickly as possible. Rather than taking the lawyers' advice, Andersen executives fired them. Instead of trying to work closely with the Justice Department leader working on the case, Andersen attempted to go over his head and seek the intervention of a deputy attorney general. Time after time, Andersen's management made missteps that left prosecutors more angry and uncertain of the firm's desire to resolve the case.

In the *crisis stage*, the options were dwindling for Andersen's leaders. To prevent dissolution, they negotiated with other firms, such as Deloitte Touche and KPMG, to acquire parts of Andersen, but negotiations stalled because of disagreements among Andersen's management and board members. As things spun increasingly out of control, factions were warring about what steps to take next. Weeks of negotiations between Andersen and the government to settle the criminal case collapsed because of miscues and missteps. The final offer from the government to resolve the case was never even considered by Andersen's management team because lawyers couldn't track them down in time to discuss it before the government's deadline. By the time the case was over, with Andersen convicted and given the maximum penalty for obstruction of justice, fewer than 2,000 of what was once an 85,000-employee firm remained on the payroll. With its reputation in tatters, its client base evaporated, and little loyalty left among its international affiliates, *dissolution* seems inevitable.[72]

As this example shows, properly managing organizational decline is necessary if an organization is to avoid dissolution. Leaders have a responsibility to detect the signs of decline, acknowledge them, implement necessary action, and reverse course. Some of the most difficult decisions pertain to **downsizing**, which refers to intentionally reducing the size of a company's workforce.

DOWNSIZING IMPLEMENTATION

BRIEFCASE

As an organization manager, keep this guideline in mind:

When layoffs are necessary, handle them with care. Treat departing employees humanely, communicate with employees and provide as much information as possible, provide assistance to displaced workers, and remember the emotional needs of survivors.

During the economic boom years of the 1990s, few managers had to be concerned with the need for downsizing. Organizations were growing and prospering, and managers were more worried about finding qualified workers than about laying people off. Today, the situation has changed. The economic downturn that began in 2000 has again made downsizing a common practice in America's corporations. In addition, downsizing is a part of many change initiatives in today's organizations.[73] Reengineering projects, mergers and acquisitions, global competition, and the trend toward outsourcing have all led to job reductions.[74]

Some researchers have found that massive downsizing has often not achieved the intended benefits and in some cases has significantly harmed the organization.[75] Nevertheless, there are times when downsizing is a necessary part of managing organizational decline. A number of techniques can help smooth the downsizing process and ease tensions for employees who leave, as well as for those who remain.[76]

1. *Communicate more, not less.* Some organizations seem to think the less that's said about a pending layoff, the better. Not so. Organizational managers should provide advance notice with as much information as possible. At 3Com Corp., managers drew up a three-stage plan as they prepared for layoffs. First, they warned employees several months ahead that layoffs were inevitable. Soon thereafter, they held on-site presentations at all locations to explain to employees why the layoffs were needed and to provide as much information as they could about what employees should expect. Employees being cut were given a full sixty days' notice (required by a new federal regulation called the Worker Adjustment and Retraining Notification Act).[77] Managers should remember that it is impossible to "overcommunicate" during turbulent times. Remaining employees need to know what is expected of them, whether future layoffs are a possibility, and what the organization is doing to help coworkers who have lost their jobs.

2. *Provide assistance to displaced workers.* The organization has a responsibility to help displaced workers cope with the loss of their jobs and get reestablished in the job market. The organization can provide training, severance packages, extended benefits, and outplacement assistance. When Motorola eliminated more than half of the jobs at its Harvard, Illinois, plant, it teamed up with the local economic development committee to find job leads for the affected workers and recruited more than forty area employers to participate in a company-sponsored job fair.[78] In addition, counseling services for both

employees and their families can ease the trauma associated with a job loss. Another key step is to allow employees to leave with dignity, giving them an opportunity to say goodbye to colleagues and meet with leaders to express their hurt and anger.

3. *Help the survivors thrive.* Leaders should remember the emotional needs of survivors, as well. Many people experience guilt, anger, confusion, and sadness after the loss of colleagues, and these feelings should be acknowledged. They might also be concerned about their own jobs and have difficulty adapting to the changes in job duties, responsibilities, and so forth. The state of Oregon hired consultant Al Siebert to help employees adapt following the elimination of more than a thousand jobs. Most people "just aren't emotionally prepared to handle major disruptions," Siebert says. Through a series of workshops, Siebert helped people acknowledge their anger and unhappiness and then helped them become "change-resilient" by developing coping skills such as flexibility, curiosity, and optimism.[79]

Even the best-managed organizations may sometimes need to lay off employees in a turbulent environment or to revitalize the organization and reverse decline. Leaders can attain positive results if they handle downsizing in a way that lets departing employees leave with dignity and enables remaining organization members to be motivated, productive, and committed to a better future.

SUMMARY AND INTERPRETATION

The material covered in this chapter contains several important ideas about organizations. Organizations evolve through distinct life cycle stages as they grow and mature. Organization structure, internal systems, and management issues are different for each stage of development. Growth creates crises and revolutions along the way toward large size. A major task of managers is to guide the organization through the entrepreneurial, collectivity, formalization, and elaboration stages of development. As organizations progress through the life cycle and grow larger and more complex, they generally take on bureaucratic characteristics, such as rules, division of labor, written records, hierarchy of authority, and impersonal procedures. Bureaucracy is a logical form of organizing that lets firms use resources efficiently. However, in many large corporate and government organizations, bureaucracy has come under attack with attempts to decentralize authority, flatten organization structure, reduce rules and written records, and create a small-company mindset. These companies are willing to trade economies of scale for responsive, adaptive organizations. Many companies are subdividing into small divisions to gain small-company advantages. Another approach to overcoming the problems of bureaucracy is to use a structural concept called the *incident command system*, which enables the organization to glide smoothly between a highly formalized, hierarchical style that is effective during times of stability and a more flexible, loosely structured one needed to respond to unexpected or volatile environmental conditions.

In large organizations, greater support is required from clerical and professional staff specialists. This is a logical outcome of employee specialization and the division of labor. By dividing an organization's tasks and having specialists perform each part, the organization can become more efficient.

All organizations, large and small, need systems for control. Managers can choose among three overall control strategies: market, bureaucratic, and clan. Bureaucratic control relies on standard rules and the rational-legal authority of managers. Market control is used where product or service outputs can be priced and competition exists. Clan control, and more recently self-control, are associated with uncertain and rapidly changing organization processes. They rely on commitment, tradition, and shared values for control. Managers may use a combination of control approaches to meet the organization's needs.

Many organizations have stopped growing, and some are declining. Organizations go through stages of decline, and it is the responsibility of managers to detect the signs of decline, implement necessary action, and reverse course. One of the most difficult decisions pertains to downsizing the workforce. To smooth the downsizing process, managers can communicate with employees and provide as much information as possible, provide assistance to displaced workers, and remember to address the emotional needs of those who remain with the organization.

Key Concepts

bureaucracy	formalization
bureaucratic control	formalization stage
centralization	incident command system
charismatic authority	life cycle
clan control	market control
collectivity stage	organizational decline
downsizing	personnel ratios
elaboration stage	rational-legal authority
entrepreneurial stage	traditional authority

Discussion Questions

1. Discuss the key differences between large and small organizations. Which kinds of organizations would be better off acting as large organizations, and which are best trying to act as big-company/small-company hybrids?
2. Why do large organizations tend to be more formalized?
3. If you were managing a department of college professors, how might you structure the department differently than if you were managing a department of bookkeepers? Why?
4. Apply the concept of life cycle to an organization with which you are familiar, such as a university or a local business. What stage is the organization in now? How did the organization handle or pass through its life cycle crises?
5. Describe the three bases of authority identified by Weber. Is it possible for each of these types of authority to function at the same time within an organization?
6. In writing about types of control, William Ouchi said, "The Market is like the trout and the Clan like the salmon, each a beautiful highly specialized species which requires uncommon conditions for its survival. In comparison, the bureaucratic method of control is the catfish—clumsy, ugly, but able to live in the widest range of environments and ultimately, the dominant species." Discuss what Ouchi meant with that analogy.
7. Government organizations often seem more bureaucratic than for-profit organizations. Could this partly be the result of the type of control used in government organizations? Explain.

8. The incident command system has been used primarily by organizations that regularly deal with crisis situations. Discuss whether this approach seems workable for a large media company that wants to reduce bureaucracy. How about for a manufacturer of cell phones?
9. Refer back to the Xerox case at the beginning of Chapter 1 and discuss how Xerox illustrates the major causes of organizational decline. In what stage of decline does Xerox seem to be?
10. Do you think a "no growth" philosophy of management should be taught in business schools? Discuss.

Chapter 9 Workbook *Control Mechanisms**

Think of two situations in your life: your work and your school experiences. How is control exerted? Fill out the tables.

ON THE JOB

Your job responsibilities	How your boss controls	Positives of this control	Negatives of this control	How you would improve control
1.				
2.				
3.				
4.				

AT THE UNIVERSITY

Items	How professor A (small class) controls	How professor B (large class) controls	How these controls influence you	What you think is a better control
1. Exams				
2. Assignments/ papers				
3. Class participation				
4. Attendance				
5. Other				

Questions

1. What are advantages and disadvantages of the various controls?
2. What happens when there is too much control? Too little?
3. Does the type of control depend on the situation and the number of people involved?
4. *Optional*: How do the control mechanisms in your tables compare to those of other students?

CASE FOR ANALYSIS   *Sunflower Incorporated**

Sunflower Incorporated is a large distribution company with more than five thousand employees and gross sales of more than $550 million (1992). The company purchases salty snack foods and liquor and distributes them to independent retail stores throughout the United States and Canada. Salty snack foods include corn chips, potato chips, cheese curls, tortilla chips, and peanuts. The United States and Canada are divided into twenty-two regions, each with its own central warehouse, salespeople, finance department, and purchasing department. The company distributes national as well as local brands and packages some items under private labels. Competition in this industry is intense. The demand for liquor has been declining, and competitors like Procter & Gamble and Frito-Lay develop new snack foods to gain market share from smaller companies like Sunflower. The head office encourages each region to be autonomous because of local tastes and practices. In the northeast United States, for example, people consume a greater percentage of Canadian whiskey and American bourbon, while in the West, they consume more light liquors, such as vodka, gin, and rum. Snack foods in the Southwest are often seasoned to reflect Mexican tastes.

Early in 1988, Sunflower began using a financial reporting system that compared sales, costs, and profits across company regions. Each region was a profit center, and top management was surprised to learn that profits varied widely. By 1990, the differences were so great that management decided some standardization was necessary. Managers believed highly profitable regions were sometimes using lower-quality items, even seconds, to boost profit margins. This practice could hurt Sunflower's image. Most regions were facing cutthroat price competition to hold market share. Triggered by price cuts by Anheuser-Busch Company's Eagle Snacks division, national distributors, such as Frito-Lay, Borden, Nabisco, Procter & Gamble (Pringles), and Standard Brands (Planters Peanuts), were pushing to hold or increase market share by cutting prices and launching new products.

As these problems accumulated, Joe Steelman, president of Sunflower, decided to create a new position to monitor pricing and purchasing practices. Loretta Williams was hired from the finance department of a competing organization. Her new title was director of pricing and purchasing, and she reported to the vice president of finance, Peter Langly. Langly gave Williams great latitude in organizing her job and encouraged her to establish whatever rules and procedures were necessary. She was also encouraged to gather information from each region. Each region was notified of her appointment by an official memo sent to the twenty-two regional directors. A copy of the memo was posted on each warehouse bulletin board. The announcement was also made in the company newspaper.

After three weeks on the job, Williams decided two problems needed her attention. Over the long term, Sunflower should make better use of information technology. Williams believed information technology could provide more information to headquarters for decision making. Top managers in the divisions were connected to headquarters by an electronic messaging system, but lower-level employees and salespeople were not connected. Only a few senior managers in about half the divisions used the system regularly.

In the short term, Williams decided fragmented pricing and purchasing decisions were a problem and these decisions should be standardized across regions. This should be undertaken immediately. As

*This case was inspired by "Frito-Lay May Find Itself in a Competition Crunch," *BusinessWeek* (July 19, 1982), 186; "Dashman Company" in Paul R. Lawrence and John A. Seiler, *Organizational Behavior and Administration: Cases, Concepts, and Research Findings* (Homewood, Ill: Irwin and Dorsey, 1965), 16–17; and Laurie M. Grossman, "Price Wars Bring Flavor to Once Quiet Snack Market," *The Wall Street Journal* (May 23, 1991), B1, B3.

a first step, she wanted the financial executive in each region to notify her of any change in local prices of more than 3 percent. She also decided that all new contracts for local purchases of more than $5,000 should be cleared through her office. (Approximately 60 percent of items distributed in the regions were purchased in large quantities and supplied from the home office. The other 40 percent were purchased and distributed within the region.) Williams believed the only way to standardize operations was for each region to notify the home office in advance of any change in prices or purchases. She discussed the proposed policy with Langly. He agreed, so they submitted a formal proposal to the president and board of directors, who approved the plan. The changes represented a complicated shift in policy procedures, and Sunflower was moving into peak holiday season, so Williams wanted to implement the new procedures right away. She decided to send an e-mail message followed by a fax to the financial and purchasing executives in each region notifying them of the new procedures. The change would be inserted in all policy and procedure manuals throughout Sunflower within four months.

Williams showed a draft of the message to Langly and invited his comments. Langly said the message was a good idea but wondered if it was sufficient. The regions handled hundreds of items and were used to decentralized decision making. Langly suggested that Williams ought to visit the regions and discuss purchasing and pricing policies with the executives. Williams refused, saying that such trips would be expensive and time-consuming. She had so many things to do at headquarters that trips were impossible. Langly also suggested waiting to implement the procedures until after the annual company meeting in three months, when Williams could meet the regional directors personally. Williams said this would take too long, because the procedures would then not take effect until after the peak sales season. She believed the procedures were needed now. The messages went out the next day.

During the next few days, e-mail replies came in from seven regions. The managers said they were in agreement and said they would be happy to cooperate.

Eight weeks later, Williams had not received notices from any regions about local price or purchase changes. Other executives who had visited regional warehouses indicated to her that the regions were busy as usual. Regional executives seemed to be following usual procedures for that time of year. She telephoned one of the regional managers and discovered that he did not know who she was and had never heard of the position called director of pricing and purchasing. Besides, he said, "we have enough to worry about reaching profit goals without additional procedures from headquarters." Williams was chagrined that her position and her suggested changes in procedure had no impact. She wondered whether field managers were disobedient or whether she should have used another communication strategy.

Chapter 9 Workshop *Windsock, Inc.* *

1. *Introduction.* Class is divided into four groups: Central Office, Product Design, Marketing/Sales, and Production. Central Office is a slightly smaller group. If groups are large enough, assign observers to each one. Central Office is given 500 straws and 750 pins. Each person reads *only* the role description relevant to that group. *Materials needed*: Plastic milk straws (500) and a box (750) of straight pins.
2. *Perform task.* Depending on length of class, step 2 may take 30 to 60 minutes. Groups perform functions and prepare for a two-minute report for "stockholders."
3. *Group reports.* Each group gives a two-minute presentation to "stockholders."
4. *Observers' reports (optional).* Observers share insights with subgroups.
5. *Class discussion.*
   a. What helped or blocked intergroup cooperation and coordination?
   b. To what extent was there open versus closed communication? What impact did that have?
   c. What styles of leadership were exhibited?
   d. What types of team interdependencies emerged?

*Adapted by Dorothy Marcic from Christopher Taylor and Saundra Taylor in "Teaching Organizational Team-Building Through Simulations," *Organizational Behavior Teaching Review* XI(3), 86–87.

Roles

Central Office

Your team is the central management and administration of WINDSOCK, INC. You are the heart and pulse of the organization, because without your coordination and resource allocation, the organization would go under. Your task is to manage the operations of the organization, not an easy responsibility because you have to coordinate the activities of three distinct groups of personnel: the Marketing/Sales group, the Production group, and the Product Design group. In addition, you have to manage resources including materials (pins and straws), time deadlines, communications, and product requirements.

In this exercise, you are to do whatever is necessary to accomplish the mission and to keep the organization operating in a harmonious and efficient manner.

WINDSOCK, INC. has a total of 30 minutes (more if instructor assigns) to design an advertising campaign and ad copy, to design the windmill, and to produce the first windmill prototypes for delivery. Good luck to you all.

Product Design

Your team is the research and product design group of WINDSOCK, INC. You are the brain and creative aspect of the operation, because without an innovative and successfully designed product, the organization would go under. Your duties are to design products that will compete favorably in the marketplace, keeping in mind function, aesthetics, cost, ease of production, and available materials.

In this exercise, you are to come up with a workable plan for a product that will be built by your production team. Your windmill must be light, portable, easy to assemble, and aesthetically pleasing. Central Office controls the budget and allocates material for your division.

WINDSOCK, INC. as an organization has a total of 30 minutes (more if instructor assigns) to design an advertising campaign, to design the windmill (your group's task), and to produce the first windmill prototypes for delivery. Good luck to you all.

Marketing/Sales

Your team is the marketing/sales group of WINDSOCK, INC. You are the backbone of the operation, because without customers and sales the organization would go under. Your task is to determine the market, develop an advertising campaign to promote your company's unique product, produce ad copy, and develop a sales force and sales procedures for both potential customers and the public at large.

For the purpose of this exercise, you may assume that a market analysis has been completed. Your team is now in a position to produce an advertising campaign and ad copy for the product. To be effective, you have to become very familiar with the characteristics of the product and how it is different from those products already on the market. The Central Office controls your budget and allocates materials for use by your division.

WINDSOCK, INC. has a total of 30 minutes (more if instructor assigns) to design an advertising campaign and ad (your group's task), to design the windmill, and to produce the first windmill prototypes for delivery. Good luck to you all.

Production

Your team is the production group of WINDSOCK, INC. You are the heart of the operation, because without a group to produce the product, the organization would go under. You have the responsibility to coordinate and produce the product for delivery. The product involves an innovative design for a windmill that is cheaper, lighter, more portable, more flexible, and more aesthetically pleasing than other designs currently available in the marketplace. Your task is to build windmills within cost guidelines, according to specifications, and within a prescribed time period, using predetermined materials.

For the purpose of this exercise, you are to organize your team, set production schedules, and build the windmills. Central Office has control over your budget and materials, as well as the specifications.

WINDSOCK, INC. has a total of thirty minutes (more if instructor assigns) to design an advertising campaign, to design the windmill, and to produce the first windmill prototypes (your group's task) for delivery. Good luck to you all.

Notes

1. Chuck Salter, "Terrorists Strike Fast . . . Interpol Has to Move Faster . . . Ron Noble Is On the Case," *Fast Company* (October 2002), 96–104.

2. James Q. Wilson, *Bureaucracy* (New York: Basic Books, 1989); Charles Perrow, *Complex Organizations: A Critical Essay* (Glenview, Ill.: Scott, Foresman, 1979), 4.

3. Tom Peters, "Rethinking Scale," *California Management Review* (Fall 1992), 7–29.

4. Matt Murray, "Critical Mass: As Huge Companies Keep Growing, CEOs Struggle to Keep Pace," *The Wall Street Journal* (February 8, 2001), A1, A6.

5. Stuart Elliott, "Advertising's Big Four: It's Their World Now," *The New York Times* (March 31, 2002), Section 3, 1, 10.

6. Donald V. Potter, "Scale Matters," *Across the Board*, (July–August 2000), 36–39.

7. James B. Treece, "Sometimes, You've Still Gotta Have Size," *BusinessWeek/Enterprise* (1993), 200–201.

8. Murray, "Critical Mass."

9. John A. Byrne and Heather Timmons, "Tough Times for a New CEO," *BusinessWeek* (October 29, 2001), 64–70; Patrick McGeehan, "Sailing Into a Sea of Trouble," *The New York Times* (October 5, 2001), C1, C4.

10. David Friedman, "Is Big Back? Or Is Small Still Beautiful?" *Inc.* (April 1998), 23–28.

11. Keith H. Hammonds, "Size Is Not a Strategy," *Fast Company* (September 2002), 78–86.

12. See Hammonds, "Size Is Not a Strategy," and Tom Brown, "How Big Is Too Big?" *Across the Board* (July–August 1999), 15–20, for a discussion.

13. Reported in John Case, "Counting Companies," *Inc.*, State of Small Business 2001 (May 29, 2001), 21–23; and Peter Drucker, "Toward the New Organization," *Executive Excellence* (February 1997), 7.

14. Bill Meyers, "Worker Shortage Forces Small Businesses Into Creative Hiring," *USA Today* (October 30, 1998), 1B, 2B.

15. Alan Deutschman, "America's Fastest Risers," *Fortune* (October 7, 1991), 46–57.

16. Ibid.

17. Gary Hamel, quoted in Hammonds, "Size Is Not a Strategy."

18. Richard A. Melcher, "How Goliaths Can Act Like Davids," *BusinessWeek/Enterprise* (1993), 192–201.

19. Edward E. Lawler III, "Rethinking Organization Size," *Organizational Dynamics* (Autumn 1997), 24–35.

20. Ibid.

21. Hammonds, "Size Is Not a Strategy."

22. John R. Kimberly, Robert H. Miles, and associates, *The Organizational Life Cycle* (San Francisco: Jossey-Bass, 1980); Ichak Adices, "Organizational Passages—Diagnosing and Treating Lifecycle Problems of Organizations," *Organizational Dynamics* (Summer 1979), 3–25; Danny Miller and Peter H. Friesen, "A Longitudinal Study of the Corporate Life Cycle," *Management Science* 30 (October 1984), 1161–1183; Neil C. Churchill and Virginia L. Lewis, "The Five Stages of Small Business Growth," *Harvard Business Review* 61 (May–June 1983), 30–50.

23. Larry E. Greiner, "Evolution and Revolution as Organizations Grow," *Harvard Business Review* 50 (July–August 1972), 37–46; Robert E. Quinn and Kim Cameron, "Organizational Life Cycles and Shifting Criteria of Effectiveness: Some Preliminary Evidence," *Management Science* 29 (1983), 33–51.

24. George Land and Beth Jarman, "Moving Beyond Breakpoint," in Michael Ray and Alan Rinzler, eds., *The New Paradigm* (New York: Jeremy P. Tarcher/Perigee Books, 1993), 250–266; Michael L. Tushman, William H. Newman, and Elaine Romanelli, "Convergence and Upheaval: Managing the Unsteady Pace of Organizational Evolution," *California Management Review* 29 (1987), 1–16.

25. Adam Lashinsky, "Google Hires a Grown-Up," *Business 2.0* (February 2002), 22.

26. David A. Whetten, "Sources, Responses, and Effects of Organizational Decline," in John R. Kimberly, Robert H. Miles, and associates, *The Organizational Life Cycle*, 342–374.

27. Brent Schlender, "Steve Jobs: The Graying Prince of a Shrinking Kingdom," *Fortune* (May 14, 2001), 118–131; Josh Quittner with Rebecca Winters, "Apple's New Core—Exclusive: How Steve Jobs Made a Sleek Machine That Could Be the Home-Digital Hub of the Future," *Time* (January 14, 2002), 46.

28. Land and Jarman, "Moving Beyond Breakpoint."

29. Mylene Mangalindan and Suein L. Hwant, "Gang of Six: Coterie of Early Hires Made Yahoo! a Hit But an Insular Place," *The Wall Street Journal* (March 9, 2001), A1, A6; Daniel Roth, "Terry Semel Thinks Yahoo Should Grow Up Already," *Fortune* (September 30, 2002), 107–113; Ralph King, "The CEO From Another Planet," *Business 2.0* (October 2002), 96–102; Brent Schlender, "How a Virtuoso Plays the Web," *Fortune* (March 6, 2000), F79–F83.

30. Richard Murphy, "Michael Dell," *Success* (January 1999), 50–53.

31. Max Weber, *The Theory of Social and Economic Organizations*, translated by A. M. Henderson and T. Parsons (New York: Free Press, 1947).

32. John Crewdson, "Corruption Viewed as a Way of Life," *Bryan-College Station Eagle* (November 28, 1982), 13A; Barry Kramer, "Chinese Officials Still Give Preference to Kin, Despite Peking Policies," *The Wall Street Journal* (October 29, 1985), 1, 21.

33. Kelly Barron, "Logistics in Brown," *Forbes* (January 10, 2000), 78–83; Scott Kirsner, "Venture Vérité: United Parcel Service," *Wired* (September 1999), 83–96; and Kathy Goode, Betty Hahn, and Cindy Seibert, *United Parcel Service: The Brown Giant* (unpublished manuscript, Texas A&M University, 1981).

34. Allen C. Bluedorn, "Pilgrim's Progress: Trends and Convergence in Research on Organizational Size and Environment," *Journal of Management Studies* 19 (Summer 1993), 163–191; John R. Kimberly, "Organizational Size and the Structuralist Perspective: A Review, Critique, and Proposal," *Administrative Science Quarterly* (1976), 571–597; Richard L. Daft and Selwyn W. Becker, "Managerial, Institutional, and Technical Influences on Administration: A Longitudinal Analysis," *Social Forces* 59 (1980), 392–413.

35. James P. Walsh and Robert D. Dewar, "Formalization and the Organizational Life Cycle," *Journal of Management Studies* 24 (May 1987), 215–231.

36. Nancy M. Carter and Thomas L. Keon, "Specialization as a Multidimensional Construct," *Journal of Management Studies* 26 (1989), 11–28; Cheng-Kuang Hsu, Robert M. March, and Hiroshi Mannari, "An Examination of the Determinants of Organizational Structure," *American Journal of Sociology* 88 (1983), 975–996; Guy Geeraerts, "The Effect of Ownership on the Organization Structure in Small Firms," *Administrative Science Quarterly* 29 (1984), 232–237; Bernard Reimann, "On the Dimensions of Bureaucratic Structure: An Empirical Reappraisal," *Administrative Science Quarterly* 18 (1973), 462–476; Richard H. Hall, "The Concept of Bureaucracy: An Empirical Assessment," *American Journal of Sociology* 69 (1963), 32–40; William A. Rushing, "Organizational Rules and Surveillance: A Proposition in Comparative Organizational Analysis," *Administrative Science Quarterly* 10 (1966), 423–443.

37. Jerald Hage and Michael Aiken, "Relationship of Centralization to Other Structural Properties," *Administrative Science Quarterly* 12 (1967), 72–91.

38. Peter Brimelow, "How Do You Cure Injelitance?" *Forbes* (August 7, 1989), 42–44; Jeffrey D. Ford and John W. Slocum, Jr., "Size, Technology, Environment and the Structure of Organizations," *Academy of Management Review* 2 (1977), 561–575; John D. Kasarda, "The Structural Implications of Social System Size: A Three-Level Analysis," *American Sociological Review* 39 (1974), 19–28.

39. Graham Astley, "Organizational Size and Bureaucratic Structure," *Organization Studies* 6 (1985), 201–228; Spyros K. Lioukas and Demitris A. Xerokostas, "Size and Administrative Intensity in Organizational Divisions," *Management Science* 28 (1982), 854–868; Peter M. Blau, "Interdependence and Hierarchy in Organizations," *Social Science Research* 1 (1972), 1–24; Peter M. Blau and R. A. Schoenherr, *The Structure of Organizations* (New York: Basic Books, 1971); A. Hawley, W. Boland, and M. Boland, "Population Size and Administration in Institutions of Higher Education," *American Sociological Review* 30 (1965), 252–255; Richard L. Daft, "System Influence on Organization Decision-Making: The Case of Resource Allocation," *Academy of Management Journal* 21 (1978), 6–22; B. P. Indik, "The Relationship between Organization Size and the Supervisory Ratio," *Administrative Science Quarterly* 9 (1964), 301–312.

40. T. F. James, "The Administrative Component in Complex Organizations," *Sociological Quarterly* 13 (1972), 533–539; Daft, "System Influence on Organization Decision-Making"; E. A. Holdaway

and E. A. Blowers, "Administrative Ratios and Organization Size: A Longitudinal Examination," *American Sociological Review* 36 (1971), 278–286; John Child, "Parkinson's Progress: Accounting for the Number of Specialists in Organizations," *Administrative Science Quarterly* 18 (1973), 328–348.

41. Richard L. Daft and Selwyn Becker, "School District Size and the Development of Personnel Resources," *Alberta Journal of Educational Research* 24 (1978), 173–187.

42. Thomas A. Stewart, "Yikes! Deadwood is Creeping Back," *Fortune* (August 18, 1997), 221–222.

43. Cathy Lazere, "Resisting Temptation: The Fourth Annual SG&A Survey," *CFO* (December 1997), 64–70.

44. Based on Gifford and Elizabeth Pinchot, *The End of Bureaucracy and the Rise of the Intelligent Organization* (San Francisco: Berrett-Koehler Publishers, 1993), 21–29.

45. Jack Rosenthal, "Entitled: A Chief for Every Occasion, and Even a Chief Chief," *New York Times Magazine* (August 26, 2001), 16.

46. Seth Godin, "Does Clinging to an Occupation Make You Better at Your Job?" *Fast Company* (April 2000), 324–326.

47. Gregory A. Bigley and Karlene H. Roberts, "The Incident Command System: High-Reliability Organizing for Complex and Volatile Task Environments," *Academy of Management Journal* 44, no. 6 (2001), 1281–1299.

48. Robert Pool, "In the Zero Luck Zone," *Forbes ASAP* (November 27, 2000), 85.

49. Based on Bigley and Roberts, "The Incident Command System."

50. Lazere, "Resisting Temptation."

51. Philip M. Padsakoff, Larry J. Williams, and William D. Todor, "Effects of Organizational Formalization on Alienation among Professionals and Nonprofessionals," *Academy of Management Journal* 29 (1986), 820–831.

52. Royston Greenwood, C. R. Hinings, and John Brown, "'P²-Form' Strategic Management: Corporate Practices in Professional Partnerships," *Academy of Management Journal* 33 (1990), 725–755; Royston Greenwood and C. R. Hinings, "Understanding Strategic Change: The Contribution of Archtypes," *Academy of Management Journal* 36 (1993), 1052–1081.

53. William G. Ouchi, "Markets, Bureaucracies, and Clans," *Administrative Science Quarterly* 25 (1980), 129–141; idem, "A Conceptual Framework for the Design of Organizational Control Mechanisms," *Management Science* 25 (1979), 833–848.

54. Weber, *The Theory of Social and Economic Organizations*, 328–340.

55. Oliver A. Williamson, *Markets and Hierarchies: Analyses and Antitrust Implications* (New York: Free Press, 1975).

56. David Wessel and John Harwood, "Capitalism is Giddy with Triumph: Is It Possible to Overdo It?" *The Wall Street Journal* (May 14, 1998), A1, A10.

57. Anita Micossi, "Creating Internal Markets," *Enterprise* (April 1994), 43–44.

58. Raymond E. Miles, Henry J. Coleman, Jr., and W. E. Douglas Creed, "Keys to Success in Corporate Redesign," *California Management Review* 37, no. 3 (Spring 1995), 128–145.

59. Micossi, "Creating Internal Markets."

60. Ouchi, "Markets, Bureaucracies, and Clans."

61. Anna Muoio, ed., "Growing Smart," *Fast Company* (August 1998), 73–83.

62. Stratford Sherman, "The New Computer Revolution," *Fortune* (June 14, 1993), 56–80.

63. Richard Leifer and Peter K. Mills, "An Information Processing Approach for Deciding Upon Control Strategies and Reducing Control Loss in Emerging Organizations," *Journal of Management* 22, no. 1 (1996), 113–137.

64. Leifer and Mills, "An Information Processing Approach for Deciding Upon Control Strategies"; Laurie J. Kirsch, "The Management of Complex Tasks in Organizations: Controlling the Systems Development Process," *Organization Science* 7, no. 1 (January–February 1996), 1–21.

65. James R. Barker, "Tightening the Iron Cage: Concertive Control in Self-Managing Teams," *Administrative Science Quarterly* 38 (1993), 408–437.

66. Kim S. Cameron, Myung Kim, and David A. Whetten, "Organizational Effects of Decline and Turbulence," *Administrative Science Quarterly* 32 (1987), 222–240.

67. Danny Miller, "What Happens After Success: The Perils of Excellence," *Journal of Management Studies* 31, no. 3 (May 1994), 325–358.

68. Leonard Greenhalgh, "Organizational Decline," in Samuel B. Bacharach, ed., *Research in the Sociology*

of Organizations 2 (Greenwich, Conn.: JAI Press, 1983), 231–276; Peter Lorange and Robert T. Nelson, "How to Recognize—and Avoid—Organizational Decline," *Sloan Management Review* (Spring 1987), 41–48.

69. Kim S. Cameron and Raymond Zammuto, "Matching Managerial Strategies to Conditions of Decline," *Human Resources Management* 22 (1983), 359–375; Leonard Greenhalgh, Anne T. Lawrence, and Robert I. Sutton, "Determinants of Workforce Reduction Strategies in Organizations," *Academy of Management Review* 13 (1988), 241–254.

70. Vanessa O'Connell, "Commercial Break: An Ad Mega-Agency Faces Harsh Realities of a Shaken Industry," *The Wall Street Journal* (October 31, 2001), A1, A4.

71. William Weitzel and Ellen Jonsson, "Reversing the Downward Spiral: Lessons from W. T. Grant and Sears Roebuck," *Academy of Management Executive* 5 (1991), 7–21; William Weitzel and Ellen Jonsson, "Decline in Organizations: A Literature Integration and Extension," *Administrative Science Quarterly* 34 (1989), 91–109.

72. Kurt Eichenwald, "Miscues, Missteps, and the Fall of Andersen," *The New York Times* (May 8, 2002), C1, C4; Ken Brown and Ianthe Jeanne Dugan, "Sad Account: Andersen's Fall from Grace Is a Tale of Greed and Miscues," *The Wall Street Journal* (June 7, 2002), A1, A6; "Accounting Firm Sentenced," *Johnson City Press* (October 17, 2002), 10.

73. William McKinley, Carol M. Sanchez, and Allen G. Schick, "Organizational Downsizing: Constraining, Cloning, Learning," *Academy of Management Executive* 9, no. 3 (1995), 32–42.

74. Gregory B. Northcraft and Margaret A. Neale, *Organizational Behavior: A Management Challenge*, 2nd ed. (Fort Worth, Tex: The Dryden Press, 1994), 626; A. Catherine Higgs, "Executive Commentary" on McKinley, Sanchez, and Schick, "Organizational Downsizing: Constraining, Cloning, Learning," 43–44.

75. James R. Morris, Wayne F. Cascio, and Clifford E. Young, "Downsizing After All These Years: Questions and Answers about Who Did It, How Many Did It, and Who Benefited From It," *Organizational Dynamics* (Winter 1999), 78–86; McKinley, Sanchez, and Schick, "Organizational Downsizing;" Stephen Doerflein and James Atsaides, "Corporate Psychology: Making Downsizing Work," *Electrical World* (September–October 1999), 41–43; Brett C. Luthans and Steven M. Sommer, "The Impact of Downsizing on Workplace Attitudes," *Group and Organization Management* 2, no. 1 (1999), 46–70.

76. These techniques are based on Bob Nelson, "The Care of the Un-Downsized," *Training and Development* (April 1997), 40–43; Shari Caudron, "Teach Downsizing Survivors How to Thrive," *Personnel Journal* (January 1996), 38; Joel Brockner, "Managing the Effects of Layoffs on Survivors," *California Management Review* (Winter 1992), 9–28; Ronald Henkoff, "Getting Beyond Downsizing," *Fortune* (January 10, 1994), 58–64; Kim S. Cameron, "Strategies for Successful Organizational Downsizing," *Human Resource Management* 33, no. 2 (Summer 1994), 189–211; Doerflein and Atsaides, "Corporate Psychology: Making Downsizing Work."

77. Matt Murray, "Stress Mounts as More Firms Announce Large Layoffs, But Don't Say Who or When" (Your Career Matters column), *The Wall Street Journal* (March 13, 2001), B1, B12.

78. Kemba J. Dunham, "The Kinder, Gentler Way to Lay Off Employees," *The Wall Street Journal* (March 13, 2001), B1, B10.

79. Caudron, "Teach Downsizing Survivors How to Thrive."

Managing Dynamic Processes

part 5

Organizational Culture and Ethical Values

chapter **10**

PSS World Medical

PSS World Medical, a specialty marketer and distributor of medical products and supplies, has thrived in a fiercely competitive industry by offering superior service and responsiveness to customers. Company practices such as same-day delivery, no minimum order sizes, and a no-hassles return policy have earned PSS a loyal following among physicians, long-term care facilities, and hospitals. But what really distinguishes the company is its employees, who approach their jobs with energy, enthusiasm, and commitment to providing the best possible service.

Founder and top executive Pat Kelly attributes his organization's success primarily to its corporate culture, which is based on the idea of personal responsibility and building an environment characterized by honesty, trust, and mutual respect. People are truly perceived as the company's most valuable asset, and how those people treat one another is as crucial a management concern as sales numbers or operating profits. The company's set of twenty core values is posted in every PSS office and serves as a foundation for everything PSS does.

One of the central values is openness and honesty. The company not only practices open book management, sharing all financial and operating information with employees, but also encourages employees to ask any question of anyone in the company without fear of punishment. When top executives visit a branch, they pass out $2 bills to anyone with a question as a fun way to get people to participate. All employees at PSS are called by their first names, and leaders see themselves as working for their employees rather than vice versa. The responsibility of leaders is to teach, guide, and develop others, helping them achieve their highest potential.

The unique cultural ritual of "Firing the Boss" shows that PSS is sincere about employee empowerment. In most cases, supervisors don't really get fired (although sometimes they do); the ritual simply provides a way to get problems out into the open, prompt better communication, and make sure leaders understand the importance of listening to and serving employees. Personal accountability is another core value, and people at all levels are given the authority to make decisions and solve problems. No one is ever fired for making an honest mistake, because taking risks and making mistakes is seen as a key to learning and growth.

PSS places great emphasis on finding the right people and then socializing them into the corporate culture through extensive training and development programs. Ongoing activities such as monthly Challenge meetings, where everyone in a branch office gets together to talk about business as well as have some fun, further support the emphasis on openness, honesty, and smooth interpersonal relationships.[1]

Caring, employee empowerment, open communication, an environment of trust and honesty, and personal responsibility—these are the values that make PSS World Medical unique. Rather than pushing and prodding people to perform, PSS creates an environment in which people want to excel and have the opportunity to do so. By creating a culture that unleashes all employees' energy and enthusiasm, PSS has grown and flourished.

Strong cultures such as the one at PSS World Medical can have a profound impact on a company, which can be either positive or negative for the organization. Negative cultural norms can damage a company just as powerfully as positive ones can strengthen it. Consider the case of Enron Corp., which failed largely because of a corporate culture that supported pushing everything to the limits: business practices, rules, personal behavior, and laws. Executives drove expensive cars, challenged employees to participate in risky competitive behavior, and often celebrated big deals by heading off to a bar or dance club. Enron's definition of the value of communication was reportedly inscribed on a Lucite cube that once sat on former Chief Financial Officer Andrew Fastow's desk: "When Enron says it's going to rip your face off, it will rip your face off."[2]

A related concept concerning the influence of norms and values on how people work together and how they treat one another and customers is called *social capital*. **Social capital** consists of the embedded trust, mutual understandings, and shared norms and values that enable members of an organization to cooperate and coordinate their activities to achieve organizational goals.[3] An organization can have either a high or a low level of social capital. One way to think of social capital is as *goodwill*. When relationships both within the organization and with customers, suppliers, and partners are based on honesty, trust, and respect, a spirit of goodwill exists and people willingly cooperate to achieve mutual benefits. A high level of social capital enables frictionless social interactions and exchanges that help to facilitate smooth organizational functioning.

Think of eBay, which relies largely on social capital to bring millions of buyers and sellers together on its Web site, leading to 2001 profits of $90 million.[4] The company builds goodwill through such mechanisms as a feedback system that enables buyers and sellers to rate one another, discussion boards that build a sense of community among site users, and regular all-day focus groups with representative buyers and sellers. Another company with high social capital is Fred Alger Management. The company lost most of its staff in the September 11, 2001, terrorist attacks on the World Trade Center. It used social capital to woo back many former employees to get the company back on its feet. Some left jobs they loved because, despite moving on in their careers, they had developed lifelong bonds with Alger. Others came out of retirement to help rebuild the firm.[5] Organizations develop such deep bonds only by being open and honest and building positive social relationships among employees and with outsiders. Relationships based on cutthroat competition, self-interest, and subterfuge, such as those at Enron, can be devastating to a company. Social capital relates to both corporate culture and ethics, which is the subject matter of this chapter.

PURPOSE OF THIS CHAPTER

This chapter explores ideas about corporate culture and associated ethical values and how these are influenced by organizations. The first section will describe the nature of corporate culture, its origins and purpose, and how to identify and interpret culture through ceremonies, stories, and symbols. We will then examine how culture reinforces the strategy and structural design the organization needs to be effective in its environment and discuss the important role of culture in creating a learning organization. Next, the chapter turns to ethical values in organizations and how managers implement the structures and systems that will influence employee behavior. We will also discuss how leaders shape culture and ethical values in a direction suitable for strategy and performance outcomes.

The chapter closes with a brief overview of the complex cultural and ethical issues that managers face in an international environment.

ORGANIZATIONAL CULTURE

The popularity of the organizational culture topic raises a number of questions. Can we identify cultures? Can culture be aligned with strategy? How can cultures be managed or changed? The best place to start is by defining culture and explaining how it can be identified in organizations.

WHAT IS CULTURE?

Culture is the set of values, norms guiding beliefs, and understandings that is shared by members of an organization and taught to new members as correct.[6] It represents the unwritten, feeling part of the organization. Everyone participates in culture, but culture generally goes unnoticed. It is only when organizations try to implement new strategies or programs that go against basic culture norms and values that they come face to face with the power of culture.

Organizational culture exists at two levels, as illustrated in Exhibit 10.1. On the surface are visible artifacts and observable behaviors—the ways people dress and act and the symbols, stories, and ceremonies organization members share. The visible elements of culture, however, reflect deeper values in the minds of organization members. These underlying values, assumptions, beliefs, and thought processes are the true culture.[7] For example, at Southwest Airlines, red "LUV" hearts are emblazoned on the company's training manuals and other materials. The hearts are a visible symbol; the underlying value is that "we are one family of people who truly care about each other." The attributes of culture display themselves in many ways but typically evolve into a patterned set of activities carried out through social interactions.[8] Those patterns can be used to interpret culture.

EMERGENCE AND PURPOSE OF CULTURE

Culture provides members with a sense of organizational identity and generates a commitment to beliefs and values that are larger than themselves. Though ideas that become part of culture can come from anywhere within the organization, an organization's culture generally begins with a founder or early leader who articulates and implements particular ideas and values as a vision, philosophy, or business strategy. For example, the culture at PSS World Medical is based on the values and guiding philosophy of Pat Kelly, who believes business should be about more than just making money. When these ideas and values lead to success, they become institutionalized, and an organizational culture emerges that reflects the vision and strategy of the founder or leader.[9]

Cultures serve two critical functions in organizations: (1) to integrate members so that they know how to relate to one another, and (2) to help the organization adapt to the external environment. **Internal integration** means that members develop a collective identity and know how to work together effectively. It is culture that guides day-to-day working relationships and determines how people communicate within the organization, what behavior is acceptable or not acceptable, and how power and status are allocated. **External adaptation**

EXHIBIT 10.1   *Levels of Corporate Culture*

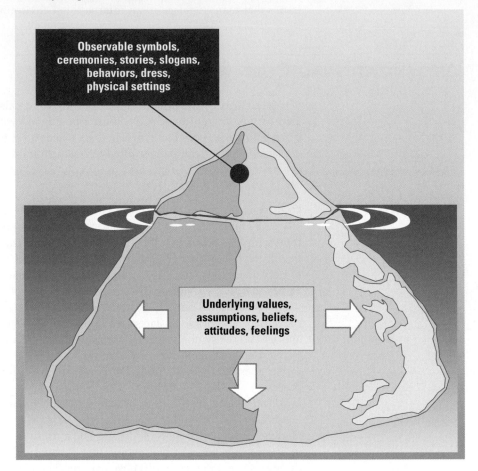

refs to how the organization meets goals and deals with outsiders. Culture helps guide the daily activities of workers to meet certain goals. It can help the organization respond rapidly to customer needs or the moves of a competitor. As discussed in this chapter's Book Mark, culture plays a key role in transforming an organization from average to truly great performance.

The organization's culture also guides employee decision making in the absence of written rules or policies.[10] Thus, both functions of culture are related to building the organization's social capital, by forging either positive or negative relationships both within the organization and with outsiders.

INTERPRETING CULTURE

To identify and interpret the content of culture requires that people make inferences based on observable artifacts. Artifacts can be studied but are hard to decipher accurately. An award ceremony in one company may have a different meaning than in another company. To decipher what is really going on in an organization requires detective work and probably some experience as an insider. Some of the typical and important observable aspects of culture are rites and ceremonies, stories, symbols, and language.

BOOK MARK *10.0* *Have You Read This Book?*

Good to Great: Why Some Companies Make the Leap...And Others Don't
By Jim Collins

How and why do some companies move from merely good to truly great long-term performance, while others can't make the leap—or if they do, can't sustain it? This is the question Jim Collins set out to answer in a six-year study that culminated in the book *Good to Great: Why Some Companies Make the Leap . . . And Others Don't.* Collins identifies eleven great companies—those that averaged returns 6.9 times the general stock market over a fifteen-year period—and compares them to a group of companies that had similar resources but failed either to make the leap or to sustain it.

A CULTURE OF DISCIPLINE
Collins identifies a number of characteristics that define truly great companies. One aspect is a culture of discipline, where everyone in the organization is focused on doing whatever is needed to keep the company successful. How is a culture of discipline built? Here are some of the key factors:

- *Level 5 leadership.* All good-to-great companies begin with a top leader who exemplifies what Collins calls Level 5 Leadership. Level 5 leaders are characterized by an almost complete lack of personal ego, coupled with a strong will and ambition for the success of the organization. They develop a strong corps of leaders throughout the organization so that when they leave, the company can grow even more successful. Values of selfishness, greed, and arrogance have no place in a great company.
- *The right values.* Leaders build a culture based on values of individual freedom and responsibility, but within a framework of organizational purpose, goals, and systems. People have the autonomy to do whatever it takes—within well-defined

boundaries and clear, consistent guidelines—to move the organization toward achieving its goals and vision.
- *The right people in the right jobs.* Leaders of good-to-great organizations look for self-disciplined people who embody values that fit the culture. These people are described using terms such as *determined, diligent, precise, systematic, consistent, focused, accountable,* and *responsible.* They are willing to go the extra mile to become the best they can be and help the organization continuously improve.
- *Knowing where to go.* Good-to-great companies base their success on a deep understanding throughout the organization of three essential ideas, conceptualized as three intersecting circles: what they can be the best in the world at, what they are deeply passionate about, and what makes economic sense for the organization. This understanding is translated into a vision and strategy that guides all actions.

THE FLYWHEEL CONCEPT
No company makes the leap from good to great in one fell swoop. The process is one of buildup followed by breakthrough, similar to pushing a giant flywheel in one direction, turn after turn, building momentum until a breakthrough is reached. Once leaders get the right people in the right jobs, support the right values, and focus on activities that fit within the three intersecting circles, people begin to see positive results, which pushes the flywheel to full momentum. As success builds on success, the organization makes the move from good to great.

From Good to Great: Why Some Companies Make the Leap . . . And Others Don't, by Jim Collins, is published by HarperBusiness.

Rites and Ceremonies. Important artifacts for culture are **rites and ceremonies**, the elaborate, planned activities that make up a special event and are often conducted for the benefit of an audience. Managers can hold rites and ceremonies to provide dramatic examples of what a company values. These are special occasions that reinforce specific values, create a bond among people for sharing an important understanding, and anoint and celebrate heroes and heroines who symbolize important beliefs and activities.[11]

Four types of rites that appear in organizations are summarized in Exhibit 10.2. *Rites of passage* facilitate the transition of employees into new social roles. *Rites of enhancement* create stronger social identities and increase the status of

EXHIBIT 10.2   *A Typology of Organizational Rites and Their Social Consequences*

Type of Rite	Example	Social Consequences
Passage	Induction and basic training, U.S. Army	Facilitate transition of persons into social roles and statuses that are new for them
Enhancement	Annual awards night	Enhance social identities and increase status of employees
Renewal	Organizational development activities	Refurbish social structures and improve organization functioning
Integration	Office holiday party	Encourage and revive common feelings that bind members together and commit them to the organization

Source: Adapted from Harrison M. Trice and Janice M. Beyer, "Studying Organizational Cultures through Rites and Ceremonials," *Academy of Management Review* 9 (1984), 653–659. Used with permission.

BRIEFCASE

As an organization manager, keep this guideline in mind:

Pay attention to corporate culture. Understand the underlying values, assumptions, and beliefs on which culture is based as well as its observable manifestations. Evaluate corporate culture based on rites and ceremonies, stories and heroes, symbols, and language.

employees. *Rites of renewal* reflect training and development activities that improve organization functioning. *Rites of integration* create common bonds and good feelings among employees and increase commitment to the organization. The following examples illustrate how these rites and ceremonies are used by top managers to reinforce important cultural values.

- In a major bank, election as an officer was seen as the key event in a successful career. A series of activities accompanied every promotion to bank officer, including a special method of notification, taking the new officer to the officers' dining room for the first time, and the new officer buying drinks on Friday after his or her notification.[12] This is a rite of passage.
- Mary Kay Cosmetics Company holds elaborate awards ceremonies, presenting gold and diamond pins, furs, and luxury cars to high-achieving sales consultants. The most successful consultants are introduced by film clips, such as the kind used to introduce award nominees in the entertainment industry. This is a rite of enhancement.
- An important event at PSS World Medical is the Blue Ribbon Tour. Twice a year, senior leaders show up at each branch unannounced for an inspection based on the company's booklet, "The Blue Ribbon Scorebook—A Foundation for PSS Culture," which details how every office is expected to look, feel, and operate. The occasion is usually a fun event, but its primary purpose is to emphasize the company's commitment to consistency in such things as cleanliness of offices and trucks, having refreshments available for guests, maintaining maintenance logs, and so forth. This is a rite of renewal.
- Whenever a Wal-Mart executive visits one of the stores, he or she leads employees in the Wal-Mart cheer: "Give me a W! Give me an A! Give me an L! Give me a squiggly! (All do a version of the twist.) Give me an M! Give me an A! Give me an R! Give me a T! What's that spell? Wal-Mart! What's that spell? Wal-Mart! Who's No. 1? THE CUSTOMER!" The cheer strengthens bonds among employees and reinforces their commitment to common goals.[13] This is a rite of integration.

Stories. **Stories** are narratives based on true events that are frequently shared among organizational employees and told to new employees to inform them about an organization. Many stories are about company **heroes** who serve as models or ideals for serving cultural norms and values. Some stories are considered **legends** because the events are historic and may have been embellished with fictional details. Other stories are **myths**, which are consistent with the values and beliefs of the organization but are not supported by facts.[14] Stories keep alive the primary values of the organization and provide a shared understanding among all employees. Examples of how stories shape culture are as follows:

- At 3M Corp., the story is told of a vice president who was fired early in his career for persisting with a new product even after his boss had told him to stop because he thought it was a stupid idea. After the worker was fired, he stayed in an unused office, working without a salary on the new product idea. Eventually he was rehired, the product was a success, and he was promoted to vice president. The story symbolizes the 3M value of persisting in what you believe in.[15]

- Employees at Prince Corp., now a division of Johnson Controls Inc., tell a story of founder Ed Prince, who was helping employees load finished materials onto a railroad car. When he discovered they needed a lubricant to effectively perform the job, he tossed the keys to his new Cadillac to a young employee he had never met, handed him a $100 bill, and asked him to go get some WD-40. The story ends with the employee returning with the product, the car, and Prince's change.[16] By telling this story, employees emphasize both the importance of anyone pitching in to help get the job done and the high value placed on trust.

Symbols. Another tool for interpreting culture is the **symbol**. A symbol is something that represents another thing. In one sense, ceremonies, stories, slogans, and rites are all symbols. They symbolize deeper values of an organization. Another symbol is a physical artifact of the organization. Physical symbols are powerful because they focus attention on a specific item. Examples of physical symbols are as follows:

- Nordstrom department store symbolizes the importance of supporting lower-level employees with the organization chart in Exhibit 10.3. Nordstrom's is known for its extraordinary customer service, and the organization chart symbolizes that managers are to support the employees who give the service rather than be managers who control them.[17]

- Symbols can also represent negative elements of corporate culture. At Enron, premium parking spots were symbols of power, wealth, and winning at any cost. At the company's London office, executives submitted blind e-mail bids for the limited spaces. One top manager paid more than $6,000 to use a well-placed company spot for a year.[18]

Language. The final technique for influencing culture is **language**. Many companies use a specific saying, slogan, metaphor, or other form of language to convey special meaning to employees. Slogans can be readily picked up and repeated by employees as well as customers of the company. Averitt Express's motto, "Our driving force is people," applies to both employees and customers. The trucking company's culture emphasizes treating employees as well as they are expected to treat customers. Drivers and customers, not top executives, are seen as the power that fuels the company's success. Other significant uses of language to shape culture are as follows:

- At PeopleSoft Inc., which sells enterprise resource planning (ERP) software, employees call themselves PeoplePeople, shop at the company PeopleStore,

EXHIBIT 10.3   *Organization Chart for Nordstrom, Inc.*

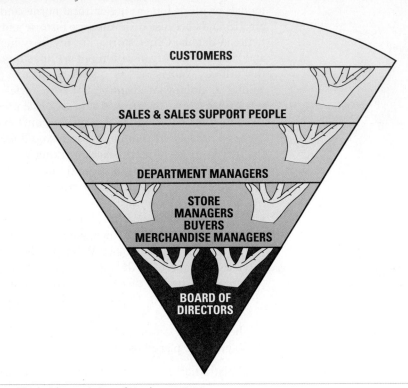

Source: Used with permission of Nordstrom, Inc.

and munch on company-funded PeopleSnacks. The use of this special lingo reinforces PeopleSoft's close-knit "family" culture.[19]

- T. J. Watson, Jr., son of the founder of International Business Machines, used the metaphor "wild ducks" to describe the type of employees needed by IBM. His point was, "You can make wild ducks tame, but you can never make tame ducks wild again."[20] Wild ducks symbolized the freedom and opportunity that must be available to keep from taming creative employees at IBM.

Recall that culture exists at two levels—the underlying values and assumptions and the visible artifacts and observable behaviors. The slogans, symbols, and ceremonies just described are artifacts that reflect underlying company values. These visible artifacts and behaviors can be used by managers to shape company values and to strengthen organizational culture.

ORGANIZATION DESIGN AND CULTURE

Corporate culture should reinforce the strategy and structural design that the organization needs to be effective within its environment. For example, if the external environment requires flexibility and responsiveness, such as the environment for emerging Internet-based companies, the culture should encourage adaptability. The correct relationship among cultural values, organizational strategy and structure, and the environment can enhance organizational performance.

Culture can be assessed along many dimensions, such as the extent of collaboration versus isolation among people and departments, the importance of control and where control is concentrated, or whether the organization's time orientation is short-range or long-range.[21] Here, we will focus on two specific dimensions: (1) the extent to which the competitive environment requires flexibility or stability; and (2) the extent to which the organization's strategic focus and strength are internal or external. Four categories of culture associated with these differences, as illustrated in Exhibit 10.4, are adaptability, mission, clan, and bureaucratic.[22] These four categories relate to the fit among culture values, strategy, structure, and the environment. Each can be successful, depending on the needs of the external environment and the organization's strategic focus.

THE ADAPTABILITY CULTURE

The **adaptability culture** is characterized by strategic focus on the external environment through flexibility and change to meet customer needs. The culture encourages entrepreneurial values, norms, and beliefs that support the capacity of the organization to detect, interpret, and translate signals from the environment into new behavior responses. This type of company, however, doesn't just react quickly to environmental changes—it actively creates change. Innovation, creativity, and risk taking are valued and rewarded.

EXHIBIT 10.4   *Relationship of Environment and Strategy to Corporate Culture*

NEEDS OF THE ENVIRONMENT

	Flexibility	Stability
External	Adaptability Culture	Mission Culture
Internal	Clan Culture	Bureaucratic Culture

STRATEGIC FOCUS

Source: Based on Daniel R. Denison and Aneil K. Mishra, "Toward a Theory of Organizational Culture and Effectiveness," *Organization Science* 6, no. 2 (March–April 1995), 204–223; R. Hooijberg and F. Petrock, "On Cultural Change: Using the Competing Values Framework to Help Leaders Execute a Transformational Strategy," *Human Resource Management* 32 (1993), 29–50; and R. E. Quinn, *Beyond Rational Management: Mastering the Paradoxes and Competing Demands of High Performance* (San Francisco: Jossey-Bass, 1988).

An example of the adaptability culture is 3M, a company whose values promote individual initiative and entrepreneurship. All new employees attend a class on risk-taking, where they are told to pursue their ideas even if it means defying their supervisors. Acxiom Corp., based in Conway, Arkansas, began changing to an adaptability culture in the early 1990s. After years of rapid growth and an explosion of interest in data management products and services, managers discovered that the company's culture, which emphasized internal efficiency, consistency in following established rules and procedures, and top-down decision making, was no longer suitable to meet the demands of the rapidly changing environment. Acxiom shifted to an external focus emphasizing the importance of employee empowerment, flexibility, and initiative.[23] Most e-commerce companies, such as eBay, Amazon.com and Buy.com, as well as companies in the marketing, electronics, and cosmetics industries, use this type of culture because they must move quickly to satisfy customers.

THE MISSION CULTURE

An organization concerned with serving specific customers in the external environment, but without the need for rapid change, is suited to the mission culture. The **mission culture** is characterized by emphasis on a clear vision of the organization's purpose and on the achievement of goals, such as sales growth, profitability, or market share, to help achieve the purpose. Individual employees may be responsible for a specified level of performance, and the organization promises specified rewards in return. Managers shape behavior by envisioning and communicating a desired future state for the organization. Because the environment is stable, they can translate the vision into measurable goals and evaluate employee performance for meeting them. In some cases, mission cultures reflect a high level of competitiveness and a profit-making orientation.

One example is PepsiCo, where former CEO Wayne Calloway set a vision to be the best consumer products company in the world. Managers who met the high performance standards were generously rewarded—first-class air travel, fully loaded company cars, stock options, bonuses, and rapid promotion. Annual performance reviews focus specifically on meeting performance goals, such as sales targets or marketing goals.[24] Another example of a mission culture is Siebel Systems, which thrives on an intense, ambitious culture. Siebel keeps employees focused on achieving high sales and profit levels. Employees who meet the demanding goals are handsomely rewarded.[25]

THE CLAN CULTURE

The **clan culture** has a primary focus on the involvement and participation of the organization's members and on rapidly changing expectations from the external environment. This culture is similar to the clan form of control described in Chapter 9. More than any other, this culture focuses on the needs of employees as the route to high performance. Involvement and participation create a sense of responsibility and ownership and, hence, greater commitment to the organization.

In a clan culture, an important value is taking care of employees and making sure they have whatever they need to help them be satisfied as well as productive. Companies in the fashion and retail industries often adopt this culture because it releases the creativity of employees to respond to rapidly changing tastes. MTW Corp., which provides Web-based software and consulting services primarily to state governments and the insurance industry, also relies on a strong clan culture to help it meet changing needs and expectations from the environment.

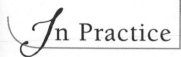

MTW CORP.

Dick Mueller and Ed Ossie built MTW Corp. around one defining characteristic: People should matter above all else, and the needs and ambitions of employees would guide the company's operations and growth.

To make sure they understand what those needs and ambitions are, leaders craft an *expectations agreement* with each employee, which spells out both professional and personal goals of each party. One value of the practice is that it makes honesty and open communication a priority right from the beginning of an employee's experience with the company. Some employees might want challenge and opportunity above everything else, whereas others highly value job flexibility to handle special family or personal needs. The expectations agreement is a two-way, ever-evolving document that stays with a person throughout his or her employment with MTW. It helps to guarantee that employees live up to their commitments as well as that managers follow through on their promises.

Employees trust managers to do what they say they'll do, which enhances their own feelings of commitment and responsibility. And the egalitarian nature of the company means no one is afraid to challenge managers if they don't live up to their side of the bargain. "I've got something I can wave at people if they don't follow through," says employee Dean Ammons. "If I have a complaint and I'm not happy, I'll knock on Ed's door." Keeping managers' doors—and minds—always open is central to the MTW culture.

Another ritual that supports the culture is the "People First" meeting, which is held two or three times a year at various company locations. The meetings begin with employees reporting on business issues, as well as what's going on in their personal lives. Next, top managers report on company-wide activities and on MTW's financial performance. All financial details are available to employees, who own more than 53 percent of the stock. Social activities and having fun are also part of the program.

MTW's people-first culture has paid off. Within three years, sales grew from $7 million to nearly $40 million. The turnover rate is 6.7 percent a year, compared to about 30 percent for the industry average. By taking care of employees and helping them meet their personal as well as professional goals, MTW has been able to adapt to competition and changing markets.[26]

THE BUREAUCRATIC CULTURE

The **bureaucratic culture** has an internal focus and a consistency orientation for a stable environment. This organization has a culture that supports a methodical approach to doing business. Symbols, heroes, and ceremonies support cooperation, tradition, and following established policies and practices as ways to achieve goals. Personal involvement is somewhat lower here, but that is outweighed by a high level of consistency, conformity, and collaboration among members. This organization succeeds by being highly integrated and efficient.

Today, most managers are shifting away from bureaucratic cultures because of a need for greater flexibility. However, one thriving new company, Pacific Edge Software, has successfully implemented some elements of a bureaucratic culture, ensuring that all its projects are on time and on budget. The husband-and-wife team of Lisa Hjorten and Scott Fuller implanted a culture of order, discipline, and control from the moment they founded the company. The emphasis on order and focus means employees can generally go home by 6:00 P.M. rather than working all night to finish an important project. Hjorten insists that the company's culture isn't rigid or uptight, just *careful*. Although sometimes being careful means being slow, so far Pacific Edge has managed to keep pace with the demands of the external environment.[27]

CULTURE STRENGTH AND ORGANIZATIONAL SUBCULTURES

A strong organizational culture can have a powerful impact on company performance. **Culture strength** refers to the degree of agreement among members of an organization about the importance of specific values. If widespread consensus exists about the importance of those values, the culture is cohesive and strong; if little agreement exists, the culture is weak.[28]

A strong culture is typically associated with the frequent use of ceremonies, symbols, stories, heroes, and slogans. These elements increase employee commitment to the values and strategy of a company. In addition, managers who want to create and maintain strong corporate cultures often give emphasis to the selection and socialization of employees. For example, PSS World Medical, described in the chapter opening, doesn't call candidates back for follow-up interviews. Requiring the candidate to take the initiative through every step of the recruiting and hiring process, which takes six to eight weeks, ensures that PSS hires the kind of people with the right values and attitudes to fit its culture. PSS invests a tremendous amount of time, care, and expense in recruiting employees and then provides them with extensive and ongoing training.

However, culture is not always uniform throughout the organization. Even in organizations that have strong cultures, there may be several sets of subcultures, particularly within large organizations. **Subcultures** develop to reflect the common problems, goals, and experiences that members of a team, department, or other unit share. An office, branch, or unit of a company that is physically separated from the company's main operations may also take on a distinctive subculture.

For example, although the dominant culture of an organization may be a mission culture, various departments may also reflect characteristics of adaptability, clan, or bureaucratic cultures. The manufacturing department of a large organization may thrive in an environment that emphasizes order, efficiency, and obedience to rules, whereas the research and development department may be characterized by employee empowerment, flexibility, and customer focus. This is similar to the concept of differentiation described in Chapter 4, where employees in manufacturing, sales, and research departments studied by Paul Lawrence and Jay Lorsch[29] developed different values with respect to time horizon, interpersonal relationships, and formality in order to perform the job of each particular department most effectively. The credit division of Pitney Bowes, a huge corporation that manufactures postage meters, copiers, and other office equipment, developed a distinctive subculture to encourage innovation and risk taking.

PITNEY BOWES CREDIT CORPORATION

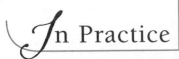

Pitney Bowes, a maker of postage meters and other office equipment, has long thrived in an environment of order and predictability. Its headquarters reflects a typical corporate environment and an orderly culture with its blank walls and bland carpeting. But step onto the third floor of the Pitney Bowes building in Shelton, Connecticut, and you might think you're at a different company. The domain of Pitney Bowes Credit Corporation (PBCC) looks more like an indoor theme park, featuring cobblestone-patterned carpets, faux gas lamps, and an ornate town square-style clock. It also has a French-style café, a 1950s-style diner, and the "Cranial Kitchen," where employees sit in cozy booths to surf the Internet or watch training videos. The friendly hallways encourage impromptu conversations, where employees can exchange information and share ideas they wouldn't otherwise share.

PBCC traditionally helped customers finance their business with the parent company. However, Matthew Kisner, PBCC's president and CEO, has worked with other managers to redefine the division as a *creator* of services rather than just a provider of services. Rather than just financing sales and leasing of existing products, PBCC now creates new services for customers to buy. For example, Purchase Power is a revolving line of credit that helps companies finance their postage costs. It was profitable within nine months and now has more than 400,000 customers. When PBCC redefined its job, it began redefining its subculture to match, by emphasizing values of teamwork, risk taking, and creativity. "We wanted a fun space that would embody our culture," Kisner says. "No straight lines, no linear thinking. Because we're a financial services company, our biggest advantage is the quality of our ideas." So far, PBCC's new approach is working. In one recent year, the division, whose 600 employees make up less than 2 percent of Pitney Bowes' total workforce, generated 36 percent of the company's net profits.[30]

Subcultures typically include the basic values of the dominant organizational culture plus additional values unique to members of the subculture. However, subcultural differences can sometimes lead to conflicts between departments, especially in organizations that do not have strong overall corporate cultures. When subcultural values become too strong and outweigh the corporate cultural values, organizational performance may suffer. Conflict will be discussed in detail in Chapter 13.

CULTURE AND THE LEARNING ORGANIZATION

One of the primary characteristics of a learning organization is a strong organizational culture. In addition, the culture of a learning organization encourages change and adaptation. A danger for many successful organizations is that the culture becomes set and the company fails to adapt as the environment changes. When organizations are successful, the values, ideas, and practices that helped attain success become institutionalized. As the environment changes, these values may become detrimental to future performance. Many organizations become victims of their own success, clinging to outmoded and even destructive values and behaviors. After decades of success at Motorola, for example, a strong culture based on internal competition among divisions and protection of turf almost destroyed the company as the environment changed and required more collaboration and information sharing to develop new Web-based products and technologies. Fortunately, CEO Christopher B. Galvin recognized the danger signs before it was too late and began a corporate makeover that included changing the insular and competitive culture. With new values of collaboration rather than competition, Motorola once again became a competitive force in the wireless industry.[31]

The impact of a strong culture is not always positive. Typically, healthy cultures not only provide for smooth internal integration but also encourage adaptation to the external environment. Nonadaptive cultures encourage rigidity and stability. One of the defining characteristics of a learning organization, introduced in Chapter 1, is a strong adaptive culture that incorporates the following values:

1. *The whole is more important than the parts and boundaries between parts are minimized.*[32] In learning organizations, people are aware of the whole system, how everything fits together, and the relationships among various organizational parts. All members consider how their actions affect other parts and the total organization. This emphasis on the whole reduces boundaries both within the organization and with other companies. Although subcultures may form, everyone's primary attitudes and behaviors reflect the organization's dominant culture. The free flow of people, ideas, and information allows coordinated action and continuous learning. At the Mayo Clinic, founded more than a century ago in Rochester, Minnesota, teamwork permeates the clinic's organizational culture. Doctors are expected to consult with doctors in other departments, with the patient, and with anyone else inside or outside the clinic who might help in dealing with any aspect of a patient's problem. Collaboration and sharing of ideas and information are incorporated into everything Mayo does, from diagnosis and surgery to policy making, strategic planning, and leadership.[33]

2. *Equality and trust are primary values.* The culture of a learning organization creates a sense of community and caring for one another. The organization is a place for creating a web of relationships that allows people to take risks and develop to their full potential. The emphasis on treating everyone with care and respect creates a climate of safety and trust that allows experimentation, frequent mistakes, and learning. Managers also emphasize honest and open communications as a way to build the trust that is a necessary component of the learning organization.

3. *The culture encourages risk taking, change, and improvement.* A basic value of a learning organization is to question the status quo. Constant questioning of assumptions opens the gates to creativity and improvement. The culture rewards and celebrates the creators of new ideas, products, and work processes. To symbolize the importance of taking risks, a learning organization culture may also reward those who fail in order to learn and grow.

The culture of a learning organization encourages openness, boundarylessness, equality, continuous improvement, and risk taking. Even though the internal culture is strong, the cultural values encourage a healthy adaptation to a changing external environment. As illustrated in Exhibit 10.5, adaptive corporate cultures have different values and behavior patterns than nonadaptive cultures.[34] In adaptive cultures, managers are concerned with customers and employees as well as the internal processes and procedures that bring about useful change. Behavior is flexible and managers initiate change when needed, even if it involves risk. In unadaptive cultures, managers are more concerned about themselves or their own special projects, and their values discourage risk taking and change. Thus, strong healthy cultures, such as those in learning companies, help organizations adapt to the external environment, whereas strong, unhealthy cultures can encourage an organization to march resolutely in the wrong direction. A strong, adaptive culture is a key factor in the success of companies such as Wal-Mart, Southwest Airlines, and Johnson & Johnson. Commerce Bank, described in this chapter's Leading by Design box, provides an excellent example of the core values and behavior patterns that characterize an adaptive corporate culture.

EXHIBIT 10.5   *Adaptive Versus Nonadaptive Corporate Cultures*

	Adaptive Corporate Cultures	**Nonadaptive Corporate Cultures**
Core Values	Managers care deeply about customers, stockholders, and employees. They also strongly value people and processes that can create useful change (for example, leadership initiatives up and down the management hierarchy).	Managers care mainly about themselves, their immediate work group, or some product (or technology) associated with that work group. They value the orderly and risk-reducing management process much more highly than leadership initiatives.
Common Behavior	Managers pay close attention to all their constituencies, especially customers, and initiate change when needed to serve their legitimate interests, even if it entails taking some risks.	Managers tend to be somewhat isolated, political, and bureaucratic. As a result, they do not change their strategies quickly to adjust to or take advantage of changes in their business environments.

Source: Adapted and reprinted with the permission of The Free Press, a division of Simon & Schuster Adult Publishing Group, from *Corporate Culture and Performance* by John P. Kotter and James L. Heskett. Copyright © 1992 by Kotter Associates, Inc. and James L. Heskett.

ETHICAL VALUES IN ORGANIZATIONS

Of the values that make up an organization's culture, ethical values are now considered among the most important. Widespread corporate accounting scandals, allegations that top managers of some organizations made personal use of company funds, and charges of insider trading have blanketed the newspapers and airwaves in recent years. In an era of terrorist attacks, sniper shootings, and war, the top stories have just as frequently been focused on issues related to corporate ethics. Top corporate managers are under scrutiny from the public as never before, and even small companies are finding a need to put more emphasis on ethics to restore trust among their customers and the community.

Strict ethical standards are becoming part of the formal policies and informal cultures of many organizations, and courses in ethics are taught in many business schools. **Ethics** is the code of moral principles and values that governs the behaviors of a person or group with respect to what is right or wrong. Ethical values set standards as to what is good or bad in conduct and decision making.[35]

Many of the recent scandals in the news have dealt with people and corporations that broke the law. But it is important to remember that ethics goes far beyond behaviors governed by law.[36] The **rule of law** arises from a set of codified principles and regulations that describe how people are required to act, are generally accepted in society, and are enforceable in the courts.[37]

The relationship between ethical standards and legal requirements is illustrated in Exhibit 10.6. Ethical standards for the most part apply to behavior not covered by the law, and the rule of law applies to behaviors not necessarily covered by ethical standards. Current laws often reflect combined moral judgments, but not all moral judgments are codified into law. The morality of aiding a drowning person, for example, is not specified by law, and driving on the right-hand side of the road has no moral basis; but in areas such as robbery or murder, rules and moral standards overlap.

EXHIBIT 10.6   *Relationship Between the Rule of Law and Ethical Standards*

Source: LaRue Tone Hosmer, *The Ethics of Management,* 2d ed. (Homewood, Ill.: Irwin, 1991).

Unethical conduct in organizations is surprisingly widespread. More than 54 percent of human resource professionals polled by the Society for Human Resource Management and the Ethics Resource Center reported observing employees lying to supervisors or coworkers, falsifying reports or records, or abusing drugs or alcohol while on the job.[38] Many people believe that if you are not breaking the law, then you are behaving in an ethical manner, but this is not always true. Many behaviors have not been codified, and managers must be sensitive to emerging norms and values about those issues. **Managerial ethics** are principles that guide the decisions and behaviors of managers with regard to whether they are right or wrong in a moral sense. The notion of **social responsibility** is an extension of this idea and refers to management's obligation to make choices and take action so that the organization contributes to the welfare and interest of society as well as to itself.[39]

Examples of the need for managerial ethics are as follows:[40]

- Top executives are considering promoting a rising sales manager who consistently brings in $70 million a year and has cracked open new markets in places like Brazil and Turkey that are important to the organization's international growth. However, female employees have been complaining for years that the manager is verbally abusive to them, tells offensive jokes, and throws temper tantrums if female employees don't do exactly as he says.
- The manager of a beauty supply store is told that she and her salespeople can receive large bonuses for selling a specified number of boxes of a new product, a permanent wave solution that costs nearly twice as much as what most of her salon customers typically use. She tells the salespeople to store the old product in the back and tell customers there's been a delay in delivery.
- The project manager for a consulting project wondered whether some facts should be left out of a report because the marketing executives paying for the report would look bad if the facts were reported.
- A North American manufacturer operating abroad was asked to make cash payments (a bribe) to government officials and was told it was consistent with local customs, despite being illegal in North America.

As these examples illustrate, ethics is about making decisions. Some issues are exceedingly difficult to resolve and often represent ethical dilemmas. An **ethical dilemma** arises in a situation concerning right and wrong where values are in conflict.[41] Right or wrong cannot be clearly identified. For example, for a salesperson at the beauty supply store, the values conflict is between being honest with customers and adhering to the boss's expectations. The manufacturing manager may feel torn between respecting and following local customs in a foreign country or adhering to U.S. laws concerning bribes. Sometimes, each alternative choice or behavior seems undesirable.

Ethical dilemmas are not easy to resolve, but choices can be aided by establishing ethical values as part of the organization's culture that provide people with guidelines for making the best decision from a moral standpoint. Long-term

LEADING BY DESIGN   *Commerce Bank*

One of the fastest-growing banks in the United States is also one of the goofiest. Commerce Bank has two costumed mascots that regularly visit branches and mingle with customers at special events. Mr. C, a jolly, oversized red letter wearing white gloves, serves as the bank's walking logo. On "Red Fridays," Mr. C joins the Wow Patrol visiting branches and taking photos of staffers and customers. The second mascot, Buzz, an exuberant giant bee, also gets in on the act, making sure employees are creating buzz within the branches. The opening of a new branch is surrounded by a carnival atmosphere, with a tent, music, family-oriented activities, and—of course—Mr. C and Buzz having their pictures taken with visitors. "It sounds juvenile, but people love getting their picture taken with Mr. C," says John Manning, vice president of the Wow Department.

The *what* department? "*Wow* is more than a word around here," Manning emphasizes. "It's a feeling that you give and get." That's right—all this silliness has a very serious purpose. Leaders rely on this playful culture to create and maintain Commerce Bank's obsession with customer service. In Commerce lingo, that means its focus on "wowing" customers. Through the company's *Kill a Stupid Rule* program, any employee who identifies a rule that prevents them from wowing customers wins $50. Each week, Dr. Wow (no one knows his or her real identity) reviews hundreds of letters and e-mails from employees and customers. Branches compete to out-wow one another and take home the coveted Hill Cup, a trophy featuring a big red letter C.

Commerce is a bank that definitely does things differently. Whereas most banks try to steer customers away from their branches, encouraging greater use of ATMs and online banking, Commerce does just the opposite, coming up with ways to lure more customers in. Branches are open seven days a week and buildings are designed to attract visitors, with floor-to-ceiling windows and historic murals on the walls. Most are open from 7:30 A.M. to 8:00 P.M.—and the company's ten-minute rule means that if you arrive at 7:20 A.M. or 8:10 P.M. you can still get service. A greeter meets you at the door, and a bright red Penny Arcade in the lobby swallows coffee cans full of loose change and spits out a receipt you can take to the teller and exchange for the full amount in bills.

Commerce Bank's unique approach is working. The number of branches nearly doubled in three years, from 96 to 185, and plans for opening forty more are in the works. Deposits in 2001 grew 38 percent to more than $10 billion. In the same year, revenues increased 34 percent and earnings rose 29 percent. Customers who are tired of being treated shabbily by other banks are enamored of Commerce's service and convenience orientation. "There's a different attitude around here, like we're all in this together," said one customer. Commerce works hard to build trust with customers and consistently deliver what it promises. And as the organization grows, what tools does Commerce plan to use to keep its focus on superior service? President and CEO Vernon Hill gives one answer: "Culture, culture, culture." Without the wow, he says, Commerce would be just another bank.

Source: Chuck Salter, "'The Problem With Most Banks Is That They Abuse Their Customers Every Day. We Want to Wow Ours,'" *Fast Company* (May 2002), 80–91.

organizational success relies largely on social capital, as described earlier in the chapter, which means companies need to build a reputation for honesty and fairness. Many companies routinely recall products even when evidence is not clear because they want to maintain a reputation for doing the right thing. Corporate culture can embrace the ethical values needed to keep the organization healthy.

SOURCES OF ETHICAL VALUES IN ORGANIZATIONS

The standards for ethical or socially responsible conduct are embodied within each employee as well as within the organization itself. In addition, external stakeholders can influence standards of what is ethical and socially responsible. The immediate forces that impinge on ethical decisions are summarized in Exhibit 10.7. Individual beliefs and values, a person's ethical decision framework, and moral development influence personal ethics. Organization culture, as we have already discussed, shapes the overall framework of values within the organization. Moreover, formal organization systems influence values and behaviors according to the organization's policy framework and reward systems.

Companies also respond to numerous stakeholders in determining what is right. They consider how their actions may be viewed by customers, government agencies, shareholders, and the general community, as well as the impact each alternative course of action may have on various stakeholders. All of these factors can be explored to understand ethical decisions in organizations.[42]

EXHIBIT 10.7   *Forces That Shape Managerial Ethics*

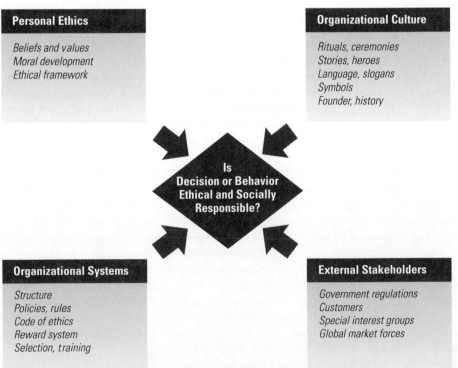

PERSONAL ETHICS

Every individual brings a set of personal beliefs and values into the workplace. Personal values and the moral reasoning that translates these values into behavior are an important aspect of ethical decision making in organizations.[43]

The family backgrounds and spiritual values of managers provide principles by which they carry out business. In addition, people go through stages of moral development that affect their ability to translate values into behavior. For example, children have a low level of moral development, making decisions and behaving to obtain rewards and avoid physical punishment. At an intermediate level of development, people learn to conform to expectations of good behavior as defined by colleagues and society. Most managers are at this level, willingly upholding the law and responding to societal expectations. At the highest level of moral development are people who develop an internal set of standards. These are self-chosen ethical principles that are more important to decisions than external expectations. Only a few people reach this high level, which can mean breaking laws if necessary to sustain higher moral principles.[44]

The other personal factor is whether managers have developed an *ethical framework* that guides their decisions. *Utilitarian theory*, for example, argues that ethical decisions should be made to generate the greatest benefits for the largest number of people. This framework is often consistent with business decisions because costs and benefits can be calculated in dollars. The *personal liberty* framework argues that decisions should be made to ensure the greatest possible freedom of choice and liberty for individuals. Liberties include freedom to act on one's conscience, free speech, due process, and the right to privacy. The *distributive justice* framework holds that moral decisions are those that promote equity, fairness, and impartiality with respect to the distribution of rewards and the administration of rules, which are essential for social cooperation.[45]

ORGANIZATIONAL CULTURE

Rarely can ethical or unethical business practices be attributed entirely to the personal ethics of a single individual. Because business practices reflect the values, attitudes, and behavior patterns of an organization's culture, ethics is as much an organizational issue as a personal one. To promote ethical behavior in the workplace, companies should make ethics an integral part of the organization's culture. At Certified Transmission Rebuilders, a small company based in Omaha, Nebraska, the culture is built on putting the customers' interests first. Employees receive ongoing in-house training to develop honest communication skills. Owner Peter Fink doesn't pay diagnosticians on commission because he doesn't want that to influence their decisions. Customers who have had their transmission repaired at Certified are asked to bring the car back in fifteen days for a free recheck to make sure everything is working right, even though the process is expensive and time consuming for the company. If Certified has to redo any work, it provides the customer with a rental car, plus the additional work, at no charge. Fink has built a highly successful business by giving customers the assurance that they're not paying for repairs they don't really need.[46]

Contrast the approach at Certified Transmission with the problems Sears faced some years ago when employees in Sears auto centers allegedly misled customers and performed unnecessary car repairs in order to earn larger commissions. Since that time, Sears has implemented an aggressive ethics and culture change program.

Organizational culture has a powerful impact on individual ethics because it helps to guide employees in making daily decisions. When the culture supports wrongdoing, it is easier for individual employees to go along. One young Enron employee explained how he slid into unethical decisions and practices in his job: "It was easy to get into, 'Well, everybody else is doing it, so maybe it isn't so bad.'"[47]

ORGANIZATIONAL SYSTEMS

The third category of influences that shape managerial ethics is formal organizational systems. This includes the basic architecture of the organization, such as whether ethical values are incorporated in policies and rules; whether an explicit code of ethics is available and issued to members; whether organizational rewards, including praise, attention, and promotions, are linked to ethical behavior; and whether ethics is a consideration in the selection and training of employees. These formal efforts can reinforce ethical values that exist in the informal culture.

Today, more and more companies are establishing formal ethics programs. For example, after being maligned by the national press and pursued by federal officials for questionable billing practices and fraud, Columbia/HCA Healthcare Corp., a large hospital chain based in Nashville, Tennessee, brought in a new management team to clean up the mess and make sure similar ethical and legal problems never happen again. When he was hired as senior vice president of ethics, compliance, and corporate responsibility, Alan R. Yuspeh found only a rudimentary compliance program and a set of perfunctory ethical guidelines that no one could understand. Yuspeh drafted a clear and concise code of conduct that emphasized the values of compassion, honesty, fairness, loyalty, respect, and kindness. He then posted it on the intranet for comment from the company's entire workforce. The final version was distributed to all 285,000 Columbia/HCA employees. In addition, Yuspeh developed a massive ethics program that includes comprehensive training for all employees and an ethics hotline that answers about 1,200 employee calls annually.[48]

EXTERNAL STAKEHOLDERS

Managerial ethics and social responsibility are also influenced by a variety of external stakeholders, groups outside the organization that have a stake in the organization's performance. Ethical and socially responsible decision making recognizes that the organization is part of a larger community and considers the impact of a decision or action on all stakeholders.[49] Important external stakeholders are government agencies, customers, and special interest groups such as those concerned with the natural environment.

Companies must operate within the limits of certain government regulations, such as safety laws, environmental protection requirements, and many other laws and regulations. Numerous companies, including Global Crossing, WorldCom, Merrill Lynch, and Xerox, have come under investigation by the Securities and Exchange Commission for alleged violations of laws related to financial controls and accounting practices. Companies in the health care industry have to respond to numerous laws and regulations, as do organizations such as schools and day care centers. Customers are another important stakeholder group. Customers are primarily concerned about the quality, safety, and availability of goods and services. For example, McDonald's has reduced trans-fatty acids in its fried foods in response to growing customer concerns about possible health risks associated with a fast-food diet.[50]

Special interest groups continue to be one of the largest stakeholder concerns that companies face. Today, those concerned with corporate responsibility to the natural environment are particularly vocal. Thus, environmentalism is becoming an integral part of organizational planning and decision making for leading companies. The concept of *sustainable development*, a dual concern for economic growth and environmental sustainability, has been gaining ground among many business leaders. The public is no longer comfortable with organizations focusing solely on profit at the expense of the natural environment. Environmental sustainability—meaning that what is taken out of the environmental system for food, shelter, clothing, energy, and other human uses is restored to the system in waste that can be reused—is a part of strategy for companies like Monsanto, Interface, IKEA, Electrolux, Scandic Hotels, and MacMillan-Bloedel. Interface, the $1-billion leader in the floor covering industry, is instituting changes that will allow the company to manufacture without pollution, waste, or fossil fuels. From the factory floor to the R&D lab, sustainability is as important a consideration at Interface as profitability. The emphasis on environmentalism hasn't hurt Interface. Over a one-year period, sales increased from $800 million to $1 billion. During that time, the amount of raw materials used by the company dropped almost 20 percent per dollar of sales.[51]

Negative values and unethical behavior can lead to serious consequences with stakeholders. For one thing, companies have a hard time attracting quality employees. The current wave of corporate scandals has prompted job-seekers to go to great lengths to check out companies' ethical standards.[52] In addition, customers who lose trust in the organization will bolt, as evidenced by the mass desertion of Arthur Andersen after the firm was accused of destroying documents related to the Enron investigation. Investors, too, will withdraw their support from the company or even sue the organization if they believe they've been lied to and cheated. By the fall of 2002, Enron and its executives had been hit with more than forty-five securities lawsuits and Tyco by at least sixty.[53]

Companies that put ethics on the back burner in favor of fast growth and short-term profits ultimately suffer. To gain and keep the trust of employees, customers, investors, and the general public, organizations put ethics first. "Just saying you're ethical isn't very useful," says Charles O. Holliday, Jr., chairman and CEO of DuPont Co. "You have to earn trust by what you do every day."[54]

HOW LEADERS SHAPE CULTURE AND ETHICS

In a study of ethics policy and practice in successful, ethical companies such as Johnson & Johnson, Boeing, and General Mills, no point emerged more clearly than the role of top management in providing commitment, leadership, and examples for ethical values.[55] The CEO and other top managers must be committed to specific values and provide constant leadership in tending and renewing those values. Values can be communicated in a number of ways—speeches, company publications, policy statements and, especially, personal actions. Top leaders are responsible for creating and sustaining a culture that emphasizes the importance of ethical behavior for all employees every day. When the CEO engages in unethical practices or fails to take firm and decisive action in response to the unethical practices of others, this attitude filters down through the organization. Formal ethics codes and training programs are worthless if leaders do not set and live up to high standards of ethical conduct.[56]

The following sections examine how managers signal and implement values through leadership as well as through the formal systems of the organization.

VALUES-BASED LEADERSHIP

The underlying value system of an organization cannot be managed in the traditional way. Issuing an authoritative directive, for example, has little or no impact on an organization's value system. Organizational values are developed and strengthened primarily through **values-based leadership**, a relationship between a leader and followers that is based on shared, strongly internalized values that are advocated and acted upon by the leader.[57] Leaders influence cultural and ethical values by clearly articulating a vision for organizational values that employees can believe in, communicating the vision throughout the organization, and institutionalizing the vision through everyday behavior, rituals, ceremonies, and symbols, as well as through organizational systems and policies. When Vic Sarni was CEO of PPG Industries, he often called himself the chief ethics officer. Sarni didn't believe in using special staff departments to investigate ethical complaints; instead, he personally headed the firm's ethics committee. This sent a powerful symbolic message that ethics was important in the organization.[58]

Leaders must remember that every statement and action has an impact on culture and values, perhaps without their realizing it. For example, a survey of readers of the magazine *The Secretary* found that employees are acutely aware of their bosses' ethical lapses. Something as simple as having a secretary notarize a document without witnessing the signature may seem insignificant, but it communicates that the manager doesn't value honesty.[59] Employees learn about values, beliefs, and goals from watching managers, just as students learn which topics are important for an exam, what professors like, and how to get a good grade from watching professors. To be effective values-based leaders, executives often use symbols, ceremonies, speeches, and slogans that match the values. Most important, actions speak louder than words, so values-based leaders "walk their talk."[60] At Baxter International Inc., a large medical products company, managers quickly yanked a product from the market when a number of people died after undergoing dialysis using a Baxter blood filter. It's a CEO's nightmare, but top leaders at Baxter did the right thing by investigating the problem, admitting their role in the deadly mistake, and providing financial compensation to families of the victims. Moreover, in atonement for the error, CEO Harry M. Jansen Kraemer Jr. slashed his annual bonus by 40 percent and the bonuses of other top executives by 20 percent.[61]

Values-based leaders engender a high level of trust and respect from employees, based not only on their stated values but also on the courage, determination, and self-sacrifice they demonstrate in upholding those values. Leaders can use this respect and trust to motivate employees toward high-level performance and a sense of purpose in achieving the organizational vision. When leaders are willing to make personal sacrifices for the sake of values, employees also become more willing to do so. This element of self-sacrifice puts a somewhat spiritual connotation on the process of leadership. Indeed, one writer in organization theory, Karl Weick, has said that, "Managerial work can be viewed as managing myth, symbols, and labels . . .; because managers traffic so often in images, the appropriate role for the manager may be evangelist rather than accountant."[62]

John Tu and David Sun, cofounders of Kingston Technology Co., provide an example of values-based leadership.

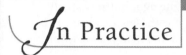

KINGSTON TECHNOLOGY CO.

"Business is not about money," says David Sun, vice president and chief operating officer of Kingston Technology Co., which manufactures memory products for personal computers, laser printers, digital cameras, and other products. "It's about relationships." Sun and his cofounder, president John Tu, strive to develop deep, caring, trusting relationships with employees. "They are part of the team," says one employee of the partnership that workers feel with leaders at Kingston. "They are not owners; they are employees. And that . . . value system is passed on."

Sun and Tu believe everyone in the company is a leader, so they share the wealth with employees. When the two sold 80 percent of Kingston to Softbank Corp. of Japan for $1.5 billion, they set aside $100 million of the proceeds for employee bonuses. The initial distribution of $38 million went to about 550 employees who were with the company at the time of its sale. Another $40 million has since been divvied up among the company's current 1,500 workers. Sun and Tu seem genuinely puzzled by people's astonishment that they would give $100 million to employees. It seems only right to them.

Despite this amazing generosity, when people talk about why they like working for Kingston, they rarely mention money and benefits. Instead, they talk about personal acts of gentleness or kindness performed by the two top leaders. There are many stories of these leaders quietly offering money, time, other resources—or just genuine concern—to employees who were dealing with family or personal troubles. This approach to leadership creates an emotional bond with employees that builds mutual trust and respect. Employees feel that they are part of a caring family. And because employees are treated with kindness, care, and respect, they pass that attitude on in their relationships with each other and with customers, suppliers, and other outsiders. Employees are highly motivated to meet organizational goals and keep the company's reputation for doing the right thing. Says one, "We try to keep the family name a good name."[63]

FORMAL STRUCTURE AND SYSTEMS

Another set of tools leaders can use to shape cultural and ethical values is the formal structure and systems of the organization. These systems have been especially effective in recent years for influencing managerial ethics.

Structure. Managers can assign responsibility for ethical values to a specific position. This not only allocates organization time and energy to the problem but symbolizes to everyone the importance of ethics. One example is an **ethics committee**, which is a cross-functional group of executives who oversee company ethics. The committee provides rulings on questionable ethical issues and assumes responsibility for disciplining wrongdoers. By appointing top-level executives to serve on the committee, the organization signals the importance of ethics in the company culture. At PPG Industries, anyone can bring a problem before the ethics committee and trust that it will be addressed quickly and confidentially.

Today, more organizations are setting up ethics departments that manage and coordinate all corporate ethics activities. These departments are headed by a **chief ethics officer**, a high-level company executive who oversees all aspects of ethics, including establishing and broadly communicating ethical standards, setting up ethics training programs, supervising the investigation of ethical problems, and advising managers on the ethical aspects of corporate decisions.[64] The title of chief ethics officer was almost unheard-of a decade ago, but recent ethical and legal problems have created a growing demand for these specialists. The Ethics Officer Association, a trade group, reports that membership soared from only twelve companies to more than seven hundred between 1992 and 2000.[65]

Ethics offices sometimes also work as counseling centers to help employees resolve difficult ethical dilemmas. The focus is as much on helping employees make the right decisions as on disciplining wrongdoers. Most ethics offices have confidential **ethics hotlines** that employees can use to seek guidance as well as report questionable behavior. One organizations calls its hotline a "Guide Line" to emphasize its use as a tool for making ethical decisions as well as reporting lapses.[66] According to Gary Edwards, president of the Ethics Resource Center, between 65 and 85 percent of calls to hotlines in the organizations he advises are calls for counsel on ethical issues. Northrup Grumman's "Openline" fields about 1,400 calls a year, of which only one-fourth are reports of misdeeds.[67]

Disclosure Mechanisms. However, the confidential hotline is also an important mechanism for employees to voice concerns about ethical practices. Holding organizations accountable depends to some degree on individuals who are willing to speak up if they suspect illegal, dangerous, or unethical activities. Organizations have to establish supportive policies and procedures to support *whistle-blowers*. **Whistle-blowing** is employee disclosure of illegal, immoral, or illegitimate practices on the part of the organization.[68] One value of corporate policy is to protect whistle-blowers so they will not be transferred to lower-level positions or fired because of their ethical concerns. A policy can also encourage whistle-blowers to stay within the organization—for instance, to quietly blow the whistle to responsible managers.[69] Whistle-blowers have the option to stop organizational activities by going to newspaper or television reporters, but as a last resort.

Although whistle-blowing has become widespread in recent years, it is still risky for employees, who can lose their jobs or be ostracized by coworkers. Sometimes managers believe a whistle-blower is out of line and think they are acting correctly to fire or sabotage that employee. As ethical problems in the corporate world increase, many companies are looking for ways to protect whistle-blowers. In addition, calls are increasing for stronger legal protection for those who report illegal or unethical business activities.[70]

When there are no protective measures, whistle-blowers suffer, and the company may continue its unethical or illegal practices. Mark Graf, a Wackenhut Services security specialist stationed at Rocky Flats nuclear facility outside Denver, Colorado, was alarmed when the company temporarily removed 450 kilograms of plutonium oxide from a vault-like room to a less secure location. After speaking to company officials and getting no response, Graf blew the whistle to outsiders. In the years that followed, Graf was consistently given unfavorable assignments, was eventually placed on administrative leave, was ordered to consult with psychologists because of his "preoccupation with security safeguards," and nearly lost his wife and family because of the stress and tension caused by this situation.[71]

Graf's story is not unusual. Many whistle-blowers suffer financial and personal loss to maintain their personal ethical standards. However, enlightened companies are striving to create a climate and a culture in which employees feel free to point out problems and managers take swift action to address concerns about unethical or illegal activities. Organizations can view whistle-blowing as a benefit to the company, helping to prevent the kind of disasters that have hit companies such as Enron, Arthur Andersen, and WorldCom, and make dedicated efforts to encourage and protect whistle-blowers.

Code of Ethics. A recent survey of *Fortune* 1000 companies found that 98 percent address issues of ethics and business conduct in formal corporate policies, and 78 percent have separate codes of ethics that are widely distributed to employees.[72] A **code of ethics** is a formal statement of the company's values concerning ethics and social responsibility; it clarifies to employees what the company stands for and its expectations for employee conduct. The code of ethics at Lockheed Martin, for example, states that the organization "aims to set the standard for ethical conduct" through adhering to the values of honesty, integrity, respect, trust, responsibility, and citizenship. The code specifies the types of behaviors expected to honor these values and encourages employees to use available company resources to help make ethical choices and decisions.[73] Codes of ethics may cover a broad range of issues, including statements of the company's guiding values, guidelines related to issues such as workplace safety, the security of proprietary information, or employee privacy, and commitments to environmental responsibility, product safety, and other matters of concern to stakeholders.

Some companies use broader values statements within which ethics is a part. These statements define ethical values as well as corporate culture and contain language about company responsibility, quality of product, and treatment of employees. A formal statement of values can serve as a fundamental organizational document that defines what the organization stands for and legitimizes value choices for employees.[74] United Technologies Corporation, GTE, and Liz Claiborne, Inc., have all established statements of cultural and ethical values. Northern Telecom's *Code of Business Conduct*, which is provided to all employees in booklet form and is also available on the Internet, is a set of standards and guidelines that illustrates how the company's core values and mission translate into ethical business practices.

Written codes of ethics are important because they clarify and formally state the company's values and expected ethical behaviors. However, it is essential that top managers support and reinforce the codes through their actions, including rewards for compliance and discipline for violations. Otherwise, a code of ethics is nothing more than a piece of paper. Indeed, one study found that companies with a written code of ethics are just as likely as those without a code to be found guilty of illegal activities.[75] Many of the companies currently in hot water with the SEC—for example, Halliburton and Arthur Andersen—had well-developed codes of ethics, but managers failed to support and enforce the ethical values.

Training Programs. To ensure that ethical issues are considered in daily decision making, companies can supplement a written code of ethics with employee training programs.[76] Most companies that place a high value on ethics include ethics training as part of their orientation and employee development seminars. At Texas Instruments, all employees go through an eight-hour ethics training course that includes case examples giving people a chance to wrestle with ethical dilemmas. In addition, TI incorporates an ethics component into every training course it offers.[77]

In an important step, ethics programs also include frameworks for ethical decision making, such as the utilitarian approach described earlier in this chapter. Learning these frameworks helps managers act autonomously and still think their way through a difficult decision. In a few companies, managers are also taught about the stages of moral development, which helps to bring them to a high level of ethical decision making. This training has been an important catalyst for establishing ethical behavior and integrity as critical components of strategic competitiveness.[78]

These formal systems and structures can be highly effective. However, they alone are not sufficient to build and sustain an ethical company. Leaders should integrate ethics into the organizational culture and support and renew ethical values through their words and actions. The Holt Companies, with headquarters in San Antonio, Texas, has very little formal structure for dealing with ethics, but the company provides a model of ethical business management.

In Practice | HOLT COMPANIES

At the Holt Companies, there is no formal ethics office, no separate ethics officer or committee. The company's executive committee serves as its ethics committee, and the designated ethics officer is the vice president of human resources. Every meeting opens with "Values in Action" stories that highlight recent values-relevant events, how they were handled, and how the company can learn from them. Most importantly, everyone in the firm, especially the CEO, Peter Holt, is expected to be responsible for ethics. Ethical values are woven into the organizational culture, and Holt continually works to renew the values and signal his total commitment to them.

Holt began developing his approach to ethics in the mid-1980s after joining the company founded by his great-grandfather a century ago. The organization has more than 1,200 employees in fourteen Texas and Ohio locations. To develop his Values-Based Leadership (VBL) process, Holt first involved the entire workforce in determining a set of core values that would guide everything the company did. The final list puts ethical values, including being honest, showing integrity, being consistent, and providing fair treatment, at the top, followed in order by values of attaining success through meeting goals, achieving continuous improvement, commitment to the long-term health of the company, and pursuing new strategic opportunities through creativity and change.

All new employees attend a two-day training program, where they learn about the values and discuss values-related cases and dilemmas. In addition, the organization presents a two-day ethics awareness course for all managers and supervisors. Peter Holt visits each of the firm's locations twice a year to conduct two-hour meetings with employees, where he discloses financial information, answers questions, and talks about the importance of each employee upholding Holt's core values every day in every action. The close involvement of the CEO and other top leaders has contributed to an environment of candor and respect between management and workers. Holt's evaluation and reward systems are also tied to the values-based leadership process. Because ethical values are entrenched in the organizational culture, Holt has not found a need for more formal systems.[79]

By integrating ethics throughout the organization, companies like Holt make personal and organizational integrity a part of day-to-day business. Holt's system was not an overnight success. It took several years to develop the level of trust needed to make it work. Only when employees are convinced that ethical values play a key role in all management decisions and actions can they become committed to making them a part of their everyday behavior.

CORPORATE CULTURE AND ETHICS IN A GLOBAL ENVIRONMENT

A Hudson Institute report, *Workforce 2020*, states, "The rest of the world matters to a degree that it never did in the past."[80] Managers are finding this to be true not only in terms of economics or human resources issues, but also in terms of cultural and ethical values. How do managers translate the ideas for developing strong corporate cultures to a complex global environment? How do they develop ethics codes or other ethical structures and systems that address the complex issues associated with doing business on a global scale?

Corporate culture and national culture are often intertwined, and the global diversity of many of today's companies presents a challenge to managers trying to build a strong organizational culture. Employees who come from different countries often have varied attitudes and beliefs that make it difficult to establish a sense of community and cohesiveness based on the corporate culture. In fact, research has indicated that national culture has a greater impact on employees than does corporate culture.[81] In addition, a recent study found that differences in national cultural values and preferences also create significant variance in ethical attitudes among people from different countries.[82]

However, in this multicultural environment some companies are developing a broad global perspective that permeates the entire organizational culture. For example, Omron, a global company with headquarters in Kyoto, Japan, has offices on each continent. However, until a few years ago, Omron had always assigned Japanese managers to head them. Today, it relies on local expertise in each geographical area and blends the insights and perspectives of local managers into a global whole. Global planning meetings are held in offices around the world. In addition, Omron established a global database and standardized its software to ensure a smooth exchange of information among its offices worldwide. It takes time to develop a broad cultural mind-set and spread it throughout the company, but firms such as Omron manage to bring a multicultural approach to every business issue.[83]

Vijay Govindarajan, a professor of international business and director of the "Global Leadership 2020" management program at Dartmouth College, offers some guidance for managers trying to build a global culture. His research indicates that, even though organizational cultures may vary widely, there are specific components that characterize a global culture. These include an emphasis on multicultural rather than national values, basing status on merit rather than nationality, being open to new ideas from other cultures, showing excitement rather than trepidation when entering new cultural environments, and being sensitive to cultural differences without being limited by them.[84]

Global ethics is also challenging today's organizations to think more broadly. Many are using a wide variety of mechanisms to support and reinforce their ethics initiatives on a global scale. One of the most useful mechanisms for building global ethics is the **social audit**, which measures and reports the ethical, social, and environmental impact of a company's operations.[85] Concerns about the labor practices and working conditions of many major U.S. corporations' overseas suppliers originally spurred the Council on Economic Priorities Accreditation Agency to propose a set of global social standards to deal with issues such as child labor, low wages, and unsafe working conditions. Today, the Social Accountability 8000, or SA 8000, is the only auditable social standard in the world. The system is designed to work like the ISO 9000 quality-auditing system of the International Standards Organization.

Many companies, such as Avon, Eileen Fisher, and Toys "R" Us, are taking steps to ensure that their factories and suppliers meet SA 8000 standards. Eileen Fisher, a clothing company, has trained all its suppliers and even picked up the bill for their SA 8000 audits.[86] Companies can also ask an outside company to perform an independent social audit to measure how well the company is living up to its ethical and social values and how it is perceived by different stakeholder groups. The Body Shop has a regular values audit to assess its performance in such areas as relationships with employees, customers, suppliers, and shareholders; environmental responsibility; and openness and honesty of its communications with the public. Three areas of particular focus are how well the company lives up to its stated commitment to animal welfare, human rights, and purchasing goods from indigenous peoples and the economically deprived.[87]

In the coming years, organizations will continue to evolve in their ability to work with varied cultures, combine them into a cohesive whole, live up to high social and ethical standards worldwide, and cope with the conflicts that may arise when working in a multicultural environment.

SUMMARY AND INTERPRETATION

This chapter covered a range of material on corporate culture, the importance of cultural and ethical values, and techniques managers can use to influence these values. Cultural and ethical values help determine the organization's social capital, and the right values can contribute to organizational success.

Culture is the set of key values, beliefs, and norms shared by members of an organization. Organizational cultures serve two critically important functions—to integrate members so that they know how to relate to one another and to help the organization adapt to the external environment. Culture can be observed and interpreted through rites and ceremonies, stories and heroes, symbols, and language.

Organizational culture should reinforce the strategy and structure that the organization needs to be successful in its environment. Four types of culture that may exist in organizations are adaptability culture, mission culture, clan culture, and bureaucratic culture. When widespread consensus exists about the importance of specific values, the organizational culture is strong and cohesive. However, even in organizations with strong cultures, several sets of subcultures may emerge, particularly in large organizations. Strong cultures can be either adaptive or nonadaptive. One of the characteristics of a learning organization is a strong, adaptive organizational culture that encourages openness, boundarylessness, equality, continuous change, and risk taking. Adaptive cultures have different values and different behavior patterns than nonadaptive cultures. Strong but unhealthy cultures can be detrimental to a company's chances for success.

An important aspect of organizational values is managerial ethics, which is the set of values governing behavior with respect to what is right or wrong. Ethical decision making in organizations is shaped by many factors: personal characteristics, which include personal beliefs, moral development, and the adoption of ethical frameworks for decision making; organizational culture, which is the extent to which values, heroes, traditions, and symbols reinforce ethical decision making; organizational systems, which pertain to the formal structure, policies, codes of ethics, and reward systems that reinforce ethical or unethical choices; and the interests and concerns of external stakeholders, which include government agencies, customers, and special interest groups.

The chapter also discussed how leaders can shape culture and ethics. One important idea is values-based leadership, which means leaders define a vision of proper values, communicate it throughout the organization, and institutionalize it through everyday behavior, rituals, ceremonies, and symbols. We also discussed formal systems that are important for shaping ethical values. Formal systems include an ethics committee, an ethics department, disclosure mechanisms for whistle-blowing, ethics training programs, and a code of ethics or values statement that specifies ethical values. As business increasingly crosses geographical and cultural boundaries, leaders face difficult challenges in establishing strong cultural and ethical values with which all employees can identify and agree. Companies that develop global cultures emphasize multicultural values, base status on merit rather than nationality, are excited about new cultural environments, remain open to ideas from other cultures, and are sensitive to different cultural values without being limited by them. Social audits are important tools for companies trying to maintain high ethical standards on a global basis.

Key Concepts

adaptability culture	legends
bureaucratic culture	managerial ethics
chief ethics officer	mission culture
clan culture	myths
code of ethics	rites and ceremonies
culture	rule of law
culture strength	social audit
ethical dilemma	social capital
ethics	social responsibility
ethics committee	stories
ethics hotlines	subcultures
external adaptation	symbol
heroes	values-based leadership
internal integration	whistle-blowing
language	

Discussion Questions

1. Describe observable symbols, ceremonies, dress, or other aspects of culture and the underlying values they represent for an organization where you have worked.
2. What might be some of the advantages of having several subcultures within an organization? The disadvantages?

3. Explain the concept of social capital. Name an organization currently in the business news that seems to have a high degree of social capital and one that seems to have a low degree.

4. Do you think a bureaucratic culture would be less employee-oriented than a clan culture? Discuss.

5. Why is values-based leadership so important to the influence of culture? Does a symbolic act communicate more about company values than an explicit statement? Discuss.

6. Are you aware of a situation where either you or someone you know was confronted by an ethical dilemma, such as being encouraged to inflate an expense account? Do you think the person's decision was affected by individual moral development or by the accepted values within the company? Explain.

7. Why is equality an important value in the culture of a learning organization? Discuss.

8. What importance would you attribute to leadership statements and actions for influencing ethical values and decision making in an organization?

9. How do external stakeholders influence ethical decision making in an organization? Discuss why globalization has contributed to more complex ethical issues for today's organizations.

10. Codes of ethics have been criticized for transferring responsibility for ethical behavior from the organization to the individual employee. Do you agree? Do you think a code of ethics is valuable for an organization?

11. Top executives at numerous technology companies, including AOL/Time Warner, Gateway, Sun Microsystems, and Cisco, made millions of dollars from the sale of stock during the "bubble years" of 1999–2001. When the bubble burst, ordinary investors lost 70 to 90 percent of their holdings. Do you see anything wrong with this from an ethical standpoint? How do you think this affects the social capital of these organizations?

Chapter 10 Workbook *Shop 'til You Drop: Corporate Culture in the Retail World* *

To understand more about corporate culture, visit two retail stores and compare them according to various factors. Go to one discount/low-end store, such as Kmart or Wal-Mart, and to one high-end store, such as Saks Fifth Avenue, Dayton/Hudson's, Goldwater's, or Dillard's. Do not interview any employees, but instead be an observer or a shopper. After your visits, fill out the following table for each store. Spend at least two hours in each store on a busy day and be very observant.

Culture Item	Discount Store	High-End Department Store
1. Mission of store: What is it, and is it clear to employees?		
2. Individual initiative: Is it encouraged?		

Culture Item	Discount Store	High-End Department Store
3. Reward system: What are employees rewarded for?		
4. Teamwork: Do people within one department or across departments work together or talk with each other?		
5. Company loyalty: Is there evidence of loyalty or of enthusiasm to be working there?		
6. Dress: Are there uniforms? Is there a dress code? How strong is it? How do you rate employees' personal appearance in general?		
7. Diversity or commonality of employees: Is there diversity or commonality in age, education, race, personality, and so on?		
8. Service orientation: Is the customer valued or tolerated?		
9. Human resource development: Is there opportunity for growth and advancement?		

Questions

1. How does the culture seem to influence employee behavior in each store?
2. What effect does employees' behavior have on customers?
3. Which store was more pleasant to be in? How does that relate to the mission of the store?

Curtis Simpson sat staring out the window of his office. What would he say to Tom Lawrence when they met this afternoon? Tom had clearly met the challenge Simpson set for him when he hired him as president of National Industrial Products a little more than a year ago, but the company seemed to be coming apart at the seams. As chairman and CEO of Simpson Industries, which had bought National several years ago, Simpson was faced with the task of understanding the problem and clearly communicating his ideas and beliefs to Lawrence.

National Industrial Products is a medium-sized producer of mechanical seals, pumps, and other flow-control products. When Simpson Industries acquired the company, it was under the leadership of Jim Carpenter, who had been CEO for almost three decades and was very well-liked by employees at National. Carpenter had always treated his employees like family. He knew most of them by name, often visited them in their homes if they were ill, and spent part of each day just chatting with workers on the factory floor. National sponsored an annual holiday party for its workers, as well as company picnics or other social events several times a year, and Carpenter was always in attendance. He considered these activities to be just as important as his visits with customers or negotiations with suppliers. Carpenter believed it was important to treat people right so they would have a sense of loyalty to the company. If business was slow, he would find something else for workers to do, even if it was just sweeping the parking lot, rather than lay people off. He figured the company couldn't afford to lose skilled workers who were so difficult to replace. "If you treat people right," he said, "they'll do a good job for you without your having to push them."

Carpenter had never set performance objectives and standards for the various departments, and he trusted his managers to run their departments as they saw fit. He offered training programs in communications and human relations for managers and team leaders several times each year. Carpenter's approach had seemed to work quite well for much of National's history. Employees were very loyal to Carpenter and the company, and there were many instances in which workers had gone above and beyond the call of duty. For example, when two National pumps that supplied water to a U.S. Navy

ship failed on a Saturday night just before the ship's scheduled departure, two employees had worked throughout the night to make new seals and deliver them for installation before the ship left port. Most of National's managers and employees had been with the company for many years, and National boasted the lowest turnover rate in the industry.

However, as the industry began to change in recent years, National's competitiveness began to decline. Four of National's major rivals had recently merged into two large companies that were better able to meet customer needs, which was one factor that led to National being acquired by Simpson Industries. Following the acquisition, National's sales and profits had continued to decline, while costs kept going up. In addition, Simpson's top executives were concerned about low productivity at National. Although they had been happy to have Carpenter stay on through the transition, within a year they had gently pressured him into early retirement. Some of the top managers believed Carpenter tolerated poor performance and low productivity in order to maintain a friendly atmosphere. "In today's world, you just can't do that," one had said. "We've got to bring in someone who can implement change and turn this company around in a hurry, or National's going to go bankrupt." That's when Tom Lawrence was brought on board, with a mandate to cut costs and improve productivity and profits.

Lawrence had a growing reputation as a young, dynamic manager who could get things done fast. He quickly began making changes at National. First, he cut costs by discontinuing the company-sponsored social activities, and he even refused to allow the impromptu birthday celebrations that had once been a regular part of life at National. He cut the training programs in communications and human relations, arguing that they were a waste of time and money. "We're not here to make people feel good," he told his managers. "If people don't want to work, get rid of them and find someone else who does." He often referred to workers who complained about the changes at National as "crybabies."

*Based on Gary Yukl, "Consolidated Products," in *Leadership in Organizations*, 4th ed. (Englewood Cliffs, N.J.: Prentice-Hall, 1998), 66–67; John M. Champion and John H. James, "Implementing Strategic Change," in *Critical Incidents in Management: Decision and Policy Issues*, 6th ed. (Homewood, Ill.: Irwin, 1989), 138–140; and William C. Symonds "Where Paternalism Equals Good Business," *BusinessWeek* (July 20, 1998), 16E4, 16E6.

Lawrence established strict performance standards for his vice presidents and department managers and ordered them to do the same for their employees. He held weekly meetings with each manager to review department performance and discuss problems. All employees were now subject to regular performance reviews. Any worker who had substandard performance was to be given one warning and then fired if performance did not improve within two weeks. And, whereas managers and sales representatives had once been paid on a straight salary basis, with seniority being the sole criterion for advancement, Lawrence implemented a revised system that rewarded them for meeting productivity, sales, and profit goals. For those who met the standards, rewards were generous, including large bonuses and perks such as company cars and first-class air travel to industry meetings. Those who fell behind were often chided in front of their colleagues to set an example, and if they didn't shape up soon, Lawrence didn't hesitate to fire them.

By the end of Lawrence's first year as president of National, production costs had been reduced by nearly 20 percent, while output was up 10 percent and sales increased by nearly 10 percent as well. However, three experienced and well-respected National managers had left the company for jobs with competitors, and turnover among production workers had increased alarmingly. In the tight labor market, replacements were not easily found. Most disturbing to Simpson were the results of a survey he had commissioned by an outside consultant. The survey indicated that morale at National was in the pits. Workers viewed their supervisors with antagonism and a touch of fear. They expressed the belief that managers are obsessed with profits and quotas and care nothing about workers' needs and feelings. They also noted that the collegial, friendly atmosphere that had made National a great place to work had been replaced by an environment of aggressive internal competition and distrust.

Simpson is pleased that Lawrence has brought National's profits and productivity up to the standards Simpson Industries expects. However, he is concerned that the low morale and high turnover will seriously damage the company in the long run. Is Lawrence correct that many of the employees at National are just being "crybabies"? Are they so accustomed to being coddled by Carpenter that they aren't willing to make the changes that are necessary to keep the company competitive in today's environment? Finally, Simpson wonders if a spirit of competition can exist in an atmosphere of collegiality and cooperativeness such as that fostered by Carpenter.

CASE FOR ANALYSIS   *Does This Milkshake Taste Funny?**

George Stein, a college student working for Eastern Dairy during the summer, was suddenly faced with an ethical dilemma. George had very little time to think about his choices, less than a minute. On the one hand, he could do what Paul told him to do, and his shift could go home on time. However, he found it tough to shake the gross mental image of all those innocent kids drinking milkshakes contaminated with pulverized maggots. If he chose instead to go against Paul, what would the guys say? He could almost hear their derisive comments already: "wimp . . . college kid . . ."

Background

George Stein had lived his entire life in various suburbs of a major city on the East Coast. His father's salary as a manager provided the family with a solid middle-class lifestyle. His mother was a homemaker. George's major interests in life were the local teenage gathering place—a drive-in restaurant—hot rod cars, and his girlfriend, Cathy. He had not really wanted to attend college, but relentless pressure by his parents convinced him to try it for a year. He chose mechanical engineering as his major, hoping there might be some similarity between being a mechanical engineer and being a mechanic. After one year of engineering school, however, he has not seen any similarity yet. Once again this summer, his parents

*This case was prepared by Roland B. Cousins, LaGrange College, and Linda E. Benitz, InterCel, Inc., as a basis for class discussion and not to illustrate either effective or ineffective handling of an administrative situation. The names of the firm and individuals and the location involved have been disguised to preserve anonymity. The situation reported is factual. The authors thank Anne T. Lawrence for her assistance in the development of this case.

had to prod and cajole him to agree to return to school in the fall. They only succeeded by promising to give their blessing to his marriage to Cathy following his sophomore year.

George had worked at menial jobs each of the last four summers to satisfy his immediate need for dating and car money. He did manage to put away a bit to be used for spending money during the school year. He had saved very little for the day that he and Cathy would start their life together, but they planned for Cathy to support them with her earnings as a secretary until George either finished or quit school.

The day after George returned home this summer, he heard that Eastern Dairy might hire summer help. He applied at the local plant the next day. Eastern Dairy was unionized, and the wages paid were over twice the minimum wage George had been paid on previous jobs, so he was quite interested in a position.

Eastern Dairy manufactured milkshake and ice cream mix for a number of customers in the metropolitan area. It sold the ice cream mix in five- and ten-gallon containers to other firms, which then added the flavoring ingredients (e.g., strawberries or blueberries), packaged and froze the mix, and sold the ice cream under their own brand names. Eastern Dairy sold the milkshake mix in five-gallon cardboard cartons, which contained a plastic liner. These packages were delivered to many restaurants in the area. The packaging was designed to fit into automatic milkshake machines used in many types of restaurants, including most fast-food restaurants and drive-ins.

George was elated when he received the call asking him to come to the plant on June 8. After a brief visit with the human resources director, at which time George filled out the necessary employment forms, he was instructed to report for work at 11 P.M. that night. He was assigned to the night shift, working from 11 P.M. until 7 A.M. six nights per week—Sunday through Friday. With the regular wages paid at Eastern Dairy, supplemented by time and one-half for eight hours of guaranteed overtime each week, George thought he could save a tidy sum before he had to return to school at the end of the first week in September.

When George reported to work, he discovered that there were no managers assigned to the night shift. The entire plant was run by a six-person crew of operators. One member of this crew, a young man named Paul Burnham, received each night's production orders from the day shift superintendent as the superintendent left for the day. Although Paul's status was no different from that of his five colleagues, the other crew members looked to him for direction. Paul passed the production orders to the mixer (who was the first stage of the production process) and kept the production records for the shift.

The production process was really quite simple. Mixes moved between various pieces of equipment (including mixing vats, pasteurizers, coolers, homogenizers, and filling machines) through stainless steel pipes suspended from the ceiling. All of the pipes had to be disassembled, thoroughly cleaned, and reinstalled by the conclusion of the night shift. This process took approximately one hour, so all the mix had to be run by 6 A.M. in order to complete the cleanup by the 7 A.M. quitting time. Paul and one other worker, Fred (the mixer), cleaned the giant mixing vats while the other four on the shift, including George, cleaned and reinstalled the pipes and filters.

George soon learned that Paul felt a sense of responsibility for completing all of the assigned work before the end of the shift. However, as long as that objective was achieved, he did not seem to care about what else went on during the shift. A great deal of story-telling and horseplay was the norm, but the work was always completed by quitting time. George was soon enjoying the easy camaraderie of the work group, the outrageous pranks they pulled on one another, and even the work itself.

George's position required that he station himself beside the conveyor in a large freezer room. He removed containers of mix as they came down the line and stacked them in the appropriate places. Periodically, Paul would decide that they had all worked hard enough and would shut down the line for a while so that they could engage in some nonwork activity like joke telling, hiding each other's lunch boxes, or "balloon" fights. The balloons were actually the five-gallon, flexible liners for the cardboard boxes in which the mix was sold.

While George did not relish being hit by an exploding bag containing five gallons of heavy mix, he found it great fun to lob one at one of his coworkers. The loss of 10 to 40 gallons of mix on a shift did not seem to concern anyone, and these fights were never curtailed.

George quickly learned that management had only two expectations of the night shift. First, the shift was expected to complete the production orders each night. Second, management expected the equipment, including the pipes, to be spotlessly clean at the conclusion of the shift. Paul told George that inspectors from the county health department would occasionally drop by unannounced at the end of the shift to inspect the vats and pipes after they had been disassembled and scrubbed. Paul also told George that management would be very upset if the inspectors registered any complaints about cleanliness.

George did join the union but saw very little evidence of its involvement in the day-to-day operations of the plant. Labor relations seemed quite amicable, and George thought of the union only when he looked at a pay stub and noticed that union dues had been deducted from his gross pay. The difference George noticed in working for Eastern Dairy compared to his previous employers was not the presence of the union but the absence of management.

The Current Situation

Things seemed to be going quite well for George on the job—until a few minutes ago. The problem first surfaced when the milkshake mix that was being run started spewing out of one of the joints in the overhead pipe network. The pumps were shut down while George disassembled the joint to see what the problem was. George removed the filter screen from the pipe at the leaking joint and saw that it was completely packed with solid matter. Closer inspection revealed that maggots were the culprits. George hurriedly took the filter to Paul to show him the blockage. Paul did not seem too concerned and told George to clean the filter and reassemble the joint. When George asked how this could have happened, Paul said maggots occasionally got into the bags of certain ingredients that were stored in a warehouse at the back of the lot. "But you do not have to worry," said Paul. "The filters will catch any solid matter."

Feeling somewhat reassured, George cleaned the filter and reassembled the pipe. But still, the image of maggots floating in a milkshake was hard to shake. And, unfortunately for George, this was not the end of it.

Shortly after the pumps were restarted, the mix began to flow out of another joint. Once again, a filter plugged with maggots was found to be the cause. For the second time, George cleaned the filter and reassembled the connection. This time Paul

seemed a bit more concerned as he noted that they barely had enough time to run the last 500 gallons remaining in the vats before they needed to clean up in preparation for the end of the shift.

Moments after the equipment was again restarted, another joint started to spew. When maggots were found to be clogging this filter, too, Paul called George over and told him to remove all five filters from the line so the last 500 gallons could be run without any filters. Paul laughed when he saw the shocked look on George's face.

"George," he said, "don't forget that all of this stuff goes through the homogenizer, so any solid matter will be completely pulverized. And when it's heated in the pasteurization process, any bacteria will be killed. No one will ever know about this, the company can save a lot of mix—that's money—and, most important, we can run this through and go home on time."

George knew that they would never get this lot packaged if they had to shut down every minute to clean filters, and there was no reason to believe it would not be this way for the rest of the run. The product had been thoroughly mixed in the mixing vats at the beginning of the process, which meant that contaminants would be distributed uniformly throughout the 500 gallons. George also knew that the 500 gallons of milkshake was very expensive. He did not think management would just want it dumped down the drain. Finally, Paul was definitely right about one thing, removing all of the filters, a ten-minute job at most, would ensure that they could get everything cleaned up and be out on time.

As George walked to the first filter joint, he felt a knot forming in his stomach as he thought of kids drinking all of the milkshakes they were about to produce. He had already decided he would not have another milkshake for at least a month, in order to be absolutely sure that this batch was no longer being served at restaurants. After all, he did not know exactly which restaurants would receive this mix. As he picked up his wrench and approached the first pipe joint that contained a filter, he still could not help wondering if he should not do or say something more.

Note: This case appeared in Paul F. Buller and Randall S. Schuler, *Managing Organizations and People*, South-Western © 2000.

Chapter 10 Workshop *The Power of Ethics**

This exercise will help you to better understand the concept of ethics and what it means to you.

1. Spend about five minutes individually answering the questions below.
2. Divide into groups of four to six members.
3. Have each group try to achieve consensus with answers to each of the four questions. For question 3, choose one scenario to highlight. You will have twenty to forty minutes for this exercise, depending on the instructor.
4. Have groups share their answers with the whole class, after which the instructor will lead a discussion on ethics and its power in business.

Questions

1. In your own words, define the concept of ethics in one or two sentences.

2. If you were a manager, how would you motivate your employees to follow ethical behavior? Use no more than two sentences.
3. Describe a situation in which you were faced with an ethical dilemma. What was your decision and behavior? How did you decide to do that? Can you relate your decision to any concept in the chapter?
4. What do you think is a powerful ethical message for others? Where did you get it from? How will it influence your behavior in the future?

*Adapted by Dorothy Marcic from Allayne Barrilleaux Pizzolatto's "Ethical Management: An Exercise in Understanding Its Power," *Journal of Management Education* 17, no. 1 (February 1993), 107–109.

Notes

1. Charles A. O'Reilly III and Jeffrey Pfeffer, "PSS World Medical: Opening the Books Boosts Commitment and Performance," *Journal of Organizational Excellence* (Spring 2001), 65–80.
2. Anita Raghavan, Kathryn Kranhold, and Alexei Barrionuevo, "Full Speed Ahead: How Enron Bosses Created a Culture of Pushing Limits," *The Wall Street Journal* (August 26, 2002), A1, A7.
3. Don Cohen and Laurence Prusak, *In Good Company: How Social Capital Makes Organizations Work* (Boston, Mass.: Harvard Business School Press, 2001), 3–4.
4. Erick Shonfeld, "eBay's Secret Ingredient," *Business 2.0* (March 2002), 52–58.
5. Ken Brown, "At Fred Alger, Close Ties Lured Back Alumni," *The Wall Street Journal* (November 15, 2001), C1, C13.
6. W. Jack Duncan, "Organizational Culture: 'Getting a Fix' on an Elusive Concept," *Academy of Management Executive* 3 (1989), 229–236; Linda Smircich, "Concepts of Culture and Organizational Analysis," *Administrative Science Quarterly* 28 (1983), 339–358; Andrew D. Brown and Ken Starkey, "The Effect of Organizational Culture on Communication and Information," *Journal of Management Studies* 31, no. 6 (November 1994), 807–828.
7. Edgar H. Schein, "Organizational Culture," *American Psychologist* 45 (February 1990), 109–119.
8. Harrison M. Trice and Janice M. Beyer, "Studying Organizational Cultures through Rites and Ceremonials," *Academy of Management Review* 9 (1984), 653–669; Janice M. Beyer and Harrison M. Trice, "How an Organization's Rites Reveal Its Culture," *Organizational Dynamics* 15 (Spring 1987), 5–24; Steven P. Feldman, "Management in Context: An Essay on the Relevance of Culture to the Understanding of Organizational Change," *Journal of Management Studies* 23 (1986), 589–607; Mary Jo Hatch, "The Dynamics of Organizational Culture," *Academy of Management Review* 18 (1993), 657–693.
9. This discussion is based on Edgar H. Schein, *Organizational Culture and Leadership*, 2d ed. (Homewood, Ill.: Richard D. Irwin, 1992); John P. Kotter and James L. Heskett, *Corporate Culture and Performance* (New York: Free Press, 1992).
10. Larry Mallak, "Understanding and Changing Your Organization's Culture," *Industrial Management* (March–April 2001), 18–24.
11. Charlotte B. Sutton, "Richness Hierarchy of the Cultural Network: The Communication of Corporate Values" (Unpublished manuscript,

Texas A&M University, 1985); Terrence E. Deal and Allan A. Kennedy, "Culture: A New Look through Old Lenses," *Journal of Applied Behavioral Science* 19 (1983), 498–505.

12. Thomas C. Dandridge, "Symbols at Work" (working paper, School of Business, State University of New York at Albany, 1978), 1.

13. Don Hellriegel and John W. Slocum, Jr., *Management*, 7th ed. (Cincinnati, Ohio: South-Western, 1996), 537.

14. Trice and Beyer, "Studying Organizational Cultures through Rites and Ceremonials."

15. Sutton, "Richness Hierarchy of the Cultural Network"; Terrence E. Deal and Allan A. Kennedy, *Corporate Cultures: The Rites and Rituals of Corporate Life* (Reading, Mass.: Addison-Wesley, 1982).

16. Mallak, "Understanding and Changing Your Organization's Culture."

17. "FYI," *Inc.* (April 1991), 14.

18. Raghavan, Kranhold, and Barrionuevo, "Full Speed Ahead."

19. Quentin Hardy, "A Software Star Sees Its 'Family' Culture Turn Dysfunctional," *The Wall Street Journal* (May 5, 1999), A1, A12; Paul Roberts, "We Are One Company, No Matter Where We Are," *Fast Company* (April–May 1998), 122–128.

20. Richard Ott, "Are Wild Ducks Really Wild: Symbolism and Behavior in the Corporate Environment" (paper presented at the Northeastern Anthropological Association, March 1979).

21. James R. Detert, Roger G. Schroeder, and John J. Mauriel, "A Framework for Linking Culture and Improvement Initiatives in Organizations," *Academy of Management Review* 25, no. 4 (2000), 850–863.

22. Based on Daniel R. Denison, *Corporate Culture and Organizational Effectiveness* (New York: Wiley, 1990), 11–15; Daniel R. Denison and Aneil K. Mishra, "Toward a Theory of Organizational Culture and Effectiveness," *Organization Science* 6, no. 2 (March–April 1995), 204–223; R. Hooijberg and F. Petrock, "On Cultural Change: Using the Competing Values Framework to Help Leaders Execute a Transformational Strategy," *Human Resource Management* 32 (1993), 29–50; R. E. Quinn, *Beyond Rational Management: Mastering the Paradoxes and Competing Demands of High Performance* (San Francisco: Jossey-Bass, 1988).

23. Daintry Duffy, "Cultural Evolution," *CIO Enterprise*, Section 2 (January 15, 1999), 44–50.

24. Brian Dumaine, "Those High Flying PepsiCo Managers," *Fortune* (April 10, 1989); L. Zinn, J. Berry, and G. Burns, "Will the Pepsi Brass Be Drinking Hemlock?" *BusinessWeek* (July 25, 1994), 31; S. Lubove, "We Have a Big Pond to Play In," *Forbes* (September 12, 1993), 216–224; J. Wolfe, "PepsiCo and the Fast Food Industry," in M. A. Hitt, R. D. Ireland, and R. E. Hoskisson, eds., *Strategic Management: Competitiveness and Globalization* (St. Paul, Minn.: West Publishing, 1995), 856–879.

25. Melanie Warner, "Confessions of a Control Freak," *Fortune* (September 4, 2000), 130–140.

26. Edward O. Welles, "Great Expectations," *Inc.* (March 2001), 68–73.

27. Rekha Balu, "Pacific Edge Projects Itself," *Fast Company* (October 2000), 371–381.

28. Bernard Arogyaswamy and Charles M. Byles, "Organizational Culture: Internal and External Fits," *Journal of Management* 13 (1987), 647–659.

29. Paul R. Lawrence and Jay W. Lorsch, *Organization and Environment* (Homewood, Ill.: Irwin, 1969).

30. Scott Kirsner, "Designed for Innovation," *Fast Company* (November 1998), 54, 56.

31. Roger O. Crockett, "A New Company Called Motorola," *BusinessWeek* (April 17, 2000), 86.

32. Mary Anne DeVanna and Noel Tichy, "Creating the Competitive Organization of the Twenty-First Century: The Boundaryless Corporation," *Human Resource Management* 29 (Winter 1990), 455–471; and Fred Kofman and Peter M. Senge, "Communities of Commitment: The Heart of Learning Organizations," *Organizational Dynamics* 22, no. 2 (Autumn 1993), 4–23.

33. Paul Roberts, "The Best Interest of the Patient is the Only Interest to be Considered," *Fast Company* (April 1999), 149–162.

34. John P. Kotter and James L. Heskett, *Corporate Culture and Performance* (New York: The Free Press, 1992).

35. Gordon F. Shea, Practical Ethics (New York: American Management Association, 1988); Linda K. Treviño, "Ethical Decision Making in Organizations: A Person–Situation Interactionist Model," *Academy of Management Review* 11 (1986), 601–617; and Linda Klebe Treviño and Katherine A. Nelson, *Managing Business Ethics:*

Straight Talk About How to Do It Right, 2nd ed. (New York: John Wiley & Sons, Inc., 1999).

36. Dawn-Marie Driscoll, "Don't Confuse Legal and Ethical Standards," *Business Ethics* (July–August 1996), 44.

37. LaRue Tone Hosmer, *The Ethics of Management*, 2d ed. (Homewood, Ill.: Irwin, 1991).

38. Geanne Rosenberg, "Truth and Consequences," *Working Woman* (July–August 1998), 79–80.

39. Eugene W. Szwajkowski, "The Myths and Realities of Research on Organizational Misconduct," in James E. Post, ed., *Research in Corporate Social Performance and Policy*, vol. 9 (Greenwich, Conn.: JAI Press, 1986), 103–122.

40. Some of these incidents are from Hosmer, *The Ethics of Management.*

41. Linda K. Treviño and Katherine A. Nelson, *Managing Business Ethics: Straight Talk about How to Do It Right*, (New York: John Wiley & Sons, Inc., 1995), 4.

42. Linda Klebe Treviño, "A Cultural Perspective on Changing and Developing Organizational Ethics," in Richard Woodman and William Pasmore, eds., *Research and Organizational Change and Development*, vol. 4 (Greenwich, Conn.: JAI Press, 1990); Lynn Sharp Paine, "Managing for Organizational Integrity," *Harvard Business Review* (March/April 1994), 106–117.

43. James Weber, "Exploring the Relationship between Personal Values and Moral Reasoning," *Human Relations* 46 (1993), 435–463.

44. L. Kohlberg, "Moral Stages and Moralization: The Cognitive-Developmental Approach," in T. Likona, ed., *Moral Development and Behavior: Theory, Research, and Social Issues* (New York: Holt, Rinehart & Winston, 1976).

45. Hosmer, *The Ethics of Management.*

46. Michael Barrier, "Doing the Right Thing," *Nation's Business* (March 1998), 33–38.

47. John A. Byrne with Mike France and Wendy Zellner, "The Environment Was Ripe for Abuse," *BusinessWeek* (February 25, 2002), 118–120.

48. Jennifer Bresnahan, "For Goodness Sake," *CIO Enterprise*, Section 2 (June 15, 1999), 54–62.

49. David M. Messick and Max H. Bazerman, "Ethical Leadership and the Psychology of Decision Making," *Sloan Management Review* (Winter 1996), 9–22; Dawn-Marie Driscoll, "Don't Confuse Legal and Ethical Standards," *Business Ethics* (July–August 1996), 44; Max B. E. Clarkson, "A Stakeholder Framework for Analyzing and Evaluating Corporate Social Performance," *Academy of Management Review* 20, no. 1 (1995), 92–117.

50. Roger Parloff, "Is Fat the Next Tobacco?" *Fortune* (February 3, 2003), 51–54.

51. Gwen Kinkead, "In the Future, People Like Me Will Go to Jail," *Fortune* (May 24, 1999), 190–200.

52. Kris Maher, "Wanted: Ethical Employer," *The Wall Street Journal* (July 9, 2002), B1, B8.

53. Jonathan D. Glater, "From Investor Fury, A Legal Bandwagon," *The New York Times* (September 15, 2002), Section 3, 1.

54. Carol Hymowitz, "CEOs Must Work Hard to Maintain Faith in the Corner Office" (In the Lead column), *The Wall Street Journal* (July 9, 2002), B1.

55. *Corporate Ethics: A Prime Business Asset* (New York: The Business Round Table, February 1988).

56. Andrew W. Singer, "The Ultimate Ethics Test," *Across the Board* (March 1992), 19–22; Ronald B. Morgan, "Self and Co-Worker Perceptions of Ethics and Their Relationships to Leadership and Salary," *Academy of Management Journal* 36, no.1 (February 1993), 200–214; Joseph L. Badaracco, Jr., and Allen P. Webb, "Business Ethics: A View From the Trenches," *California Management Review* 37, no. 2 (Winter 1995), 8–28.

57. This discussion is based on Robert J. House, Andre Delbecq, and Toon W. Taris, "Value Based Leadership: An Integrated Theory and an Empirical Test" (working paper).

58. Treviño and Nelson, *Managing Business Ethics*, 201.

59. Barrier, "Doing the Right Thing."

60. Thomas J. Peters and Robert H. Waterman, Jr., *In Search of Excellence* (New York: Harper & Row, 1982).

61. Michael Arndt, "How Does Harry Do It?" *BusinessWeek* (July 22, 2002), 66–67.

62. Karl E. Weick, "Cognitive Processes in Organizations," in B. M. Staw, ed., *Research in Organizations*, vol. 1 (Greenwich, Conn.: JAI Press, 1979), 42.

63. Richard Osborne, "Kingston's Family Values," *IndustryWeek* (August 13, 2001), 51–54.

64. Alan Yuspeh, "Do the Right Thing," *CIO* (August 1, 2000), 56–58.

65. Amy Zipkin, "Getting Religion on Corporate Ethics," *The New York Times* (October 18, 2000), C1, C10.

66. Treviño and Nelson, *Managing Business Ethics*, 212.

67. Beverly Geber, "The Right and Wrong of Ethics Offices," *Training* (October 1995), 102–118.

68. Janet P. Near and Marcia P. Miceli, "Effective Whistle-Blowing," *Academy of Management Review* 20, no. 3 (1995), 679–708.

69. Richard P. Nielsen, "Changing Unethical Organizational Behavior," *Academy of Management Executive* 3 (1989), 123–130.

70. Jene G. James, "Whistle-Blowing: Its Moral Justification," in Peter Madsen and Jay M. Shafritz, eds., *Essentials of Business Ethics* (New York: Meridian Books, 1990), 160–190; Janet P. Near, Terry Morehead Dworkin, and Marcia P. Miceli, "Explaining the Whistle-Blowing Process: Suggestions from Power Theory and Justice Theory," *Organization Science* 4 (1993), 393–411.

71. Susan Orenstein, "Exposing Your Superiors: A Practical Guide," *Business 2.0* (April 2002), 112–113.

72. Linda Klebe Treviño, Gary R. Weaver, David G. Gibson, and Barbara Ley Toffler, "Managing Ethics and Legal Compliance: What Works and What Hurts?" *California Management Review* 41, no. 2 (Winter 1999), 131–151.

73. "Setting the Standard," accessed at Lockheed Martin's Web site, *http://www.lockheedmartin.com/exeth/html/code/code* html, on August 7, 2001.

74. Carl Anderson, "Values-Based Management," *Academy of Management Executive* 11, no. 4 (1997), 25–46.

75. Ronald E. Berenbeim, *Corporate Ethics Practices* (New York: The Conference Board, 1992).

76. James Weber, "Institutionalizing Ethics into Business Organizations: A Model and Research Agenda," *Business Ethics Quarterly* 3 (1993), 419–436.

77. Mark Henricks, "Ethics in Action," *Management Review* (January 1995), 53–55; Dorothy Marcic, *Management and the Wisdom of Love* (San Francisco: Jossey-Bass, 1997); Beverly Geber, "The Right and Wrong of Ethics Offices," *Training* (October 1995), 102–118.

78. Susan J. Harrington, "What Corporate America Is Teaching about Ethics," *Academy of Management Executive* 5 (1991), 21–30.

79. Treviño and Nelson, *Managing Business Ethics*, 2nd. ed., 274–283.

80. Richard W. Judy and Carol D'Amico, *Workforce 2020: Work and Workers in the 21st Century* (Indianapolis, Ind.: Hudson Institute, 1997).

81. S. C. Schneider, "National Vs. Corporate Culture: Implications for Human Resource Management," *Human Resource Management* (Summer 1988), 239.

82. Terence Jackson, "Cultural Values and Management Ethics: A 10-Nation Study," *Human Relations* 54, no. 10 (2001), 1267–1302.

83. Gail Dutton, "Building a Global Brain," *Management Review* (May 1999), 34–38.

84. Ibid.

85. Homer H. Johnson, "Corporate Social Audits— This Time Around," *Business Horizons* (May– June 2001), 29–36.

86. Cassandra Kegler, "Holding Herself Accountable," *Working Woman* (May 2001), 13; Louisa Wah, "Treading the Sacred Ground," *Management Review* (July–August 1998), 18–22.

87. Johnson, "Corporate Social Audits."

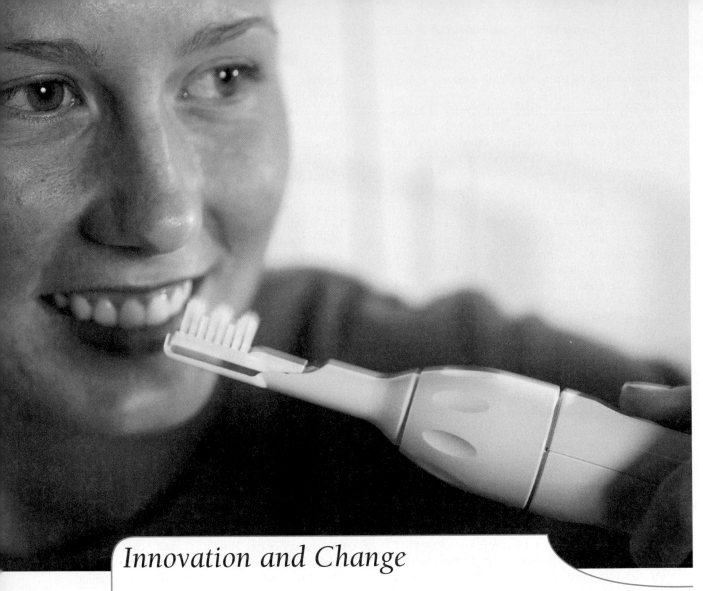

Innovation and Change

chapter
11

Innovate or Perish: The Strategic Role of Change
Incremental Versus Radical Change • *Strategic Types of Change*

Elements for Successful Change

Technology Change
The Ambidextrous Approach • *Techniques for Encouraging Technology Change*

New Products and Services
New Product Success Rate • *Reasons for New Product Success* • *Horizontal Linkage Model* • *Achieving Competitive Advantage: The Need for Speed*

Strategy and Structure Change
The Dual-Core Approach • *Organization Design for Implementing Administrative Change*

Culture Change
Forces for Culture Change • *OD Culture Change Interventions*

Strategies for Implementing Change
Leadership for Change • *Barriers to Change* • *Techniques for Implementation*

Summary and Interpretation

Procter & Gamble

What a concept! Create a snazzy-looking battery-powered toothbrush, name it the SpinBrush, and sell it for $5. It was one of Procter & Gamble's hottest new product launches in years—but Procter & Gamble didn't have a thing to do with inventing the product. P&G broke out of its insular culture and make-it-here mentality when it bought the SpinBrush business from a group of entrepreneurs—and then brought them on board to manage it.

P&G has long insisted on controlling every step, from developing a new product to pricing and promotion decisions. But its best-selling new products in recent years have come from outside the company. With the Crest SpinBrush, P&G combined the giant company's strengths in marketing and distribution with the innovative thinking and risk-taking abilities of a small start-up company. When P&G bought the start-up, the tiny company's entrepreneurs were also hired to keep the new business from getting swallowed up in the slow-moving P&G bureaucracy. The venture team had full authority to bend any rule that interfered with the creative development and marketing of the SpinBrush and any spin-off products. A lot of decisions went against traditional Procter & Gamble approaches to business. For example, the company typically introduces a new product with a massive advertising campaign and slaps a high enough price on the product to carry the costs. But keeping the cost low had been one of the entrepreneurs' goals from the beginning. "If [the price] had gone to $7.99, we wouldn't have gone forward," said one. P&G didn't even advertise SpinBrush for the first seven months, relying on a "Try Me" button that allowed consumers to turn the brush on in the store. Shoppers tried it and liked it. Sales of the SpinBrush zoomed; within no time it was the country's best-selling toothbrush, electric or manual. P&G now sells the product in about thirty-five countries and has added a multitude of innovative models and features. Procter & Gamble CEO A. G. Lafley knows that innovative and creative ideas can sometimes get lost in a huge company like P&G. So he has increased efforts to identify new product ideas outside the company, bring them in, and give teams the power and ability to work around the bureaucracy.[1]

Today, every company must change and innovate to survive. New discoveries and inventions quickly replace standard ways of doing things. Companies like Procter & Gamble are searching for any innovation edge they can find. Some companies, like 3M, the maker of Post-it Notes, Thinsulate insulation, Scotch-Brite scouring pads, and thousands or other products, are known for innovation. 3M's culture supports a risk-taking and entrepreneurial spirit that keeps it bubbling over with new ideas and new products. However, many large, established companies have a hard time being entrepreneurial and continually look for ways to encourage change and innovation to keep pace with changes in the external environment.

The pace of change is revealed in the fact that the parents of today's college-age students grew up without voice mail, compact discs, videogames, debit cards, cellular phones, and laser checkout systems in supermarkets. The idea of communicating instantly with people around the world via the Internet was unimaginable to many people as recently as a decade ago.

PURPOSE OF THIS CHAPTER

This chapter will explore how organizations change and how managers direct the innovation and change process. The next section describes the difference between incremental and radical change, the four types of change—technology, product, structure, people—occurring in organizations, and how to manage change successfully. The organization structure and management approach for facilitating each type of change is then discussed. Management techniques for influencing both the creation and implementation of change are also covered.

INNOVATE OR PERISH: THE STRATEGIC ROLE OF CHANGE

If there is one theme or lesson that emerges from previous chapters, it is that organizations must run fast to keep up with changes taking place all around them. Large organizations must find ways to act like small, flexible organizations. Manufacturing firms need to reach out for new, flexible manufacturing technology and service firms for new information technology. Today's organizations must poise themselves to innovate and change, not only to prosper but merely to survive in a world of increased competition.[2] As illustrated in Exhibit 11.1, a number of environmental forces drive this need for major organizational change. Powerful forces associated with advancing technology, international economic integration, the maturing of domestic markets, and the shift to capitalism in formerly communist regions have brought about a globalized economy that impacts every business, from the largest to the smallest, creating more threats as well as more opportunities. To recognize and manage the threats and take advantage of the opportunities, today's companies are undergoing dramatic changes in all areas of their operations.

As we have seen in previous chapters, many organizations are responding to global forces by adopting self-directed teams and horizontal structures that enhance communication and collaboration, streamlining supply and distribution channels, and overcoming barriers of time and place through e-business. Others become involved in joint ventures or consortia to exploit opportunities and extend operations or markets internationally. Some adopt structural innovations such as the modular approach to focus on their core competencies while outside specialists handle other activities. In addition, today's organizations face a need for dramatic strategic and cultural change and for rapid and continuous innovations in technology, services, products, and processes.

Change, rather than stability, is the norm today. Whereas change once occurred incrementally and infrequently, today it is dramatic and constant. A key element of the success of companies such as 3M Corporation, Starbucks Coffee, and PepsiCo has been their passion for creating change.

INCREMENTAL VERSUS RADICAL CHANGE

The changes used to adapt to the environment can be evaluated according to scope—that is, the extent to which changes are incremental or radical for the organization.[3] As summarized in Exhibit 11.2, **incremental change** represents a series of continual progressions that maintain the organization's general equilibrium and often affect only one organizational part. **Radical change**, by contrast,

EXHIBIT 11.1   *Forces Driving the Need for Major Organizational Change*

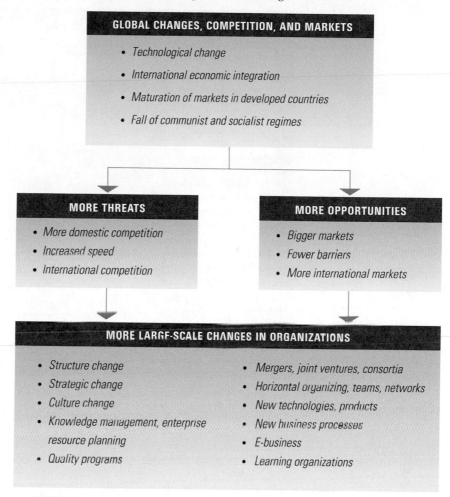

GLOBAL CHANGES, COMPETITION, AND MARKETS

- *Technological change*
- *International economic integration*
- *Maturation of markets in developed countries*
- *Fall of communist and socialist regimes*

MORE THREATS

- *More domestic competition*
- *Increased speed*
- *International competition*

MORE OPPORTUNITIES

- *Bigger markets*
- *Fewer barriers*
- *More international markets*

MORE LARGE-SCALE CHANGES IN ORGANIZATIONS

- *Structure change*
- *Strategic change*
- *Culture change*
- *Knowledge management, enterprise resource planning*
- *Quality programs*

- *Mergers, joint ventures, consortia*
- *Horizontal organizing, teams, networks*
- *New technologies, products*
- *New business processes*
- *E-business*
- *Learning organizations*

Source: Based on John P. Kotter, *The New Rules: How to Succeed in Today's Post-Corporate World* (New York: The Free Press, 1995).

breaks the frame of reference for the organization, often transforming the entire organization. For example, an incremental change is the implementation of sales teams in the marketing department, whereas a radical change is shifting the entire organization from a vertical to a horizontal structure, with all employees who work on specific core processes brought together in teams rather than being separated into functional departments such as marketing, finance, production, and so forth.

For the most part, incremental change occurs through the established structure and management processes, and it may include technology improvements—such as the introduction of flexible manufacturing systems—or product improvements—such as Procter & Gamble's addition to Tide detergent of cleaning agents that protect colors and fabrics. Radical change involves the creation of a new structure and new management processes. The technology is likely to be breakthrough, and new products thereby created will establish new markets.

As we have just discussed, there is a growing emphasis on the need for radical change because of today's turbulent, unpredictable environment.[4] One example of

EXHIBIT 11.2   *Incremental Versus Radical Change*

Source: Based on Alan D. Meyer, James B. Goes, and Geoffrey R. Brooks, "Organizations in Disequilibrium: Environmental Jolts and Industry Revolutions," in George Huber and William H. Glick, eds., *Organizational Change and Redesign* (New York: Oxford University Press, 1992), 66–111; and Harry S. Dent, Jr., "Growth through New Product Development," *Small Business Reports* (November 1990), 30–40.

radical change was the revolution at Motorola that achieved an astounding Six Sigma quality (only 3.4 mistakes per million parts produced). This level of quality, previously considered impossible, became the new norm.

Corporate transformations and turnarounds, such as Larry Bossidy's turnaround of Allied Signal or Lou Gerstner's transformation of IBM, are also considered radical change. Major turnarounds involve changes in all areas of the organization, including structure, management systems, culture, technology, and products or services.

STRATEGIC TYPES OF CHANGE

Managers can focus on four types of change within organizations to achieve strategic advantage. These four types of change are summarized in Exhibit 11.3 as products and services, strategy and structure, culture, and technology. We touched on overall leadership and organizational strategy in Chapter 2 and in the previous chapter on corporate culture. These factors provide an overall context within which the four types of change serve as a competitive wedge to achieve an advantage in the international environment. Each company has a unique configuration of products and services, strategy and structure, culture, and technologies that can be focused for maximum impact upon the company's chosen markets.[5]

EXHIBIT 11.3   *The Four Types of Change Provide a Strategic Competitive Wedge*

Source: Joseph E. McCann, "Design Principles for an Innovating Company," *Academy of Management Executive* 5 (May 1991), 76–93. Used by permission.

Technology changes are changes in an organization's production process, including its knowledge and skill base, that enable distinctive competence. These changes are designed to make production more efficient or to produce greater volume. Changes in technology involve the techniques for making products or services. They include work methods, equipment, and work flow. For example, a technology change at UPS was the implementation of the DIAD (Delivery Information Acquisition Device). When a customer signs for a package on a computerized clipboard, the device automatically zaps the information to the Web site, where the sender can verify that the package has been delivered before the driver even gets back to the truck.[6]

Product and service changes pertain to the product or service outputs of an organization. New products include small adaptations of existing products or entirely new product lines. New products and services are normally designed to increase the market share or to develop new markets, customers, or clients. As part of the transformation at IBM, top managers shifted the organization toward providing clients with information management solutions rather than just selling them computers.

Strategy and structure changes pertain to the administrative domain in an organization. The administrative domain involves the supervision and management of the organization. These changes include changes in organization structure, strategic management, policies, reward systems, labor relations, coordination devices, management information and control systems, and accounting and budgeting systems. Structure and system changes are usually top-down, that is, mandated by top management, whereas product and technology changes may often come from the bottom up. A system change instituted by management in a university might be a new merit pay plan. Corporate downsizing and the shift to horizontal teams are other examples of top-down structure change.

Culture changes refer to changes in the values, attitudes, expectations, beliefs, abilities, and behavior of employees. Culture changes pertain to changes in how employees think; these are changes in mind-set rather than technology, structure, or products.

The four types of change in Exhibit 11.3 are interdependent—a change in one often means a change in another. A new product may require changes in the production technology, or a change in structure may require new employee skills. For example, when Shenandoah Life Insurance Company acquired new computer technology to process claims, the technology was not fully utilized until clerks were restructured into teams of five to seven members that were compatible with the technology. The structural change was an outgrowth of the technology change. Organizations are interdependent systems, and changing one part often has implications for other organization elements.

ELEMENTS FOR SUCCESSFUL CHANGE

Regardless of the type or scope of change, there are identifiable stages of innovation, which generally occur as a sequence of events, though innovation stages may overlap.[7] In the research literature on innovation, **organizational change** is considered the adoption of a new idea or behavior by an organization.[8] **Organizational innovation**, in contrast, is the adoption of an idea or behavior that is new to the organization's industry, market, or general environment.[9] The first organization to introduce a new product is considered the innovator, and organizations that copy are considered to adopt changes. For purposes of managing change, however, the terms *innovation* and *change* will be used interchangeably because the **change process** within organizations tends to be identical whether a change is early or late with respect to other organizations in the environment.

Innovations typically are assimilated into an organization through a series of steps or elements. Organization members first become aware of a possible innovation, evaluate its appropriateness, and then evaluate and choose the idea.[10] The required elements of successful change are summarized in Exhibit 11.4. For a change to be successfully implemented, managers must make sure each element occurs in the organization. If one of the elements is missing, the change process will fail.

BRIEFCASE

As an organization manager, keep this guideline in mind:

Make sure every change undertaken has a definite need, idea, adoption decision, implementation strategy, and resources. Avoid failure by not proceeding until each element is accounted for.

1. *Ideas.* No company can remain competitive without new ideas; change is the outward expression of those ideas.[11] An idea is a new way of doing things. It may be a new product or service, a new management concept, or a new procedure for working together in the organization. Ideas can come from within or from outside the organization. Internal creativity is a dramatic element of organizational change. **Creativity** is the generation of novel ideas that may meet perceived needs or respond to opportunities. Jim Brown at Honeywell came up with an idea that became the Fram SureDRAIN Fast Access Oil Change System, a valve-and-hose device that enables do-it-yourselfers to drain their old oil directly into a container without the danger of spilling it all over themselves and the garage floor.[12] Some techniques for spurring internal creativity are to increase the diversity within the organization, make sure employees have plenty of opportunities to interact with people different

EXHIBIT 11.4   *Sequence of Elements for Successful Change*

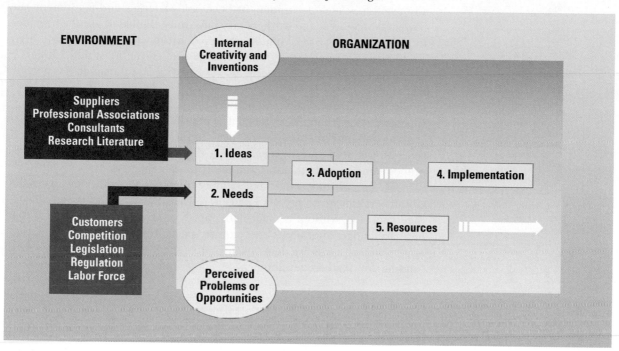

from themselves, give employees time and freedom for experimentation, and support risk taking and making mistakes.[13] Many of today's best organizations are finding ways to encourage creativity among all employees. Google, the search-engine company based in Mountain View, California, believes everyone should spend part of their time thinking up new ideas, as described in this chapter's Leading by Design box.

2. *Need.* Ideas are generally not seriously considered unless there is a perceived need for change. A perceived need for change occurs when managers see a gap between actual performance and desired performance in the organization. Managers try to establish a sense of urgency so that others will understand the need for change. Sometimes a crisis provides an undoubted sense of urgency. For example, Midwest Contract Furnishings, a small firm that designs and fabricates hotel interiors, faced a crisis when its largest customer, Renaissance Hotels, was sold to Marriott, which did interior designing in-house. Midwest lost 80 percent of its revenues virtually overnight.[14] In many cases, however, there is no crisis, so managers have to recognize a need and communicate it to others.[15] In addition, although many ideas are generated to meet perceived needs, innovative companies encourage the constant development of new ideas that may stimulate consideration of problems or new opportunities.

3. *Adoption.* Adoption occurs when decision makers choose to go ahead with a proposed idea. Key managers and employees need to be in agreement to support the change. For a major organizational change, the decision might require the signing of a legal document by the board of directors. For a small change, adoption might occur with informal approval by a middle manager.

4. *Implementation*. Implementation occurs when organization members actually use a new idea, technique, or behavior. Materials and equipment may have to be acquired, and workers may have to be trained to use the new idea. Implementation is a very important step because without it, previous steps are to no avail. Implementation of change is often the most difficult part of the change process. Until people use the new idea, no change has actually taken place.

5. *Resources*. Human energy and activity are required to bring about change. Change does not happen on its own; it requires time and resources, for both creating and implementing a new idea. Employees have to provide energy to see both the need and the idea to meet that need. Someone must develop a proposal and provide the time and effort to implement it.

3M has an unwritten but widely understood rule that its 8,300 researchers can spend up to 15 percent of their time working on any idea of their choosing, without management approval. Most innovations go beyond ordinary budget allocations and require special funding. At 3M, exceptionally promising ideas become "pacing programs" and receive high levels of funding for further development.[16] Some companies use task forces, as

LEADING BY DESIGN   *Google*

Google quickly became the most popular search engine on the Internet with its smarter, faster approach to providing users with what they are looking for. But to maintain that success, managers knew the company needed a steady stream of new ideas and a systematic way to capture and develop them.

Product manager Marissa Mayer suggested that the company come up with new ideas the same way its search engine scours the Web. To provide users with the best Web search experience possible, Google searches far and wide, combing through billions of documents. Then it ranks the search results by relevance and zaps them to the user fast. The idea search process works much the same way by casting a wide net across Google's 300-plus employees. The process begins with an easy-to-use intranet. Even employees with limited technology expertise can quickly set up a page of ideas. "We never say, 'This group should innovate and the rest should just do their jobs,'" says Jonathan Rosenberg, vice president of product management. "Everyone spends a fraction of [the] day on R&D." The intranet has also tapped into more ideas from technologically savvy Google employees who may not be very vocal or assertive in meetings. Mayer says some engineers had lots of good ideas but were shy about putting them forth in open meetings. Now, employees can post their ideas on the intranet and see what kind of response they get.

Mayer searches the site each day to see what ideas are generating the most excitement and comments. Once a week, she sits down with a team to hash over the ideas and flesh out at least six or seven that can be taken to the next level of development. Examples of ideas that have been implemented are a news search feature and a pilot project that keeps track of persistent Web searches. The emphasis at the meeting is on speed and focus. People hone in on the ideas that seem the most promising and the most doable and then take action. Usually, the person who came up with the idea is put in charge of implementing it.

Google's idea search works because it provides both a free-form environment and a structured environment for finding ideas and acting on them. The intranet taps into ideas from all across the company by giving people an easy, comfortable, and safe way to post ideas that they might not be willing to share any other way. Some less technologically oriented people, for example, might be reluctant to express their ideas to a team of engineers, but these ideas may be some of the most creative ones because they provide a new way of looking at things. Next, the structured approach of the weekly meetings provides a way for the most promising ideas to get fast-tracked into development.

Source: Fara Warner, "How Google Searches Itself," *Fast Company* (July 2002), 50–52.

described in Chapter 3, to focus resources on a change. Others set up seed funds or venture funds that employees with promising ideas can tap into. Fluke Corporation, which manufactures electronic testing devices, creates teams of workers and gives them a hundred days and $100,000 to generate proposals for new business opportunities.[17]

One point about Exhibit 11.4 is especially important. Needs and ideas are listed simultaneously at the beginning of the change sequence. Either may occur first. Many organizations adopted the computer, for example, because it seemed a promising way to improve efficiency. Today's search for a vaccine against the AIDS virus, on the other hand, was stimulated by a severe need. Whether the need or the idea occurs first, for the change to be accomplished, each of the steps in Exhibit 11.4 must be completed.

TECHNOLOGY CHANGE

In today's business world, any company that isn't continually developing, acquiring, or adapting new technology will likely be out of business in a few years. However, organizations face a contradiction when it comes to technology change, for the conditions that promote new ideas are not generally the best for implementing those ideas for routine production. An innovative organization is characterized by flexibility, empowered employees, and the absence of rigid work rules.[18] As discussed earlier in this book, an organic, free-flowing organization is typically associated with change and is considered the best organization form for adapting to a chaotic environment.

The flexibility of an organic organization is attributed to people's freedom to be creative and introduce new ideas. Organic organizations encourage a bottom-up innovation process. Ideas bubble up from middle- and lower-level employees because they have the freedom to propose ideas and to experiment. A mechanistic structure, in contrast, stifles innovation with its emphasis on rules and regulations, but it is often the best structure for efficiently producing routine products. The challenge for organizations is to create both organic and mechanistic conditions within themselves to achieve both innovation and efficiency. To attain both aspects of technological change, many organizations use the ambidextrous approach.

THE AMBIDEXTROUS APPROACH

Recent thinking has refined the idea of organic versus mechanistic structures with respect to innovation creation versus innovation utilization. For example, sometimes an organic structure generates innovative ideas but is not the best structure for using those ideas.[19] In other words, the initiation and the utilization of change are two distinct processes. Organic characteristics such as decentralization and employee freedom are excellent for initiating ideas; but these same conditions often make it hard to implement a change because employees are less likely to comply. Employees can ignore the innovation because of decentralization and a generally loose structure.

How does an organization solve this dilemma? One approach is for the organization to be *ambidextrous*—to incorporate structures and management processes that are appropriate to both the creation and the use of innovation.[20]

The organization can behave in an organic way when the situation calls for the initiation of new ideas and in a mechanistic way to implement and use the ideas.

A study of long-established Japanese companies such as Honda and Canon that have succeeded in breakthrough innovations found that these companies use an **ambidextrous approach**.[21] To develop ideas related to a new technology, the companies assign teams of young staff members who are not entrenched in the "old way of doing things" to work on the project. The teams are headed by an esteemed elder and are charged with doing whatever is needed to develop new ideas and products, even if it means breaking rules that are important in the larger organization for implementing the new ideas. Another example of the ambidextrous approach is the Freudenberg-NOK auto-parts factory in Ligonier, Indiana. Shifting teams of twelve, including plant workers, managers, and outsiders, each spend three days creating ideas to cut costs and boost productivity in various sections of the plant. At the end of the three days, team members go back to their regular jobs, and a new team comes in to look for even more improvements. Over a year's time, there are approximately forty of these GROWTTH (Get Rid of Waste Through Team Harmony) teams roaming through the sprawling factory. Management has promised that no one will be laid off as a result of suggestions from GROWTTH teams, which further encourages employees to both create and use innovations.[22]

TECHNIQUES FOR ENCOURAGING TECHNOLOGY CHANGE

Freudenberg-NOK has created both organic and mechanistic conditions in the factory. Some of the techniques used by companies to maintain an ambidextrous approach are switching structures, separate creative departments, venture teams, and corporate entrepreneurship.

Switching Structures. **Switching structures** means an organization creates an organic structure when such a structure is needed for the initiation of new ideas.[23] Some of the ways organizations have switched structures to achieve the ambidextrous approach are as follows.

- Philips Corporation, a building materials producer based in Ohio, each year creates up to 150 transient teams—made up of members from various departments—to develop ideas for improving Philips products and work methods. After five days of organic brainstorming and problem solving, the company reverts to a more mechanistic basis to implement the changes.[24]
- Gardetto's, a family-run snack-food business, sends small teams of workers to Eureka Ranch, where they may engage in a Nerf gun battle to set the tone for fun and freedom and then participate in brainstorming exercises with the idea of generating as many new ideas as possible by the end of the day. After two and a half days, the group returns to the regular organizational structure to put the best of the ideas into action.[25]
- Boeing Company's "moonshine shops" work outside the traditional factory structure and are staffed by mavericks who aren't afraid of being unconventional. Robert Harms is a Boeing moonshine shop mechanic who came up with the idea of modifying a hay loader to get bulky passenger seats from the factory floor up thirteen feet to the door of a plane without having to use an overhead crane. Before the contraption went to work, Harms arrived at work one day to find a note that read, "Idiots running amok." That sign now serves as inspiration for the moonshine shops because the shops' unconventional ideas are helping Boeing build planes more cheaply, faster, and better.[26]

- The NUMMI plant, a Toyota subsidiary located in Fremont, California, creates a separate, organically organized, cross-functional subunit, called the Pilot Team, to design production processes for new car and truck models. When the model they are preparing moves into production, workers return to their regular jobs on the shop floor.[27]

Each of these organizations found creative ways to be ambidextrous, establishing organic conditions for developing new ideas in the midst of more mechanistic conditions for implementing and using those ideas.

Creative Departments. In many large organizations the initiation of innovation is assigned to separate **creative departments**.[28] Staff departments, such as research and development, engineering, design, and systems analysis, create changes for adoption in other departments. Departments that initiate change are organically structured to facilitate the generation of new ideas and techniques. Departments that use those innovations tend to have a mechanistic structure more suitable for efficient production. Exhibit 11.5 indicates how one department is responsible for creation and another department implements the innovation.

The Nokia Ventures Organization (NVO) illustrates how creativity and entrepreneurial spirit can coexist with discipline and controls. NVO's purpose is to initiate, test, and develop new ideas that go beyond Nokia's existing technologies and may be implemented anywhere in the organization. Once a project is developed and appears viable, it is integrated into one of Nokia's established businesses or set up as a new division. "What we do is up [to] somebody else to take further," says Markus Lindqvist, NVO's director of business development.[29]

A related type of creative department is the **idea incubator**, an increasingly popular way to facilitate the development of new ideas within the organization. An idea incubator provides a safe harbor where ideas from employees throughout the organization can be developed without interference from company bureaucracy or politics.[30] The incubator gives people throughout the organization a place to go rather than having to shop a new idea all over the company and hope someone will pay attention. Companies as diverse as Boeing, Adobe Systems, Ziff-Davis, and United Parcel Service are using incubators to support the development of creative ideas.

Venture Teams. **Venture teams** are a technique used to give free rein to creativity within organizations. Venture teams are often given a separate location and facilities so they are not constrained by organizational procedures. A venture team is like a small company within a large company. Monsanto, Exxon, Levi-Strauss, and

EXHIBIT 11.5   *Division of Labor Between Departments to Achieve Changes in Technology*

numerous other organizations have used the venture team concept to free creative people from the bureaucracy of a large corporation. Most established companies that have successfully established Internet-based operations have set them up as venture teams so they have the freedom and authority to explore and develop the new technology.

At 3M, venture teams are referred to as *action teams*. An employee with a promising new product idea is allowed to recruit team members from throughout the company. These people may end up running the newly created division if the idea is successful.[31] Action teams and venture teams are kept small so they have autonomy and no bureaucracy emerges.

One type of venture team is called a *skunkworks*.[32] A **skunkworks** is a separate, small, informal, highly autonomous, and often secretive group that focuses on breakthrough ideas for the business. The original skunkworks was created by Lockheed Martin more than fifty years ago and is still in operation. The essence of a skunkworks is that highly talented people are given the time and freedom to let creativity reign.

A variation of the venture team concept is the **new-venture fund**, which provides financial resources for employees to develop new ideas, products, or businesses. In order to tap into its employees' entrepreneurial urges, Lockheed Martin allows workers to take up to two years' unpaid leave to explore a new idea, using company labs and equipment and paying company rates for health insurance. If the idea is successful, the corporation's venture fund invests about $250,000 in the start-up company. One successful start-up is Genase, which created an enzyme that "stone-washes" denim.[33]

Corporate Entrepreneurship.   Corporate entrepreneurship attempts to develop an internal entrepreneurial spirit, philosophy, and structure that will produce a higher-than-average number of innovations.[34] Corporate entrepreneurship may involve the use of creative departments and new venture teams, but it also attempts to release the creative energy of all employees in the organization. The most important outcome is to facilitate **idea champions**. These go by a variety of names, including *advocate*, *intrapreneur*, or *change agent*. Idea champions provide the time and energy to make things happen. They fight to overcome natural resistance to change and to convince others of the merit of a new idea.[35] Peter Drucker suggests that idea champions need not be within the organization and that fostering potential idea champions among regular customers can be a highly successful approach.[36] An example is Anglian Water, where every innovation project has a sponsor or champion who is a customer seeking a solution to a specific problem.[37] The importance of the idea champion is illustrated by a fascinating fact discovered by Texas Instruments: When TI reviewed fifty successful and unsuccessful technical projects, it discovered that every failure was characterized by the absence of a volunteer champion. There was no one who passionately believed in the idea, who pushed the idea through every obstacle to make it work. Texas Instruments took this finding so seriously that now its number-one criterion for approving new technical projects is the presence of a zealous champion.[38]

Companies encourage idea champions by providing freedom and slack time to creative people. IBM, General Electric, and 3M allow employees to develop new technologies without company approval. Known as *bootlegging*, the unauthorized research often pays big dividends. As one IBM executive said, "We wink at it. It pays off. It's just amazing what a handful of dedicated people can do when they are really turned on."[39]

Idea champions usually come in two types. The **technical** or **product champion** is the person who generates or adopts and develops an idea for a technological innovation and is devoted to it, even to the extent of risking position or prestige. The **management champion** acts as a supporter and sponsor to shield and promote an idea within the organization.[40] The management champion sees the potential application and has the prestige and authority to get it a fair hearing and to allocate resources to it. Technical and management champions often work together because a technical idea will have a greater chance of success if a manager can be found to sponsor it. Numerous studies have identified the importance of idea champions as a factor in the success of new products.[41] The Finnish cell phone giant Nokia relies on idea champions for its record of monster new product hits.

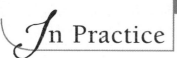

NOKIA

Erkki Kuisma was conducting radio frequency research at Nokia when he came up with what seemed like a crazy idea—why not hide a cell phone's antenna inside the phone? Kuisma tinkered around with his idea and eventually cut the antenna off an existing phone model and patched the hole by remodeling the plastic casing after melting it with a blow-dryer. Then, he devised an antenna from a square piece of copper tape and inserted it inside the phone. It worked.

But Kuisma's idea immediately hit resistance among executives at Nokia, who were afraid customers would doubt the phone's power without a visible antenna. Kuisma's boss, Yrjö Neuvo, went to work next, waging daily warfare against the hierarchy to champion the new idea. He'd corner executives in lobbies and meeting rooms, showing them the prototype and talking about its potential. He also coached Kuisma on how to support the idea to doubters, since the inventor's commitment to the project could make a substantial difference within Nokia. The internal antenna debuted in Nokia's 8800 series, which became one of the most profitable products in Nokia's history. The innovation was quickly copied by competitors.

Many other crazy ideas have bubbled up from Nokia's culture of *uninhibited dabbling*, including user-changeable cell-phone covers, the first one-chip phone, the first compact battery with power that would last 100 hours, and the first chat room for text messaging. Yrjö, head of research and development at Nokia, fosters an entrepreneurial spirit by encouraging people to try crazy things and never shrink from making mistakes. Technical champions at Nokia know that no idea is too harebrained to get a hearing from Yrjö, who will do whatever it takes as a management champion to get higher-ups to pay attention too.[42]

NEW PRODUCTS AND SERVICES

Although the ideas just discussed are important to product and service as well as technology changes, there are other factors that also need to be considered. In many ways, new products and services are a special case of innovation because they are used by customers outside the organization. Since new products are designed for sale in the environment, uncertainty about the suitability and success of an innovation is very high.

NEW PRODUCT SUCCESS RATE

Research has explored the enormous uncertainty associated with the development and sale of new products.[43] To understand what this uncertainty can mean to organizations, just consider such flops as RCA's VideoDisc player, which lost an estimated $500 million, or Time Incorporated's *TV-Cable Week*, which lost $47 million. Pfizer Inc. invested more than $70 million in the development and testing of an anti-aging drug before it flopped in the final testing stages.[44] Developing and producing products that fail is a part of business in all industries. Packaged food companies spend billions on research and development for new products such as Kraft's Rip-Ums, a fun pull-apart cheese snack, P.B. Slices, Kennedy Foods' answer to making peanut butter easy, or ConAgra's Squeez 'n Go portable pudding, but hundreds of new food products fail each year. Organizations take the risk because product innovation is one of the most important ways companies adapt to changes in markets, technologies, and competition.[45]

Experts estimate that about 80 percent of new products fail upon introduction and another 10 percent disappear within five years. Considering that it can cost $50 million or more to successfully launch a new product, new product development is a risky, high-stakes game for organizations. Nevertheless, more than 25,000 new products appeared in one recent year alone, including more than 5,000 new toys.[46]

A survey some years ago examined two hundred projects in nineteen chemical, drug, electronics, and petroleum laboratories to learn about success rates.[47] To be successful, the new product had to pass three stages of development: technical completion, commercialization, and market success. The findings about success rates are given in Exhibit 11.6. On the average, only 57 percent of all projects undertaken in the R&D laboratories achieved technical objectives, which means all technical problems were solved and the projects moved on to production. Of all projects that were started, less than one-third (31 percent) were fully marketed and commercialized. Several projects failed at this stage because production estimates or test market results were unfavorable.

Finally, only 12 percent of all projects originally undertaken achieved economic success. Most of the commercialized products did not earn sufficient returns to cover the cost of development and production. This means that only about one project in eight returned a profit to the company.

REASONS FOR NEW PRODUCT SUCCESS

The next question to be answered by research was, Why are some products more successful than others? Why did a product such as Frappuccino succeed in the marketplace while others such as Miller Clear Beer and Frito-Lay's lemonade failed? Further studies indicated that innovation success was related

EXHIBIT 11.6   *Probability of New Product Success*

	Probability
Technical completion (technical objectives achieved)	.57
Commercialization (full-scale marketing)	.31
Market success (earns economic returns)	.12

Source: Based on Edwin Mansfield, J. Rapaport, J. Schnee, S. Wagner, and M. Hamburger, *Research and Innovation in Modern Corporations* (New York: Norton, 1971), 57.

to collaboration between technical and marketing departments. Successful new products and services seemed to be technologically sound and also carefully tailored to customer needs.[48] A study called Project SAPPHO examined seventeen pairs of new product innovations, with one success and one failure in each pair, and concluded the following.

1. Successful innovating companies had a much better understanding of customer needs and paid much more attention to marketing.
2. Successful innovating companies made more effective use of outside technology and outside advice, even though they did more work in-house.
3. Top management support in the successful innovating companies was from people who were more senior and had greater authority.

Thus, there is a distinct pattern of tailoring innovations to customer needs, making effective use of technology, and having influential top managers support the project. These ideas taken together indicate that the effective design for new product innovation is associated with horizontal linkage across departments.

HORIZONTAL LINKAGE MODEL

The organization design for achieving new product innovation involves three components—departmental specialization, boundary spanning, and horizontal linkages. These components are similar to the information linkage mechanisms in Chapter 3 and the differentiation and integration ideas in Chapter 4. Exhibit 11.7 illustrates these components in the **horizontal linkage model**.

Specialization. The key departments in new product development are R&D, marketing, and production. The specialization component means that the personnel in all three of these departments are highly competent at their own tasks. The three departments are differentiated from each other and have skills, goals, and attitudes appropriate for their specialized functions.

EXHIBIT 11.7   *Horizontal Linkage Model for New Product Innovations*

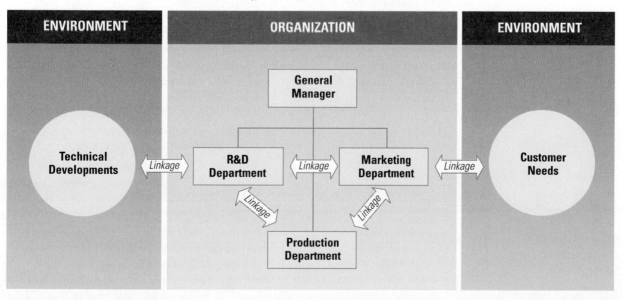

Boundary Spanning. This component means each department involved with new products has excellent linkage with relevant sectors in the external environment. R&D personnel are linked to professional associations and to colleagues in other R&D departments. They are aware of recent scientific developments. Marketing personnel are closely linked to customer needs. They listen to what customers have to say, and they analyze competitor products and suggestions by distributors. For example, Kimberly-Clark had amazing success with Huggies Pull-Ups because marketing researchers worked closely with customers in their own homes and recognized the emotional appeal of pull-on diapers for toddlers. By the time competitors caught on, Kimberly-Clark was selling $400 million worth of Huggies annually.[49]

Horizontal Linkages. This component means that technical, marketing, and production people share ideas and information. Research people inform marketing of new technical developments to learn whether the developments are applicable to customers. Marketing people provide customer complaints and information to R&D to use in the design of new products. People from both R&D and marketing coordinate with production because new products have to fit within production capabilities so costs are not exorbitant. The decision to launch a new product is ultimately a joint decision among all three departments.

Toyota is using a new product development technique called *oobeya* (ooh-bay-yah), which in Japanese means "big open office." The idea behind *oobeya* is to change the way people think about product innovation and development by changing how they share information. Toyota brings together people from all parts of the company—design, engineering, manufacturing, logistics, marketing, and so forth—once a month for two years before a new product goes into production so they can share information and discuss how to make the product better, cut costs, reduce mistakes, and smooth production. "There are no taboos in *oobeya*," explains Takeshi Yoshida, chief engineer for the 2003 Corolla. "Everyone in that room is an expert. They all have a part to play in building the car."[50] IBM's market researchers worked side by side with designers, engineers, and manufacturing personnel, as well as representatives from procurement, logistics, and other departments, to produce IBM's hot-selling Think Pad laptop computer.[51]

Most companies strive to foster a high level of communication and coordination from the beginning of the product design and development process. The Brady Corporation, which makes high-end industrial tools, shifted its product development approach to meet new competition from low-cost providers. Brady now has people from sales, marketing, engineering, and manufacturing work together to design a new product. Often, the entire team sits in on customer focus group sessions to help them create new tools with the most needed features and functions.[52] Mattel is using a new approach to improve horizontal collaboration and come up with hot new toys that connect with children as well as their parents.

MATTEL

Participants in Mattel's Project Platypus sometimes spend their days dropping eggs from a fourteen-foot ladder or throwing stuffed bunnies at one another. It is all part of the process of getting people to think outside the box and come up with creative ideas for new toys.

With Project Platypus, people from a variety of functional areas leave their regular jobs for three months and move out of Mattel headquarters to a separate location where they work collaboratively on new product ideas. According to Ivy Ross, head of Mattel's girls design division, exercises such as devising a method to prevent an egg from breaking when dropped fourteen feet or throwing stuffed animals at a colleague to release inhibitions are ways to get people to think differently, open their minds, and pick up on consumer trends and marketplace changes. Mattel goofed big-time when it missed the girl-empowerment trend of the late 1990s, and Ross wants to make sure it doesn't happen again.

Project Platypus is also designed to encourage group bonding, so that people will continue to share ideas and collaborate once the creative ideas move further into product development and production. Previously, product development at Mattel involved a lot of "baton passing," as Ross puts it. Mattel now wants everyone to collaborate in a design and development process where there's a sense of shared ownership and accomplishment. Participants in the project work in a huge open space with no walls or cubicles. Desks are on wheels to encourage spontaneous sharing and collaboration. Team members can post their sketched ideas on the walls and invite others to add suggestions. The first Project Platypus effort is a new toy called Ello, a hybrid between a construction set and an activity kit. Ello sets consist of interconnected pieces that enable children to build anything from jewelry to buildings. Platypus groups are continuing their work to develop two to three new product ideas a year.[53]

Companies such as Mattel, IBM, Brady, and Toyota use the concept of horizontal linkage to achieve competitive advantage. Famous innovation failures such as McDonald's Arch Deluxe, Procter & Gamble's Fit produce wash, or the baby-food company Gerber's Singles for Adults—usually violate the horizontal linkage model. Employees fail to connect with customer needs and market forces or internal departments fail to adequately share needs and coordinate with one another. Recent research has confirmed a connection between effective boundary spanning that keeps the organization in touch with market forces, smooth coordination among departments, and successful product development.[54]

Cross-functional teams such as those at Mattel and Brady increase both the amount and the variety of information for new product development, enabling the design of products that meet customer needs and circumventing manufacturing and marketing problems.[55] Many organizations are also bringing customers and suppliers into the product development process. During the development of the Boeing 777, flight attendants, pilots, and engineers from major airlines, as well as representatives from key suppliers, worked closely with Boeing employees to make sure the new plane was designed for maximum functionality and compatibility with suppliers.[56]

ACHIEVING COMPETITIVE ADVANTAGE: THE NEED FOR SPEED

The rapid development of new products is becoming a major strategic weapon in the shifting international marketplace.[57] To remain competitive, companies are learning to develop ideas into new products and services incredibly fast. Whether the approach is called the horizontal linkage model, concurrent engineering, companies without walls, the parallel approach, or simultaneous coupling of departments, the point is the same—get people working together simultaneously on a project rather than in sequence. Many companies are learning to sprint to market with new products.

Time-based competition means delivering products and services faster than competitors, giving companies a competitive edge. As one expert says, the old adage to provide the best value for the least cost has been updated to "provide the most value for the least cost in the least elapsed time."[58] Moen has made speed a top priority. By using the Internet to collaborate on new designs among various functional departments and with suppliers, Moen's teams take a new kitchen or bath faucet from drawing board to store shelf in only sixteen months. The time savings means Moen's teams can work on three times as many projects as previously and introduce up to 15 new designs a year for today's fashion-conscious consumers. The speedy development of new products has helped Moen move from third place in market share to a tie for first with rival Delta Faucet Company.[59] Similarly, General Motors has cut its time from concept to production on a new vehicle model down to a mere eighteen months. Not so long ago, it took GM an astounding four years to complete that process. The company made the transformation by using advanced virtual reality design systems, collaborative software, and a horizontal, integrated design process that provides a seamless information link from design and engineering to the production plant. Suppliers are also brought into the product development loop, collaborating with GM engineers in real time over a private computer network. The new approach to product development has given GM a speed advantage over competitors in the design and production of hot new car models that capitalize on fashion trends and capture the market for younger car buyers.[60]

Another critical issue is designing products that can compete on a global scale and successfully marketing those products internationally. Companies such as Quaker Oats, Häagen Dazs, and Levi's are trying to improve horizontal communication and collaboration across geographical regions, recognizing that they can pick up winning product ideas from customers in other countries. A new Häagen Dazs flavor, *dulce de leche*, developed primarily for sale in Argentina, has quickly become a favorite in the United States.[61]

Many new product development teams today are global teams because organizations have to develop products that will meet diverse needs of consumers all over the world.[62] GM's collaborative, computer-based product development system enables engineers and suppliers from all over the world to work together on a project. Ford Motor Company also uses an intranet and global teleconferencing to link car design teams around the world into a single unified group. To make global product development faster and more effective at Black & Decker, new products are developed by cross-functional project delivery teams, which are answerable to a global business unit team.[63] When companies enter the arena of intense international competition, horizontal coordination across countries is essential to new product development.

STRATEGY AND STRUCTURE CHANGE

The preceding discussion focused on new production processes and products, which are based in the technology of an organization. The expertise for such innovation lies within the technical core and professional staff groups, such as research and engineering. This section turns to an examination of structural and strategy changes.

All organizations need to make changes in their strategies, structures, and administrative procedures from time to time. In the past, when the environment was relatively stable, most organizations focused on small, incremental changes to solve immediate problems or take advantage of new opportunities. However, over the past decade, companies throughout the world have faced the need to make radical changes in strategy, structure, and management processes to adapt to new competitive demands.[64] Many organizations are cutting out layers of management and decentralizing decision making. There is a strong shift toward more horizontal structures, with teams of frontline workers empowered to make decisions and solve problems on their own. Some companies are breaking totally away from traditional organization forms and shifting toward modular strategies and structures. Numerous companies are reorganizing and shifting their strategies as the expansion of e-business changes the rules. For example, online banking, credit cards, and ATMs are affecting the role of branch banks. Global competition and rapid technological change will likely lead to even greater strategy-structure realignments over the next decade.

These types of changes are the responsibility of the organization's top managers, and the overall process of change is typically different from the process for innovation in technology or new products.

THE DUAL-CORE APPROACH

The **dual-core approach** to organizational change compares administrative and technical changes. Administrative changes pertain to the design and structure of the organization itself, including restructuring, downsizing, teams, control systems, information systems, and departmental grouping. Research into administrative change suggests two things. First, administrative changes occur less frequently than do technical changes. Second, administrative changes occur in response to different environmental sectors and follow a different internal process than do technology-based changes.[65] The dual-core approach to organizational change identifies the unique processes associated with administrative change.[66]

Organizations—schools, hospitals, city governments, welfare agencies, government bureaucracies, and many business firms—can be conceptualized as having two cores: a *technical core* and an *administrative core*. Each core has its own employees, tasks, and environmental domain. Innovation can originate in either core.

The administrative core is above the technical core in the hierarchy. The responsibility of the administrative core includes the structure, control, and coordination of the organization itself and concerns the environmental sectors of government, financial resources, economic conditions, human resources, and competitors. The technical core is concerned with the transformation of raw materials into organizational products and services and involves the environmental sectors of customers and technology.[67]

The point of the dual-core approach is that many organizations—especially not-for-profit and government organizations—must adopt frequent administrative changes and need to be structured differently from organizations that rely on frequent technical and product changes for competitive advantage.

ORGANIZATION DESIGN FOR IMPLEMENTING ADMINISTRATIVE CHANGE

The findings from research comparing administrative and technical change suggest that a mechanistic organization structure is appropriate for frequent administrative changes, including changes in goals, strategy, structure, control systems, and personnel.[68] For example, administrative changes in policy, regulations, or control systems are more critical than technical changes in many government organizations that are bureaucratically structured. Organizations that successfully adopt many administrative changes often have a larger administrative ratio, are larger in size, and are centralized and formalized compared with organizations that adopt many technical changes.[69] The reason is the top-down implementation of changes in response to changes in the government, financial, or legal sectors of the environment. If an organization has an organic structure, lower-level employees have more freedom and autonomy and, hence, may resist top-down initiatives. An organic structure is more often used when changes in organizational technology or products are important to the organization.

The innovation approaches associated with administrative versus technical change are summarized in Exhibit 11.8. Technical change, such as changes in production techniques and innovation technology for new products, is facilitated by an organic structure, which allows ideas to bubble upward from lower- and middle-level employees. Organizations that must adopt frequent administrative changes, in contrast, tend to use a top-down process and a mechanistic structure. For example, policy changes, such as the adoption of no-smoking policies, sexual harassment policies, or new safety procedures, are facilitated by a top-down approach. Downsizing and restructuring are nearly always managed top down, such as when the president of Oracle Corp. split the sales force into two teams (one focused on selling database software and the other on selling applications), cut out two levels of management, and placed himself directly in charge of U.S. sales.[70]

For organizations that must adopt frequent administrative changes, a mechanistic structure may be appropriate. Research into civil service reform found that the implementation of administrative innovation was extremely difficult in organizations that had an organic technical core. The professional employees in a decentralized agency could resist civil service changes. By contrast, organizations that were considered more bureaucratic in the sense of high formalization and centralization adopted administrative changes readily.[71]

What about business organizations that are normally technologically innovative in bottom-up fashion but suddenly face a crisis and need to reorganize? Or a technically innovative, high-tech firm that must reorganize frequently to

EXHIBIT 11.8   *Dual-Core Approach to Organization Change*

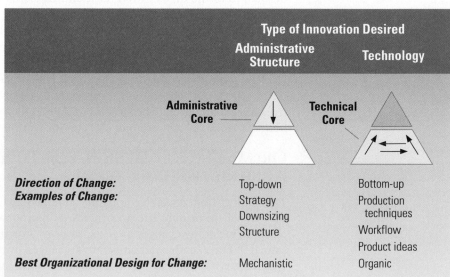

accommodate changes in production technology or the environment? Technically innovative firms may suddenly have to restructure, reduce the number of employees, alter pay systems, disband teams, or form a new division.[72] The answer is to use a top-down change process. The authority for strategy and structure change lies with top management, who should initiate and implement the new strategy and structure to meet environmental circumstances. Employee input may be sought, but top managers have the responsibility to direct the change.

At GTE Corporation (now Verizon), top managers implemented a new human resources strategy using a top-down approach, although the organization typically encourages freedom and flexibility for technical innovation. Managers knew they needed new techniques for managing and measuring employees' contributions to achieving business goals to keep pace in the volatile telecommunications industry. They first devised a new human resource (HR) strategy based on five concepts—talent, leadership, customer support and service, organization integration for knowledge management, and developing HR competencies. Next, managers created and implemented an HR measurement model, based on the balanced scorecard model of control described in Chapter 8, in order to measure and track employee performance against business objectives.[73]

Some top-down changes, particularly those related to restructuring and downsizing, can be painful for employees, so top managers should move quickly and authoritatively to make them as humane as possible.[74] A study of successful corporate transformations, which frequently involve painful changes, found that managers followed a fast, focused approach. When top managers spread difficult changes such as downsizing over a long time period, employee morale suffers and the change is much less likely to lead to positive outcomes.[75]

Top managers should also remember that top-down change means initiation of the idea occurs at upper levels and is implemented downward. It does not mean that lower-level employees are not educated about the change or allowed to participate in it. Dan Caulfield, founder of Hire Quality Inc., learned the hard way that there are right ways and wrong ways to manage top-down administrative change.

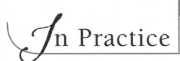

HIRE QUALITY INC.

Employees laughed when Dan Caulfield stormed through the headquarters of Hire Quality carrying a large waste barrel, snatching Post-it notes off of computer monitors, crumpling spreadsheets, and tossing in reports. But the laughter stopped when he soaked the trash heap with lighter fluid and set it ablaze. Some employees saw months of work go up in flames. One worker even quit the company because of the incident.

Caulfield now realizes that his method of implementing a change to a totally paperless office may have been counterproductive. However, at the time he felt he needed something dramatic to get people to stop using paper and start taking advantage of the $400,000 information technology system he had installed. A job-placement business like Hire Quality is driven by speed and high volume, and Caulfield felt that the tons of paper were getting in the way of performance. The company screens about 35,000 candidates and sends out 3,000 or more résumés a month. There was no way Caulfield could afford the number of staff it would take to handle everything on a paper-only basis. Hire Quality's paperless system includes a massive database that can store information on 200,000 job candidates and be searched by more than 150 possible fields, making it a snap to match candidates with potential jobs. Caulfield also instituted a policy of allowing job candidates to register only electronically, and clients such as FedEx and Bell Atlantic send job postings electronically. Almost every desk has a scanner so that any paper that comes into the office can be automatically converted to an electronic file.

Caulfield's mistake was that he failed to educate employees and allow them to be involved in the change to a paperless system. Rather than communicating with workers about the importance of switching to electronic files, he assessed fines of a few cents up to a dollar for using the fax machine, making copies, or printing résumés. Employees rebelled against the harsh tactics. Today, Caulfield is trying to tone down his brutal implementation and work gradually to implement change.[76]

Caulfield recognized that it is the responsibility of top managers to implement administrative changes downward. However, his overly aggressive approach backfired and Caulfield saw the need to educate and communicate with employees.

CULTURE CHANGE

Organizations are made up of people and their relationships with one another. Changes in strategy, structure, technologies, and products do not happen on their own, and changes in any of these areas involve changes in people as well. Employees must learn how to use new technologies, or market new products, or work effectively in a team-based structure.

Sometimes achieving a new way of thinking requires a focused change in the underlying corporate culture values and norms. Changing corporate culture fundamentally shifts how work is done in an organization and generally leads to renewed commitment and empowerment of employees and a stronger bond between the company and its customers.[77]

FORCES FOR CULTURE CHANGE

A number of recent trends have contributed to a need for cultural makeovers at companies such as Electronic Data Systems (EDS), Alberto-Culver, Marriott, and IBM. Some of the primary changes requiring a shift in culture and employee mindset are reengineering and the move toward horizontal forms of organizing, greater employee and customer diversity, and the shift to the learning organization.

Reengineering and Horizontal Organizing. As described in Chapter 3, reengineering involves redesigning a vertical organization along its horizontal workflows. This changes the way managers and employees have to think about how work is done and requires greater focus on employee empowerment, collaboration, information sharing, and meeting customer needs. In his book *The Reengineering Revolution*, Michael Hammer refers to people change as "the most perplexing, annoying, distressing, and confusing part" of reengineering.[78] Managers may confront powerful emotions as employees react to rapid, massive change with fear or anger.

In the horizontal organization, managers and frontline workers need to understand and embrace the concepts of teamwork, empowerment, and cooperation. Managers shift their thinking to view workers as colleagues rather than cogs in a wheel; and workers learn to accept not only greater freedom and power, but also the higher level of responsibility that comes with them. Mutual trust, risk taking, and tolerance for mistakes become key cultural values in the horizontal organization.

Diversity. Diversity is a fact of life for today's organizations, and many are implementing new recruiting, mentoring, and promotion methods, diversity training programs, tough policies regarding sexual harassment and racial discrimination, and new benefits programs that respond to a more diverse workforce. However, if the underlying culture of an organization does not change, all other efforts to support diversity will fail. Managers at Mitsubishi are still struggling with this reality. Even though the company settled a sexual harassment lawsuit filed by women at its Normal, Illinois, plant, established a zero tolerance policy, and fired workers who were guilty of blatant sexual or racial harassment, employees said the work environment at the plant remained deeply hostile to women and minorities. Incidents of blatant harassment declined, but women and minority workers still felt threatened and powerless because the culture that allowed the harassment to occur had not changed.[79]

The Learning Organization. The learning organization involves breaking down boundaries both within and between organizations to create companies that are focused on knowledge sharing and continuous learning. Recall from Chapter 1 that shifting to a learning organization involves changes in a number of areas. For example, structures become horizontal and involve empowered teams working directly with customers. There are few rules and procedures for performing tasks, and knowledge and control of tasks are located with employees rather than supervisors. Information is broadly shared rather than being concentrated with top managers. In addition, employees, customers, suppliers, and partners all play a role in determining the organization's strategic direction. Clearly, all of these changes require new values, new attitudes, and new ways of thinking and working together. A learning organization cannot exist without a culture that supports openness, equality, adaptability, and employee participation.

One organization that has undergone culture change to support greater information sharing, collaboration, and adaptability is Electronic Data Systems (EDS).

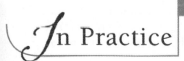

ELECTRONIC DATA SYSTEMS

Electronic Data Systems (EDS) pioneered the information technology services industry, but by the time Dick Brown took over as chairman and CEO, the company was floundering. Brown quickly learned why. On his first day of work, when Brown asked a phone technician why his phone wasn't working, the technician explained that the previous CEO had the lines cut to avoid disruptive incoming calls. Brown knew he had to "reconnect" the company—and fast.

The new CEO made it clear that the old culture of isolationism, information hoarding, rampant individualism, slow response time, and separation between managers and employees on the front lines was no longer acceptable. He implemented a number of company initiatives designed to foster a company-wide culture based on quick feedback, open communication, and rapid response.

One technique is the *monthly performance call,* during which 125 of EDS's top worldwide executives join in a conference call to review the past month's operational details. Executives know if they don't meet their targets, they'll have to explain to everyone why. The calls also emphasize the importance of sharing information and helping one another perform better.

Brown also began personally visiting customers to show a commitment to customer service and responsiveness. The company's structure was changed to focus everyone on the client and provide stronger horizontal integration. Information and reward systems were altered to support teamwork and collaboration all across the organization.

"At the old EDS, the culture was 'Fix the problem yourself,'" says one manager. Now, rather than fighting among themselves to win new business or outdo one another, employees at EDS are focused on collaborating to better serve clients and beat the competition. A more open, adaptable culture has helped EDS reap increases in sales, profits, and market share. The company's famous "Cat Herders" Super Bowl commercial was a symbol of the cultural changes at EDS. In the commercial, rugged cowboys are herding 10,000 house cats under big open skies, accompanied by a stirring musical score. The commercial allowed EDS to poke a little bit of fun at itself. At the same time, it symbolized the company's commitment to riding herd over clients' technological problems. Thus, the commercial was an outward representation of the substantial changes in employee attitudes and how people work with each other and with clients.[80]

OD CULTURE CHANGE INTERVENTIONS

Managers use a variety of approaches and techniques for changing corporate culture, some of which we discussed in Chapter 10. One method of quickly bringing about culture change is known as **organization development**, which focuses on the human and social aspects of the organization as a way to improve the organization's ability to adapt and solve problems. Organization development (OD) emphasizes the values of human development, fairness, openness, freedom from coercion, and individual autonomy that allows workers to perform the job as they see fit, within reasonable organizational constraints.[81] In the 1970s, OD evolved as a separate field that applied the behavioral sciences in a process of planned organization-wide change, with the goal of increasing organizational effectiveness. Today, the concept has been enlarged to examine how people and groups can change to a learning organization culture in a complex and turbulent environment. Organization development is not a step-by-step procedure to solve a specific problem but a process of fundamental change in the human and social systems of the organization, including organizational culture.[82]

OD uses knowledge and techniques from the behavioral sciences to create a learning environment through increased trust, open confrontation of problems, employee empowerment and participation, knowledge and information sharing, the design of meaningful work, cooperation and collaboration between groups, and the full use of human potential.

OD interventions involve training of specific groups or of everyone in the organization. For OD intervention to be successful, senior management in the organization must see the need for OD and provide enthusiastic support for the change. Techniques used by many organizations for improving people skills through OD include the following.

Large Group Intervention. Most early OD activities involved small groups and focused on incremental change. However, in recent years, there has been growing interest in the application of OD techniques to large group settings, which are more attuned to bringing about radical or transformational change in organizations operating in complex environments.[83] The **large group intervention** approach[84] brings together participants from all parts of the organization—often including key stakeholders from outside the organization as well—in an off-site setting to discuss problems or opportunities and plan for change. A large-group intervention might involve fifty to five hundred people and last for several days. The off-site setting limits interference and distractions, enabling participants to focus on new ways of doing things. General Electric's "Work Out" program, an ongoing process of solving problems, learning, and improving, begins with large-scale off-site meetings that get people talking across functional, hierarchical, and organizational boundaries. Hourly and salaried workers come together from many different parts of the organization and join with customers and suppliers to discuss and solve specific problems.[85] The process forces a rapid analysis of ideas, the creation of solutions, and the development of a plan for implementation. Over time, Work Out creates a culture where ideas are rapidly translated into action and positive business results.[86]

Team Building.   **Team building** promotes the idea that people who work together can work as a team. A work team can be brought together to discuss conflicts, goals, the decision-making process, communication, creativity, and leadership. The team can then plan to overcome problems and improve results. Team-building activities are also used in many companies to train task forces, committees, and new product development groups. These activities enhance communication and collaboration and strengthen the cohesiveness of organizational groups and teams.

Interdepartmental Activities.   Representatives from different departments are brought together in a mutual location to expose conflict, diagnose its causes, and plan improvements in communication and coordination. This type of intervention has been applied to union–management conflict, headquarters–field office conflict, interdepartmental conflict, and mergers.[87]

One current area in which OD can provide significant value is in spurring culture change toward valuing diversity.[88] In addition, today's organizations are continuously adapting to environmental uncertainty and increasing global competition, and OD interventions can respond to these new realities as companies strive to create greater capability for learning and growth.[89]

STRATEGIES FOR IMPLEMENTING CHANGE

Managers and employees can think of inventive ways to improve the organization's technology, creative ideas for new products and services, fresh approaches to strategies and structures, or ideas for fostering adaptive cultural values, but until the ideas are put into action, they are worthless to the organization. Implementation is the most crucial part of the change process, but it is also the most difficult. Change is frequently disruptive and uncomfortable for managers as well as employees. The Book Mark explores how managers can improve change implementation by understanding the emotional aspects of the change process. Change is complex, dynamic, and messy, and implementation requires strong and persistent leadership. In this final section, we will briefly discuss the role of leadership for change, some reasons for resistance to change, and techniques that managers can use to overcome resistance and successfully implement change.

LEADERSHIP FOR CHANGE

The need for change within organizations and the need for leaders who can successfully manage change continues to grow. As we discussed in Chapter 1, coping with rapid change is one of the greatest challenges facing today's

BOOK MARK *11.0* *Have You Read This Book?*

The Change Monster: The Human Forces That Fuel or Foil Corporate Transformation and Change
By Jeanie Daniel Duck

The change monster is lurking in every organization, just waiting to gobble up unsuspecting managers who are striving to implement new strategies, accomplish reorganizations, or complete mergers. Jeanie Daniel Duck uses the term *change monster* in her book by the same name to refer to all the complex human emotions and social dynamics that emerge during major change efforts. Many managers, she says, simplify or ignore the people issues of change, a sure prescription for failure.

MASTERING THE CHANGE CURVE
Duck says that major organizational change typically follows a change curve—a roller-coaster ride that brings out myriad unexpected and conflicting emotions.

- *Stagnation.* This is the period during which the organization has lost direction or is moving in the wrong direction. The change monster is generally quiet—people feel comfortable and safe. However, it is the job of managers to recognize stagnation and create a sense of urgency for change.
- *Preparation.* "In Preparation," Duck writes, "the change monster is rudely awakened from its hibernating slumber and stretches itself, causing all kinds of emotional tremors. . . ." This is the period during which change leaders define and refine their vision for change and begin to involve others in the change process. Emotions range from excitement and hopefulness to anxiety and betrayal. Everyone is jittery and distracted.
- *Implementation.* This phase is the actual tactical start of the change journey, and as such is the longest and typically the most painful. There is an explosion of emotions, both positive and negative, in the organization. During this phase,

employees often feel in limbo. Everything has changed, and yet the changes haven't been solidified. Many people feel uncertain about their ability to function in the new environment.

- *Determination.* During this period, Duck says, the change monster is roaming the hallways, ready to do its worst damage. Many managers think the change has been accomplished and turn their attention elsewhere right at the time when reinforcement is most needed. People often exhibit *retroactive resistance*, a sort of change fatigue and a desire to revert to the old way of doing things.
- *Fruition.* Ahhhh . . . the time when all the hard work pays off at last. In this phase, the changes have become a part of the accepted way of doing things. The whole organization may feel new and different. Employees have gained confidence and are optimistic and energized. The change monster has been corralled.

COMING FULL CIRCLE
It is the goal of every change initiative to reach fruition. But Duck cautions that a new period of stagnation is just around the corner. When an organization accomplishes a major change, people need to take time to bask in the success. But managers must be on guard that basking doesn't turn to napping. Managers can teach their organizations how to perpetually adapt and help them muster the will to do so. "When an organization sees itself as a hearty band of monster slayers, change becomes a challenge they're ready to meet rather than a threat that signals retreat."

The Change Monster: The Human Forces That Fuel or Foil Corporate Transformation and Change, by Jeanie Daniel Duck, is published by Crown Business.

organizations. They need leaders who can clearly recognize the need for change and make it happen, who can develop and communicate a vision for what the organization can be and provide the motivation and guidance to take it there. Leaders who can effect the kind of continuous adaptation needed in today's world recognize that change is painful for employees, and they learn to put themselves in their employees' shoes and develop partnerships that make successful change possible.[90]

Successful change can happen only when employees are willing to devote the time and energy needed to reach new goals as well as endure possible stress and hardship. Having a clearly communicated vision that embodies flexibility and openness to new ideas, methods, and styles sets the stage for a change-oriented organization and helps employees cope with the chaos and tension associated with change.[91] Leaders also build organization-wide commitment by taking employees through three stages of the change commitment process, illustrated in Exhibit 11.9.[92] In the first stage, *preparation*, employees hear about the change through memos, meetings, speeches, or personal contact and become aware that the change will directly affect their work. In the second stage, *acceptance*, leaders should help employees develop an understanding of the full impact of the change and the positive outcomes of making the change. When employees perceive the change as positive, the decision to implement is made. In the third stage, the true *commitment* process begins. The commitment stage involves the steps of installation and institutionalization. Installation is a trial process for the change, which gives leaders an opportunity to discuss problems and employee concerns and build commitment to action. In the final step, institutionalization, employees view the change not as something new but as a normal and integral part of organizational operations.

The pressures on organizations to change will likely increase over the next few decades. Leaders must develop the personal qualities, skills, and methods needed to help their companies remain competitive. Indeed, some management experts argue that to survive the upheaval of the early twenty-first century, managers must turn their organizations into *change leaders* by using the present to actually create the future—breaking industry rules, creating new market space, and routinely abandoning outmoded products, services, and processes to free up resources to build the future.[93]

EXHIBIT 11.9   *Stages of Commitment to Change*

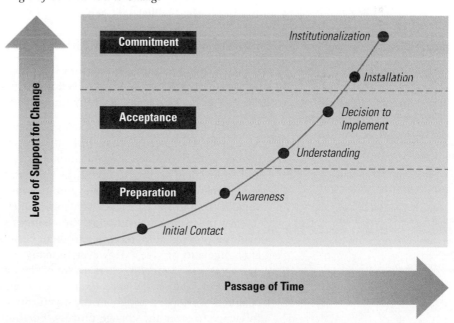

Source: Adapted from Daryl R. Conner, *Managing at the Speed of Change* (New York: Villard Books, 1992), 148. Used with permission.

BARRIERS TO CHANGE

Visionary leadership is crucial for change; however, leaders should expect to encounter resistance as they attempt to take the organization through the three stages of the change commitment process. It is natural for people to resist change, and many barriers to change exist at the individual and organizational levels.[94]

1. *Excessive focus on costs.* Management may possess the mind-set that costs are all-important and may fail to appreciate the importance of a change that is not focused on costs—for example, a change to increase employee motivation or customer satisfaction.
2. *Failure to perceive benefits.* Any significant change will produce both positive and negative reactions. Education may be needed to help managers and employees perceive more positive than negative aspects of the change. In addition, if the organization's reward system discourages risk taking, a change process might falter because employees think that the risk of making the change is too high.
3. *Lack of coordination and cooperation.* Organizational fragmentation and conflict often result from the lack of coordination for change implementation. Moreover, in the case of new technology, the old and new systems must be compatible.
4. *Uncertainty avoidance.* At the individual level, many employees fear the uncertainty associated with change. Constant communication is needed so that employees know what is going on and understand how it impacts their jobs.
5. *Fear of loss.* Managers and employees may fear the loss of power and status—or even their jobs. In these cases, implementation should be careful and incremental, and all employees should be involved as closely as possible in the change process.

Implementation can typically be designed to overcome many of the organizational and individual barriers to change.

TECHNIQUES FOR IMPLEMENTATION

Top leaders articulate the vision and set the tone, but managers and employees throughout the organization are involved in the process of change. A number of techniques can be used to successfully implement change.[95]

BRIEFCASE

As an organization manager, keep this guideline in mind:

Lead employees through the three stages of commitment to change—preparation, acceptance, and commitment—and use techniques to achieve successful implementation. These include obtaining top management support, implementing the change in a series of steps, assigning change teams or idea champions, and overcoming resistance by actively communicating with workers and encouraging their participation in the change process.

1. *Establish a sense of urgency for change.* Once managers identify a true need for change, they need to thaw resistance by creating a sense of urgency that change is really needed. Organizational crises can help unfreeze employees and make them willing to invest the time and energy needed to adopt new techniques or procedures. For example, American Airlines has lost billions since 2001, and top managers have undertaken a massive change effort to try to save the company. Although the changes will be painful, the crisis has made employees more receptive to them because otherwise the organization is not likely to survive.[96] However, in many cases there is no public crisis and managers have to make others aware of the need for change.
2. *Establish a coalition to guide the change.* Change managers have to build a coalition of people throughout the organization who have enough power and influence to steer the change process. For implementation to be successful, there must be a shared commitment to the need and possibilities for change. Top management support is crucial for any major change project, and lack of

top management support is one of the most frequent causes of implementation failure.[97] In addition, the coalition should involve lower-level supervisors and middle managers from across the organization. For smaller changes, the support of influential managers in the affected departments is important.

3. *Create a vision and strategy for change.* Leaders who have taken their companies through major successful transformations often have one thing in common: they focus on formulating and articulating a compelling vision and strategy that will guide the change process. Even for a small change, a vision of how the future can be better and strategies to get there are important motivations for change.

4. *Find an idea that fits the need.* Finding the right idea often involves search procedures—talking with other managers, assigning a task force to investigate the problem, sending out a request to suppliers, or asking creative people within the organization to develop a solution. The creation of a new idea requires organic conditions. This is a good opportunity to encourage employee participation, because employees need the freedom to think about and explore new options.[98] ALLTEL set up a program called Team Focus to gather input from all employees. In twenty group meetings over a period of two weeks, managers gathered 2,800 suggestions, which they then narrowed down to 170 critical action items that specifically addressed problems that were affecting employee morale and performance.[99]

5. *Develop plans to overcome resistance to change.* Many good ideas are never used because managers failed to anticipate or prepare for resistance to change by consumers, employees, or other managers. No matter how impressive the performance characteristics of an innovation, its implementation will conflict with some interests and jeopardize some alliances in the organization. To increase the chance of successful implementation, management must acknowledge the conflict, threats, and potential losses perceived by employees. Several strategies can be used by managers to overcome the resistance problem:

   • *Alignment with needs and goals of users.* The best strategy for overcoming resistance is to make sure change meets a real need. Employees in R&D often come up with great ideas that solve nonexistent problems. This happens because initiators fail to consult with the intended users. Resistance can be frustrating for managers, but moderate resistance to change is good for an organization. Resistance provides a barrier to frivolous changes or to change for the sake of change. The process of overcoming resistance to change normally requires that the change be good for its users.

   • *Communication and training.* Communication means informing users about the need for change and the consequences of a proposed change, preventing rumors, misunderstanding, and resentment. In one study of change efforts, the most commonly cited reason for failure was that employees learned of the change from outsiders. Top managers concentrated on communicating with the public and shareholders but failed to communicate with the people who would be most intimately involved and most affected by the change—their own employees.[100] Open communication often gives management an opportunity to explain what steps will be taken to ensure that the change will have no adverse consequences for employees. Training is also needed to help employees understand and cope with their role in the change process.

   • *An environment that affords psychological safety.* Psychological safety means that people feel a sense of confidence that they will not be embarrassed or rejected by others in the organization. People need to feel secure and capable of making the changes that are asked of them.[101] Change requires that people be willing to take risks and do things differently, but many people are fearful of trying something new if they think they might be embarrassed by mistakes or failure. Managers support psychological safety by creating a climate of trust and mutual respect in the organization. "Not being afraid someone is laughing at you helps you take genuine risks," says Andy Law, one of the founders of St. Luke's, an advertising agency based in London.[102]

- *Participation and involvement.* Early and extensive participation in a change should be part of implementation. Participation gives those involved a sense of control over the change activity. They understand it better, and they become committed to successful implementation. One study of the implementation and adoption of technology systems at two companies showed a much smoother implementation process at the company that introduced the new technology using a participatory approach.[103] The team-building and large-group intervention activities described earlier can be effective ways to involve employees in a change process.

- *Forcing and coercion.* As a last resort, managers may overcome resistance by threatening employees with loss of jobs or promotions or by firing or transferring them. In other words, management power is used to overwhelm resistance. In most cases, this approach is not advisable because it leaves people angry at change managers, and the change may be sabotaged. However, this technique may be needed when speed is essential, such as when the organization faces a crisis. It may also be required for needed administrative changes that flow from the top down, such as downsizing the workforce.[104]

6. *Create change teams.* Throughout, this chapter has discussed the need for resources and energy to make change happen. Separate creative departments, new venture groups, or an ad hoc team or task force are ways to focus energy on both creation and implementation. A separate department has the freedom to create a new technology that fits a genuine need. A task force can be created to see that implementation is completed. The task force can be responsible for communication, involvement of users, training, and other activities needed for change.

7. *Foster idea champions.* One of the most effective weapons in the battle for change is the idea champion. The most effective champion is a volunteer champion who is deeply committed to a new idea. The idea champion sees that all technical activities are correct and complete. An additional champion, such as a manager sponsor, may also be needed to persuade people about implementation, even using coercion if necessary.

SUMMARY AND INTERPRETATION

Organizations face a dilemma. Managers prefer to organize day-to-day activities in a predictable, routine manner. However, change—not stability—is the natural order of things in today's global environment. Thus, organizations need to build in change as well as stability, to facilitate innovation as well as efficiency.

Most change in organizations is incremental, but there is a growing emphasis on the need for radical change. Four types of change—technology, products and services, strategy and structure, and culture—may give an organization a competitive edge, and managers can make certain each of the necessary ingredients for change is present.

For technical innovation, which is of concern to most organizations, an organic structure that encourages employee autonomy works best because it encourages a bottom-up flow of ideas. Other approaches are to establish a separate department charged with creating new technical ideas, establish venture teams or idea incubators, and encourage idea champions. New products and services generally require cooperation among several departments, so horizontal linkage is an essential part of the innovation process.

For changes in strategy and structure, a top-down approach is typically best. These innovations are in the domain of top administrators who take responsibility for restructuring, for downsizing, and for changes in policies, goals, and control systems.

Culture changes are also generally the responsibility of top management. Some recent trends that may create a need for broad-scale culture change in the organization are reengineering, the shift to horizontal forms of organizing, greater organizational diversity, and the learning organization. All of these changes require significant shifts in employee and manager attitudes and ways of working together. One method for bringing about this level of culture change is organization development (OD). OD focuses on the human and social aspects of the organization and uses behavioral science knowledge to bring about changes in attitudes and relationships.

Finally, the implementation of change can be difficult. Strong leadership is needed to guide employees through the turbulence and uncertainty and build organizationwide commitment to change. A number of barriers to change exist, including excessive focus on cost, failure to perceive benefits, lack of organizational coordination, and individual uncertainty avoidance and fear of loss. Managers can thoughtfully plan how to deal with resistance to increase the likelihood of success. Techniques that will facilitate implementation are to establish a sense or urgency that change is needed, create a powerful coalition to guide the change, formulate a vision and strategy to achieve the change, and overcome resistance by aligning with the needs and goals of users, including users in the change process, providing psychological safety and, in rare cases, forcing the innovation if necessary. Change teams and idea champions are also effective.

Key Concepts

ambidextrous approach
change process
creative departments
creativity
culture changes
dual-core approach
horizontal linkage model
idea champions
idea incubator
incremental change
large group intervention
management champion
new-venture fund

organization development
organizational change
organizational innovation
product and service changes
radical change
skunkworks
strategy and structure changes
switching structures
team building
technical or product champion
technology changes
time-based competition
venture teams

Discussion Questions

1. How is the management of radical change likely to differ from the management of incremental change?

2. How are organic characteristics related to changes in technology? To administrative changes?

3. Describe the dual-core approach. How does administrative change normally differ from technology change? Discuss.

4. How might organizations manage the dilemma of needing both stability and change? Discuss.

5. Why do organizations experience resistance to change? What steps can managers take to overcome this resistance?

6. "Bureaucracies are not innovative." Discuss.

7. A noted organization theorist said, "Pressure for change originates in the environment; pressure for stability originates within the organization." Do you agree? Discuss.

8. Of the five elements required for successful change, which element do you think managers are most likely to overlook? Discuss.

9. How do the underlying values of organization development compare to the values underlying other types of change? Why do the values underlying OD make it particularly useful in shifting to a learning organization?

10. The manager of R&D for a drug company said only 5 percent of the company's new products ever achieve market success. He also said the industry average is 10 percent and wondered how his organization might increase its success rate. If you were acting as a consultant, what advice would you give him concerning organization structure?

11. Review the stages of commitment to change illustrated in Exhibit 11.9 and the seven techniques for implementing change discussed at the end of the chapter. At which stage of change commitment would each of the seven techniques most likely be used?

Chapter 11 Workbook   *Innovation Climate**

In order to examine differences in the level of innovation encouragement in organizations, you will be asked to rate two organizations. The first should be an organization in which you have worked, or the university. The second should be someone else's workplace, that of a family member, a friend, or an acquaintance. You will have to interview that person to answer the questions on the next page. You should put your own answers in column A, your interviewee's answers in column B, and what you think would be the ideal in column C.

*Adapted by Dorothy Marcic from Susanne G. Scott and Reginald A. Bruce, "Determinants of Innovative Behavior: A Path Model of Individual Innovation in the Workplace," *Academy of Management Journal* 37, no. 3 (1994), 580–607.

Innovation Measures

Item of Measure	A Your Organization	B Other Organization	C Your Ideal
Score items 1–5 on this scale: 1 = *don't agree at all* to 5 = *agree completely*			
1. Creativity is encouraged here.*			
2. People are allowed to solve the same problems in different ways.*			
3. I get to pursue creative ideas.#			
4. The organization publicly recognizes and also rewards those who are innovative.#			
5. Our organization is flexible and always open to change.*			
Score items 6–10 on the *opposite* scale: 1 = *agree completely* to 5 = *don't agree at all*			
6. The primary job of people here is to follow orders that come from the top.*			
7. The best way to get along here is to think and act like the others.*			
8. This place seems to be more concerned with the status quo than with change.*			
9. People are rewarded more if they don't rock the boat.#			
10. New ideas are great, but we don't have enough people or money to carry them out.#			

Note: *Starred items indicate the organization's innovation climate.
         # Pound-sign items show resource support.

Questions

1. What comparisons in terms of innovative climates can you make between these two organizations?
2. How might productivity differ between a climate that supports innovation and a climate that does not?
3. Where would you rather work? Why?

Shoe Corporation of Illinois produces a line of women's shoes that sell in the lower-price market for $27.99 to $29.99 per pair. Profits averaged twenty-five cents to thirty cents per pair ten years ago, but according to the president and the controller, labor and materials costs have risen so much in the intervening period that profits today average only thirty cents to fifty cents per pair.

Production at both the company's plants totals 12,500 pairs per day. The two factories are located within a radius of sixty miles of Chicago: one at Centerville, which produces 4,500 pairs per day, and the other at Meadowvale, which produces 8,000 pairs per day. Company headquarters is located in a building adjacent to the Centerville plant.

It is difficult to give an accurate picture of the number of items in the company's product line. Shoes change in style perhaps more rapidly than any other style product, including garments. This is so chiefly because it is possible to change production processes quickly and because, historically, each company, in attempting to get ahead of competitors, gradually made style changes ever more frequently. At present, including both major and minor style changes, SCI offers 100 to 120 different products to customers each year.

A partial organizational chart, showing the departments involved in this case, appears in Exhibit 11.10.

Competitive Structure of the Industry

Very large general shoe houses, such as International and Brown, carry a line of women's shoes and are able to undercut prices charged by Shoe Corporation of Illinois, principally because of the policy in the big companies of producing large numbers of "stable" shoes, such as the plain pump and the loafer. They do not attempt to change styles as rapidly as their smaller competitors. Thus, without constant changes in production processes and sales presentations, they are able to keep costs substantially lower.

Charles F. Allison, the president of Shoe Corporation of Illinois, feels that the only way for a small independent company to be competitive is to change styles frequently, taking advantage of the flexibility of a small organization to create designs that appeal to customers. Thus, demand can be created, and a price set high enough, to make a profit. Allison, incidentally,

appears to have an artistic talent in styling and a record of successful judgments in approving high-volume styles over the years.

Regarding how SCI differs from its large competitors, Allison has said:

You see, Brown and International Shoe Company both produce hundreds of thousands of the same pair of shoes. They store them in inventory at their factories. Their customers, the large wholesalers and retailers, simply know their line and send in orders. They do not have to change styles nearly as often as we do. Sometimes I wish we could do that, too. It makes for a much more stable and orderly system. There is also less friction between people inside the company. The salespeople always know what they're selling; the production people know what is expected of them. The plant personnel are not shook up so often by someone coming in one morning and tampering with their machine lines or their schedules. The styling people are not shook up so often by the plant saying, "We can't do your new style the way you want it."

To help SCI be even more competitive against larger firms, Allison recently created an e-commerce department. Although his main interest was in marketing over the Internet, he also hoped new technology would help reduce some of the internal friction by giving people an easier way to communicate. He invested in a sophisticated new computer system and hired consultants to set up a company intranet and provide a few days' training to upper and middle managers. Katherine Olsen came on board as director of e-commerce, charged primarily with coordinating Internet marketing and sales. When she took the job, she had visions of one day offering consumers the option of customized shoe designs. However, Olsen was somewhat surprised to learn that most employees still refused to use the intranet even for internal communication and coordination. The process for deciding on new styles, for example, had not changed since the 1970s.

*Written by Charles E. Summer. Copyright 1978. Revised with permission.

EXHIBIT 11.10   *Partial Organization Chart of Shoe Corporation of Illinois*

Major Style Changes

The decision about whether to put a certain style into production requires information from a number of different people. Here is what typically happens in the company. It may be helpful to follow the organization chart in tracing the procedure.

M. T. Lawson, the styling manager, and his designer, John Flynn, originate most of the ideas about shape, size of heel, use of flat sole or heels, and findings (the term used for ornaments attached to, but not part of, the shoes—bows, straps, and so forth). They get their ideas principally from reading style and trade magazines or by copying top-flight designers. Lawson corresponds with publications and friends in large stores in New York, Rome, and Paris in order to obtain pictures and samples of up-to-the-minute style innovations. Although he uses e-mail occasionally, Lawson prefers telephone contact and receiving drawings or samples by overnight mail. Then, he and Flynn discuss various ideas and come up with design options.

When Lawson decides on a design, he takes a sketch to Allison, who either approves or disapproves it. If Allison approves, he (Allison) then passes the sketch on to L. K. Shipton, the sales manager, to find out what lasts (widths) should be chosen. Shipton, in turn, forwards the design to Martin Freeman, a statistician in the sales department, who maintains summary information on customer demand for colors and lasts.

To compile this information, Freeman visits salespeople twice a year to get their opinions on the colors and lasts that are selling best, and he keeps records of shipments by color and by last. For these needs, he simply totals data that are sent to him by the shipping foreman in each of the two plants.

When Freeman has decided on the lasts and colors, he sends Allison a form that lists the colors and lasts in which the shoe should be produced. Allison, if he approves this list, forwards the information to Lawson, who passes it on to Jenna Richards, an expert pattern maker. Richards makes a paper pattern and then constructs a prototype in leather and paper. She sends this to Lawson, who in turn approves or disapproves it. He forwards any approved prototype to Allison. Allison, if he, too, approves, notifies Lawson, who takes the prototype to Paul Robbins, assistant to the superintendent of the Centerville plant. Only this plant produces small quantities of new or experimental shoe styles. This is referred to as a "pilot run" by executives at the plant.

Robbins then literally carries the prototype through the six production departments of the plant—from cutting to finishing—discussing it with each foreman, who in turn works with employees on the machines in having a sample lot of several thousand pairs made.

When the finished lot is delivered by the finishing foreman to the shipping foreman (because of the importance of styling, Allison has directed that each foreman personally deliver styling goods in process to the foreman of the next department), the latter holds the inventory in storage and sends one pair each to Allison and Lawson. If they approve of the finished product, Allison instructs the shipping foreman to mail samples to each of the company's twenty-two salespeople throughout the country. Olsen also receives samples, photos, and drawings to post on the Web page and gauge customer interest. Salespeople have instructions to take the samples immediately (within one week) to at least ten customers. Orders for already-established shoes are normally sent to Ralph Ferguson, a clerk in Shipton's office, who records them and forwards them to the plant superintendents for production. However, salespeople have found by experience that Martin Freeman has a greater interest in the success of new "trials," so they rush these orders to him by overnight mail, and he in turn places the first orders for a new style in the interoffice mail to the plant superintendents. He then sends off a duplicate of the order, mailed in by the salespeople, to Ferguson for entering in his statistical record of all orders received by the company.

Three weeks after the salespeople receive samples, Allison requires Ralph Ferguson to give him a tabulation of orders. At that time, he decides whether the salespeople and the Web page should push the item and the superintendents should produce large quantities, or whether he will tell them that although existing orders will be produced, the item will be discontinued in a short time.

The procedures outlined here have, according to Allison:

> . . . worked reasonably well. The average time from when Lawson decides on a design until we notify the Centerville plant to produce the pilot run is two weeks to a month. Of course, if we could speed that up, it would make the company just that much more secure in staying in the game against the big companies, and in taking

sales away from our competitors. There seems to be endless bickering among people around here involved in the styling phase of the business. That's to be expected when you have to move fast—there isn't much time to stop and observe all of the social amenities. I have never thought that a formal organization chart would be good in this company—we've worked out a customary system here that functions well.

M.T. Lawson, manager of styling, said that within his department all work seems to get out in minimum time; he also stated that both Flynn and Richards are good employees and skilled in their work. He mentioned that Flynn had been in to see him twice in the last year:

. . . to inquire about his (Flynn's) future in the company. He is thirty-three years old and has three children. I know that he is eager to make money, and I assured him that over the years we can raise him right along from the $50,000 we are now paying. Actually, he has learned a lot about shoe styles since we hired him from the design department of a fabric company six years ago.

John Flynn revealed:

I was actually becoming dissatisfied with this job. All shoe companies copy styles—it's generally accepted practice within the industry. But I've picked up a real feel for designs, and several times I've suggested that the company make all its own original styles. We could make SCI a style leader and also increase our volume. When I ask Lawson about this, he says it takes too much time for the designer to create originals—that we have all we can handle to do research in trade magazines and maintain contracts feeding us the results of experts. Beside, he says our styles are standing the test of the marketplace.

Projects X and Y

Flynn also said that he and Martin Freeman had frequently talked about the styling problem. They felt that:

Allison is really a great president, and the company surely would be lost without him. However, we've seen times when he lost a lot of money on bad judgments in styles. Not many times—perhaps six or seven times in the last 18 months.

Also, he is, of course, extremely busy as president of the corporation. He must look after everything from financing from the banks to bargaining with the union. The result is that he is sometimes unavailable to do his styling approvals for several days, or even two weeks. In a business like this, that kind of delay can cost money. It also makes him slightly edgy. It tends, at times when he has many other things to do, to make him look quickly at the styles we submit, or the prototypes Richards makes, or even the finished shoes that are sent for approval by the shipping foreman. Sometimes I worry that he makes two kinds of errors. He simply rubber-stamps what we've done, which makes sending these things to him simply a waste of time. At other times he makes snap judgments of his own, overruling those of us who have spent so much time and expertise on the shoe. We do think he has good judgment, but he himself has said at times that he wishes he had more time to concentrate on styling and approval of prototypes and final products.

Flynn further explained (and this was corroborated by Freeman) that the two had worked out two plans, which they referred to as "project X" and "project Y." In the first, Flynn created an original design that was not copied from existing styles. Freeman then gave special attention to color and last research for the shoe and recommended a color line that didn't exactly fit past records on consumer purchases—but one he and Flynn thought would have "great consumer appeal." This design and color recommendation were accepted by Lawson and Allison; the shoe went into production and was one of the three top sellers during the calendar year. The latter two men did not know that the shoe was styled in a different way from the usual procedure.

The result of a second, similar project (Y) was put into production the next year, but this time sales were discontinued after three weeks.

Problem Between Lawson and Robbins

Frequently, perhaps ten to twelve times a year, disagreement arises between Mel Lawson, manager of styling, and Paul Robbins, assistant to the superintendent of the Centerville plant. Robbins said:

The styling people don't understand what it means to produce a shoe in the quantities that we do, and to make the changes in production that we have to. They dream up a style quickly, out of thin air. They do not realize that we have a lot of machines that have to be adjusted and that some things they dream up take much longer on certain machines than others, thus creating a bottleneck in the production line. If they put a bow or strap in one position rather than another, it may mean we have to keep people idle on later machines while there is a pileup on the sewing machines on which this complicated little operation is performed. This costs the plant money. Furthermore, there are times when they get the prototype here late, and either the foremen and I work overtime or the trial run won't get through in time to have new production runs on new styles, to take the plant capacity liberated by our stopping production on old styles. Lawson doesn't know much about production and sales and the whole company. I think all he does is to bring shoes down here to the plant, sort of like a messenger boy. Why should he be so hard to get along with? He isn't getting paid any more than I am, and my position in the plant is just as important as his.

Lawson, in turn, said that he has a difficult time getting along with Robbins:

> There are many times when Robbins is just unreasonable. I take prototypes to him five or six times a month, and other minor style changes to him six or eight times. I tell him every time that we have problems in getting these ready, but he knows only about the plant, and telling him doesn't seem to do any good. When we first joined the company, we got along all right, but he has gotten harder and harder to get along with.

Other Problems

Ralph Ferguson, the clerk in the sales department who receives orders from salespeople and forwards totals for production schedules to the two plant superintendents, has complained that the salespeople and Freeman are bypassing him in their practice of sending experimental shoe orders to Freeman. He insisted that his job description (one of only two written descriptions in the company) gives him responsibility for receiving all orders throughout the company and for maintaining historical statistics on shipments.

Both the salespeople and Freeman, on the other hand, said that before they started the new practice

(that is, when Ferguson still received the experimental shoe orders), there were at least eight or ten instances a year when these were delayed from one to three days on Ferguson's desk. They reported that Ferguson just wasn't interested in new styles, so the salespeople "just started sending them to Freeman." Ferguson acknowledged that there were times of short delay, but there were good reasons for them:

> They (the salespeople and Freeman) are so interested in new designs, colors, and lasts that they can't understand the importance of a systematic handling of the whole order procedure, including both old and new shoe styles. There must be accuracy. Sure, I give some priority to experimental orders, but sometimes when rush orders for existing company products are piling up, and when there's a lot of planning I have to do to allocate production between Centerville and Meadowvale, I decide which comes first—processing of these, or processing the experimental shoe orders. Shipton is my boss, not the salespeople or Freeman. I'm going to insist that these orders come to me.

The Push for New Technology

Katherine Olsen believes many of these problems could be solved through better use of technology. She has approached Charles Allison several times about the need to make greater use of the expensive and sophisticated computer information systems he had installed. Although Allison always agrees with her, he has so far done nothing to help solve the problem. Olsen thinks the new technology could dramatically improve coordination at SCI:

> Everyone needs to be working from the same data at the same time. As soon as Lawson and Flynn come up with a new design, it should be posted on the intranet so all of us can be informed. And everyone needs access to sales and order information, production schedules, and shipping deadlines. If everyone—from Allison down to the people in the production plants—was kept up to date throughout the entire process, we wouldn't have all this confusion and bickering. But no one around here wants to give up any control—they all have their own little operations and don't want to share information with anyone else. For example, I sometimes don't even know there's a new style in

the works until I get finished samples and photos. No one seems to recognize that one of the biggest advantages of the Internet is to help stay ahead of changing styles. I know that Flynn has a good feel for design, and we're not taking advantage of his abilities. But I also have information and ideas that could help this company keep pace with changes and really stand out from the crowd. I don't know how long we expect to remain competitive using this cumbersome, slow-moving process and putting out shoes that are already behind the times.

CASE FOR ANALYSIS   *Southern Discomfort**

Jim Malesckowski remembers the call of two weeks ago as if he just put down the telephone receiver: "I just read your analysis and I want you to get down to Mexico right away," Jack Ripon, his boss and chief executive officer, had blurted in his ear. "You know we can't make the plant in Oconomo work anymore—the costs are just too high. So go down there, check out what our operational costs would be if we move, and report back to me in a week."

As president of the Wisconsin Specialty Products Division of Lamprey, Inc., Jim knew quite well the challenge of dealing with high-cost labor in a third-generation, unionized U.S. manufacturing plant. And although he had done the analysis that led to his boss's knee-jerk response, the call still stunned him. There were 520 people who made a living at Lamprey's Oconomo facility, and if it closed, most of them wouldn't have a chance of finding another job in the town of 9,900 people.

Instead of the $16-per-hour average wage paid at the Oconomo plant, the wages paid to the Mexican workers—who lived in a town without sanitation and with an unbelievably toxic effluent from industrial pollution—would amount to about $1.60 an hour on average. That would be a savings of nearly $15 million a year for Lamprey, to be offset in part by increased costs for training, transportation, and other matters.

After two days of talking with Mexican government representatives and managers of other companies in the town, Jim had enough information to develop a set of comparative figures of production and shipping costs. On the way home, he started to outline the report, knowing full well that unless some miracle occurred, he would be ushering in a blizzard of pink slips for people he had come to appreciate.

The plant in Oconomo had been in operation since 1921, making special apparel for persons suffering from injuries and other medical conditions.

Jim had often talked with employees who would recount stories about their fathers or grandfathers working in the same Lamprey company plant—the last of the original manufacturing operations in town.

But friendship aside, competitors had already edged past Lamprey in terms of price and were dangerously close to overtaking it in product quality. Although both Jim and the plant manager had tried to convince the union to accept lower wages, union leaders resisted. In fact, on one occasion when Jim and the plant manager tried to discuss a cell manufacturing approach, which would cross-train employees to perform up to three different jobs, local union leaders could barely restrain their anger. Jim thought he sensed an underlying fear, meaning the union reps were aware of at least some of the problems, but he had been unable to get them to acknowledge this and move on to open discussion.

A week has passed and Jim just submitted his report to his boss. Although he didn't specifically bring up the point, it was apparent that Lamprey could put its investment dollars in a bank and receive a better return than what its Oconomo operation is currently producing.

Tomorrow, he'll discuss the report with the CEO. Jim doesn't want to be responsible for the plant's dismantling, an act he personally believes would be wrong as long as there's a chance its costs can be lowered. "But Ripon's right," he says to himself. "The costs are too high, the union's unwilling to cooperate, and the company needs to make a better return on its investment if it's to continue at all. It sounds right but feels wrong. What should I do?"

*Doug Wallace, "What Would You Do?" *Business Ethics* (March/April 1996), 52–53. Reprinted with permission from *Business Ethics*, P. O. Box 8439, Minneapolis, MN 55408, 612-879-0695.

Notes

1. Robert Berner, "Why P&G's Smile Is So Bright," *BusinessWeek* (August 12, 2002), 58–60.

2. Based on John P. Kotter, *Leading Change* (Boston, Mass.: Harvard Business School Press, 1996), 18–20.

3. David A. Nadler and Michael L. Tushman, "Organizational Frame Bending: Principles for Managing Reorientation," *Academy of Management Executive* 3 (1989), 194–204; Michael L. Tushman and Charles A. O'Reilly III, "Ambidextrous Organizations: Managing Evolutionary and Revolutionary Change," *California Management Review* 38, no. 4 (Summer 1996), 8–30.

4. William A. Davidow and Michael S. Malone, *The Virtual Corporation* (New York: HarperBusiness, 1992); Gregory G. Dess, Abdul M. A. Rasheed, Kevin J. McLaughlin, and Richard L. Priem, "The New Corporate Architecture," *Academy of Management Executive* 9, no. 3 (1995), 7–20.

5. Joseph E. McCann, "Design Principles for an Innovating Company," *Academy of Management Executive* 5 (May 1991), 76–93.

6. Kelly Barron, "Logistics in Brown," *Forbes* (January 10, 2000), 78–83; Scott Kirsner, "Venture Vérité: United Parcel Service," *Wired* (September 1999), 83–96.

7. Richard A. Wolfe, "Organizational Innovation: Review, Critique and Suggested Research Directions," *Journal of Management Studies* 31, no. 3 (May 1994), 405–431.

8. John L. Pierce and Andre L. Delbecq, "Organization Structure, Individual Attitudes and Innovation," *Academy of Management Review* 2 (1977), 27–37; Michael Aiken and Jerald Hage, "The Organic Organization and Innovation," *Sociology* 5 (1971), 63–82.

9. Richard L. Daft, "Bureaucratic versus Non-bureaucratic Structure in the Process of Innovation and Change," in Samuel B. Bacharach, ed., *Perspectives in Organizational Sociology: Theory and Research* (Greenwich, Conn.: JAI Press, 1982), 129–166.

10. Alan D. Meyer and James B. Goes, "Organizational Assimilation of Innovations: A Multilevel Contextual Analysis," *Academy of Management Journal* 31 (1988), 897–923.

11. Richard W. Woodman, John E. Sawyer, and Ricky W. Griffin, "Toward a Theory of Organizational Creativity," *Academy of Management Review* 18 (1993), 293–321; Alan Farnham, "How to Nurture Creative Sparks," *Fortune* (January 10, 1994), 94–100.

12. Robert Barker, "The Art of Brainstorming," *BusinessWeek* (August 26, 2002), 168–169.

13. Robert I. Sutton, "Weird Ideas That Spark Innovation," *MIT Sloan Management Review* (Winter 2002), 83–87; Barker, "The Art of Brainstorming"; Gary A. Steiner, ed., *The Creative Organization* (Chicago, Ill.: University of Chicago Press, 1965), 16–18; James Brian Quinn, "Managing Innovation: Controlled Chaos," *Harvard Business Review* (May–June 1985), 73–84.

14. Michael Barrier, "Managing Workers in Times of Change," *Nation's Business* (May 1998), 31–34.

15. Kotter, *Leading Change*, 20–25; John P. Kotter, "Leading Change," *Harvard Business Review* (March–April 1995), 59–67.

16. L. D. DiSimone, comments about 3M in "How Can Big Companies Keep the Entrepreneurial Spirit Alive?" *Harvard Business Review* (November–December 1995), 184–185; Thomas A. Stewart, "3M Fights Back," *Fortune* (February 1996), 94–99.

17. Eric Matson, "Here, Innovation Is No Fluke," *Fast Company* (August–September 1977), 42–44.

18. D. Bruce Merrifield, "Intrapreneurial Corporate Renewal," *Journal of Business Venturing* 8 (September 1993), 383–389; Linsu Kim, "Organizational Innovation and Structure," *Journal of Business Research* 8 (1980), 225–245; Tom Burns and G. M. Stalker, *The Management of Innovation* (London: Tavistock Publications, 1961).

19. James Q. Wilson, "Innovation in Organization: Notes toward a Theory," in James D. Thompson, ed., *Approaches to Organizational Design* (Pittsburgh, Penn.: University of Pittsburgh Press, 1966), 193–218.

20. Michael L. Tushman and Charles A. O'Reilly III, "Building an Ambidextrous Organization: Forming Your Own 'Skunk Works,'" *Health Forum Journal* 42, no. 2 (March–April 1999), 20–23; J. C. Spender and Eric H. Kessler, "Managing the Uncertainties of Innovation: Extending Thompson (1967)," *Human Relations* 48, no. 1 (1995), 35–56; Robert B. Duncan, "The Ambidextrous Organization: Designing Dual

Structures for Innovation," in Ralph H. Killman, Louis R. Pondy, and Dennis Slevin, eds., *The Management of Organization*, vol. 1 (New York: North-Holland, 1976), 167–188.

21. Tushman and O'Reilly, "Building an Ambidextrous Organization."

22. James B. Treece, "Improving the Soul of an Old Machine," *BusinessWeek* (October 25, 1993), 134–36.

23. Edward F. McDonough III and Richard Leifer, "Using Simultaneous Structures to Cope with Uncertainty," *Academy of Management Journal* 26 (1983), 727–735.

24. John McCormick and Bill Powell, "Management for the 1990s," *Newsweek* (April 25, 1988), 47–48.

25. Todd Datz, "Romper Ranch," *CIO Enterprise* Section 2 (May 15, 1999), 39–52.

26. J. Lynn Lunsford, "Lean Times: With Airbus on Its Tail, Boeing Is Rethinking How It Builds Planes," *The Wall Street Journal* (September 2001), A1, A16.

27. Paul S. Adler, Barbara Goldoftas, and David I. Levine, "Ergonomics, Employee Involvement, and the Toyota Production System: A Case Study of NUMMI's 1993 Model Introduction," *Industrial and Labor Relations Review* 50, no. 3 (April 1997), 416–437.

28. Judith R. Blau and William McKinley, "Ideas, Complexity, and Innovation," *Administrative Science Quarterly* 24 (1979), 200–219.

29. Jonathan D. Day, Paul Y. Mang, Ansgar Richter, and John Roberts, "The Innovative Organization: Why New Ventures Need More Than a Room of Their Own," *The McKinsey Quarterly* no. 2 (2001), 21–31.

30. Sherri Eng, "Hatching Schemes," *The Industry Standard* (November 27–December 4, 2000), 174–175.

31. Russell Mitchell, "Masters of Innovation: How 3M Keeps Its New Products Coming," *BusinessWeek* (April 10, 1989), 58–63.

32. Christopher Hoenig, "Skunk Works Secrets," *CIO* (July 1, 2000), 74–76.

33. Phaedra Hise, "New Recruitment Strategy: Ask Your Best Employees to Leave," *Inc.* (July 1997), 2.

34. Daniel F. Jennings and James R. Lumpkin, "Functioning Modeling Corporate Entrepreneurship: An Empirical Integrative Analysis," *Journal of Management* 15 (1989), 485–502.

35. Jane M. Howell and Christopher A. Higgins, "Champions of Technology Innovation," *Administrative Science Quarterly* 35 (1990), 317–341; Jane M. Howell and Christopher A. Higgins, "Champions of Change: Identifying, Understanding, and Supporting Champions of Technology Innovations," *Organizational Dynamics* (Summer 1990), 40–55.

36. Peter F. Drucker, "Change Leaders," *Inc.* (June 1999), 65–72; Peter F. Drucker, *Management Challenges for the 21st Century* (New York: HarperBusiness, 1999).

37. Stuart Crainer and Des Dearlove, "Water Works," *Management Review* (May 1999), 39–43.

38. Thomas J. Peters and Robert H. Waterman, Jr., *In Search of Excellence* (New York: Harper & Row, 1982).

39. Ibid., p. 205.

40. Peter J. Frost and Carolyn P. Egri, "The Political Process of Innovation," in L. L. Cummings and Barry M. Staw, eds., *Research in Organizational Behavior*, vol. 13 (New York: JAI Press, 1991), 229–295; Jay R. Galbraith, "Designing the Innovating Organization," *Organizational Dynamics* (Winter 1982), 5–25; Marsha Sinatar, "Entrepreneurs, Chaos, and Creativity—Can Creative People Really Survive Large Company Structure?" *Sloan Management Review* (Winter 1985), 57–62.

41. See Lionel Roure, "Product Champion Characteristics in France and Germany," *Human Relations* 54, no. 5 (2001), 663–682 for a recent review of the literature related to product champions.

42. Paul Kaihla, "Nokia's Hit Factory," *Business 2.0* (August 2002), 66–70.

43. Christopher Power with Kathleen Kerwyn, Ronald Grover, Keith Alexander, and Robert D. Hof, "Flops," *BusinessWeek* (August 16, 1993), 76–82; Modesto A. Maidique and Billie Jo Zirger, "A Study of Success and Failure in Product Innovation: The Case of the U.S. Electronics Industry," *IEEE Transactions in Engineering Management* 31 (November 1984), 192–203.

44. Scott Hensley, "Bleeding Cash: Pfizer 'Youth Pill' Ate Up $71 Million Before It Flopped," *The Wall Street Journal* (May 2, 2002), A1, A8.

45. Deborah Dougherty and Cynthia Hardy, "Sustained Product Innovation in Large, Mature Organizations: Overcoming Innovation-to-Organization Problems," *Academy of Management Journal* 39, no. 5 (1996), 1120–1153.

46. Cliff Edwards, "Many Products Have Gone Way of the Edsel," *Johnson City Press* (May 23, 1999), 28, 30; Paul Lukas, "The Ghastliest Product Launches," *Fortune* (March 16, 1998), 44; Robert McMath, *What Were They Thinking? Marketing Lessons I've Learned from Over 80,000 New-Product Innovations and Idiocies* (New York: Times Business, 1998).

47. Edwin Mansfield, J. Rapaport, J. Schnee, S. Wagner, and M. Hamburger, *Research and Innovation in Modern Corporations* (New York: Norton, 1971); Antonio J. Bailetti and Paul F. Litva, "Integrating Customer Requirements into Product Designs," *Journal of Product Innovation Management* 12 (1995), 3–15.

48. Shona L. Brown and Kathleen M. Eisenhardt, "Product Development: Past Research, Present Findings, and Future Directions," *Academy of Management Review* 20, no. 2 (1995), 343–378; F. Axel Johne and Patricia A. Snelson, "Success Factors in Product Innovation: A Selective Review of the Literature," *Journal of Product Innovation Management* 5 (1988), 114–128; Science Policy Research Unit, University of Sussex, *Success and Failure in Industrial Innovation* (London: Centre for the Study of Industrial Innovation, 1972).

49. Dorothy Leonard and Jeffrey F. Rayport, "Spark Innovation Through Empathic Design," *Harvard Business Review* (November–December 1997), 102–113.

50. Fara Warner, "In a Word, Toyota Drives for Innovation," *Fast Company* (August 2002), 36–38.

51. Ira Sager, "The Man Who's Rebooting IBM's PC Business," *BusinessWeek* (July 24, 1995), 68–72.

52. Jason Gertzen, "Brady Corp. Streamlines Development Process," *The Milwaukee Journal Sentinel*, *http://www.jsonline.com* (March 10, 2002), accessed on August 8, 2002.

53. Lisa Bannon, "Think Tank in Toyland," *The Wall Street Journal* (June 6, 2002), B1, B3.

54. Kenneth B. Kahn, "Market Orientation, Interdepartmental Integration, and Product Development Performance," *The Journal of Product Innovation Management* 18 (2001), 314–323.

55. Brown and Eisenhardt, "Product Development; Dan Dimancescu and Kemp Dwenger, "Smoothing the Product Development Path," *Management Review* (January 1996), 36–41.

56. Melissa A. Schilling and Charles W. L. Hill, "Managing the New Product Development Process," *Academy of Management Executive* 12, no. 3 (1998), 67–81.

57. Kathleen M. Eisenhardt and Behnam N. Tabrizi, "Accelerating Adaptive Processes: Product Innovation in the Global Computer Industry," *Administrative Science Quarterly* 40 (1995), 84–110; Dougherty and Hardy, "Sustained Product Innovation in Large, Mature Organizations"; Karne Bronikowski, "Speeding New Products to Market," *Journal of Business Strategy* (September–October 1990), 34–37.

58. George Stalk, Jr., "Time and Innovation," *Canadian Business Review* (Autumn 1993), 15–18.

59. Faith Keenan, "Opening the Spigot," *Business-Week e.biz* (June 4, 2001), EB17–EB20.

60. Steve Konicki, "Time Trials," *Information Week* (June 3, 2002), 36–44.

61. David Leonhardt, "It Was a Hit in Buenos Aires—So Why Not Boise?" *BusinessWeek* (September 7, 1998), 56, 58.

62. Edward F. McDonough III, Kenneth B. Kahn, and Gloria Barczak, "An Investigation of the Use of Global, Virtual, and Colocated New Product Development Teams," *The Journal of Product Innovation Management* 18 (2001), 110–120.

63. Dimancescu and Dwenger, "Smoothing the Product Development Path."

64. Raymond E. Miles, Henry J. Coleman, Jr., and W. E. Douglas Creed, "Keys to Success in Corporate Redesign," *California Management Review* 37, no. 3 (Spring 1995), 128–145.

65. Fariborz Damanpour and William M. Evan, "Organizational Innovation and Performance: The Problem of 'Organizational Lag,'" *Administrative Science Quarterly* 29 (1984), 392–409; David J. Teece, "The Diffusion of an Administrative Innovation," *Management Science* 26 (1980), 464–470; John R. Kimberly and Michael J. Evaniski, "Organizational Innovation: The Influence of Individual, Organizational and Contextual Factors on Hospital Adoption of Technological and Administrative Innovation," *Academy of Management Journal* 24 (1981), 689–713; Michael K. Moch and Edward V. Morse, "Size, Centralization, and Organizational Adoption of Innovations," *American Sociological Review* 42 (1977), 716–725; Mary L. Fennell, "Synergy, Influence, and Information in the

Adoption of Administrative Innovation," *Academy of Management Journal* 27 (1984), 113–129.

66. Richard L. Daft, "A Dual-Core Model of Organizational Innovation," *Academy of Management Journal* 21 (1978), 193–210.

67. Daft, "Bureaucratic versus Nonbureaucratic Structure"; Robert W. Zmud, "Diffusion of Modern Software Practices: Influence of Centralization and Formalization," *Management Science* 28 (1982), 1421–1431.

68. Daft, "A Dual-Core Model of Organizational Innovation"; Zmud, "Diffusion of Modern Software Practices."

69. Fariborz Damanpour, "The Adoption of Technological, Administrative, and Ancillary Innovations: Impact of Organizational Factors," *Journal of Management* 13 (1987), 675–688.

70. Steve Hamm, "Is Oracle Finally Seeing Clearly?" *BusinessWeek* (August 3, 1998), 86–88.

71. Gregory H. Gaertner, Karen N. Gaertner, and David M. Akinnusi, "Environment, Strategy, and the Implementation of Administrative Change: The Case of Civil Service Reform," *Academy of Management Journal* 27 (1984), 525–543.

72. Claudia Bird Schoonhoven and Mariann Jelinek, "Dynamic Tension in Innovative, High Technology Firms: Managing Rapid Technology Change Through Organization Structure," in Mary Ann Von Glinow and Susan Albers Mohrman, eds., *Managing Complexity in High Technology Organizations* (New York: Oxford University Press, 1990), 90–118.

73. Garrett Walker and J. Randolph MacDonald, "Designing and Implementing an HR Scorecard," *Human Resource Management* 40, no. 4 (Winter 2001), 365–377.

74. David Ulm and James K. Hickel, "What Happens after Restructuring?" *Journal of Business Strategy* (July–August 1990), 37–41; John L. Sprague, "Restructuring and Corporate Renewal: A Manager's Guide," *Management Review* (March 1989), 34–36.

75. Stan Pace, "Rip the Band-Aid Off Quickly," *Strategy & Leadership* 30, no. 1 (2002), 4–9.

76. Joshua Macht, "Pulp Addiction," *Inc. Technology* no. 1 (1997), 43–46.

77. Benson L. Porter and Warrington S. Parker, Jr., "Culture Change," *Human Resource Management* 31 (Spring–Summer 1992), 45–67.

78. Quoted in Anne B. Fisher, "Making Change Stick," *Fortune* (April 17, 1995), 122.

79. Reed Abelson, "Can Respect Be Mandated? Maybe Not Here," *The New York Times* (September 10, 2000).

80. Bill Breen, "How EDS Got Its Groove Back," *Fast Company* (October 2001), 106–116.

81. W. Warner Burke, "The New Agenda for Organization Development," in Wendell L. French, Cecil H. Bell, Jr., and Robert A. Zawacki, *Organization Development and Transformation: Managing Effective Change* (Burr Ridge, Ill.: Irwin McGraw-Hill, 2000), 523–535.

82. W. Warner Burke, *Organization Development: A Process of Learning and Changing*, 2nd ed. (Reading, Mass.: Addison-Wesley, 1994); Wendell L. French and Cecil H. Bell, Jr., "A History of Organization Development," in French, Bell, and Zawacki, *Organization Development and Transformation*, 20–42.

83. French and Bell, "A History of Organization Development."

84. The information on large-group intervention is based on Kathleen D. Dannemiller and Robert W. Jacobs, "Changing the Way Organizations Change: A Revolution of Common Sense," *The Journal of Applied Behavioral Science* 28, no. 4 (December 1992), 480–498; and Barbara B. Bunker and Billie T. Alban, "Conclusion: What Makes Large Group Interventions Effective?" *The Journal of Applied Behavioral Science* 28, no. 4 (December 1992), 570–591; Marvin R. Weisbord, "Inventing the Future: Search Strategies for Whole System Improvements," in French, Bell, and Zawacki, *Organization Development and Transformation*, 242–250.

85. J. Quinn, "What a Workout!" *Performance* (November 1994), 58–63; Bunker and Alban, "Conclusion: What Makes Large Group Interventions Effective?"

86. Dave Ulrich, Steve Kerr, and Ron Ashkenas, with Debbie Burke and Patrice Murphy, *The GE Work-Out: How to Implement GE's Revolutionary Method for Busting Bureaucracy and Attacking Organizational Problems—Fast!* (New York: McGraw-Hill, 2002).

87. Paul F. Buller, "For Successful Strategic Change: Blend OD Practices with Strategic Management," *Organizational Dynamics* (Winter 1988), 42–55.

88. Richard S. Allen and Kendyl A. Montgomery, "Applying an Organizational Development Approach to Creating Diversity," *Organizational Dynamics* 30, no. 2 (2001), 149–161.

89. Jyotsna Sanzgiri and Jonathan Z. Gottlieb, "Philosophic and Pragmatic Influences on the Practice of Organization Development, 1950–2000," *Organizational Dynamics* (Autumn 1992), 57–69.

90. Kotter, *Leading Change*; Paul Strebel, "Why Do Employees Resist Change?" *Harvard Business Review* (May–June 1996), 86–92; Michael Beer and Russell A. Eisenstat, "Developing an Organization Capable of Implementing Strategy and Learning," *Human Relations* 49, no. 5 (1996), 597–619.

91. Ronald Recardo, Kathleen Molloy, and James Pellegrino, "How the Learning Organization Manages Change," *National Productivity Review* (Winter 1995/96), 7–13.

92. Based on Daryl R. Conner, *Managing at the Speed of Change* (New York: Villard Books, 1992), 146–160.

93. Drucker, *Management Challenges for the 21st Century*; Tushman and O'Reilly, "Ambidextrous Organizations"; Gary Hamel and C. K. Prahalad, "Seeing the Future First," *Fortune* (September 4, 1994), 64–70; Linda Yates and Peter Skarzynski, "How Do Companies Get to the Future First?" *Management Review* (January 1999), 16–22.

94. Based on Carol A. Beatty and John R. M. Gordon, "Barriers to the Implementation of CAD/CAM Systems," *Sloan Management Review* (Summer 1988), 25–33.

95. These techniques are based partly on John P. Kotter's eight-stage model of planned organizational change, Kotter, *Leading Change*, 20–25.

96. Scott McCartney, "Clipped Wings: American Airlines To Retrench in Bid to Beat Discount Carriers," *The Wall Street Journal* (August 13, 2002), A1, A8; Christine Y. Chen, "American Airlines: Blastoff or Bust? *Fortune* (October 28, 2002), 37.

97. Everett M. Rogers and Floyd Shoemaker, *Communication of Innovations: A Cross Cultural Approach*, 2d ed. (New York: Free Press, 1971); Stratford P. Sherman, "Eight Big Masters of Innovation," *Fortune* (October 15, 1984), 66–84.

98. Richard L. Daft and Selwyn W. Becker, *Innovation in Organizations* (New York: Elsevier, 1978); John P. Kotter and Leonard A. Schlesinger, "Choosing Strategies for Change," *Harvard Business Review* 57 (1979), 106–114.

99. Jim Cross, "Back to the Future," *Management Review* (February 1999), 50–54.

100. Peter Richardson and D. Keith Denton, "Communicating Change," *Human Resource Management* 35, no. 2 (Summer 1996), 203–216.

101. Edgar H. Schein and Warren Bennis, *Personal and Organizational Change Via Group Methods* (New York: Wiley, 1965); Amy Edmondson, "Psychological Safety and Learning Behavior in Work Teams," *Administrative Science Quarterly* 44 (1999), 350–383.

102. Diane L. Coutu, "Creating the Most Frightening Company on Earth, An Interview with Andy Law of St. Luke's," *Harvard Business Review* (September–October 2000), 143–150.

103. Philip H. Mirvis, Amy L. Sales, and Edward J. Hackett, "The Implementation and Adoption of New Technology in Organizations: The Impact on Work, People, and Culture," *Human Resource Management* 30 (Spring 1991), 113–139; Arthur E. Wallach, "System Changes Begin in the Training Department," *Personnel Journal* 58 (1979), 846–848, 872; Paul R. Lawrence, "How to Deal with Resistance to Change," *Harvard Business Review* 47 (January–February 1969), 4–12, 166–176.

104. Dexter C. Dunphy and Doug A. Stace, "Transformational and Coercive Strategies for Planned Organizational Change: Beyond the O.D. Model," *Organizational Studies* 9 (1988), 317–334; Kotter and Schlesinger, "Choosing Strategies for Change."

Decision-Making Processes

Definitions

Individual Decision Making
Rational Approach • Bounded Rationality Perspective

Organizational Decision Making
Management Science Approach • Carnegie Model • Incremental Decision Process Model

The Learning Organization
Combining the Incremental Process and Carnegie Models • Garbage Can Model

Contingency Decision-Making Framework
Problem Consensus • Technical Knowledge About Solutions • Contingency Framework

Special Decision Circumstances
High-Velocity Environments • Decision Mistakes and Learning • Escalating Commitment

Summary and Interpretation

LOOK INSIDE

Avon Products

Andrea Jung stepped into the CEO job at Avon several years ago with a vision to make Avon as big in the beauty business as Walt Disney Co. is in entertainment. Her plan to rebuild the organization from the ground up hit a few snags early on, as the company's global army of independent sales consultants resisted changes that might cut into their sales and profits. However, Jung used her skill and savvy to smooth ruffled feathers and successfully implement a series of decisions that have cut costs, boosted sales, and actually expanded the corps of "Avon ladies" who push lipsticks and nail polish to their friends, relatives, or women they meet at the grocery store. Even in a time of economic uncertainty, Avon's share price is near its all-time high, double what it was when Jung took over.

Despite the success, Jung is now facing a big problem. Her decision to sell a costlier line of cosmetics in retail stores has been a flop. Jung hoped the push into retail sales would boost Avon's image, transforming Middle America's cosmetics brand into a sophisticated, modern line that would attract affluent customers. But Avon's beComing line has had trouble attracting even retail partners, much less new customers. Sears dropped the beComing line shortly before its launch, and Jung has yet to find another retailer despite negotiations with several department store chains. So far, the line has been sold only at J.C. Penney—and only in 92 of the company's more than 1,000 stores. In its first year, beComing reaped only $30 million in retail sales, a disappointing performance considering Jung had predicted $100 million. Jung's chances of hitting a goal of $500 million in sales by 2005 look pretty dim.

On a positive note, the beComing line seems to have actually boosted Avon's sales of its less expensive products through its direct sales force, an advantage to the independent sales reps. However, Jung still believes a retail presence is critical to Avon's growth and that the company will eventually find the right mix of products, pricing, marketing, and retail partners to make the decision pay off.[1]

Every organization grows, prospers, or fails as a result of decisions by its managers, and decisions can be risky and uncertain, without any guarantee of success. Sometimes, decision making is a trial-and-error process, as at Avon, where top managers will continue to search for appropriate ways to expand Avon's brand into a wider market. Decision making is done amid constantly changing factors, unclear information, and conflicting points of view. Hewlett-Packard CEO Carly Fiorina accomplished a merger with Compaq, but she still faces opposition from shareholders, customers, and employees who question whether the decision was a good one. The merger has produced some early successes, but there's no guarantee that the merged company can flourish.[2] Similarly, at Ford Motor Company, CEO Bill Ford is being pushed and pulled by people both within and outside the company who have conflicting ideas about how to revive the struggling automaker. Ford has to weigh many opinions, absorb massive amounts of information, and evaluate complex, ever-changing circumstances when making decisions on how to put Ford back on the road to prosperity and prestige.[3]

Many organizational decisions are complete failures. Consider CompUSA's decision to establish a separate and distinct online brand through a Web site called Cozone. The confusing name, the lack of brand recognition, the failure to take advantage of cooperative marketing opportunities, and the refusal to allow merchandise bought online to be returned to CompUSA retail stores all helped to doom the spinoff, which fell apart after only six months.[4]

Yet managers also make many successful decisions every day. Meg Whitman made eBay today's model of what an Internet company should be by steering clear of get-rich-quick schemes and keeping the company focused on nurturing its community of buyers and sellers. Finland's Nokia became a leader in the cellular phone industry because managers decided to sell off unrelated businesses such as tires, paper, and aluminum and concentrate the company's resources on electronics.[5]

PURPOSE OF THIS CHAPTER

At any time, an organization may be identifying problems and implementing alternatives for hundreds of decisions. Managers and organizations somehow muddle through these processes.[6] The purpose here is to analyze these processes to learn what decision making is actually like in organizational settings. Decision-making processes can be thought of as the brain and nervous system of an organization. Decision making is the end use of the information and control systems described in Chapter 8. Decisions are made about organization strategy, structure, innovation, and acquisitions. This chapter explores how organizations can and should make decisions about these issues.

The first section defines decision making. The next section examines how individual managers make decisions. Then several models of organizational decision making are explored. Each model is used in a different organizational situation. The final section in this chapter combines the models into a single framework that describes when and how they should be used and discusses special issues, such as decision mistakes.

DEFINITIONS

Organizational decision making is formally defined as the process of identifying and solving problems. The process has two major stages. In the **problem identification** stage, information about environmental and organizational conditions is monitored to determine if performance is satisfactory and to diagnose the cause of shortcomings. The **problem solution** stage is when alternative courses of action are considered and one alternative is selected and implemented.

Organizational decisions vary in complexity and can be categorized as programmed or nonprogrammed.[7] **Programmed decisions** are repetitive and well defined, and procedures exist for resolving the problem. They are well structured because criteria of performance are normally clear, good information is available about current performance, alternatives are easily specified, and there is relative certainty that the chosen alternative will be successful. Examples of programmed decisions include decision rules, such as when to replace an office copy machine, when to reimburse managers for travel expenses, or whether an applicant has sufficient qualifications for an assembly-line job. Many companies adopt rules based on experience with programmed decisions. For example, general pricing rules in the restaurant industry are that food is marked up three times direct cost, beer four times, and liquor six times. A rule for large hotels staffing banquets is to allow one server per thirty guests for a sit-down function and one server per forty guests for a buffet.[8]

Nonprogrammed decisions are novel and poorly defined, and no procedure exists for solving the problem. They are used when an organization has not seen a problem before and may not know how to respond. Clear-cut decision criteria do not exist. Alternatives are fuzzy. There is uncertainty about whether a proposed solution will solve the problem. Typically, few alternatives can be developed for a nonprogrammed decision, so a single solution is custom-tailored to the problem.

Many nonprogrammed decisions involve strategic planning, because uncertainty is great and decisions are complex. Recent examples of nonprogrammed decisions come from the airline industry, which is suffering an industry-wide recession due to continuing fears of terrorism and the war with Iraq. To better compete with low-fare rivals such as AirTran, JetBlue, and Southwest, Donald Carty, CEO of American Airlines, has undertaken a sweeping overhaul that includes grounding planes, cutting more than 7,000 jobs, eliminating some services, and fundamentally changing the way American connects passengers at "hub" airports. Meanwhile, Delta's top executives have decided to launch a new, low-cost unit (as yet unnamed) to fend off the greater competition.[9] These leaders had to make difficult decisions about how to pull these major airlines out of trouble, but there is tremendous uncertainty about whether the changes will be successful.

Particularly complex nonprogrammed decisions have been referred to as "wicked" decisions, because simply defining the problem can turn into a major task. Wicked problems are associated with manager conflicts over objectives and alternatives, rapidly changing circumstances, and unclear linkages among decision elements. Managers dealing with a wicked decision may hit on a solution that merely proves they failed to correctly define the problem to begin with.[10]

Today's managers and organizations are dealing with a higher percentage of nonprogrammed decisions because of the rapidly changing business environment. As outlined in Exhibit 12.1, today's environment has increased both the number and complexity of decisions that have to be made and has created a need for new decision-making processes. Managers in rapidly changing e-business departments, for example, often have to make quick decisions based on very limited information. Another example is globalization. The trend toward moving production to low-wage countries has managers all over corporate America struggling with ethical decisions concerning working conditions in the Third World and the loss of manufacturing jobs in small American communities. In one Tennessee community where the unemployment rate is 18 percent, six hundred workers lost their jobs because the company decided to send garment manufacturing overseas.[11]

INDIVIDUAL DECISION MAKING

Individual decision making by managers can be described in two ways. First is the **rational approach**, which suggests how managers should try to make decisions. Second is the **bounded rationality perspective**, which describes how decisions actually have to be made under severe time and resource constraints. The rational approach is an ideal managers may work toward but never reach.

EXHIBIT 12.1   *Decision Making in Today's Environment*

Today's Business Environment

- *Demands more large-scale change via new strategies, reengineering, restructuring, mergers, acquisitions, downsizing, new product or market development, and so on*

Decisions Made Inside the Organization

- *Are based on bigger, more complex, more emotionally charged issues*
- *Are made more quickly*
- *Are made in a less certain environment, with less clarity about means and outcomes*
- *Require more cooperation from more people involved in making and implementing decisions*

A New Decision-Making Process

- *Is required because no one individual has the information needed to make all major decisions*
- *Is required because no one individual has the time and credibility needed to convince lots of people to implement the decision*
- *Relies less on hard data as a basis for good decisions*
- *Is guided by a powerful coalition that can act as a team*
- *Permits decisions to evolve through trial and error and incremental steps as needed*

Reprinted by permission of Harvard Business School Press. From *Leading Change* by John P. Kotter. Boston, MA, 1996, p. 56. Copyright © 1996 by the Harvard Business School Publishing Corporation, all rights reserved.

RATIONAL APPROACH

The rational approach to individual decision making stresses the need for systematic analysis of a problem followed by choice and implementation in a logical, step-by-step sequence. The rational approach was developed to guide individual decision making because many managers were observed to be unsystematic and arbitrary in their approach to organizational decisions. Although the rational model is an ideal not fully achievable in the real world of uncertainty, complexity, and rapid change highlighted in Exhibit 12.1, the model does help managers think about decisions more clearly and rationally. Managers should use systematic procedures to make decisions whenever possible. When managers have a deep understanding of the rational decision-making process, it can help them make better decisions even when there is a lack of clear information. The authors of a recent book on decision making use the example of the U.S. Marines, who have a reputation for handling complex problems quickly and decisively. However, the Marines are trained to quickly go through a series of mental routines that help them analyze the situation and take action.[12]

According to the rational approach, decision making can be broken down into eight steps, as illustrated in Exhibit 12.2. and demonstrated by the department store Marshall Field's.[13]

EXHIBIT 12.2   *Steps in the Rational Approach to Decision Making*

1. *Monitor the decision environment.* In the first step, a manager monitors internal and external information that will indicate deviations from planned or acceptable behavior. He or she talks to colleagues and reviews financial statements, performance evaluations, industry indices, competitors' activities, and so forth. For example, during the pressure-packed five-week Christmas season, Linda Koslow, general manager of Marshall Field's Oakbrook, Illinois, store, checks out competitors around the mall, eyeing whether they are marking down merchandise. She also scans printouts of her store's previous day's sales to learn what is or is not moving.[14]

2. *Define the decision problem.* The manager responds to deviations by identifying essential details of the problem: where, when, who was involved, who was affected, and how current activities are influenced. For Koslow, this means defining whether store profits are low because overall sales are less than expected or because certain lines of merchandise are not moving as expected.

3. *Specify decision objectives.* The manager determines what performance outcomes should be achieved by a decision.

4. *Diagnose the problem.* In this step, the manager digs below the surface to analyze the cause of the problem. Additional data might be gathered to facilitate this diagnosis. Understanding the cause enables appropriate treatment. For

Koslow at Marshall Field's, the cause of slow sales might be competitors' marking down of merchandise or Marshall Field's failure to display hot-selling items in a visible location.

5. *Develop alternative solutions.* Before a manager can move ahead with a decisive action plan, he or she must have a clear understanding of the various options available to achieve desired objectives. The manager may seek ideas and suggestions from other people. Koslow's alternatives for increasing profits could include buying fresh merchandise, running a sale, or reducing the number of employees.

6. *Evaluate alternatives.* This step may involve the use of statistical techniques or personal experience to gauge the probability of success. The merits of each alternative are assessed as well as the probability that it will reach the desired objectives.

7. *Choose the best alternative.* This step is the core of the decision process. The manager uses his or her analysis of the problem, objectives, and alternatives to select a single alternative that has the best chance for success. At Marshall Field's, Koslow may choose to reduce the number of staff as a way to meet the profit goals rather than increase advertising or markdowns.

8. *Implement the chosen alternative.* Finally, the manager uses managerial, administrative, and persuasive abilities and gives directions to ensure that the decision is carried out. The monitoring activity (step 1) begins again as soon as the solution is implemented. For Linda Koslow, the decision cycle is a continuous process, with new decisions made daily based on monitoring her environment for problems and opportunities.

The first four steps in this sequence are the problem identification stage, and the next four steps are the problem solution stage of decision making, as indicated in Exhibit 12.2. A manager normally goes through all eight steps in making a decision, although each step may not be a distinct element. Managers may know from experience exactly what to do in a situation, so one or more steps will be minimized. The following In Practice illustrates how the rational approach is used to make a decision about a personnel problem.

ALBERTA CONSULTING

In Practice

1. *Monitor the decision environment.* It is Monday morning, and Joe DeFoe, Alberta's accounts receivable supervisor, is absent again.

2. *Define the decision problem.* This is the fourth consecutive Monday DeFoe has been absent. Company policy forbids unexcused absenteeism, and DeFoe has been warned about his excessive absenteeism on the last two occasions. A final warning is in order but can be delayed, if warranted.

3. *Specify decision objectives.* DeFoe should attend work regularly and establish the invoice collection levels of which he is capable. The time period for solving the problem is two weeks.

4. *Diagnose the problem.* Discreet discussions with DeFoe's coworkers and information gleaned from DeFoe indicate that DeFoe has a drinking problem. He apparently uses Mondays to dry out from weekend benders. Discussion with other company sources confirms that DeFoe is a problem drinker.

5. *Develop alternative solutions.* (1) Fire DeFoe. (2) Issue a final warning without comment. (3) Issue a warning and accuse DeFoe of being alcoholic to let him know you are aware of his problem. (4) Talk with DeFoe to see if he will discuss his drinking. If he

admits he has a drinking problem, delay the final warning and suggest that he enroll in Alberta's new employee assistance program for help with personal problems, including alcoholism. (5) Talk with DeFoe to see if he will discuss his drinking. If he does not admit he has a drinking problem, let him know that the next absence will cost him his job.

6. *Evaluate alternatives.* The cost of training a replacement is the same for each alternative. Alternative 1 ignores cost and other criteria. Alternatives 2 and 3 do not adhere to company policy, which advocates counseling where appropriate. Alternative 4 is designed for the benefit of both DeFoe and the company. It might save a good employee if DeFoe is willing to seek assistance. Alternative 5 is primarily for the benefit of the company. A final warning might provide some initiative for DeFoe to admit he has a drinking problem. If so, dismissal might be avoided, but further absences will no longer be tolerated.

7. *Choose the best alternative.* DeFoe does not admit that he has a drinking problem. Choose alternative 5.

8. *Implement the chosen alternative.* Write up the case and issue the final warning.[15]

In the preceding example, issuing the final warning to Joe DeFoe was a programmed decision. The standard of expected behavior was clearly defined, information on the frequency and cause of DeFoe's absence was readily available, and acceptable alternatives and procedures were described. The rational procedure works best in such cases, when the decision maker has sufficient time for an orderly, thoughtful process. Moreover, Alberta Consulting had mechanisms in place to implement the decision, once made.

When decisions are nonprogrammed, ill-defined, and piling on top of one another, the individual manager should still try to use the steps in the rational approach, but he or she often will have to take shortcuts by relying on intuition and experience. Deviations from the rational approach are explained by the bounded rationality perspective.

BOUNDED RATIONALITY PERSPECTIVE

The point of the rational approach is that managers should try to use systematic procedures to arrive at good decisions. When organizations are facing little competition and are dealing with well-understood issues, managers generally use rational procedures to make decisions.[16] Yet research into managerial decision making shows that managers often are unable to follow an ideal procedure. Decisions often must be made very quickly. Time pressure, a large number of internal and external factors affecting a decision, and the ill-defined nature of many problems make systematic analysis virtually impossible. Managers have only so much time and mental capacity and, hence, cannot evaluate every goal, problem, and alternative. The attempt to be rational is bounded (limited) by the enormous complexity of many problems. There is a limit to how rational managers can be. For example, an executive in a hurry may have a choice of fifty ties on a rack but will take the first or second one that matches his suit. The executive doesn't carefully weigh all fifty alternatives because the short amount of time and the large number of plausible alternatives would be overwhelming. The manager simply selects the first tie that solves the problem and moves on to the next task.

Not only are large organizational decisions too complex to fully comprehend, but many other constraints impinge on the decision maker, as illustrated in Exhibit 12.3. The circumstances are ambiguous, requiring social support, a

EXHIBIT 12.3   *Constraints and Trade-offs During Nonprogrammed Decision Making*

Source: Adapted from Irving L. Janis, *Crucial Decisions* (New York: Free Press, 1989); and A. L. George, *Presidential Decision Making in Foreign Policy: The Effective Use of Information and Advice* (Boulder, Colo.: Westview Press, 1980).

shared perspective on what happens, and acceptance and agreement. For example, in a study of the decision making surrounding the Cuban missile crisis, the executive committee in the White House knew a problem existed but was unable to specify exact goals and objectives. The act of discussing the decision led to personal objections and finally to the discovery of desired objectives that helped clarify the desired course of action and possible consequences.[17]

Corporate culture and ethical values also influence decision making, as discussed in Chapter 10. For example, this chapter's Leading by Design box describes how the founder of software company Motek created a culture where decisions are made based on a primary goal of improving the lives of employees and customers. In addition, managers throughout an organization often make decisions within a context of trying to please upper managers, people who are perceived to have power within the organization, or others they respect and want to emulate.[18] Personal constraints—such as decision style, work pressure, desire for prestige, or simple feelings of insecurity—may constrain either the search for alternatives or the acceptability of an alternative. All of these factors constrain a perfectly rational approach that should lead to an obviously ideal choice.[19] Even seemingly simple decisions, such as selecting a job on graduation from college, can quickly become so complex that a bounded rationality approach is used. Graduating students have been known to search for a job until they have two or three acceptable job offers, at which point their search activity rapidly diminishes. Hundreds of firms may be available for interviews, and two or three job offers are far short of the maximum number that would be possible if students made the decision based on perfect rationality.

The bounded rationality perspective is often associated with intuitive decision processes. In **intuitive decision making**, experience and judgment rather than sequential logic or explicit reasoning are used to make decisions.[20]

Intuition is not arbitrary or irrational because it is based on years of practice and hands-on experience, often stored in the subconscious. When managers use their intuition based on long experience with organizational issues, they more rapidly perceive and understand problems, and they develop a gut feeling or hunch about which alternative will solve a problem, speeding the decision-making process.[21] The value of intuition for effective decision making is supported by a growing body of research from psychology, organizational science, and other disciplines.[22] Indeed, many universities are offering courses in creativity and intuition so business students can learn to understand and rely on these processes.

In a situation of great complexity or ambiguity, previous experience and judgment are needed to incorporate intangible elements at both the problem identification and problem solution stages.[23] A study of manager problem finding showed that thirty of thirty-three problems were ambiguous and ill-defined.[24] Bits and scraps of unrelated information from informal sources

LEADING BY DESIGN   *Motek*

At Motek, which makes software that tracks the movement of goods in warehouses, no one is permitted to work past 5 p.m. or on weekends. Everyone gets five weeks of vacation, plus ten paid holidays, and people get to choose their own assignments and vote on the size of their pay raises and bonuses.

When Ann Price founded Motek, she wanted to create a company whose primary mission was to improve the lives of its employees and customers rather than to reward shareholders or investors. She decided early on to take a long-term approach to business. "We know we're revolutionizing the warehouse automation industry," Price says. "We know we'll get there. But instead of doing it in five years, we'll do it in ten and have a life along the way." Her emphasis on treating people well has guided every major company decision as Motek grows and changes.

Decision making at Motek is a democratic process. Every Monday morning, the company's technical staff gathers to discuss what needs to be done that week, poring over a to-do list of hundreds of tasks. Rather than having a manager determine which people should perform which jobs, individuals volunteer for various chores and decide among themselves the best way to accomplish all the work. "We decide what happens," explains employee Ran Ever-Hadani. "Things are rarely decreed from above." If someone sees that all the tasks can't be completed by Friday, he or she is expected to give a

Thursday-afternoon alert, which gives others time to pitch in and help or move the job to the following week and inform the customer. Customers rarely complain because Motek has developed such strong bonds of loyalty that they know the job will be done right and within an acceptable time frame.

Motek's democratic decision making also applies to pay rates and bonuses. Everyone except the CIO and sales manager makes one of three salaries at Motek, and the highest is only $30,000 more than the lowest. Employees recently had an opportunity to vote on increasing their compensation by distributing profits, but they decided instead to look to the long run and pay down company debt. Each founding employee has been promised 1 percent of Motek's value when it is sold to a large company, which Price believes could happen within the next few years.

Price has emphasized hiring the right people, socializing them into the corporate culture, providing them with complete information, and then trusting them to make their own decisions. It's a decision formula that seems to be working. As Motek continues to grow, Price's challenge will be maintaining an environment that encourages the kind of decisions that create both happy employees and a successful organization.

Source: Ellyn Spragins, "Is This the Best Company to Work for Anywhere?" *FSB* (November 2002), 66–70.

resulted in a pattern in the manager's mind. The manager could not prove a problem existed but knew intuitively that a certain area needed attention. A too-simple view of a complex problem is often associated with decision failure,[25] and research shows managers are more likely to respond intuitively to a perceived threat to the organization than to an opportunity.[26] Intuition plays an increasingly important role in problem identification in today's fast-paced and uncertain business environment. A study of sixty managers from a variety of industries found that nearly half said they rely on intuition often for organizational decision making, while another 30 percent reported using intuition sometimes.[27]

Intuitive processes are also used in the problem solution stage. Executives frequently make decisions without explicit reference to the impact on profits or to other measurable outcomes.[28] As we saw in Exhibit 12.3, many intangible factors—such as a person's concern about the support of other executives, fear of failure, and social attitudes—influence selection of the best alternative. These factors cannot be quantified in a systematic way, so intuition guides the choice of a solution. Managers may make a decision based on what they sense to be right rather than on what they can document with hard data.

Bob Lutz helped put the shine back on Chrysler by relying on intuitive decision making regarding new car models. For example, the Dodge Viper, which was a smashing success for the company in the 1990s, would never have been made if Lutz (then the company's president) hadn't pushed ahead despite opposition and criticism. In explaining his decision, Lutz said that "it just felt right."[29]

Another example is Jodie Foster, who is known for making good decisions based on gut feelings at her production company, Egg Pictures. Foster made her movie debut at the age of eight, and her manager–mother involved her in almost all decision making regarding roles, script changes, and so forth. "She understands Hollywood almost mathematically," said one producer.[30] Thus, intuition may be thought of as *recognition* because when managers develop a depth of experience and knowledge in a particular area, problem recognition and problem solution often come almost effortlessly as a recognition of information that has largely been forgotten by the conscious mind.[31]

However, managers may walk a fine line between two extremes: on the one hand, making arbitrary decisions without careful study, and on the other, relying obsessively on numbers and rational analysis.[32] Remember that the bounded rationality perspective and the use of intuition apply mostly to nonprogrammed decisions. The novel, unclear, complex aspects of nonprogrammed decisions mean hard data and logical procedures are not available. A study of executive decision making found that managers simply could not use the rational approach for nonprogrammed decisions, such as when to buy a CT scanner for an osteopathic hospital or whether a city had a need for and could reasonably adopt an enterprise resource planning system.[33] In those cases, managers had limited time and resources, and some factors simply couldn't be measured and analyzed. Trying to quantify such information could cause mistakes because it may oversimplify decision criteria. Intuition can also balance and supplement rational analysis to help organization leaders make better decisions. At Paramount Pictures, a top management team has combined intuition and analysis to keep the studio consistently profitable.

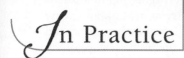

Sherry Lansing, chairwoman of Paramount Pictures, and her boss, Jonathan Dolgen, chairman of the Viacom Entertainment Group, make a powerful team. Unlike many studios, which lose money despite successful box-office films, Paramount has consistently turned a profit every year since Lansing and Dolgen were put in charge.

As a former independent producer, Lansing relies on her experience and intuition to pick good scripts and the right actors to make them work. Consider 1994's *Forrest Gump*. "It was a film about a guy on a bench," said Lansing. "It was one of the riskiest films ever made." But Lansing's intuition told her that Tom Hanks sitting on a bench talking about life being "like a box of chocolates" would work, and the film reaped $329 million at the box office. More recent successes under the leadership of Lansing and Dolgen include *Along Came a Spider*, *Vanilla Sky*, and *Lara Croft: Tomb Raider*. Dolgen, a former lawyer, provides the analytical side of the partnership. Dolgen's intelligence and careful attention to details help Paramount generate consistently good returns. Sometimes, his analysis suggests that a risk is just not worth taking, even though it means the studio turns down a potential blockbuster. In fact, some critics argue that Paramount is too cautious, but Dolgen's influence has helped the company turn out a string of well-planned, well-executed, and reliable hits.

Lansing and Dolgen are considered one of the most effective management teams in Hollywood. They have combined their natural strengths—one intuitive, the other analytical—to make good decisions that have kept Paramount consistently successful in a difficult, high-risk, unpredictable business. "Since I have been here, they have not disappointed once," said Mel Karmazin, Viacom's president. "If not the best, they are among the best at turning out profitable films."[34]

ORGANIZATIONAL DECISION MAKING

Organizations are composed of managers who make decisions using both rational and intuitive processes; but organization-level decisions are not usually made by a single manager. Many organizational decisions involve several managers. Problem identification and problem solution involve many departments, multiple viewpoints, and even other organizations, which are beyond the scope of an individual manager.

The processes by which decisions are made in organizations are influenced by a number of factors, particularly the organization's own internal structures as well as the degree of stability or instability of the external environment.[35] Research into organization-level decision making has identified four types of organizational decision-making processes: the management science approach, the Carnegie model, the incremental decision process model, and the garbage can model.

MANAGEMENT SCIENCE APPROACH

The **management science approach** to organizational decision making is the analog to the rational approach by individual managers. Management science came into being during World War II.[36] At that time, mathematical and statistical techniques were applied to urgent, large-scale military problems that were beyond the ability of individual decision makers. Mathematicians, physicists, and operations researchers used systems analysis to develop artillery trajectories, antisubmarine strategies, and bombing strategies such as salvoing (discharging multiple shells simultaneously). Consider the problem of a battleship trying to sink an enemy ship several miles away. The calculation for aiming the battleship's guns should consider distance, wind speed, shell size, speed and direction of both ships, pitch and roll of the firing ship, and curvature of the earth. Methods for performing such calculations using trial and error and intuition are not accurate, take far too long, and may never achieve success.

This is where management science came in. Analysts were able to identify the relevant variables involved in aiming a ship's guns and could model them with the use of mathematical equations. Distance, speed, pitch, roll, shell size, and so on could be calculated and entered into the equations. The answer was immediate, and the guns could begin firing. Factors such as pitch and roll were soon measured mechanically and fed directly into the targeting mechanism. Today, the human element is completely removed from the targeting process. Radar picks up the target, and the entire sequence is computed automatically.

Management science yielded astonishing success for many military problems. This approach to decision making diffused into corporations and business schools, where techniques were studied and elaborated. Today, many corporations have assigned departments to use these techniques. The computer department develops quantitative data for analysis. Operations research departments use mathematical models to quantify relevant variables and develop a quantitative representation of alternative solutions and the probability of each one solving the problem. These departments also use such devices as linear programming, Bayesian statistics, PERT charts, and computer simulations.

Management science is an excellent device for organizational decision making when problems are analyzable and when the variables can be identified and measured. Mathematical models can contain a thousand or more variables, each one relevant in some way to the ultimate outcome. Management science techniques have been used to correctly solve problems as diverse as finding the right spot for a church camp, test-marketing the first of a new family of products, drilling for oil, and radically altering the distribution of telecommunications services.[37] Other problems amenable to management science techniques are the scheduling of airline employees, ambulance technicians, telephone operators, and turnpike toll collectors.[38] The NBC television network, a subsidiary of the General Electric Company, uses management science techniques to create optimum advertising schedules.

In Practice

NATIONAL BROADCASTING COMPANY (NBC)

For television viewers, the NBC network may seem like it's in the business of providing entertainment, but management's primary goal is to provide eyeballs (audiences) for advertisers. Each broadcast year, NBC managers have to develop a detailed advertising plan and schedule that meets advertisers' desires in terms of cost, target audience, program mix, and other factors. In addition, the plan has to meet NBC management's goal of maximizing revenues for the available amount of inventory (advertising slots).

Traditionally, sales plans were developed manually, a grueling and time-consuming process that usually required a great deal of rework because the initial plan rarely met customers' requirements or management's goals. In addition, since up to 80 percent of airtime inventory is sold during a brief two- to three-week period at the beginning of the broadcast year, planners had to work twelve to sixteen hours a day to keep up. A new computer-based sales-plan-generation system solved these problems by generating sales plans quickly and making optimal use of available advertising slots.

When a customer (advertiser) request is received, planners enter all the information into the sales-plan-generation system, including the budgeted amount the customer is willing to pay for a total package of commercials, the number of people the customer wants to reach and the targeted demographic categories, how the budget is to be distributed over the four quarters of the year, the number of weeks in the program year, the unit lengths of the commercials, the shows in the program schedule that the customer is interested in, and so forth. One of the primary goals of the system is to use as little premium inventory (i.e., airtime during peak periods or on highly popular shows) as possible to satisfy each client's requirements. NBC management ranks the shows and weeks of the year by their importance, and these data, along with the availability of inventory during each week, are also entered in the system. The system formulates each sales plan to use the least amount of premium inventory subject to meeting client requirements, airtime availability constraints, and product conflict constraints (such that ads for Coke and Pepsi, for example, do not air during the same commercial break).

Today, NBC sales personnel in New York, Los Angeles, Chicago, and Detroit use the sales-plan-generation system. Using management science has generated optimal plans that have met customer requirements yet saved millions of dollars of premium inventory, which NBC can use to lure new customers who will pay a premium to advertise on the hottest shows. The time needed to produce a sales plan has been cut from four hours to about twenty minutes, which gives the sales force more time to work with customers. In addition, service has been improved because of fewer errors, less rework, and quicker response time.[39]

Management science can accurately and quickly solve problems that have too many explicit variables for human processing. This system is at its best when applied to problems that are analyzable, are measurable, and can be structured in a logical way. Increasingly sophisticated computer technology and software programs are allowing the expansion of management science to cover a broader range of problems than ever before. For example, the Kellogg Company uses enterprise resource planning and a sophisticated computer-based system called Kellogg Planning System (KPS) to make operational decisions that achieve systematic coordination and optimization of its global production and distribution of breakfast cereal and other foods.[40] In addition, KPS helps Kellogg make tactical decisions on budgeting, capacity expansion or reassignment, and other critical management problems.

Management science has also produced many failures.[41] In recent years, many banks have begun using computerized scoring systems to rate those applying for credit, but some argue that human judgment is needed to account for extenuating circumstances. In one case, a member of the Federal Reserve Board, the agency that sets interest rates and regulates banks, was denied a Toys "R" Us credit card based on his computerized score.[42] One problem with the management science approach is that quantitative data are not rich and do not convey tacit knowledge, as discussed in Chapter 8. Informal cues that indicate the existence of problems have to be sensed on a more personal basis by managers.[43] The most sophisticated mathematical analyses are of no value if the important factors cannot be quantified and included in the model. Such things as competitor reactions, consumer tastes, and product warmth are qualitative dimensions. In these situations, the role of management science is to supplement manager decision making.

Quantitative results can be given to managers for discussion and interpretation along with their informal opinions, judgment, and intuition. The final decision can include qualitative factors as well as quantitative calculations.

CARNEGIE MODEL

The **Carnegie model** of organizational decision making is based on the work of Richard Cyert, James March, and Herbert Simon, who were all associated with Carnegie-Mellon University.[44] Their research helped formulate the bounded rationality approach to individual decision making as well as provide new insights about organizational decisions. Until their work, research in economics assumed that business firms made decisions as a single entity, as if all relevant information were funneled to the top decision maker for a choice. Research by the Carnegie group indicated that organization-level decisions involved many managers and that a final choice was based on a coalition among those managers. A **coalition** is an alliance among several managers who agree about organizational goals and problem priorities.[45] It could include managers from line departments, staff specialists, and even external groups, such as powerful customers, bankers, or union representatives.

Management coalitions are needed during decision making for two reasons. First, organizational goals are often ambiguous, and operative goals of departments are often inconsistent. When goals are ambiguous and inconsistent, managers disagree about problem priorities. They must bargain about problems and build a coalition around the question of which problems to solve.

The second reason for coalitions is that individual managers intend to be rational but function with human cognitive limitations and other constraints, as described earlier. Managers do not have the time, resources, or mental capacity to identify all dimensions and to process all information relevant to a decision. These limitations lead to coalition-building behavior. Managers talk to each other and exchange points of view to gather information and reduce ambiguity. People who have relevant information or a stake in a decision outcome are consulted. Building a coalition will lead to a decision that is supported by interested parties.

The process of coalition formation has several implications for organizational decision behavior. First, decisions are made to satisfice rather than to optimize problem solutions. **Satisficing** means organizations accept a satisfactory rather than a maximum level of performance, enabling them to achieve several goals simultaneously. In decision making, the coalition will accept a solution that is perceived as satisfactory to all coalition members. Second, managers are concerned with immediate problems and short-run solutions. They engage in what Cyert and March called problemistic search.[46] **Problemistic search** means managers look around in the immediate environment for a solution to quickly resolve a problem. Managers don't expect a perfect solution when the situation is ill-defined and conflict-laden. This contrasts with the management science approach, which assumes that analysis can uncover every reasonable alternative. The Carnegie model says search behavior is just sufficient to produce a satisfactory solution and that managers typically adopt the first satisfactory solution that emerges. Third, discussion and bargaining are especially important in the problem identification stage of decision making. Unless coalition members perceive a problem, action will not be taken. The decision process described in the Carnegie model is summarized in Exhibit 12.4.

EXHIBIT 12.4   *Choice Processes in the Carnegie Model*

The Carnegie model points out that building agreement through a managerial coalition is a major part of organizational decision making. This is especially true at upper management levels. Discussion and bargaining are time-consuming, so search procedures are usually simple and the selected alternative satisfices rather than optimizes problem solution. When problems are programmed—are clear and have been seen before—the organization will rely on previous procedures and routines. Rules and procedures prevent the need for renewed coalition formation and political bargaining. Nonprogrammed decisions, however, require bargaining and conflict resolution.

To support a U.S.-led campaign against terrorism and a war with Iraq, President George W. Bush has tried to take a lesson from his father, who was known as a consummate coalition builder. The elder Bush always sought a broad-based coalition at the start of any important decision process, such as that regarding the Persian Gulf War.[47] The younger president has been criticized for being more aggressive in pushing his own priorities and opinions, but negative reactions have led him to engage in stronger coalition-building behavior before making and implementing major decisions concerning homeland security and overseas campaigns.

Organizations suffer when managers are unable to build a coalition around goals and problem priorities, as illustrated by the case of Encyclopaedia Britannica.

ENCYCLOPAEDIA BRITANNICA

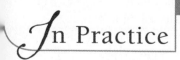

In Practice

For most of its 231-year history, the *Encyclopaedia Britannica* had been viewed as an illustrious repository of cultural and historical knowledge—almost a national treasure. Generations of students and librarians relied on the *Britannica*—but that was before CD-ROMs and the Internet became the study tools of choice. Suddenly, the thirty-two-volume collection of encyclopedias, stretching four feet on a bookshelf and costing as much as a personal computer, seemed destined to fade into history.

When Swiss-based financier Joseph Safra bought Britannica, he discovered one of the reasons. For nearly a decade, managers had bickered over goals and priorities. Some top executives believed the company needed to invest more in electronic media, but others supported Britannica's traditional direct-to-home sales force. Eventually, the company's Compton unit, a CD-ROM pioneer now being used by millions of consumers, was sold, leaving Britannica without any presence in the new market. In the 1980s, Microsoft had approached Britannica to develop a CD-ROM encyclopedia; when it didn't work out, Microsoft went with Funk & Wagnalls and developed Encarta. Microsoft arranged to have Encarta preinstalled on PCs, so the CD-ROM was essentially free to new PC buyers. When Britannica finally came out with its CD-ROM version, however, it was priced at a staggering $1,200. The squabbling among managers, owners, and editors about product development, pricing, distribution, and other important decisions contributed to the company's decline.

The first step in Safra's turnaround strategy was to install a new top management team, led by one of his longtime advisors. The team immediately coalesced around the important problem of establishing a presence in the world of electronic media. With this goal, the company rushed out a revamped, lower-cost CD-ROM package and launched the Britannica.com Web site, which allows users to call up encyclopedia entries online as well as get a list of links to related Web sites. The team also created a separate digital media division to focus on new product development, such as for wireless Web technology. Managers are looking toward the wireless Web as the best route to a successful future and have teamed up with numerous wireless carriers and licensed Britannica's content to other Web sites.

Building a coalition focused on common goals rather than having managers pushing and pulling in different directions has gotten Britannica off the critical list by helping it cross the bridge to the digital era. Now, managers are in the process of evaluation to see what new decisions need to be made to help the company thrive in the digital world.[48]

The Carnegie model is particularly useful at the problem identification stage. However, a coalition of key department managers is also important for smooth implementation of a decision, particularly a major reorganization. Top executives at Britannica realize the importance of building coalitions for decision making to keep the company moving forward. When top managers perceive a problem or want to make a major decision, they need to reach agreement with other managers to support the decision.[49]

INCREMENTAL DECISION PROCESS MODEL

Henry Mintzberg and his associates at McGill University in Montreal approached organizational decision making from a different perspective. They identified twenty-five decisions made in organizations and traced the events associated with these decisions from beginning to end.[50] Their research identified each step in the decision sequence. This approach to decision making, called the **incremental decision process model**, places less emphasis on the political and social factors described in the Carnegie model, but tells more about the structured sequence of activities undertaken from the discovery of a problem to its solution.[51]

Sample decisions in Mintzberg's research included choosing which jet aircraft to acquire for a regional airline, developing a new supper club, developing a new container terminal in a harbor, identifying a new market for a deodorant, installing a controversial new medical treatment in a hospital, and firing a star radio announcer.[52] The scope and importance of these decisions are revealed in the length of time taken to complete them. Most of these decisions took more

BRIEFCASE

As an organization manager, keep this guideline in mind:

Take risks and move the company ahead by increments when a problem is defined but solutions are uncertain. Try solutions step by step to learn whether they work.

than a year, and one-third of them took more than two years. Most of these decisions were nonprogrammed and required custom-designed solutions.

One discovery from this research is that major organization choices are usually a series of small choices that combine to produce the major decision. Thus, many organizational decisions are a series of nibbles rather than a big bite. Organizations move through several decision points and may hit barriers along the way. Mintzberg called these barriers *decision interrupts*. An interrupt may mean an organization has to cycle back through a previous decision and try something new. Decision loops or cycles are one way the organization learns which alternatives will work. The ultimate solution may be very different from what was initially anticipated.

The pattern of decision stages discovered by Mintzberg and his associates is shown in Exhibit 12.5. Each box indicates a possible step in the decision sequence. The steps take place in three major decision phases: identification, development, and selection.

Identification Phase. The identification phase begins with *recognition*. Recognition means one or more managers become aware of a problem and the need to make a decision. Recognition is usually stimulated by a problem or an opportunity. A problem exists when elements in the external environment change or when internal performance is perceived to be below standard. In the case of firing a radio announcer, comments about the announcer came from listeners, other announcers, and advertisers. Managers interpreted these cues until a pattern emerged that indicated a problem had to be dealt with.

The second step is *diagnosis*, in which more information is gathered if needed to define the problem situation. Diagnosis may be systematic or informal, depending upon the severity of the problem. Severe problems do not allow time for extensive diagnosis; the response must be immediate. Mild problems are usually diagnosed in a more systematic manner.

Development Phase. In the development phase, a solution is shaped to solve the problem defined in the identification phase. The development of a solution takes one of two directions. First, *search* procedures may be used to seek out alternatives within the organization's repertoire of solutions. For example, in the case of firing a star announcer, managers asked what the radio station had done the last time an announcer had to be let go. To conduct the search, organization participants may look into their own memories, talk to other managers, or examine the formal procedures of the organization.

The second direction of development is to *design* a custom solution. This happens when the problem is novel so that previous experience has no value. Mintzberg found that in these cases, key decision makers have only a vague idea of the ideal solution. Gradually, through a trial-and-error process, a custom-designed alternative will emerge. Development of the solution is a groping, incremental procedure, building a solution brick by brick.

Selection Phase. The selection phase is when the solution is chosen. This phase is not always a matter of making a clear choice among alternatives. In the case of custom-made solutions, selection is more an evaluation of the single alternative that seems feasible.

Evaluation and choice may be accomplished in three ways. The *judgment* form of selection is used when a final choice falls upon a single decision maker, and the choice involves judgment based upon experience. In analysis, alternatives

EXHIBIT I 2.5   *The Incremental Decision Process Model*

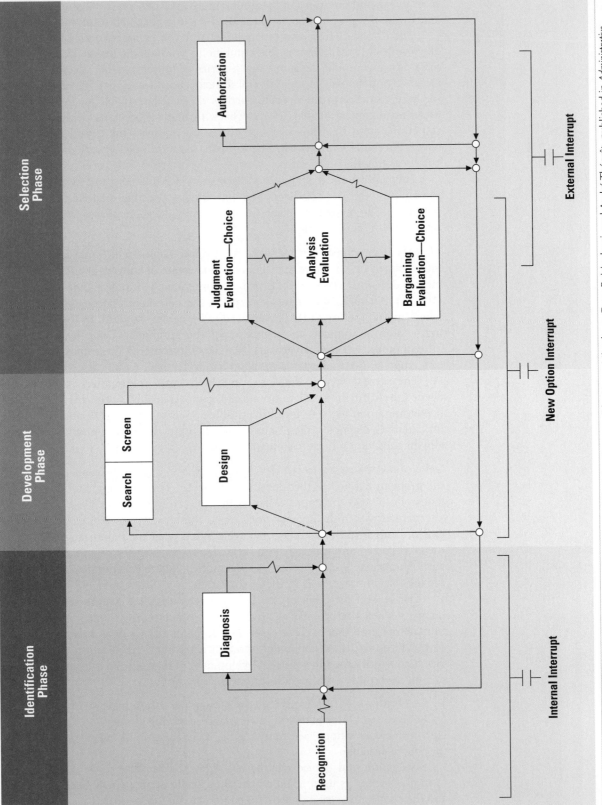

Source: Adapted and reprinted from "The Structure of Unstructured Decision Processes" by Henry Mintzberg, Duru Raisinghani, and André Théorêt, published in *Administrative Science Quarterly* 21, no. 2 (1976), 266, by permission of *The Administrative Science Quarterly*. Copyright © 1976 Cornell University.

are evaluated on a more systematic basis, such as with management science techniques. Mintzberg found that most decisions did not involve systematic analysis and evaluation of alternatives. *Bargaining* occurs when selection involves a group of decision makers. Each decision maker may have a different stake in the outcome, so conflict emerges. Discussion and bargaining occur until a coalition is formed, as in the Carnegie model described earlier.

When a decision is formally accepted by the organization, *authorization* takes place. The decision may be passed up the hierarchy to the responsible hierarchical level. Authorization is often routine because the expertise and knowledge rest with the lower decision makers who identified the problem and developed the solution. A few decisions are rejected because of implications not anticipated by lower-level managers.

Dynamic Factors. The lower part of the chart in Exhibit 12.5 shows lines running back toward the beginning of the decision process. These lines represent loops or cycles that take place in the decision process. Organizational decisions do not follow an orderly progression from recognition through authorization. Minor problems arise that force a loop back to an earlier stage. These are decision interrupts. If a custom-designed solution is perceived as unsatisfactory, the organization may have to go back to the very beginning and reconsider whether the problem is truly worth solving. Feedback loops can be caused by problems of timing, politics, disagreement among managers, inability to identify a feasible solution, turnover of managers, or the sudden appearance of a new alternative. For example, when a small Canadian airline made the decision to acquire jet aircraft, the board authorized the decision, but shortly after, a new chief executive was brought in who canceled the contract, recycling the decision back to the identification phase. He accepted the diagnosis of the problem but insisted upon a new search for alternatives. Then a foreign airline went out of business and two used aircraft became available at a bargain price. This presented an unexpected option, and the chief executive used his own judgment to authorize the purchase of the aircraft.[53]

Because most decisions take place over an extended period of time, circumstances change. Decision making is a dynamic process that may require a number of cycles before a problem is solved. An example of the incremental process and cycling that can take place is illustrated in Gillette's decision to create a new razor.

GILLETTE COMPANY

In Practice

The Gillette Company uses incremental decision making to perfect the design of razors such as the Sensor and the Mach3. While searching for a new idea to increase sales in Gillette's mature shaving market, researchers at the company's British research lab came up with a bright idea to create a razor with three blades to produce a closer, smoother, more comfortable shave (recognition and diagnosis). Ten years later, the Mach3 reached the market, after thousands of shaving tests, numerous design modifications, and a development and tooling cost of $750 million.

The technical demands of building a razor with three blades that would follow a man's face and also be easy to clean had several blind alleys. Engineers first tried to find established techniques (search, screen), but none fit the bill. Eventually a prototype called Manx was built (design), and in shaving tests it "beat the pants off" Gillette's Sensor Excel, the company's best-selling razor at the time. However, Gillette's CEO insisted that the razor had to have a radically new blade edge so the razor could use thinner blades (internal interrupt), so engineers began looking for new technology that could produce a stronger blade (search, screen). Eventually, the new edge, known as DLC for diamond-like carbon coating, would be applied atom by atom with chipmaking technology (design). The next problem was manufacturing (diagnosis), which required an entirely new process to handle the complexity of the triple-bladed razor (design). Although the board gave the go-ahead to develop manufacturing equipment (judgment, authorization), some members became concerned because the new blades, which are three times stronger than stainless steel, would last longer and cause Gillette to sell fewer cartridges (internal interrupt). The board eventually made the decision to continue with the new blades, which would have a blue indicator strip that would fade to white and signal when it's time for a new cartridge. The board gave final approval for production of the Mach3 to begin in the fall of 1997.

The new razor was introduced in the summer of 1998 and began smoothly sliding off shelves. Gillette recovered its huge investment in record time. Now Gillette is starting the process of searching for the next shaving breakthrough all over again, using new technology that can examine a razor blade at the atomic level and high-speed video that can capture the act of cutting a single whisker. The company will move ahead in increments to create its next major shaving product, projected for release in 2006.[54]

At Gillette, the identification phase occurred because executives were aware of the need for a new razor and became alert to the idea of using three blades to produce a closer shave. The development phase was characterized by the trial-and-error custom design leading to the Mach3. During the selection phase, certain approaches were found unacceptable, causing Gillette to cycle back and redesign the razor, including using thinner, stronger blades. Advancing once again to the selection phase, the Mach3 passed the judgment of top executives and board members, and manufacturing and marketing budgets were quickly authorized. This decision took more than a decade, finally reaching completion in the summer of 1998.

THE LEARNING ORGANIZATION

At the beginning of this chapter, we discussed how the rapidly changing business environment is creating greater uncertainty for decision makers. Some organizations that are particularly affected by this trend are shifting to the learning organization concept. These organizations are marked by a tremendous amount of uncertainty at both the problem identification and problem solution stages. Two approaches to decision making have evolved to help managers cope with this uncertainty and complexity. One approach is to combine the Carnegie and incremental process models just described. The second is a unique approach called the garbage can model.

COMBINING THE INCREMENTAL PROCESS AND CARNEGIE MODELS

The Carnegie description of coalition building is especially relevant for the problem identification stage. When issues are ambiguous, or if managers disagree about problem severity, discussion, negotiation, and coalition building are needed. Once agreement is reached about the problem to be tackled, the organization can move toward a solution.

The incremental process model tends to emphasize the steps used to reach a solution. After managers agree on a problem, the step-by-step process is a way of trying various solutions to see what will work. When problem solution is unclear, a trial-and-error solution may be designed. For example, executives from three of the world's largest music companies formed a coalition to provide online consumers with a legal alternative to the digital piracy of Internet song-swapping services. However, making the joint venture MusicNet an appealing choice has been a challenge. As originally conceived, the service didn't provide music lovers with the features they wanted, so managers are taking an incremental approach to try to make MusicNet more user friendly. As one executive put it, "This is a business of trial and error."[55]

The two models do not disagree with one another. They describe how organizations make decisions when either problem identification or solution is uncertain. The application of these two models to the stages in the decision process is illustrated in Exhibit 12.6. When both parts of the decision process are highly uncertain simultaneously, which is often the case in learning organizations, the organization is in an extremely difficult position. Decision processes in that situation may be a combination of Carnegie and incremental process models, and this combination may evolve into a situation described in the garbage can model.

GARBAGE CAN MODEL

The **garbage can model** is one of the most recent and interesting descriptions of organizational decision processes. It is not directly comparable to the earlier models, because the garbage can model deals with the pattern or flow of multiple decisions within organizations, whereas the incremental and Carnegie models focus on how a single decision is made. The garbage can model helps you think of the whole organization and the frequent decisions being made by managers throughout.

Organized Anarchy. The garbage can model was developed to explain the pattern of decision making in organizations that experience extremely high uncertainty, such as the growth and change required in a learning organization. Michael Cohen, James March, and Johan Olsen, the originators of the model, called the highly uncertain conditions an **organized anarchy**, which is an extremely organic organization.[56] Organized anarchies do not rely on the normal vertical hierarchy of authority and bureaucratic decision rules. They result from three characteristics:

EXHIBIT 12.6   *Learning Organization Decision Process When Problem Identification and Problem Solution Are Uncertain*

Problem Identification

When problem identification is uncertain, Carnegie model *applies*

Political and social process is needed

Build coalition, seek agreement, and resolve conflict about goals and problem priorities

Problem Solution

When problem solution is uncertain, incremental process model *applies*

Incremental, trial-and-error process is needed

Solve big problems in little steps

Recycle and try again when blocked

1. *Problematic preferences*. Goals, problems, alternatives, and solutions are ill-defined. Ambiguity characterizes each step of a decision process.
2. *Unclear, poorly understood technology*. Cause-and-effect relationships within the organization are difficult to identify. An explicit database that applies to decisions is not available.
3. *Turnover*. Organizational positions experience turnover of participants. In addition, employees are busy and have only limited time to allocate to any one problem or decision. Participation in any given decision will be fluid and limited.

An organized anarchy is characterized by rapid change and a collegial, non-bureaucratic environment. No organization fits this extremely organic circumstance all the time, although learning organizations and today's Internet-based companies may experience it much of the time. Many organizations will occasionally find themselves in positions of making decisions under unclear, problematic circumstances. The garbage can model is useful for understanding the pattern of these decisions.

Streams of Events. The unique characteristic of the garbage can model is that the decision process is not seen as a sequence of steps that begins with a problem and ends with a solution. Indeed, problem identification and problem solution may not be connected to each other. An idea may be proposed as a solution when no problem is specified. A problem may exist and never generate a solution. Decisions are the outcome of independent streams of events within the organization. The four streams relevant to organizational decision making are as follows:

1. *Problems*. Problems are points of dissatisfaction with current activities and performance. They represent a gap between desired performance and current activities. Problems are perceived to require attention. However, they are distinct from solutions and choices. A problem may lead to a proposed solution or it may not. Problems may not be solved when solutions are adopted.
2. *Potential solutions*. A solution is an idea somebody proposes for adoption. Such ideas form a flow of alternative solutions through the organization. Ideas may be brought into the organization by new personnel or may be invented by existing personnel. Participants may simply be attracted to certain ideas and push them as logical choices regardless of problems. Attraction to an idea may cause an employee to look for a problem to which the idea can be attached and, hence, justified. The point is that solutions exist independent of problems.
3. *Participants*. Organization participants are employees who come and go throughout the organization. People are hired, reassigned, and fired. Participants vary widely in their ideas, perception of problems, experience, values, and training. The problems and solutions recognized by one manager will differ from those recognized by another manager.
4. *Choice opportunities*. Choice opportunities are occasions when an organization usually makes a decision. They occur when contracts are signed, people are hired, or a new product is authorized. They also occur when the right mix of participants, solutions, and problems exists. Thus, a manager who happened to learn of a good idea may suddenly become aware of a problem to which it applies and, hence, can provide the organization with a choice opportunity. Match-ups of problems and solutions often result in decisions.

With the concept of four streams, the overall pattern of organizational decision making takes on a random quality. Problems, solutions, participants, and choices all flow through the organization. In one sense, the organization is a large garbage can in which these streams are being stirred, as illustrated in Exhibit 12.7. When a problem, solution, and participant happen to connect at one point, a decision may be made and the problem may be solved; but if the solution does not fit the problem, the problem may not be solved. Thus, when viewing the organization as a whole and considering its high level of uncertainty, one sees problems arise that are not solved and solutions tried that do not work. Organization decisions are disorderly and not the result of a logical, step-by-step sequence. Events may be so ill-defined and complex that decisions, problems, and solutions act as independent events. When they connect, some problems are solved, but many are not.[57]

Consequences. There are four specific consequences of the garbage can decision process for organizational decision making:

1. *Solutions may be proposed even when problems do not exist.* An employee might be sold on an idea and might try to sell it to the rest of the organization. An example was the adoption of computers by many organizations during the 1970s. The computer was an exciting solution and was pushed by both computer manufacturers and systems analysts within organizations.

Exhibit 12.7   *Illustration of Independent Streams of Events in the Garbage Can Model of Decision Making*

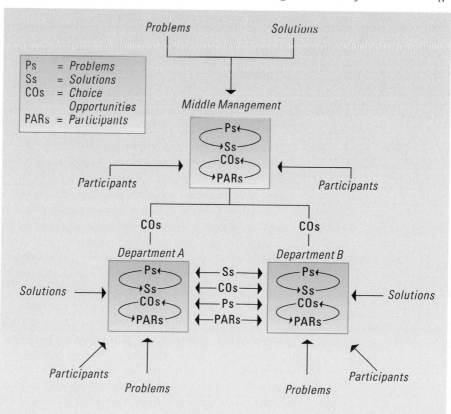

The computer did not solve any problems in those initial applications. Indeed, some computers caused more problems than they solved.

2. *Choices are made without solving problems.* A choice such as creating a new department may be made with the intention of solving a problem; but, under conditions of high uncertainty, the choice may be incorrect. Moreover, many choices just seem to happen. People decide to quit, the organization's budget is cut, or a new policy bulletin is issued. These choices may be oriented toward problems but do not necessarily solve them.

3. *Problems may persist without being solved.* Organization participants get used to certain problems and give up trying to solve them; or participants may not know how to solve certain problems because the technology is unclear. A university in Canada was placed on probation by the American Association of University Professors because a professor had been denied tenure without due process. The probation was a nagging annoyance that the administrators wanted to remove. Fifteen years later, the nontenured professor died. The probation continues because the university did not acquiesce to the demands of the heirs of the association to reevaluate the case. The university would like to solve the problem, but administrators are not sure how, and they do not have the resources to allocate to it. The probation problem persists without a solution.

4. *A few problems are solved.* The decision process does work in the aggregate. In computer simulation models of the garbage can model, important problems were often resolved. Solutions do connect with appropriate problems and participants so that a good choice is made. Of course, not all problems are resolved when choices are made, but the organization does move in the direction of problem reduction.

The effects of independent streams and the rather chaotic decision processes of the garbage can model can be seen in the production of the classic film *Casablanca.*

CASABLANCA

In Practice

The public flocked to see *Casablanca* when it opened in 1942. The film won Academy Awards for best picture, best screenplay, and best director, and is recognized today by film historians and the public alike as a classic. But up until the filming of the final scene, no one involved in the production of the now-famous story even knew how it was going to end.

Everybody Comes to Rick's wasn't a very good play, but when it landed on Hal Wallis's desk at Warner Brothers, Wallis spotted some hot-from-the-headlines potential, purchased the rights, and changed the name to *Casablanca* to capitalize on the geographical mystique the story offered. A series of negotiations led to casting Humphrey Bogart as Rick, even though studio chief Jack Warner questioned his romantic appeal. The casting of Ingrid Bergman as Ilsa was largely by accident. A fluke had left an opening in her usually booked schedule. The screenplay still wasn't written.

Filming was chaotic. Writers made script changes and plot revisions daily. Actors were unsure of how to develop their characterizations, so they just did whatever seemed right at the time. For example, when Ingrid Bergman wanted to know which man should get most of her on-screen attention, she was told, "We don't know yet—just play it, well...in between." Scenes were often filmed blindly with no idea of how they were supposed to fit in the overall story. Amazingly, even when it came time to shoot the climactic final scene, no one involved in the production seemed to know who would "get the girl"; a legend still persists that two versions were written. During filming, Bogart disagreed with director Michael Curtiz's view that Rick should kiss Ilsa good-bye, and Hal Wallis was summoned to mediate. Because the cast received their scripts only hours before filming began, they couldn't remember their lines, causing continual delays.

Some industry analysts predicted disaster, but the haphazard process worked. Ingrid Bergman played it "in between" just right. Bogart's characterization of Rick was perfect. The tale of love and glory and heartbreaking romance couldn't have been told better than it was in *Casablanca*. In addition, fortuitous circumstances outside the studio contributed to the film's commercial success. Just eighteen days before the premiere on Thanksgiving Day, 1942, the Allies invaded North Africa and fought the Battle of Casablanca. Then, when the film opened nationwide, President Franklin D. Roosevelt and Prime Minister Winston Churchill presided over the Casablanca Conference, a historical coincidence that was clearly a boon to the film, helping to push its initial gross to $3.7 million.[58]

The production of *Casablanca* was not a rational process that started with a clear problem and ended with a logical solution. Many events occurred by chance and were intertwined, which characterizes the garbage can model. Everyone from the director to the actors continuously added to the stream of new ideas for the story. Some solutions were connected to emerging problems: the original script arrived just when Hal Wallis was looking for topical stories; and Bergman was surprisingly available to be cast in the role of Ilsa. The actors (participants) daily made personal choices regarding characterization that proved to be perfect for the story line. Other events that contributed to *Casablanca's* success were not even connected to the film—for example, the invasion of North Africa only eighteen days before the premiere. Overall, the production of *Casablanca* had a random, chancy flavor that is characteristic of the garbage can model. As evidenced by the film's huge success and continuing popularity after more than fifty years, the random, garbage can decision process did not hurt the film or the studio.

The garbage can model, however, doesn't always work—in the movies or in organizations. A similar haphazard process during the filming of *Waterworld* led to the most expensive film in Hollywood history and a decided box-office flop for Universal Pictures.[59]

CONTINGENCY DECISION-MAKING FRAMEWORK

This chapter has covered several approaches to organizational decision making, including management science, the Carnegie model, the incremental decision process model, and the garbage can model. It has also discussed rational and intuitive decision processes used by individual managers. Each decision approach is a relatively accurate description of the actual decision process, yet all differ from each other. Management science, for example, reflects a different set of decision assumptions and procedures than does the garbage can model.

One reason for having different approaches is that they appear in different organizational situations. The use of an approach is contingent on the organization setting. Two characteristics of organizations that determine the use of decision approaches are (1) problem consensus and (2) technical knowledge about the means to solve those problems.[60] Analyzing organizations along these two dimensions suggests which approach will be used to make decisions.

PROBLEM CONSENSUS

Problem consensus refers to the agreement among managers about the nature of a problem or opportunity and about which goals and outcomes to pursue. This variable ranges from complete agreement to complete disagreement. When managers agree, there is little uncertainty—the problems and goals of the organization are clear, and so are standards of performance. When managers disagree, organization direction and performance expectations are in dispute, creating a situation of high uncertainty. One example of problem uncertainty occurred at Wal-Mart stores regarding the issue of parking lot patrols. Some managers presented evidence that golf-cart patrols significantly reduced auto theft, assault, and other crimes in the stores' lots and increased business because they encouraged more nighttime shopping. These managers argued that the patrols should be used, but others believed the patrols were not needed and were too expensive, emphasizing that parking lot crime was a society problem rather than a store problem.[61]

Problem consensus tends to be low when organizations are differentiated, as described in Chapter 4. Recall that uncertain environments cause organizational departments to differentiate from one another in goals and attitudes to specialize in specific environmental sectors. This differentiation leads to disagreement and conflict about organizational goals and problem priorities. When differentiation among departments or divisions is high, managers must make a special effort to build coalitions during decision making.

Problem consensus is especially important for the problem identification stage of decision making. When problems are clear and agreed on, they provide clear standards and expectations for performance. When problems are not agreed on, problem identification is uncertain and management attention must be focused on gaining agreement about goals and priorities.

TECHNICAL KNOWLEDGE ABOUT SOLUTIONS

Technical knowledge refers to understanding and agreement about how to solve problems and reach organizational goals. This variable can range from complete agreement and certainty to complete disagreement and uncertainty about cause-effect relationships leading to problem solution. One example of low technical knowledge occurred at PepsiCo's 7-Up division. Managers agreed on the problem to be solved—they wanted to increase market share from 6 percent to 7 percent. However, the means for achieving this increase in market share were not known or agreed on. A few managers wanted to use discount pricing in supermarkets. Other managers believed they should increase the number of soda fountain outlets in restaurants and fast-food chains. A few other managers insisted that the best approach was to increase advertising through radio and television. Managers did not know what would cause an increase in market share. Eventually, the advertising judgment prevailed at 7-Up, but it did not work very well. The failure of its decision reflected 7-Up's low technical knowledge about how to solve the problem.

When means are well understood, the appropriate alternatives can be identified and calculated with some degree of certainty. When means are poorly understood, potential solutions are ill-defined and uncertain. Intuition, judgment, and trial and error become the basis for decisions.

CONTINGENCY FRAMEWORK

Exhibit 12.8 describes the **contingency decision-making framework**, which brings together the two dimensions of problem consensus and technical knowledge about solutions. Each cell represents an organizational situation that is appropriate for the decision-making approaches described in this chapter.

Cell 1. In cell 1 of Exhibit 12.8, rational decision procedures are used because problems are agreed on, and cause–effect relationships are well understood so there is little uncertainty. Decisions can be made in a computational manner. Alternatives can be identified and the best solution adopted through analysis and calculations. The rational models described earlier in this chapter, both for individuals and for the organization, are appropriate when problems and the means for solving them are well defined.

Cell 2. In cell 2, there is high uncertainty about problems and priorities, so bargaining and compromise are used to reach consensus. Tackling one problem might mean the organization must postpone action on other issues. The priorities given to respective problems are decided through discussion, debate, and coalition building.

Managers in this situation should use broad participation to achieve consensus in the decision process. Opinions should be surfaced and discussed until compromise is reached. The organization will not otherwise move forward as an integrated unit. In the case of Wal-Mart, managers will discuss conflicting opinions about the benefits and costs of parking lot patrols.

EXHIBIT 12.8   *Contingency Framework for Using Decision Models*

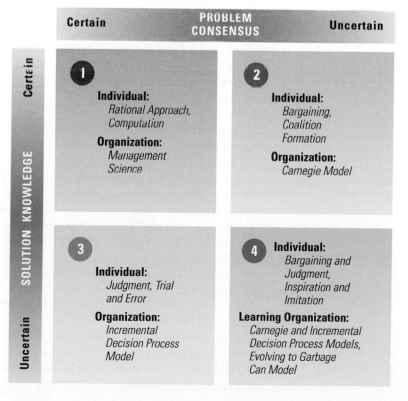

The Carnegie model applies when there is dissension about organizational problems. When groups within the organization disagree, or when the organization is in conflict with constituencies (government regulators, suppliers, unions), bargaining and negotiation are required. The bargaining strategy is especially relevant to the problem identification stage of the decision process. Once bargaining and negotiation are completed, the organization will have support for one direction.

Cell 3. In a cell 3 situation, problems and standards of performance are certain, but alternative technical solutions are vague and uncertain. Techniques to solve a problem are ill defined and poorly understood. When an individual manager faces this situation, intuition will be the decision guideline. The manager will rely on past experience and judgment to make a decision. Rational, analytical approaches are not effective because the alternatives cannot be identified and calculated. Hard facts and accurate information are not available.

The incremental decision process model reflects trial and error on the part of the organization. Once a problem is identified, a sequence of small steps enables the organization to learn a solution. As new problems arise, the organization may recycle back to an earlier point and start over. Eventually, over a period of months or years, the organization will acquire sufficient experience to solve the problem in a satisfactory way. Solving the engineering and manufacturing problems for the Mach3 razor, described earlier, is an example of a cell 3 situation. Gillette engineers had to use trial and error to develop an efficient manufacturing process.

The situation in cell 3, of senior managers agreeing about problems but not knowing how to solve them, occurs frequently in business organizations. If managers use incremental decisions in such situations, they will eventually acquire the technical knowledge to accomplish goals and solve problems.

Cell 4. The situation in cell 4, characterized by high uncertainty about both problems and solutions, is difficult for decision making. An individual manager making a decision under this high level of uncertainty can employ techniques from both cell 2 and cell 3. The manager can attempt to build a coalition to establish goals and priorities and use judgment or trial and error to solve problems. Additional techniques, such as inspiration and imitation, also may be required. **Inspiration** refers to an innovative, creative solution that is not reached by logical means. Inspiration sometimes comes like a flash of insight, but—similar to intuition—it is often based on deep knowledge and understanding of a problem that the unconscious mind has had time to mull over.[62] **Imitation** means adopting a decision tried elsewhere in the hope that it will work in this situation.

For example, in one university, accounting department faculty were unhappy with their current circumstances but could not decide on the direction the department should take. Some faculty members wanted a greater research orientation, whereas others wanted greater orientation toward business firms and accounting applications. The disagreement about goals was compounded because neither group was sure about the best technique for achieving its goals. The ultimate solution was inspirational on the part of the dean. An accounting research center was established with funding from major accounting firms. The funding was used to finance research activities for faculty interested in basic research and to provide contact with business firms for other faculty. The solution provided a common goal and unified people within the department to work toward that goal.

When an entire organization is characterized by high uncertainty regarding both problems and solutions, as in learning organizations, elements of the garbage can model will appear. Managers may first try techniques from both cells 2 and 3, but logical decision sequences starting with problem identification and ending with problem solution will not occur. Potential solutions will precede problems as often as problems precede solutions. In this situation, managers should encourage widespread discussion of problems and idea proposals to facilitate the opportunity to make choices. Eventually, through trial and error, the organization will solve some problems.

Research has found that decisions made following the prescriptions of the contingency decision-making framework tend to be more successful. However, the study noted that nearly six of ten strategic management decisions failed to follow the framework, leading to a situation in which misleading or missing information decreased the chance of an effective decision choice.[63] Managers can use the contingency framework in Exhibit 12.8 to improve the likelihood of successful organizational decisions.

SPECIAL DECISION CIRCUMSTANCES

In a highly competitive world beset by global competition and rapid change, decision making seldom fits the traditional rational, analytical model. Today's managers have to make high-stakes decisions more often and faster than ever before In an environment that is increasingly less predictable. This chapter's Book Mark describes some new decision-making skills that managers can develop in order to make fast, frequent, and effective decisions in this new environment.

Three issues of particular concern for today's decision makers are coping with high-velocity environments, learning from decision mistakes, and avoiding escalating commitment

HIGH-VELOCITY ENVIRONMENTS

BRIEFCASE

As an organization manager, keep this guideline in mind:

Track real-time information, build multiple alternatives simultaneously, and try to involve everyone—but move ahead anyway when making decisions in a high-velocity environment.

In some industries today, the rate of competitive and technological change is so extreme that market data are either unavailable or obsolete, strategic windows open and shut quickly, perhaps within a few months, and the cost of poor decisions is company failure. Recent research has examined how successful companies make decisions in these **high-velocity environments**, especially to understand whether organizations abandon rational approaches or have time for incremental implementation.[64]

A comparison of successful with unsuccessful decisions in high-velocity environments found the following patterns:

- Successful decision makers tracked information in real time to develop a deep and intuitive grasp of the business. Two to three intense meetings per week with all key players were usual. Decision makers tracked operating statistics about cash, scrap, backlog, work in process, and shipments to constantly feel the pulse of what was happening. Unsuccessful firms were more concerned with future planning and forward-looking information, with only a loose grip on immediate happenings.

- During a major decision, successful companies began immediately to build multiple alternatives. Implementation sometimes ran in parallel before they finally settled on a final choice. Companies that made decisions slowly developed just one alternative, moving to another only after the first one failed.

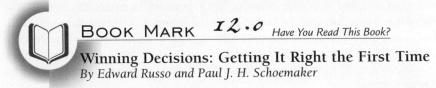

BOOK MARK   *12.0*   *Have You Read This Book?*

Winning Decisions: Getting It Right the First Time
By Edward Russo and Paul J. H. Schoemaker

"Whether you work in business, government, professional services, education, or the not-for-profit sector, the same scenario probably reigns. High speed rules decision making as well as everything else. . . . Whatever their role and organization, most professionals have to make a decision 'now'—followed by another decision 'now,' followed by yet another one." This introduction to *Winning Decisions*, by Edward Russo and Paul Schoemaker, probably sounds familiar to most decision makers. How can managers possibly make winning decisions in an environment characterized by rapid change, uncertainty, information overload, and high pressure?

BECOMING AN EXPERT DECISION MAKER
Although intuition, past experience, and common sense all play an important role in decision making, they alone are not enough. Managers can develop skills in four areas that will help them make better decisions in a fast-paced world.

- *Framing decisions.* A frame of reference is a perspective or a way of looking at something. The way managers frame a problem has a tremendous influence on the options they consider and the solutions they choose. For example, managers at *Encyclopaedia Britannica* missed a chance to become a powerful force on the Internet by making decisions within a limited print-book publisher frame. To make better decisions, managers need to be aware of the frames they are using and develop multiple frames that capture the essence of the problem and broaden the decision-making perspective.
- *Gathering intelligence.* Most people tend to collect information that supports their own biases rather than focusing on turning information into genuine insight that can guide an effective decision. Managers must learn to ask the right questions, properly interpret the answers, and recognize when it's time to end the search and move on.
- *Reaching conclusions.* This is where the decision maker has to determine how to act on the intelligence that's been gathered. The authors argue for using systematic tools and techniques rather than relying heavily on intuition and rules of thumb. Intuition and experience, they believe, are best applied to framing questions and gathering intelligence; the final choice calls for discipline.
- *Learning from experience.* Managers often make good decisions based on their experience making bad ones. Making mistakes is inevitable in fast-paced environments, but learning from those mistakes is a key step to more effective decision making in the future.

CONCLUSION
In addition to offering interesting insight into decision making in the real world, this book provides a practical way for managers to improve their skills through the use of how-to guides, case studies, and worksheets. Each chapter is sprinkled with mini-lessons, one-sentence maxims that capture a key concept or learning point from the chapter. The authors point out that their process is not a recipe but a conceptual approach that requires both discipline and creativity.

Winning Decisions: Getting It Right the First Time, by Edward Russo and Paul J. H. Schoemaker, is published by Currency/Doubleday.

- Fast, successful decision makers sought advice from everyone and depended heavily on one or two savvy, trusted colleagues as counselors. Slow companies were unable to build trust and agreement among the best people.
- Fast companies involved everyone in the decision and tried for consensus; but if consensus did not emerge, the top manager made the choice and moved ahead. Waiting for everyone to be on board created more delays than was warranted. Slow companies delayed decisions to achieve a uniform consensus.
- Fast, successful choices were well integrated with other decisions and the overall strategic direction of the company. Less successful choices considered the decision in isolation from other decisions; the decision was made in the abstract.[65]

When speed matters, a slow decision is as ineffective as the wrong decision. As we discussed in Chapter 11, speed is a crucial competitive weapon in a growing number of industries, and companies can learn to make decisions fast. To improve the chances of a good decision under high-velocity conditions, some organizations stimulate constructive conflict through a technique called **point–counterpoint**, which divides decision makers into two groups and assigns them different, often competing responsibilities.[66] The groups develop and exchange proposals and debate options until they arrive at a common set of understandings and recommendations. A consensus may not be reached, but the exercise gives everyone a chance to consider options and state their opinions, and it gives top managers a broader understanding. Typically, those involved support the final choice. However, if a very speedy decision is required, top managers are willing to make the decision and move forward.

DECISION MISTAKES AND LEARNING

Organizational decisions result in many errors, especially when made in conditions of great uncertainty. Managers simply cannot determine or predict which alternative will solve a problem. In these cases, the organization must make the decision—and take the risk—often in the spirit of trial and error. If an alternative fails, the organization can learn from it and try another alternative that better fits the situation. Each failure provides new information and insight. The point for managers is to move ahead with the decision process despite the potential for mistakes. "Chaotic action is preferable to orderly inaction."[67]

In many cases, managers have been encouraged to instill a climate of experimentation, even foolishness, to facilitate creative decision making. If one idea fails, another idea should be tried. Failure often lays the groundwork for success, as when technicians at 3M developed Post-it Notes based on a failed product—a not-very-sticky glue. Companies such as PepsiCo believe that if all their new products succeed, they're doing something wrong, not taking the necessary risks to develop new markets.[68]

Only by making mistakes can managers and organizations go through the process of **decision learning** and acquire sufficient experience and knowledge to perform more effectively in the future. Robert Townsend, who was president at Avis Corporation, gives the following advice:

> Admit your mistakes openly, maybe even joyfully. Encourage your associates to do likewise by commiserating with them. Never castigate. Babies learn to walk by falling down. If you beat a baby every time he falls down, he'll never care much for walking.
>
> My batting average on decisions at Avis was no better than a .333. Two out of every three decisions I made were wrong. But my mistakes were discussed openly and most of them corrected with a little help from my friends.[69]

ESCALATING COMMITMENT

A much more dangerous mistake is to persist in a course of action when it is failing. Research suggests that organizations often continue to invest time and money in a solution despite strong evidence that it is not working. Two explanations are given for why managers **escalate commitment** to a failing decision. The first is that managers block or distort negative information when they are personally responsible for a negative decision. They simply don't know when to pull the

BRIEFCASE

As an organization manager, keep this guideline in mind:

Do not persist in a course of action that is failing. Some actions will not work if uncertainty is high, so encourage organizational learning by readily trying new alternatives. Seek information and evidence that indicates when a course of action is failing, and allocate resources to new choices rather than to unsuccessful ventures.

plug. In some cases, they continue to throw good money after bad even when a strategy seems incorrect and goals are not being met.[70]

Consider the increasing investment of the Canadian Imperial Bank of Commerce in the ill-fated Canary Wharf project, an $8 billion development in London's remote Docklands area. CIBC had already lent over $1 billion for Canary Wharf to the now-failed Olympia & York Developments Ltd. and its subsidiaries. Despite plenty of negative information that led CEO Al Flood to pronounce Canary Wharf a project that "would not meet our lending criteria today," CIBC invested an additional $36 million in the project. Flood said the move was designed to "protect our investment…and try to make the project work."[71]

A second explanation for escalating commitment to a failing decision is that consistency and persistence are valued in contemporary society. Consistent managers are considered better leaders than those who switch around from one course of action to another. Even though organizations learn through trial and error, organizational norms value consistency. These norms may result in a course of action being maintained, resources being squandered, and learning being inhibited. Emphasis on consistent leadership was partly responsible for the Long Island Lighting Company's refusal to change course in the construction of the Shoreham Nuclear Power Plant, which was eventually abandoned—after an investment of more than $5 billion—without ever having begun operation. Shoreham's cost was estimated at $75 million when the project was announced in 1966, but by the time a construction permit was granted, LILCO had already spent $77 million. Opposition to nuclear power was growing. Critics continued to decry the huge sums of money being pumped into Shoreham. Customers complained that LILCO was cutting back on customer service and maintenance of current operations. Shoreham officials, however, seemed convinced that they would triumph in the end; their response to criticism was, "If people will just wait until the end, they are going to realize that this is a hell of an investment."

The end came in 1989, when a negotiated agreement with New York led LILCO to abandon the $5.5 billion plant in return for rate increases and a $2.5 billion tax write-off. By the time Governor Mario Cuomo signed an agreement with the company, LILCO had remained firmly committed to a losing course of action for more than twenty-three years.[72]

Failure to admit a mistake and adopt a new course of action is far worse than an attitude that encourages mistakes and learning. Based on what has been said about decision making in this chapter, one can expect companies to be ultimately successful in their decision making by adopting a learning approach toward solutions. They will make mistakes along the way, but they will resolve uncertainty through the trial-and-error process.

SUMMARY AND INTERPRETATION

The single most important idea in this chapter is that most organizational decisions are not made in a logical, rational manner. Most decisions do not begin with the careful analysis of a problem, followed by systematic analysis of alternatives, and finally implementation of a solution. On the contrary, decision processes are characterized by conflict, coalition building, trial and error, speed, and mistakes. Managers operate under many constraints that limit rationality; hence, intuition and hunch often are the criteria for choice.

Another important idea is that individuals make decisions, but organizational decisions are not made by a single individual. Organizational decision making is a social process. Only in rare circumstances do managers analyze problems and find solutions by themselves. Many problems are not clear, so widespread discussion and coalition building take place. Once goals and priorities are set, alternatives to achieve those goals can be tried. When a manager does make an individual decision, it is often a small part of a larger decision process. Organizations solve big problems through a series of small steps. A single manager may initiate one step but should be aware of the larger decision process to which it belongs.

The greatest amount of conflict and coalition building occurs when problems are not agreed on. Priorities must be established to indicate which goals are important and what problems should be solved first. If a manager attacks a problem other people do not agree with, the manager will lose support for the solution to be implemented. Thus, time and activity should be spent building a coalition in the problem identification stage of decision making. Then the organization can move toward solutions. Under conditions of low technical knowledge, the solution unfolds as a series of incremental trials that will gradually lead to an overall solution.

The most novel description of decision making is the garbage can model. This model describes how decision processes can seem almost random in highly organic organizations such as learning organizations. Decisions, problems, ideas, and people flow through organizations and mix together in various combinations. Through this process, the organization gradually learns. Some problems may never be solved, but many are, and the organization will move toward maintaining and improving its level of performance.

Finally, many organizations must make decisions with speed, which means staying in immediate touch with operations and the environment. Moreover, in an uncertain world, organizations will make mistakes, and mistakes made through trial and error should be encouraged. Encouraging trial-and-error increments facilitates organizational learning. On the other hand, an unwillingness to change from a failing course of action can have serious negative consequences for an organization. Norms for consistency and the desire to prove one's decision correct can lead to continued investment in a useless course of action.

Key Concepts

bounded rationality perspective	nonprogrammed decisions
Carnegie model	organizational decision making
coalition	organized anarchy
contingency decision-making framework	point–counterpoint
decision learning	problem consensus
escalating commitment	problem identification
garbage can model	problem solution
high-velocity environments	problemistic search
imitation	programmed decisions
incremental decision process model	rational approach
inspiration	satisficing
intuitive decision making	technical knowledge
management science approach	

Discussion Questions

1. A professional economist once told his class, "An individual decision maker should process all relevant information and select the economically rational alternative." Do you agree? Why or why not?
2. Why is intuition used in decision making? Can you think of a time when you used intuition to make a decision?
3. The Carnegie model emphasizes the need for a political coalition in the decision-making process. When and why are coalitions necessary?
4. What are the three major phases in Mintzberg's incremental decision process model? Why might an organization recycle through one or more phases of the model?
5. An organization theorist once told her class, "Organizations never make big decisions. They make small decisions that eventually add up to a big decision." Explain the logic behind this statement.
6. Why would managers in high-velocity environments worry more about the present than the future? Discuss.
7. How does problem consensus affect decision-making processes in an organization?
8. Describe the four streams of events in the garbage can model of decision making. Why are they considered to be independent?
9. Are there decision-making situations in which managers should be expected to make the correct decision? Are there situations in which decision makers should be expected to make mistakes? Discuss.
10. Why are decision mistakes usually accepted in organizations but penalized in college courses and exams that are designed to train managers?

Chapter 12 Workbook *Decision Styles**

Think of some recent decisions that have influenced your life. Choose two significant decisions that you made and two decisions that other people made. Fill out the following table, using Exhibit 12.8 to determine decision styles.

*Adapted by Dorothy Marcic from "Action Assignment" in Jennifer M. Howard and Lawrence M. Miller, *Team Management* (Miller Consulting Group, 1994), p. 205.

Your decisions	Approach used	Advantages and disadvantages	Your recommended decision style
1.			
2.			
Decisions by others			
1.			
2.			

Questions

1. How can a decision approach influence the outcome of the decision? What happens when the approach fits the decision? When it doesn't fit?

2. How can you know what approach is best?

CASE FOR ANALYSIS   *Cracking the Whip**

Harmon Davidson stared dejectedly at the departing figure of his management survey team leader. Their meeting had not gone well. Davidson had relayed to Al Pitcher complaints about his handling of the survey. Pitcher had responded with adamant denial and unveiled scorn.

Davidson, director of headquarters management, was prepared to discount some of the criticism as resentment of outsiders meddling with "the way we've always done business," exacerbated by the turbulence of continual reorganization. But Davidson could hardly ignore the sheer volume of complaints or his high regard for some of their sources.

"Was I missing danger signals about Pitcher from the start?" Davidson asked himself. "Or was I just giving a guy I didn't know a fair chance with an inherently controversial assignment?"

With his division decimated in the latest round of downsizing at the Department of Technical Services (DTS) earlier that year, Davidson had been asked to return to the headquarters management office after a five-year hiatus. The director, Walton Drummond, had abruptly taken early retirement.

One of the first things Davidson had learned about his new job was that he would be responsible for a comprehensive six-month survey of the headquarters management structure and processes. The DTS secretary had promised the survey to the White House as a prelude to the agency's next phase of management reform. Drummond had already picked the five-person survey team consisting of two experienced management analysts, a promising younger staff member, an intern, and Pitcher, the team leader. Pitcher was fresh from the Treasury Department, where he had participated in a similar survey. But having gone off after retirement for an extended mountain-climbing expedition in Asia, Drummond was unavailable to explain his survey plans or any understandings he had reached with Pitcher.

Davidson had been impressed with Pitcher's energy and motivation. He worked long hours, wrote voluminously if awkwardly, and was brimming with the latest organizational theory. Pitcher had other characteristics, however, that were disquieting. He seemed uninterested in DTS's history and culture and was paternalistic toward top managers, assuming they were unsophisticated and unconcerned about modern management.

A series of presurvey informational briefings for headquarters office heads conducted by Davidson and Pitcher seemed to go swimmingly. Pitcher deferred to his chief on matters of philosophy and confined his remarks to schedule and procedures. He closed his segment on a friendly note, saying, "If we do find opportunities for improvement, we'll try to have recommendations for you."

But the survey was barely a week old when the director of management received his first call from an outraged customer. It was the assistant secretary for public affairs, Erin Dove, and she was not speaking in her usual upbeat tones. "Your folks have managed to upset my whole supervisory staff with their comments about how we'll have to change our organization and methods," she said. "I thought you were going through a fact-finding study. This guy Pitcher sounds like he wants to remake DTS headquarters overnight. Who does he think he is?"

When Davidson asked him about the encounter with public affairs, Pitcher expressed puzzlement that a few summary observations shared with supervisors in the interest of "prompt informal feedback" had been interpreted as such disturbing conclusions. "I told them we'll tell them how to fix it," he reassured his supervisor.

* This case was prepared by David Hornestay and appeared in *Government Executive*, August 1998, 45–46, as part of a series of case studies examining workplace dilemmas confronting federal managers. Reprinted by permission of *Government Executive*.

"Listen, Al," Davidson remonstrated gently. "These are very accomplished managers who aren't used to being told they have to fix anything. This agency's been on a roll for years, and the need for reinvention isn't resonating all that well yet. We've got to collect and analyze the information and assemble a convincing case for change, or we'll be spinning our wheels. Let's hold off on the feedback until you and I have reviewed it together."

But two weeks later, Technology Development Director Phil Canseco, an old and treasured colleague, was on Davidson's doorstep looking as unhappy as Erin Dove had sounded on the phone. "Harmon, buddy, I think you have to rein in this survey team a bit," he said. "Several managers who were scheduled for survey interviews were working on a 24-hour turn-around to give a revised project budget to the Appropriations subcommittee that day. My deputy says Pitcher was all put out about postponing interviews and grumbled about whether we understood the new priorities. Is he living in the real world?"

Canseco's comments prompted Davidson to call a few of his respected peers who had dealt with the survey team. With varying degrees of reluctance, they all criticized the team leader and, in some cases, team members, as abrasive and uninterested in the rationales offered for existing structure and processes.

And so Davidson marshaled all of his tact for a review with the survey team leader. But Pitcher was in no mood for either introspection or reconsideration. He took the view that he had been brought in to spearhead a White House-inspired management improvement initiative in a glamour agency that had never had to think much about efficiency. He reminded Davidson that even he had conceded that managers were due some hard lessons on this score. Pitcher didn't see any way to meet his deadline except by adhering to a rigorous schedule, since he was working with managers disinclined to cooperate with an outsider pushing an unpopular exercise. He felt Davidson's role was to hold the line against unwarranted criticisms from prima donnas trying to discredit the survey.

Many questions arose in Davidson's mind about the survey plan and his division's capacity to carry it out. Had they taken on too much with too little? Had the right people been picked for the survey team? Had managers and executives, and even the team, been properly prepared for the survey?

But the most immediate question was whether Al Pitcher could help him with these problems.

CASE FOR ANALYSIS   The Dilemma of Aliesha State College: Competence Versus Need*

Until the 1980s, Aliesha was a well-reputed, somewhat sleepy state teachers college located on the outer fringes of a major metropolitan area. Then with the rapid expansion of college enrollments, the state converted Aliesha to a four-year state college (and the plans called for its becoming a state university with graduate work and perhaps even with a medical school in the 1990s). Within ten years, Aliesha grew from 1,500 to 9,000 students. Its budget expanded even faster than the enrollment, increasing twenty-fold during that period.

The only part of Aliesha that did not grow was the original part, the teachers college; there enrollment actually went down. Everything else seemed to flourish. In addition to building new four-year schools of liberal arts, business, veterinary medicine, and dentistry, Aliesha developed many community service programs. Among them were a rapidly growing evening program, a mental health clinic, and a speech therapy center for children with speech defects—the only one in the area. Even within education one area grew—the demonstration high school attached to the old teachers college. Even though the high school enrolled only 300 students, its teachers were the leading experts in teacher education, and it was considered the best high school in the whole area.

Then, in 1986, the budget was suddenly cut quite sharply by the state legislature. At the same time the faculty demanded and got a fairly hefty raise in salary. It was clear that something had to give—the budget deficit was much too great to be covered by ordinary cost reductions. When the faculty committee sat down with the president and the board of trustees, two candidates for abandonment emerged after long and heated wrangling: the speech therapy program and the demonstration high school. Both cost about the same—and both were extremely expensive.

"The Dilemma of Aliesha State College: Competence Versus Need" (pp. 23–24), from *Management Cases* by Peter F. Drucker. Copyright © 1977 by Peter F. Drucker. Reprinted by permission of the author.

The speech therapy clinic, everyone agreed, addressed itself to a real need and one of high priority. But—and everyone had to agree as the evidence was overwhelming—it did not do the job. Indeed, it did such a poor, sloppy, disorganized job that pediatricians, psychiatrists, and psychologists hesitated to refer their patients to the clinic. The reason was that the clinic was a college program run to teach psychology students rather than to help children with serious speech impediments.

The opposite criticism applied to the high school. No one questioned its excellence and the impact it made on the education students who listened in on its classes and on many young teachers in the area who came in as auditors. But what need did it fill? There were plenty of perfectly adequate high schools in the area.

"How can we justify," asked one of the psychologists connected with the speech clinic, "running an unnecessary high school in which each child costs as much as a graduate student at Harvard?"

"But how can we justify," asked the dean of the school of education, himself one of the outstanding teachers in the demonstration high school, "a speech clinic that has no results even though each of its patients costs the state as much as one of our demonstration high school students, or more?"

Notes

1. Katarzyna Moreno, "UnbeComing," *Forbes* (June 10, 2002), 151–152; Nanette Byrnes, "Avon: The New Calling," *BusinessWeek* (September 18, 2000), 136–148.

2. Adam Lashinsky, "Now for the Hard Part," *Fortune* (November 18, 2002), 94–106.

3. Betsy Morris, "Can Ford Save Ford?" *Fortune* (November 18, 2002), 52–63.

4. Kim Girard, "Cozone in the Ozone," *Business 2.0* (June 27, 2000), 90–95.

5. Saul Hansell, "Meg Whitman and eBay, Net Survivors," *The New York Times* (May 5, 2002), 1, 17; Linda Yates and Peter Skarzynski, "How Do Companies Get to the Future First?" *Management Review* (January 1999), 16–22.

6. Charles Lindblom, "The Science of 'Muddling Through,'" *Public Administration Review* 29 (1954), 79–88.

7. Herbert A. Simon, *The New Science of Management Decision* (Englewood Cliffs, N.J.: Prentice-Hall, 1960), 1–8.

8. Paul J. H. Schoemaker and J. Edward Russo, "A Pyramid of Decision Approaches," *California Management Review* (Fall 1993), 9–31.

9. Scott McCartney, "Clipped Wings: American Airlines to Retrench in Bid to Beat Discount Carriers," *The Wall Street Journal* (August 13, 2002), A1, A8; "Delta to Start Low-Cost Airline," AP story in *The Johnson City Press* (November 17, 2002), 22.

10. Michael Pacanowsky, "Team Tools for Wicked Problems," *Organizational Dynamics* 23, no. 3 (Winter 1995), 36–51.

11. Doug Wallace, "What Would You Do? Southern Discomfort," *Business Ethics* (March/April 1996), 52–53; Renee Elder, "Apparel Plant Closings Rip Fabric of Community's Employment," *The Tennessean* (November 3, 1996), 1E.

12. Karen Dillon, "The Perfect Decision" (an interview with John S. Hammond and Ralph L. Keeney), *Inc.* (October 1998), 74–78; John S. Hammond and Ralph L. Keeney, *Smart Choices: A Practical Guide to Making Better Decisions* (Boston, Mass.: Harvard Business School Press, 1998).

13. Earnest R. Archer, "How to Make a Business Decision: An Analysis of Theory and Practice," *Management Review* 69 (February 1980), 54–61; Boris Blai, "Eight Steps to Successful Problem Solving," *Supervisory Management* (January 1986), 7–9.

14. Francine Schwadel, "Christmas Sales' Lack of Momentum Test Store Managers' Mettle," *The Wall Street Journal* (December 16, 1987), 1.

15. Adapted from Archer, "How to Make a Business Decision," 59–61.

16. James W. Dean, Jr., and Mark P. Sharfman, "Procedural Rationality in the Strategic Decision-Making Process," *Journal of Management Studies* 30 (1993), 587–610.

17. Paul A. Anderson, "Decision Making by Objection and the Cuban Missile Crisis," *Administrative Science Quarterly* 28 (1983), 201–222.

18. Art Kleiner, "Core Group Therapy," *Strategy & Business*, Issue 27 (Second Quarter, 2002), 26–31.

19. Irving L. Janis, *Crucial Decisions: Leadership in Policymaking and Crisis Management* (New York: The Free Press, 1989); Paul C. Nutt, "Flexible Decision Styles and the Choices of Top Executives," *Journal of Management Studies* 30 (1993), 695–721.

20. Herbert A. Simon, "Making Management Decisions: The Role of Intuition and Emotion," *Academy of Management Executive* 1 (February 1987), 57–64; Daniel J. Eisenberg, "How Senior Managers Think," *Harvard Business Review* 62 (November–December 1984), 80–90.

21. Sefan Wally and J. Robert Baum, "Personal and Structural Determinants of the Pace of Strategic Decision Making," *Academy of Management Journal* 37, no. 4 (1994), 932–956; Orlando Behling and Norman L. Eckel, "Making Sense Out of Intuition," *Academy of Management Executive* 5, no. 1 (1991), 46–54.

22. Gary Klein, *Intuition at Work: Why Developing Your Gut Instincts Will Make You Better at What You Do* (New York: Doubleday, 2002); Milorad M. Novicevic, Thomas J. Hench, and Daniel A. Wren, "'Playing By Ear . . . In An Incessant Din of Reasons': Chester Barnard and the History of Intuition in Management Thought," *Management Decision* 40, no. 10 (2002), 992–1002; Alden M. Hayashi, "When to Trust Your Gut," *Harvard Business Review* (February 2001), 59–65; Brian R. Reinwald, "Tactical Intuition," *Military Review* 80, no. 5 (September–October 2000), 78–88; Thomas A. Stewart, "How to Think with Your Gut," *Business 2.0* (November 2002), accessed at *http://www.business2.com/articles* on November 7, 2002; Bill Breen, "What's Your Intuition?" *Fast Company* (September 2000), 290–300; Henry Mintzberg and Frances Westley, "Decision Making: It's Not What You Think," *MIT Sloan Management Review* (Spring 2001), 89–93.

23. Thomas F. Issack, "Intuition: An Ignored Dimension of Management," *Academy of Management Review* 3 (1978), 917–922.

24. Marjorie A. Lyles, "Defining Strategic Problems: Subjective Criteria of Executives," *Organizational Studies* 8 (1987), 263–280; Marjorie A. Lyles and Ian I. Mitroff, "Organizational Problem Formulation: An Empirical Study," *Administrative Science Quarterly* 25 (1980), 102–119.

25. Marjorie A. Lyles and Howard Thomas, "Strategic Problem Formulation: Biases and Assumptions Embedded in Alternative Decision-Making Models," *Journal of Management Studies* 25 (1988), 131–145.

26. Susan E. Jackson and Jane E. Dutton, "Discerning Threats and Opportunities," *Administrative Science Quarterly* 33 (1988), 370–387.

27. Lisa A. Burke and Monica K. Miller, "Taking the Mystery Out of Intuitive Decision Making," *Academy of Management Executive* 13, no. 4 (1999), 91–99.

28. Ross Stagner, "Corporate Decision-Making: An Empirical Study," *Journal of Applied Psychology* 53 (1969), 1–13.

29. Hayashi, "When to Trust Your Gut."

30. Suzanna Andrews, "Calling the Shots," *Working Woman* (November 1995), 30–35, 90.

31. Michael L. Ray and Rochelle Myers, *Creativity in Business* (Garden City, N.J.: Doubleday, 1986).

32. Ann Langley, "Between 'Paralysis By Analysis' and 'Extinction By Instinct,'" *Sloan Management Review* (Spring 1995), 63–76.

33. Paul C. Nutt, "Types of Organizational Decision Processes," *Administrative Science Quarterly* 29 (1984), 414–450.

34. Geraldine Fabrikant, "The Paramount Team Puts Profit Over Splash," *The New York Times* (June 30, 2002), 1, 15.

35. Nandini Rajagopalan, Abdul M. A. Rasheed, and Deepak K. Datta, "Strategic Decision Processes: Critical Review and Future Decisions," *Journal of Management* 19 (1993), 349–384; Paul J. H. Schoemaker, "Strategic Decisions in Organizations: Rational and Behavioral Views," *Journal of Management Studies* 30 (1993), 107–129; Charles J. McMillan, "Qualitative Models of Organizational Decision Making," *Journal of Management Studies* 5 (1980), 22–39; Paul C. Nutt, "Models for Decision Making in Organizations and Some Contextual Variables Which Stimulate Optimal Use," *Academy of Management Review* 1 (1976), 84–98.

36. Hugh J. Miser, "Operations Analysis in the Army Air Forces in World War II: Some Reminiscences," *Interfaces* 23 (September–October 1993), 47–49; Harold J. Leavitt, William R. Dill, and Henry B. Eyring, *The Organizational World* (New York: Harcourt Brace Jovanovich, 1973), chap. 6.

37. Stephen J. Huxley, "Finding the Right Spot for a Church Camp in Spain," *Interfaces* 12 (October

1982), 108–114; James E. Hodder and Henry E. Riggs, "Pitfalls in Evaluating Risky Projects," *Harvard Business Review* (January–February 1985), 128–135.

38. Edward Baker and Michael Fisher, "Computational Results for Very Large Air Crew Scheduling Problems," *Omega* 9 (1981), 613–618; Jean Aubin, "Scheduling Ambulances," *Interfaces* 22 (March–April, 1992), 1–10.

39. Srinivas Bollapragada, Hong Cheng, Mary Phillips, Marc Garbiras, Michael Scholes, Tim Gibbs, and Mark Humphreville, "NBC's Optimization Systems Increase Revenues and Productivity," *Interfaces* 32, no. 1 (January–February 2002), 47–60.

40. Gerald Brown, Joseph Keegan, Brian Vigus, and Kevin Wood, "The Kellogg Company Optimizes Production, Inventory, and Distribution," *Interfaces* 31, no. 6 (November–December 2001), 1–15.

41. Harold J. Leavitt, "Beyond the Analytic Manager," *California Management Review* 17 (1975), 5–12; C. Jackson Grayson, Jr., "Management Science and Business Practice," *Harvard Business Review* 51 (July–August 1973), 41–48.

42. David Wessel, "A Man Who Governs Credit Is Denied a Toys 'R' Us Card," *The Wall Street Journal* (December 14, 1995), B1.

43. Richard L. Daft and John C. Wiginton, "Language and Organization," *Academy of Management Review* (1979), 179–191.

44. Based on Richard M. Cyert and James G. March, *A Behavioral Theory of the Firm* (Englewood Cliffs, N.J.: Prentice-Hall, 1963); and James G. March and Herbert A. Simon, *Organizations* (New York: Wiley, 1958).

45. William B. Stevenson, Joan L. Pearce, and Lyman W. Porter, "The Concept of 'Coalition' in Organization Theory and Research," *Academy of Management Review* 10 (1985), 256–268.

46. Cyert and March, *A Behavioral Theory of the Firm*, 120–222.

47. Ann Reilly Dowd, "How Bush Decided," *Fortune* (February 11, 1991), 45–46.

48. Pui-Wing Tam, "One for the History Books: The Tale of How Britannica Is Trying to Leap from the Old Economy Into the New One," *The Wall Street Journal* (December 11, 2000), R32; Richard A. Melcher, "Dusting Off the *Britannica*," *BusinessWeek* (October 20, 1997), 143–146.

49. Lawrence G. Hrebiniak, "Top–Management Agreement and Organizational Performance," *Human Relations* 35 (1982), 1139–1158; Richard P. Nielsen, "Toward a Method for Building Consensus during Strategic Planning," *Sloan Management Review* (Summer 1981), 29–40.

50. Based on Henry Mintzberg, Duru Raisinghani, and André Théorêt, "The Structure of 'Unstructured' Decision Processes," *Administrative Science Quarterly* 21 (1976), 246–275.

51. Lawrence T. Pinfield, "A Field Evaluation of Perspectives on Organizational Decision Making," *Administrative Science Quarterly* 31 (1986), 365–388.

52. Mintzberg *et al.* "The Structure of 'Unstructured' Decision Processes."

53. Ibid., 270.

54. William C. Symonds with Carol Matlack, "Gillette's Edge," *BusinessWeek* (January 19, 1998), 70–77; William C. Symonds, "Would You Spend $1.50 for a Razor Blade?" *BusinessWeek* (April 27, 1998), 46

55. Anna Wilde Mathews, Martin Peers, and Nick Wingfield, "Off-Key: The Music Industry Is Finally Online, But Few Listen," *The Wall Street Journal* (May 7, 2002), A1, A20.

56. Michael D. Cohen, James G. March, and Johan P. Olsen, "A Garbage Can Model of Organizational Choice," *Administrative Science Quarterly* 17 (March 1972), 1–25; Michael D. Cohen and James G. March, *Leadership and Ambiguity: The American College President* (New York: McGraw-Hill, 1974).

57. Michael Masuch and Perry LaPotin, "Beyond Garbage Cans: An AI Model of Organizational Choice," *Administrative Science Quarterly* 34 (1989), 38–67.

58. David Krouss, "Casablanca," *Sky* (November 1992), 82–91.

59. Thomas R. King, "Why 'Waterworld,' with Costner in Fins, Is Costliest Film Ever," *The Wall Street Journal* (January 31, 1995), A1.

60. Adapted from James D. Thompson, *Organizations in Action* (New York: McGraw-Hill, 1967), chap. 10; and McMillan, "Qualitative Models of Organizational Decision Making," 25.

61. Louise Lee, "Courts Begin to Award Damages to Victims of Parking-Area Crime," *The Wall Street Journal* (April 23, 1997), A1, A8.

62. Mintzberg and Wheatley, "Decision Making: It's Not What You Think."

63. Paul C. Nutt, "Selecting Decision Rules for Crucial Choices: An Investigation of the Thompson Framework," *The Journal of Applied Behavioral Science* 38, no. 1 (March 2002), 99–131; Paul C. Nutt, "Making Strategic Choices," *Journal of Management Studies* 39, no. 1 (January 2002), 67–95.

64. L. J. Bourgeois III and Kathleen M. Eisenhardt, "Strategic Decision Processes in High Velocity Environments: Four Cases in the Microcomputer Industry," *Management Science* 34 (1988), 816–835.

65. Kathleen M. Eisenhardt, "Speed and Strategic Course: How Managers Accelerate Decision Making," *California Management Review* (Spring 1990), 39–54.

66. David A. Garvin and Michael A. Roberto, "What You Don't Know About Making Decisions," *Harvard Business Review* (September 2001), 108–116.

67. Karl Weick, *The Social Psychology of Organizing*, 2d ed. (Reading, Mass.: Addison-Wesley, 1979), 243.

68. Christopher Power with Kathleen Kerwin, Ronald Grover, Keith Alexander, and Robert D. Hof, "Flops," *BusinessWeek* (August 16, 1993), 76–82.

69. Robert Townsend, *Up the Organization* (New York: Knopf, 1974), 115.

70. Helga Drummond, "Too Little Too Late: A Case Study of Escalation in Decision Making," *Organization Studies* 15, no. 4 (1994), 591–607; Joel Brockner, "The Escalation of Commitment to a Failing Course of Action: Toward Theoretical Progress," *Academy of Management Review* 17 (1992), 39–61; Barry M. Staw and Jerry Ross, "Knowing When to Pull the Plug," *Harvard Business Review* 65 (March–April 1987), 68–74; Barry M. Staw, "The Escalation of Commitment to a Course of Action," *Academy of Management Review* 6 (1981), 577–587.

71. Shona McKay, "When Good People Make Bad Choices," *Canadian Business* (February 1994), 52–55.

72. Jerry Ross and Barry M. Staw, "Organizational Escalation and Exit: Lessons from the Shoreham Nuclear Power Plant," *Academy of Management Journal* 36 (1993), 701–732.

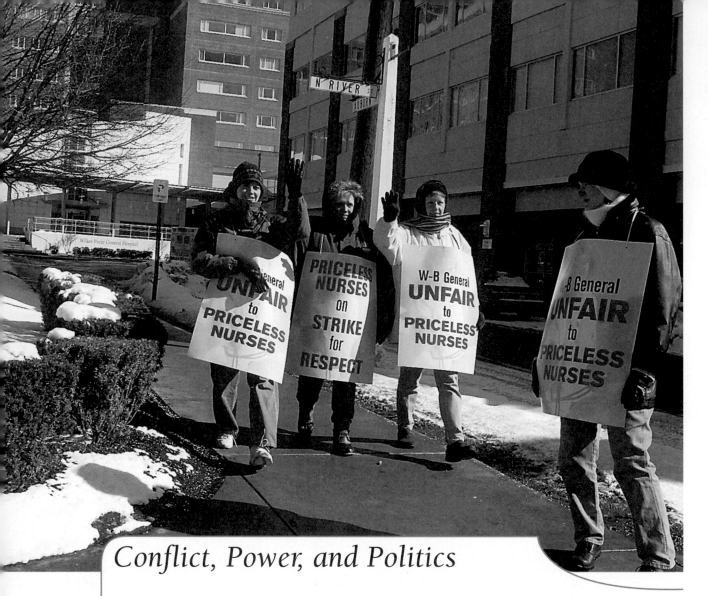

Conflict, Power, and Politics

chapter 13

Pacific Medical Center

Roger Simpson, head of the largest radiology group in the San Francisco area, had worked at Pacific Medical Center for more than fifteen years when Pacific was acquired by a huge, for-profit health care corporation. Like other health care professionals, Simpson and members of his group had long provided radiology services for other hospitals in the region, including Pacific's biggest local competitor. However, Adam Schiff, the hospital's new administrator, who came in with a goal of strengthening Pacific as a for-profit business, quickly issued an ultimatum, not only to radiologists but to pathologists and emergency room doctors as well: practice only at Pacific or leave. The new rules threw health care professionals into severe conflict with hospital administrators. The doctors saw themselves as independent practitioners, while administrators viewed doctors as part of the hospital's assets. Although many other hospital-based doctor groups eventually gave in to Schiff's demands, Simpson and his group made the decision to fight. The forty-five members of the group, five of whom practice nearly full-time at Pacific, say they have tried to hash out a compromise, but Schiff insisted that the doctors who practiced at Pacific must break off totally from the group.

The conflict between Schiff and Simpson illustrates a power struggle that is going on all over America as large, for-profit corporations take control of more and more hospitals. Traditionally, hospitals would give an exclusive contract to a radiology or pathology group in return for an agreement that the group would staff the hospital twenty-four hours a day year-round. However, doctors were also free to forge similar relationships with other hospitals and clinics, as long as they met their obligations to each one. Schiff's demands, according to Paul Ginsburg, president of the Center for Studying Health System Change, are "a reflection of the shifting market power from physicians to hospitals." While Simpson and members of his group have continued to practice at their outpatient facility and at other hospitals and clinics in addition to Pacific, the chief of physician services has made it clear that the doctors will ultimately have to make a choice.[1]

Like Pacific Medical Center, all organizations are a complex mix of individuals and groups pursuing various goals and interests. Conflict is a natural and inevitable outcome of the close interaction of people who may have diverse opinions and values, pursue different objectives, and have differential access to information and resources within the organization. Individuals and groups will use power and political activity to handle their differences and manage conflict.[2]

Too much conflict can be harmful to an organization. However, conflict can also be a positive force because it challenges the status quo, encourages new ideas and approaches, and leads to change.[3] Some degree of conflict occurs in all human relationships—between friends, romantic partners, and teammates as well as between parents and children, teachers and students, and bosses and employees. Conflict is not necessarily a negative force; it results from the normal interaction of varying human interests. Within organizations, individuals and groups frequently have different interests and goals they wish to achieve through the organization. In learning organizations, which encourage a democratic push and pull of ideas, the forces of conflict, power, and politics may be particularly evident. Managers in all organizations regularly deal with conflict and struggle with decisions about how to get the most out of employees, enhance job satisfaction and team identification, and realize high organizational performance.

PURPOSE OF THIS CHAPTER

This chapter will discuss the nature of conflict and the use of power and political tactics to manage and reduce conflict among individuals and groups. The notion of conflict has appeared in previous chapters. In Chapter 3, we talked about horizontal linkages such as task forces and teams that encourage collaboration among functional departments. Chapter 4 introduced the concept of differentiation, which means that different departments pursue different goals and may have different attitudes and values. Chapter 10 discussed the emergence of subcultures, and in Chapter 12, coalition building was proposed as one way to resolve disagreements among departments.

The first sections of this chapter explore the nature of intergroup conflict, characteristics of organizations that contribute to conflict, and the use of a political versus a rational model of organization to manage conflicting interests. Subsequent sections examine individual and organizational power, the vertical and horizontal sources of power for managers and other employees, and how power is used to attain organizational goals. The latter part of the chapter looks at politics, which is the application of power and authority to achieve desired outcomes. We will also discuss some tactics managers can use to enhance collaboration among people and departments.

INTERGROUP CONFLICT IN ORGANIZATIONS

Intergroup conflict requires three ingredients: group identification, observable group differences, and frustration. First, employees have to perceive themselves as part of an identifiable group or department.[4] Second, there has to be an observable group difference of some form. Groups may be located on different floors of the building, members may have different social or educational backgrounds, or members may work in different departments. The ability to identify oneself as a part of one group and to observe differences in comparison with other groups is necessary for conflict.[5]

The third ingredient is frustration. Frustration means that if one group achieves its goal, the other will not; it will be blocked. Frustration need not be severe and only needs to be anticipated to set off intergroup conflict. Intergroup conflict will appear when one group tries to advance its position in relation to other groups. **Intergroup conflict** can be defined as the behavior that occurs among organizational groups when participants identify with one group and perceive that other groups may block their group's goal achievement or expectations.[6] Conflict means that groups clash directly, that they are in fundamental opposition. Conflict is similar to competition but more severe. **Competition** means rivalry among groups in the pursuit of a common prize, while conflict presumes direct interference with goal achievement.

Intergroup conflict within organizations can occur horizontally across departments or vertically between different levels of the organization.[7] For example, the production department of a manufacturing company may have a dispute with quality control because new quality procedures reduce production efficiency. Teammates may argue about the best way to accomplish tasks and achieve goals. Workers may clash with bosses about new work methods, reward systems, or job assignments. Another typical area of conflict is between groups such as unions and management or franchise owners and headquarters. Franchise owners for McDonald's, Taco Bell, Burger King, and KFC have clashed with headquarters because of the increase of company-owned stores in neighborhoods that compete directly with franchisees.[8] The Communication Workers of America local recently fought with Verizon Communications over issues such as wage increases and working hours, ultimately forcing the company to limit mandatory overtime.[9]

Conflict can also occur between different divisions or business units within an organization, such as between the auditing and consulting units of big firms such as PriceWaterhouseCoopers and Deloitte Touche.[10] In global organizations, conflicts between regional managers and business division managers, among different divisions, or between divisions and headquarters are common because of the complexities of international business, as described in Chapter 6.

SOURCES OF CONFLICT

Some specific organizational characteristics can generate conflict. These **sources of intergroup conflict** are goal incompatibility, differentiation, task interdependence, and limited resources. These characteristics of organizational relationships are determined by the contextual factors of environment, size, technology, strategy and goals, and organizational structure, which have been discussed in previous chapters. These characteristics, in turn, help shape the extent to which a rational model of behavior versus a political model of behavior is used to accomplish objectives.

Goal Incompatibility. Goal incompatibility is probably the greatest cause of intergroup conflict in organizations.[11] The goals of each department reflect the specific objectives members are trying to achieve. The achievement of one department's goals often interferes with another department's goals. University police, for example, have a goal of providing a safe and secure campus. They can achieve their goal by locking all buildings on evenings and weekends and not distributing keys. Without easy access to buildings, however, progress toward the science department's research goals will proceed slowly. On the other hand, if scientists come and go at all hours and security is ignored, police goals for security will not be met. Goal incompatibility throws the departments into conflict with each other.

The potential for conflict is perhaps greater between marketing and manufacturing than between other departments because the goals of these two departments are frequently at odds. Exhibit 13.1 shows examples of goal conflict between typical marketing and manufacturing departments. Marketing strives to increase the breadth of the product line to meet customer tastes for variety. A broad product line means short production runs, so manufacturing has to bear higher costs.[12] Other areas of goal conflict are quality, cost control, and new products. Goal incompatibility exists among departments in most organizations.

EXHIBIT I 3. I   *Marketing-Manufacturing Areas of Potential Goal Conflict*

Goal Conflict	MARKETING versus Operative goal is customer satisfaction	MANUFACTURING Operative goal is production efficiency
Conflict Area	**Typical Comment**	**Typical Comment**
1. Breadth of product line	"Our customers demand variety."	"The product line is too broad—all we get are short, uneconomical runs."
2. New product introduction	"New products are our lifeblood."	"Unnecessary design changes are prohibitively expensive."
3. Product scheduling	"We need faster response. Our lead times are too long."	"We need realistic customer commitments that don't change like wind direction."
4. Physical distribution	"Why don't we ever have the right merchandise in inventory?"	"We can't afford to keep huge inventories."
5. Quality	"Why can't we have reasonable quality at lower cost?"	"Why must we always offer options that are too expensive and offer little customer utility?"

Source: Based on Benson S. Shapiro, "Can Marketing and Manufacturing Coexist?" *Harvard Business Review* 55 (September–October 1977), 104–114; and Victoria L. Crittenden, Lorraine R. Gardiner, and Antonie Stam, "Reducing Conflict Between Marketing and Manufacturing," *Industrial Marketing Management* 22 (1993), 299–309.

Differentiation.   Differentiation was defined in Chapter 4 as "the differences in cognitive and emotional orientations among managers in different functional departments." Functional specialization requires people with specific education, skills, attitudes, and time horizons. For example, people may join a sales department because they have ability and aptitude consistent with sales work. After becoming members of the sales department, they are influenced by departmental norms and values.

Departments or divisions within an organization often differ in values, attitudes, and standards of behavior, and these subcultural differences lead to conflicts.[13] Consider an encounter between a sales manager and an R&D scientist about a new product:

> The sales manager may be outgoing and concerned with maintaining a warm, friendly relationship with the scientist. He may be put off because the scientist seems withdrawn and disinclined to talk about anything other than the problems in which he is interested. He may also be annoyed that the scientist seems to have such freedom in choosing what he will work on. Furthermore, the scientist is probably often late for appointments, which, from the salesman's point of view, is no way to run a business. Our scientist, for his part, may feel uncomfortable because the salesman seems to be pressing for immediate answers to technical questions that will take a long time to investigate. All the discomforts are concrete manifestations of the relatively wide differences between these two men in respect to their working and thinking styles. . . .[14]

A lack of trust within the organization can magnify these natural differences and increase the potential for conflict among departments and with top managers, as the new CEO of Advanced Cardiovascular Systems discovered. Her solution was to build a new culture of honesty, as discussed in this chapter's Leading by Design.

Task Interdependence.   Task interdependence refers to the dependence of one unit on another for materials, resources, or information. As described in Chapter 7 on technology, pooled interdependence means little interaction; sequential interdependence means the output of one department goes to the next department; and reciprocal interdependence means departments mutually exchange materials and information.[15]

Generally, as interdependence increases, the potential for conflict increases.[16] In the case of pooled interdependence, units have little need to interact. Conflict is at a minimum. Sequential and reciprocal interdependence require employees to spend time coordinating and sharing information. Employees must communicate frequently, and differences in goals or attitudes will surface. Conflict is especially likely to occur when agreement is not reached about the

LEADING BY DESIGN   *Advanced Cardiovascular Systems (ACS)*

Advanced Cardiovascular Systems (now Guidant Corporation) was the darling of the medical devices industry. The company, owned by pharmaceutical giant Eli Lilly, reached $100 million in sales within five years of launching its first product and revolutionized the field of angioplasty by producing one innovation after another. But when Ginger Graham took over as president and CEO of the medical device manufacturer, she realized that something was terribly wrong. Even though top managers were still touting ACS's strong internal and external relationships as key to the company's success, the reality was that these relationships were increasingly marked by conflict and discord rather than harmony and cooperation.

When Graham gave her first address to the company, she decided to tell the truth: "I've always heard about what a wonderful company ACS is," she began, "but frankly, that's not what I see. What I see is deteriorating morale, disillusioned customers, and finger-pointing. I see a place where R&D and manufacturing are practically at war. You folks in sales blame manufacturing. R&D blames marketing. We're all so busy blaming each other that nothing gets done." The response of employees—standing and cheering their approval—confirmed Graham's suspicions. People just wanted to hear that someone at the top knew the truth and was willing to admit it. From that moment, Graham began building a culture at ACS where everyone feels free to tell the truth without fear of negative consequences.

ACS has established a number of practices that foster open and honest communications. To start, Graham reversed the top-down communication structure in an immediately visible way. Each top manager was assigned a coach from lower ranks of the organization. The coaches were trained to ask questions and gather specific information from everyone throughout the organization about the manager's openness and honest communication skills. Managers met with their coaches once a quarter. Because it had support from the top, the coaching program worked to close the communication gap between managers and employees. Managers also began sharing all information with employees—good and bad—and asking for their help in solving company problems. Employees who went above and beyond the call of duty to meet organizational goals were recognized and rewarded.

Rallying everyone around company goals rather than departmental goals helped alleviate much of the tension and conflict between departments. The war between R&D and manufacturing, however, had become so entrenched that stronger methods were needed. Even though it cost the company dearly, Graham shut down product development altogether while representatives from R&D, manufacturing, clinical, and marketing worked with a professional facilitator to confront the issues head-on and come up with a new approach to product development. The process meant that no new products went out the door for eighteen months, but the results were worth it. The company now repeatedly launches innovative new products every year, can produce enough to supply the entire market in a matter of weeks, completes clinical studies in record-setting time, and has improved quality while cutting costs.

Source: Ginger L. Graham, "If You Want Honesty, Break Some Rules," *Harvard Business Review* (April 2002), 42–47.

coordination of services to each other. Greater interdependence means departments often exert pressure for a fast response because departmental work has to wait on other departments.[17]

Limited Resources. Another major source of conflict involves competition between groups for what members perceive as limited resources.[18] Organizations have limited money, physical facilities, staff resources, and human resources to share among departments. In their desire to achieve goals, groups want to increase their resources. This throws them into conflict. Managers may develop strategies, such as inflating budget requirements or working behind the scenes, to obtain a desired level of resources. Resources also symbolize power and influence within an organization. The ability to obtain resources enhances prestige. Departments typically believe they have a legitimate claim on additional resources. However, exercising that claim results in conflict. For example, in almost every organization, conflict occurs during the annual budget exercise, often creating political activity.

RATIONAL VERSUS POLITICAL MODEL

The sources of intergroup conflict are listed in Exhibit 13.2. The degree of goal incompatibility, differentiation, interdependence, and conflict over limited resources determines whether a rational or political model of behavior is used within the organization to accomplish goals. When goals are in alignment, there is little differentiation, departments are characterized by pooled interdependence, and resources seem abundant, managers can use a **rational model** of organization, as outlined in Exhibit 13.2. As with the rational approach to decision making described in Chapter 12, the rational model of organization is an ideal that is not fully achievable in the real world, though managers strive to use rational processes whenever possible. In the rational organization, behavior is not random or accidental. Goals are clear and choices are made in a logical way. When a decision is needed, the goal is defined, alternatives are identified, and the choice with the

EXHIBIT 13.2   *Sources of Conflict and Use of Rational Versus Political Model*

Sources of Potential Intergroup Conflict	When Conflict is Low, Rational Model Describes Organization		When Conflict is High, Political Model Describes Organization
• Goal incompatibility • Differentiation • Task interdependence • Limited resources	Consistent across participants	Goals	Inconsistent, pluralistic within the organization
	Centralized	Power and control	Decentralized, shifting coalitions and interest groups
	Orderly, logical, rational	Decision process	Disorderly, result of bargaining and interplay among interests
	Norm of efficiency	Rules and norms	Free play of market forces; conflict is legitimate and expected
	Extensive, systematic, accurate	Information	Ambiguous; information used and withheld strategically

highest probability of success is selected. The rational model is also characterized by centralized power and control, extensive information systems, and an efficiency orientation.[19] The opposite view of organizational processes is the **political model**, also described in Exhibit 13.2. When differences are great, organization groups have separate interests, goals, and values. Disagreement and conflict are normal, so power and influence are needed to reach decisions. Groups will engage in the push and pull of debate to decide goals and reach decisions. Information is ambiguous and incomplete. The political model particularly describes organizations that strive for democracy and participation in decision making by empowering workers. Purely rational procedures do not work in democratic organizations, such as learning organizations.

Both rational and political processes are normally used in organizations. In most organizations, neither the rational model nor the political model characterizes things fully, but each will be used some of the time. Managers may strive to adopt rational procedures but will find that politics is needed to accomplish objectives. The political model means managers learn to acquire, develop, and use power to accomplish objectives.

POWER AND ORGANIZATIONS

Power is an intangible force in organizations. It cannot be seen, but its effect can be felt. Power is often defined as the potential ability of one person (or department) to influence other persons (or departments) to carry out orders[20] or to do something they would not otherwise have done.[21] Other definitions stress that power is the ability to achieve goals or outcomes that power holders desire.[22] The achievement of desired outcomes is the basis of the definition used here: **Power is the ability** of one person or department in an organization to influence other people to bring about desired outcomes. It is the potential to influence others within the organization but with the goal of attaining desired outcomes for power holders.

Power exists only in a relationship between two or more people, and it can be exercised in either vertical or horizontal directions. The source of power often derives from an exchange relationship in which one position or department provides scarce or valued resources to other departments. When one person is dependent on another person, a power relationship emerges in which the person with the resources has greater power.[23] When power exists in a relationship, the power holders can achieve compliance with their requests. Powerful individuals are often able to get bigger budgets for their departments, more favorable production schedules, and more control over the organization's agenda.[24]

INDIVIDUAL VERSUS ORGANIZATIONAL POWER

In popular literature, power is often described as a personal characteristic, and a frequent topic is how one person can influence or dominate another person.[25] You probably recall from an earlier management or organizational behavior course that managers have five sources of personal power.[26] *Legitimate power* is the authority granted by the organization to the formal management position a manager holds. *Reward power* stems from the ability to bestow rewards—promotion, raise, pat on the back—to other people. The authority to punish or recommend punishment is called *coercive power*. *Expert power* derives from a person's greater skill or knowledge about the tasks being performed. The last one, *referent power*, derives from personal characteristics such that people admire the manager and want to be like or identify with the manager out of respect and admiration. Each of these sources may be used by individuals within organizations.

Power in organizations, however, is often the result of structural characteristics.[27] Organizations are large, complex systems that contain hundreds, even thousands, of people. These systems have a formal hierarchy in which some tasks are more important regardless of who performs them. In addition, some positions have access to greater resources, or their contribution to the organization is more critical. Thus, the important power processes in organizations reflect larger organizational relationships, both horizontal and vertical, and organizational power usually is vested in the position, not in the person.

POWER VERSUS AUTHORITY

Anyone in an organization can exercise power to achieve desired outcomes. In 1994, when the Discovery Channel wanted to extend its brand beyond cable television, Tom Hicks began pushing for a focus on the emerging Internet. Even though Discovery's CEO favored exploring interactive television, Hicks organized a grassroots campaign that eventually persuaded the CEO to focus instead on Web publishing, indicating that Hicks had power within the organization. Today, Hicks runs Discovery Channel Online.[28]

The concept of formal authority is related to power but is narrower in scope. **Authority** is also a force for achieving desired outcomes, but only as prescribed by the formal hierarchy and reporting relationships. Three properties identify authority:

1. *Authority is vested in organizational positions*. People have authority because of the positions they hold, not because of personal characteristics or resources.
2. *Authority is accepted by subordinates*. Subordinates comply because they believe position holders have a legitimate right to exercise authority.[29] In most North American organizations, employees accept that supervisors can legitimately tell them what time to arrive at work, the tasks to perform while they're there, and what time they can go home.
3. *Authority flows down the vertical hierarchy*.[30] Authority exists along the formal chain of command, and positions at the top of the hierarchy are vested with more formal authority than are positions at the bottom.

Organizational power can be exercised upward, downward, and horizontally in organizations. Formal authority is exercised downward along the hierarchy and is the same as vertical power and legitimate power. In the following sections, we will examine vertical and horizontal sources of power for employees throughout the organization.

VERTICAL SOURCES OF POWER

All employees along the vertical hierarchy have access to some sources of power. Although a large amount of power is typically allocated to top managers by the organization structure, employees throughout the organization often obtain power disproportionate to their formal positions and can exert influence in an upward direction, as Tom Hicks did at the Discovery Channel. There are four major sources of vertical power: formal position, resources, control of decision premises and information, and network centrality.[31]

Formal Position. Certain rights, responsibilities, and prerogatives accrue to top positions. People throughout the organization accept the legitimate right of top managers to set goals, make decisions, and direct activities. Thus, the power from formal position is sometimes called legitimate power.[32] Senior managers often use symbols and language to perpetuate their legitimate power. For example, Adam Schiff, administrator of Pacific Medical Center, described in the chapter opening, symbolized his formal power by issuing a newsletter with his photo on the cover and airing a 24-hour-a-day video to welcome patients and announce that "we don't waste dollars."

The amount of power provided to middle managers and lower-level participants can be built into the organization's structural design. The allocation of power to middle managers and staff is important because power enables employees to be productive. When job tasks are nonroutine, and when employees participate in self-directed teams and problem-solving task forces, this encourages employees to be flexible and creative and to use their own discretion. Allowing people to make their own decisions increases their power. Power is also increased when a position encourages contact with high-level people. Access to powerful people and the development of a relationship with them provide a strong base of influence.[33] For example, in some organizations a secretary to the vice president has more power than a department head because the secretary has access to the senior executive on a daily basis.

The logic of designing positions for more power assumes that an organization does not have a limited amount of power to be allocated among high-level and low-level employees. The total amount of power in an organization can be increased by designing tasks and interactions along the hierarchy so everyone has more influence. If the distribution of power is skewed too heavily toward the top, research suggests the organization will be less effective.[34]

Resources. Organizations allocate huge amounts of resources. Buildings are constructed, salaries are paid, and equipment and supplies are purchased. Each year, new resources are allocated in the form of budgets. These resources are allocated downward from top managers. Top managers often own stock, which gives them property rights over resource allocation. However, in many of today's organizations, employees throughout the organization also share in ownership, which increases their power.

In most cases, top managers control the resources and, hence, can determine their distribution. Resources can be used as rewards and punishments, which are additional sources of power. Resource allocation also creates a dependency relationship. Lower-level participants depend on top managers for the financial and physical resources needed to perform their tasks. Top management can exchange resources in the form of salaries and bonuses, personnel, promotion, and physical facilities for compliance with the outcomes they desire. Throughout the 1990s, the power of employees over top management grew because of the tight labor market and booming economy. Managers offered high salaries, attractive bonuses, and employee-friendly work environments to retain experienced employees who had many options in the job market. Today, however, the situation has reversed. "You can't get an extra $10,000 because you breathed last year," says Scott Turicchi, executive vice president of J2 Global Communications. Today, J2 and many other companies are tying bonuses closely to goal accomplishment at all levels of the organization.[35]

Control of Decision Premises and Information. Control of **decision premises** means that top managers place constraints on decisions made at lower levels by specifying a decision frame of reference and guidelines. In one sense, top managers make big decisions, whereas lower-level participants make small decisions. Top management decides which goal an organization will try to achieve, such as increased market share. Lower-level participants then decide how the goal is to be reached. In one company, top management appointed a committee to select a new marketing vice president. The CEO provided the committee with detailed qualifications that the new vice president should have. He also selected people to serve on the committee. In this way, the CEO shaped the decision premises within which the marketing vice president would be chosen. Top manager actions and decisions such as these place limits on the decisions of lower-level managers and thereby influence the outcome of their decisions.[36]

The control of information can also be a source of power. Managers in today's organizations recognize that information is a primary business resource and that by controlling what information is collected, how it is interpreted, and how it is shared, they can influence how decisions are made.[37] In many of today's companies, especially in learning organizations, information is openly and broadly shared, which increases the power of people throughout the organization.

However, top managers generally have access to more information than do other employees. This information can be released as needed to shape the decision outcomes of other people. In one organization, Clark, Ltd., the senior information technology manager controlled information given to the board of directors and thereby influenced the board's decision to purchase a large server and computer system.[38] The board of directors had formal authority to decide from which company the system would be purchased. The management services group was asked to recommend which of six computer manufacturers should receive the order. Jim Kenny was in charge of the management services group, and Kenny disagreed with other managers about which system to purchase. As shown in Exhibit 13.3, other managers had to go through Kenny to have their viewpoints heard by the board. Kenny shaped the board's thinking toward selecting the system he preferred by controlling information given to them.

Middle managers and lower-level employees may also have access to information that can increase their power. A secretary to a senior executive can often control information that other people want and will thus be able to influence those people. Top executives depend on people throughout the organization for information about problems or opportunities. Middle managers or lower-level employees may manipulate the information they provide to top managers in order to influence decision outcomes.

Network Centrality. **Network centrality** means being centrally located in the organization and having access to information and people that are critical to the company's success. Top executives often increase their power by surrounding themselves with a network of loyal subordinates and using the network to learn about events throughout the organization.[39] They can use their central positions to build alliances and wield substantial power in the organization. The following In Practice illustrates a successful power play that followed the merger of Morgan Stanley and Dean Witter, where the Dean Witter boss gained complete power over the newly merged firm by surrounding himself with loyal allies and edging out his Morgan Stanley counterpart.

EXHIBIT 13.3   *Information Flow for Computer Decision at Clark, Ltd.*

Source: Andrew M. Pettigrew, *The Politics of Organizational Decision-Making* (London: Tavistock, 1973), 235, with permission.

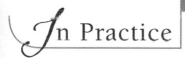

MORGAN STANLEY DEAN WITTER

The merger of Morgan Stanley and Dean Witter was one that both sides wanted badly. Morgan Stanley, with a list of blue-chip clients stretching back to the nineteenth century, yearned for a retail brokerage network, while retail brokerage firm Dean Witter needed an image makeover that Morgan could provide. As negotiations drew to an end, Dean Witter's long-time head, Philip Purcell, argued that since his firm was technically the acquirer in the deal, it was only right that the first CEO come from Dean Witter. Morgan's heir apparent, John Mack, who was well liked and respected in the industry, agreed to the terms, saying the merger was too important to make an issue over the top job.

Morgan's then-CEO and chairman, Richard Fisher, cautioned Mack to guard against losing too much power to Purcell, and the three hammered out an informal arrangement whereby Purcell would run the company for approximately five years and then Mack would succeed him. But the Morgan managers soon began to suspect that Purcell was out to gain all the power for himself. He quickly installed trusted Dean Witter veterans in key positions and often supported them over higher-level Morgan managers. Mack was put in charge of the core retail brokerage business, with the former head of the unit, James Higgins, reporting to him. However, Higgins continued to deal directly with Purcell, and the two successfully resisted any efforts Mack made for change in the business. Purcell gradually shifted more and more aspects of the business away from Mack and to his trusted aides. Frustrated, Mack launched a campaign to have himself named co-CEO, but the balance of power had already swung too far toward Purcell. A series of departures from the board, including Mack's biggest supporter, Richard Fisher, allowed Purcell to appoint new directors who were loyal to him and would support his proposals for management changes over those of Mack.

Defeated at every turn, Mack announced he was leaving, perhaps in a desperate move to work out an arrangement whereby he would have greater power. Instead, Purcell urged that they work out the details of the resignation as quickly as possible. When the dust settled at Morgan Stanley Dean Witter, Phillip Purcell had gained complete control of the firm, with all core operations reporting directly to him. Mack gave a short departure speech to the staff and, after a standing ovation, he was gone.[40]

By surrounding himself with trusted allies within the firm and on the board, Purcell developed sufficient network centrality to gradually push his rival for the top job out of the firm. Middle managers and lower-level employees can also use the ideas of network centrality. For example, several years ago at Xerox, Cindy Casselman, who had little formal power and authority, began selling her idea for an intranet site to managers all over the company. Working behind the scenes, Casselman gradually gained the power she needed to make her vision a reality— and win a promotion.[41]

Employees also have more power when their jobs are related to current areas of concern or opportunity. When a job pertains to pressing organizational problems, power is more easily accumulated. For example, managers at all levels who possess crisis leadership skills are gaining more power in today's world of terrorist attacks, anthrax scares, and general uncertainty. Managers and employees who stepped in to quickly solve problems in the wake of the September 11, 2001, attacks on the World Trade Center have increased their power within the organization. A communications manager at Empire Blue Cross and Blue Shield, for instance, acted on his own, working around the clock to get phone lines and voice mail restored.[42]

Employees increase their network centrality by becoming knowledgeable and expert about certain activities or by taking on difficult tasks and acquiring specialized knowledge that makes them indispensable to managers above them. People who show initiative, work beyond what is expected, take on undesirable but important projects, and show interest in learning about the company and industry often find themselves with influence. Physical location also helps because some locations are in the center of things. Central location lets a person be visible to key people and become part of important interaction networks.

HORIZONTAL SOURCES OF POWER

Horizontal power pertains to relationships across departments. All vice presidents are usually at the same level on the organization chart. Does this mean each department has the same amount of power? No. Horizontal power is not defined by the formal hierarchy or the organization chart. Each department makes a unique contribution to organizational success. Some departments will have greater say and will achieve their desired outcomes, whereas others will not. For example, Charles Perrow surveyed managers in several industrial firms.[43] He bluntly asked, "Which department has the most power?" among four major departments: production, sales and marketing, research and development, and finance and accounting. Partial survey results are given in Exhibit 13.4. In most firms, sales had the greatest power. In a few firms, production was also quite powerful. On average, the sales and production departments were more powerful than R&D and finance, although substantial variation existed. Differences in the amount of horizontal power clearly occurred in those firms. Today, information technology departments have growing power in many organizations.

EXHIBIT 13.4   *Ratings of Power Among Departments in Industrial Firms*

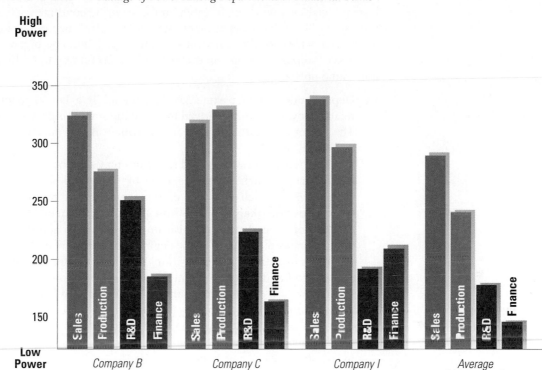

Source: Charles Perrow, "Departmental Power and Perspective in Industrial Firms," in Mayer N. Zald, ed., *Power in Organizations* (Nashville, Tenn.: Vanderbilt University Press, 1970), 64.

Horizontal power is difficult to measure because power differences are not defined on the organization chart. However, some initial explanations for departmental power differences, such as those shown in Exhibit 13.4, have been found. The theoretical concept that explains relative power is called strategic contingencies.[44]

Strategic Contingencies. **Strategic contingencies** are events and activities both inside and outside an organization that are essential for attaining organizational goals. Departments involved with strategic contingencies for the organization tend to have greater power. Departmental activities are important when they provide strategic value by solving problems or crises for the organization. For example, if an organization faces an intense threat from lawsuits and regulations, the legal department will gain power and influence over organizational decisions because it copes with such a threat. If product innovation is the key strategic issue, the power of R&D can be expected to be high.

The strategic contingency approach to power is similar to the resource dependence model described in Chapters 4 and 5. Recall that organizations try to reduce dependency on the external environment. The strategic contingency approach to power suggests that the departments most responsible for dealing with key resource issues and dependencies in the environment will become most powerful.

Power Sources. Jeffrey Pfeffer and Gerald Salancik, among others, have been instrumental in conducting research on the strategic contingency theory.[45] Their findings indicate that a department rated as powerful may possess one or more of the characteristics illustrated in Exhibit 13.5.[46] In some organizations these five **power sources** overlap, but each provides a useful way to evaluate sources of horizontal power.

1. **Dependency**. Interdepartmental dependency is a key element underlying relative power. Power is derived from having something someone else wants. The power of department A over department B is greater when department B depends on A.[47]

   Materials, information, and resources may flow between departments in one direction, such as in the case of sequential task interdependence (Chapter 7). In such cases, the department receiving resources is in a lower power position than the department providing them. The number and strength of dependencies are also important. When seven or eight departments must come for help to the engineering department, for example, engineering is in a strong power position. In contrast, a department that depends on many other departments is in a low power position.

   Likewise, a department in an otherwise low power position might gain power through dependencies. If a factory cannot produce without the expertise of maintenance workers to keep the machines working, the maintenance department is in a strong power position because they have control over a strategic contingency.

EXHIBIT 13.5   *Strategic Contingencies That Influence Horizontal Power Among Departments*

2. **Financial resources**. There's a new golden rule in the business world: "The person with the gold makes the rules."[48] Control over resources is an important source of power in organizations. Money can be converted into other kinds of resources that are needed by other departments. Money generates dependency; departments that provide financial resources have something other departments want. Departments that generate income for an organization have greater power. Exhibit 13.4 showed sales as the most powerful unit in most industrial firms. This is because salespeople find customers and bring in money, thereby removing an important problem for the organization. An ability to provide financial resources also explains why certain departments are powerful in other organizations, such as universities.

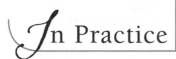

UNIVERSITY OF ILLINOIS

You might expect budget allocation in a state university to be a straightforward process. The need for financial resources can be determined by such things as the number of undergraduate students, the number of graduate students, and the number of faculty in each department.

In fact, resource allocation at the University of Illinois is not clear-cut. The University of Illinois has a relatively fixed resource inflow from state government. Beyond that, important resources come from research grants and the quality of students and faculty. University departments that provide the most resources to the university are rated as having the most power. Some departments have more power because of their resource contribution to the university. Departments that generate large research grants are more powerful because research grants contain a sizable overhead payment to university administration. This overhead money pays for a large share of the university's personnel and facilities. The size of a department's graduate student body and the national prestige of the department also add to power. Graduate students and national prestige are nonfinancial resources that add to the reputation and effectiveness of the university.

How do university departments use their power? Generally, they use it to obtain even more resources from the rest of the university. Very powerful departments receive university resources, such as graduate student fellowships, internal research support, and summer faculty salaries, far in excess of their needs based on the number of students and faculty.[49]

As shown in the example of the University of Illinois, power accrues to departments that bring in or provide resources that are highly valued by an organization. Power enables those departments to obtain more of the scarce resources allocated within the organization. "Power derived from acquiring resources is used to obtain more resources, which in turn can be employed to produce more power—the rich get richer."[50]

3. **Centrality**. Centrality reflects a department's role in the primary activity of an organization.[51] One measure of centrality is the extent to which the work of the department affects the final output of the organization. For example, the production department is more central and usually has more power than staff groups (assuming no other critical contingencies). Centrality is associated with power because it reflects the contribution made to the organization. The corporate finance department of an investment bank generally has more power than the stock research department. By contrast, in the manufacturing firms described in Exhibit 13.4, finance tends to be low in power. When the finance department has the limited task of recording money and

expenditures, it is not responsible for obtaining critical resources or for producing the products of the organization.

√ 4. **Nonsubstitutability.** Power is also determined by nonsubstitutability, which means that a department's function cannot be performed by other readily available resources. If an employee cannot be easily replaced, his or her power is greater. If an organization has no alternative sources of skill and information, a department's power will be greater. This can be the case when management uses outside consultants. Consultants might be used as substitutes for staff people to reduce the power of staff groups.

The impact of substitutability on power was studied for programmers in computer departments.[52] When computers were first introduced, programming was a rare and specialized occupation. Programmers controlled the use of organizational computers because they alone possessed the knowledge to program them. Over a period of about ten years, computer programming became a more common activity. People could be substituted easily, and the power of programming departments dropped.

√ 5. **Coping with Uncertainty.** Elements in the environment can change swiftly and can be unpredictable and complex. In the face of uncertainty, little information is available to managers on appropriate courses of action. Departments that reduce this uncertainty for the organization will increase their power.[53] When market research personnel accurately predict changes in demand for new products, they gain power and prestige because they have reduced a critical uncertainty. But forecasting is only one technique. Sometimes uncertainty can be reduced by taking quick and appropriate action after an unpredictable event occurs.

Departments can cope with critical uncertainties by (1) obtaining prior information, (2) prevention, and (3) absorption.[54] *Obtaining prior information* means a department can reduce an organization's uncertainty by forecasting an event. Departments increase their power through *prevention* by predicting and forestalling negative events. *Absorption* occurs when a department takes action after an event to reduce its negative consequences. In the following case, the industrial relations department increased its power by absorbing a critical uncertainty. It took action after the event to reduce uncertainty for the organization.

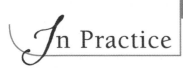

CRYSTAL MANUFACTURING

Although union influence has been declining in recent years, unions are still actively seeking to extend their membership to new organizations. A new union is a crucial source of uncertainty for many manufacturing firms. It can be a countervailing power to management in decisions concerning wages and working conditions.

In 1998, the workers in Crystal Manufacturing Company voted to become part of the Glassmakers Craft Union. Management had been aware of union organizing activities, but it had not taken the threat seriously. No one had acted to forecast or prevent the formation of a union.

The presence of the union had potentially serious consequences for Crystal. Glassmaking is a delicate and expensive manufacturing process. The float-glass process cannot be shut down even temporarily except at great expense. A strike or walkout would mean financial disaster. Therefore, top management decided that establishing a good working relationship with the union was critically important.

The industrial relations department was assigned to deal with the union. This department was responsible for coping with the uncertainties created by the new union. The industrial relations group quickly developed expertise in union relationships. It became the contact point on industrial relations matters for managers throughout the organization. Industrial relations members developed a network throughout the organization and could bypass the normal chain of command on issues they considered important. Industrial relations had nearly absolute knowledge and control over union relations.

In Crystal Manufacturing Company, the industrial relations unit coped with the critical uncertainty by absorption. It took action to reduce the uncertainty after it appeared. This action gave the unit increased power.

Horizontal power relationships in organizations change as strategic contingencies change. For example, in recent years, giant retailers such as Wal-Mart and Winn-Dixie have created new problems for magazine publishers by refusing to sell issues that contain cover photos or stories that might be objectionable to some customers. Some magazine publishers have agreed to provide advance copies so retailers can spot controversial material ahead of time and decline the issue. "If you don't let them know in advance," one circulation director said, "they will delist the title and never carry it again." These demands from powerful retailers are creating new uncertainties and strategic issues for magazine publishers such as Hearst Corp., Miller Publishing Group, and AOL Time Warner.[55] For their part, large retailers attempting to build new stores are facing fresh challenges from community activists fighting urban sprawl. Wal-Mart managers estimate that activists block at least two or three new stores a year.[56] Departments that help organizations cope with these new strategic issues will have greater power.

POLITICAL PROCESSES IN ORGANIZATIONS

Politics, like power, is intangible and difficult to measure. It is hidden from view and is hard to observe in a systematic way. Two surveys uncovered the following reactions of managers toward political behavior.[57]

1. Most managers have a negative view toward politics and believe that politics will more often hurt than help an organization in achieving its goals.
2. Managers believe political behavior is common to practically all organizations.
3. Most managers think political behavior occurs more often at upper rather than lower levels in organizations.
4. Political behavior arises in certain decision domains, such as structural change, but is absent from other decisions, such as handling employee grievances.

Based on these surveys, politics seems more likely to occur at the top levels of an organization and around certain issues and decisions. Moreover, managers do not approve of political behavior. The remainder of this chapter explores more fully what is political behavior, when it should be used, the type of issues and decisions most likely to be associated with politics, and some political tactics that may be effective.

DEFINITION

Power has been described as the available force or potential for achieving desired outcomes. *Politics* is the use of power to influence decisions in order to achieve those outcomes. The exercise of power and influence has led to two ways to define politics—as self-serving behavior or as a natural organizational decision process. The first definition emphasizes that politics is self-serving and involves activities that are not sanctioned by the organization.[58]

In this view, politics involves deception and dishonesty for purposes of individual self-interest and leads to conflict and disharmony within the work environment. This dark view of politics is widely held by laypeople. Recent studies have shown that workers who perceive this kind of political activity at work within their companies often have related feelings of anxiety and job dissatisfaction. Studies also support the belief that inappropriate use of politics is related to low employee morale, inferior organizational performance, and poor decision making.[59] This view of politics explains why managers in the surveys described above did not approve of political behavior.

Although politics can be used in a negative, self-serving way, the appropriate use of political behavior can serve organizational goals.[60] The second view sees politics as a natural organizational process for resolving differences among organizational interest groups.[61] Politics is the process of bargaining and negotiation that is used to overcome conflicts and differences of opinion. In this view, politics is similar to the coalition-building decision processes defined in Chapter 12 on decision making.

The organization theory perspective views politics as described in the second definition—as a normal decision-making process. Politics is simply the activity through which power is exercised in the resolution of conflicts and uncertainty. Politics is neutral and is not necessarily harmful to the organization. The formal definition of organizational politics is as follows: **organizational politics** involves activities to acquire, develop, and use power and other resources to obtain the preferred outcome when there is uncertainty or disagreement about choices.[62]

Political behavior can be either a positive or a negative force. Politics is the use of power to get things accomplished—good things as well as bad. Uncertainty and conflict are natural and inevitable, and politics is the mechanism for reaching agreement. Politics includes informal discussions that enable participants to arrive at consensus and make decisions that otherwise might be stalemated or unsolvable.

WHEN IS POLITICAL ACTIVITY USED?

Politics is a mechanism for arriving at consensus when uncertainty is high and there is disagreement over goals or problem priorities. Recall the rational versus political models described in Exhibit 13.2. The political model is associated with conflict over goals, shifting coalitions and interest groups, ambiguous information, and uncertainty. Thus, political activity tends to be most visible when managers confront nonprogrammed decisions, as discussed in Chapter 12, and is related to the Carnegie model of decision making. Because managers at the top of an organization generally deal with more nonprogrammed decisions than do managers at lower levels, more political activity will appear. Moreover, some issues are associated with inherent disagreement. Resources, for example, are critical for the survival and effectiveness of departments, so resource allocation often becomes a

BRIEFCASE

As an organization manager, keep this guideline in mind:

Expect and allow for political behavior in organizations. Politics provides the discussion and clash of interests needed to crystallize points of view and to reach a decision. Build coalitions, expand networks, control decision premises, enhance legitimacy, and make a direct appeal to attain desired outcomes.

political issue. Rational methods of allocation do not satisfy participants. Three **domains of political activity** (areas in which politics plays a role) in most organizations are structural change, management succession, and resource allocation.

Structural reorganizations strike at the heart of power and authority relationships. Reorganizations such as those discussed in Chapter 3 change responsibilities and tasks, which also affects the underlying power base from strategic contingencies. For these reasons, a major reorganization can lead to an explosion of political activity.[63] Managers may actively bargain and negotiate to maintain the responsibilities and power bases they have. Mergers and acquisitions also frequently create tremendous political activity. The acquisition by Hewlett-Packard of Compaq Computer is a prime example. The political battle between Walter Hewlett, an H-P cofounder's son who opposed the acquisition, and H-P CEO Carly Fiorina brought brass-knuckle campaign politics to Wall Street. The two sides established "war rooms," deployed rapid response units, set up Web sites run by online political consulting firms, and spent tens of millions of dollars on advertisements to woo shareholders to their respective points of view.[64]

Organizational changes such as hiring new executives, promotions, and transfers have great political significance, particularly at top organizational levels where uncertainty is high and networks of trust, cooperation, and communication among executives are important.[65] Hiring decisions can generate uncertainty, discussion, and disagreement. Managers can use hiring and promotion to strengthen network alliances and coalitions by putting their own people in prominent positions.

The third area of political activity is resource allocation. Resource allocation decisions encompass all resources required for organizational performance, including salaries, operating budgets, employees, office facilities, equipment, use of the company airplane, and so forth. Resources are so vital that disagreement about priorities exists, and political processes help resolve the dilemmas.

USING POWER, POLITICS, AND COLLABORATION

One theme in this chapter has been that power in organizations is not primarily a phenomenon of the individual. It is related to the resources departments command, the role departments play in an organization, and the environmental contingencies with which departments cope. Position and responsibility more than personality and style determine a manager's influence on outcomes in the organization.

Power is used through individual political behavior, however. Individual managers seek agreement about a strategy to achieve their departments' desired outcomes. Individual managers negotiate decisions and adopt tactics that enable them to acquire and use power. In addition, managers develop ways to increase cooperation and collaboration within the organization to reduce damaging conflicts.

To fully understand the use of power within organizations, it is important to look at both structural components and individual behavior.[66] Although the power comes from larger organizational forms and processes, the political use of power involves individual-level activities. This section briefly summarizes tactics that managers can use to increase the power base of their departments, political tactics they can use to achieve desired outcomes, and tactics for increasing collaboration. These tactics are summarized in Exhibit 13.6.

Exhibit 13.6   *Power and Political Tactics in Organizations*

Tactics for Increasing the Power Base	Political Tactics for Using Power	Tactics for Enhancing Collaboration
1. Enter areas of high uncertainty.	1. Build coalitions.	1. Create integration devices.
2. Create dependencies.	2. Expand networks.	2. Use confrontation and negotiation.
3. Provide scarce resources.	3. Control decision premises.	3. Schedule intergroup consultation.
4. Satisfy strategic contingencies.	4. Enhance legitimacy and expertise.	4. Practice member rotation.
	5. Make a direct appeal.	5. Create superordinate goals.

TACTICS FOR INCREASING POWER

Four **tactics for increasing power** for the organization are as follows:

1. *Enter areas of high uncertainty.* One source of departmental power is to cope with critical uncertainties.[67] If department managers can identify key uncertainties and take steps to remove those uncertainties, the department's power base will be enhanced. Uncertainties could arise from stoppages on an assembly line, from the quality demanded of a new product, or from the inability to predict a demand for new services. Once an uncertainty is identified, the department can take action to cope with it. By their very nature, uncertain tasks will not be solved immediately. Trial and error will be needed, which is to the advantage of the department. The trial-and-error process provides experience and expertise that cannot easily be duplicated by other departments.

2. *Create dependencies.* Dependencies are another source of power.[68] When the organization depends on a department for information, materials, knowledge, or skills, that department will hold power over the others. This power can be increased by incurring obligations. Doing additional work that helps out other departments will obligate the other departments to respond at a future date. The power accumulated by creating a dependency can be used to resolve future disagreements in the department's favor. An equally effective and related strategy is to reduce dependency on other departments by acquiring necessary information or skills. Information technology departments have created dependencies in many organizations because of the rapid changes in this area. Employees in other departments depend on the information technology unit to master complex software programs, changing use of the Internet, and other advances so that they will have the information they need to perform effectively.

3. *Provide scarce resources.* Resources are always important to organizational survival. Departments that accumulate resources and provide them to an organization in the form of money, information, or facilities will be powerful. An earlier In Practice described how university departments with the greatest power are those that obtain external research funds for contributions to university overhead. Likewise, sales departments are powerful in industrial firms because they bring in financial resources.

4. *Satisfy strategic contingencies.* The theory of strategic contingencies says that some elements in the external environment and within the organization are especially important for organizational success. A contingency could be a critical event, a task for which there are no substitutes, or a central task that

is interdependent with many others in the organization. An analysis of the organization and its changing environment will reveal strategic contingencies. To the extent that contingencies are new or are not being satisfied, there is room for a department to move into those critical areas and increase its importance and power.

In summary, the allocation of power in an organization is not random. Power is the result of organizational processes that can be understood and predicted. The abilities to reduce uncertainty, increase dependency on one's own department, obtain resources, and cope with strategic contingencies will all enhance a department's power. Once power is available, the next challenge is to use it to attain helpful outcomes.

POLITICAL TACTICS FOR USING POWER

The use of power in organizations requires both skill and willingness. Many decisions are made through political processes because rational decision processes do not fit. Uncertainty or disagreement is too high. **Political tactics for using power** to influence decision outcomes include the following:

1. *Build coalitions.* Coalition building means taking the time to talk with other managers to persuade them to your point of view.[69] Most important decisions are made outside formal meetings. Managers discuss issues with each other and reach agreements on a one-to-one basis. Effective managers are those who huddle, meeting in groups of twos and threes to resolve key issues.[70] An important aspect of coalition building is to build good relationships. Good interpersonal relationships are built on liking, trust, and respect. Reliability and the motivation to work with others rather than exploit others are part of coalition building.[71]

2. *Expand networks.* Networks can be expanded (1) by reaching out to establish contact with additional managers and (2) by co-opting dissenters. The first approach is to build new alliances through the hiring, transfer, and promotion process. Placing in key positions people who are sympathetic to the outcomes of the department can help achieve departmental goals.[72] On the other hand, the second approach, co-optation, is the act of bringing a dissenter into one's network. One example of co-optation involved a university committee whose membership was based on promotion and tenure. Several female professors who were critical of the tenure and promotion process were appointed to the committee. Once a part of the administrative process, they could see the administrative point of view and learned that administrators were not as evil as suspected. Co-optation effectively brought them into the administrative network.[73]

3. *Control decision premises.* To control decision premises means to constrain the boundaries of a decision. One technique is to choose or limit information provided to other managers. A common method is simply to put your department's best foot forward, such as selectively presenting favorable criteria. A variety of statistics can be assembled to support the departmental point of view. A university department that is growing rapidly and has a large number of students can make claims for additional resources by emphasizing its growth and large size. Such objective criteria do not always work, but they are a valuable step.

Decision premises can be further influenced by limiting the decision process. Decisions can be influenced by the items put on an agenda for an important meeting or even by the sequence in which items are discussed.[74] Items discussed last, when time is short and people want to leave, will receive less attention than those discussed early. Calling attention to specific problems and suggesting alternatives also will affect outcomes. Stressing a specific problem to get it—rather than problems not relevant to your department—on the agenda is an example of agenda setting.

4. *Enhance legitimacy and expertise.* Managers can exert the greatest influence in areas in which they have recognized legitimacy and expertise. If a request is within the task domain of a department and is consistent with the department's vested interest, other departments will tend to comply. Members can also identify external consultants or other experts within the organization to support their cause.[75] For example, a financial vice president in a large retail firm wanted to fire the director of human resource management. She hired a consultant to evaluate the human resource management projects undertaken to date. A negative report from the consultant provided sufficient legitimacy to fire the director, who was replaced with a director loyal to the financial vice president.

5. *Make a direct appeal.* If managers do not ask, they seldom receive. Political activity is effective only when goals and needs are made explicit so the organization can respond. Managers should bargain aggressively and be persuasive. An assertive proposal may be accepted because other managers have no better alternatives. Moreover, an explicit proposal will often receive favorable treatment because other alternatives are ambiguous and less well defined. Effective political behavior requires sufficient forcefulness and risk taking to at least ask for what you need to achieve desired outcomes.

The use of power, however, should not be obvious.[76] If one formally draws upon his or her power base in a meeting by saying, "My department has more power, so the rest of you have to do it my way," the power will be diminished. Power works best when it is used quietly. To call attention to power is to lose it. Explicit claims for power are made by the powerless, not by the powerful. People know who has power. There is substantial agreement on which departments are more powerful. Explicit claims to power are not necessary and can even harm the department's cause.

When using any of the preceding tactics, recall that most people think self-serving behavior hurts rather than helps an organization. If managers are perceived to be throwing their weight around or pursuing goals that are self-serving rather than beneficial to the organization, they will lose respect. On the other hand, managers must recognize the relational and political aspect of their work. It is not sufficient to be rational and technically competent. Politics is a way to reach agreement. This chapter's Book Mark describes some basic psychological principles that underlie successful political influence tactics. Managers can use this understanding to assert influence and get things done within the organization. When managers ignore political tactics, they may find themselves failing without understanding why. This is partly the reason Tim Koogle failed to accomplish a key acquisition at Yahoo!

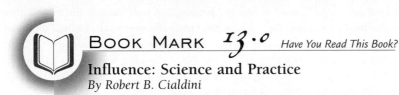

BOOK MARK *13.0* *Have You Read This Book?*

Influence: Science and Practice
By Robert B. Cialdini

Managers use a variety of political tactics to influence others and bring about desired outcomes. In his book *Influence: Science and Practice*, Robert Cialdini examines the social and psychological pressures that cause people to respond favorably to these various tactics. Over years of study, Cialdini, Regents' Professor of Psychology at Arizona State University, has identified some basic influence principles, "those that work in a variety of situations, for a variety of practitioners, on a variety of topics, for a variety of prospects."

INFLUENCE PRINCIPLES

Having a working knowledge of the basic set of persuasion tools can help managers predict and influence human behavior, which is valuable for interacting with colleagues, employees, customers, partners, and even friends. Some basic psychological principles that govern successful influence tactics are:

- *Reciprocity.* The principle of reciprocity refers to the sense of obligation people feel to give back in kind what they have received. For example, a manager who does favors for others creates in them a sense of obligation to return the favors in the future. Smart managers find ways to be helpful to others, whether it be helping a colleague finish an unpleasant job or offering compassion and concern for a subordinate's personal problems.

- *Liking.* People say yes more often to those they like. Companies such as Tupperware Corp. have long understood that familiar faces and congenial characteristics sell products. In-home Tupperware parties allow customers to buy from a friend instead of an unknown salesperson. Salespeople in all kinds of companies often try to capitalize on this principle by finding interests they share with customers as a way to establish rapport. In general, managers who are pleasant,

generous with praise, cooperative, and considerate of others' feelings find that they have greater influence.

- *Credible authority.* Legitimate authorities are particularly influential sources. However, research has discovered that the key to successful use of authority is to be knowledgeable, credible, and trustworthy. Managers who become known for their expertise, who are honest and straightforward with others, and who inspire trust can exert greater influence than those who rely on formal position alone.

- *Social validation.* One of the primary ways people decide what to do in any given situation is to consider what others are doing. That is, people examine the actions of others to validate correct choices. For instance, when homeowners were shown a list of neighbors who had donated to a local charity during a fundraiser, the frequency of contributions increased dramatically. By demonstrating, or even implying, that others have already complied with a request, managers gain greater cooperation.

THE PROCESS OF SOCIAL INFLUENCE

Because life as a manager is all about influencing others, learning to be genuinely persuasive is a valuable management skill. Cialdini's book helps managers understand the basic psychological rules of persuasion—how and why people are motivated to change their attitudes and behaviors. When managers use this understanding in an honest and ethical manner, they improve their effectiveness and the success of their organizations.

Influence: Science and Practice (4th edition), by Robert B. Cialdini, is published by Allyn & Bacon.

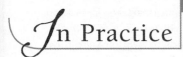

In Practice

YAHOO!

In late March of 2000, Yahoo! began negotiating to buy online auction leader eBay Inc. Tim Koogle, Yahoo!'s CEO at the time, was fully in support of the deal, believing it would enable the company to beef up its e-commerce revenues and bring needed new blood to the increasingly insular Yahoo! culture. But the deal never happened, and while Yahoo!'s fortunes flagged, eBay's revenues and net income continued to climb.

What happened? Jeffrey Mallett, Yahoo!'s president, opposed the acquisition of eBay, and he used political tactics to quash it. Koogle had always been a consensus-style manager.

He believed the top leaders would debate the pros and cons of the acquisition and arrive at the best decision. In addition, he felt sure the merits of the eBay deal would ultimately win the day. But Mallett, who insiders say was already angling to take over the CEO job, began courting cofounders Jerry Yang and David Filo. Eventually, he convinced them that the eBay culture was a poor fit with Yahoo! With Koogle outnumbered, the deal fell apart. A former Yahoo! manager called it management by persuasion.

By failing to build a coalition, Koogle allowed Mallett to control this important decision. It's only one example of several that ultimately led to Koogle being pushed out as CEO. Despite Mallett's political moves, he was passed over for the top job in favor of an outsider who board members hope can turn the struggling company around. Koogle took the decision to seek a new CEO calmly and blamed himself for not keeping a closer eye on Mallett.[77]

TACTICS FOR ENHANCING COLLABORATION

Power and political tactics are important means for getting things done within organizations. Most organizations today have at least moderate interunit conflict. An additional approach in many organizations is to overcome conflict by stimulating cooperation and collaboration among departments to support the attainment of organizational goals. **Tactics for enhancing collaboration** include the following:

1. *Create integration devices.* As described in Chapter 3, teams, task forces, and project managers who span the boundaries between departments can be used as integration devices. Bringing together representatives from conflicting departments in joint problem-solving teams is an effective way to enhance collaboration because representatives learn to understand each other's point of view.[78] Sometimes a full-time integrator is assigned to achieve cooperation and collaboration by meeting with members of the respective departments and exchanging information. The integrator has to understand each group's problems and must be able to move both groups toward a solution that is mutually acceptable.[79]

   Teams and task forces reduce conflict and enhance cooperation because they integrate people from different departments. Integration devices can also be used to enhance cooperation between labor and management, as the example of Aluminum Company of America and the International Association of Machinists illustrates.

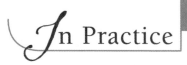

ALUMINUM COMPANY OF AMERICA/INTERNATIONAL ASSOCIATION OF MACHINISTS

When representatives from the International Association of Machinists (IAM) approached David Groetsch, president of a division of Aluminum Company of America (Alcoa), and offered to help create a new work system, Groetsch immediately agreed to give it a try. Alcoa managers joined union leaders for a week-long course at the union's school in Maryland, where they learned how to set up a labor–management partnership and spur productivity. Working together, labor and management studied everything from the history of high-performance systems to new accounting methods to help measure them. Following the course, the union sent experts free of charge to help union leaders and managers from manufacturing to marketing create teams and joint decision-making councils.

The IAM is at the forefront of a revolutionary change in the relationship between labor and management. After decades of suspicion about company-sponsored teams, many unions are now actively embracing the concept of partnership. According to Groetsch, relationships on the shop floor at Alcoa have improved because each side better understands the other's concerns. "The days of 1950s-style table-banging aren't gone yet," says Arthur C. Coia, former president of the Laborers' International Union of North America, whose union is also involved in cooperative ventures.[80] However, the use of integration devices is dramatically improving cooperative relationships between labor and management.

Labor–management teams, which are designed to increase worker participation and provide a cooperative model for solving union–management problems, are increasingly being used at companies such as Goodyear, Ford Motor Company, and Xerox. In the steel industry, companies such as USX and Wheeling-Pittsburgh Steel Corp. have signed pacts that give union representatives seats on the board.[81] Although unions continue to battle over traditional issues such as wages, these integration devices are creating a level of cooperation that many managers would not have believed possible just a few years ago.

2. *Use confrontation and negotiation.* **Confrontation** occurs when parties in conflict directly engage one another and try to work out their differences. **Negotiation** is the bargaining process that often occurs during confrontation and that enables the parties to systematically reach a solution. These techniques bring appointed representatives from the departments together to work out a serious dispute.

   Confrontation and negotiation involve some risk. There is no guarantee that discussions will focus on a conflict or that emotions will not get out of hand. However, if members are able to resolve the conflict on the basis of face-to-face discussions, they will find new respect for each other, and future collaboration becomes easier. The beginnings of relatively permanent attitude change are possible through direct negotiation.

   Confrontation is successful when managers engage in a *win–win strategy*. Win–win means both departments adopt a positive attitude and strive to resolve the conflict in a way that will benefit each other.[82] Ron Shapiro and Mark Jankowski, who negotiate deals for star athletes, suggest that each side should clearly identify, in descending order of importance, what it truly wants out of the negotiation and then try to do the same thing for the other side, eventually determining how the two sides' interests mesh.[83] If the negotiations deteriorate into a strictly win–lose strategy (each group wants to defeat the other), the confrontation will be ineffective. The differences between win–win and win–lose strategies of negotiation are shown in Exhibit 13.7. With a win–win strategy—which includes defining the problem as mutual, communicating openly, and avoiding threats—understanding can be changed while the dispute is resolved.

   One type of negotiation, used to resolve a disagreement between workers and management, is referred to as **collective bargaining**. The bargaining process is usually accomplished through a union and results in an agreement that specifies each party's responsibilities for the next two to three years.

3. *Schedule intergroup consultation.* When conflict is intense and enduring, and department members are suspicious and uncooperative, top managers may intervene as third parties to help resolve the conflict or bring in third-party consultants from outside the organization.[84] This process, sometimes called *workplace mediation*, is a strong intervention to reduce conflict because it involves bringing the disputing parties together and allowing each side to

EXHIBIT 13.7   *Negotiating Strategies*

Win–Win Strategy	Win–Lose Strategy
1. Define the conflict as a mutual problem.	1. Define the problem as a win–lose situation.
2. Pursue joint outcomes.	2. Pursue own group's outcomes.
3. Find creative agreements that satisfy both groups.	3. Force the other group into submission.
4. Be open, honest, and accurate in communicating the group's needs, goals, and proposals.	4. Be deceitful, inaccurate, and misleading in communicating the group's needs, goals, and proposals.
5. Avoid threats (to reduce the other's defensiveness).	5. Use threats (to force submission).
6. Communicate flexibility of position.	6. Communicate strong commitment (rigidity) regarding one's position.

Source: Adapted from David W. Johnson and Frank P. Johnson, *Joining Together: Group Theory and Group Skills* (Englewood Cliffs, N.J.: Prentice-Hall, 1975), 182–183.

present its version of the situation. The technique has been developed by such psychologists as Robert Blake, Jane Mouton, and Richard Walton.[85]

Department members attend a workshop, which may last for several days, away from day-to-day work problems. This approach is similar to the OD approach described in Chapter 11 on innovation and change. The conflicting groups are separated, and each group is invited to discuss and make a list of its perceptions of itself and the other group. Group representatives publicly share these perceptions, and together the groups discuss the results.

Intergroup consultation can be quite demanding for everyone involved. It is fairly easy to have conflicting groups list perceptions and identify discrepancies. However, exploring their differences face-to-face and agreeing to change is more difficult. If handled correctly, these sessions can help department employees understand each other much better and lead to improved attitudes and better working relationships for years to come.

4. *Practice member rotation.* Rotation means individuals from one department can be asked to work in another department on a temporary or permanent basis. The advantage is that individuals become submerged in the values, attitudes, problems, and goals of the other department. In addition, individuals can explain the problems and goals of their original departments to their new colleagues. This enables a frank, accurate exchange of views and information.

Rotation works slowly to reduce conflict but is very effective for changing the underlying attitudes and perceptions that promote conflict.[86]

5. *Create shared mission and superordinate goals.* Another strategy is for top management to create a shared mission and establish superordinate goals that require cooperation among departments.[87] As discussed in Chapter 10, organizations with strong, adaptive cultures, where employees share a larger vision for their company, are more likely to have a united, cooperative workforce. Recent studies have shown that when employees from different departments see that their goals are linked together, they will openly share

resources and information.[88] To be effective, superordinate goals must be substantial, and employees must be granted the time and incentives to work cooperatively in pursuit of the superordinate goals rather than departmental subgoals.

Perhaps the most powerful superordinate goal is company survival. If an organization is about to fail and jobs will be lost, groups forget their differences and try to save the organization. At Harley-Davidson Inc., for example, internal relationships as well as union–management relationships dramatically improved after top executives made it clear that the company was facing extinction. Harley-Davidson now applies the concept of self-directed work teams from the shop floor to the executive suite, and the workers closest to the job have the authority and responsibility to do their jobs as they see fit. In addition, all workers attend eighty hours of training, which includes training in communication and conflict resolution. The company negotiated agreements with its two unions, the International Association of Machinists and Aerospace Workers and the United Paperworkers International, to share a commitment to making Harley a high-performance organization. The new level of cooperation helped the company weather the turbulence and rise again to the pinnacle of American business success.[89]

SUMMARY AND INTERPRETATION

The central message of this chapter is that conflict, power, and politics are natural outcomes of organizing. Differences in goals, backgrounds, and tasks are necessary for organizational excellence, but these differences can throw groups into conflict. Managers use power and politics to manage and resolve conflict. Two views of organization were presented. The rational model of organization assumes that organizations have specific goals and that problems can be logically solved. The other view, the political model of organization, is the basis for much of the chapter. This view assumes that the goals of an organization are not specific or agreed upon. Departments have different values and interests, so managers come into conflict. Decisions are made on the basis of power and political influence. Bargaining, negotiation, persuasion, and coalition building decide outcomes.

The chapter also discussed the vertical and horizontal sources of power. Vertical sources of power include formal position, resources, control of decision premises, and network centrality. In general, managers at the top of the organizational hierarchy have more power than people at lower levels. However, positions all along the hierarchy can be designed to increase the power of employees. As organizations face increased competition and environmental uncertainty, top executives are finding that increasing the power of middle managers and lower-level employees can help the organization be more competitive. Research into horizontal power processes has revealed that certain characteristics make some departments more powerful than others. Such factors as dependency, resources, and nonsubstitutability determine the influence of departments.

Managers can use political tactics such as coalition building, expanded networks, and control of decision premises to help departments achieve desired outcomes. Many people distrust political behavior, fearing that it will be used for selfish ends that benefit the individual but not the organization. However, politics is often needed to achieve the legitimate goals of a department or organization. Three areas in which politics often play a role are structural change, management succession, and resource allocation because these are areas of high uncertainty. Although conflict and political behavior are natural and can be used for beneficial purposes, managers also strive to enhance collaboration so that conflict between groups does not become too strong. Tactics for enhancing collaboration include integration devices, confrontation and negotiation, intergroup consultation, member rotation, and shared mission and superordinate goals.

Key Concepts

authority	network centrality
centrality	nonsubstitutability
collective bargaining	organizational politics
competition	political model
confrontation	political tactics for using power
coping with uncertainty	power
decision premises	power sources
dependency	rational model
domains of political activity	sources of intergroup conflict
financial resources	strategic contingencies
intergroup conflict	tactics for enhancing collaboration
labor–management teams	tactics for increasing power
negotiation	

Discussion Questions

1. Briefly describe how differences in tasks, personal background, and training lead to conflict among groups. How does task interdependence lead to conflict among groups?

2. Discuss why some conflict is considered beneficial to organizations.

3. In a learning organization, are decisions more likely to be made using the rational or political model of organization? Discuss.

4. What is the difference between power and authority? Is it possible for a person to have formal authority but no real power? Discuss.

5. Explain how control over decision premises gives power to a person.

6. In Exhibit 13.4, research and development has greater power in company B than in the other firms. Discuss possible strategic contingencies that give R&D greater power in this firm.

7. State University X receives 90 percent of its financial resources from the state and is overcrowded with students. It is trying to pass regulations to limit student enrollment. Private University Y receives 90 percent of its income from student tuition and has barely enough students to make ends meet. It is actively recruiting students for next year. In which university will students have greater power? What implications will this have for professors and administrators? Discuss.

8. Do you believe it is possible to increase the total amount of power in an organization by delegating power to employees? Explain.

9. The engineering college at a major university brings in three times as many government research dollars as does the rest of the university combined.

Engineering appears wealthy and has many professors on full-time research status. Yet, when internal research funds are allocated, engineering gets a larger share of the money, even though it already has substantial external research funds. Why would this happen?

10. Which do you believe would have a greater long-term impact on changing employee attitudes toward increased collaboration—intergroup consultation or confrontation and negotiation? Discuss.

Chapter 13 Workbook *How Do You Handle Conflict?**

Think of some disagreements you have had with a friend, relative, manager, or coworker. Then indicate how frequently you engage in each of the following behaviors. There are no right or wrong answers. Respond to all items using the scale. The responses from 1 to 7 are

SCALE

Always	Very often	Often	Sometimes	Seldom	Very seldom	Never
1	2	3	4	5	6	7

____   1.   I blend my ideas to create new alternatives for resolving a disagreement.

____   2.   I shy away from topics that are sources of disputes.

____   3.   I make my opinion known in a disagreement.

____   4.   I suggest solutions that combine a variety of viewpoints.

____   5.   I steer clear of disagreeable situations.

____   6.   I give in a little on my ideas when the other person also gives in.

____   7.   I avoid the other person when I suspect that he or she wants to discuss a disagreement.

____   8.   I integrate arguments into a new solution from the issues raised in a dispute.

____   9.   I will go 50–50 to reach a settlement.

____   10.   I raise my voice when I'm trying to get the other person to accept my position.

____   11.   I offer creative solutions in discussions of disagreements.

____   12.   I keep quiet about my views in order to avoid disagreements.

____   13.   I give in if the other person will meet me halfway.

____   14.   I downplay the importance of a disagreement.

____   15.   I reduce disagreements by making them seem insignificant.

____   16.   I meet the other person at a midpoint in our differences.

____   17.   I assert my opinion forcefully.

____   18.   I dominate arguments until the other person understands my position.

____   19.   I suggest we work together to create solutions to disagreements.

____   20.   I try to use the other person's ideas to generate solutions to problems.

____   21.   I offer trade-offs to reach solutions in disagreements.

---

* From "How Do You Handle Conflict?" in Robert E. Quinn et al., *Becoming a Master Manager* (New York: Wiley, 1990), 221–223. Copyright © 1990 by John Wiley & Sons, Inc. This material is used by permission of John Wiley & Sons, Inc.

_____ 22. I argue insistently for my stance.

_____ 23. I withdraw when the other person confronts me about a controversial issue.

_____ 24. I sidestep disagreements when they arise.

_____ 25. I try to smooth over disagreements by making them appear unimportant.

_____ 26. I insist my position be accepted during a disagreement with the other person.

_____ 27. I make our differences seem less serious.

_____ 28. I hold my tongue rather than argue with the other person.

_____ 29. I ease conflict by claiming our differences are trivial.

_____ 30. I stand firm in expressing my viewpoints during a disagreement.

Scoring and Interpretation: Three categories of conflict-handling strategies are measured in this instrument: solution-oriented, nonconfrontational, and control. By comparing your scores on the following three scales, you can see which of the three is your preferred conflict-handling strategy.

To calculate your three scores, add the individual scores for the items and divide by the number of items measuring the strategy. Then subtract each of the three mean scores from seven.

> *Solution-oriented:* Items 1, 4, 6, 8, 9, 11, 13, 16, 19, 20, 21 (Total = 11)
> *Nonconfrontational:* Items 2, 5, 7, 12, 14, 15, 23, 24, 25, 27, 28, 29 (Total = 12)
> *Control:* Items 3, 10, 17, 18, 22, 26, 30 (Total = 7)

Solution-oriented strategies tend to focus on the problem rather than on the individuals involved. Solutions reached are often mutually beneficial, with neither party defining himself or herself as the winner and the other party as the loser.

Nonconfrontational strategies tend to focus on avoiding the conflict by either avoiding the other party or by simply allowing the other party to have his or her way. These strategies are used when there is more concern with avoiding a confrontation than with the actual outcome of the problem situation.

Control strategies tend to focus on winning or achieving one's goals without regard for the other party's needs or desires. Individuals using these strategies often rely on rules and regulations in order to win the battle.

Questions

1. Which strategy do you find easiest to use? Most difficult? Which do you use more often?
2. How would your answers have differed if the other person was a friend, family member, or co-worker?
3. What is it about the conflict situation or strategy that tells you which strategy to use in dealing with a conflict situation?

CASE FOR ANALYSIS   *The Daily Tribune**

The *Daily Tribune* is the only daily newspaper serving a six-county region of eastern Tennessee. Even though its staff is small and it serves a region of mostly small towns and rural areas, the *Tribune* has won numerous awards for news coverage and photojournalism from the Tennessee Press Association and other organizations.

Rick Arnold became news editor almost fifteen years ago. He has spent his entire career with the *Tribune* and feels a great sense of pride that it has been recognized for its journalistic integrity and balanced coverage of issues and events. The paper has

been able to attract bright, talented young writers and photographers thanks largely to Rick's commitment and his support of the news staff. In his early years, the news room was a dynamic, exciting place to work—reporters thrived on the fast pace and the chance to occasionally scoop the major daily paper in Knoxville.

---

*This case was inspired by G. Pascal Zachary, "Many Journalists See a Growing Reluctance to Criticize Advertisers," *The Wall Street Journal* (February 6, 1992), A1, A9; and G. Bruce Knecht, "Retail Chains Emerge as Advance Arbiters of Magazine Content," *The Wall Street Journal* (October 22, 1997), A1, A13.

But times have changed at the *Daily Tribune*. Over the past five years or so, the advertising department has continued to grow, in terms of both staff and budget, while the news department has begun to shrink. "Advertising pays the bills," publisher John Freeman reminded everyone at this month's managers' meeting. "Today, advertisers can go to direct mail, cable television, even the Internet, if they don't like what we're doing for them."

Rick has regularly clashed with the advertising department regarding news stories that are critical of major advertisers, but the conflicts have increased dramatically over the past few years. Now, Freeman is encouraging greater "horizontal collaboration," as he calls it, asking that managers in the news department and the ad department consult with one another regarding issues or stories that involve the paper's major advertisers. The move was prompted in part by a growing number of complaints from advertisers about stories they deemed unfair. "We print the news," Freeman said, "and I understand that sometimes we've got to print things that some people won't like. But we've got to find ways to be more advertiser-friendly. If we work together, we can develop strategies that both present good news coverage and serve to attract more advertisers."

Rick left the meeting fuming, and he didn't fail to make his contempt for the new "advertiser-friendly" approach known to all, including the advertising manager, Fred Thomas, as he headed down the hallway back to the newsroom. Lisa Lawrence, his managing editor, quietly agreed but pointed out that advertisers were readers too, and the newspaper had to listen to all its constituencies. "If we don't handle this carefully, we'll have Freeman and Thomas in here dictating to us what we can write and what we can't." Lawrence has worked with Rick since he first came to the paper, and even though the two have had their share of conflicts, the relationship is primarily one of mutual respect and trust. "Let's just be careful," she emphasized. "Read the stories about big advertisers a little more carefully, make sure we can defend whatever we print, and it will all work out. I know this blurring of the line between advertising and editorial rubs you the wrong way, but Thomas is a reasonable man. We just need to keep him in the loop."

Late that afternoon, Rick received a story from one of his corresponding reporters that had been in the works for a couple of days. East Tennessee Healthcorp (ETH), which operated a string of health clinics throughout the region, was closing three of its rural clinics because of mounting financial woes. The reporter, Elisabeth Fraley, who lived in one of the communities, had learned about the closings from her neighbor, who worked as an accountant for ETH, before the announcement had been made just this afternoon. Fraley had written a compelling human-interest story about how the closings would leave people in two counties with essentially no access to health care, while clinics in larger towns that didn't really need them were being kept open. She had carefully interviewed both former patients of the clinics as well as ETH employees, including the director of one of the clinics and two high-level managers at the corporate office, and she had carefully documented her sources. After this morning's meeting, Rick knew he should run the story by Lisa Lawrence, since East Tennessee Healthcorp was one of the *Tribune's* biggest advertisers, but Lawrence had left for the day. And he simply couldn't bring himself to consult with the advertising department—that political nonsense was for Lawrence to handle. If he held the story for Lawrence's approval, it wouldn't make the Sunday edition. His only other option was to write a brief story simply reporting the closings and leaving out the human interest aspect. Rick was sure the major papers from Knoxville and other nearby cities would have the report in their Sunday papers, but none of them would have the time to develop as comprehensive and interesting an account as Fraley had presented. With a few quick strokes of the pen to make some minor editorial changes, Rick sent the story to production.

When he arrived at work the next day, Rick was called immediately to the publisher's office. He knew it was bad news for Freeman to be in on a Sunday. After some general yelling and screaming, Rick learned that tens of thousands of copies of the Sunday paper had been destroyed and a new edition printed. The advertising manager had called Freeman at home in the wee hours of Sunday morning and informed him of the ETH story, which was appearing the same day the corporation was running a full-page ad touting its service to the small towns and rural communities of East Tennessee.

"The story's accurate, and I assumed you'd want to take advantage of a chance to scoop the big papers," Rick began, but Freeman cut his argument short with his favorite line: "When you assume," he screamed, "you make an ass out of you and me. You could have just reported the basic facts without implying that the company doesn't care about the people of this region. The next time something like this happens, you'll find yourself and your reporters standing in the unemployment line!"

Rick had heard it before, but somehow this time he almost believed it. "What happened to the days when the primary purpose of a newspaper was to present the news?" Rick mumbled. "Now, it seems we have to dance to the tune played by the ad department."

Pierre Dux sat quietly in his office considering the news. A third appointment to regional management had been announced and, once again, the promotion he had expected had been given to someone else. The explanations seemed insufficient this time. Clearly, this signaled the end to his career at INCO. Only one year ago, the company president had arrived at Dux's facility with national press coverage to publicize the success of his innovations in the management of manufacturing operations. The intervening year had brought improved operating results and further positive publicity for the corporation but a string of personal disappointments for Pierre Dux.

Four years earlier, the INCO manufacturing plant had been one of the least productive of the thirteen facilities operating in Europe. Absenteeism and high employee turnover were symptoms of the low morale among the work group. These factors were reflected in mediocre production levels and the worst quality record in INCO. Pierre Dux had been in his current position one year and had derived his only satisfaction from the fact that these poor results might have been worse had he not instituted minor reforms in organizational communication. These allowed workers and supervisors to vent their concerns and frustrations. Although nothing substantial had changed during that first year, operating results had stabilized, ending a period of rapid decline. But this honeymoon was ending. The expectation of significant change was growing, particularly among workers who had been vocal in expressing their dissatisfaction and suggesting concrete proposals for change.

The change process, which had begun three years before, had centered on a redesign of production operations from a single machine-paced assembly line to a number of semiautonomous assembly teams. Although the change had been referred to as the INCO "Volvo project" or "INCO's effort at Japanese-style management," it had really been neither of these. Rather, it had been the brainchild of a group of managers, led by Dux, who believed that both productivity and working conditions in the plant could be improved through a single effort. Of course, members of the group had visited other so-called innovative production facilities, but the new work groups and job classifications had been designed with the particular products and technology at INCO in mind.

After lengthy discussions among the management group, largely dedicated to reaching agreement on the general direction that the new project would take, the actual design began to emerge. Equally lengthy discussions (often referred to as negotiations) with members of the workforce, supervisors, and representatives of the local unions were part of the design process. The first restructuring into smaller work groups was tried in an experimental project that received tentative approval from top management in INCO headquarters and a "wait and see" response from the union. The strongest initial resistance had come from the plant engineers. They were sold neither on the new structure nor on the process of involving the workforce in the design of operating equipment and production methods. Previously, the engineering group had itself fulfilled these functions, and it felt the present problems were a result of a lack of skill among employees or managerial unwillingness to make the system work.

The experiment was staffed by volunteers supported by a few of the better-trained workers in the plant. The latter were necessary to ensure a start-up of the new equipment, which had been modified from the existing technology on the assembly line.

The initial experiment met with limited success. Although the group was able to meet the productivity levels of the existing line within a few weeks, critics of the new plan attributed the low level of success to the unrepresentative nature of the experimental group or

*This case was prepared by Michael Brimm, Associate Professor of INSEAD. It is intended to be used as a basis for class discussion rather than to illustrate either effective or ineffective handling of an administrative situation. Copyright © 1983 INSEAD Foundation, Fontainebleau, France. Revised 1987.

the newness of the equipment on which they were working. However, even this limited success attracted the attention of numerous people at INCO headquarters and in other plants. All were interested in seeing the new experiment. Visits soon became a major distraction, and Dux declared a temporary halt to permit the project to proceed, although this produced some muttering at headquarters about his "secretive" and "uncooperative" behavior.

Because of the experiment's success, Dux and his staff prepared to convert the entire production operation to the new system. The enthusiasm of workers in the plant grew as training for the changeover proceeded. In fact, a group of production workers asked to help with the installation of the new equipment as a means of learning more about its operation.

Dux and his staff were surprised at the difficulties encountered at this phase. Headquarters seemed to drag its feet in approving the necessary funding for the changeover. Even after the funding was approved, there was a stream of challenges to minor parts of the plan. "Can't you lay the workers off during the changeover?" "Why use workers on overtime to do the changeover when you could hire temporary workers more cheaply?" These criticisms reflected a lack of understanding of the basic operating principles of the new system, and Dux rejected them.

The conversion of the entire assembly line to work groups was finally achieved, with the local management group making few concessions from their stated plans. The initial change and the first days of operation were filled with crises. The design process had not anticipated many of the problems that arose with full-scale operations. However, Dux was pleased to see managers, staff, and workers clustered together at the trouble areas, fine-tuning the design when problems arose. Just as the start-up finally appeared to be moving forward, a change in product specifications from a headquarters group dictated additional changes in the design of the assembly process. The new changes were handled quickly and with enthusiasm by the workforce. While the period was exhausting and seemingly endless to those who felt responsible for the change, the new design took only six months to reach normal operating levels (one year had been forecast as the time needed to reach that level—without the added requirement for a change in product specifications).

Within a year, Dux was secure that he had a major success on his hands. Productivity and product quality measures for the plant had greatly improved. In this relatively short period his plant had moved from the worst, according to these indicators, to the third most productive in the INCO system. Absenteeism had dropped only slightly, but turnover had been reduced substantially. Morale was not measured formally but was considered by all members of the management team to be greatly improved. Now, after three years of full operations, the plant was considered the most productive in the entire INCO system.

Dux was a bit surprised when no other facility in INCO initiated a similar effort or called upon him for help. Increases of the early years had leveled off, with the peak being achieved in the early part of year three. Now the facility seemed to have found a new equilibrium. The calm of smoother operations had been a welcome relief to many who had worked so hard to launch the new design. For Dux it provided the time to reflect on his accomplishment and think about his future career.

It was in this context that he considered the news that he had once again been bypassed for promotion to the next level in the INCO hierarchy.

Notes

1. This example is based on an incident reported in Monica Langley, "Columbia Tells Doctors at Hospital to End Their Outside Practice," *The Wall Street Journal* (May 2, 1997), A1, A6.
2. Lee G. Bolman and Terrence E. Deal, *Reframing Organizations: Artistry, Choice, and Leadership* (San Francisco: Jossey-Bass, 1991).
3. Paul M. Terry, "Conflict Management," *The Journal of Leadership Studies* 3, no. 2 (1996), 3–21; Kathleen M. Eisenhardt, Jean L. Kahwajy, and L. J. Bourgeois III, "How Management Teams Can Have a Good Fight," *Harvard Business Review* (July–August 1997), 77–85.
4. Clayton T. Alderfer and Ken K. Smith, "Studying Intergroup Relations Imbedded in Organizations," *Administrative Science Quarterly* 27 (1982), 35–65.
5. Muzafer Sherif, "Experiments in Group Conflict," *Scientific American* 195 (1956), 54–58; Edgar H. Schein, *Organizational Psychology*, 3d ed. (Englewood Cliffs, N.J.: Prentice-Hall, 1980).

6. M. Afzalur Rahim, "A Strategy for Managing Conflict in Complex Organizations," *Human Relations* 38 (1985), 81–89; Kenneth Thomas, "Conflict and Conflict Management," in M.D. Dunnette, ed., *Handbook of Industrial and Organizational Psychology* (Chicago, Ill. Rand McNally, 1976); Stuart M. Schmidt and Thomas A. Kochan, "Conflict: Toward Conceptual Clarity," *Administrative Science Quarterly* 13 (1972), 359–370.

7. L. David Brown, "Managing Conflict Among Groups," in David A. Kolb, Irwin M. Rubin, and James M. McIntyre, eds., *Organizational Psychology*: *A Book of Readings* (Englewood Cliffs, N.J.: Prentice-Hall, 1979), 377–389; Robert W. Ruekert and Orville C. Walker, Jr., "Interactions between Marketing and R&D Departments in Implementing Different Business Strategies," *Strategic Management Journal* 8 (1987), 233–248.

8. Amy Barrett, "Indigestion at Taco Bell," *BusinessWeek* (December 14, 1994), 66–67; Greg Burns, "Fast-Food Fight," *BusinessWeek* (June 2, 1997), 34–36.

9. Aaron Bernstein with Michael Arndt, Wendy Zellner, and Peter Coy, "Too Much Corporate Power?" *BusinessWeek* (September 11, 2000), 144–158.

10. Nanette Byrnes, with Mike McNamee, Ronald Grover, Joann Muller, and Andrew Park, "Auditing Here, Consulting Over There," *BusinessWeek* (April 8, 2002), 34–36.

11. Thomas A. Kochan, George P. Huber, and L. L. Cummings, "Determinants of Intraorganizational Conflict in Collective Bargaining in the Public Sector," *Administrative Science Quarterly* 20 (1975), 10–23.

12. Victoria L. Crittenden, Lorraine R. Gardiner, and Antonie Stam, "Reducing Conflict Between Marketing and Manufacturing," *Industrial Marketing Management* 22 (1993), 299–309; Benson S. Shapiro, "Can Marketing and Manufacturing Coexist?" *Harvard Business Review* 55 (September–October 1977), 104–114.

13. Eric H. Neilsen, "Understanding and Managing Intergroup Conflict," in Jay W. Lorsch and Paul R. Lawrence, eds., *Managing Group and Intergroup Relations* (Homewood, Ill.: Irwin and Dorsey, 1972), 329–343; Richard E. Walton and John M. Dutton, "The Management of Interdepartmental Conflict: A Model and Review," *Administrative Science Quarterly* 14 (1969), 73–84.

14. Jay W. Lorsch, "Introduction to the Structural Design of Organizations," in Gene W. Dalton, Paul R. Lawrence, and Jay W. Lorsch, eds., *Organization Structure and Design* (Homewood, Ill.: Irwin and Dorsey, 1970), 5.

15. James D. Thompson, *Organizations in Action* (New York: McGraw-Hill, 1967), 54–56.

16. Walton and Dutton, "The Management of Interdepartmental Conflict."

17. Joseph McCann and Jay R. Galbraith, "Inter-departmental Relations," in Paul C. Nystrom and William H. Starbuck, eds., *Handbook of Organizational Design*, vol. 2 (New York: Oxford University Press, 1981), 60–84.

18. Roderick M. Cramer, "Intergroup Relations and Organizational Dilemmas: The Role of Categorization Processes," in L. L. Cummings and Barry M. Staw, eds., *Research in Organizational Behavior*, vol. 13 (New York: JAI Press, 1991), 191–228; Neilsen, "Understanding and Managing Intergroup Conflict"; Louis R. Pondy, "Organizational Conflict: Concepts and Models," *Administrative Science Quarterly* 12 (1968), 296–320.

19. Jeffrey Pfeffer, *Power in Organizations* (Marshfield, Mass.: Pitman, 1981).

20. Robert A. Dahl, "The Concept of Power," *Behavioral Science* 2 (1957), 201–215.

21. W. Graham Astley and Paramjit S. Sachdeva, "Structural Sources of Intraorganizational Power: A Theoretical Synthesis," *Academy of Management Review* 9 (1984), 104–113; Abraham Kaplan, "Power in Perspective," in Robert L. Kahn and Elise Boulding, eds., *Power and Conflict in Organizations* (London: Tavistock, 1964), 11–32.

22. Gerald R. Salancik and Jeffrey Pfeffer, "The Bases and Use of Power in Organizational Decision-Making: The Case of the University," *Administrative Science Quarterly* 19 (1974), 453–473.

23. Richard M. Emerson, "Power-Dependence Relations," *American Sociological Review* 27 (1962), 31–41.

24. Rosabeth Moss Kanter, "Power Failure in Management Circuits," *Harvard Business Review* (July–August 1979), 65–75.

25. Examples are Robert Greene and Joost Elffers, *The 48 Laws of Power* (New York: Viking, 1999); Jeffrey J. Fox, *How to Become CEO* (New York: Hyperion, 1999).

26. John R. P. French, Jr., and Bertram Raven, "The Bases of Social Power," in *Group Dynamics*, D. Cartwright and A. F. Zander, eds. (Evanston, Ill.: Row Peterson, 1960), 607–623.

27. Ran Lachman, "Power from What? A Reexamination of Its Relationships with Structural Conditions," *Administrative Science Quarterly* 34 (1989), 231–251; Daniel J. Brass, "Being in the Right Place: A Structural Analysis of Individual Influence in an Organization," *Administrative Science Quarterly* 29 (1984), 518–539.

28. Michael Warshaw, "The Good Guy's Guide to Office Politics," *Fast Company* (April–May 1998), 157–178.

29. A. J. Grimes, "Authority, Power, Influence, and Social Control: A Theoretical Synthesis," *Academy of Management Review* 3 (1978), 724–735.

30. Astley and Sachdeva, "Structural Sources of Intraorganizational Power."

31. Jeffrey Pfeffer, *Managing with Power: Politics and Influence in Organizations* (Boston, Mass. Harvard Business School Press, 1992).

32. Robert L. Peabody, "Perceptions of Organizational Authority," *Administrative Science Quarterly* 6 (1962), 479.

33. Richard S. Blackburn, "Lower Participant Power: Toward a Conceptual Integration," *Academy of Management Review* 6 (1981), 127–131.

34. Kanter, "Power Failure in Management Circuits," 70.

35. Carol Hymowitz, "Managers Are Starting to Gain More Clout Over Their Employees" (In the Lead column), *The Wall Street Journal* (January 30, 2001), B1.

36. Pfeffer, *Power in Organizations*.

37. Erik W. Larson and Jonathan B. King, "The Systemic Distortion of Information: An Ongoing Challenge to Management," *Organizational Dynamics* 24, no. 3 (Winter 1996), 49–61; Thomas H. Davenport, Robert G. Eccles, and Lawrence Prusak, "Information Politics," *Sloan Management Review* (Fall 1992), 53–65.

38. Andrew M. Pettigrew, *The Politics of Organizational Decision-Making* (London: Tavistock, 1973).

39. Astley and Sachdeva, "Structural Sources of Intraorganizational Power"; Noel M. Tichy and Charles Fombrun, "Network Analysis in Organizational Settings," *Human Relations* 32 (1979), 923–965.

40. Charles Gasparino and Anita Raghavan, "Survivor: How Dean Witter Boss Got the Upper Hand in Merger with Morgan," *The Wall Street Journal* (March 22, 2001), A1, A6.

41. Warshaw, "The Good Guy's Guide to Office Politics."

42. Carol Hymowitz, "Companies Experience Major Power Shifts as Crises Continue" (In the Lead column), *The Wall Street Journal* (October 9, 2001), B1.

43. Charles Perrow, "Departmental Power and Perspective in Industrial Firms," in Mayer N. Zald, ed., *Power in Organizations* (Nashville, Tenn.: Vanderbilt University Press, 1970), 59–89.

44. D. J. Hickson, C. R. Hinings, C. A. Lee, R. E. Schneck, and J. M. Pennings, "A Strategic Contingencies Theory of Intraorganizational Power," *Administrative Science Quarterly* 16 (1971), 216–229; Gerald R. Salancik and Jeffrey Pfeffer, "Who Gets Power—and How They Hold onto It: A Strategic-Contingency Model of Power," *Organizational Dynamics* (Winter 1977), 3–21.

45. Pfeffer, *Managing with Power*; Salancik and Pfeffer, "Who Gets Power"; C. R. Hinings, D. J. Hickson, J. M. Pennings, and R. E. Schneck, "Structural Conditions of Intraorganizational Power," *Administrative Science Quarterly* 19 (1974), 22–44.

46. Carol Stoak Saunders, "The Strategic Contingencies Theory of Power: Multiple Perspectives," *Journal of Management Studies* 27 (1990), 1–18; Warren Boeker, "The Development and Institutionalization of Sub-Unit Power in Organizations," *Administrative Science Quarterly* 34 (1989), 388–510; Irit Cohen and Ran Lachman, "The Generality of the Strategic Contingencies Approach to Sub-Unit Power," *Organizational Studies* 9 (1988), 371–391.

47. Emerson, "Power-Dependence Relations."

48. Pfeffer, *Managing with Power*.

49. Jeffrey Pfeffer and Gerald Salancik, "Organizational Decision-Making as a Political Process: The Case of a University Budget," *Administrative Science Quarterly* (1974), 135–151.

50. Salancik and Pfeffer, "Bases and Use of Power in Organizational Decision-Making," 470.

51. Hickson et al., "A Strategic Contingencies Theory."

52. Pettigrew, *The Politics of Organizational Decision-Making*.

53. Hickson et al., "A Strategic Contingencies Theory."

54. Ibid.

55. G. Bruce Knecht, "Retail Chains Emerge as Advance Arbiters of Magazine Content," *The Wall Street Journal* (October 22, 1997), A1, A13.

56. Bernstein, "Too Much Corporate Power?"

57. Jeffrey Gantz and Victor V. Murray, "Experience of Workplace Politics," *Academy of Management Journal* 23 (1980), 237–251; Dan L. Madison, Robert W. Allen, Lyman W. Porter, Patricia A. Renwick, and Bronston T. Mayes, "Organizational Politics: An Exploration of Managers' Perception," *Human Relations* 33 (1980), 79–100.

58. Gerald R. Ferris and K. Michele Kacmar, "Perceptions of Organizational Politics," *Journal of Management* 18 (1992), 93–116; Parmod Kumar and Rehana Ghadially, "Organizational Politics and its Effects on Members of Organizations," *Human Relations* 42 (1989), 305–314; Donald J. Vredenburgh and John G. Maurer, "A Process Framework of Organizational Politics," *Human Relations* 37 (1984), 47–66; Gerald R. Ferris, Dwight D. Frink, Maria Carmen Galang, Jing Zhou, Michele Kacmar, and Jack L. Howard, "Perceptions of Organizational Politics: Prediction, Stress-Related Implications, and Outcomes," *Human Relations* 49, no. 2 (1996), 233–266.

59. Ferris et al., "Perceptions of Organizational Politics: Prediction, Stress-Related Implications, and Outcomes"; John J. Voyer, "Coercive Organizational Politics and Organizational Outcomes: An Interpretive Study," *Organization Science* 5, no. 1 (February 1994), 72–85; James W. Dean, Jr., and Mark P. Sharfman, "Does Decision Process Matter? A Study of Strategic Decision-Making Effectiveness," *Academy of Management Journal* 39, no. 2 (1996), 368–396.

60. Jeffrey Pfeffer, *Managing With Power: Politics and Influence in Organizations* (Boston, Mass.: Harvard Business School Press, 1992).

61. Amos Drory and Tsilia Romm, "The Definition of Organizational Politics: A Review," *Human Relations* 43 (1990), 1133–1154; Vredenburgh and Maurer, "A Process Framework of Organizational Politics."

62. Pfeffer, *Power in Organizations*, p. 70.

63. Madison et al., "Organizational Politics"; Jay R. Galbraith, *Organizational Design* (Reading, Mass.: Addison-Wesley, 1977).

64. Pui-Wing Tam and Scott Thurm, "Hard Drive: H-P Struggle Brings Smashmouth Politics to Corporate World," *The Wall Street Journal* (March 5, 2002), A1, A10.

65. Gantz and Murray, "Experience of Workplace Politics"; Pfeffer, *Power in Organizations*.

66. Daniel J. Brass and Marlene E. Burkhardt, "Potential Power and Power Use: An Investigation of Structure and Behavior," *Academy of Management Journal* 38 (1993), 441–470.

67. Hickson et al., "A Strategic Contingencies Theory."

68. Pfeffer, *Power in Organizations*.

69. Ibid.

70. V. Dallas Merrell, *Huddling: The Informal Way to Management Success* (New York: AMACON, 1979).

71. Vredenburgh and Maurer, "A Process Framework of Organizational Politics."

72. Ibid.

73. Pfeffer, *Power in Organizations*.

74. Ibid.

75. Ibid.

76. Kanter, "Power Failure in Management Circuits"; Pfeffer, *Power in Organizations*.

77. Ben Elgin, "Inside Yahoo!" *BusinessWeek* (May 21, 2001), 114–122.

78. Robert R. Blake and Jane S. Mouton, "Overcoming Group Warfare," *Harvard Business Review* (November–December 1984), 98–108.

79. Blake and Mouton, "Overcoming Group Warfare"; Paul R. Lawrence and Jay W. Lorsch, "New Management Job: The Integrator," *Harvard Business Review* 45 (November–December 1967), 142–151.

80. Aaron Bernstein, "Look Who's Pushing Productivity," *BusinessWeek* (April 7, 1997), 72–75.

81. Ibid.

82. Robert R. Blake, Herbert A. Shepard, and Jane S. Mouton, *Managing Intergroup Conflict in Industry* (Houston: Gulf Publishing, 1964); Doug Stewart, "'Expand the Pie Before You Divvy It Up,'" *Smithsonian* (November 1997), 78–90.

83. Ron Shapiro and Mark Jankowski, with James Dale, *The Power of Nice—How to Negotiate So Everyone Wins, Especially You!* (New York: John Wiley & Sons, 1998).

84. Patrick S. Nugent, "Managing Conflict: Third-Party Interventions for Managers," *Academy of Management Executive* 16, no. 1 (2002), 139–155.

85. Blake and Mouton, "Overcoming Group Warfare"; Schein, *Organizational Psychology*; Blake, Shepard, and Mouton, *Managing Intergroup Conflict in Industry*; Richard E. Walton, *Interpersonal Peacemaking: Confrontation and Third-Party Consultations* (Reading, Mass.: Addison-Wesley, 1969).

86. Neilsen, "Understanding and Managing Intergroup Conflict"; McCann and Galbraith, "Interdepartmental Relations."

87. Neilsen, "Understanding and Managing Intergroup Conflict"; McCann and Galbraith, "Interdepartmental Relations"; Sherif et al., *Intergroup Conflict and Cooperation*.

88. Dean Tjosvold, Valerie Dann, and Choy Wong, "Managing Conflict between Departments to Serve Customers," *Human Relations* 45 (1992), 1035–1054.

89. Gina Imperato, "Harley Shifts Gears," *Fast Company* (June–July 1997), 104–113.

INTEGRATIVE CASES

INTEGRATIVE CASE 1.0 *It Isn't So Simple: Infrastructure Change at Royce Consulting**

The lights of the city glittered outside Ken Vincent's twelfth-floor office. After nine years of late nights and missed holidays, Ken was in the executive suite with the words "Associate Partner" on the door. Things should be easier now, but the proposed changes at Royce Consulting had been more challenging than he had expected. "I don't understand," he thought. "At Royce Consulting our clients, our people, and our reputation are what count, so why do I feel so much tension from the managers about the changes that are going to be made in the office? We've analyzed why we have to make the changes. Heck, we even got an outside person to help us. The administrative support staff are pleased. So why aren't the managers enthusiastic? We all know what the decision at tomorrow's meeting will be—Go! Then it will all be over. Or will it?" Ken thought as he turned out the lights.

Background

Royce Consulting is an international consulting firm whose clients are large corporations, usually with long-term contracts. Royce employees spend weeks, months, and even years working under contract at the client's site. Royce consultants are employed by a wide range of industries, from manufacturing facilities to utilities to service businesses. The firm has over 160 consulting offices located in 65 countries. At this location Royce employees included 85 staff members, 22 site managers, 9 partners and associate partners, 6 administrative support staff, 1 human resource professional, and 1 financial support person.

For the most part, Royce Consulting hired entry-level staff straight out of college and promoted from within. New hires worked on staff for five or six years; if they did well, they were promoted to manager. Managers were responsible for maintaining client contracts and assisting partners in creating proposals for future engagements. Those who were not promoted after six or seven years generally left the company for other jobs.

Newly promoted managers were assigned an office, a major perquisite of their new status. During the previous year, some new managers had been forced to share an office because of space limitations. To minimize the friction of sharing an office, one of the managers was usually assigned to a long-term project out of town. Thus, practically speaking, each manager had a private office.

Infrastructure and Proposed Changes

Royce was thinking about instituting a hoteling office system—also referred to as a "nonterritorial" or "free-address" office. A hoteling office system made offices available to managers on a reservation or drop-in basis. Managers are not assigned a permanent office; instead, whatever materials and equipment the manager needs are moved into the temporary office. These are some of the features and advantages of a hoteling office system:

- No permanent office assigned
- Offices are scheduled by reservations
- Long-term scheduling of an office is feasible
- Storage space would be located in a separate file room
- Standard manuals and supplies would be maintained in each office
- Hoteling coordinator is responsible for maintaining offices
- A change in "possession of space"
- Eliminates two or more managers assigned to the same office
- Allows managers to keep the same office if desired
- Managers would have to bring in whatever files they needed for their stay
- Information available would be standardized regardless of office
- Managers do not have to worry about "housekeeping issues"

The other innovation under consideration was an upgrade to state-of-the-art electronic office technology. All managers would receive a new notebook computer with updated communications capability to use Royce's integrated and proprietary software. Also, as

---

*Presented to and accepted by the Society for Case Research. All rights reserved to the authors and SCR.

This case was prepared by Sally Dresdow of the University of Wisconsin at Green Bay and Joy Benson of the University of Illinois at Springfield and is intended to be used as a basis for class discussion. The views represented here are those of the case authors and do not necessarily reflect the views of the Society for Case Research. The authors' views are based on their own professional judgments. The names of the organization, individuals, and location have been disguised to preserve the organization's request for anonymity.

part of the electronic office technology, an electronic filing system was considered. The electronic filing system meant information regarding proposals, client records, and promotional materials would be electronically available on the Royce Consulting network.

The administrative support staff had limited experience with many of the application packages used by the managers. While they used word processing extensively, they had little experience with spreadsheets, communications, or graphics packages. The firm had a graphics department and the managers did most of their own work, so the administrative staff did not have to work with those application software packages.

Work Patterns

Royce Consulting was located in a large city in the Midwest. The office was located in the downtown area, but it was easy to get to. Managers assigned to in-town projects often stopped by for a few hours at various times of the day. Managers who were not currently assigned to client projects were expected to be in the office to assist on current projects or work with a partner to develop proposals for new business.

In a consulting firm, managers spend a significant portion of their time at client sites. As a result, the office occupancy rate at Royce Consulting was about 40 to 60 percent. This meant that the firm paid lease costs for offices that were empty approximately half of the time. With the planned growth over the next ten years, assigning permanent offices to every manager, even in doubled-up arrangements, was judged to be economically unnecessary given the amount of time offices were empty.

The proposed changes would require managers and administrative support staff to adjust their work patterns. Additionally, if a hoteling office system was adopted, managers would need to keep their files in a centralized file room.

Organizational Culture

Royce Consulting had a strong organizational culture, and management personnel were highly effective at communicating it to all employees.

Stability of Culture

The culture at Royce Consulting was stable. The leadership of the corporation had a clear picture of who they were and what type of organization they were. Royce Consulting had positioned itself to be a leader in all areas of large business consulting. Royce

Consulting's CEO articulated the firm's commitment to being client-centered. Everything that was done at Royce Consulting was because of the client.

Training

New hires at Royce Consulting received extensive training in the culture of the organization and the methodology employed in consulting projects. They began with a structured program of classroom instruction and computer-aided courses covering technologies used in the various industries in which the firm was involved. Royce Consulting recruited top young people who were aggressive and who were willing to do whatever was necessary to get the job done and build a common bond. Among new hires, camaraderie was encouraged along with a level of competition. This kind of behavior continued to be cultivated throughout the training and promotion process.

Work Relationships

Royce Consulting employees had a remarkably similar outlook on the organization. Accepting the culture and norms of the organization was important for each employee. The norms of Royce Consulting revolved around high performance expectations and strong job involvement.

By the time people made manager, they were aware of what types of behaviors were acceptable. Managers were formally assigned the role of coach to younger staff people, and they modeled acceptable behavior. Behavioral norms included when they came into the office, how late they stayed at the office, and the type of comments they made about others. Managers spent time checking on staff people and talking with them about how they were doing.

The standard for relationships was that of professionalism. Managers knew they had to do what the partners asked and they were to be available at all times. A norms survey and conversations made it clear that people at Royce Consulting were expected to help each other with on-the-job problems, but personal problems were outside the realm of sanctioned relationships. Personal problems were not to interfere with performance on a job. To illustrate, vacations were put on hold and other kinds of commitments were set aside if something was needed at Royce Consulting.

Organizational Values

Three things were of major importance to the organization: its clients, its people, and its reputation. There was a strong client-centered philosophy communicated and practiced. Organization members sought to meet and exceed customer expectations. Putting clients first was stressed. The management of Royce Consulting listened to its clients and made adjustments to satisfy the client.

The reputation of Royce Consulting was important to those leading the organization. They protected and enhanced it by focusing on quality services delivered by quality people. The emphasis on clients, Royce Consulting personnel, and the firm's reputation was cultivated by developing a highly motivated, cohesive, and committed group of employees.

Management Style and Hierarchical Structure

The company organization was characterized by a directive style of management. The partners had the final word on all issues of importance. It was common to hear statements like "Managers are expected to solve problems, and do whatever it takes to finish the job" and "Whatever the partners want, we do." Partners accepted and asked for managers' feedback on projects, but in the final analysis, the partners made the decisions.

Current Situation

Royce Consulting had an aggressive five-year plan that was predicated on a continued increase in business. Increases in the total number of partners, associate partners, managers, and staff were forecast. Additional office space would be required to accommodate the growth in staff; this would increase rental costs at a time when Royce's fixed and variable costs were going up.

The partners, led by managing partner Donald Gray and associate partner Ken Vincent, believed that something had to be done to improve space utilization and the productivity of the managers and administrative personnel. The partners approved a feasibility study of the innovations and their impact on the company.

The ultimate decision makers were the partner group who had the power to approve the concepts and commit the required financial investment. A planning committee consisted of Ken Vincent, the human resources person, the financial officer, and an outside consultant, Mary Schrean.

The Feasibility Study

Within two working days of the initial meeting, all the partners and managers received a memo announcing the hoteling office feasibility study. The memo included a brief description of the concept and stated that it would include an interview with the staff. By this time, partners and managers had already heard about the possible changes and knew that Gray was leaning toward hoteling offices.

Interviews with the Partners

All the partners were interviewed. One similarity in the comments was that they thought the move to hoteling offices was necessary but they were glad it would not affect them. Three partners expressed concern about managers' acceptance of the change to a hoteling system. The conclusion of each partner was that if Royce Consulting moved to hoteling offices, with or without electronic office technology, the managers would accept the change. The reason given by the partners for such acceptance was that the managers would do what the partners wanted done.

The partners all agreed that productivity could be improved at all levels of the organization: in their own work as well as among the secretaries and the managers. Partners acknowledged that current levels of information technology at Royce Consulting would not support the move to hoteling offices and that advances in electronic office technology needed to be considered.

Partners viewed all filing issues as secondary to both the office layout change and the proposed technology improvement. What eventually emerged, however, was that ownership and control of files was a major concern, and most partners and managers did not want anything centralized.

Interviews with the Managers

Personal interviews were conducted with all ten managers who were in the office. During the interviews, four of the managers asked Schrean whether the change to hoteling offices was her idea. The managers passed the question off as a joke; however, they expected a response from her. She stated that she was there as an adviser, that she had not generated the idea, and that she would not make the final decision regarding the changes.

The length of time that these managers had been in their current positions ranged from six months to five years. None of them expressed positive feelings about the hoteling system, and all of them referred to how hard they had worked to make manager and gain an office of their own. Eight managers spoke of the status that the office gave them and the convenience of having a permanent place to keep their information and files. Two of the managers said they did not care so much about the status but were concerned about the convenience. One manager said he would come in less frequently if he did not have his own office. The managers believed that a change to hoteling offices would decrease their productivity. Two managers stated that they did not care how much money Royce Consulting would save on lease costs; they wanted to keep their offices.

However, for all the negative comments, all the managers said that they would go along with whatever the partners decided to do. One manager stated that if Royce Consulting stays busy with client projects, having a permanently assigned office was not a big issue.

During the interviews every manager was enthusiastic and supportive of new productivity tools, particularly the improved electronic office technology. They believed that new computers and integrated software and productivity tools would definitely improve their productivity. Half the managers stated that updated technology would make the change to hoteling offices "a little less terrible," and they wanted their secretaries to have the same software as they did.

The managers' responses to the filing issue varied. The volume of files managers had was in direct proportion to their tenure in that position: The longer a person was a manager, the more files he or she had. In all cases, managers took care of their own files, storing them in their offices and in whatever filing drawers were free.

As part of the process of speaking with managers, their administrative assistants were asked about the proposed changes. Each of the six thought that the electronic office upgrade would benefit the managers, although they were somewhat concerned about what would be expected of them. Regarding the move to hoteling offices, each said that the managers would hate the change, but that they would agree to it if the partners wanted to move in that direction.

Results of the Survey

A survey developed from the interviews was sent to all partners, associate partners, and managers two weeks after the interviews were conducted. The completed survey was returned by 6 of the 9 partners and associate partners and 16 of the 22 managers. This is what the survey showed.

Work Patterns. It was "common knowledge" that managers were out of the office a significant portion of their time, but there were no figures to substantiate this belief, so the respondents were asked to provide data on where they spent their time. The survey results indicated that partners spent 38 percent of their time in the office, 54 percent at client sites, 5 percent at home, and 3 percent in other places, such as airports. Managers reported spending 32 percent of their time in the office, 63 percent at client sites, 4 percent at home, and 1 percent in other places.

For 15 workdays, the planning team also visually checked each of the 15 managers' offices four times each day: at 9 a.m., 11 a.m., 2 p.m., and 4 p.m. These times were selected because initial observations indicated that these were the peak occupancy times. An average of six offices (40 percent of all manager offices) were empty at any given time; in other words, there was a 60 percent occupancy rate.

Alternative Office Layouts. One of the alternatives outlined by the planning committee was a continuation of and expansion of shared offices. Eleven of the managers responding to the survey preferred shared offices to hoteling offices. Occasions when more than one manager was in the shared office at the same time were infrequent. Eight managers reported 0 to 5 office conflicts per month; three managers reported 6 to 10 office conflicts per month. The type of problems encountered with shared offices included not having enough filing space, problems in directing telephone calls, and lack of privacy.

Managers agreed that having a permanently assigned office was an important perquisite. The survey confirmed the information gathered in the interviews about managers' attitudes: All but two managers preferred shared offices over hoteling, and managers believed their productivity would be negatively impacted. The challenges facing Royce Consulting if they move to hoteling offices centered around tradition and managers' expectations, file accessibility and organization, security and privacy issues, unpredictable work schedules, and high-traffic periods.

Control of Personal Files. Because of the comments made during the face-to-face interviews, survey respondents were asked to rank the importance of having personal control of their files. A 5-point scale was used, with 5 being "strongly agree" and 1 being "strongly disagree." Here are the responses.

Respondents	Sample	Rank
Partners	6	4.3
Managers:		
0–1 year	5	4.6
2–3 years	5	3.6
4+ years	6	4.3

Electronic Technology. Royce Consulting had a basic network system in the office that could not accommodate the current partners and managers working at a remote site. The administrative support staff had a separate network, and the managers and staff could not communicate electronically. Of managers responding to the survey, 95 percent wanted to use the network but only 50 percent could actually do so.

Option Analysis

A financial analysis showed that there were significant cost differences between the options under consideration:

Option 1: Continue private offices with some office sharing

- Lease an additional floor in existing building; annual cost, $360,000
- Build out the additional floor (i.e., construct, furnish, and equip offices and work areas): one-time cost, $600,000

Option 2: Move to hoteling offices with upgraded office technology

- Upgrade office electronic technology: one-time cost, $190,000

Option 1 was expensive because under the terms of the existing lease Royce had to commit to an entire floor if it wanted additional space. Hoteling offices showed an overall financial advantage of $360,000 per year and a one-time savings of $410,000 over shared or individual offices.

The Challenge

Vincent met with Mary Schrean to discuss the upcoming meeting of partners and managers, where they would present the results of the study and a proposal for action. Included in the report were proposed layouts for both shared and hoteling offices. Vincent and Gray were planning to recommend a hoteling office system, which would include storage areas, state-of-the-art electronic office technology for managers and administrative support staff, and centralized files. The rationale for their decision emphasized the amount of time that managers were out of the office and the high cost of maintaining the status quo and was built around the following points:

1. Royce's business is different: offices are empty from 40 to 60 percent of the time.
2. Real estate costs continue to escalate.
3. Projections indicate there will be increased need for offices and cost-control strategies as the business develops.
4. Royce Consulting plays a leading role in helping organizations implement innovation.

"It's still a go," thought Vincent as he and the others returned from a break. "The cost figures support it and the growth figures support it. It's simple—or is it? The decision is the easy part. What is it about Royce Consulting that will help or hinder its acceptance? In the long run, I hope we strengthen our internal processes and don't hinder our effectiveness by going ahead with these simple changes."

INTEGRATIVE CASE 2.0   *Custom Chip, Inc.**

Introduction

It was 7:50 on Monday morning. Frank Questin, product engineering manager at Custom Chip, Inc., was sitting in his office making a TO DO list for the day. From 8:00 to 9:30 a.m., he would have his weekly meeting with his staff of engineers. After the meeting, Frank thought he would begin developing a proposal for solving what he called "Custom Chip's manufacturing documentation problem"—inadequate technical information regarding the steps to manufacture many of the company's products. Before he could finish his TO DO list, he answered a phone call from Custom Chip's human resource manager, who asked him about the status of two overdue performance appraisals and reminded him that this day marked Bill Lazarus's fifth-year anniversary with the company. Following this call, Frank hurried off to the Monday morning meeting with his staff.

Frank had been product engineering manager at Custom Chip for fourteen months. This was his first management position, and he sometimes questioned his effectiveness as a manager. Often he could not complete the tasks he set out for himself due to interruptions and problems brought to his attention by others. Even though he had not been told exactly what results he was supposed to accomplish, he had a nagging feeling that he should have achieved more after these fourteen months. On the other hand, he thought maybe he was functioning pretty well in some of his areas of responsibility given the complexity of the problems his group handled and the unpredictable changes in the semiconductor industry—changes caused not only by rapid advances in technology, but also by increased foreign competition and a recent downturn in demand.

Company Background

Custom Chip, Inc., was a semiconductor manufacturer specializing in custom chips and components used in radars, satellite transmitters, and other radio frequency devices. The company had been founded in 1977 and had grown rapidly with sales exceeding $25 million in 1986. Most of the company's 300 employees were located in the main plant in Silicon Valley, but overseas manufacturing facilities in Europe and the Far East were growing in size and importance. These overseas facilities assembled the less complex, higher-volume products. New products and the more complex ones were assembled in the main plant. Approximately one-third of the assembly employees were in overseas facilities.

While the specialized products and markets of Custom Chip provided a market niche that had thus far shielded the company from the major downturn in the semiconductor industry, growth had come to a standstill. Because of this, cost reduction had become a high priority.

The Manufacturing Process

Manufacturers of standard chips have long production runs of a few products. Their cost per unit is low and cost control is a primary determinant of success. In contrast, manufacturers of custom chips have extensive product lines and produce small production runs of special applications. Custom Chip, Inc., for example, had manufactured over 2,000 different products in the last five years. In any one quarter the company might schedule 300 production runs for different products, as many as one-third of which might be new or modified products that the company had not made before. Because they must be efficient in designing and manufacturing many product lines, all custom chip manufacturers are highly dependent on their engineers. Customers are often first concerned with whether Custom Chip can design and manufacture the needed product *at all*; second, with whether they can deliver it on time; and only third, with cost.

After a product is designed, there are two phases to the manufacturing process. (See Exhibit 1.) The first is wafer fabrication. This is a complex process in which circuits are etched onto the various layers added to a silicon wafer. The number of steps that the wafer goes through plus inherent problems in controlling various chemical processes make it very difficult to meet the exacting specifications required for the final wafer. The wafers, which are typically "just a few" inches in diameter when the fabrication process is complete, contain hundreds, sometimes thousands, of tiny identical die. Once the wafer has been tested and sliced up to produce these die, each die will be used as a circuit component.

*Copyright Murray Silverman, San Francisco State University. Reprinted by permission.

EXHIBIT I   *Manufacturing Process*

Pre-production

- *Application engineers design and produce prototype*
- *Product engineers translate design into manufacturing instructions*

Production

- *Wafer fabrication*

Circuits are etched onto layers added to . . .

. . . a silicon wafer.

Wafer is tested and then cut up into "die."

8 – 12 weeks

- *Assembly*

  Die, wires, and other components are attached to circuits.

4 – 6 weeks

If the completed wafer passes the various quality tests, it moves on to the assembly phase. In assembly, the die from the wafers, very small wires, and other components are attached to a circuit in a series of precise operations. This finished circuit is the final product of Custom Chip, Inc.

Each product goes through many independent and delicate operations, and each step is subject to operator or machine error. Due to the number of steps and tests involved, the wafer fabrication takes eight to twelve weeks and the assembly process takes four to six weeks. Because of the exacting specifications, products are rejected for the slightest flaw. The likelihood that every product starting the run will make it through all of the processes and still meet specifications is often quite low. For some products, average yield[1] is as low as 40 percent, and actual yields can vary considerably from one run to another. At Custom Chip, the average yield for all products is in the 60 to 70 percent range.

Because it takes so long to make a custom chip, it is especially important to have some control of these yields. For example, if a customer orders one thousand units of a product and typical yields for that product average 50 percent, Custom Chip will schedule a starting batch of 2,200 units. With this approach, even if the yield falls as low as 45.4 percent (45.4 percent of 2,200 is 1,000) the company can still meet the order. If the actual yield falls below 45.4 percent, the order will not be completed in that run, and a very small, costly run of the item will be needed to complete the order. The only way the company can effectively control these yields and stay on schedule is for the engineering groups and operations to cooperate and coordinate their efforts efficiently.

Role of the Product Engineer

The product engineer's job is defined by its relationship to applications engineering and operations. The applications engineers are responsible for designing and developing prototypes when incoming orders are for new or modified products. The product engineer's role is to translate the applications engineering group's design into a set of manufacturing instructions and then to work alongside manufacturing to make sure that engineering-related problems get solved. The product engineers' effectiveness is ultimately measured by their ability to control yields on their assigned products. The organization chart in Exhibit 2 shows the engineering and operations departments. Exhibit 3 summarizes the roles and objectives of manufacturing, applications engineering, and product engineering.

The product engineers estimate that 70 to 80 percent of their time is spent in solving day-to-day manufacturing problems. The product engineers have cubicles in a room directly across the hall from the manufacturing facility. If a manufacturing supervisor has a question regarding how to build a product during a run, that supervisor will call the engineer assigned to that product. If the engineer is available, he or she will go to the manufacturing floor to help answer the question. If the engineer is not available, the production run may be stopped and the product put aside so that other orders can be manufactured. This results in delays and added costs. One reason that product engineers are consulted is that documentation—the instructions for manufacturing the product—is unclear or incomplete.

The product engineer will also be called if a product is tested and fails to meet specifications. If a product fails to meet test specifications, production stops, and the engineer must diagnose the problem and attempt to find a solution. Otherwise, the order for that product may be only partially met. Test failures

EXHIBIT 2   *Custom Chip, Inc., Partial Organization Chart*

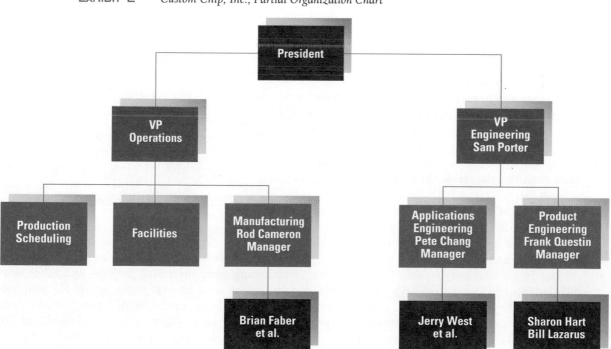

EXHIBIT 3   *Departmental Roles and Objectives*

Department	Role	Primary Objective
Applications Engineering	Designs and develops prototypes for new or modified products	Satisfy customer needs through innovative designs
Product Engineering	Translates designs into manufacturing instructions and works alongside manufacturing to solve "engineering-related" problems	Maintain and control yields on assigned products
Manufacturing	Executes designs	Meet productivity standards and time schedules

are a very serious problem, which can result in considerable cost increases and schedule delays for customers. Products do not test properly for many reasons, including operator errors, poor materials, a design that is very difficult to manufacture, a design that provides too little margin for error, or a combination of these.

On a typical day, the product engineer may respond to half a dozen questions from the manufacturing floor, and two to four calls to the testing stations. When interviewed, the engineers expressed a frustration with this situation. They thought they spent too much time solving short-term problems, and, consequently, they were neglecting other important parts of their jobs. In particular, they felt they had little time in which to:

- *Coordinate with applications engineers during the design phase.* The product engineers stated that their knowledge of manufacturing could provide valuable input to the applications engineer. Together they could improve the manufacturability and thus, the yields of the new or modified product.
- *Engage in yield improvement projects.* This would involve an in-depth study of the existing process for a specific product in conjunction with an analysis of past product failures.
- *Accurately document the manufacturing steps for their assigned products, especially for those that tend to have large or repeat orders.* They said that the current state of the documentation is very poor. Operators often have to build products using only a drawing showing the final circuit, along with a few notes scribbled in the margins. While experienced operators and supervisors may be able to work with this information, they often make incorrect guesses and assumptions.

Inexperienced operators may not be able to proceed with certain products because of this poor documentation.

Weekly Meeting

As manager of the product engineering group, Frank Questin had eight engineers reporting to him, each responsible for a different set of Custom Chip products. According to Frank:

> When I took over as manager, the product engineers were not spending much time together as a group. They were required to handle operations problems on short notice. This made it difficult for the entire group to meet due to constant requests for assistance from the manufacturing area.
>
> I thought that my engineers could be of more assistance and support to each other if they all spent more time together as a group, so one of my first actions as a manager was to institute a regularly scheduled weekly meeting. I let the manufacturing people know that my staff would not respond to requests for assistance during the meeting.

The meeting on this particular Monday morning followed the usual pattern. Frank talked about upcoming company plans, projects, and other news that might be of interest to the group. He then provided data about current yields for each product and commended those engineers who had maintained or improved yields on most of their products. This initial phase of the meeting lasted until about 8:30 a.m. The remainder of the meeting was a meandering discussion of a variety of topics. Since there was no agenda, engineers felt comfortable in raising issues of concern to them.

The discussion started with one of the engineers describing a technical problem in the assembly of one of his products. He was asked a number of questions and given some advice. Another engineer raised the topic of a need for new testing equipment and described a test unit he had seen at a recent demonstration. He claimed the savings in labor and improved yields from this machine would allow it to pay for itself in less than nine months. Frank immediately replied that budget limitations made such a purchase unfeasible, and the discussion moved into another area. They briefly discussed the increasing inaccessibility of the applications engineers and then talked about a few other topics.

In general, the engineers valued these meetings. One commented that:

> The Monday meetings give me a chance to hear what's on everyone's mind and to find out about and discuss company-wide news. It's hard to reach any conclusions because the meeting is a freewheeling discussion. But I really appreciate the friendly atmosphere with my peers.

Coordination with Applications Engineers

Following the meeting that morning, an event occurred that highlighted the issue of the inaccessibility of the applications engineers. An order of 300 units of custom chip 1210A for a major customer was already overdue. Because the projected yield of this product was 70 percent, they had started with a run of 500 units. A sample tested at one of the early assembly points indicated a major performance problem that could drop the yield to below 50 percent. Bill Lazarus, the product engineer assigned to the 1210A, examined the sample and determined that the problem could be solved by redesigning the wiring. Jerry West, the applications engineer assigned to that product category, was responsible for revising the design. Bill tried to contact Jerry, but he was not immediately available, and didn't get back to Bill until later in the day. Jerry explained that he was on a tight schedule trying to finish a design for a customer who was coming into town in two days, and could not get to "Bill's problem" for a while.

Jerry's attitude that the problem belonged to product engineering was typical of the applications engineers. From their point of view there were a number of reasons for making the product engineers' needs for assistance a lower priority. In the first place, applications engineers were rewarded and acknowledged primarily for satisfying customer needs through designing new and modified products. They got little recognition for solving manufacturing problems. Second, applications engineering was perceived to be more glamorous than product engineering because of opportunities to be credited with innovative and groundbreaking designs. Finally, the size of the applications engineering group had declined over the past year, causing the workload on each engineer to increase considerably. Now they had even less time to respond to the product engineers' requests.

When Bill Lazarus told Frank about the situation, Frank acted quickly. He wanted this order to be in process again by tomorrow, and he knew manufacturing was also trying to meet this goal. He walked over to see Pete Chang, head of applications engineering (see the organizational chart in Exhibit 2). Meetings like this with Pete to discuss and resolve interdepartmental issues were common.

Frank found Pete at a workbench talking with one of his engineers. He asked Pete if he could talk to him in private, and they walked to Pete's office.

Frank: We've got a problem in manufacturing in getting out an order of 1210As. Bill Lazarus is getting little or no assistance from Jerry West. I'm hoping you can get Jerry to pitch in and help Bill. It should take no more than a few hours of his time.

Pete: I do have Jerry on a short leash trying to keep him focused on getting out a design for Teletronics. We can't afford to show up empty-handed at our meeting with them in two days.

Frank: Well, we are going to end up losing one customer in trying to please another. Can't we satisfy everyone here?

Pete: Do you have an idea?

Frank: Can't you give Jerry some additional support on the Teletronics design?

Pete: Let's get Jerry in here to see what we can do.

Pete brought Jerry back to the office, and together they discussed the issues and possible solutions. When Pete made it clear to Jerry that he considered the problem with the 1210As a priority, Jerry offered to work on the 1210A problem with Bill. He said, "This will mean I'll have to stay a few hours past 5:00 this evening, but I'll do what's required to get the job done."

Frank was glad he had developed a collaborative relationship with Pete. He had always made it a point to keep Pete informed about activities in the product engineering group that might affect the applications engineers. In addition, he would often chat with Pete informally over coffee or lunch in the company cafeteria. This relationship with Pete made Frank's job easier. He wished he had the same rapport with Rod Cameron, the manufacturing manager.

Coordination with Manufacturing

The product engineers worked closely on a day-to-day basis with the manufacturing supervisors and workers. The problems between these two groups stemmed from an inherent conflict between their objectives (see Exhibit 3). The objective of the product engineers was to maintain and improve yields. They had the authority to stop production of any run that did not test properly. Manufacturing, on the other hand, was trying to meet productivity standards and time schedules. When a product engineer stopped a manufacturing run, he or she was possibly preventing the manufacturing group from reaching its objectives.

Rod Cameron, the current manufacturing manager, had been promoted from his position as a manufacturing supervisor a year ago. His views on the product engineers:

> The product engineers are perfectionists. The minute a test result looks a little suspicious they want to shut down the factory. I'm under a lot of pressure to get products out the door. If they pull a few $50,000 orders off the line when they are within a few days of reaching shipping, I'm liable to miss my numbers by $100,000 that month.
>
> Besides that, they are doing a lousy job of documenting the manufacturing steps. I've got a lot of turnover, and my new operators need to be told or shown exactly what to do for each product. The instructions for a lot of our products are a joke.

At first, Frank found Rod very difficult to deal with. Rod found fault with the product engineers for many problems and sometimes seemed rude to Frank when they talked. For example, Rod might tell Frank to "make it quick; I haven't got much time." Frank tried not to take Rod's actions personally, and through persistence was able to develop a more amicable relationship with him. According to Frank:

> Sometimes, my people will stop work on a product because it doesn't meet test results at that stage of manufacturing. If we study the situation, we might be able to maintain yields or even save an entire run by adjusting the manufacturing procedures. Rod tries to bully me into changing my engineers' decisions. He yells at me or criticizes the competence of my people, but I don't allow his temper or ravings to influence my best judgment in a situation. My strategy in dealing with Rod is to try not to respond defensively to him. Eventually he cools down, and we can have a reasonable discussion of the situation.

Despite this strategy, Frank could not always resolve his problems with Rod. On these occasions, Frank took the issue to his own boss, Sam Porter, the vice president in charge of engineering. However, Frank was not satisfied with the support he got from Sam. Frank said:

> Sam avoids confrontations with the operations VP. He doesn't have the influence or clout with the other VPs or the president to do justice to engineering's needs in the organization.

Early that afternoon, Frank again found himself trying to resolve a conflict between engineering and manufacturing. Sharon Hart, one of his most effective product engineers, was responsible for a series of products used in radars—the 3805A–3808A series. Today she had stopped a large run of 3806As. The manufacturing supervisor, Brian Faber, went to Rod Cameron to complain about the impact of this stoppage on his group's productivity. Brian felt that yields were low on that particular product because the production instructions were confusing to his operators, and that even with clearer instructions, his operators would need additional training to build it satisfactorily. He stressed that the product engineer's responsibility was to adequately document the production instructions and provide training. For these reasons, Brian asserted that product engineering, and not manufacturing, should be accountable for the productivity loss in the case of these 3806As.

Rod called Frank to his office, where he joined the discussion with Sharon, Brian, and Rod. After listening to the issues, Frank conceded that product engineering had responsibility for documenting and training. He also explained, even though everyone was aware of it, that the product engineering group had been operating with reduced staff for over a year now, so training and documentation were lower priorities. Because of this staffing situation, Frank suggested that manufacturing and product engineering work together and pool their limited resources to solve the documentation and training problem. He was especially interested in using a few of the long-term experienced workers to assist in training newer workers. Rod and Brian opposed his suggestion. They did not want to take experienced operators off of the line because it would decrease productivity. The meeting ended when Brian stormed out, saying that Sharon had better get the 3806As up and running again that morning.

Frank was particularly frustrated by this episode with manufacturing. He knew perfectly well that his group had primary responsibility for documenting the manufacturing steps for each product. A year ago he told Sam Porter that the product engineers needed to update and standardize all of the documentation for manufacturing products. At that time, Sam told Frank that he would support his efforts to develop the documentation, but would not increase his staff. In fact, Sam had withheld authorization to fill a recently vacated product engineering slot. Frank was reluctant to push the staffing issue because of Sam's adamance about reducing costs. "Perhaps," Frank thought, "if I develop a proposal clearly showing the benefits of a documentation program in manufacturing and detailing the steps and resources required to implement the program, I might be able to convince Sam to provide us with more resources." But Frank could never find the time to develop that proposal. And so he remained frustrated.

Later in the Day

Frank was reflecting on the complexity of his job when Sharon came to the doorway to see if he had a few moments. Before he could say "Come in," the phone rang. He looked at the clock. It was 4:10 p.m.

Pete was on the other end of the line with an idea he wanted to try out on Frank, so Frank said he could call him back shortly. Sharon was upset, and told him that she was thinking of quitting because the job was not satisfying for her.

Sharon said that although she very much enjoyed working on yield improvement projects, she could find no time for them. She was tired of the applications engineers acting like "prima donnas," too busy to help her solve what they seemed to think were mundane day-to-day manufacturing problems. She also thought that many of the day-to-day problems she handled wouldn't exist if there was enough time to document manufacturing procedures to begin with.

Frank didn't want to lose Sharon, so he tried to get into a frame of mind where he could be empathetic to her. He listened to her and told her that he could understand her frustration in this situation. He told her the situation would change as industry conditions improved. He told her that he was pleased that she felt comfortable in venting her frustrations with him, and he hoped she would stay with Custom Chip.

After Sharon left, Frank realized that he had told Pete that he would call back. He glanced at the TO DO list he had never completed, and realized that he hadn't spent time on his top priority—developing a proposal relating to solving the documentation problem in manufacturing. Then, he remembered that he had forgotten to acknowledge Bill Lazarus's fifth-year anniversary with the company. He thought to himself that his job felt like a roller coaster ride, and once again he pondered his effectiveness as a manager.

Notes

1. Yield refers to the ratio of finished products that meet specifications relative to the number that initially entered the manufacturing process.

"To make money and have fun." W. L. Gore

The First Day on the Job

Bursting with resolve, Jack Dougherty, a newly minted M.B.A. from the College of William and Mary, reported to his first day at W. L. Gore & Associates on July 26, 1976. He presented himself to Bill Gore, shook hands firmly, looked him in the eye, and said he was ready for anything.

Jack was not ready, however, for what happened next. Gore replied, "That's fine, Jack, fine. Why don't you look around and find something you'd like to do?" Three frustrating weeks later he found that something: trading in his dark blue suit for jeans, he loaded fabric into the mouth of a machine that laminated the company's patented GORE-TEX®[1] membrane to fabric. By 1982, Jack had become responsible for all advertising and marketing in the fabrics group. This story is part of the folklore of W. L. Gore & Associates.

Today the process is more structured. Regardless of the job for which they are hired, new Associates[2] take a journey through the business before settling into their own positions. A new sales Associate in the fabrics division may spend six weeks rotating through different areas before beginning to concentrate on sales and marketing. Among other things the newcomer learns is how GORE-TEX fabric is made, what it can and cannot do, how Gore handles customer complaints, and how it makes its investment decisions.

Anita McBride related her early experience at W. L. Gore & Associates this way: "Before I came to Gore, I had worked for a structured organization. I came here, and for the first month it was fairly structured because I was going through training and this is what we do and this is how Gore is and all of that. I went to Flagstaff for that training. After a month I came down to Phoenix and my sponsor said, 'Well, here's your office; it's a wonderful office,' and 'Here's your desk,' and walked away. And I thought, 'Now what do I do?' You know, I was waiting for a memo or something, or a job description. Finally after another month I was so frustrated, I felt, 'What have I gotten myself into?' And so I went to my sponsor and I said, 'What the heck do you want from me? I need something from you.' And he said, 'If you don't know what you're supposed to do, examine your commitment, and opportunities.'"

Company Background

W. L. Gore & Associates was formed by the late Wilbert L. Gore and his wife in 1958. The idea for the business sprang from his personal, organizational, and technical experiences at E. I. DuPont de Nemours, and, particularly, his discovery of a chemical compound with unique properties. The compound, now widely know as GORE-TEX, has catapulted W. L. Gore & Associates to a high ranking on the *Forbes* 1998 list of the 500 largest private companies in the United States, with estimated revenues of more than $1.1 billion. The company's avant-garde culture and people management practices resulted in W. L. Gore being ranked as the seventh best company to work for in America by *Fortune* in a January 1998 article.

Wilbert Gore was born in Meridian, Idaho, near Boise in 1912. By age six, according to his own account, he was an avid hiker in the Wasatch Mountain Range in Utah. In those mountains, at a church camp, he met Genevieve, his future wife. In 1935, they got married—in their eyes, a partnership. He would make breakfast and Vieve, as everyone called her, would make lunch. The partnership lasted a lifetime.

He received both a bachelor of science in chemical engineering in 1933 and a master of science in physical chemistry in 1935 from the University of Utah. He began his professional career at American Smelting and Refining in 1936. He moved to Remington Arms Company in 1941 and then to E. I. DuPont de Nemours in 1945. He held positions as research supervisor and head of operations research. While at DuPont, he worked on a team to develop applications for polytetrafluoroethylene, referred to as PTFE in the scientific community and known as "Teflon" by DuPont's consumers. (Consumers know it under other names from other companies.) On this team Wilbert Gore, called Bill by everyone, felt a sense of excited commitment, personal fulfillment, and self-direction. He followed the development of computers and transistors and felt that PTFE had the ideal insulating characteristics for use with such equipment.

*Prepared by Frank Shipper, Department of Management and Marketing, Franklin P. Perdue School of Business, Salisbury State University and Charles C. Manz, Nirenberg Professor of Business Leadership, School of Management, University of Massachusetts. Used with permission.

He tried many ways to make a PTFE-coated ribbon cable without success. A breakthrough came in his home basement laboratory while he was explaining the problem to his nineteen-year-old son, Bob. The young Gore saw some PTFE sealant tape made by 3M and asked his father, "Why don't you try this tape?" Bill then explained that everyone knew that you cannot bond PTFE to itself. Bob went on to bed.

Bill Gore remained in his basement lab and proceeded to try what everyone knew would not work. At about 4 a.m. he woke up his son, waving a small piece of cable around and saying excitedly, "It works, it works." The following night father and son returned to the basement lab to make ribbon cable coated with PTFE. Because the breakthrough idea came from Bob, the patent for the cable was issued in Bob's name.

For the next four months Bill Gore tried to persuade DuPont to make a new product—PTFE-coated ribbon cable. By this time in his career Bill Gore knew some of the decision makers at DuPont. After talking to a number of them, he came to realize that DuPont wanted to remain a supplier of raw materials and not a fabricator.

Bill and his wife, Vieve, began discussing the possibility of starting their own insulated wire and cable business. On January 1, 1958, their wedding anniversary, they founded W. L. Gore & Associates. The basement of their home served as their first facility. After finishing dinner that night, Vieve turned to her husband of twenty-three years and said, "Well, let's clear up the dishes, go downstairs, and get to work."

Bill Gore was forty-five years old with five children to support when he left DuPont. He put aside a career of seventeen years, and a good, secure salary. To finance the first two years of the business, he and Vieve mortgaged their house and took $4,000 from savings. All their friends told them not to do it.

The first few years were rough. In lieu of salary, some of their employees accepted room and board in the Gore home. At one point eleven Associates were living and working under one roof. One afternoon, while sifting PTFE powder, Vieve received a call from the City of Denver's water department. The caller indicated that he was interested in the ribbon cable, but wanted to ask some technical questions. Bill was out running some errands. The caller asked for the product manager. Vieve explained that he was out at the moment. Next he asked for the sales manager and finally, the president. Vieve explained that they were

also out. The caller became outraged and hollered, "What kind of company is this anyway?" With a little diplomacy the Gores were able eventually to secure an order for $100,000. This order put the company on a profitable footing and it began to take off.

W. L. Gore & Associates continued to grow and develop new products, primarily derived from PTFE. Its best-known product would become GORE-TEX fabric. In 1986, Bill Gore died while backpacking in the Wind River Mountains of Wyoming. He was then Chairman of the Board. His son, Bob, continued to occupy the position of president. Vieve remained as the only other officer, secretary-treasurer.

Company Products

In 1998 W. L. Gore & Associates has a fairly extensive line of high-tech products that are used in a variety of applications, including electronic, waterproofing, industrial filtration, industrial seals, and coatings.

Electronic & Wire Products

Gore electronic products have been found in unconventional places where conventional products will not do—in space shuttles, for example, where Gore wire and cable assemblies withstand the heat of ignition and the cold of space. In addition, they have been found in fast computers, transmitting signals at up to 93 percent of the speed of light. Gore cables have even gone underground, in oil-drilling operations, and underseas, on submarines that require superior microwave signal equipment and no-fail cables that can survive high pressure. The Gore electronic products division has a history of anticipating future customer needs with innovative products. Gore electronic products have been well received in industry for their ability to last under adverse conditions. For example, Gore has become, according to Sally Gore, leader in Human Resources and Communications, "one of the largest manufacturers of ultrasound cable in the world, the reason being that Gore's electronic cables' signal transmission is very, very accurate and it's very thin and extremely flexible and has a very, very long flex life. That makes it ideal for things like ultrasound and many medical electronic applications."

Medical Products

The medical division began on the ski slopes of Colorado. Bill was skiing with a friend, Dr. Ben Eiseman of Denver General Hospital. As Bill Gore told the story: "We were just to start a run when I absentmindedly pulled a small tubular section of GORE-TEX out of my pocket and looked at it. 'What is that stuff?' Ben asked. So I told him about its properties. 'Feels great,' he said. 'What do you use it for?' 'Got no idea,' I said. 'Well give it to me,' he said, 'and I'll try it in a vascular graft on a pig.' Two weeks later, he called me up. Ben was pretty excited. 'Bill,' he said, 'I put it in a pig and it works. What do I do now?' I told him to get together with Pete Cooper in our Flagstaff plant, and let them figure it out." Not long after, hundreds of thousands of people throughout the world began walking around with GORE-TEX vascular grafts.

GORE-TEX's expanded PTFE proved to be an ideal replacement for human tissue in many situations. In patients suffering from cardiovascular disease the diseased portion of arteries has been replaced by tubes of expanded PTFE—strong, biocompatible structures capable of carrying blood at arterial pressures. Gore has a strong position in this product segment. Other Gore medical products have included patches that can literally mend broken hearts by sealing holes, and sutures that allow for tissue attachment and offer the surgeon silk-like handling coupled with extreme strength. In 1985, W. L. Gore & Associates won Britain's Prince Philip Award for Polymers in the Service of Mankind. The award recognized especially the lifesaving achievements of the Gore medical products team.

Two recently developed products by this division are a new patch material that is intended to incorporate more tissue into the graft more quickly and the GORE™ RideOn®[3] Cable System for bicycles. According to Amy LeGere of the medical division, "All the top pro riders in the world are using it. It was introduced just about a year ago and it has become an industry standard." This product had a positive cash flow very soon after its introduction. Some Associates who were also outdoor sports enthusiasts developed the product and realized that Gore could make a great bicycle cable that would have 70 percent less friction and need no lubrication. The Associates maintain that the profitable development, production, and marketing of such specialized niche products are possible because of the lack of bureaucracy and associated overhead, Associate commitment, and the use of product champions.

Industrial Products
The output of the industrial products division has included sealants, filter bags, cartridges, clothes, and coatings. Industrial filtration products, such as GORE-TEX filter bags, have reduced air pollution and recovered valuable solids from gases and liquids more completely than alternatives—and they have done so economically. In the future they may make coal-burning plants completely smoke-free, contributing to a cleaner environment. The specialized and critical applications of these products, along with Gore's reputation for quality, have had a strong influence on industrial purchasers.

This division has developed a unique joint sealant—a flexible cord of porous PTFE—that can be applied as a gasket to the most complex shapes, sealing them to prevent leakage of corrosive chemicals, even at extreme temperature and pressure. Steam valves packed with GORE-TEX have been sold with a lifetime guarantee, provided the valve is used properly. In addition, this division has introduced Gore's first consumer product—GLIDE®[4]—a dental floss. "That was a product that people knew about for a while and they went the route of trying to persuade industry leaders to promote the product, but they didn't really pursue it very well. So out of basically default almost, Gore decided, Okay, they're not doing it right. Let's go in ourselves. We had a champion, John Spencer, who took that and pushed it forward through the dentists' offices and it just skyrocketed. There were many more people on the team but it was basically getting that one champion who focused on that product and got it out. They told him it 'couldn't be done,' 'It's never going to work,' and I guess that's all he needed. It was done and it worked," said Ray Wnenchak of the industrial products division. Amy LeGere added, "The champion worked very closely with the medical people to understand the medical market like claims and labeling so that when the product came out on the market it would be consistent with our medical products. And that's where, when we cross divisions, we know whom to work with and with whom we combine forces so that the end result takes the strengths of all of our different teams." As of 1998, GLIDE has captured a major portion of the dental floss market and the mint flavor is the largest-selling variety in the U.S. market based on dollar volume.

Fabric Products
The Gore fabrics division has supplied laminates to manufacturers of foul weather gear, ski wear, running suits, footwear, gloves, and hunting and fishing garments. Firefighters and U.S. Navy pilots have worn

GORE-TEX fabric gear, as have some Olympic athletes. The U.S. Army adopted a total garment system built around a GORE-TEX fabric component. Employees in high-tech clean rooms also wear GORE-TEX garments.

GORE-TEX membrane has 9 billion pores randomly dotting each square inch and is feather-light. Each pore is 700 times larger than a water vapor molecule, yet thousands of times smaller than a water droplet. Wind and water cannot penetrate the pores, but perspiration can escape.

As a result, fabrics bonded with GORE-TEX membrane are waterproof, windproof, and breathable. The laminated fabrics bring protection from the elements to a variety of products—from survival gear to high-fashion rainwear. Other manufacturers, including 3M, Burlington Industries, Akzo Nobel Fibers, and DuPont, have brought out products to compete with GORE-TEX fabrics. Earlier, the toughest competition came from firms that violated the patents on GORE-TEX. Gore successfully challenged them in court. In 1993, the basic patent on the process for manufacturing ran out. Nevertheless, as Sally Gore explained, "what happens is you get an initial process patent and then as you begin to create things with this process you get additional patents. For instance we have patents protecting our vascular graft, different patents for protecting GORE-TEX patches, and still other patents protecting GORE-TEX industrial sealants and filtration material. One of our patent attorneys did a talk recently, a year or so ago, when the patent expired and a lot of people were saying, Oh, golly, are we going to be in trouble! We would be in trouble if we didn't have any patents. Our attorney had this picture with a great big umbrella, sort of a parachute, with Gore under it. Next he showed us lots of little umbrellas scattered all over the sky. So you protect certain niche markets and niche areas, but indeed competition increases as your initial patents expire." Gore, however, has continued to have a commanding position in the active-wear market.

To meet a variety of customer needs, Gore introduced a new family of fabrics in the 1990s (Exhibit 1). The introduction posed new challenges. According to Bob Winterling, "we did such a great job with the brand GORE-TEX that we actually have hurt ourselves in many ways. By that I mean it has been very difficult for us to come up with other new brands, because many people didn't even know Gore. We are the GORE-TEX company. One thing we decided to change about Gore four or five years ago was instead of being the GORE-TEX company we wanted to become the Gore company and that underneath the Gore company we had an umbrella of products that fall out of being the great Gore company. So it was a shift in how we positioned GORE-TEX. Today GORE-TEX is stronger than ever as it's turned out, but now we've ventured into such things as WindStopper®[5] fabric that is very big in the golf market. It could be a sweater or a fleece piece or even a knit shirt with the WindStopper behind it or closer

EXHIBIT 1 *Gore's Family of Fabrics*

Brand Name	Activity/Conditions	Breathability	Water Protection	Wind Protection
GORE-TEX®	rain, snow, cold, windy	very breathable	waterproof	windproof
Immersion™ technology	for fishing and paddle sports	very breathable	waterproof	windproof
Ocean technology	for offshore and coastal sailing	very breathable	waterproof	windproof
WindStopper®	cool/cold, windy	very breathable	no water resistance	windproof
Gore Dryloft™	cold, windy, light precipitation	extremely breathable	water-resistant	windproof
Activent™	cool/cold, windy, light precipitation	extremely breathable	water-resistant	windproof

to your skin and what it does is it stops the wind. It's not waterproof; it's water resistant. What we've tried to do is position the Gore name and beneath that all of the great products of the company."

W. L. Gore & Associates' Approach to Organization and Structure

W. L. Gore & Associates has never had titles, hierarchy, or any of the conventional structures associated with enterprises of its size. The titles of president and secretary-treasurer continue to be used only because they are required by the laws of incorporation. In addition, Gore has never had a corporate-wide mission or code of ethics statement, nor has Gore ever required or prohibited business units from developing such statements for themselves. Thus, the Associates of some business units who have felt a need for such statements have developed them on their own. When questioned about this issue, one Associate stated, "The company belief is that (1) its four basic operating principles cover ethical practices required of people in business; (2) it will not tolerate illegal practices." Gore's management style has been referred to as unmanagement. The organization has been guided by Bill's experiences on teams at DuPont and has evolved as needed.

For example, in 1965 W. L. Gore & Associates was a thriving company with a facility on Paper Mill Road in Newark, Delaware. One Monday morning in the summer, Bill Gore was taking his usual walk through the plant. All of a sudden he realized that he did not know everyone in the plant. The team had become too big. As a result, he established the practice of limiting plant size to approximately two hundred Associates. Thus was born the expansion policy of "Get big by staying small." The purpose of maintaining small plants was to accentuate a close-knit atmosphere and encourage communication among Associates in a facility.

At the beginning of 1998 W. L. Gore & Associates consisted of over forty-five plants worldwide with approximately seven thousand Associates. In some cases, the plants are grouped together on the same site (as in Flagstaff, Arizona, with ten plants). Overseas, Gore's manufacturing facilities are located in Scotland, Germany, and China, and the company has two joint ventures in Japan (see Exhibit 2). In addition, it has sales facilities located in fifteen other countries. Gore manufactures electronic, medical, industrial, and fabric products. In addition, it has numerous sales offices worldwide, including offices in Eastern Europe and Russia.

EXHIBIT 2   *International Locations of W. L. Gore & Associates*

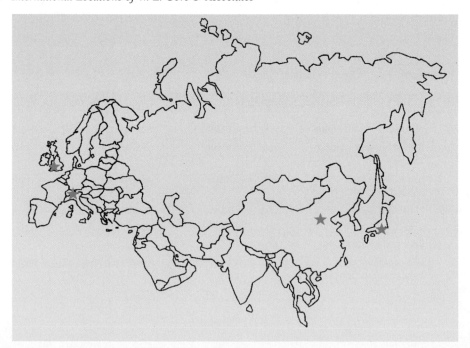

The Lattice Organization

W. L. Gore & Associates has been described not only as unmanaged, but also as unstructured. Bill Gore referred to the structure as a lattice organization (see Exhibit 3). The characteristics of this structure are:

1. Direct lines of communication—person to person—no intermediary
2. No fixed or assigned authority
3. Sponsors, not bosses
4. Natural leadership defined by followership
5. Objectives set by those who must "make them happen"
6. Tasks and functions organized through commitments

The structure within the lattice is complex and evolves from interpersonal interactions, self commitment to group-known responsibilities, natural leadership, and group-imposed discipline. Bill Gore once explained the structure this way: "Every successful organization has an underground lattice. It's where the news spreads like lightning, where people can go around the organization to get things done." An analogy might be drawn to a structure of constant cross-area teams—the equivalent of quality circles going on all the time. When a puzzled interviewer told Bill that he was having trouble understanding how planning and accountability worked, Bill replied with a grin: "So am I. You ask me how it works? Every which way."

The lattice structure has not been without its critics. As Bill Gore stated, "I'm told from time to time that a lattice organization can't meet a crisis well because it takes too long to reach a consensus when there are no bosses. But this isn't true. Actually, a lattice by its very nature works particularly well in a crisis. A lot of useless effort is avoided because there is no rigid management hierarchy to conquer before you can attack a problem."

The lattice has been put to the test on a number of occasions. For example, in 1975, Dr. Charles Campbell of the University of Pittsburgh reported that a GORE-TEX arterial graft had developed an aneurysm. If the bubble-like protrusion continued to expand, it would explode.

Obviously, this life-threatening situation had to be resolved quickly and permanently. Within only a few days of Dr. Campbell's first report, he flew to Newark to present his findings to Bill and Bob Gore and a few other Associates. The meeting lasted two hours. Dan Hubis, a former policeman who had joined Gore to develop new production methods, had an idea before the meeting was over. He returned to his work area to try some different pro-

EXHIBIT 3   *The Lattice Structure*

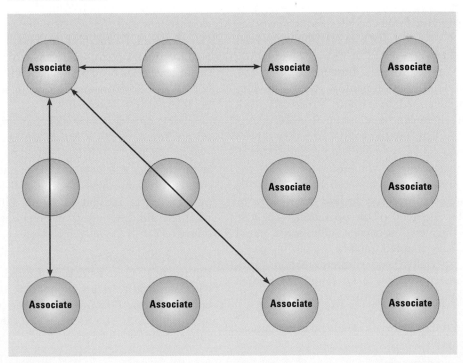

duction techniques. After only three hours and twelve tries, he had developed a permanent solution. In other words, in three hours a potentially damaging problem to both patients and the company was resolved. Furthermore, Hubis's redesigned graft went on to win widespread acceptance in the medical community.

Eric Reynolds, founder of Marmot Mountain Works Ltd. of Grand Junction, Colorado, and a major Gore customer, raised another issue: "I think the lattice has its problems with the day-to-day nitty-gritty of getting things done on time and out the door. I don't think Bill realizes how the lattice system affects customers. I mean, after you've established a relationship with someone about product quality, you can call up one day and suddenly find that someone new to you is handling your problem. It's frustrating to find a lack of continuity." He went on to say: "But I have to admit that I've personally seen at Gore remarkable examples of people coming out of nowhere and excelling."

When Bill Gore was asked if the lattice structure could be used by other companies, he answered: "No. For example, established companies would find it very difficult to use the lattice. Too many hierarchies would be destroyed. When you remove titles and positions and allow people to follow who they want, it may very well be someone other than the person who has been in charge. The lattice works for us, but it's always evolving. You have to expect problems." He maintained that the lattice system worked best when it was put in place in start-up companies by dynamic entrepreneurs.

Not all Gore Associates function well in this unstructured work environment, especially initially. For those accustomed to a more structured work environment, there can be adjustment problems. As Bill Gore said: "All our lives most of us have been told what to do, and some people don't know how to respond when asked to do something—and have the very real option of saying no—on their job. It's the new Associate's responsibility to find out what he or she can do for the good of the operation." The vast majority of the new Associates, after some initial floundering, have adapted quickly.

Others, especially those who require more structured working conditions, have found that Gore's flexible workplace is not for them. According to Bill, for those few, "It's an unhappy situation, for both the Associate and the sponsor. If there is no contribution, there is no paycheck."

As Anita McBride, an Associate in Phoenix, noted: "It's not for everybody. People ask me do we have turnover, and yes we do have turnover. What you're seeing looks like utopia, but it also looks extreme. If you finally figure the system, it can be real exciting. If you can't handle it, you gotta go. Probably by your own choice, because you're going to be so frustrated." Overall, the Associates appear to have responded positively to the Gore system of unmanagement and unstructure. And the company's lattice organization has proven itself to be good from a bottom-line perspective. Bill estimated the year before he died that "the profit per Associate is double" that of DuPont.

Features of W. L. Gore's Culture

Outsiders have been struck by the degree of informality and humor in the Gore organization. Meetings tend to be only as long as necessary. As Trish Hearn, an Associate in Newark, Delaware, said, "No one feels a need to pontificate." Words such as "responsibilities" and "commitments" are commonly heard, whereas words such as "employees," "subordinates," and "managers" are taboo in the Gore culture. This is an organization that has always taken what it does very seriously, without its members taking themselves too seriously.

For a company of its size, Gore has always had a very short organizational pyramid. As of 1995 the pyramid consists of Bob Gore, the late Bill Gore's son, as president and Vieve, Bill Gore's widow, as secretary-treasurer. He has been the chief executive officer for more than twenty years. No second-in-command or successor has been designated. All the other members of the Gore organization were, and continue to be, referred to as Associates.

Some outsiders have had problems with the idea of no titles. Sarah Clifton, an Associate at the Flagstaff facility, was being pressed by some outsiders as to what her title was. She made one up and had it printed on some business cards: SUPREME COMMANDER (see Exhibit 4). When Bill Gore learned what she did, he loved it and recounted the story to others.

Leaders, Not Managers

Within W. L. Gore & Associates, the various people who take lead roles are thought of as being leaders, not managers. Bill Gore described in an internal memo the kinds of leadership and the role of leadership as follows:

EXHIBIT 4   *The Supreme Commander*

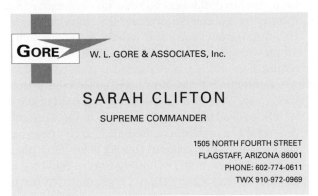

GORE ▸   W. L. GORE & ASSOCIATES, Inc.

SARAH CLIFTON

SUPREME COMMANDER

1505 NORTH FOURTH STREET
FLAGSTAFF, ARIZONA 86001
PHONE: 602-774-0611
TWX 910-972-0969

1. The Associate who is recognized by a team as having a special knowledge, or experience (for example, this could be a chemist, computer expert, machine operator, salesman, engineer, lawyer). This kind of leader gives the team *guidance in a special area*.

2. The Associate the team looks to for coordination of individual activities in order to achieve the agreed-upon objectives of the team. The role of this leader is to persuade team members to *make the commitments* necessary for success (commitment seeker).

3. The Associate who proposes necessary objectives and activities and seeks agreement and team *consensus on objectives*. This leader is perceived by the team members as having a good grasp of how the objectives of the team fit in with the broad objective of the enterprise. This kind of leader is often also the "commitment-seeking" leader in 2 above.

4. The leader who evaluates relative contribution of team members (in consultation with other sponsors), and reports these contribution evaluations to a compensation committee. This leader may also participate in the compensation committee on relative contribution and pay and *reports changes in compensation* to individual Associates. This leader is then also a compensation sponsor.

5. *Product specialists* who coordinate the research, manufacturing, and marketing of one product type within a business, interacting with team leaders and individual Associates who have commitments regarding the product type. They are respected for their knowledge and dedication to their products.

6. *Plant leaders* who help coordinate activities of people within a plant.

7. *Business leaders* who help coordinate activities of people in a business.

8. *Functional leaders* who help coordinate activities of people in a "functional" area.

9. *Corporate leaders* who help coordinate activities of people in different businesses and functions and who try to promote communication and cooperation among all Associates.

10. *Entrepreneuring Associates* who organize new teams for new businesses, new products, new processes, new devices, new marketing efforts, new or better methods of all kinds. These leaders invite other Associates to "sign up" for their project.

It is clear that leadership is widespread in our lattice organization and that it is continually changing and evolving. The situation that leaders are frequently *also* sponsors should not imply that these are different activities and responsibilities.

Leaders are not authoritarians, managers of people, or supervisors who tell us what to do or forbid us to do things; nor are they "parents" to whom we transfer our own self-responsibility. However, they do often advise us of the consequences of actions we have done or propose to do. Our actions result in contributions, or lack of contribution, to the success of our enterprise. Our pay depends on the magnitude of our contributions. This is the basic discipline of our lattice organization.

Egalitarian and Innovative

Other aspects of the Gore culture have been aimed at promoting an egalitarian atmosphere, such as parking lots with no reserved parking spaces except for customers and disabled workers or visitors and dining areas—only one in each plant—set up as focal points for Associate interaction. As Dave McCarter of Phoenix explained: "The design is no accident. The lunchroom in Flagstaff has a fireplace in the middle. We want people to like to be here." The location of a plant is also no accident. Sites have been selected on the basis of transportation access, a nearby university, beautiful surroundings, and climate appeal. Land cost has never been a primary consideration. McCarter justified the selection by stating: "Expanding is not costly in the long run. The loss of money is what you make happen by stymieing people into a box."

Bob Gore is a champion of Gore culture. As Sally Gore related, "We have managed surprisingly to maintain our sense of freedom and our entrepreneurial spirit. I think what we've found is that we had to develop new ways to communicate with Associates because you can't communicate with six thousand people the way that you can communicate with five hundred people. It just can't be done. So we have developed a newsletter that we didn't have before. One of the most important communication mediums that we developed, and this was Bob Gore's idea, is a digital voice exchange which we call our Gorecom. Basically everyone has a mailbox and a password. Lots of companies have gone to e-mail and we use e-mail, but Bob feels very strongly that we're very much an oral culture and there's a big difference between cultures that are predominantly oral and predominantly written. Oral cultures encourage direct communication, which is, of course, something that we encourage."

In rare cases an Associate "is trying to be unfair," in Bill's own words. In one case the problem was chronic absenteeism and in another, an individual was caught stealing. "When that happens, all hell breaks loose," said Bill Gore. "We can get damned authoritarian when we have to."

Over the years, Gore & Associates has faced a number of unionization drives. The company has neither tried to dissuade Associates from attending an organizational meeting nor retaliated when flyers were passed out. As of 1995, none of the plants had been organized. Bill believed that no need existed for third-party representation under the lattice structure. He asked the question, "Why would Associates join a union when they own the company? It seems rather absurd."

Commitment has long been considered a two-way street. W. L. Gore & Associates has tried to avoid layoffs. Instead of cutting pay, which in the Gore culture would be disastrous to morale, the company has used a system of temporary transfers within a plant or cluster of plants and voluntary layoffs. Exhibit 7 at the end of this case example contains excerpts of interviews with two Gore Associates that further indicate the nature of the culture and work environment at W. L. Gore and Associates.

W. L. Gore & Associates' Sponsor Program

Bill Gore knew that products alone did not a company make. He wanted to avoid smothering the company in thick layers of formal "management." He felt that hierarchy stifled individual creativity. As the company grew, he knew that he had to find a way to assist new people and to follow their progress. This was particularly important when it came to compensation. W. L. Gore & Associates developed its "sponsor" program to meet these needs.

When people apply to Gore, they are initially screened by personnel specialists. As many as ten

EXHIBIT 5   *Growth of Gore's Sales vs. Gross Domestic Product*

	1989	1990	1991	1992	1993	1994	1995	1996	1997
Gore	600	660	700	750	804	828	958	1064	1160
G.D.P.	5438.7	5743.8	5916.7	6244.4	6553	6935.7	7265.4	7636	8079.9

references might be contacted on each applicant. Those who meet the basic criteria are interviewed by current Associates. The interviews have been described as rigorous by those who have gone through them. Before anyone is hired, an Associate must agree to be his or her sponsor. The sponsor is to take a personal interest in the new Associate's contributions, problems, and goals, acting as both a coach and an advocate. The sponsor tracks the new Associate's progress, helping and encouraging, dealing with weaknesses, and concentrating on strengths. Sponsoring is not a short-term commitment. All Associates have sponsors and many have more than one. When individuals are hired initially, they are likely to have a sponsor in their immediate work area. If they move to another area, they may have a sponsor in that work area. As Associates' commitments change or grow, they may acquire additional sponsors. Because the hiring process looks beyond conventional views of what makes a good Associate, some anomalies have occurred. Bill Gore proudly told the story of "a very young man" of 84 who walked in, applied, and spent five very good years with the company. The individual had thirty years of experience in the industry before joining Gore. His other Associates had no problems accepting him, but the personnel computer did. It insisted that his age was 48. The individual success stories at Gore have come from diverse backgrounds.

An internal memo by Bill Gore described three roles of sponsors:

1. *Starting sponsor*—a sponsor who helps a new Associate get started on a first job, or a present Associate get started on a new job.
2. *Advocate sponsor*—a sponsor who sees that an Associate's accomplishments are recognized.
3. *Compensation sponsor*—a sponsor who sees to it that an Associate is fairly paid for contributions to the success of the enterprise.

A single person can perform any one or all three kinds of sponsorship. Quite frequently, a sponsoring Associate is a good friend and it is not unknown for two Associates to sponsor each other.

Compensation Practices

Compensation at W. L. Gore & Associates has taken three forms: salary, profit sharing, and an Associates' Stock Ownership Program (ASOP).[6] Entry-level salary has been in the middle for comparable jobs.

According to Sally Gore: "We do not feel we need to be the highest paid. We never try to steal people away from other companies with salary. We want them to come here because of the opportunities for growth and the unique work environment." Associates' salaries have been reviewed at least once a year and more commonly twice a year. The reviews are conducted by a compensation team at each facility, with sponsors for the Associates acting as their advocates during the review process. Prior to meeting with the compensation committee, the sponsor checks with customers or Associates familiar with the person's work to find out what contribution the Associate has made. The compensation team relies heavily on this input. In addition, the compensation team considers the Associate's leadership ability and willingness to help others develop to their fullest.

Profit sharing follows a formula based on economic value added (EVA). Sally Gore had the following to say about the adoption of a formula: "It's become more formalized, and in a way, I think that's unfortunate because it used to be a complete surprise to receive a profit share. The thinking of the people like Bob Gore and other leaders was that maybe we weren't using it in the right way and we could encourage people by helping them know more about it and how we made profit-share decisions. The fun of it before was people didn't know when it was coming and all of a sudden you could do something creative about passing out checks. It was great fun and people would have a wonderful time with it. The disadvantage was that Associates then did not focus much on, 'What am I doing to create another profit share?' By using EVA as a method of evaluation for our profit share, we know at the end of every month how much EVA was created that month. When we've created a certain amount of EVA, we then get another profit share. So everybody knows and everyone says, 'We'll do it in January,' so it is done. Now Associates feel more part of the happening to make it work. What have you done? Go make some more sales calls, please! There are lots of things we can do to improve our EVA and everybody has a responsibility to do that." Every month EVA is calculated and every Associate is informed. John Mosko of electronic products commented, "... (EVA) lets us know where we are on the path to getting one (a profit share). It's very critical—every Associate knows."

Annually, Gore also buys company stock equivalent to a fixed percent of the Associates' annual incomes, placing it in the ASOP retirement fund.

Thus, an Associate can become a stockholder after being at Gore for a year. Gore's ASOP ensures Associates participate in the growth of the company by acquiring ownership in it. Bill Gore wanted Associates to feel that they themselves are owners. One Associate stated, "This is much more important than profit sharing." In fact, some long-term Associates (including a twenty-five-year veteran machinist) have become millionaires from the ASOP.

W. L. Gore & Associates' Guiding Principles and Core Values

In addition to the sponsor program, Bill Gore articulated four guiding principles:

1. Try to be fair.
2. Encourage, help, and allow other Associates to grow in knowledge, skill, and scope of activity and responsibility.
3. Make your own commitments, and keep them.
4. Consult with other Associates before taking actions that may be "below the water line."

The four principles have been referred to as Fairness, Freedom, Commitment, and Waterline. The *waterline* terminology is drawn from an analogy to ships. If someone pokes a hole in a boat above the water line, the boat will be in relatively little real danger. If someone, however, pokes a hole below the water line, the boat is in immediate danger of sinking. "Water line" issues must be discussed across teams and plants before decisions are made.

The operating principles were put to a test in 1978. By this time word about the qualities of GORE-TEX fabric was being spread throughout the recreational and outdoor markets. Production and shipment had begun in volume. At first a few complaints were heard. Next some of the clothing started coming back. Finally, much of the clothing was being returned. The trouble was that the GORE-TEX fabric was leaking. Waterproofing was one of the major properties responsible for GORE-TEX fabric's success. The company's reputation and credibility were on the line.

Peter W. Gilson, who led Gore's fabrics division, recalled: "It was an incredible crisis for us at that point. We were really starting to attract attention; we were taking off—and then this." In the next few months, Gilson and a number of his Associates made a number of those below-the-water-line decisions.

First, the researchers determined that oils in human sweat were responsible for clogging the pores in the GORE-TEX fabric and altering the surface tension of the membrane. Thus, water could pass through. They also discovered that a good washing could restore the waterproof property. At first this solution, known as the "Ivory Snow solution," was accepted. A single letter from "Butch," a mountain guide in the Sierras, changed the company's position. Butch described what happened while he was leading a group: "My parka leaked and my life was in danger." As Gilson noted, "That scared the hell out of us. Clearly our solution was no solution at all to someone on a mountaintop." All the products were recalled. Gilson remembered: "We bought back, at our own expense, a fortune in pipeline material—anything that was in the stores, at the manufacturers, or anywhere else in the pipeline."

In the meantime, Bob Gore and other Associates set out to develop a permanent fix. One month later, a second-generation GORE-TEX fabric had been developed. Gilson, furthermore, told dealers that if a customer ever returned a leaky parka, they should replace it and bill the company. The replacement program alone cost Gore roughly $4 million.

The popularity of GORE-TEX outerwear took off. Many manufacturers now make numerous pieces of apparel such as parkas, gloves, boots, jogging outfits, and wind shirts from GORE-TEX laminate. Sometimes when customers are dissatisfied with a garment, they return them directly to Gore. Gore has always stood behind any product made of GORE-TEX fabric. Analysis of the returned garments found that the problem was often not the GORE-TEX fabric. The manufacturer, "... had created a design flaw so that the water could get in here or get in over the zipper and we found that when there was something negative about it, everyone knew it was GORE-TEX. So we had to make good on products that we were not manufacturing. We now license the manufacturers of all our GORE-TEX fabric products. They pay a fee to obtain a license to manufacture GORE-TEX products. In return we oversee the manufacture and we let them manufacture only designs that we are sure are guaranteed to keep you dry, that really will work. Then it works for them and for us—a win-win for them as well as for us," according to Sally Gore.

To further ensure quality, Gore & Associates has its own test facility including a rain room for garments made from GORE-TEX. Besides a rain/storm test, all garments must pass abrasion and washing machine tests. Only the garments that pass these tests will be licensed to display the GORE-TEX label.

Research and Development

Like everything else at Gore, research and development has always been unstructured. Even without a formal R&D department, the company has been issued many patents, although most inventions have been held as proprietary or trade secrets. For example, few Associates are allowed to see GORE-TEX being made. Any Associate can, however, ask for a piece of raw PTFE (known as a silly worm) with which to experiment. Bill Gore believed that all people had it within themselves to be creative.

One of the best examples of Gore inventiveness occurred in 1969. At the time, the wire and cable division was facing increased competition. Bill Gore began to look for a way to straighten out the PTFE molecules. As he said, "I figured out that if we ever unfold those molecules, get them to stretch out straight, we'd have a tremendous new kind of material." He thought that if PTFE could be stretched, air could be introduced into its molecular structure. The result would be greater volume per pound of raw material with no effect on performance. Thus, fabricating costs would be reduced and profit margins would be increased. Going about this search in a scientific manner, Bob Gore heated rods of PTFE to various temperatures and then slowly stretched them. Regardless of the temperature or how carefully he stretched them, the rods broke.

Working alone late one night after countless failures, Bob in frustration stretched one of the rods violently. To his surprise, it did not break. He tried it again and again with the same results. The next morning Bob demonstrated his breakthrough to his father, but not without some drama. As Bill Gore recalled: "Bob wanted to surprise me so he took a rod and stretched it slowly. Naturally, it broke. Then he pretended to get mad. He grabbed another rod and said, 'Oh, the hell with this,' and gave it a pull. It didn't break—he'd done it." The new arrangement of molecules not only changed the wire and cable division, but led to the development of GORE-TEX fabric.

Bill and Vieve did the initial field-testing of GORE-TEX fabric the summer of 1970. Vieve made a hand-sewn tent out of patches of GORE-TEX fabric. They took it on their annual camping trip to the Wind River Mountains in Wyoming. The very first night in the wilderness, they encountered a hail storm. The hail tore holes in the top of the tent, and the bottom filled up like a bathtub from the rain. Undaunted, Bill Gore stated: "At least we knew from all the water that the tent was waterproof. We just needed to make it stronger, so it could withstand hail."

Gore Associates have always been encouraged to think, experiment, and follow a potentially profitable idea to its conclusion. At a plant in Newark, Delaware, Fred L. Eldreth, an Associate with a third-grade education, designed a machine that could wrap thousands of feet of wire a day. The design was completed over a weekend. Many other Associates have contributed their ideas through both product and process breakthroughs.

Even without an R&D department, innovation and creativity continue at a rapid pace at Gore & Associates. The year before he died, Bill Gore claimed that "the creativity, the number of patent applications and innovative products is triple" that of DuPont.

Development of Gore Associates

Ron Hill, an Associate in Newark, noted that Gore "will work with Associates who want to advance themselves." Associates have been offered many in-house training opportunities, not only in technical and engineering areas but also in leadership development. In addition, the company has established cooperative education programs with universities and other outside providers, picking up most of the costs for the Gore Associates. The emphasis in Associate development, as in many parts of Gore, has always been that the Associate must take the initiative.

Marketing Approaches and Strategy

Gore's business philosophy incorporates three beliefs and principles: (1) that the company can and should offer the best-valued products in the markets and market segments where it chooses to compete, (2) that buyers in each of its markets should appreciate the caliber and performance of the items it manufactures, and (3) that Gore should become a leader with unique expertise in each of the product categories where it competes. To achieve these outcomes, the company's approach to marketing (it has no formally organized marketing department) is based on the following principles:

1. *Marketing a product requires a leader, or product champion.* According to Dave McCarter: "You

marry your technology with the interests of your champions, since you've got to have champions for all these things no matter what. And that's the key element within our company. Without a product champion you can't do much anyway, so it is individually driven. If you get people interested in a particular market or a particular product for the marketplace, then there is no stopping them." Bob Winterling of the Fabrics Division elaborated further on the role and importance of the product champion.

> The product champion is probably the most important resource we have at Gore for the introduction of new products. You look at that bicycle cable. That could have come out of many different divisions of Gore, but it really happened because one or two individuals said, "Look, this can work. I believe in it; I'm passionate about it; and I want it to happen." And the same thing with GLIDE floss. I think John Spencer in this case—although there was a team that supported John, let's never forget that—John sought the experts out throughout the organization. But without John making it happen on his own, GLIDE floss would never have come to fruition. He started with a little chain of drugstores here, Happy Harry's I think, and we put a few cases in and we just tracked the sales and that's how it all started. Who would have ever believed that you could take what we would have considered a commodity product like that, sell it direct for $3–$5 apiece. That is so unGorelike it's incredible. So it comes down to people and it comes down to the product champion to make things happen.

2. *A product champion is responsible for marketing the product through commitments with sales representatives.* Again, according to Dave McCarter: "We have no quota system. Our marketing and our sales people make their own commitments as to what their forecasts have been. There is no person sitting around telling them that is not high enough, you have to increase it by 10 percent, or whatever somebody feels is necessary. You are expected to meet your commitment, which is your forecast, but nobody is going to tell you to change it.... There is no order of command, no chain involved. These are groups of independent people who come together to make unified commitments to do something and sometimes when

they can't make those agreements... you may pass up a marketplace... but that's OK, because there's much more advantage when the team decides to do something."

3. *Sales Associates are on salary, not commission.* They participate in the profit sharing and ASOP plans in which all other Associates participate. As in other areas of Gore, individual success stories have come from diverse backgrounds. Dave McCarter related another success of the company relying on a product champion as follows:

> I interviewed Sam one day. I didn't even know why I was interviewing him actually. Sam was retired from AT&T. After twenty-five years, he took the golden parachute and went down to Sun Lakes to play golf. He played golf a few months and got tired of that. He was selling life insurance. I sat reading the application; his technical background interested me.... He had managed an engineering department with six hundred people. He'd managed manufacturing plants for AT&T and had a great wealth of experience at AT&T. He said, "I'm retired. I like to play golf but I just can't do it every day, so I want to do something else. Do you have something around here I can do?" I was thinking to myself, "This is one of these guys I would sure like to hire but I don't know what I would do with him." The thing that triggered me was the fact that he said he sold insurance and here is a guy with a high degree of technical background selling insurance. He had marketing experience, international marketing experience. So, the bell went off in my head that we were trying to introduce a new product into the marketplace that was a hydrocarbon leak protection cable. You can bury it in the ground and in a matter of seconds it could detect a hydrocarbon-like gasoline. I had a couple of other guys working on the product who hadn't been very successful with marketing it. We were having a hard time finding a customer. Well, I thought, that kind of product would be like selling insurance. If you think about it, why should you protect your tanks? It's an insurance policy that things are not leaking into the environment. That has implications, big-time monetary. So, actually, I said, "Why don't you come back Monday? I have just the thing for you." He

did. We hired him; he went to work, a very energetic guy. Certainly a champion of the product, he picked right up on it, ran with it singlehanded. . . .

Now it's a growing business. It certainly is a valuable one too for the environment. In the implementation of its marketing strategy, Gore has relied on cooperative and word-of-mouth advertising. Cooperative advertising has been especially used to promote GORE-TEX fabric products. These high-dollar, glossy campaigns include full-color ads and dressing the sales force in GORE-TEX garments. A recent slogan used in the ad campaigns has been, "If it doesn't say GORE-TEX, it's not." Some retailers praise the marketing and advertising efforts as the best. Leigh Gallagher, managing editor of *Sporting Goods Business* magazine, describes Gore & Associates' marketing as "unbeatable."

Gore has stressed cooperative advertising because the Associates believe positive experiences with any one product will carry over to purchases of other and more GORE-TEX fabric products. Apparently, this strategy has paid off. When the Grandoe Corporation introduced GORE-TEX gloves, its president, Richard Zuckerwar, noted: "Sports activists have had the benefit of GORE-TEX gloves to protect their hands from the elements. . . . With this handsome collection of gloves . . . you can have warm, dry hands without sacrificing style." Other clothing manufacturers and distributors who sell GORE-TEX garments include Apparel Technologies, Lands' End, Austin Reed, Hudson Trail Outfitters, Timberland, Woolrich, North Face, L.L. Bean, and Michelle Jaffe.

The power of these marketing techniques extends beyond consumer products. According to Dave McCarter: "In the technical end of the business, company reputation probably is most important. You have to have a good reputation with your company." He went on to say that without a good reputation, a company's products would not be considered seriously by many industrial customers. In other words, the sale is often made before the representative calls. Using its marketing strategies, Gore has been very successful in securing a market leadership position in a number of areas, ranging from waterproof outdoor clothing to vascular grafts. Its market share of waterproof, breathable fabrics is estimated to be 90 percent.

Adapting to Changing Environmental Forces

Each of Gore's divisions has faced from time to time adverse environmental forces. For example, the fabric division was hit hard when the fad for jogging suits collapsed in the mid-1980s. The fabric division took another hit from the recession of 1989. People simply reduced their purchases of high-end athletic apparel. By 1995, the fabric division was the fastest-growing division of Gore again.

The electronic division was hit hard when the mainframe computer business declined in the early 1990s. By 1995, that division was seeing a resurgence for its products partially because that division had developed some electronic products for the medical industry. As can be seen, not all the forces have been negative.

The aging population of America has increased the need for health care. As a result, Gore has invested in the development of additional medical products and the medical division is growing.

W. L. Gore & Associates' Financial Performance

As a closely held private corporation, W. L. Gore has kept its financial information as closely guarded as proprietary information on products and processes. It has been estimated that Associates who work at Gore own 90 percent of the stock. According to Shanti Mehta, an Associate, Gore's returns on assets and sales have consistently ranked it among the top 10 percent of the *Fortune* 500 companies. According to another source, W. L. Gore & Associates has been doing just fine by any financial measure. For thirty-seven straight years (from 1961 to 1997) the company has enjoyed profitability and positive return on equity. The compounded growth rate for revenues at W. L. Gore & Associates from 1969 to 1989 was more than 18 percent, discounted for inflation.[7] In 1969, total sales were about $6 million; by 1989, the figure was $600 million. As should be expected with the increase in size, the percentage increase in sales has slowed over the last seven years (Exhibit 6). The company projects sales to reach $1.4 billion in 1998. Gore financed this growth without long-term debt unless it made sense. For example, "We used to have some industrial revenue bonds where, in essence, to build facilities the government allows banks to lend you money tax-free. Up to a couple of years ago we were borrowing money through industrial revenue bonds. Other than that, we are totally debt-free. Our money is generated out of the operations of the business, and frankly we're looking for new things to invest in. I know that's a challenge for all of us today," said Bob Winterling. *Forbes* magazine estimates Gore's operating profits for 1993, 1994, 1995, 1996, and 1997 to be $120, $140, $192, $213, and $230 million, respectively (Exhibit 6). Bob Gore predicts that the company will reach $2 billion in sales by 2001.

Recently, the company purchased Optical Concepts Inc., a laser, semiconductor technology company, of Lompoc, California. In addition, Gore & Associates is investing in test-marketing a new product, guitar strings, which was developed by its Associates.

When asked about cost control, Sally Gore had the following to say:

You have to pay attention to cost or you're not an effective steward of anyone's money, your own or anyone else's. It's kind of interesting, we started manufacturing medical products in 1974 with the vascular graft and it built from there. The Gore vascular graft is the Cadillac or BMW or the Rolls Royce of the business. There is absolutely no contest, and our medical products division became

very successful. People thought this was Mecca. Nothing had ever been manufactured that was so wonderful. Our business expanded enormously, rapidly out there (Flagstaff, Arizona) and we had a lot of young, young leadership. They spent some time thinking they could do no wrong and that everything they touched was going to turn to gold.

They have had some hard knocks along the way and discovered it wasn't as easy as they initially thought it was. And that's probably good learning for everyone somewhere along the way. That's not how business works. There's a lot of truth in that old saying that you learn more from your failures than you do your successes. One failure goes a long way toward making you say, Oh, wow!

Acknowledgments

Many sources were helpful in providing background material for this case. The most important sources of all were the W. L. Gore Associates, who generously shared their time and viewpoints about the company. They provided many resources, including internal documents, and added much to this case through sharing their personal experiences as well as ensuring that the case accurately reflected the Gore company and culture.

EXHIBIT 6   *Operating and Net Profits of W. L. Gore & Associates*

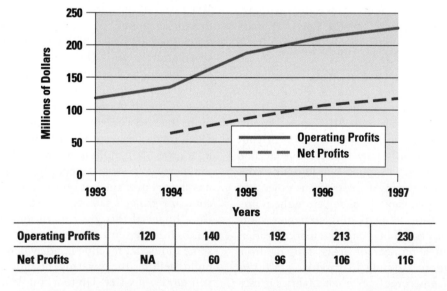

	1993	1994	1995	1996	1997
Operating Profits	120	140	192	213	230
Net Profits	NA	60	96	106	116

Data from *Forbes* Magazine's Annual Report on the 500 Largest Private Companies in the U.S.

Excerpts from Interviews with Associates

The first excerpt is from an Associate that was formerly with IBM and has been with Gore for two years:

Q. What is the difference between being with IBM and Gore?

A. I spent twenty-four years working for IBM, and there's a big difference. I can go ten times faster here at Gore because of the simplicity of the lattice organization. Let me give you an example. If I wanted to purchase chemicals at IBM (I am an industrial chemist), the first thing I would need to do is get accounting approval, then I would need at least two levels of managers' approval, then a secretary to log in my purchase and the purchase order would go to Purchasing where it would be assigned a buyer. Some time could be saved if you were willing to "walk" the paperwork through the approval process, but even after computerizing the process, it typically would take one month from the time you initiated the purchase requisition till the time the material actually arrived. Here they have one simple form. Usually, I get the chemicals the next day and a copy of the purchase order will arrive a day or two after that. It happens so fast. I wasn't used to that.

Q. Do you find that a lot more pleasant?

A. Yeah, you're unshackled here. There's a lot less bureaucracy that allows you to be a lot more productive. Take Lab Safety, for example. In my lab at IBM, we were cited for not having eyewash taped properly. The first time, we were cited for not having a big enough area taped off. So we taped off a bigger area. The next week the same eyewash was cited again, because the area we taped off was three inches too short in one direction. We retaped it and the following week, it got cited again for having the wrong color tape. Keep in mind that the violation was viewed as serious as a pail of gasoline next to a lit Bunsen burner. Another time I had the dubious honor of being selected the functional safety representative in charge of getting the function's labs ready for a Corporate Safety Audit. (The function was a third level in the pyramidal organization—(1) department, (2) project, and (3) function.) At the same time I was working on developing a new surface mount package. As it turned out, I had no time to work on development, and the function spent a lot of time and money getting ready for the Corporate Auditors who in the end never showed. I'm not belittling the importance of safety, but you really don't need all that bureaucracy to be safe.

The second interview is with an Associate who is a recent engineering graduate:

Q. How did you find the transition coming here?

A. Although I never would have expected it to be, I found my transition coming to Gore to be rather challenging. What attracted me to the company was the opportunity to "be my own boss" and determine my own commitments. I am very goal-oriented, and enjoy taking a project and running with it—all things that you are able to do and encouraged to do within the Gore culture. Thus, I thought, a perfect fit!

However, as a new Associate, I really struggled with where to focus my efforts—I was ready to make my own commitments, but to what?! I felt a strong need to be sure that I was working on something that had value, something that truly needed to be done. While I didn't expect to have the "hottest" project, I did want to make sure that I was helping the company to "make money" in some way.

At the time, though, I was working for a plant that was pretty typical of what Gore was like when it was originally founded—after my first project (which was designed to be a "quick-win"—a project with meaning, but one that had a definite end point), I was told, "Go find something to work on." While I could have found something, I wanted to find something with at least a small degree of priority! Thus, the whole process of finding a project was very frustrating for me—I didn't feel that I had the perspective to make such a choice and ended up in many conversations with my sponsor about what would be valuable....

In the end, of course, I did find that project—and it did actually turn out to be a good investment for Gore. The process to get there, though, was definitely trying for someone as inexperienced as I was—so much ground would have been gained by suggesting a few projects to me and then letting me choose from that smaller pool.

What's really neat about the whole thing, though, is that my experience has truly made a difference. Due in part to my frustrations, my plant now provides college grads with more guidance on their first several projects. (This guidance obviously becomes less and less critical as each Associate grows within Gore.) Associates still are choosing their own commitments, but they're doing so with additional perspective, and the knowledge that they are making a contribution to Gore—which is an important thing within our culture. As I said, though, it was definitely rewarding to see that the company was so responsive, and to feel that I had helped to shape someone else's transition!

Notes

1. GORE-TEX is a registered trademark of W. L. Gore & Associates.
2. In this case the word *Associates* is used and capitalized because in W. L. Gore & Associates' literature the word is always used instead of *employees* and is capitalized. In fact, case writers were told that Gore "never had 'employees'—always 'Associates.'"
3. GORE RideOn is a registered trademark of W. L. Gore & Associates.
4. Glide is a registered trademark of W. L. Gore & Associates.
5. WindStopper is a registered trademark of W. L. Gore & Associates.
6. Similar legally to an ESOP (Employee Stock Ownership Plan). Again, Gore simply has never allowed the word *employee* in any of its documentation.
7. In comparison, only 11 of the 200 largest companies in the *Fortune* 500 had positive ROE each year from 1970 to 1988 and only 2 other companies missed a year. The revenue growth rate for these 13 companies was 5.4 percent, compared with 2.5 percent for the entire *Fortune* 500.

References

Aburdene, Patricia, and John Nasbitt. *Re-inventing the Corporation* (New York: Warner Books, 1985).

Angrist, S. W. "Classless Capitalists," *Forbes* (May 9, 1983), 123–24.

Franlesca, L. "Dry and Cool," *Forbes* (August 27, 1984), 126.

Hoerr, J. "A Company Where Everybody Is the Boss," *Business Week* (April 15, 1985), 98.

Levering, Robert. *The 100 Best Companies to Work for in America*. See the chapter on W. L. Gore & Associates, Inc. (New York: Signet, 1985.)

McKendrick, Joseph. "The Employees as Entrepreneur," *Management World* (January 1985), 12–13.

Milne, M. J. "The Gorey Details," *Management Review* (March 1985), 16–17.

Posner, B. G. "The First Day on the Job," *Inc.* (June 1986), 73–75.

Price, Debbie M. "GORE-TEX style," *Baltimore Sun* (April 20, 1997), 1D & 4D.

Price, Kathy. "Firm Thrives Without Boss," *AZ Republic* (February 2, 1986).

Rhodes, Lucien. "The Un-manager," *Inc.* (August 1982), 34.

Simmons, J. "People Managing Themselves: Un-management at W. L. Gore Inc.," *The Journal for Quality and Participation* (December 1987), 14–19.

"The Future Workplace," *Management Review* (July 1986), 22–23.

Trachtenberg, J. A. "Give Them Stormy Weather," *Forbes* (March 24, 1986), 172–174.

Ward, Alex. "An All-Weather Idea," *The New York Times Magazine* (November 10, 1985), Sec. 6.

Weber, Joseph. "No Bosses. And Even 'Leaders' Can't Give Orders," *BusinessWeek* (December 10, 1990), 196–197.

"Wilbert L. Gore," *IndustryWeek* (October 17, 1983), 48–49.

In the fall of 1995, Bill Sanko, president of XEL Communications, Inc., strolled around in the new 115,000-square-foot facility with its spacious conference rooms and computer-based skills training center, into which the company had just moved. Their former facility had been a 53,000-square-foot building that just could not accommodate XEL's growth. During the upcoming round of strategic planning sessions, Bill wondered how XEL and its management team would decide to grapple with the two-edged sword of rapid growth. Would it be possible for XEL to maintain its entrepreneurial culture while it experienced rapid growth? Would it find the resources necessary to sustain growth without harming its culture? From where?

XEL Communications, Inc.

XEL Communications, Inc.[1]—located in the outskirts of Denver, Colorado—designed and manufactured various telecommunications products for a number of companies—primarily large U.S. telephone operating companies. Originally a division within GTE headed by Bill Sanko, it was in the process of being closed when Bill and a few key managers persuaded GTE to sell the division to them. In July 1984, Sanko and fellow managers signed a letter of intent to buy the division from GTE. Two months later, the bill of sale was signed, and XEL Communications, Inc., became an independent company. Ironically, GTE remained as one of XEL's major customer accounts.

In terms of overall financial performance, XEL was profitable. Its revenues increased from $16.8 million in 1992 to $23.6 million in 1993 and $52.3 million in 1994—over a threefold increase in three years. In 1996, XEL employed approximately 300 people.

XEL designed and manufactured more than 300 individual products that enabled network operators to upgrade existing infrastructures and cost-effectively enhance the speed and functionality of their networks while reducing operating expenses and overhead costs. The firm's products provided access to telecommunications services and automated monitoring and maintenance of network performance, and extended the distance over which network operators were able to offer their services.[2] For example, XEL produced equipment that "conditioned" existing lines to make

them acceptable for business use and sold products that facilitated the transmission of data and information over phone lines. Driving the need for XEL's products was the keen interest in electronic data transference: "Businesses are more and more dependent on the transfer of information," Bill Sanko noted. In addition, more businesses, including XEL, were operating by taking and filling orders through electronic data exchanges. Instead of dialing in to inside salespeople, businesses often accessed databases directly.

One of XEL's strengths was its ability to adapt one manufacturer's equipment to another's. XEL provided the bits and pieces of telecommunications equipment to the "network," allowing the smooth integration of disparate transmission pieces. XEL also sold central office transmission equipment and a full range of mechanical housings, specialty devices, power supplies, and shelves.

In 1995, XEL began developing a hybrid fiber/cable broadband modem for use by cable television firms seeking to provide enhanced data communication services over their network facilities. Cable modems were one of the hottest new products in telecommunications. The devices would enable computers to send and receive information about one hundred times faster than standard modems used with phone lines. Given that 34 million homes had personal computers, cable modems were seen as a surefire way to exploit the personal computer (PC) boom and the continuing convergence of computers and television. Media analysts estimated that cable modem users would rise to 11.8 million by the end of 2005 from a handful in 1996.[3]

"Business customers and their changing telecommunications needs drive the demand for XEL's products. That, in turn, presents a challenge to the company," said Sanko. Sanko cited the constant stream of new products developed by XEL—approximately two per month—as the driving force behind

*This case was prepared by Professors Robert P. McGowan and Cynthia V. Fukami, Daniels College of Business, as a basis for classroom discussion rather than to illustrate either effective or ineffective handling of an administrative situation. Copyright © 1995 by the authors: © 1997 by the Case Center, Daniels College of Business, University of Denver. Published by South-Western College Publishing.

For information regarding this and other CaseNet* cases, please visit CaseNet* on the World Wide Web at *http://casenet.thomson.com*.

the growth. Throughout the industry, product life-cycle times were getting even shorter. Before the breakup of the Bell System in 1984, transmission switches and other telecommunications devices enjoyed a thirty- to forty-year life. In 1995, with technology moving so fast, XEL's products had about a three-year to five-year life.

XEL sold products to all of the Regional Bell Operating Companies (RBOCs), as well as such companies as GTE and Centel. Railroads, with their own telephone networks, were also customers. In addition to its domestic business, products were sold in Canada, Mexico, and Central and South America.[4] XEL's field salespeople worked with engineers to satisfy client requests for specific services. Over a period of time, the salespeople developed a rapport with these engineers, providing XEL with new product leads.

With all the consolidations and ventures in telecommunications, those who watched the industry often concluded that the overall market would become more difficult. Sanko believed, however, that "out of change comes opportunity. The worst-case scenario would be a static situation. Thus, a small company, fast to respond to customer needs and able to capitalize on small market niches, will be successful. Often, a large company like AT&T will forsake a smaller market and XEL will move in. Also, XEL's size allows it to design a project in a very short time."

Sanko watched federal legislation keenly. The Telecommunications Act of 1996, which removed numerous barriers to competition, had clearly changed the rules of the game. Consequently, said Sanko, "we need to expand our market and be prepared to sell to others as the regulatory environment changes." The joint venture between Time Warner and US West also signaled that telephone and cable companies would be pooling their resources to provide a broader array of information services. As for the future, Sanko saw "a lot of opportunities we can't even now imagine."

The XEL Vision

A feature that set XEL apart from other companies was its strong, healthy corporate culture. Developing a culture of innovation and team decision making was instrumental in providing the results XEL prided itself on.[5] An early attempt to define culture in a top-down fashion was less successful than the management team had hoped,[6] so the team had embarked on a second journey to determine what their core values were and what they would like the company to look like in five years. The team had then gone off-site for several days and finalized the XEL Vision statement (Exhibit 1). By the summer of 1987, the statement had been signed by members of the senior team and been hung up by the bulletin board. Employees were not required to sign the statement, but were free to do so when each was ready.

Julie Rich, vice president of human resources, described the management team's approach to getting the rest of the organization to understand as well as become comfortable with the XEL Vision: "Frequently, organizations tend to take a combination top-down/bottom-up approach in instituting cultural change. That is, the top level will develop a statement about values and overall vision. They will then communicate it down to the bottom level and hope that results will percolate upward through the middle levels. Yet it is often the middle level of management which is most skeptical, and they will block it or resist change. We decided to take a 'cascade' approach in which the process begins at the top and gradually cascades from one level to the next so that the critical players are slowly acclimated to the process. We also did a number of other things—including sending a copy of the vision statement to the homes of the employees and dedicating a section of the company newspaper to communicate what key sections of the vision mean from the viewpoint of managers and employees."

The vision statement became a living symbol of the XEL culture and the degree to which XEL embraced and empowered its employees. When teams or managers made decisions, they routinely brought out the XEL Vision document so workers might consult various parts of the statement to help guide and direct decisions. According to Julie, the statement was used to help evaluate new products, emphasize quality (a specific XEL strategic objective was to be the top quality vendor for each product), support teams, and drive the performance-appraisal process.

The XEL Vision was successfully implemented as a key first step; but it was far from being a static document. Key XEL managers continually revisited the statement to ensure that it became a reflection of where they wanted to go, not where they had been. Julie believed this regular appraisal was a large factor in the success of the vision. "Our values are the key," Julie explained. "They are strong, they

EXHIBIT I   *The XEL Vision*

XEL will become the leader in our selected telecommunications markets through innovation in products and services. Every XEL product and service will be rated Number One by our customers.

XEL will set the standards by which our competitors are judged. We will be the best, most innovative, responsive designer, manufacturer and provider of quality products and services as seen by customers, employees, competitors, and suppliers.*

We will insist upon the highest quality from everyone in every task.

We will be an organization where each of us is a self-manager who will:
- initiate action, commit to, and act responsibly in achieving objectives
- be responsible for XEL's performance
- be responsible for the quality of individual and team output
- invite team members to contribute based on experience, knowledge and ability

We will:
- be ethical and honest in all relationships
- build an environment where creativity and risk taking is promoted
- provide challenging and satisfying work
- ensure a climate of dignity and respect for all
- rely on interdepartmental teamwork, communications and cooperative problem solving to attain common goals**
- offer opportunities for professional and personal growth
- recognize and reward individual contribution and achievement
- provide tools and services to enhance productivity
- maintain a safe and healthy work environment

XEL will be profitable and will grow in order to provide both a return to our investors and rewards to our team members.

XEL will be an exciting and enjoyable place to work while we achieve success.

*Responsiveness to customers' new product needs as well as responding to customers' emergency delivery requirements have been identified as key strategic strengths. Therefore, the vision statement has been updated to recognize this important element.
**The importance of cooperation and communication was emphasized with this update of the Vision Statement.

are truly core values, and they are deeply held." Along with the buy-in process, the workers also saw that the managers experimented with the statement, which reflected the strong entrepreneurial nature of XEL's founders—a common bond that they all shared. They were not afraid of risk, or of failure, and this spirit was reinforced in all employees through the vision itself, as well as through the yearly process of revisiting the statement. Once a year, Bill Sanko sat with all employees and directly challenged (and listened to direct challenges to) the XEL Vision. From 1987 to 1995, only two relatively minor additions had altered the original statement.

Which Path to Choose

When the 1995 annual strategic planning process got under way, XEL was in good shape on any one of a number of indicators. Profits were growing, new products were being developed, the culture and vision of the company were strong, employee morale was high, and the self-directed work teams were achieving exceptional quality.[7] Rapid growth, however, was also presenting a challenge. Would it be possible for XEL to maintain its entrepreneurial culture in the face of rapid growth? Could they sustain their growth without harming their culture? Would they find the resources necessary to sustain the growth? From where?

As the strategic planning retreat progressed, three options seemed apparent to the team. First, they could stay the course and remain privately held. Second, they could initiate a public offering of stock. Third, they could seek a strategic partnership. Which would be the right choice for XEL?

Staying the Course

The most obvious option was to do nothing. Bill Sanko indicated that the management team did not favor staying the course and remaining privately held. "We had a venture capitalist involved who, after being with us for ten years, wanted out. In addition, the founders—ourselves—also wanted out from a financial standpoint. You also have to understand that one of the original founders, Don Donnelly, had passed away; and his estate was looking to make his investment more liquid. So, there were a lot things that converged at the same time."

Once they determined they would not remain privately held, Bill mentioned that the decision boiled down to two main avenues: XEL would do an initial public offering and go public, or it would find a strategic partner. "To guide us in this process, we decided to retain the services of an outside party; we talked to about a dozen investment houses. In October 1994, we decided to hire Alex Brown, a long time investment house out of Baltimore. What we liked about this firm was that they had experience with doing both options—going public or finding a partner."

Going Public

One avenue open to XEL was initiating a public offering of stock. Alex Brown advised them of the pluses and minuses of this option. Sanko reviewed their recommendations:

> The plus side for XEL doing an initial public offering was that technology was really hot about this time [October 1994]. In addition, we felt that XEL would be valued pretty highly in the market. The downside of going public was that XEL was really not a big firm, and institutional investors usually like doing offerings of firms that generate revenues of over $100 million. Another downside was that you had to deal with analysts, and their projections become your plan, which really turned me off. Also, shareholders want a steady and predictable rate of return. Technology stocks are not steady—there are frequent ups and downs in this marketplace—caused by a number

of factors, such as a major telecommunications company deciding not to upgrade at the last minute or Congress considering sweeping regulatory changes. Finally, Alex Brown felt that the stock would have traded thinly. This, coupled with SEC restrictions on trading, made the option of going public less desirable.

Strategic Partnership

After taking these factors into account, Sanko said,

> . . . we decided to take the third path and look for a potential partner. But you have to also note that there was always the first option available as a safety valve. We could not do anything and stay the way we were. That's the nice thing about all of this. We were not under any pressure to go public or seek a partner. We could also wait and do one of these things later on. So, we had the luxury of taking our time.
>
> In terms of finding a potential partner, there were certain key items that we wanted Alex Brown to consider in helping us in this process. The first was that we, management, wanted to remain with XEL. We had really grown XEL as a business and were not interested in going off and doing something else. The second key item was that we were not interested in being acquired by someone who was interested in consolidating our operations with theirs, closing this facility and moving functions from here to there. To us, this would destroy the essence of XEL. The third item was that we wanted a partner that would bring something to the table but would not try to micromanage our business.

The Case Against Strategic Partnership

In the 1990s, "merger mania" swept the United States. In the first nine months of 1995, the value of all announced mergers and acquisitions reached $248.5 billion, surpassing the record full-year volume of $246.9 billion reached in 1988. This volume occurred in the face of strong evidence that over the past thirty-five years, mergers and acquisitions had hurt organizations more than they had helped.[8] Among the reasons for failure in mergers and acquisitions were the following:

- Inadequate due diligence
- Lack of strategic rationale
- Unrealistic expectations of possible synergies

- Paying too much
- Conflicting corporate cultures
- Failure to move quickly to meld the two companies

Nevertheless, there had been successful mergers and acquisitions. Most notably, small and midsized deals had been found to have a better chance for success. Michael Porter argued that the best acquisitions were "gap-filling," that is, a deal in which one company bought another to strengthen its product line or expand its territory, including globally. Anslinger and Copeland argued that successful acquisitions were more likely when preacquisition managers were kept in their positions, big incentives were offered to top-level executives so that their net worths were on the line, and the holding company was kept flat (that is, the business was kept separate from other operating units and retained a high degree of autonomy).[9]

More often than not, however, the deal was won or lost after it was done. Bad post-merger planning and integration could doom the acquisition. "While there is clearly a role for thoughtful and well-conceived mergers in American business, all too many don't meet that description."[10]

Choosing a Partner

"With these issues in mind, Alex Brown was able to screen out possible candidates," said Sanko. "In January, 1995, this plan was presented to our board of directors for approval, and by February, we had developed the 'book' about XEL that was to be presented to these candidates. We then had a series of meetings with the candidates in the conference room at our new facility. The interesting aside on these meetings was that, often, senior management from some of these firms didn't know what pieces of their business that they still had or had gotten rid of. We did not see this as a good sign."

One of the firms with which XEL met was Gilbert Associates, based in Reading, Pennsylvania. Gilbert Associates was founded in the 1940s as an engineering and construction firm, primarily in the area of power plants. They embarked on a strategy of reinventing themselves by divesting their energy-related companies and becoming a holding company whose subsidiaries operated in the high-growth markets of telecommunications and technical services. Gilbert also owned a real estate management-and-development subsidiary. After due diligence and due deliberation, Gilbert was chosen by the management

team as XEL's strategic partner. The letter of intent was signed on October 5, 1995, and the deal was closed on October 27, 1995. Gilbert paid $30 million in cash.[11]

Why was Gilbert chosen as the partner from among six or seven suitors? Not because they made the highest bid. XEL was attracted to Gilbert by three factors: (1) Gilbert's long-term strategy to enter the telecommunications industry, (2) its intention of keeping XEL as a separate, autonomous company, and (3) its willingness to pay cash (as opposed to stock or debt). "It was a clean deal," said Sanko.

The deal was also attractive because it was structured with upside potential. XEL was given realistic performance targets for the next three years. If these targets were achieved, and Sanko had every expectation that they would be, approximately $6-$8 million would be earned. Gilbert did not place a cap on the upside.

In spite of the attractive financial package, more was necessary to seal the deal. "At the end of the day," said Sanko, "culture, comfort, and trust—those were more important than money." It was important to XEL's board that Gilbert presented a good fit. Sanko was encouraged because he felt comfortable with Gilbert's chief executive officer. Vice president of Human Resources Julie Rich also noted, "The management team was to remain intact. Gilbert recognized that the XEL Vision was part of our success and our strength. They wanted to keep it going."

As one way of gaining confidence in Gilbert, Bill Sanko personally spoke with the CEOs of other companies Gilbert had recently acquired. In these conversations, Sanko was assured that Gilbert would keep its promises.

Timothy S. Cobb, chair, president, and CEO of Gilbert Associates, commented at the time of the acquisition: "This transaction represented the first clear step toward the attainment of our long-term strategy of focusing on the higher margin areas of telecommunications and technical services. XEL's superior reputation for quality throughout the industry, its innovative design and manufacturing capabilities, and its focus on products aimed at the emerging information highway markets, will serve us well as we seek to further penetrate this important segment of the vast communications market."[12]

Cobb continued, "We see long-term growth opportunities worldwide for XEL's current proprietary and Original Equipment Manufacturer [OEM] products as well as for the powerful new products being developed. These products fall into two families: (1) fiber-optic network interfaces designed specifically to meet the needs of telephone companies, interexchange carriers (e.g., AT&T, Sprint, MCI), and specialized network carriers installing fiber-optic facilities, and (2) a hybrid fiber/cable broadband modem for use by cable television firms seeking to provide enhanced data communications services over their network facilities. Going forward, we expect to leverage Gilbert's knowledge and relationships with the RBOCs to significantly increase sales to those important customers, while also utilizing our GAI-Tronics subsidiary's established international sales organization to further penetrate the vast global opportunities which exist. As a result, revenues from Gilbert Associates' growing telecommunications segment could represent over half of our total revenues by the end of 1996."

Timothy Cobb had come to Gilbert from Ameritech, an RBOC which covered the Midwestern United States. He had been president of GAI-Tronics Corporation, an international supplier of industrial communication equipment, a subsidiary of Gilbert, prior to his appointment as Gilbert's CEO.

Bill Sanko offered, "When all the dust had settled, the one firm that we really felt good about was Gilbert.... Gilbert is an interesting story in itself. Ironically, they had contacted us in August, 1994, based on the advice of their consultant who had read about us in an *Inc.* magazine article. Unfortunately, at the time, they did not have the cash to acquire us since they were in the process of selling off one of their divisions. In the intervening period, Gilbert Associates divested itself of one of its companies, Gilbert/Commonwealth. This sale provided needed funds for the acquisition of XEL."

Once Sanko was confident that the deal would go, but before the letter of intent was signed, the pending acquisition was announced to the management team, and a general meeting was held with all employees. SEC regulations prohibited sharing particular information (and common sense seconded this directive), but Sanko and his associates felt it was important to keep employees informed before the letter was signed.

During the meeting, Sanko told the employees that the board was "seriously considering" an offer. Sanko assured the employees that the suitor was not a competitor, and that he felt that the suitor was a good fit in culture and values. Sanko reiterated that this partnership would give XEL the resources it needed to grow. Questions were not allowed because of SEC regulations. Employees left the meeting concerned and somewhat nervous, but members of the management team and Julie Rich were positioned in the audience and made themselves available to talk.

During the closing of the deal, Sanko held another general meeting, attended by Timothy Cobb, where more detailed information was shared with employees. Managers had been informed in a pre-meeting so that they would be prepared to meet with their teams directly following the general meeting.

Employees wanted to know about Gilbert. They wanted to know simple information, such as where Gilbert was located and what businesses it was in. They also wanted to know strategic plans, such as whether Gilbert had plans to consolidate manufacturing operations. Finally, they wanted to know about the near future of XEL—they wanted to know if their benefits would change, if they would still have profit sharing, and if the management team would stay in place. "We have a track record of being open," says Sanko. "Good news or bad is always shared. This history stemmed much of the rumor mill."

In the next few weeks, Tim Cobb returned to hold a series of meetings with the management team and with a focus group of thirty employees representing a cross-section of the organization. Cobb also met with managers and their spouses at an informal reception. Sanko wanted to ease the management team into the realization that they were now part of a larger whole in Gilbert. He asked Cobb to make the same presentation to XEL that he was currently making to stockholders throughout the country—a presentation that emphasized the role XEL would play in the long-term strategy of Gilbert.

Going Forward

The human resource systems remained in place with no changes. The management bonus system would change slightly because it included stock options, which were no longer available. XEL's internal advisory board, the "management team," remained intact, but XEL's external advisory board was disbanded. Bill Sanko reported to Gilbert's chairman.

XEL's strategic plan was to follow the process it already had in place, and which was not unlike Gilbert's. The cycle did not change: Gilbert expected XEL's next strategic plan in early November 1996.

XEL's strategic objectives also remained the same. Nothing was put on hold. Plans were still in place to penetrate Brazil, Mexico, and South America.[13] Sanko hoped to capitalize on the synergies of Gilbert's existing international distribution network. XEL met with Gilbert's international representatives to see if this was an avenue for XEL to gain a more rapid presence in South America. Finally, XEL was planning to move into Radio Frequency (RF) engineering and manufacturing, potentially opening the door for wireless support.

Whether XEL would grow depended on the success of these new ventures. In 1996, slight growth was forecasted. But if these new markets really took off, Julie Rich was concerned about hiring enough people in Colorado when the labor market was approaching full employment. Julie considered more creative ways of attracting new hires: for example, by offering more flexible scheduling, or by hiring unskilled workers and training them internally. A new U.S. Department of Education grant to test computer-based training systems was being implemented. Nevertheless, employment was strong in the Denver metro area in 1996, and migration to Colorado had slowed. It would be a challenge to staff XEL if high growth became the business strategy.

Approximately six weeks after the acquisition, Sanko noted that few changes had taken place. Now that they were a publicly held company, there was a great deal more interest in meeting quarterly numbers. "If there has been a change," said Sanko, "it is that there is more attention to numbers." Julie Rich noted

that there had been no turnover in the six-week period following the acquisition. She took this calm in the workforce as a sign that things were going well so far.

One reason things went well was that the management team had all worked for GTE prior to the spin-off of XEL. Having all worked for a large public company, they did not experience a terrible culture shock when the Gilbert acquisition took place. Time would tell if the remaining XEL employees would feel the same way.

As Sanko awaited Cobb's upcoming visit, he wondered how to prepare for the event and for the year ahead. He wondered whether XEL would attempt new ventures into RF technology, or how the planned fiber/cable broadband modem would progress. He wondered whether Gilbert's experience in selling in South America would prove valuable for XEL's international strategy. In addition, he wondered how he could encourage XEL and its employees to become members of Gilbert's "team." Would XEL's vision survive the new partnership?

Finally, according to one study of CEO turnover after acquisition, 80 percent of acquired CEOs left their companies by the sixth year after the acquisition, but 87 percent of those who did leave, did so within two years. The key factor in their turnover was post-acquisition autonomy.[14] After nearly twelve years as the captain of his own ship, Sanko wondered what his own future, and the future of the XEL management team, would hold.

Notes

1. For additional information on XEL Communications, Inc., and the key strategic issues facing XEL, see Robert P. McGowan and Cynthia V. Fukami, "XEL Communications, Inc. (A)," Daniels College of Business, University of Denver © 1995, published by South-Western Publishing.
2. *PR Newsletter* (October 5, 1995).
3. Bill Menezes "Modern Times," *Rocky Mountain News* (April 28, 1996).
4. *PR Newswire* (October 5, 1995).
5. John Sheridan, "America's Best Plants: XEL Communications," *IndustryWeek* (October 16, 1995).
6. See McGowan and Fukami, "XEL Communications, Inc. (A)," for a larger discussion of corporate culture at XEL.
7. Sheridan, "America's Best Plants."
8. Philip Zweig "The Case Against Mergers," *BusinessWeek* (October 30, 1995).
9. Patricia Anslinger and Thomas Copeland, "Growth Through Acquisitions: A Fresh Look," *Harvard Business Review* (January–February 1996).
10. Zweig, "The Case Against Mergers."
11. Dina Bunn "XEL to be Sold in $30 Million Deal," *Rocky Mountain News* (October 27, 1995).
12. *PR Newswire* (October 5, 1995).
13. For more information on XEL's global penetration, see McGowan and Allen, "XEL Communications, Inc. (B): Going Global."
14. Kim A. Stewart, "After the Acquisition: A Study of Turnover of Chief Executives of Target Companies," doctoral dissertation, University of Houston, 1992.

INTEGRATIVE CASE 5.0 *National Bank of San Francisco**

The National Bank of San Francisco operates seven branches that receive deposits and make loans to both businesses and individual depositors. Deposits have grown from $14 million to $423 million within the past twenty years, and the directors have opened more branches as population and business activity in the Bay Area have increased.

The Bank has generally been characterized by aggressive marketing including giveaway promotions for new deposits and extremely competitive interest rates on loans. President E. F. Wellington has prided himself on his ability to appoint entrepreneurial branch managers and loan officers who have pushed new business development.

In response to a question at a board meeting two years ago concerning a noticeable rate of increase in operating and overhead expenses, Wellington announced that he would undertake a study of ways the bank might lower, or at least hold the line on, these costs.

Shortly thereafter, he called in James Nicholson, one of his two assistants, described the general problem of reducing costs, and told him that the bank had reached the size where it needed someone to devote full time to operating methods and facilities. He said that he had talked this matter over with Ms. Simmons, manager of personnel, and that both of them had agreed "that you would be ideal for this position." He also explained that Ms. Simmons would be simultaneously promoted to vice president and put in charge of all equipment purchases, the maintenance of all bank buildings, and personnel relations. "Simmons and I feel that you might have a permanent advisory committee made up of one person from each branch, and that such a group can be really effective in deciding on ways to utilize our banking buildings and equipment, and our people, more effectively. Unless you have some objection, each of the branch managers will appoint a representative to meet with you regularly."

Within three months of the original reference to the subject at the directors' meeting, Simmons had been promoted to vice president, Nicholson received the title of manager of personnel and equipment planning, and all branch managers had appointed, at Wellington's request, an employee to what became known as the "systems committee." At the present time, two years later, the committee appears to have taken its work seriously, as evidenced by:

1. a record of regular meetings held over a period of eighteen months;
2. the transcripts of those meetings and exhibits, which show that all seven committee members entered the discussions;
3. seventeen recommendations in writing, supported by a total of 1,800 pages of research data and reasoning;
4. the fact that meetings often lasted four to five hours, extending after working hours; and
5. the statements of all seven members of the committee to the effect that they enjoyed the work, felt that they were accomplishing something for the bank, and had personally enjoyed being on the committee with the other members.

All members have also expressed their high regard for Jim Nicholson and feel that he has done a good job.

The seventeen recommendations cover such matters as salary scales, a policy on days off for personal business, a policy on central purchasing of janitorial supplies, and a recommendation that certain models of personal computers and software be adopted uniformly in all branches.

Office Space and Furnishings

About a year ago, both Simmons and Nicholson had made inspection trips to the branches and had come to the conclusion that there was much wasted space in branch offices and that this situation had been brought about principally because office personnel and clerical personnel had been, over a period of years, buying equipment—such as desks, telephone stands, and extra tables—that pleased them personally but that, in many instances, was also "too large and expensive" for what the bank needed to keep up its public appearance. In addition, loan officers in some branches had succeeded in having the managers construct walls for unnecessary private offices. Nicholson had obtained the services of the bank's architect and also of systems engineers from two large equipment manufacturers; together they made a "general estimate, to be confirmed by further fact-finding" that the bank could save $80,000 a year over a thirty-year period if (1) furniture were to be standardized with functional equipment that was modest in design but

*Written by Charles E. Summer. Copyright 1978. Used with permission.

met the essential requirements of dignity for the branches and if (2) henceforth, only branch managers could have private offices.

Before the meeting of the systems committee last week, Simmons expressed concern to Nicholson that his committee had not taken up these two problems.

> Your committee could have done some real research on these questions. I hope that you will put them on the agenda right away and agree, let's say in six months, on standard layouts and equipment. You and I both know, for instance, that the loan officers at San Mateo and Menlo Park have entirely too much space, should not be in those large offices, and perhaps should have three standard pieces of equipment—a desk, chair, and small bookcase. There should be no telephone stands like those that were purchased there last year for $90 each.

Relations with Branch Managers

Branch managers have been kept informed of the committee's general work over the eighteen-month period. Most managers selected a loan officer (assistant manager) to represent them, and these officers made a real effort to let their managers know what was going on. Dick May, representative of the Burlingame branch, reports that he has been spending at least an hour a week with his boss telling him what the committee is doing and asking for his ideas. Janice Strickland of the Market Street branch says that she has been able to confer briefly with her boss about once a week on the subjects the committee is working on. Other members report that they, too, have been able to keep their managers informed and that the latter exhibit a good deal of interest in the committee's work. In all cases except Burlingame, however, representatives say that their managers quite naturally do not have the time to go into the details of committee recommendations and that they, the managers, have not been particularly aggressive or enthusiastic about putting any of these recommendations into effect.

The committee has talked about the best way to get its recommendations adopted. Dick May claims that his manager is ready to put many of them into effect immediately and that it is up to each representative to convince his or her own manager. All others say they believe that the president should issue the recommendations as instructions over his signature. The reason given by Strickland is typical:

> We're convinced that the recommendations are best for the bank, but the managers just won't buy them. The only way to get the managers to carry them out is to have Mr. Wellington lay them out as official and let it be known that they are going to be put into effect. Of course, they would have to be acknowledged as being drawn up by the Department of Personnel and Equipment, with some advice from our committee.

James Nicholson reported in his own weekly meeting with the president that it looked as if it is going to be "rather touchy" to get managers to accept the recommendations. Mr. Wellington thereupon stated that his own knowledge of the committee recommendations was rather sketchy, even though he had discussed them in part with Nicholson each week for a year. He therefore decided to call a meeting of all branch managers and committee members at the same time so that he and everyone concerned could be acquainted in detail with them. This meeting took place one week ago.

Informal Comments of Branch Managers

Most of the branch managers dropped in to the officers' dining room for lunch before the meeting. After the usual banter, the conversation naturally drifted onto the proposals of the systems committee.

> Sure hope my secretary likes those new computers. I can't spell, and if Sally left I'd be sunk.

> So what, Karen, you always talk better than you write.

> Say, I sure hated to come in here this afternoon. Ever since Smedley Scott became president of Menlo Laboratories I've been trying to convince him to do all his banking with us. Had to break a date with him, and in my office, too. If we start spending all our time buying mops, our development program goes out the window.

> How are you making out with your two (officer) trainees, Carl? I have a smart one coming right along, but she won't be happy under the proposed salary schedule.

> The best employee we have came from the credit department a year ago. He sure gets around. Tennis matches, hospital drives, U.N. meetings; always on the go. I thought of him when I read that proposal for days off. How do you decide when a guy like that is working? Granted his work gets behind sometimes. That's better than drawing pay for just sitting at his desk. I get a kick out of bringing a young employee like that

along. And he is building a lot of goodwill for the bank in my area.

Well, I kind of like that days-off rule. It would save a lot of complaints and conversation about grandfather's weak heart.

It might be just fine for you, Tyson, but not so good for Ann. Why not let each manager decide? After all, each of us is paid to run our branch in the best interests of the bank, and we wouldn't be in our present positions if we weren't doing it. What do you think, Oscar?

Guess I have longer service than any of the rest of you. It will be thirty-nine years in September. But I'd say there isn't a manager who doesn't run his branch just as though it was his own business.

And the record is not bad either. Deposits are going up and the bank is making money.

It's making money that counts. (This from a manager of one of the slower-growing branches.)

I heard from somebody about a year ago that the committee was going to study office space and equipment and that someone figured they could save $1 million over a period of years. But apparently they didn't get around to that.

Don't worry. We're building a real base for the future. By the way, did you see the latest report on Zenith?

Just before the meeting with the systems committee, Simmons called Jim Nicholson into her office to have a brief discussion of the recommendations. The two read over the list of seventeen final recommendations; then Nicholson explained briefly the reasons why each recommendation was made and how it would help the bank to reduce costs.

The Meeting of the Committee and Branch Managers

The meeting started at 2 p.m. and was scheduled to last until 5 p.m., but actually ran over until 6 p.m. The committee, branch managers, Wellington, and Simmons were present. Wellington opened the meeting by stating that its purpose was to study the committee recommendations and, it was hoped, to arrive at a decision on whether they should be accepted and put into effect.

In fact, however, after a reading of the seventeen recommendations, the entire meeting was taken up by a discussion of the first two recommendations.

1. It is recommended that the following pay scales be adopted for clerical and nonofficer personnel in all branches. (This was followed by a list of positions and grades—the bank had had some uniformity before, but the recommendations specified absolute uniformity and also changed some of the classifications, thus meaning, for instance, that head tellers would in the future receive more than head bookkeepers, whereas both had received the same in the past.)

2. Employees should be allowed two days per year off with pay for miscellaneous personal business, such days to be granted at the discretion of managers. Because of the possibility of abuse of this privilege, days in excess of two must be taken without pay. This limitation does not apply to sickness or death in the immediate family.

In the discussion, the branch managers found a great many points on which (a) they disagreed among themselves, and (b) they agreed among themselves but disagreed with the committee. For instance, they all agreed that uniformity was in the interest of the bank but disagreed on many of the salary scales and classifications. On this point, they cited many instances in which one competent employee would feel hurt if the scales were arranged in the way the committee recommended.

The committee members had talked confidentially among themselves before the meeting and agreed that Jim Nicholson must be the one to present the findings and, by and large, the one to defend them. This plan was carried out, and after the meeting, the president remarked to Jim that

…the combined thinking of the managers, with all of their experience, made quite an impression on Simmons and me. We have confidence in you, and you know that, but I can't help but wonder if your committee really worked out the "best" recommendation for all on this salary matter. If you had, why couldn't you convince the managers instead of raising all of the criticism?

Yesterday, Wellington and Simmons met to consider the recommendations privately. Simmons again expressed the same idea that Wellington passed on to Nicholson, wondering out loud whether the committee should be sent back to do more research on the recommendations. Both were concerned that two years had elapsed since the committee was established without any recommendations having been accepted and put into effect.

INTEGRATIVE CASE 6.0   *The Audubon Zoo, 1993**

The Audubon Zoo was the focus of national concern in the early 1970s, with well-documented stories of animals kept in conditions that were variously termed an "animal ghetto,"[1] "the New Orleans anti-quarium," and even "an animal concentration camp."[2] In 1971, the Bureau of Governmental Research recommended a $5.6 million zoo improvement plan to the Audubon Park Commission and the City Council of New Orleans. The local *Times Picayune* commented on the new zoo: "It's not going to be quite like the Planet of the Apes situation in which the apes caged and studied human beings but something along those broad general lines."[3] The new zoo confined people to bridges and walkways while the animals roamed amidst grass, shrubs, trees, pools, and fake rocks. The gracefully curving pathways, generously lined with luxuriant plantings, gave the visitor a sense of being alone in a wilderness, although crowds of visitors might be only a few yards away.

The Decision

The Audubon Park Commission launched a $5.6 million development program, based on the Bureau of Governmental Research plan for the zoo, in March 1972. A bond issue and a property tax dedicated to the zoo were put before the voters on November 7, 1972. When it passed by an overwhelming majority, serious discussions began about what should be done. The New Orleans City Planning Commission finally approved the master plan for the Audubon Park Zoo in September 1973. But the institution of the master plan was far from smooth.

The Zoo Question Goes Public

Over two dozen special interests were ultimately involved in choosing whether to renovate/expand the existing facilities or move to another site. Expansion became a major community controversy. Some residents opposed the zoo expansion, fearing "loss of green space" would affect the secluded character of the neighborhood. Others opposed the loss of what they saw as an attractive and educational facility.

Most of the opposition came from the zoo's affluent neighbors. Zoo Director John Moore ascribed the criticism to "a select few people who have the money and power to make a lot of noise." He went on to say, "[T]he real basis behind the problem is that the neighbors who live around the edge of the park have a selfish concern because they want the park as their private backyard." Legal battles over the expansion plans continued until early 1976. At that time, the 4th Circuit Court of Appeals ruled that the expansion was legal.[4] An out-of-court agreement with the zoo's neighbors (the Upper Audubon Association) followed shortly.

Physical Facilities

The expansion of the Audubon Park Zoo took it from fourteen to fifty-eight acres. The zoo was laid out in geographic sections: the Asian Domain, World of Primates, World's Grasslands, Savannah, North American Prairie, South American Pampas, and Louisiana Swamp, according to the zoo master plan developed by the Bureau of Governmental Research. Additional exhibits included the Wisner Discovery Zoo, Sea Lion exhibit, and Flight Cage. Exhibit 1 is a map of the new zoo.

Purpose of the Zoo

The main outward purpose of the Audubon Park Zoo was entertainment. Many of the promotional efforts of the zoo were aimed at creating an image of the zoo as an entertaining place to go. Obviously, such a campaign was necessary to attract visitors to the zoo. Behind the scenes, the zoo also preserved and bred many animal species, conducted research, and educated the public. The mission statement of the Audubon Institute is given in Exhibit 2.

New Directions

A chronology of major events in the life of the Audubon Zoo is given in Exhibit 3. One of the first significant changes made was the institution of an admission charge in 1972. Admission to the zoo had been free to anyone prior to the adoption of the renovation plan. Ostensibly, the initial purpose behind instituting the admission charge was to prevent vandalism,[5] but the need for additional income was also apparent. Despite the institution of and increases in admission charges, attendance increased dramatically (see Exhibit 4).

*By Claire J. Anderson, Old Dominion University, and Caroline Fisher, Loyola University, New Orleans. © 1993, 1991, 1989, 1987, Claire J. Anderson and Caroline Fisher. This case was designed for classroom discussion only, not to depict effective or ineffective handling of administrative situations.

EXHIBIT I   *The Audubon Park Zoo*

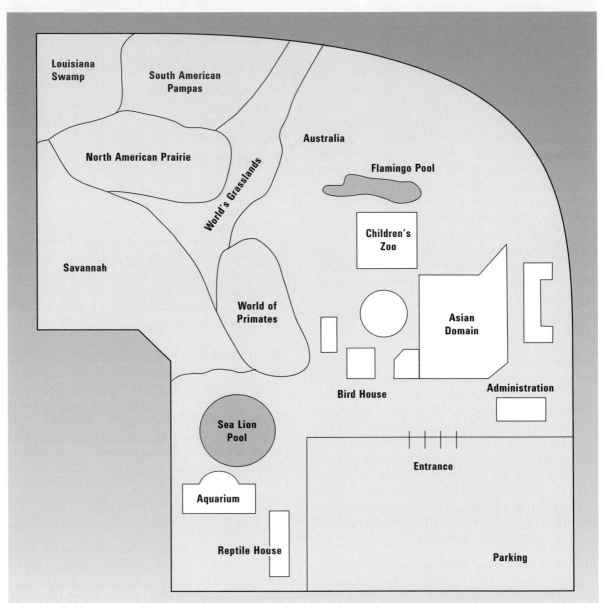

Operations

Friends of the Zoo

The Friends of the Zoo was formed in 1974 and incorporated in 1975 with four hundred members. The stated purpose of the group was to increase support and awareness of the Audubon Park Zoo. Initially, the Friends of the Zoo tried to increase interest in and commitment to the zoo, but its activities increased dramatically over the following years to where it was involved in funding, operating, and governing the zoo.

The Friends of the Zoo had a 24-member governing board. Yearly elections were held for six members of the board, who served four-year terms. The board oversaw the policies of the zoo and set guidelines for memberships, concessions, fund-raising, and marketing. Actual policy making and operations were controlled by the Audubon Park Commission, however, which set zoo hours, admission prices, and so forth.

Through its volunteer programs, the Friends of the Zoo staffed many of the zoo's programs. Members

EXHIBIT 2   *Audubon Institute Mission Statement*

The mission of the Audubon Institute is to cultivate awareness and appreciation of life and the earth's resources and to help conserve and enrich our natural world. The Institute's primary objectives toward this are:

Conservation: To participate in the global effort to conserve natural resources by developing and maintaining captive stocks of endangered plants, animals, and marine life, and by cooperating with related projects in the wild.

Education: To impart knowledge and understanding of the interaction of nature and man through programs, exhibits, and publications and to encourage public participation in global conservation efforts.

Research: To foster the collection and dissemination of scientific information that will enhance the conservation and educational objectives of the facilities of the Audubon Institute.

Economics: To ensure long-range financial security by sound fiscal management and continued development, with funding through creative means that encourage corporate, foundation, and individual support.

Leadership: To serve as a model in the civic and professional communities. To foster a spirit of cooperation, participation, and pride.

Source: The Audubon Institute

EXHIBIT 3   *Chronology of Major Events for the Zoo*

1972   Voters approved a referendum to provide tax dollars to renovate and expand the Zoo. The first Zoo-To-Do was held. An admission charge was instituted.
1973   The City Planning Commission approved the initial master plan for the Audubon Park Zoo calling for $3.4 million for upgrading. Later phases called for an additional $2.1 million.
1974   Friends of the Zoo formed with 400 members to increase support and awareness of the Zoo.
1975   Renovations began with $25 million in public and private funds; 14 acres to be expanded to 58 acres.
1976   The Friends of the Zoo assumed responsibility for concessions.
1977   John Moore went to Albuquerque; Ron Forman took over as Park and Zoo director.
1980   First full-time education staff assumed duties at the Zoo.
1981   Contract signed allowing New Orleans Steamboat Company to bring passengers from downtown to the Park.
1981   Delegates from the American Association of Zoological Parks and Aquariums ranked the Audubon Zoo as one of the top three zoos of its size in America.
1981   Zoo accredited.
1982   The Audubon Park Commission reorganized under Act 352, which required the Commission to contract with a nonprofit organization for the daily management of the Park.
1985   The Zoo was designated as a Rescue Center for Endangered and Threatened Plants.
1986   Voters approved a $25 million bond issue for the Aquarium.
1988   The Friends of the Zoo became the Audubon Institute.
1990   The Aquarium of the Americas opened in September.

Source: The Audubon Institute

EXHIBIT 4   *Admission Charges*

Admission Charges		
Year	Adult	Child
1972	$0.75	$0.25
1978	1.00	0.50
1979	1.50	0.75
1980	2.00	1.00
1981	2.50	1.25
1982	3.00	1.50
1983	3.50	1.75
1984	4.00	2.00
1985	4.50	2.00
1986	5.00	2.50
1987	5.50	2.50
1988	5.50	2.50
1989	6.00	3.00
1990	6.50	3.00
1991	7.00	3.25

	Admission	
Year	Number of Paid Admissions	Number of Member Admissions
1972	163,000	
1973	310,000	
1974	345,000	
1975	324,000	
1976	381,000	
1977	502,000	
1978	456,000	
1979	561,000	
1980	707,000	
1981	741,000	
1982	740,339	78,950
1983	835,044	118,665
1984	813,025	128,538
1985	856,064	145,020
1986	916,865	187,119
1987	902,744	193,926
1988	899,181	173,313
1989	711,709	239,718
1990	725,469	219,668

Source: The Audubon Institute

of the Friends of the Zoo served as "edZOOcators," education volunteers who were specially trained to conduct interpretive educational programs, and "Zoo Area Patrollers," who provided general information at the zoo and helped with crowd control. Other volunteers assisted in the commissary, the Animal Health Care Center, and the Wild Bird Rehabilitation Center or helped with membership, public relations, graphics, clerical work, research, or horticulture.

In 1988, the name of the Friends of the Zoo was changed to the Audubon Institute to reflect its growing interest in activities beyond the zoo alone. It planned to promote the development of other facilities and manage these facilities once they were a reality.

Fund-Raising. The Audubon Park Zoo and the Friends of the Zoo raised funds through five major types of activities: Friends of the Zoo membership, concessions, "Adopt an Animal," "Zoo-To-Do," and capital fund drives. Zoo managers from around the country came to the Audubon Park Zoo for tips on fund-raising.

Membership. Membership in the Friends of the Zoo was open to anyone. The membership fees increased over the years as summarized in Exhibit 5, yet the number of members increased steadily from the original 400 members in 1974 to 38,000 members in 1990, but declined to 28,000 in 1992. Membership allowed free entry to the Audubon Park Zoo and many other zoos around the United States. Participation in Zoobilations (annual members only evenings at the zoo) and the many volunteer programs described earlier were other benefits of membership.

Expanding membership required a special approach to marketing the zoo. Chip Weigand, director of marketing for the zoo, stated:

> ... [I]n marketing memberships we try to encourage repeat visitations, the feeling that one can visit as often as one wants, the idea that the zoo changes from visit to visit and that there are good reasons to make one large payment or donation for a membership card, rather than paying for each visit.... [T]he overwhelming factor is a good zoo that people want to visit often, so that a membership makes good economical sense.

Results of research on visitors to the zoo are contained in Exhibits 6 and 7.

In 1985, the zoo announced a new membership designed for business, the Audubon Zoo Curator Club, with four categories of membership: bronze, $250; silver, $500; gold, $1,000; and platinum, $2,500 and more.

Concessions. The Friends of the Zoo took over the Audubon Park Zoo concessions for refreshments and gifts in 1976 through a public bidding process. The concessions were run by volunteer members of the Friends of the Zoo and all profits went directly to the zoo. Before 1976, concession rentals brought in $1,500 in a good year. Profits from operation of the concessions by the Friends of the Zoo brought in $400,000 a year by 1980 and almost $700,000 in profits in 1988. In 1993, FOTZ was considering leasing the concessions to a third-party vendor.

Adopt an Animal. Zoo Parents paid a fee to "adopt" an animal, the fee varying with the animal chosen. Zoo Parents' names were listed on a large sign inside the zoo. They also had their own annual celebration, Zoo Parents Day.

Exhibit 5   *Membership Fees and Membership*

Year	Family Membership Fees	Individual Membership Fees	Number of Memberships
1979	$20	$10	1,000
1980	20	10	7,000
1981	20	10	11,000
1982	25	15	18,000
1983	30	15	22,000
1984	35	20	26,000
1985	40	20	27,000
1986	45	25	28,616
1987	45	25	29,318
1988	45	25	33,314
1989	49	29	36,935
1990	49	29	38,154

Source: The Audubon Institute

EXHIBIT 6   *Respondent Characteristics of Zoo Visitors According to Visitation Frequency (in %)*

Respondent Characteristic	Number of Zoo Visits Over Past Two Years			
	Four or More	Two or Three	One or None	Never Visited
Age				
Under 27	26	35	31	9
27 to 35	55	27	15	3
36 to 45	48	32	11	9
46 to 55	18	20	37	25
Over 55	27	29	30	14
Marital status				
Married	41	28	20	11
Not married	30	34	24	13
Children at home				
Yes	46	30	15	9
No	34	28	27	12
Interested in visiting New Orleans Aquarium				
Very, with emphasis	47	26	18	9
Very, without emphasis	45	24	23	12
Somewhat	28	37	14	11
Not too	19	32	27	22
Member of Friends of the Zoo				
Yes	67	24	6	4
No, but heard of it	35	30	24	12
Never heard of it	25	28	35	13
Would you be interested in joining FOTZ (non-members only)?				
Very/somewhat	50	28	14	8
No/don't know	33	29	26	12

Source: The Audubon Institute

Zoo-To-Do. Zoo-To-Do was an annual black-tie fund-raiser held with live music, food and drink, and original, high-class souvenirs, such as posters or ceramic necklaces. Admission tickets, limited to 3,000 annually, were priced starting at $100 per person. A raffle was conducted in conjunction with the Zoo-To-Do, with raffle items varying from an opportunity to be zoo curator for a day to the use of a Mercedes-Benz for a year. Despite the rather stiff price, the Zoo-To-Do was a popular sellout every year. Local restaurants and other businesses donated most of the necessary supplies, decreasing the cost of the affair. In 1985, the Zoo-To-Do raised almost $500,000 in one night, more money than any other nonmedical fund-raiser in the county.[6]

Advertising

The Audubon Zoo launched impressive marketing campaigns in the 1980s. The zoo received ADDY awards from the New Orleans Advertising Club year after year.[7] In 1986, the film *Urban Eden*, produced by Alford Advertising and Buckholtz Productions Inc. in New Orleans, finished first among fifty entries in the "documentary films, public relations" category of the Eighth Annual Houston International Film Festival. The first-place Gold Award recognized the film for vividly portraying Audubon Zoo as a conservation, rather than a confining, environment.

During the same year, local television affiliates of ABC, CBS and NBC produced independent TV spots using the theme: "One of the World's Greatest Zoos

EXHIBIT 7   *Relative Importance of Seven Reasons Respondent Does Not Visit the Zoo More Often (in %)*

Reason (Closed-Ended)	Very Imp. w/ Emphasis	Very Imp. w/o Emphasis	Somewhat Important	Unimportant
The distance of the Zoo from where you live	7	11	21	60
The cost of a Zoo visit	4	8	22	66
Not being all that interested in Zoo animals	2	12	18	67
The parking problems on weekends	7	11	19	62
The idea that you get tired of seeing the same exhibits over and over	5	18	28	49
It's too hot during summer months	25	23	22	30
Just not having the idea occur to you	8	19	26	48

Source: The Audubon Institute

Is in Your Own Backyard...Audubon Zoo!" Along with some innovative views of the Audubon Zoo being in someone's "backyard," local news anchor personalities enjoyed "monkeying around" with the animals, and the zoo enjoyed some welcome free exposure.[8]

In 1993 the marketing budget was over $800,000, including group sales, public relations, advertising, and special events. Not included in this budget was developmental fund-raising or membership. Percentage breakdowns of the marketing budget can be found in Exhibit 8.

The American Association of Zoological Parks and Aquariums reported that most zoos find the majority of their visitors live within a single population center in close proximity to the park.[9] Thus, to sustain attendance over the years, zoos must attract the same visitors repeatedly. A large number of the zoo's promotional programs and special events were aimed at just that.

Progress was slow among non-natives. For example, Simon & Schuster, a reputable publishing firm, in its 218-page [Frommer's] *1983–84 Guide to New Orleans*, managed only a three-word allusion to a "very nice zoo." A 1984 study found that only 36 percent of the visitors were tourists, and even this number was probably influenced to some extent by an overflow from the World's Fair.

Promotional Programs

The Audubon Park Zoo and the Friends of the Zoo conducted a multitude of very successful promotional programs. The effect was to have continual parties and celebrations going on, attracting a variety of people to the zoo (and raising additional revenue). Exhibit 9 lists the major annual promotional programs conducted by the zoo.

In addition to these annual promotions, the zoo scheduled concerts of well-known musicians, such as Irma Thomas, Pete Fountain, The Monkees, and Manhattan Transfer, and other special events throughout the year. As a result, a variety of events occurred each month.

Many educational activities were conducted all year long. These included (1) a junior zookeeper program for seventh and eighth graders, (2) a student intern program for high school and college students, and (3) a ZOOmobile that took live animals to such locations as special education classes, hospitals, and nursing homes.

Admission Policy

The commission recommended the institution of an admission charge. Arguments generally advanced against such a charge held that it results in an overall decline in attendance and a reduction of nongate revenues. Proponents held that gate charges control vandalism, produce greater revenues, and result in

EXHIBIT 8   *1991 Marketing Budget*

Marketing

General and Administrative	$ 30,900
Sales	96,300
Public Relations	109,250
Advertising	304,800
Special Events	157,900
TOTAL	$699,150

Public Relations

Education, Travel, and Subscriptions	$ 5,200
Printing and Duplicating	64,000
Professional Services	15,000
Delivery and Postage	3,000
Telephone	1,250
Entertainment	2,000
Supplies	16,600
Miscellaneous	2,200
TOTAL	$109,250

Advertising

Media	$244,000
Production	50,000
Account Service	10,800
TOTAL	$304,800

Special Events

General and Administrative	$ 27,900
LA Swamp Fest	35,000
Earthfest	25,000
Ninja Turtle Breakfast	20,000
Jazz Search	15,000
Fiesta Latina	10,000
Crescent City Cats	10,000
Other Events	15,000
TOTAL	$157,900

Source: The Audubon Institute

increased public awareness and appreciation of the facility. In the early 1970s, no major international zoo charged admission, and 73 percent of the 125 zoos in the United States charged admission.

The commission argued that there is no such thing as a free zoo; someone must pay. If the zoo is tax-supported, then locals carry a disproportionate share of the cost. At the time, neighboring Jefferson Parish was growing by leaps and bounds and surely would bring a large, nonpaying [constituency] to the new zoo. Further, since most zoos are tourist attractions, tourists should pay since they contribute little to the local tax revenues.

The average yearly attendance for a zoo may be estimated using projected population figures multiplied by a "visitor generating factor." The average visitor generating factor of fourteen zoos similar in size and climate to the Audubon Zoo was 1.34, with a rather wide range from a low of 0.58 in the cities of Phoenix and Miami to a high of 2.80 in Jackson, Mississippi.

Attracting More Tourists and Other Visitors

A riverboat ride on the romantic paddle wheeler *Cotton Blossom* took visitors from downtown New Orleans to the zoo. Originally, the trip began at a dock in the French Quarter, but it was later moved to a dock immediately adjacent to New Orleans' newest attraction, the Riverwalk, a Rouse development, on the site of the 1984 Louisiana World Exposition. Not only was the riverboat ride great fun, it also lured tourists and conventioneers from the downtown attractions of the French Quarter and the new Riverwalk to the zoo, some six miles upstream. A further allure of the riverboat ride was a return trip to downtown on the New Orleans Streetcar, one of the few remaining trolley cars in the United States. The Zoo Cruise not only drew more visitors but also generated additional revenue through landing fees paid by the New Orleans Steamboat Company and [helped keep] traffic out of uptown New Orleans.[10]

Financial

The zoo's ability to generate operating funds has been ascribed to the dedication of the Friends of the Zoo, continuing increases in attendance, and creative special events and programs. A history of adequate operating funds allowed the zoo to guarantee capital donors that their gifts would be used to build and maintain top-notch exhibits. A comparison of the 1989 and 1990 Statements of Operating Income and Expense for the Audubon Institute is in Exhibit 10.

Capital Fund Drives

The Audubon Zoo Development Fund was established in 1973. Corporate/industrial support of the zoo has been very strong—many corporations have underwritten construction of zoo displays and facili-

EXHIBIT 9   Selected Audubon Park Zoo Promotional Programs

Month	Activity
March	**Louisiana Black Heritage Festival**. A two-day celebration of Louisiana's black history and its native contributions through food, music, and arts and crafts.
March	**Earth Fest**. The environment and our planet are the focus of this fun-filled and educational event. Recycling, conservation displays, and puppet shows.
April	**Jazz Search**. This entertainment series is aimed at finding the best new talent in the area with the winners featured at the New Orleans Jazz & Heritage Festival.
April	**Zoo-To-Do for kids**. At this "pint-sized" version of the Zoo-To-Do, fun and games abound for kids.
May	**Zoo-To-Do**. Annual black tie fund-raiser featuring over 100 of New Orleans' finest restaurants and three music stages.
May	**Irma Thomas Mother's Day Concert**. The annual celebration of Mother's Day with a buffet.
August	**Lego Invitational**. Architectural firms turn thousands of Lego pieces into original creations.
September	**Fiesta Latina**. Experience the best the Hispanic community has to offer through music, cuisine, and arts and crafts.
October	**Louisiana Swamp Festival**. Cajun food, music, and crafts highlight this four-day salute to Louisiana's bayou country; features hands on contact with live swamp animals.
October	**Boo at the Zoo**. This annual Halloween extravaganza features games, special entertainment, trick or treat, a haunted house, and the Zoo's Spook Train.

Source: The Audubon Institute

ties. A partial list of major corporate sponsors is in Exhibit 11. A sponsorship was considered to be for the life of the exhibit. The development department operated on a 12 percent overhead rate, which meant 88 cents of every dollar raised went toward the projects. By 1989, the master plan for development was 75 percent complete. The fund-raising goal for the zoo in 1989 was $1,500,000.

Management

The Zoo Director
Ron Forman, Audubon Zoo director, was called a "zoomaster extraordinaire" and was described by the press as a "cross between Doctor Doolittle and the Wizard of Oz," as a "practical visionary," and as "serious, but with a sense of humor."[11] A native New Orleanian...Forman quit an MBA program to join the city government as an administrative assistant and found himself doing a business analysis project on the Audubon Park. Once the city was committed

to a new zoo, Forman was placed on board as an assistant to the zoo director, John Moore. In early 1977, Moore gave up the battle between the "animal people" and the "people people,"[12] and Forman took over as park and zoo director.

Forman was said to bring an MBA-meets-menagerie style to the zoo, which was responsible for transforming it from a public burden into an almost completely self-sustaining operation. The result not only benefited the citizens of the city but also added a major tourist attraction to the economically troubled city of the 1980s.

Staffing
The zoo used two classes of employees, civil service, through the Audubon Park Commission, and noncivil service. The civil service employees included the curators and zookeepers. They fell under the jurisdiction of the city civil service system but were paid out of the budget of the Friends of the Zoo. Employees who worked in public relations, advertising, concessions,

EXHIBIT 10   *The Audubon Institute, Inc. The Audubon Park and Zoological Garden Statement of Operating Income and Expenses*

	1989	1990 (Zoo)	1990 (Aquarium)
Operating Income			
Admissions	$2,952,000	$3,587,000	$3,664,000
Food and Gift Operations	2,706,000	3,495,500	711,000
Membership	1,476,000	1,932,000	2,318,000
Recreational Programs	410,000	396,000	0
Visitor Services	246,000	218,000	0
Other	410,000	32,000	650,000
TOTAL INCOME	$8,200,000	$9,660,500	$7,343,000
Operating Expenses			
Maintenance	$1,394,000	$1,444,000	$1,316,000
Educational/Curatorial	2,296,000	2,527,500	2,783,000
Food and Gift Operations	1,804,000	2,375,000	483,000
Membership	574,000	840,000	631,000
Recreational	328,000	358,000	362,000
Marketing	410,000	633,000	593,000
Visitor Services	574,000	373,000	125,000
Administration	820,000	1,110,000	1,050,000
TOTAL EXPENSES	$8,200,000	$9,660,500	$7,343,000

EXHIBIT 11   *Major Corporate Sponsors*

Amoco Foundation
American Express
Anheuser-Busch, Inc.
Arthur Andersen and Company
J. Aron Charitable Foundation, Inc.
Bell South Corporation
BP America
Chevron USA, Inc.
Conoco, Inc.
Consolidated Natural Gas Corporation
Entergy Corporation
Exxon Company, USA
Freeport-McMoRan, Inc.
Host International, Inc.
Kentwood Spring Water

Louisiana Coca-Cola Bottling Company, Ltd.
Louisiana Land and Exploration Company
Martin Marietta Manned Space Systems
McDonald's Operators of New Orleans
Mobil Foundation, Inc.
National Endowment for the Arts
National Science Foundation
Ozone Spring Water
Pan American Life Insurance Company
Philip Morris Companies Inc.
Shell Companies Foundation, Inc.
Tenneco, Inc.
Texaco USA
USF&G Corporation
Wendy's of New Orleans, Inc.

Source: The Audubon Institute

fund-raising, and so on were hired through the Friends of the Zoo and were not part of the civil service system. See Exhibit 12 for further data on staffing patterns.

The Zoo in the Late 1980s

A visitor to the new Audubon Park Zoo could quickly see why New Orleanians were so proud of their zoo. In a city that was termed among the dirtiest in the nation, the zoo was virtually spotless. This was a result of adequate staffing and the clear pride of both those who worked at and those who visited the zoo. One of the first points made by volunteers guiding school groups was that anyone seeing a piece of trash on the ground must pick it up.[13] A 1986 city poll showed that 93 percent of the citizens surveyed gave the zoo a high approval rating—an extremely high rating for any public facility.

Kudos came from groups outside the local area as well. Delegates from the American Association of Zoological Parks and Aquariums ranked the Audubon Park Zoo as one of the three top zoos of its size in America. In 1982, the American Association of Nurserymen gave the zoo a Special Judges Award for its use of plant materials. In 1985, the Audubon Park Zoo received the Phoenix Award from the Society of American Travel Writers for its achievements in conservation, preservation, and beautification.

By 1987, the zoo was virtually self-sufficient. The small amount of money received from government grants amounted to less than 10 percent of the budget. The master plan for the development of the zoo was 75 percent complete, and the reptile exhibit was scheduled for completion in the fall. The organization had expanded with a full complement of professionals and managers. (See Exhibit 13 for the organizational structure of the zoo.)

While the zoo made great progress in fifteen years, all was not quiet on the political front. In a court battle, the city won over the state on the issue of who wielded ultimate authority over Audubon Park and Zoo. Indeed, the zoo benefited from three friendly mayors in a row, starting with Moon Landrieu, who championed the new zoo, to Ernest "Dutch" Morial, to Sidney Barthelemy who threw his support to both the zoo and the aquarium proposal championed by Ron Forman.

EXHIBIT 12   *Employee Structure*

Year	Number of Paid Employees	Number of Volunteers
1972	36	
1973	49	
1974	69	
1975	90	
1976	143	
1977	193	
1978	184	
1979	189	
1980	198	
1981	245	
1982	305	
1983	302	56
1984	419	120
1985	454	126
1986	426	250
1987	431	300
1988	462	310
1989	300	270
1990	450	350

Source: The Audubon Institute

The Future

New Directions for the Zoo

Zoo Director Ron Forman demonstrated that zoos have almost unlimited potential. A 1980 New Orleans magazine article cited some of Forman's ideas, ranging from a safari train to a breeding center for rare animals. The latter has an added attraction as a potential money-maker since an Asiatic lion cub, for example, sells for around $10,000. This wealth of ideas was important because expanded facilities and programs are required to maintain attendance at any public attraction. The most ambitious of Forman's ideas was for an aquarium and riverfront park to be located at the foot of Canal Street.

Although the zoo enjoyed political support in 1992, New Orleans was still suffering from a high unemployment rate and a generally depressed economy resulting from the slump in the oil industry. Some economists predicted the beginning of a gradual turnaround in 1988, but any significant improvement in the economy was still forecasted to be years away in 1993. (A few facts about New Orleans are given in Exhibit 14.) In addition, the zoo operated in a city where many attractions competed for the leisure dollar of citizens and visitors. The Audubon Zoological Garden had to vie with the French Quarter, Dixieland jazz, the Superdome, and even the greatest of all attractions in the city—Mardi Gras.

The New Orleans Aquarium

In 1986, Forman and a group of supporters proposed the development of an aquarium and riverfront park to the New Orleans City Council. In November 1986, the electorate voted to fund an aquarium and a riverfront park by a 70 percent margin—one of the largest margins the city has ever given to any tax proposal. Forman[14] hailed this vote of confidence from the citizens as a mandate to build a world-class aquarium that would produce new jobs, stimulate the local economy, and create an educational resource for the children of the city.

The Aquarium of the Americas opened in September 1990. The $40 million aquarium project was located providing a logical pedestrian link for visitors between [major] attractions of the Riverwalk and the Jax Brewery, a shopping center in the French Quarter. Management of the aquarium was placed under the Audubon Institute, the same organization that ran the Audubon Zoo. A feasibility study prepared by Harrison Price Company[15] projected a probable 863,000 visitors by the year 1990, with 75 percent of the visitors coming from outside the metropolitan area. That attendance figure was reached in only four months and six days from the grand opening. Attendance remained strong through 1992, after a slight drop from the initial grand opening figures.

Meanwhile, the zoo had its own future to plan. The new physical facilities and professional care paid off handsomely in increased attendance and new animal births. But the zoo could not expand at its existing location because of lack of land within the city. Forman and the zoo considered several alternatives. One was little "neighborhood" zoos to be located all over the city. A second was a special survival center, a separate breeding area to be located outside the city boundaries where land was available.

Forman presented ... plans for a project called Riverfront 2000, which included expansion of the aquarium, the Woldenberg Riverfront Park, a species survival center, an arboretum, an insectarium, a natural history museum, and a further expansion of the zoo. With the zoo running smoothly, the staff seemed to need new challenges to tackle, and the zoo needed new facilities or programs to continue to increase attendance.

EXHIBIT 13   *Audubon Park Commission*

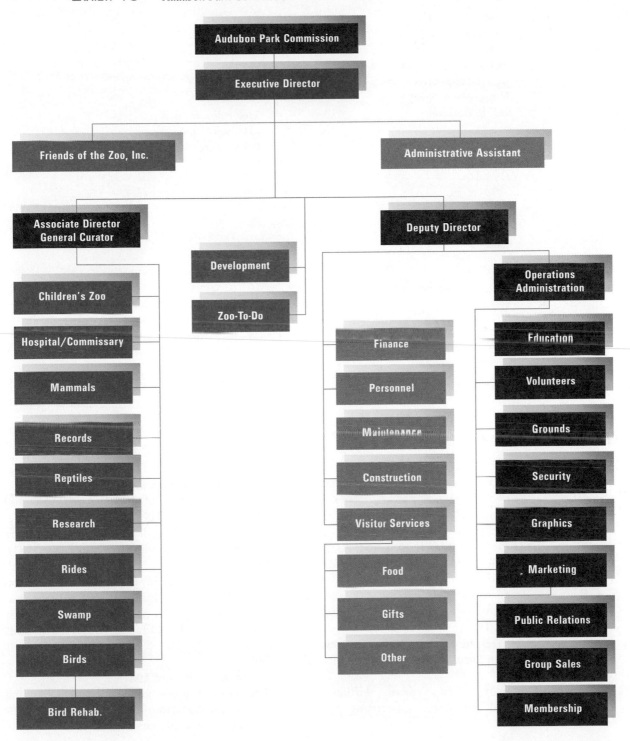

EXHIBIT 14   *A Few Facts About the New Orleans MSA*

Population	1,324,400
Households	489,900
Median Age	30.8 years
Median Household EBI	$29,130
Average Temperature	70 degrees
Average Annual Rainfall	63 inches
Average Elevation	5 feet below sea level
Area	363.5 square miles
	199.4 square miles of land

Major Economic Activities

Tourism (5 million visitors per year)

Oil and Gas Industry

The Port of New Orleans (170 million tons of cargo/year)

Taxes

State Sales Tax	4.0%
Parish (County) Sales Tax	5.0% (Orleans)
State Income Tax	2.1%–2.6% on first $20,000
	3.0%–3.5% on next $30,000
	6.0% on $51,000 and over

Parish property tax of 126.15 mills (Orleans) is based on 10% of appraised value over $75,000 homestead exemption.

Source: Sales and Marketing Management. South Central Bell Yellow Pages, 1991.

Notes

1. Millie Ball, "The New Zoo of '82," *Dixie Magazine, Sunday Times Picayune* (June 24, 1979).
2. Merikaye Presley, "Neighbors Objecting to Audubon Zoo Expansion Project in Midst of Work," *Times Picayune* (March 30, 1975), A3.
3. "Zoo Expansion Is Ruled Illegal," *Times Picayune* (January 20, 1976).
4. Ibid.
5. "Society Seeks Change at Zoo," *Times Picayune* (April 29, 1972), D25.
6. "Zoo Thrives Despite Tough Times in New Orleans," *Jefferson Business* (August 1985), A1.
7. Ibid.
8. Sharon Donovan, "New Orleans Affiliates Monkey Around for Zoo," *Advertising Age* (March 17, 1986).
9. Karen Sausmann, ed., *Zoological Park and Aquarium Fundamentals* (Wheeling, W. Va.: American Association of Zoological Parks and Aquariums, 1982), 111.
10. Diane Luope, "Riverboat Rides to Zoo Are Planned," *Times Picayne* (November 30, 1981), A17.
11. Steve Brooks, "Don't Say 'No Can Do' to Audubon Zoo Chief," *Jefferson Business* (May 5, 1986), 1
12. Ross Yuchey, "No Longer Is Heard a Discouraging Word at the Audubon Zoo," *New Orleans* (August 1980), 53.
13. Ibid., 49.
14. "At the Zoo" (Winter 1987).
15. "Feasibility Analysis and Conceptual Planning for a Major Aquarium Attraction," prepared for the City of New Orleans (March 1985).

References

Ball, Millie. "The New Zoo of '82," *Dixie Magazine, Sunday Times Picayune* (June 24, 1978).

Beaulieu, Lovell. "It's All Happening at the Zoo," *Sunday Times Picayune* (January 28, 1978).

Brooks, Steve. "Don't Say 'No Can Do' to Audubon Zoo Chief," *Jefferson Business* (May 5, 1986).

Bureau of Governmental Research, City of New Orleans, "Audubon Park Zoo Study, Part I, Zoo Improvement Plan" (New Orleans, La.: Bureau of Governmental Research, August 1971).

Bureau of Governmental Research, City of New Orleans, "Audubon Park Zoo Study, Part II, An Operational Analysis," (New Orleans, La.: Bureau of Governmental Research, August 1971).

Donovan, S. "The Audubon Zoo: A Dream Come True," *New Orleans* (May 1986), 52–66.

"Feasibility Analysis and Conceptual Planning for a Major Aquarium Attraction," prepared for the City of New Orleans (March 1985).

Forman, R., J. Logsdon, and J. Wilds. "Audubon Park: An Urban Eden" (New Orleans, La.: The Friends of the Zoo, 1985.)

Poole, Susan. *Frommer's 1983–84 Guide to New Orleans,* (New York: Simon & Schuster, 1983).

Sausmann, Karen, ed., *Zoological Park and Aquarium Fundamentals* (Wheeling, WVa.: American Association of Zoological Parks and Aquariums, 1982).

Yuchey, Ross "No Longer Is Heard a Discouraging Word at the Audubon Zoo," *New Orleans* (August 1980), 49–60.

Zuckerman, S., ed. *Great Zoos of the World* (Boulder, Co.: Westview Press, 1980).

INTEGRATIVE CASE 7.0   *Dowling Flexible Metals**

In 1960, Bill Dowling, a "machine-tool set-up man" for a large auto firm, became so frustrated with his job that he quit to form his own business. The manufacturing operation consisted of a few general-purpose metalworking machines that were set up in Dowling's garage. Space was such a constraint that it controlled the work process. For example, if the cutting press was to be used with long stock, the milling machines would have to be pushed back against the wall and remain idle. Production always increased on rain-free, summer days since the garage doors could be opened and a couple of machines moved out onto the drive. Besides Dowling, who acted as salesman, accountant, engineer, president, manufacturing representative, and working foreman, members of the original organization were Eve Sullivan, who began as a part-time secretary and payroll clerk; and Wally Denton, who left the auto firm with Bill. The workforce was composed of part-time moonlighters, full-time machinists for other firms, who were attracted by the job autonomy that provided experience in setting up jobs and job processes, where a high degree of ingenuity was required.

The first years were touch and go, with profits being erratic. Gradually the firm began to gain a reputation for being ingenious at solving unique problems and for producing a quality product on, or before, deadlines. The "product" consisted of fabricating dies for making minor component metal parts for automobiles and a specified quantity of the parts. Having realized the firm was too dependent on the auto industry and that sudden fluctuations in auto sales could have a drastic effect on the firm's survival, Dowling began marketing their services toward manufacturing firms not connected with the auto industry. Bids were submitted for work that involved legs for vending machines, metal trim for large appliances, clamps and latches for metal windows, and display racks for small power hand tools.

As Dowling Flexible Metals became more diversified, the need for expansion forced the company to borrow building funds from the local bank, which enabled construction of a small factory on the edge of town. As new markets and products created a need for increasingly more versatile equipment and a larger workforce, the plant has since expanded twice until it is now three times its original size.

In 1980, Dowling Flexible Metals hardly resembles the garage operation of the formative years. The firm now employs approximately thirty full-time journeymen and apprentice machinists, a staff of four engineers that were hired about three years ago, and a full-time office secretary subordinate to Eve Sullivan, the office manager. The rapid growth has created problems that in 1980 have not been resolved. Bill Dowling, realizing his firm is suffering from growing pains, has asked you to "take a look at the operation and make recommendations as to how things could be run better." You begin the consulting project by interviewing Dowling, other key people in the firm, and workers out in the shop who seem willing to express their opinions about the firm.

Bill Dowling, Owner-President

"We sure have come a long way from that first setup in my garage. On a nice day we would get everything all spread out in the drive and then it would start pouring cats and dogs—so we would have to move back inside. It was just like a one-ring circus. Now it seems like a three-ring circus. You would think that with all that talent we have here and all the experience, things would run smoother. Instead, it seems I am putting in more time than ever and accomplishing a whole lot less in a day's time.

"It's not like the old days. Everything has gotten so complicated and precise in design. When you go to a customer to discuss a job you have to talk to six kids right out of engineering school. Every one of them has a calculator—they don't even carry slide rules anymore—and all they can talk is fancy formulas and how we should do our job. It just seems I spend more time with customers and less time around the shop than I used to. That's why I hired the engineering staff—to interpret specifications, solve engineering problems, and draw blueprints. It still seems all the problems are solved out on the shop floor by guys like Walt and Tom, just like always. Gene and the other engineers are necessary, but they don't seem to be working as smoothly with the guys on the floor as they should.

"One of the things I would like to see us do in the future is to diversify even more. Now that we have the capability, I am starting to bid jobs that require the computerized milling machine process tape. This involves devising a work process for

*This case was prepared by Floyd G. Willoughby, Oakland University, Rochester, MI. © by Floyd G. Willoughby. Reprinted by permission.

milling a part on a machine and then making a computer process tape of it. We can then sell copies of the tape just like we do dies and parts. These tapes allow less skilled operators to operate complicated milling machines without the long apprenticeship of a tradesman. All they have to do is press buttons and follow the machine's instructions for changing the milling tools. Demand is increasing for the computerized process tapes.

"I would like to see the firm get into things like working with combinations of bonded materials such as plastics, fiberglass, and metals. I am also starting to bid jobs involving the machining of plastics and other materials beside metals."

Wally Denton, Shop Foreman, First Shift

"Life just doesn't seem to be as simple as when we first started in Bill's garage. In those days he would bring a job back and we would all gather round and decide how we were going to set it up and who would do it. If one of the moonlighters was to get the job, either Bill or I would lay the job out for him when he came in that afternoon. Now, the customers' ideas get processed through the engineers and we, out here in the shop, have to guess just exactly what the customer had in mind.

"What some people around here don't understand is that I am a partner in this business. I've stayed out here in the shop because this is where I like it and it's where I feel most useful. When Bill isn't here, I'm always around to put out fires. Between Eve, Gene, and myself we usually make the right decision.

"With all this diversification and Bill spending a lot of time with customers, I think we need to get somebody else out there to share the load."

Thomas McNull, Shop Foreman, Second Shift

"In general, I agree with Wally that things aren't as simple as they used to be, but I think, given the amount of jobs we are handling at any one time, we run the ship pretty smoothly. When the guys bring problems to me that require major job changes, I get Wally's approval before making the changes. We haven't had any difficulty in that area.

"Where we run into problems is with the engineers. They get the job when Bill brings it back. They decide how the part should be made and by what process, which in turn pretty much restricts what type of dies we have to make. Therein lies the bind.

Oftentimes we run into a snag following the engineers' instructions. If it's after five o'clock, the engineers have left for the day. We, on the second shift, either have to let the job sit until the next morning or solve the problem ourselves. This not only creates bad feeling between the shop personnel and the engineers, but it makes extra work for the engineers because they have to draw up new plans.

"I often think we have the whole process backwards around here. What we should be doing is giving the job to the journeymen—after all, these guys have a lot of experience and know-how—then give the finished product to the engineers to draw up. I'll give you an example. Last year we got a job from a vending machine manufacturer. The job consisted of fabricating five sets of dies for making those stubby little legs for vending machines, plus five hundred of the finished legs. Well, the engineers figured the job all out, drew up the plans, and sent it out to us. We made the first die to specs, but when we tried to punch out the leg on the press, the metal tore. We took the problem back to the engineers, and after the preliminary accusations of who was responsible for the screwup, they changed the raw material specifications. We waited two weeks for delivery of the new steel, then tried again. The metal still tore. Finally, after two months of hassle, Charlie Oakes and I worked on the die for two days and finally came up with a solution. The problem was that the shoulders of the die were too steep for forming the leg in just one punch. We had to use two punches (see Exhibit 1). The problem was the production process, not the raw materials. We spent four months on that job and ran over our deadline. Things like that shouldn't happen."

Charlie Oakes, Journeyman Apprentice

"Really, I hate to say anything against this place because it is a pretty good place to work. The pay and benefits are pretty good and because it is a small shop our hours can be somewhat flexible. If you have a doctor's appointment you can either come in late or stay until you get your time in or punch out and come back. You can work as much overtime as you want to.

"The thing I'm kind of disappointed about is that I thought the work would be more challenging. I'm just an apprentice, but I've only got a year to go in my program before I can get my journeyman's card, and I think I should be handling more jobs on my own. That's why I came to work here. My dad was one of the original moonlighters here. He told

EXHIBIT 1   *Two-Stage Production Process*

me about how interesting it was when he was here. I guess I just expected the same thing."

Gene Jenkins, Chief Engineer

"I imagine the guys out in the shop have already told you about 'The Great Vending Machine Fiasco.' They'll never let us forget that. However, it does point out the need for better coordination around here. The engineers were hired as engineers, not as drafters, which is just about all we do. I'm not saying we should have the final say on how the job is designed, because there is a lot of practical experience out in that shop; but just as we haven't their expertise, neither do they have ours. There is a need for both, the technical skill of the engineers and the practical experience of the shop.

"One thing that would really help is more information from Bill. I realize Bill is spread pretty thin but there are a lot of times he comes back with a job, briefs us, and we still have to call the customer about details because Bill hasn't been specific enough or asked the right questions of the customer. Engineers communicate best with other engineers. Having an engineering function gives us a competitive advantage over our competition. In my opinion, operating as we do now, we are not maximizing that advantage.

"When the plans leave here we have no idea what happens to those plans once they are out in the shop. The next thing we know, we get a die or set of dies that doesn't even resemble the plans we sent out in the shop. We then have to draw up new plans to fit the dies. Believe me, it's not only discouraging, but it really makes you wonder what your job is around

here. It's embarrassing when a customer calls to check on the status of the job and I have to run out in the shop, look up the guy handing the job, and get his best estimate of how the job is going."

Eve Sullivan, Office Manager

"One thing is for sure, life is far from dull around here. It seems Bill is either dragging in a bunch of plans or racing off with the truck to deliver a job to a customer.

"Really, Wally and I make all the day-to-day decisions around here. Of course, I don't get involved in technical matters. Wally and Gene take care of those, but if we are shorthanded or need a new machine, Wally and I start the ball rolling by getting together the necessary information and talking to Bill the first chance we get. I guess you could say that we run things around here by consensus most of time. If I get a call from a customer asking about the status of a job, I refer the call to Gene because Wally is usually out in the shop.

"I started with Bill and Wally twenty years ago, on a part-time basis, and somehow the excitement has turned into work. Joan, the office secretary, and I handle all correspondence, bookkeeping, payroll, insurance forms, and everything else besides run the office. It's just getting to be too hectic—I just wish the job was more fun, the way it used to be."

Having listened to all concerned, you returned to Bill's office only to find him gone. You tell Eve and Wally that you will return within one week with your recommendations.

Exhibit 2   *Dowling Flexible Metals Organizational Chart*

INTEGRATIVE CASE 8.1   *Littleton Manufacturing (A)**

Rule #1 for business organizations: People, not structure, make a business work or fail. Blindly following organizational concepts that have worked elsewhere is a sure way to waste talent and get poor results. Organizational change alone achieves nothing, while dedicated people can make any structure work. This doesn't mean that organizational changes shouldn't happen. But design any changes to get the most out of people in the company's unique circumstances. Top management should never dictate change as a cure-all to avoid facing fundamental problems.

> Quotation from the *Harvard Business Review* (title and author uncited) posted on the wall of Bill Larson, Plant Manager of Littleton Manufacturing

On June 21, 1990, Paul Winslow, the director of human resources at Littleton Manufacturing, was told by his boss, Bill Larson, to put together a team of employees to address a number of issues that Larson thought were hurting Littleton's bottom line. Winslow's assignment had come about as a result of his making a presentation on those problems to Larson. Larson had then met with his executive staff, and he and Winslow had subsequently gone to the plant's Quality Steering Committee to discuss what to do. They decided to form a Human Resources Process Improvement Team (PIT) to prioritize the issues and propose a corrective course of action. Winslow, who had been at the plant for seventeen years, had been asked by Larson to chair the PIT.

The Quality Steering Committee decided that the PIT should include two representatives each from Sales and Marketing, Fabrication, and Components. Two managers from each of these areas were chosen, including Dan Gordon, the fabrication manufacturing manager, and Phil Hanson, the components manufacturing manager. There were no supervisors or hourly employees on the team.

At the first meeting, the PIT discussed the six widely recognized problem areas that Winslow had identified to Larson. Each member's assignment for the next meeting, on June 28, was to prioritize the issues and propose an action plan.

The Problems

A course in management and organizational studies carried out by students at a nearby college had started the chain of events that led to the formation of the Human Resources PIT. In late 1989, Winslow was approached by a faculty member at a local college who was interested in using Littleton as a site for a field-project course. Because of ongoing concerns about communication at the plant by all levels, Winslow asked that the students assess organizational communication at Littleton. Larson gave his approval, and in the spring of 1990 the students carried out the project, conducting individual and group interviews with employees at all levels of the plant.

Winslow and his staff combined the results of the students' assessment with the results of an in-house survey done several years earlier. The result was the identification of six problem areas that they thought were critical for the plant to address:

- Lack of organizational unity
- Lack of consistency in enforcing rules and procedures
- Supervisor's role poorly perceived
- Insufficient focus on Littleton's priorities
- Change is poorly managed
- Lack of a systematic approach to training

The Company

Littleton Manufacturing, located in rural Minnesota, was founded in 1925. In 1942, Littleton was bought by Brooks Industries, a major manufacturer of domestic appliances and their components. At that time, Littleton manufactured custom-made and precision-machined components from special metals for a variety of industries.

In 1983, through the purchase of a larger competitor, Frühling, Inc., Brooks was able to increase its domestic market share from 8 percent to about 25 percent. Brooks then decided to have only one facility produce the components that were used in most of the products it made in the United States. The site chosen was Littleton Manufacturing. To do this, Brooks added a whole new business (Components) to Littleton's traditional activity. To accommodate the new line, a building of 80,000 square feet was added

*By David E. Whiteside, organizational development consultant. This case was written at Lewiston-Auburn College of the University of Southern Maine with the cooperation of management, solely for the purpose of stimulating student discussion. Data are based on field research; all events are real, although the names of organizations, locations, and individuals have been disguised. Faculty members in nonprofit institutions are encouraged to reproduce this case for distribution to their students without charge or written permission. All other rights reserved jointly to the author and the North American Case Research Association (NACRA). Copyright © 1994 by the *Case Research Journal* and David E. Whiteside.

to the old Littleton plant, bringing the total to 220,000 square feet of plant space. Because of the addition of this new business, Littleton went from 150 employees in 1984 to 600 in 1986. In mid-1990, there were about 500 employees.

The older part of the plant (the Fabrication side) manufactured its traditional custom-made products and sold them to a variety of industrial customers. It also supplied the newer side of the plant (the Components side) with a variety of parts that were further processed and used to make electrical components. These components were used by all other Brooks plants in the assembly of domestic appliances that were sold worldwide. About 95 percent of the products made on the Components side of the plant originated on the Fabrication side.

The plant was also headquarters for Brooks Industries' sales and marketing department, known as the "commercial group," which had worldwide sales responsibilities for products made by the Fabrication side. These included international and domestic sales of products to several industries, including the semiconductor, consumer electronics, and nuclear furnace industry. This group marketed products made not only by Littleton Manufacturing but also those made by Brooks's other fourteen plants, all located in the United States.

Bill Larson, the plant manager, reported to the executive vice president of manufacturing of Brooks, whose corporate office was in Chicago, Illinois. Larson met once a month with his boss and the other plant managers. Reporting directly to Larson were

six functional line managers and the manager of the Quality Improvement System (QIS). This group of seven managers, known as the "staff," met weekly to plan and discuss how things were going. (See Exhibit 1 for an organizational chart.)

In December 1989, there were 343 hourly and 125 salaried employees at the plant. About 80 percent of the workforce was under 45. Seventy-seven percent were male, and 23 percent were female. Seventy-six percent had been at the plant 10 years or less. All of the hourly workers were represented by the Teamsters union.

The Financial Picture

Brooks Industries

Brooks was the second largest producer of its kind of domestic appliances in the United States. Its three core business units were commercial/industrial, consumer, and original equipment manufacturing. The major U.S. competitors for its domestic appliances were Eagleton, Inc., and Universal Appliances, Inc. In the United States, Eagleton's market share was 17 percent; Brooks had about 23 percent; and Universal Appliances and a number of small companies had the remaining 30 percent. However, U.S. manufacturers were facing increasing competition, primarily based on lower prices, from companies in Asia and eastern Europe.

In 1989, Brooks's sales declined 4 percent, and in 1990, they declined another 5 percent, to $647 million. Their 1989 annual report contained the

EXHIBIT 1   *Littleton Manufacturing Organizational Chart*

following statement about the company's financial condition: "There was fierce competition...which led to a decline in our share of a stable market and a fall in prices, resulting in a lower level of sales.... With sales volume showing slower growth, we failed to reduce our costs proportionately and there was underutilization of capacity." In May 1990, after announcing unexpected first-quarter losses, Brooks started a corporation-wide efficiency drive, including planned layoffs of 16 percent of its workforce, a corporate restructuring, and renewed emphasis on managerial accountability for bottom-line results.

Because of its worsening financial condition, for the past few years Brooks had been reducing the resources available to Littleton. For example, Larson's budget for salaries had been increased by only 4 percent each year for the past several years. As a result, supervisors and middle managers complained strongly that recent salary increases had been too little and that plant salaries were too low. They also felt that the forced-ranking performance appraisal system used by the plant, which was based on a bell curve, did not reward good performance adequately. One middle manager commented: "All we get now for good performance is a card and a turkey." In April 1990, the company cut Littleton's capital budget by half and stipulated that any new project involving nonessential items had to have a one-year payback.

In addition, in both 1988 and 1989 Brooks had charged the Littleton plant around $300,000 for various services provided, such as technical support, but in 1990 this charge was increased by $1 million. Many of the Littleton plant managers felt that this was done to help offset Brooks's deteriorating financial condition and were frustrated by it. Indicating that he thought Brooks was using Littleton as a cash cow, one staff member said, "The more profitable we get, the more corporate will charge us."

Many managers, especially those on the Fabrication side, felt that even though they had made money for the plant, corporate's increase in charges nullified their success and hard work. A number of managers on the Fabrication side also feared that if their operation did not do well financially, the company might close it down.

In discussing the increasing lack of resources available from corporate and the plant's own decline in profits, Larson said: "There needs to be a change in the way people here think about resources. They have to

think more in terms of efficiency." He was proud of the fact that the company had achieved its goal of reducing standard costs by 1 percent for each of the past three years and that in 1990 cost reductions would equal 5 percent of production value. He thought that if the company reduced the number of reworks, costs could be lowered by another 20 to 30 percent.

Littleton Manufacturing

The Fabrication and the Components operations at Littleton Manufacturing were managed as cost centers by Brooks while the commercial group was a profit center. (A *profit center* is a part of an organization that is responsible for accumulating revenues as well as costs. A *cost center* is an organizational division or unit of activity in which accounts are maintained containing direct costs for which the center's head is responsible.) In 1989 and 1990, the Fabrication side of Littleton had done well in terms of budgeted costs, while the Components side had incurred significant losses for both years.

Littleton's net worth increased from $319,000 in 1989 to $3,094,000 in 1990 due to the addition of a new Fabrication-side product that was sold on the external market and had required no additional assets or resources. In 1990, sales for the plant as a whole were $41,196,000, with an operating profit of 3.7 percent, down from 7.3 percent in 1989. Larson estimated that the current recession, which was hurting the company, would lower sales in 1991 by 10 percent. Exhibit 2 presents an operating statement for Littleton Manufacturing from 1988 to 1990.

The Quality Improvement System

In 1985, corporate mandated a total quality management effort, the Quality Improvement System (QIS), which replaced the quality circles that the plant had instituted in 1980. Posted throughout the plant was a Quality Declaration, which had been developed by Larson and his staff. It read:

> We at Littleton Manufacturing are dedicated to achieving lasting quality. This means that each of us must understand and meet the requirements of our customers and co-workers. We all must continually strive for improvement and error-free work in all we do—in every job...on time...all the time.

Bill Larson was enthusiastic about QIS. He saw QIS as a total quality approach affecting not just products but all of the plant's processes, one that would

EXHIBIT 2   *Littleton Manufacturing Operating Profit Statement*

	1988	1989	1990
Fabrication			
Sales	$16,929	$18,321	$19,640
Direct costs	11,551	11,642	11,701
Contribution margin	5,378	6,679	7,939
% of sales	31.8%	36.5%	40.4%
All other operating costs	4,501	4,377	4,443
Operating profit	877	2,301	3,496
% to sales	5.2%	12.6%	17.8%
Components			
Sales	$20,468	$15,590	$21,556
Direct costs	16,049	10,612	18,916
Contribution margin	4,419	4,978	2,640
% of sales	21.6%	31.9%	12.2%
All other operating costs	4,824	4,797	4,628
Operating profit	(405)	180	(1,988)
% to sales	−2.0%	1.2%	−9.2%
Total Littleton Manufacturing			
Sales	$37,397	$33,911	$41,196
Direct costs	27,599	22,254	30,617
Contribution margin	9,798	11,657	10,579
% to sales	26.2%	34.4%	25.7%
All other operating costs	9,326	9,175	9,071
Operating profit	472	2,482	1,508
% to sales	1.3%	7.3%	3.7%

Note: Changes in Operating Profit from year to year are posted to retained earnings (net worth) account on the corporate balance sheet. It must be noted, however, that the balance sheet figures include the impact of headquarters, national organization changes, and extraordinary income from other operations, which are not reflected on the operating profit statement shown above.

Source: Controller, Littleton Manufacturing

require a long-term effort at changing the culture at the plant. He felt that QIS was already reaping benefits in terms of significant improvements in quality, and that the system had also greatly helped communication at the plant.

In the QIS all employees were required to participate in Departmental Quality Teams (DQTs) that met in groups of six to twelve every two weeks for at least an hour to identify ways to improve quality. Most hourly employees were on only one DQT; middle managers were, on average, on three DQTs. Some managers were on as many as six. The results of each team's efforts were exhibited in graphs and charts by their work area and updated monthly. There were about sixty teams in the plant.

The leader from each Departmental Quality Team, a volunteer, served also as a member of a Quality Improvement Team (QIT), whose goals were to support the DQTs and help them link their goals to the company's goals. QITs consisted of six to eight people; each was chaired by a member of the executive staff. These staff members, along with Bill Larson, composed the Quality Steering Committee (QSC) for the plant. The QSC's job was to oversee the direction and implementation of the Quality Improvement System for the plant and to coordinate with corporate's quality improvement programs. The QSC also sometimes formed corrective action teams to work on special projects. Unlike DQTs, which were composed of employees from a single department or work area, corrective action teams had members from different functions or departments. By 1986, there were nine corrective action teams, but by 1989, none were functioning. When asked about them, Winslow said, "I'm not sure what happened to them. They just sort of died out."

Larson and most managers believed that the QIS had improved quality. On most of its Fabrication products, the company competed on the basis of quality and customer service, and the vice president of sales and marketing thought that their quality was the best in the industry. In 1988 and 1989, the plant won several Brooks awards for quality and was publicly cited by a number of customers for quality products.

Hourly employees in general also thought that QIS had improved quality, although they were less enthusiastic about the system than management. A number of hourly employees complained that since participation was mandatory, many groups were held back by unmotivated members. They thought participation should be voluntary. Another complaint was that there was inadequate training for group leaders, with the result that some groups were not productive.

In the spring of 1990, the company decided that the QIS effort was "stagnating" and that DQTs should be changed to include members from different departments. It was thought that this would improve communication and coordination between departments and lead to further improvements in quality, productivity, and on-time delivery. DQTs became known is IDQTs (Interdepartmental Quality Teams). IDQTs were scheduled to begin in November 1990. In addition, the company decided to begin Process Improvement Teams (PITs), which would focus on various ongoing processes at the plant, such as budgeting and inventory management. A PIT, composed of managers from different functions, would not be ongoing but only last as long as it took to achieve its particular goals.

How Different Levels Perceived the Problems

In order to choose the issues to tackle first and to devise a tentative plan for addressing them, Winslow reflected on the background information he had on the six problem areas that he and his staff had identified on the basis of their own analysis and the students' assessment of organizational communication.

A Lack of Organizational Unity

People often talked about "this side of the wall and that side of the wall" in describing the plant. They were referring to the wall separating the newer Components side and the older Fabrication side of the plant. (Some parts of the Fabrication side had been built in the twenties.) The Components side was brighter, cleaner, and more open, and, in summer, it was cooler. In comparing the two sides, one manager said, "At the end of the shift in Fabrication, you come out looking like you've been through the wringer." On the whole, the equipment in the Components side was also newer, with most of it dating from the 1970s and 1980s and some of it state-of-the-art machinery that was developed at the plant. Much of the equipment on the Fabrication side went back to the 1950s and 1960s. These differences in age meant that, in general, the machinery on the Fabrication side required more maintenance.

It was generally agreed that Components jobs were cleaner and easier, and allowed more social interaction. On the Fabrication side many of the machines could run only two to three hours before needing attention, whereas on the Components side the machines might run for days without worker intervention. On the Fabrication side, because of the placement of the machines and the need for frequent maintenance, people tended to work more by themselves and to "be on the go all the time." It was not uncommon for senior hourly employees in Fabrication to request a transfer to Components.

Hourly workers described Components as "a country club" compared to the Fabrication side. Many attributed this to how the different sides were managed. Enforcement of rules was more lax on the Components side. For example, rules requiring safety shoes and goggles were not as strictly enforced, and some operators were allowed to eat on the job.

One Human Resources staff member described Components supervisors as "laid-back about sticking to the rules" and those in Fabrication as "sergeants." He saw the manufacturing manager of Fabrication, Dan Gordon, as having a clear vision of what he wanted for the Fabrication side and a definite plan on how to get there. He also saw Gordon as keeping a tight rein on his supervisors and holding them accountable. The same Human Resources employee described the factory manager of Components, Phil Hanson, as dealing with things as they came up—as more reactive. Hanson allowed his supervisors more freedom and did not get involved on the floor unless there was a problem. When there was a problem, however, he reacted strongly and swiftly. For example, to combat a recent tendency for employees to take extended breaks, he had begun posting supervisors outside of the bathrooms right before and after scheduled breaks.

Bill Larson attributed the differences in the two sides "to the different performance and accountability needs dictated by their business activities and by the corporate office." Components met the internal production needs of Brooks by supplying all of the other Brooks plants with a product that they, in turn, used to manufacture a household product that sold in the millions each year. Fabrication, however, had to satisfy the needs of a variety of industrial customers while competing on the open market. Larson felt that Fabrication had to have a more entrepreneurial ethic than Components because "Fabrication lives or dies by how they treat their customers—they have to woo them and interact well with them," whereas Components had a ready-made market.

Larson also thought that some of the differences were due to the fact that the plant was "held prisoner by what goes on in corporate." Although the corporate office set financial targets for both sides of the plant, it exercised more control over the financial and productivity goals of the Components side because no other Brooks plant was in the Fabrication business and Brooks understood the Components business much better. In addition, corporate was dependent on the Components side for the standardized parts—primarily wire coils—used in many of its finished products. The Components side produced as many as 2 million of some of these small parts a day.

Larson also indicated that the requirements for the number of workers on the two sides of the plant were different. For example, depending on what business was like for each side, the overtime requirements could vary. Hourly employees on the side of the plant that had more overtime felt the side that was working less was getting "easier" treatment. Larson knew that the overtime disparity was due to need, not preferential treatment of one side over the other, but as he put it: "You can talk your head off, but you're not going to be able to explain it to them to their satisfaction. So that causes a lot of frustration among the ranks down there."

The Manager of QIS traced the differences between the Fabrication side and the Components side to the consolidation at Littleton of all of Brooks's production of wire coils needed for its domestic appliances after Brooks bought Frühling, Inc., in 1984. Most of the upper managers hired to start the Components business were brought in from Frühling,

and, as he put it, "They had a different way of doing things. It wasn't a tightly run ship." He said that some of the old managers at the plant wondered about the wisdom of bringing in managers from a company that had not been successful. People asked, "Why use them here? They must have been part of what was wrong." One Fabrication manager added that the manager brought in to start the Components business, Bob Halperin, had the view: "We're going to start a new business here and do whatever is necessary to make it run and to hell with Littleton Manufacturing policies." Also, when the new Components business was started, its manager reported directly to the Brooks corporate office and not to the plant manager. In 1986 the structure was changed so that the factory manager of Components reported to the Littleton Manufacturing plant manager.

A union steward at the plant attributed some of the differences between the two sides to the fact that the workforce on the Components side tended to be younger and had more women with young children (67 percent of the hourly women in the plant worked in Components). The demands of raising children, he thought, resulted in the women needing to take more time off from work. One of the Fabrication supervisors thought that since the supervisors on the Components side were younger, they expected more from management and were more outspoken, especially about how much an hour they should be paid. A number of these supervisors had also been brought in from Frühling, and were not originally from Littleton.

Lack of Consistency in Enforcing Rules and Procedures

A major complaint of both hourly and salaried workers was the inconsistent application of policies and procedures. Although most people mentioned the differences from one side of the plant to the other, there were also differences from one department to another. As the chief union steward put it, "This is the number-one problem here—nobody is the same!" Some Components supervisors were letting people take longer breaks and going for breaks earlier than they were supposed to. Some supervisors allowed hourly employees to stand around and talk for a while before getting them to start their machines. In some departments on the Components side, employees were allowed to gather in the bathrooms and "hang out" anywhere from five to twenty minutes before quitting time. The chief steward cited an example where, contrary to previous policy, some workers on the Components side were allowed to have radios. "When people on the Fabrication side found out," he said, "they went wild."

Some other examples of inconsistencies cited by employees were as follows:

1. Fighting in the plant was supposed to result in automatic dismissal, but the Human Resources administrator recalled two incidents of fighting where the people involved were not disciplined.

2. Another incident that had been much discussed throughout the plant involved an employee who was "caught in a cloud of marijuana smoke" by his supervisor. Since the supervisor did not observe the man smoking but just smelled the marijuana, the person was only given a written warning. One manager said, "We need to take a stand on these things. We need to make a statement. That way we would gain some respect." Describing the same incident, another manager said, "It makes us close to thinking we're giving them (hourly employees) the key to the door."

3. Several people also mentioned the case of a mother who claimed she missed work several times because of doctors' appointments for her children and was suspended for three days, which they compared with the case of an operator who also missed work several times, and was suspected of drug or alcohol abuse, but was not disciplined.

In discussing differences in the enforcement of safety regulations throughout the plant, the administrator of plant safety and security said that when he confronted people who were wearing sneakers, often they would just say they forgot to wear their safety shoes. He said, "If I had to punish everyone, I'd be punishing 50 to 100 people a day."

There were also differences in absenteeism for the two sides of the plant. Absenteeism on the Components side was around 2.2 percent, whereas it was slightly less than 1 percent on the Fabrication side. Some attributed this to a looser enforcement of the rules governing absenteeism by supervisors on the Components side.

Winslow had tried to estimate the annual cost of failure to enforce the rules governing starting and stopping work. His estimate was that the plant was losing $2,247.50 per day, for a total of $539,400 a year. Winslow's memo detailing how he arrived at his overall estimate had been part of his presentation to Larson; it is included as Exhibit 3. Although Winslow had not said so in the memo, he later estimated that 70 percent of the total loss occurred on the Components side of the plant.

Supervisors complained that when they tried to discipline subordinates, they often did not feel confident of backing by management. They referred to incidents where they had disciplined hourly employees only to have their decisions changed by management or the Human Resources department. One supervisor told of an incident in which he tried to fire someone in accordance with what he thought was company policy, but the termination was changed to a suspension. He was told he had been too harsh. In a subsequent incident he had another decision overruled and was told he had been too lenient. He said, "We feel our hands are tied; we're not sure what we can do." Supervisors' decisions that were changed were usually communicated directly to the union by the Human Resources department. In these instances, the supervisors felt they wound up with "egg on their faces."

Winslow attributed some of these problems to a lack of communication regarding the company's policies and procedures. He thought that if the supervisors understood company policy better, their decisions would not need to be changed so frequently. There was no Human Resources policy manual, for example, although the work rules were contained in the union contract.

Dan Gordon disagreed with the view that these problems were a result of the supervisors' lack of understanding of the plant's policies and procedures. He claimed: "Ninety-nine percent of the supervisors know the policies but they lack the skills and willingness to enforce them. Just like a police officer needs to be trained to read a prisoner his rights, the supervisors need to be taught to do their jobs." He thought that in some of the cases where a supervisor's decision was changed, the supervisor had made a mistake in following the proper disciplinary procedure. Then, when the supervisor's decision was overturned, no explanation was provided, so the supervisor would be left with his or her own erroneous view of what happened.

The Human Resources administrator thought that some of the supervisors were reluctant to discipline or confront people because "They're afraid to hurt people's feelings and want to stay on their good side."

EXHIBIT 3   *Memo from Paul Winslow to Bill Larson*

MEMORANDUM

From: Paul Winslow, Director of Human Resources

To: Bill Larson

Subject: Estimated Cost of Loss of Manufacturing Time

Date: 6/18/90

Loss of Manufacturing Time*

(Based on 348 Hourly Employees)

Delay at start of shift	10 minutes × 25% (87)	= 14.50 hours
Washup before AM break	5 minutes × 75% (261)	= 21.75 hours
Delayed return from break	10 minutes × 50% (174)	= 29.00 hours
Early washup—lunch	avg. 10 minutes × 50% (174)	= 29.00 hours
Daily return from lunch	10 minutes × 25% (87)	= 14.50 hours
Early washup before PM break	5 minutes × 75% (261)	= 21.75 hours
Delayed return from break	10 minutes × 50% (174)	= 29.00 hours
Early washup—end of shift	5 minutes × 75% (261)	= 65.25 hours
	Total	= 224.75 hours/day

Cost: 224.75 × avg. $10 hr. = $2,247.50/day

240 days × $2,247.50 = $539,400.00/year

*1.   Does not include benefits.

  2.   Does not include overtime abuses.

  3.   Does not include instances of employees exiting building while punched in.

Supervisor's Role Is Poorly Perceived

On the first shift in Fabrication there were about 70 hourly workers and 7 supervisors, and in Components there were about 140 hourly workers and 11 supervisors. Supervisors were assisted by group leaders, hourly employees who were appointed by the company and who received up to an extra 10 cents an hour.

All levels of the plant were concerned about the role of supervisors. "Supervisors feel like a nobody," said one senior manager. In the assessment of organizational communication done by the students, hourly employees, middle managers, and supervisors all reported that supervisors had too much to do and that this limited their effectiveness. A typical observation by one hourly employee was: "The supervisors can't be out on the floor because of meetings and paperwork. They have a tremendous amount of things on their mind. . . . The supervisor has become a paperboy, which prevents him from being able to do his job." In speaking about how busy the supervisors were and how they responded to suggestions by hourly employees, another hourly person said, "The supervisor's favorite word is, 'I forgot.'"

Supervisors also wanted more involvement in decision making. "You will! You will! You will!" is the way one supervisor characterized the dominant decision-making style of managers at the plant. He thought that most managers expected supervisors to just do what they were told to do. "We have a lot of responsibility but little authority," was how another supervisor put it. Many supervisors felt that they were ordered to do things by their managers, but when something went wrong, they were blamed.

Another factor contributing to the low morale of supervisors was a perceived lack of the resources that they felt were necessary to do a good job. Many complained that they were often told there was no money to make changes to improve things. They also complained of too few engineering, housekeeping, and maintenance personnel. Some supervisors thought there were too few supervisors on the second and third shifts. They thought this resulted in inadequate supervision and allowed some hourly workers to goof off, since the employees knew when these few supervisors would and would not be around.

The combination of these factors—job overload, too much paperwork, lack of authority, not enough involvement in decision making, lack of resources to make changes, inadequate training, and few rewards—made it difficult to find hourly people at the plant who would accept an offer to become a supervisor.

In discussing the role of supervisors, Larson said, "We don't do a good job of training our supervisors. We tell them what we want and hold them accountable, but we don't give them the personal tools for them to do what we want them to do. They need to have the confidence and ability to deal with people and to hold them accountable without feeling badly." He continued by praising one supervisor who he thought was doing a good job. In particular, Larson felt, this supervisor's subordinates knew what to expect from him. This person had been a chief petty officer in the Navy for many years, and Larson thought this had helped him feel comfortable enforcing rules. Reflecting on this, he said, "Maybe we should just look for people with military backgrounds to be supervisors."

Insufficient Focus on Littleton's Priorities

The phrase "insufficient focus on Littleton's priorities" reflected two concerns expressed by employees. First, there was a lack of understanding of Littleton's goals. Second, there was a questioning of the plant's commitment to these goals. However, various levels saw these matters differently.

Although the plant had no mission statement, senior managers said that they thought that they understood Littleton's priorities. A typical senior management description of the plant's goals was, "To supply customers with quality products on time at the lowest possible cost in order to make a profit."

Each year, Larson and the executive staff developed a four-year strategic plan for Littleton. Sales and marketing would first project the amounts and types of products that they thought they could sell. Then manufacturing would look at the machine and labor capabilities of the plant. The sales projections and capabilities were then adjusted as necessary. Throughout the process, goals were set for improving quality and lowering costs. Larson then took the plan to Brooks for revision and/or approval. Next, Larson turned the goals in the strategic plan into specific objectives for each department. These departmental objectives were used to set measurable objectives for each executive staff member. These then formed the basis for annual performance appraisals. Because of this process, all of the executive staff felt that they

knew what was expected of them and how their jobs contributed to achieving the company's goals.

At the same time, both senior and middle managers thought there was insufficient communication and support from corporate headquarters. They mentioned not knowing enough about corporate's long-term plans for the company. A number of the managers on the Fabrication side wondered about corporate's commitment to the Fabrication business. They thought that if their operation did not do well financially, the company might end it. In discussing the status of the Fabrication side of the plant, Gordon said that Brooks considered it a "noncore business." The Quality Assurance manager felt that corporate was not providing enough support and long-term direction for the QIS. Winslow was concerned about the lack of consistency in corporate's Human Resources policies and felt that he did not have enough say in corporate Human Resources planning efforts.

All levels below the executive staff complained that they did not have a good understanding of Littleton's own long-range goals. Some middle managers thought there was a written, long-range plan for the company but others disagreed. One member of the executive staff reported that as far as he knew, the entire strategic plan was seen only by the executive staff, although some managers would see the portions of it that concerned their departments. He also reported that the strategic plan was never discussed at operations review meetings. Most hourly employees said that they relied on the grapevine for information about "the big picture." In discussing the flow of information at the plant, one union steward said, "Things get lost in the chain of command." He said he got more than 80 percent of his information from gossip on the floor.

The primary mechanism used to communicate Littleton's goals and the plant's status with regard to achieving them was the operations review meeting held once a month by the plant manager, to which all salaried employees were ostensibly invited. At these meetings, usually attended by about eighty people, the plant manager provided figures on how closely the plant had hit selected business indicators. At one recent and typical meeting, for example, the Manager of QIS described various in-place efforts to improve quality. Bill Larson then reviewed the numbers. He presented data on budgeted versus actual production, variances between budgeted and actual manufacturing costs, profits, the top ten products in sales, standard margins on various products, shipments of products, information on backlogs, and the top ten customers.[1] When he asked for questions at the end of his presentation, there were none.

The students' organizational assessment reported that all levels appreciated the intent of the operations review meetings, but there were a number of concerns. Everyone interviewed wanted more two-way communication but thought the size and format of the meetings inhibited discussion. Middle managers thought the meetings focused too much on what had happened and not enough on the future. As one manager said: "It's like seeing Lubbock in the rearview mirror. We want to know where we're going—not where we've been. We want to know what's coming up, how it's going to affect our department, and what we can do to help." Others, including some of the executive staff, complained about the difficulty of understanding the financial jargon. Some hourly employees interviewed did not know there were operations review meetings, and others did not know what was discussed at them.

A number of middle managers in manufacturing thought that having regular departmental meetings would improve communication within their departments. They also said that they would like to see minutes of the executive staff meetings.

When interviewed by the students for their assessment of organizational communication, a number of middle managers, supervisors, and hourly workers thought the company was not practicing what it preached with regard to its stated goals. A primary goal was supposed to be a quality product; however, they reported that there was too much emphasis on "hitting the numbers," or getting the required number of products shipped, even if there were defects. They said this especially occurred toward the end of the month when production reports were submitted. One worker's comment reflected opinions held by many hourly employees: "Some foremen are telling people to push through products that are not of good quality. This passes the problem from one department to another and the end result is a lousy product. They seem too interested in reaching the quota and getting the order out on time rather than quality. It's a big problem because when the hourly workers believe that quality isn't important, they start not to care about their work. They pass it on to the next guy, and the next guy gets mad."

The perception by a number of hourly workers that their suggestions to improve quality were not responded to because of a lack of money also resulted in their questioning the company's commitment to quality.

Change Is Poorly Managed

Most of the employees interviewed by the students thought there were too many changes at the plant and that the numerous changes resulted in confusion.

1. QIS was initiated in 1985.
2. In 1986, 100 hourly employees were laid off.
3. In 1984, there were 154 managers; in 1990, there were 87 managers.
4. In 1989, corporate initiated a restructuring that changed the reporting relationships of several senior managers.
5. In 1989, as part of QIS, the plant began using statistical process control techniques and began efforts to attain ISO certification. (ISO is an internationally recognized certification of excellence.)
6. In 1989, a new production and inventory control system was introduced, with the help of a team of outside consultants who were at the plant for almost a year studying its operations.
7. In 1990, the Components side reorganized its production flow.

A number of complaints were voiced about the effect of all the changes. People felt that some roles and responsibilities were not clear. There was a widespread belief that the reasons for changes were not communicated well enough and that people found out about changes affecting them too late. In addition, many were uncertain how long a new program, once started, would be continued. Larson thought that many hourly employees were resistant to the changes being made because they thought the changes would require more work for them and they were already "running all the time." One union steward observed, "There's never a gradual easing in of things here." A middle manager said: "We're mandated for speed. We pride ourselves on going fast. We rush through today to get to tomorrow."

Larson thought the culture of the plant was gradually changing due to the implementation of QIS, but he noted that a lot of time had to be spent giving the employees reasons for changes.

Dan Gordon thought the plant needed to "communicate change in a single voice." He said that Larson's style was to leave it to the staff to tell others about upcoming changes. He commented, "By the time it gets to the last person, it's lost something." He felt that Larson needed to communicate changes to those on lower levels in person.

The QIS manager thought that Brooks did not provide enough resources and support for changes at the plant. In explaining his view of corporate's approach to change, he said, "Step one is to not give much. Step two is to not give anything. Step three is they take what's left away." Another middle manager commented, "We're always being asked to do more with less, but the requirements by corporate don't get cut back."

A frequently mentioned example of change that was frustrating to many people was the introduction of the Manufacturing Assisted Production and Inventory Control System (MAPICS) in 1989. MAPICS was a computerized system that was supposed to keep track of materials, productivity, and labor efficiency. Theoretically, it tracked orders from time of entry to payment of the bill, and one could find out where an order was at any point in the system by calling it up on a computer. However, the system was time-consuming (data had to be entered manually by the supervisors), and was not as well suited to the Fabrication side of the plant as it was to the Components side, where production was more standardized. One senior manager commented, "MAPICS was sold as the savior for the supervisors, and the company was supposed to get all of the data it needed. But it's never happened. It's only half-installed, and there are systems problems and input problems." Recently, there had been some question as to whether MAPICS was giving an accurate inventory count.

Hourly workers felt put upon by the way in which changes were made. One person said, "We were all of a sudden told to start monitoring waste and then all of a sudden we were told to stop." Another said, "One day the MAPICS room is over here, and then the next day it's over there. They also put a new system in the stockroom, and we didn't know about it." Many resented the outside consultants that had been brought in by corporate, reporting that they did not know why the consultants were brought in or what they were doing. They feared that the consultants' recommendations might result in layoffs.

Hourly people felt that a lot of their information about upcoming changes came through the grapevine. "Rumors fly like crazy" is the way one hourly person described communication on the floor. Another said, "The managers don't walk through the plant much. We only see them when things are going bad."

In discussing communication about changes, one middle manager said: "It's a standing joke. The hourly know what's going to happen before we do." One steward said, "Lots of times, you'll tell the supervisors something that's going to happen and they will be surprised. It raises hell with morale and creates unstable working conditions. But nine out of ten times it's true."

Hourly workers also felt that they were not involved enough in management decisions about changes to be made. One hourly worker said, "They don't ask our input. We could tell them if something is not going to work. They should keep us informed. We're not idiots."

Lack of a Systematic Approach to Training

The company had carried out a well-regarded training effort when employees were hired to begin the Components side of the plant and when the QIS program was started. In addition, every two years each employee went through refresher training for the QIS. There was no other formal company training or career development at the plant.

Hourly employees and supervisors in particular complained about the lack of training. One hourly employee expressed the predominant view: "When you start work here, it's sink or swim." In discussing the promotion of supervisors, the chief union steward said he did not know how people got to be supervisors and that as far as he knew there was no training that one had to have to become a supervisor.

When they were hired, new hourly and salaried employees attended an orientation session in which they were informed about benefits, attendance policies, their work schedule, parking regulations, and safety issues. After the orientation session, further training for new salaried employees was left up to individual departments. Standard practice was for the department supervisor to assign the hourly person to an experienced hourly operator for one-on-one job training for two weeks. Winslow expressed some of his reservations about this approach by commenting, "You don't know if the department is assigning the best person to train the new employee or if they always use the same person for training."

The Human Resources department had no separate training budget. Individual departments, however, did sometimes use their money for training and counted the money used as a variance from their budgeted goals. The training that did occur with some regularity tended to be technical training for maintenance personnel.

When asked to explain why there was not more training, Winslow replied, "We would like to do more but we haven't been able to because of the cost and staffing issues." For example, in 1986 Winslow's title was manager of training and development, and he had been responsible for the training program for all of the new employees hired to begin the Components unit. After the initial training was completed, he requested that the plant provide ongoing training for Components operators. However, his request was turned down by Larson, who did not want to spend the money. Winslow also recalled the over 160 hours he had spent the previous year developing a video training package for hourly workers in one part of the Components side of the plant. He said that the program had been piloted, but when it came time to send people through the training course, production management was unwilling to let people take time off the floor.

Winslow also cited a lack of support from corporate as a factor in the plant's sporadic training efforts. At one time Brooks had employed a director of training for its plants, but in 1987, the person left and the company never hired anyone to replace him. Now, Brooks had no training department; each plant was expected to provide its own training. The training Brooks did provide, according to Winslow, was for the "promising manager" and was purchased from an outside vendor.

Top Management

As he sat in his office thinking about what to do, Winslow knew that any plan would have to be acceptable to Larson, Gordon, and Hanson—the plant manager and the two factory managers—and he spent some time thinking about their management styles.

Bill Larson was in his late forties, had a B.S. in mechanical engineering, and had started at Littleton in 1970. He had been plant manager since 1983. His direct reports considered him bright, analytical, and down to earth. When asked once how he would describe himself to someone who didn't know him, he said, "I keep my emotions out of things. I can remember when I was in the Army, standing at attention in my dress blues at the Tomb of the Unknown Soldier. People would come up a foot from my face

and look me in the eye and try to get me to blink. But I was able to remove myself from that. I wouldn't even see it." He added that he had built most of his own home and repaired his own equipment, including the diesels on a cabin cruiser he used to own. Being raised on a farm in the rural Midwest, he said he learned at an early age how to repair equipment with baling wire to keep it going.

Although Larson was considered accessible by the executive staff, he rarely got out on the floor to talk to people. Many managers saw him as a "numbers" person who readily sprinkled his conversations about the plant with quantitative data about business indicators, variances, budgeted costs, etc. In referring to his discomfort discussing personal things, he somewhat jokingly said about himself, "I can talk on the phone for about thirty-five seconds and then I can't talk any longer."

In describing his own management style, Larson said, "I like to support people and get them involved. I like to let them know what I am thinking and what they need to accomplish. I like to let ideas come from them. I want them to give me recommendations, and if I feel they're OK, I won't change them. They need to be accountable, but I don't want them to feel I'm looking over their shoulders. I don't want to hamper their motivation." He estimated that 40 percent of his job responsibility consisted of managing change.

Dan Gordon, who was 38, had been at Littleton for fifteen years and had been manufacturing manager of Fabrication for seven years. In describing himself, he said, "I'm a stickler for details, and I hate to not perform well. My superiors tell me I'm a Theory X manager and that I have a strong personality—that I can intimidate people."

In speaking about how much he communicated with hourly employees, Gordon said that he didn't do enough of it, adding that "Our platters are all so loaded, we don't spend as much time talking to people as we should." He said he seldom walked through the plant and never talked to hourly workers one-on-one. Once a year, though, he met formally with all the hourly employees on the Fabrication side to have an operations review meeting like the salaried people had in order to discuss what the plant was doing, profits, new products, etc. "The hourly people love it," he reported.

Reflecting on why he didn't communicate more with hourly workers, Gordon said, "Since the accounting department's data depends, in part, on our data collection, a lot of my time is eaten up with this. Maybe I'm too busy with clerical activities to be more visible." He based his management decisions on documented data and regularly studied the financial and productivity reports issued by the accounting department. He said he would like to see the supervisors go around in the morning to just talk to people but acknowledged that they had too many reports to fill out and too many meetings to attend.

When asked to explain what one needed to do to succeed as a manager at Littleton, Gordon answered, "You have to get things done. Bill Larson wants certain things done within a certain time span. If you do this, you'll succeed."

Phil Hanson, in his early fifties, had been at Littleton for seven years. He was hired as materials manager for Components and was promoted to Components factory manager in mid-1989. Phil estimated that he spent 50 percent of his time on the factory floor talking to people. He felt it gave him a better insight as to what was going on at the plant and created trust. He thought that too many of the managers at the plant were "office haunts"—they felt it was beneath them to talk with hourly workers. It appeared to other managers that Hanson often made decisions based on what he learned in informal conversations with hourly employees. He tried to delegate as much as he could to his managers. When asked what a manager had to do to succeed there, he said, "You have to be a self-starter and make things happen."

Winslow remembered how a few years ago, when he was manager of training and development, the executive staff had gone to one of those management development workshops where you find out about your management style. All of the staff had scored high on the authoritarian end of the scale.

This triggered a memory of a recent debate in which he had passed along a suggestion by his staff to the executive staff to "do something nice for the workers on the floor." To celebrate the arrival of summer, his staff wanted the company to pay for buying hamburgers, hot dogs, and soft drinks so the workers could have a cookout during their lunch break. Those on the executive staff who resisted the idea cited the "jellybean theory of management." As one manager explained it, "If you give a hungry bear jellybeans, you can keep it happy and get it to do what you want. But watch out when you run out of jellybeans! You're going to have a helluva angry bear to deal with!" The jelly bean argument carried the day, and the cookout was not held.

Recommendation Time

As Winslow turned on the computer to write down his recommendations concerning the six problem areas, he recalled how Larson had reacted when the students made their presentation on organizational communication at Littleton. After praising the students' efforts, Larson had said, in an offhanded way, "This mainly confirms what we already knew. Most of this is not a surprise." Winslow was hopeful that now some of these issues would be addressed.

One potential sticking point, he knew, was the need for the meetings that would be necessary to discuss the problems and plan a strategy. People were already strapped for time and complaining about the number of meetings. Yet unless they took time to step back and look at what they were doing, nothing would change.

On a more hopeful note, he recalled that Larson had been impressed when the Human Resources staff emphasized in their presentation to him that these issues were impacting Littleton's bottom line. Winslow felt that the decline in sales and profits at Brooks, the increasing domestic and foreign competition, the current recession, and declining employee morale made it even more important that the issues be dealt with. People at all levels of the plant were starting to worry about the possibility of more layoffs.

Notes

1. At Littleton, the manufacturing, engineering, and accounting departments estimated the standard labor costs for making each of the plant's products and a budget was prepared based on those estimates. The budgeted costs were plant goals. A variance is the difference between actual and standard costs. A variance could be positive (less than) or negative (greater than) with respect to the budgeted costs.

INTEGRATIVE CASE 8.2   *Littleton Manufacturing (B)**

Winslow met with his staff to develop a list of proposed corrective actions. Exhibit 1 is the memo that Winslow sent, in June 1990, to the Human Resources PIT, outlining suggested corrective actions. (The action steps were not prioritized.)

The PIT did not meet to discuss what to do about the six issues identified by the Human Resources department until the middle of September. The first issue the PIT decided to address was the inconsistent application of disciplinary policies and procedures. They chose this issue first because they thought that if this could be improved, many of the other issues would be resolved as well.

The PIT decided to first find out how well supervisors understood the work rules and the extent to which they had different interpretations of them. To do this they developed a quiz covering Littleton's twenty-eight work rules and gave the quiz to all supervisors. One question, for example, was "If you came in and found an employee who had just dozed off at his/her workstation, what would you do?" The supervisor then had to choose from several alternatives. This question was followed by, "If you came in and found an employee away from the job and asleep on top of some packing materials, what would you do?" Again, there was a choice of several responses. After taking the exam, the answers were discussed and the correct answer explained by Winslow and the Human Resources staff. The results revealed to the PIT that there was much less knowledge of these rules and how to apply them than management had expected.

The PIT then theorized that a number of supervisors were not comfortable with confronting employees about their failure to follow the company's policies and procedures, especially the wearing of safety shoes and goggles. They decided to seek the assistance of an outside consultant to help them develop a training program for the supervisors. However, on September 1, 1991, as a continuation of its "efficiency drive," Brooks had imposed a freeze on salaries and a reduction in travel, and prohibited the use of outside consultants at all of its plants. When Winslow asked Bill Larson for approval to hire the consultant, he was reminded that because of the freeze they would have to do the training in-house.

As a consequence, Winslow began a series of meetings with union stewards and supervisors—called "Sup and Stew" meetings—to discuss what the work rules were, different interpretations of them, and how violations of work rules should be handled. For scheduling reasons, it was planned so that half of the supervisors and the stewards would attend each meeting. These meetings were held biweekly for over a year. Winslow believed that the meetings were helping to clarify and support the role of the supervisors and were beginning to have a positive effect on the enforcement of policies and procedures.

In 1991, because the plants that bought the wire coils made by Components had excess finished goods inventory, Brooks shut them down for a month during the Christmas holidays, leading Littleton to eliminate 125 positions from the Components side for the same month, to reduce production. "If we hadn't," Winslow said, "we would have had a horrendous amount of inventory." The employees filling those positions had, in general, less seniority than their counterparts from Fabrication, and no one from the Fabrication side was laid off. A few of the more senior employees from the Components side were hired to work on the Fabrication side. At the time of the layoffs, business on the Fabrication side was booming. In January, the plant started rehiring the laid-off workers, and by the end of June, all of them had been rehired.

In November 1991, Bill Larson learned that he had cancer, and in June 1992, he died. Because of Larson's illness, the lack of resources, and time pressures, there was no formal attempt to address any of the issues identified by Winslow other than inconsistent enforcement of policies and procedures.

The new plant manager, Bob Halperin, took over in the fall of 1992; Halperin had been managing another Brooks plant in the south for three years. One of the reasons he was chosen was his familiarity with Littleton. He had been at Littleton as an industrial engineer from 1973 to 1980, when he left to manage another facility. In 1984 he was sent back to Littleton to start and manage Components. He held this position for four years before leaving to manage the plant in the southern United States.

*By David E. Whiteside, organizational development consultant. This case was written at Lewiston-Auburn College of the University of Southern Maine with the cooperation of management, solely for the purpose of stimulating student discussion. Data are based on field research; all events are real, although the names of organizations, locations, and individuals have been disguised. Faculty members in nonprofit institutions are encouraged to reproduce this case for distribution to their students without charge or written permission. All other rights reserved jointly to the author and the North American Case Research Association (NACRA). Copyright © 1994 by the *Case Research Journal* and David E. Whiteside.

EXHIBIT I   *Memorandum from Paul Winslow to Human Resources*

MEMORANDUM

From: Paul Winslow, Director of Human Resources

To: Human Resources Process Improvement Team

Subject: Proposed Corrective Actions

Date: 6/14/90

Lack of Organizational Unity

1. Use job shadowing or rotation to help people understand each other's jobs, e.g., do this across functions.
2. Reformat the Operations Review meetings, e.g., have a program committee.
3. Have a smaller group forum, e.g., have supervisors from the two sides meet.
4. Provide teamwork training for salaried employees.

Lack of Consistency in Enforcing Rules and Procedures

1. Hold meetings with department managers and supervisors to discuss how to enforce policies and procedures. Have these led by Bill Larson.
2. Develop a policy and procedures review and monitoring system.

Supervisor's Role Poorly Perceived

1. Have department managers meet with supervisors to determine priorities or conflicts between priorities.
2. Have supervisory training for all manufacturing supervisors.
3. Time assessment. (How is their time being spent?)

Insufficient Focus on Littleton's Priorities

1. Use the in-house newsletter to communicate priorities.
2. Develop an internal news sheet.
3. Have a question box for questions to be answered at Operations Review meetings.
4. Have a restatement of Littleton's purpose (do at Operations Review).
5. Have an Operations Review for hourly workers.
6. Use payroll stuffers to communicate information about goals.
7. Hold department meetings; have the manager of the department facilitate the meeting.

Change Is Poorly Managed

1. Provide training in managing change.
2. Communicate changes.

Lack of a Systematic Approach to Training

1. Establish annual departmental training goals.
2. Link training goals to organizational priorities.
3. Have a systematic approach to training the hourly workforce.
4. Have a training plan for each salaried employee.
5. Have an annual training budget.

HR Dept.

6/90

Shortly after Halperin arrived, Winslow acquainted him with the problem areas defined the previous year, gave him a copy of the (A) case, and met with him to discuss the issues. At that time, although Winslow felt that progress had been made on having more consistent enforcement of policies and procedures from one side of the plant to the other, he did not feel much had changed with regard to the other issues. With the exception of the Sup and Stew meetings, none of the specific action steps recommended by him and his staff had been implemented.

GLOSSARY

adaptability/entrepreneurial culture a culture characterized by strategic focus on the external environment through flexibility and change to meet customer needs.

administrative principles a closed systems management perspective that focuses on the total organization and grows from the insights of practitioners.

ambidextrous approach a characteristic of an organization that can behave both in an organic and a mechanistic way.

analyzability a dimension of technology in which work activities can be reduced to mechanical steps and participants can follow an objective, computational procedure to solve problems.

analyzer a business strategy that seeks to maintain a stable business while innovating on the periphery.

authority a force for achieving desired outcomes that is prescribed by the formal hierarchy and reporting relationships.

balanced scorecard a comprehensive management control system that balances traditional financial measures with operational measures relating to an organization's critical success factors.

benchmarking process whereby companies find out how others do something better than they do and then try to imitate or improve on it.

boundary spanning roles activities that link and coordinate an organization with key elements in the external environment.

bounded rationality perspective how decisions are made when time is limited, a large number of internal and external factors affect a decision, and the problem is ill-defined.

buffering roles activities that absorb uncertainty from the environment.

bureaucracy an organizational framework marked by rules and procedures, specialization and division of labor, hierarchy of authority, technically qualified personnel, separate position and incumbent, and written communications and records.

bureaucratic control the use of rules, policies, hierarchy of authority, written documentation, standardization, and other bureaucratic mechanisms to standardize behavior and assess performance.

bureaucratic culture a culture that has an internal focus and a consistency orientation for a stable environment.

bureaucratic organization a perspective that emphasizes management on an impersonal, rational basis through such elements as clearly defined authority and responsibility, formal record-keeping, and uniform application of standard rules.

Carnegie model organizational decision making involving many managers and a final choice based on a coalition among those managers.

centrality a trait of a department whose role is in the primary activity of an organization.

centralization refers to the level of hierarchy with authority to make decisions.

change process the way in which changes occur in an organization.

chaos theory a scientific theory that suggests that relationships in complex, adaptive systems are made up of numerous interconnections that create unintended effects and render the environment unpredictable.

charismatic authority based in devotion to the exemplary character or heroism of an individual and the order defined by him or her.

chief ethics officer high-level company executive who oversees all aspects of ethics, including establishing and broadly communicating ethical standards, setting up ethics training programs, supervising the investigation of ethical problems, and advising managers in the ethical aspects of corporate decisions.

clan control the use of social characteristics, such as corporate culture, shared values, commitments, traditions, and beliefs, to control behavior.

clan culture a culture that focuses primarily on the involvement and participation of the organization's members and on rapidly changing expectations from the external environment.

closed system a system that is autonomous, enclosed, and not dependent on its environment.

coalition an alliance among several managers who agree through bargaining about organizational goals and problem priorities.

coercive forces external pressures such as legal requirements exerted on an organization to adopt structures, techniques, or behaviors similar to other organizations.

collaborative network an emerging perspective whereby organizations allow themselves to become dependent on other organizations to increase value and productivity for all.

collective bargaining the negotiation of an agreement between management and workers.

collectivity stage the life cycle phase in which an organization has strong leadership and begins to develop clear goals and direction.

competing values approach a perspective on organizational effectiveness that combines diverse indicators of performance that represent competing management values.

competition rivalry between groups in the pursuit of a common prize.

confrontation a situation in which parties in conflict directly engage one another and try to work out their differences.

consortia groups of firms that venture into new products and technologies.

contextual dimensions traits that characterize the whole organization, including its size, technology, environment, and goals.

contingency a theory meaning one thing depends on other things; the organization's situation dictates the correct management approach.

contingency decision-making framework a perspective that brings together the two organizational dimensions of problem consensus and technical knowledge about solutions.

continuous process production a completely mechanized manufacturing process in which there is no starting or stopping.

cooptation occurs when leaders from important sectors in the environment are made part of an organization.

coping with uncertainty a source of power for a department that reduces uncertainty for other departments by obtaining prior information, prevention, and absorption.

core technology the work process that is directly related to the organization's mission.

craft technology technology characterized by a fairly stable stream of activities but in which the conversion process is not analyzable or well understood.

creative departments organizational departments that initiate change, such as research and development, engineering, design, and systems analysis.

creativity the generation of novel ideas that may meet perceived needs or respond to opportunities.

culture the set of values, guiding beliefs, norms, and ways of thinking that are shared by members of an organization and are taught to new members as correct.

culture changes changes in the values, attitudes, expectations, beliefs, abilities, and behavior of employees.

culture strength the degree of agreement among members of an organization about the importance of specific values.

data the input of a communication channel.

data mining software that uses sophisticated decision-making processes to search raw data for patterns and relationships that may be significant.

data warehousing the use of a huge database that combines all of an organization's data and allows users to access the data directly, create reports, and obtain answers to "what-if" questions.

decision learning a process of recognizing and admitting mistakes that allows managers and organizations to acquire the experience and knowledge to perform more effectively in the future.

decision premises constraining frames of reference and guidelines placed by top managers on decisions made at lower levels.

decision support system a system that enables managers at all levels of the organization to retrieve, manipulate, and display information from integrated databases for making specific decisions.

defender a business strategy that seeks stability or even retrenchment rather than innovation or growth.

departmental grouping a structure in which employees share a common supervisor and resources, are jointly responsible for performance, and tend to identify and collaborate with each other.

differentiation the cognitive and emotional differences among managers in various functional departments of an organization and formal structure differences among these departments.

direct interlock a situation that occurs when a member of the board of directors of one company sits on the board of another.

divisional grouping a grouping in which people are organized according to what the organization produces.

divisional structure the structuring of the organization according to individual products, services, product groups, major projects, or profit centers; also called product structure or strategic business units.

domain an organization's chosen environmental field of activity.

domains of political activity areas in which politics plays a role. Three domains in organizations are structural change, management succession, and resource allocation.

domestic stage the first stage of international development in which a company is domestically oriented while managers are aware of the global environment.

downsizing intentionally reducing the size of a company's workforce by laying off employees.

dual-core approach an organizational change perspective that identifies the unique processes associated with administrative change compared to those associated with technical change.

e-business any business that takes place by digital processes over a computer network rather than in physical space.

effectiveness the degree to which an organization achieves its goals.

efficiency the amount of resources used to produce a unit of output.

elaboration stage the organizational life cycle phase in which the red tape crisis is resolved through the development of a new sense of teamwork and collaboration.

electronic data interchange (EDI) the linking of organizations through computers for the transmission of data without human interference.

empowerment power sharing; the delegation of power or authority to subordinates.

engineering technology technology in which there is substantial variety in the tasks performed, but activities are usually handled on the basis of established formulas, procedures, and techniques.

enterprise resource planning (ERP) sophisticated computerized systems that collect, process, and provide information about a company's entire enterprise, including order processing, product design, purchasing, inventory, manufacturing, distribution, human resources, receipt of payments, and forecasting of future demand.

entrepreneurial stage the life cycle phase in which an organization is born and its emphasis is on creating a product and surviving in the marketplace.

escalating commitment persisting in a course of action when it is failing; occurs because managers block or distort negative information and because consistency and persistence are valued in contemporary society.

ethical dilemma when each alternative choice or behavior seems undesirable because of a potentially negative ethical consequence.

ethics the code of moral principles and values that governs the behavior of a person or group with respect to what is right or wrong.

ethics committee a group of executives appointed to oversee company ethics.

executive information system (EIS) interactive systems that help top managers monitor and control organizational operations by processing and presenting data in usable form.

explicit knowledge formal, systematic knowledge that can be codified, written down, and passed on to others in documents or general instructions.

external adaptation the manner in which an organization meets goals and deals with outsiders.

extranet a private information network.

feedback control model a control cycle that involves setting goals, establishing standards of performance, measuring actual performance and comparing it to standards, and changing activities as needed based on the feedback.

flexible manufacturing systems (FMS) using computers to link together manufacturing components such as robots, machines, product design, and engineering analysis to enable fast switching from one product to another.

focus an organization's dominant perspective value, which may be internal or external.

focus strategy a strategy in which an organization concentrates on a specific regional market or buyer group.

formalization the degree to which an organization has rules, procedures, and written documentation.

formalization stage the phase in an organization's life cycle involving the installation and use of rules, procedures, and control systems.

functional grouping the placing together of employees who perform similar functions or work processes or who bring similar knowledge and skills to bear.

functional matrix a structure in which functional bosses have primary authority and product or project managers simply coordinate product activities.

functional structure the grouping of activities by common function.

garbage can model model that describes the pattern or flow of multiple decisions within an organization.

general environment includes those sectors that may not directly affect the daily operations of a firm but will indirectly influence it.

generalist an organization that offers a broad range of products or services and serves a broad market.

global company a company that no longer thinks of itself as having a home country.

global geographic structure a form in which an organization divides its operations into world regions, each of which reports to the CEO.

global matrix structure a form of horizontal linkage in an international organization in which both product and geographical structures are implemented simultaneously to achieve a balance between standardization and globalization.

global product structure a form in which product divisions take responsibility for global operations in their specific product areas.

global stage the stage of international development in which the company transcends any one country.

global teams work groups made up of multinational members whose activities span multiple countries; also called transnational teams.

globalization strategy the standardization of product design and advertising strategy throughout the world.

goal approach an approach to organizational effectiveness that is concerned with output and whether the organization achieves its output goals.

Hawthorne Studies a series of experiments on worker productivity begun in 1924 at the Hawthorne plant of Western Electric Company in Illinois; attributed employees' increased output to managers' better treatment of them during the study.

heroes organizational members who serve as models or ideals for serving cultural norms and values.

high-velocity environments industries in which competitive and technological change is so extreme that market data is either unavailable or obsolete, strategic windows open and shut quickly, and the cost of poor decisions is company failure.

horizontal grouping the organizing of employees around core work processes rather than by function, product, or geography.

horizontal linkage the amount of communication and coordination that occurs horizontally across organizational departments.

horizontal linkage model a model of the three components of organizational design needed to achieve new product innovation: departmental specialization, boundary spanning, and horizontal linkages.

horizontal structure a structure that virtually eliminates both the vertical hierarchy and departmental boundaries by organizing teams of employees around core work processes; the end-to-end work, information, and material flows that provide value directly to customers.

human relations emphasis an aspect of the competing values model that incorporates the values of an internal focus and a flexible structure.

hybrid structure a structure that combines characteristics of various structural approaches (functional, divisional, geographical, horizontal) tailored to specific strategic needs.

idea champions organizational members who provide the time and energy to make things happen; sometimes called "advocates," "intrapreneurs," and "change agents."

idea incubator safe harbor where ideas from employees throughout the organization can be developed without interference from company bureaucracy or politics.

imitation the adoption of a decision tried elsewhere in the hope that it will work in the present situation.

incident command system developed to maintain the efficiency and control benefits of bureaucracy yet prevent the problems of slow response to crises.

incremental change a series of continual progressions that maintain an organization's general equilibrium and often affect only one organizational part.

incremental decision process model a model that describes the structured sequence of activities undertaken from the discovery of a problem to its solution.

indirect interlock a situation that occurs when a director of one company and a director of another are both directors of a third company.

information that which alters or reinforces understanding.

information reporting systems the most common form of management information system, these computerized systems provide managers with reports that summarize data and support day-to-day decision making.

inspiration an innovative, creative solution that is not reached by logical means.

institutional environment norms and values from stakeholders (customers, investors, boards, government etc.) that organizations try to follow in order to please stakeholders.

institutional perspective an emerging view that holds that under high uncertainty, organizations imitate others in the same institutional environment.

institutional similarity the emergence of common structures, management approaches, and behaviors among organizations in the same field.

integrated enterprise an organization that uses advanced information technology to enable close coordination within the company as well as with suppliers, customers, and partners.

integration the quality of collaboration between departments of an organization.

integrator a position or department created solely to coordinate several departments.

intellectual capital the sum of an organization's knowledge, experience, understanding, processes, innovations and discoveries.

intensive technologies a variety of products or services provided in combination to a client.

interdependence the extent to which departments depend on each other for resources or materials to accomplish their tasks.

intergroup conflict behavior that occurs between organizational groups when participants identify with one group and perceive that other groups may block their group's goal achievements or expectations.

interlocking directorate a formal linkage that occurs when a member of the board of directors of one company sits on the board of another company.

internal integration a state in which organization members develop a collective identity and know how to work together effectively.

internal process approach an approach that looks at internal activities and assesses effectiveness by indicators of internal health and efficiency.

internal process emphasis an aspect of the competing values model that reflects the values of internal focus and structural control.

international division a division that is equal in status to other major departments within a company and has its own hierarchy to handle business in various countries.

international stage the second stage of international development, in which the company takes exports seriously and begins to think multidomestically.

interorganizational relationships the relatively enduring resource transactions, flows, and linkages that occur among two or more organizations.

intranet a private, companywide information network that uses the communications protocols and standards of the Internet but is accessible only to people within the company.

intuitive decision making the use of experience and judgment rather than sequential logic or explicit reasoning to solve a problem.

job design the assignment of goals and tasks to be accomplished by employees.

job enlargement the designing of jobs to expand the number of different tasks performed by an employee.

job enrichment the designing of jobs to increase responsibility, recognition, and opportunities for growth and achievement.

job rotation moving employees from job to job to give them a greater variety of tasks and alleviate boredom.

job simplification the reduction of the number and difficulty of tasks performed by a single person.

joint optimization the goal of the sociotechnical systems approach, which states that an organization will function best only if its social and technical systems are designed to fit the needs of one another.

joint venture a separate entity for sharing development and production costs and penetrating new markets that is created with two or more active firms as sponsors.

knowledge a conclusion drawn from information that has been linked to other information and compared to what is already known.

knowledge management the efforts to systematically find, organize, and make available a company's intellectual capital and to foster a culture of continuous learning and knowledge sharing so that organizational activities build on existing knowledge.

labor management teams a cooperative approach designed to increase worker participation and provide a cooperative model for union-management problems.

language slogans, sayings, metaphors, or other expressions that convey a special meaning to employees.

large group intervention an approach that brings together participants from all parts of the organization (and may include outside stakeholders as well) to discuss problems or opportunities and plan for change.

large-batch production a manufacturing process characterized by long production runs of standardized parts.

lean manufacturing uses highly trained employees at every stage of the production process who take a painstaking approach to details and continuous problem solving to cut waste and improve quality.

learning organization an organization in which everyone is engaged in identifying and solving problems, enabling the organization to continuously experiment, improve, and increase its capability.

legends stories of events based in history that may have been embellished with fictional details.

legitimacy the general perspective that an organization's actions are desirable, proper, and appropriate within the environment's system of norms, values, and beliefs.

level of analysis in systems theory, the subsystem on which the primary focus is placed; four levels of analysis normally characterize organizations.

liaison role the function of a person located in one department who is responsible for communicating and achieving coordination with another department.

life cycle a perspective on organizational growth and change that suggests organizations are born, grow older, and eventually die.

long-linked technology the combination within one organization of successive stages of production, with each stage using as its inputs the production of the preceding stage.

low-cost leadership a strategy that tries to increase market share by emphasizing low cost when compared with competitors.

management champion a manager who acts as a supporter and sponsor of a technical champion to shield and promote an idea within the organization.

management control systems the formalized routines, reports, and procedures that use information to maintain or alter patterns in organizational activity.

management information system a comprehensive, computerized system that provides information and supports day-to-day decision making.

management science approach organizational decision making that is the analog to the rational approach by individual managers.

managerial ethics principles that guide the decisions and behaviors of managers with regard to whether they are morally right or wrong.

market control a situation that occurs when price competition is used to evaluate the output and productivity of an organization.

mass customization the use of computer-integrated systems and flexible work processes to enable companies to mass produce a variety of products or services designed to exact customer specification.

matrix structure a strong form of horizontal linkage in which both product and functional structures (horizontal and vertical) are implemented simultaneously.

mechanistic an organization system marked by rules, procedures, a clear hierarchy of authority, and centralized decision making.

mediating technology the provision of products or services that mediate or link clients from the external environment and allow each department to work independently.

meso theory a new approach to organization studies that integrates both micro and macro levels of analysis.

mimetic forces under conditions of uncertainty, the pressure to copy or model other organizations that appear successful in the environment.

mission the organization's reason for its existence.

mission culture a culture that places emphasis on a clear vision of the organization's purpose and on the achievement of specific goals.

modular grouping organization that is a loosely connected cluster of separate components.

modular structure the firm subcontracts many or most of its major processes to separate companies and coordinates their activities from a small headquarters organization.

multidomestic company a company that deals with competitive issues in each country independent of other countries.

multidomestic strategy one in which competition in each country is handled independently of competition in other countries.

multifocused grouping a structure in which an organization embraces two or more structural grouping alternatives simultaneously.

multinational stage the stage of international development in which a company has marketing and production facilities in many countries and more than one-third of its sales outside its home country.

myths stories that are consistent with the values and beliefs of the organization but are not supported by facts.

negotiation the bargaining process that often occurs during confrontation and enables the parties to systematically reach a solution.

network centrality top managers increase their power by locating themselves centrally in an organization and surrounding themselves with loyal subordinates.

networking linking computers within or between organizations.

new-venture fund a fund that provides financial resources to employees to develop new ideas, products, or businesses.

niche a domain of unique environmental resources and needs.

noncore technology a department work process that is important to the organization but is not directly related to its central mission.

nonprogrammed decisions novel and poorly defined, these are used when no procedure exists for solving the problem.

nonroutine technology technology in which there is high task variety and the conversion process is not analyzable or well understood.

nonsubstitutability a trait of a department whose function cannot be performed by other readily available resources.

normative forces pressures to adopt structures, techniques, or management processes because they are considered by the community to be up-to-date and effective.

official goals the formally stated definition of business scope and outcomes the organization is trying to achieve; another term for mission.

open system a system that must interact with the environment to survive.

open systems emphasis an aspect of the competing values model that reflects a combination of external focus and flexible structure.

operative goals descriptions of the ends sought through the actual operating procedures of the organization; these explain what the organization is trying to accomplish.

organic an organization system marked by free-flowing, adaptive processes, an unclear hierarchy of authority, and decentralized decision making.

organization development a behavioral science field devoted to improving performance through trust, open confrontation of problems, employee empowerment and participation, the design of meaningful work, cooperation between groups, and the full use of human potential.

organization theory a macro approach to organizations that analyzes the whole organization as a unit.

organizational behavior a micro approach to organizations that focuses on the individuals within organizations as the relevant units for analysis.

organizational change the adoption of a new idea or behavior by an organization.

organizational decision making the organizational process of identifying and solving problems.

organizational decline a condition in which a substantial, absolute decrease in an organization's resource base occurs over a period of time.

organizational ecosystem a system formed by the interaction of a community of organizations and their environment, usually cutting across traditional industry lines.

organizational environment all elements that exist outside the boundary of the organization and have the potential to affect all or part of the organization.

organizational form an organization's specific technology, structure, products, goals, and personnel.

organizational goal a desired state of affairs that the organization attempts to reach.

organizational innovation the adoption of an idea or behavior that is new to an organization's industry, market, or general environment.

organizational politics activities to acquire, develop, and use power and other resources to obtain one's preferred outcome when there is uncertainty or disagreement about choices.

organizations social entities that are goal-directed, deliberately structured activity systems linked to the external environment.

organized anarchy extremely organic organizations characterized by highly uncertain conditions.

personnel ratios the proportions of administrative, clerical, and professional support staff.

point-counter point a decision-making technique that divides decision makers into two groups and assigns them different, often competing responsibilities.

political model a definition of an organization as being made up of groups that have separate interests, goals, and values in which power and influence are needed to reach decisions.

political tactics for using power these include building coalitions, expanding networks, controlling decision premises, enhancing legitimacy and expertise, and making a direct appeal.

pooled interdependence the lowest form of interdependence among departments, in which work does not flow between units.

population a set of organizations engaged in similar activities with similar patterns of resource utilization and outcomes.

population ecology model a perspective in which the focus is on organizational diversity and adaptation within a community or population of organizations.

power the ability of one person or department in an organization to influence others to bring about desired outcomes.

power sources there are five sources of horizontal power in organizations: dependency, financial resources, centrality, nonsubstitutability, and the ability to cope with uncertainty.

problem consensus the agreement among managers about the nature of problems or opportunities and about which goals and outcomes to pursue.

problem identification the decision-making stage in which information about environmental and organizational conditions is monitored to determine if performance is satisfactory and to diagnose the cause of shortcomings.

problem solution the decision-making stage in which alternative courses of action are considered and one alternative is selected and implemented.

problemistic search occurs when managers look around in the immediate environment for a solution to resolve a problem quickly.

process organized group of related tasks and activities that work together to transform inputs into outputs that create value for customers.

product and service changes changes in an organization's product or service outputs.

product matrix a variation of the matrix structure in which project or product managers have primary authority and functional managers simply assign technical personnel to projects and provide advisory expertise.

programmed decisions repetitive and well-defined procedures that exist for resolving problems.

prospector a business strategy characterized by innovation, risk taking, seeking out new opportunities, and growth.

radical change a breaking of the frame of reference for an organization, often creating a new equilibrium because the entire organization is transformed.

rational approach a process of decision making that stresses the need for systematic analysis of a problem followed by choice and implementation in a logical sequence.

rational goal emphasis an aspect of the competing values model that reflects values of structural control and external focus.

rational model a description of an organization characterized by a rational approach to decision making, extensive and reliable information systems, central power, a norm of optimization, uniform values across groups, little conflict, and an efficiency orientation.

rational-legal authority based on employees' belief in the legality of rules and the right of those in authority to issue commands.

reactor a business strategy in which environmental threats and opportunities are responded to in an ad hoc fashion.

reasons organizations grow growth occurs because it is an organizational goal, it is necessary to attract and keep quality managers, or it is necessary to maintain economic health.

reciprocal interdependence the highest level of interdependence, in which the output of one operation is the input of a second, and the output of the second operation is the input of the first (for example, a hospital).

reengineering redesigning a vertical organization along its horizontal workflows and processes.

resource dependence a situation in which organizations depend on the environment but strive to acquire control over resources to minimize their dependence.

resource-based approach an organizational perspective that assesses effectiveness by observing how successfully the organization obtains, integrates, and manages valued resources.

retention the preservation and institutionalization of selected organizational forms.

rites and ceremonies the elaborate, planned activities that make up a special event and often are conducted for the benefit of an audience.

role a part in a dynamic social system that allows an employee to use his or her discretion and ability to achieve outcomes and meet goals.

routine technology technology characterized by little task variety and the use of objective, computational procedures.

rule of law that which arises from a set of codified principles and regulations that describe how people are required to act, are generally accepted in society, and are enforceable in the courts.

satisficing the acceptance by organizations of a satisfactory rather than a maximum level of performance.

scientific management a classical approach that claims decisions about organization and job design should be based on precise, scientific procedures.

sectors subdivisions of the external environment that contain similar elements.

selection the process by which organizational variations are determined to fit the external environment; variations that fail to fit the needs of the environment are "selected out" and fail.

sequential interdependence a serial form of interdependence in which the output of one operation becomes the input to another operation.

service technology technology characterized by simultaneous production and consumption, customized output, customer participation, intangible output, and being labor intensive.

simple-complex dimension the number and dissimilarity of external elements relevant to an organization's operation.

Six Sigma quality standard that specifies a goal of no more than 3.4 defects per million parts; expanded to refer to a set of control procedures that emphasize the relentless pursuit of higher quality and lower costs.

skunkworks a separate, small, informal, highly autonomous, and often secretive group that focuses on breakthrough ideas for the business.

small-batch production a manufacturing process, often custom work, that is not highly mechanized and relies heavily on the human operator.

social audit measures and reports the ethical, social, and environmental impact of a company's operations.

social responsibility management's obligation to make choices and take action so that the organization contributes to the welfare and interest of society as well as itself.

sociotechnical systems approach an approach that combines the needs of people with the needs of technical efficiency.

sources of intergroup conflict factors that generate conflict, including goal incompatibility, differentiation, task interdependence, and limited resources.

specialist an organization that has a narrow range of goods or services or serves a narrow market.

stable-unstable dimension the state of an organization's environmental elements.

stakeholder any group within or outside an organization that has a stake in the organization's performance.

stakeholder approach also called the constituency approach, this perspective assesses the satisfaction of stakeholders as an indicator of the organization's performance.

stories narratives based on true events that are frequently shared among organizational employees and told to new employees to inform them about an organization.

strategic contingencies events and activities inside and outside an organization that are essential for attaining organizational goals.

strategy the current set of plans, decisions, and objectives that have been adopted to achieve the organization's goals.

strategy and structure changes changes in the administrative domain of an organization, including structure, policies, reward systems, labor relations, coordination devices, management information control systems, and accounting and budgeting.

structural dimensions descriptions of the internal characteristics of an organization

structure the formal reporting relationships, groupings, and systems of an organization.

struggle for existence a principle of the population ecology model that holds that organizations are engaged in a competitive struggle for resources and fighting to survive.

subcultures cultures that develop within an organization to reflect the common problems, goals, and experiences that members of a team, department, or other unit share.

subsystems divisions of an organization that perform specific functions for the organization's survival; organizational subsystems perform the essential functions of boundary spanning, production, maintenance, adaptation, and management.

switching structures an organization creates an organic structure when such a structure is needed for the initiation of new ideas.

symbol something that represents another thing.

symptoms of structural deficiency signs of the organizational structure being out of alignment, including delayed or poor-quality decision making, failure to respond innovatively to environmental changes, and too much conflict.

system a set of interacting elements that acquires inputs from the environment, transforms them, and discharges outputs to the external environment.

tacit knowledge knowledge that is based on personal experience, intuition, rules of thumb, and judgment, and cannot be easily codified and passed on to others in written form.

tactics for enhancing collaboration techniques such as integration devices, confrontation and negotiation, intergroup consultation, member rotation, and shared mission and superordinate goals that enable groups to overcome differences and work together.

tactics for increasing power these include entering areas of high uncertainty, creating dependencies, providing resources, and satisfying strategic contingencies.

task a narrowly defined piece of work assigned to a person.

task environment sectors with which the organization interacts directly and that have a direct effect on the organization's ability to achieve its goals.

task force a temporary committee composed of representatives from each department affected by a problem.

team building activities that promote the idea that people who work together can work together as a team.

teams permanent task forces often used in conjunction with a full-time integrator.

technical champion a person who generates or adopts and develops an idea for a technological innovation and is devoted to it, even to the extent of risking position or prestige; also called product champion.

technical complexity the extent of mechanization in the manufacturing process.

technical knowledge understanding and agreement about how to solve problems and reach organizational goals.

technology the tools, techniques, and actions used to transform organizational inputs into outputs.

technology changes changes in an organization's production process, including its knowledge and skills base, that enable distinctive competence.

traditional authority based in the belief in traditions and the legitimacy of the status of people exercising authority through those traditions.

transaction processing systems (TPS) automation of the organization's routine, day-to-day business transactions.

transnational model a form of horizontal organization that has multiple centers, subsidiary managers who initiate strategy and innovations for the company as a whole, and unity and coordination achieved through corporate culture and shared vision and values.

uncertainty occurs when decision makers do not have sufficient information about environmental factors and have a difficult time predicting external changes.

values-based leadership a relationship between a leader and followers that is based on shared values that are advocated and acted upon by the leader.

variation appearance of new organizational forms in response to the needs of the external environment; analogous to mutations in biology.

variety in terms of tasks, the frequency of unexpected and novel events that occur in the conversion process.

venture teams a technique to foster creativity within organizations in which a small team is set up as its own company to pursue innovations.

vertical information system the periodic reports, written information, and computer-based communications distributed to managers.

vertical linkages communication and coordination activities connecting the top and bottom of an organization.

virtual team made up of organizationally or geographically dispersed members who are linked through advanced information and communications technologies. Members frequently use the Internet and collaborative software to work together, rather than meeting face-to-face.

whistle-blowing employee disclosure of illegal, immoral, or illegitimate practices on the part of the organization.